WHAT PEOPLE ARE SAYING ABOUT

ZINNOPHOBIA

I've been waiting for this book! Howard Zinn's remarkably passionate and erudite work has attracted a huge readership, even while it has also been the target of shrill attacks by both politicians and academics, and not only rightwing academics. Now finally David Detmer has stepped up to the plate on Zinn's behalf with a calm and careful dissection of the logic and evidence, and Zinn emerges as he should, unscathed and indeed triumphant!

Frances Fox Piven, Distinguished Professor of Political Science and Sociology at the Graduate School, CUNY, author of *Challenging Authority: How Ordinary People Change America*

In his life and work, Howard Zinn made an immeasurable contribution to a more educated, enlightened, and civilized generation of Americans, more aware of the authentic history of their country and inspired by his example of courage and integrity. While justly honored and admired for his accomplishments, these also aroused bitter resentment and anger in certain circles, and he was subjected to venomous, contemptible attacks. The critiques and vituperation are subjected to rigorous and informed exposure and refutation in this spirited and comprehensive defense of one of the most admirable figures of the modern period. A major contribution to bringing Zinn's great contributions to even broader ng features of intellectual and pol le interest.

D1292552

Noam Chomsky, Institute Prof cs Emeritus, MIT, author of *Who Rules the World?*

David Detmer, a philosopher, has done what no historian to date has accomplished—he has undertaken a systematic examination of Zinn's critics' arguments against him and basically has dismantled them. In the process he offers a clinic on how to evaluate the validity of other people's arguments.... Detmer has done justice to the complexity of Howard Zinn's work and has evaluated Zinn's critics fairly, if unsparingly.... The book is written in clear and compelling prose—it would be accessible to undergraduate students and could be used in History methods classes, in courses on critical thinking, and I would not be averse to assigning it in a graduate seminar.

Susan Curtis, Professor of History and American Studies, Purdue University

Detmer offers a fascinating look at the anti-liberal prejudices of Mitch Daniels, a powerful politician turned university president. He exposes the uneducated foundation of Daniels' hatred for Howard Zinn, and...reveals insights about broader attacks on intellectual freedom. But this is also a hopeful story, because the revelation of Daniels' attempted censorship sparked a new wave of interest in Zinn's work and the opportunity to examine his writings and his critics.

John K. Wilson, author, *President Trump Unveiled: Exposing the Bigoted Billionaire*

Zinnophobia

The Battle Over History in Education,
Politics, and Scholarship

First published by Zero Books, 2018
Zero Books is an imprint of John Hunt Publishing Ltd., No. 3 East St., Alresford,
Hampshire SO24 9EE, UK
office1@jhpbooks.net
www.johnhuntpublishing.com
www.zero-books.net

For distributor details and how to order please visit the 'Ordering' section on our website.

Text copyright: David Detmer 2017

ISBN: 978 1 78535 678 0
978 1 78535 679 7 (ebook)
Library of Congress Control Number: 2017932885

A CIP catalogue record for this book is available from the British Library.

Design: Stuart Davies

Printed and bound by CPI Group (UK) Ltd, Croydon, CR0 4YY, UK

We operate a distinctive and ethical publishing philosophy in all
areas of our business, from our global network of authors to
production and worldwide distribution.

CONTENTS

Preface	1
Abbreviations	8
Chapter 1: The Daniels–Zinn Controversy	17
Assessing Daniels's Claims and Arguments	21
Chapter 2: Bias and Objectivity in History	60
Who Was Howard Zinn?	62
Anti-Americanism	89
Bias	96
Objectivity	113
Chapter 3: Zinn's Critics	141
Sam Wineburg	142
David Greenberg	200
David J. Bobb	235
Mary Grabar	237
Eugene D. Genovese	246
Robert Paquette	251
David Horowitz	271
Michael Kazin	308
Daniel J. Flynn	332
Oscar Handlin	378
"frankly speaking"	417
Michael Kammen	419
The Editors of the *National Review*	429
Rich Lowry	433
Roger Kimball	438
Jill Lepore	451
Michael C. Moynihan	453
Arthur M. Schlesinger, Jr.	474

Kevin Mattson   480
Benno Schmidt   482
Gabriel Schoenfeld   484
Rick Shenkman   489
The Weekly Standard   492
Peter Wood   495
Sean Wilentz   502
Endnotes   514
Index   576

Also by David Detmer
Freedom as a Value
Challenging Postmodernism: Philosophy and the
Politics of Truth
Sartre Explained
Phenomenology Explained

Preface

Howard Zinn's *A People's History of the United States*, a perennial bestseller, offers a version of American history that differs substantially from previous accounts. Instead of the standard story, in which the wise and heroic deeds of presidents, Supreme Court justices, military and business leaders, and various other wealthy and powerful elites are celebrated, Zinn makes the case that, whenever progressive change has occurred, it has resulted from the struggles of ordinary people—those who have participated in popular movements agitating for peace, for racial and sexual equality, for improved working conditions, and for environmental protection, among other similar causes. And in opposition to the triumphalist bias of the more orthodox histories, in which the misdeeds of the powerful are either sanitized or erased altogether, Zinn shines a spotlight on official acts of enslaving Africans, slaughtering Indians, lying, breaking promises, violating treaties, trashing the Constitution, exploiting workers, bombing or massacring civilians, assassinating foreign leaders, sabotaging elections, and propping up brutal puppet dictators, among other transgressions.

Unsurprisingly, Zinn's book has provoked strong, and widely divergent, reactions. As the continuing success of the book testifies (it was first published in 1980 and remains a bestseller 37 years later) many readers warmly welcome Zinn's work. These include students of history who celebrate it as a vital corrective to the omissions and distortions of the standard surveys; radicals and political activists who are inspired by it; women, racial and ethnic minorities, and economically disadvantaged persons who are delighted to see their contributions to history recognized; and victims (or the children or grandchildren of victims) of U.S. power who appreciate seeing their victimization documented and its moral significance acknowledged.

But the reaction of many other readers (and non-readers who know of Zinn's book only by reputation) has been one of loathing. Such has been the typical response of political conservatives, the wealthy and powerful, many mainstream historians, and everyone else whose sense of "patriotism" engenders a commitment to the idea that our nation's leaders, traditions, and institutions are uniquely great and moral. Accordingly, Zinn's work has received a great deal of harsh criticism.

And sometimes the negative reaction has taken the form of something stronger than mere criticism: attempted suppression. As a case in point, the event that sparked the writing of this book was the 2013 revelation that Mitch Daniels, the president of my university, Purdue (I am a professor of philosophy at one of its campuses), had in 2010, when he was Governor of my state (Indiana), attempted to ban the teaching of *A People's History of the United States* in the state's public schools, an incident that is described in some detail in this book.

But the central focus of the book, as its title indicates, is not the Daniels/Zinn incident but rather the extraordinarily severe criticisms, indeed denunciations, that Zinn has received from some of his fellow historians and from a few other writers and scholars. Indeed, when Daniels's actions came to light, through the publication of emails that he had intended to keep private, a substantial portion of the defense that he offered consisted simply of quoting the blistering invective of Zinn's critics, many of whom, Daniels was quick to point out, were "experts."

Though I knew, prior to learning of Daniels's actions, that Zinn was controversial and had been harshly criticized in some quarters, I had never read the works in which those criticisms are stated. Though I admired Zinn, once I turned to those writings I fully expected to find in them, given how eminent many of these critics were, together with the severity of their language, documentation that his work contained significant flaws. After all, though Zinn struck me as a highly competent and principled person (I knew him personally, as he was one of my teachers when I was an undergraduate student at Boston University in the 1970s, and I had also read his books), I understood that he is a human being, and that human beings are fallible. Moreover, I recognized that history is difficult, and that a project as ambitious as writing a 688-page account of the full sweep of American history is one that would present many possibilities for error. And surely, I reasoned, Pulitzer prize-winning historians at Ivy League universities would not be so reckless and irresponsible as to issue such strongly-worded condemnations as they had unless they could produce the goods to back up their charges. Thus, when I began to read their critiques I fully expected to find within them documentation that Zinn had gotten some facts wrong, or committed some logical blunders, or misinterpreted some data, or employed some faulty methodology, or omitted information that undermined some of his claims, or committed some other definite and specific errors. Additionally, even in cases where no particular error could be identified, I expected to find interesting, intelligent arguments for evaluating some set of facts differently than Zinn did, or thoughtful criticisms of his explicitly stated criteria of selection (that is, of what to include, what to omit, and what to emphasize when choosing among the vast mass of historical data), or some other lucid and perceptive argument, based on a competent grasp of Zinn's text, and of the arguments he has provided in support of his historical methods, that there is some deficiency in his approach, his theorizing, or his ways of drawing conclusions from historical evidence.

Instead, and to my surprise, what I found, over and over again, is that Zinn's harsh critics (I'm not talking about those who articulate normal, moderately-worded scholarly disagreements, but rather those Daniels cited, that is, those who regard Zinn's work with contempt, and who, for example, call it "lousy," or characterize *A People's History* as a "deranged fairy tale") produce incompetent work—work that, while it occasionally scores an

3

isolated minor point or two against Zinn, nonetheless can be fairly characterized, on the whole, as uncomprehending, larded with errors, and not up to the quality standards one would expect in a term paper submitted for credit by a college freshman for an introductory level course. This book attempts to document that these critics, one after another, commit the following scholarly mistakes: misquoting Zinn; paraphrasing him inaccurately; taking his words out of context; accusing him of saying things he has never said; accusing him of never having said things that he has in fact said repeatedly; claiming that some idea or theory or explanation "has never occurred to him" when in fact he discusses and analyzes it extensively; saying that he is "unable to grasp" some concept or theory that in fact he explains far more clearly and completely than the critic does; indicting him for presenting a one-sided account of some issue or event while ignoring everything he says on other sides of the issue or event in question; accusing him of oversimplifying an issue or event while ignoring or denying all of the subtleties, nuances, and complications that can be found in his discussion; presenting criticisms of him that he himself has anticipated and addressed in his writings, but in doing so failing even to acknowledge, let alone adequately addressing or satisfactorily answering, his replies to those criticisms; failing to address his theorizing about historiography, including his explicit arguments in support of his principles of selection; compounding that error by issuing criticisms that are based on misunderstandings of his project, where those misunderstandings, in turn, are based on either misunderstandings (or, more often, complete ignorance) of his arguments about historiography; criticizing him for "admitting" that he was "biased," or for rejecting "objectivity," without either explaining what he meant by such statements or quoting his own explanations, and without acknowledging his repeated insistence that they did not entail any loosening of the scholarly obligation to achieve factual accuracy or to refrain from omitting information that would be damaging to one's thesis; ignoring all of the distinctions he draws in explaining his approach to history—such as the distinction between universal values and parochial values, between ultimate values and instrumental values, between preconceived questions and preconceived answers, and distinctions among different senses of "objectivity"—and then advancing criticisms that make sense only against a background of ignorance of those distinctions; committing clear, demonstrable factual errors; committing obvious and crude logical fallacies; and, above all else, issuing strongly-worded criticisms that are not backed up with any evidence or argument of any kind. I am tempted to add, sarcastically, the old joke line: "aside from that, they do a terrific job!" But that, alas, would be far too generous. For the list just offered includes only those errors that are committed repeatedly, and by several critics. Sadly, as a list of all of the errors of the Zinnophobes, it fails even to approach completeness.

The structure of this book can be laid out simply. It tells the story of the Daniels–Zinn affair and refutes Daniels's claims about Zinn (Chapter One), offers a brief account of Zinn's life and work, and discusses his ideas on historiography (especially his analyses of bias and objectivity) (Chapter Two), and concludes with an extended, detailed defense of his work against 25 of his most prominent critics (Chapter Three). The Daniels–Zinn incident is thus used as a kind of jumping off point from which to consider such issues as censorship, academic freedom, propaganda, objectivity, historiography, contemporary intellectual standards, and the place of politics in scholarly research and teaching, in addition to the merits of Howard Zinn's approach to history.

As I write these words, in late January 2017, recent events in U.S. political history have demonstrated how far much of our culture has drifted away from any concern for high standards of critical thinking: the idea that our beliefs should be well grounded in a logically competent appraisal of relevant evidence. One way of approaching the issue is to recognize that beliefs tend to issue in actions, and that actions grounded in true beliefs are more likely to lead to success than are actions grounded in falsehoods. When our beliefs are false people tend to get hurt: we go to war without good reason; we enact educational policies that are ineffective; we adopt a diet that is not conducive to health; we react to social problems, such as crime, poverty, and environmental degradation, with policies that make things worse rather than better. At the risk of sounding pretentious, I would suggest that each of us, and perhaps especially scholars, should make some effort to try to nudge our culture in the direction of greater care and scrupulousness in matters of handling evidence, and in the formulation and articulation of beliefs. I offer this book in that spirit.

I would like to thank those who have helped me with this project. I have benefited from discussing some of the ideas in this book with past and present colleagues at Purdue, including (with apologies to anyone I may have overlooked) Neil Florek, Phyllis Bergiel, Renee Conroy, Sam Zinaich, Eugene Schlossberger, Howard Cohen, John Rowan, Michael Dobberstein, Sam Dobberstein, David Nalbone, Tony Elmendorf, Elsa Weber, Rita Brusca-Vega, Pat Jacoby, Saul Lerner, Kathy Tobin, Susan Curtis, and Kim Scipes. I am also grateful to my Purdue colleagues in philosophy for twice giving me the opportunity to make a public presentation of some of the findings presented in this book. Some audience members at these presentations helped me by asking good questions or by offering incisive comments or criticisms, for which I thank them.

Also deserving of thanks are Steve Walsh, formerly of Lakeshore Public Radio, and Ron Harlow of WJOB radio in Hammond, Indiana for inviting me on their programs to discuss the issues raised in this book. I am fond of quoting Harlow's rejoinder to a hostile listener (it is a call-in show) who complained that he was sick and tired of hearing people "whine about genocide." Harlow's quick reply: "That's right. Walk it off, genocide victims. Just walk it off!"

I would also like to thank Jerry Davich of the *Post-Tribune* newspaper in northwest Indiana for writing a couple of columns, the first on one of my public presentations about the Daniels–Zinn affair, and the second on the voluminous mail he received in response to the first column. He also put me in touch with some of my critics among his readers, which led to some fruitful exchanges.

It is my pleasure to thank several other friends for their advice and encouragement in connection with this project. Bill Martin responded to my first public presentation on the Daniels–Zinn incident by suggesting that the material was worth pursuing as a book project. And John Wachala and Connie Sowa-Wachala have been especially supportive. Connie took it upon herself to use her contacts as a former journalist to get the press interested in my work, with the result that my first lecture on this topic was well publicized, drew a huge crowd, and was the subject of articles in several newspapers. She also suggested Zero Books as a publisher for my work. And she and John have both helped to keep the project alive by their continued interest in and enthusiasm for it throughout all phases of its development.

I am also very grateful to Noam Chomsky, Susan Curtis, and Frances Fox Piven for taking the time to read all or substantial portions of this book, and for offering helpful, and very generous, comments on it. I hasten to add that the standard disclaimer applies in this case. It must not be assumed that anyone named above agrees with everything I say in this book. I am the one who is to blame for its faults.

Finally, as always, my biggest thanks go to Kerri and Arlo. They make life worth living, and make me proud every day.

Abbreviations

The following abbreviations are used for works that are repeatedly cited in the text.

APH   Howard Zinn, *A People's History of the United States*, Thirty-Fifth Anniversary Edition (New York: HarperCollins, 2015).

ATW   Howard Zinn, *Artists in Times of War* (New York: Seven Stories Press, 2003).

AW   Alice Walker, "Saying Goodbye to My Friend Howard Zinn," *Boston Globe* (January 31, 2010); http://www. boston.com/ae/books/articles/2010/01/31/alice_walker_s ays_goodbye_to_her_friend_howard_zinn/

AWS   Stephen Bird, Adam Silver, and Joshua C. Yesnowitz, eds., *Agitation with a Smile: Howard Zinn's Legacies and The Future of Activism* (Boulder, CO: Paradigm Publishers, 2013).

BAT   "Fulgencio Batista—Military Coup and Second Presidency (1952–1959)—Batista, Fidel Castro, and The Cuban Revolution"; http://www.liquisearch.com/fulg encio_batista/military_coup_and_second_presi- dency_1952–1959/batista_fidel_castro_and_the_cuban_r evolution

BLL   "bin Laden links to the CIA"; http://www.911 myths.com/html/bin_ladin_links_to_the_cia.html

CAV   Alfred A. Cave, *The Pequot War* (Amherst, MA: University of Massachusetts Press, 1996).

COL   Hayleigh Colombo, "Mitch Daniels Disputes Copycat Claim," *Lafayette Journal & Courier* (July 24, 2013); http://hcolombo28.weebly.com/work-samples/mitch- daniels-disputes-copycat-claim

CP   David Detmer, *Challenging Postmodernism: Philosophy and the Politics of Truth* (Amherst, NY: Humanity Books, 2003).

CSZ   Howard Zinn, "The Case of Sacco and Vanzetti," in HZS 121–31.

CW   Howard Zinn, "The Politics of History in the Era of the Cold War," in Noam Chomsky et al., *The Cold War & The University* (New York: The New Press, 1997), 35–72.

DC   David Colapinto (essay on Zinn as a teacher); http://zinnedproject.org/why/howard-zinn-our-favorite-teacher/david-colapinto/

DDT   Tom LoBianco, "Daniels Denies Trying to Quash Academic Freedom," *San Diego Union-Tribune* (July 17, 2013); http://www.utsandiego.com/news/2013/jul/17/daniels-denies-trying-to-quash-academic-freedom/

DOD   John K. Wilson, "The Defenders of Daniels" (July 26, 2013); http://academeblog.org/2013/07/26/the-defenders-of-daniels/

DOI   Howard Zinn, *Declarations of Independence* (New York: HarperCollins, 1990).

DUB   Martin Duberman, *Howard Zinn: A Life on the Left* (New York: The New Press, 2012).

EAS   Stuart Easterling, "Defending Howard Zinn" (February 11, 2010); http://socialistworker.org/2010/02/11/defending-howard-zinn

ELL   Daniel Ellsberg, *Secrets: A Memoir of Vietnam and the Pentagon Papers* (New York: Viking, 2002).

EMA   Mitch Daniels and Associates (Zinn emails); http://hosted.ap.org/specials/interactives/documents/daniels1.pdf

FC   Free Exchange on Campus, "Facts Count: An Analysis of David Horowitz's *The Professors: The 101 Most Dangerous Academics in America*" (May 2006); http://cdn.publicinterestnetwork.org/assets/woUsLGhMMPR98xFTxvDWyw/Facts_Count-Report.pdf

FLY   Daniel J. Flynn, "Master of Deceit" (June 3, 2003); http://archive.frontpagemag.com/readArticle.aspx?ARTI D=17914

FOH   Howard Zinn, *The Future of History* (Monroe, ME: Common Courage Press, 1999).

FTQ   Howard Zinn, *Failure to Quit* (Monroe, ME: Common Courage Press, 1993).

FUT   Howard Zinn, "The Future of History," in FOH 93–154.

GLA   Grammy "Lifetime Achievement Award"; https://www.grammy.org/recording-academy/awards/lifetime-awards

GM   *"Grey Matters Interviews Howard Zinn,"* in ODE 123–36.

GRA   Mary Grabar, "The 'Bad History' of Howard Zinn and the Brainwashing of America"; http://www.marygrabar.com/PDF%20Articles/ZinnReportKincaidFullArial.pdf

GRE   David Greenberg, "Agit-Prof: Howard Zinn's influential mutilations of American history," *The New Republic* (March 25, 2013), 44–9.

GW   Steve Coll, *Ghost Wars* (New York: Penguin, 2004).

HAN   Oscar Handlin, "Arawaks," *The American Scholar*, Vol. 49, No. 4 (Autumn 1980), 546, 548, 550; https://d3ae ncwbm6zmht.cloudfront.net/asset/97521/A_Handlin_19 80.pdf

HCD   John K. Wilson, "The Historians Cited by Mitch Daniels Denounce Him" (July 19, 2013); http://academeblog.org/2013/07/19/the-historians-cited-by-mitch-daniels-denounce-him/

HPE   Howard Zinn, "History as Private Enterprise," in POH 15–34.

HRZ   Oscar Handlin (Response to Howard Zinn's reply to Handlin's review of APH), *The American Scholar*, Vol. 50, No. 3 (Summer 1981), 432.

HUP   Howard Zinn, *The Historic Unfulfilled Promise* (San Francisco: City Lights, 2012).

HZS   Howard Zinn, *Howard Zinn Speaks: Collected Speeches 1963–2009*, edited by Anthony Arnove (Chicago: Haymarket Books, 2012).

IFE   Howard Zinn, "Introduction to the First Edition" of POH, 1–3.

IH   Michael Kammen, "The Insubordinate Historian: The Life and Legacy of Howard Zinn," *Los Angeles Review of Books* (November 29, 2012); https://lareviewofbooks. org/review/the-insubordinate-historian-the-life-and-legacy-of-howard-zinn

JAS   Scott Jaschik, "The Governor's Bad List" (July 17, 2013); https://www.insidehighered.com/news/2013/07/17/e-mails-reveal-mitch-daniels-governor-tried-ban-howard-zinn-book

JFK   John F. Kennedy, "Speech at Democratic Dinner, Cincinnati, Ohio, October 6, 1960"; http://www.presidency.ucsb.edu/ws/?pid=25660

JOY   Davis D. Joyce, *Howard Zinn: A Radical American Vision* (Amherst, NY: Prometheus, 2003).

KAZ   Michael Kazin, "Howard Zinn's History Lessons," *Dissent* (Spring 2004); https://www.dissentmagazine.org/article/howard-zinns-history-lessons

KIM   Roger Kimball, "Mitch Daniels vs. Howard Zinn. Daniels Wins" (July 20, 2013); http://pjmedia.com/rogerkimball/2013/07/20/mitch-daniel-vs-howard-zinn-daniels-wins/

KFP   Howard Zinn, "Knowledge as a Form of Power," in POH 5–14.

KRE   Howard Zinn, *Some Truths Are Not Self-Evident*, ed. Richard Kreitner (New York: The Nation, 2014).

KTR   Mitch Daniels, *Keeping the Republic: Saving America by Trusting Americans* (New York: Sentinel, 2011).

KYS   Alison Kysia, "Bashing Howard Zinn: A Critical Look at One of the Critics," Zinn Education Project (November

18, 2013); http://zinnedproject.org/2013/11/bashing-ho
ward-zinn-a-critical-look-at-one-of-the-critics/

LAK   Jacob Laksin, "Discounting the Facts (June 15, 2006);
http://archive.frontpagemag.com/readArticle.aspx?ARTI
D=4039

LEF   Harry G. Lefever, *Undaunted By the Fight: Spelman College
and the Civil Rights Movement 1957–1967* (Macon, GA:
Mercer University Press, 2005).

LET   Howard Zinn, "Letter" to *Dissent* (Summer 2004), 110.

LIN   Douglas O. Linder, "The Trials of 'The Scottsboro Boys'";
http://law2.umkc.edu/faculty/projects/ftrials/scottsboro/
SB_acct.html

LMT   James W. Loewen, *Lies My Teacher Told Me: Everything
Your American History Textbook Got Wrong*, revised and
updated edition (New York: Touchstone, 2007).

LOB   Tom LoBianco, "AP Exclusive: Daniels Looked to Censor
Opponents" (July 17, 2013); http://bigstory.ap.org/arti
cle/ap-exclusive-daniels-looked-censor-opponents

LOC   Howard Zinn, "1492–1992: The Legacy of Columbus," in
HZS 77–90.

MC   Edward S. Herman and Noam Chomsky, "Legitimizing
versus Meaningless Third World Elections: El Salvador,
Guatemala, and Nicaragua," in *Manufacturing Consent:
The Political Economy of the Mass Media* (New York:
Pantheon, 2002), 87–142.

MDF   John K. Wilson, "Why Mitch Daniels Must Be Fired"
(July 17, 2013); http://academeblog.org/2013/07/17
/whymitch-daniels-must-be-fired/

MIL   Marjorie Miller, "An Experts' History of Howard Zinn,"
Los Angeles Times (February 1, 2010); http://articles.lati
mes.com/2010/feb/01/opinion/la-oe-miller1-2010feb01

MIS   Howard Zinn, *Marx in Soho* (Cambridge, MA: South End
Press, 1999).

MKR   Michael Kazin, review of Howard Zinn, *Declarations of*

Independence, in *The Journal of American History.* Vol. 78, No. 3 (December 1991), 1034–5.

MOY   Michael C. Moynihan, "The People's Historian?," *Reason* (February 3, 2010); http://reason.com/archives/2010/02/0 3/the-peoples-historian

NAS   Gary B. Nash et al, *History on Trial: Culture Wars and the Teaching of the Past* (New York: Knopf, 1997).

NG   Ben Bradley et al, eds., *Por Amor Al Pueblo: Not Guilty!* (White River Junction, VT: Front Porch Publishing, 1986).

NOV   Peter Novick, *That Noble Dream: The "Objectivity Question" and the American Historical Profession* (New York: Cambridge University Press, 1988).

NR   Howard Zinn, "The New Radicalism," in ZR 620–32.

NYT   Howard Powell, "Howard Zinn, Historian, Dies at 87," *New York Times* (January 27, 2010); http://www.nytimes. com/2010/01/28/us/28zinn.html?_r=0

ODE   Howard Zinn, *On Democratic Education* (Boulder, CO: Paradigm Publishers, 2005).

OH   Howard Zinn, *On History* (New York: Seven Stories Press, 2001).

OHM   Howard Zinn, "Objective History a Myth," *Michigan Daily* (December 13, 1988); https://news.google.com/ newspapers?nid=2706&dat=19881213&id=D_5JAAAAIB AJ&sjid=Mh4NAAAAIBAJ&pg=3807,5164615&hl=en

OLM   Susan Curtis and Kristina Bross, "An Open Letter to Mitch Daniels" (July 22, 2013); http://academeblog.org /2013/07/23/an-open-letter-to-mitch-daniels-from-90-purdue-professors/

OTO   Howard Zinn, "Objections to Objectivity," in FTQ 29–42.

OZ   Howard Zinn with David Barsamian, *Original Zinn: Conversations on History and Politics* (New York: Harper Perennial, 2006).

PA   Howard Zinn, *Postwar America: 1945–1971* (Indianapolis: Bobbs-Merrill, 1973).

PA1   Robert Paquette, "Mitch Daniels Unmasks Howard Zinn's Propagandizing" (August 5, 2013); http://www.seethruedu.com/updatesmitch-daniels-unmasks-howard-zinns-propagandizing/

PA2   Robert Paquette, "Mitch Daniels v. Howard Zinn, Part 2" (August 25, 2013); http://www.seethruedu.com/update smitch-daniels-v-howard-zinn-part-2/

PAC   Harry Kreisler, *Political Awakenings: Conversations with History* (New York: The New Press, 2010).

PGC   Howard Zinn, *A Power Governments Cannot Suppress* (San Francisco: City Lights, 2007).

POC   Roger Kimball, "Professor of Contempt," *National Review* (February 3, 2010); http://www.nationalreview.com/articl e/229071/professor-contempt-roger-kimball

POH   Howard Zinn, *The Politics of History*, second edition (Urbana, IL: University of Illinois Press, 1990).

REE   Howard Zinn, "A People's History of the United States," in HZS 91–113. (Note: Despite sharing a title with Zinn's famous book, this is a different item—a speech delivered at Reed College in Portland, Oregon, November 20, 1995.)

REV   John K. Wilson, review of David Horowitz and Jacob Laksin, *One-Party Classroom: How Radical Professors at America's Top Colleges Indoctrinate Students and Undermine Our Democracy*, in *Academe* (September–October 2009); http://www.aaup.org/article/skim-book#.VoPDwhE4n-Y

RIL   J.B.S. Riley, "You'll Never Believe It" (July 24, 2013); http://doghouseriley.blogspot.com/2013/07/youll-never-believe-it.html

RPF   Mitch Daniels, "Response to Purdue Faculty" (July 23, 2013); http://academeblog.org/2013/07/23/mitch-daniels-responds-to-purdue-faculty/

SAP   Mitch Daniels, "Statement to the Associated Press: 'I Will Stand by My Statements'" (July 17, 2013); http://arc

hive.jconline.com/article/20130717/NEWS0501/30717001
8/Mitch-Daniels-statement-Associated-Press

SPD   Mitch Daniels, "A Statement from President Daniels" (July 17, 2013); http://www.purdue.edu/president/mes sages/130717-statement.html

SWH   Robert Cohen, "The Second Worst History Book in Print? Rethinking *A People's History of the United States*," *Reviews in American History*, Vol. 42, No. 2 (June 2014).

TAV   Howard Zinn, "Thinking About Vietnam: Political Theory and Human Life," in HZS 21–39.

TAW   Howard Zinn, *Terrorism and War* (New York: Seven Stories Press, 2002).

THP   Howard Zinn, *Three Plays: The Political Theater of Howard Zinn: Emma, Marx in Soho, Daughter of Venus* (Boston: Beacon, 2010).

TIZ   Timothy Patrick McCarthy, "Introduction: The People's Historian," in Timothy Patrick McCarthy, ed., *The Indispensable Zinn* (New York: The New Press, 2012), xv–xxxi.

TP   David Horowitz, *The Professors: The 101 Most Dangerous Academics in America* (Washington, DC: Regnery, 2006).

TVR   William L. Griffen and John Marciano, *Teaching the Vietnam War* (Montclair, NJ: Allanheld, Osmun, 1979).

UOS   Howard Zinn, "The Uses of Scholarship." http://www. kritischestudenten.nl/wp-content/uploads/2012/09/ Howard-Zinn-The-Uses-of-Scholarship.pdf

USP   United States Postal Service, "African-Americans on Stamps" (January 2004); https://about.usps.com/publica-tions/pub354.pdf

VAA   Marvin E. Gettleman et al, eds., *Vietnam and America*, Second Edition (New York: Grove Press, 1995).

VLW   Howard Zinn, *Vietnam: The Logic of Withdrawal* (Boston: Beacon Press, 1967).

WAR   Jon Ward, "Mitch Daniels: I'm 'More Devoted To

Academic Freedom' Than Critics in Howard Zinn Controversy" (October 30, 2013); http://www.huffingtonpost.com/2013/10/30/mitch-daniels-howardzinn_n_4178180.html.

WAZ   Robert Cohen, "When Assessing Zinn, Listen to the Voices of Teachers and Students," *History News Network* (January 6, 2013); http://historynewsnetwork.org/article/149974

WCP   Howard Zinn, "Who Controls the Past Controls the Future," in FTQ 3–21.

WIN   Sam Wineburg, "Undue Certainty: Where Howard Zinn's *A People's History* Falls Short," *American Educator* (Winter 2012–2013), 27–34; https://www.aft.org/sites/default/files/periodicals/Wineburg.pdf

YCB   Howard Zinn, *You Can't Be Neutral on a Moving Train: A Personal History of Our Times* (Boston: Beacon Press, 1994).

ZCH   Eric Foner, "Zinn's Critical History," *The Nation* (February 22, 2010), in KRE 211–13.

ZR   Howard Zinn, *The Zinn Reader* (New York: Seven Stories Press, 1997.)

ZRH   Howard Zinn (Reply to Oscar Handlin's review of APH), *The American Scholar*, Vol. 50, No. 3 (Summer 1981), 431–2.

Chapter 1

The Daniels–Zinn Controversy

On June 21, 2012 the Purdue University Board of Trustees unanimously selected Mitch Daniels, who was at the time the governor of Indiana, to be the University's new President.[1] Daniels subsequently took office in January 2013, upon completion of his term as governor. His selection attracted a great deal of criticism, primarily on two grounds. First, Daniels lacked any of the academic qualifications typically required of university presidents: he did not have a Ph.D. or comparable research degree; he had no teaching experience; and he had never published any peer reviewed scholarly research.[2] Secondly, the trustees who selected him to this position, for which he lacked the customary qualifications, owed their own positions as trustees to him—as governor, he had appointed eight of them to the Board of Trustees, and had re-appointed the other two.[3]

The controversy intensified on July 17, 2013, when the Associated Press, having obtained them through a Freedom of Information Act request, published some of Daniels's emails from February 2010 (LOB).[4] The emails revealed that while Daniels was governor of Indiana he privately instructed his subordinates to make sure that a book he did not like, Howard Zinn's *A People's History of the United States*, would not be "in use anywhere in Indiana." As an alternative to Zinn's text, Daniels expressed a preference for a book by a fellow Republican politician, William Bennett, and asked his staff to do what it could to see that Bennett's work, *America: The Last Best Hope*, would become "the textbook of choice in our state."[5]

Daniels's initial email was sent at 10:54 AM on February 9, 2010 to Tony Bennett (not the singer, but the Indiana State Superintendent of Schools) and copied to Todd Huston (former

Chief of Staff for the Indiana Department of Education), Scott Jenkins (Senior Education Policy Director), and David Shane (Republican donor and member of the state school board). Under the subject heading "Howard Zinn," the email reads as follows:

> This terrible anti-American academic finally passed away. The obits and commentaries mentioned that his book "A People's History of the United States" is "the textbook of choice in high schools and colleges around the country." It is a truly execrable, anti-factual piece of disinformation that misstates American history on every page.
>
> Can someone assure me that it is not in use anywhere in Indiana? If it is, how do we get rid of it before more young people are force-fed a totally false version of our history?

Twenty-four minutes later Jenkins posted a reply, in which he informed Daniels that Zinn's text was indeed being used in a course at Indiana University on "Social Movements in America: Labor, Civil Rights, and Feminism." Though Jenkins provided no information about the course aside from its title and the claim that "Zinn along with other anti American leftist readings are prominently featured," Daniels needed only three minutes to reach the conclusion that "This crap should not be accepted for any credit by the state," and that "No student will be any better taught because someone sat through this session." He then inquired, "Which board has jurisdiction over what counts and what doesn't?" A brief back-and-forth on bureaucratic technicalities immediately ensued, during which Daniels again demanded to know "Who will take charge?" Shane suggested that Bennett and Indiana Commissioner for Higher Education Teresa Lubbers could undertake a review of university courses across the state, a process that, he assured Daniels, "would force to daylight a lot of excrement." Just seven minutes later, Daniels endorsed the plan: "Go for it. Disqualify propaganda and highlight (if there is any) the more useful offerings."

In response to criticism, once the emails were made public, Daniels defended his actions, noting that "we must not falsely teach American history in our schools." And he redoubled his criticism of Zinn, calling him a "fraud," saying that he was "by his own admission a biased writer" (SAP), insisting that his book "represents a falsified version of history" (SPD), accusing him of having "purposely falsified American history," and asserting that "his books have no more place in Indiana history classrooms than phrenology or Lysenkoism would in our biology classes or the 'Protocols of the Elders of Zion' in world history courses" (SAP). Further, he offered the following, more specific, criticism: "Prof. Zinn's disdain for the idea of objective truth went far beyond American history. In his essay, 'The Uses of Scholarship,' Prof. Zinn criticized 'disinterested scholarship,' 'objective study' and the 'scientific method' across the disciplines, thus attacking the foundations of Purdue's entire research enterprise" (RPF).

To support his harsh criticisms of Zinn, Daniels also claimed that a consensus of opinion among professional historians supported his position,[6] that Zinn's book "has been criticized all across the ideological spectrum, including by so many who share his strongly negative view of the American experiment" (RPF), and that "no one credible defended his versions of history."[7] More expansively, he argued that

No one need take my word that my concerns were well-founded. Respected scholars and communicators of all ideologies agree that the work of Howard Zinn was irredeemably slanted and unsuited for teaching to school-children. Arthur M. Schlesinger said, "I don't take him very seriously. He's a polemicist, not a historian." Socialist historian Michael Kazin judged Zinn's work as "bad history, albeit tilted with virtuous intentions" and said the book was more suited to a "conspiracy monger's website than to a work of scholarship." Reviewing the text in *The American Scholar*, Harvard University professor Oscar Handlin denounced "the deranged quality of his fairy tale, in which the incidents are made to fit the legend, no matter how intractable the evidence of American history." Stanford history education expert Sam Wineburg cautioned that exposing children to a heavily filtered and weighted interpretation such as Zinn's work is irresponsible when "we are talking about how we educate the young, those who do not yet get the interpretive game." Many more such condemnations by persons of political viewpoints different from my own are available on request.[8]

But the heart of Daniels's defense consisted of three rather startling assertions. First, he claimed that in his Zinn emails he had been speaking exclusively about K-12 classrooms, and that his questions and concerns "had nothing to do with higher education at all" (SPD). Or again, "My only concern in two e-mail questions years ago was what was being taught to middle school children in their formative lessons in American history. My questions expressed no interest in higher education" (RPF). Second, he asserted that his emails "proposed absolutely no censorship of any person or viewpoint" (SPD), adding that "I have never made any suggestion that any university cease teaching whatever its faculty pleases, or cease using any book.... Most important, no one tried to 'censor' anyone's right to express any opinion they might hold. As many others have observed, this was a careless and inappropriate use of that inflammatory word" (RPF). Third, he claimed that his actions "infringed on no one's academic freedom" (SPD), "had nothing to do with academic freedom on campus" (WAR), and carried "no implication for academic freedom" (JAS).

Further, Daniels pointed out that his emails did not lead to any actions. There was no need to ban Zinn's book from Indiana public school K-12 classrooms, since his subordinates found "that no Hoosier school district had inflicted [it] on its students" (SAP), because "apparently every school board in the state to date shares and has adopted" Daniels's own evaluation of the book (RPF). Similarly, but this time for unspecified reasons, nothing was done about the Indiana University course, discussed in the initial emails, that featured Zinn on its reading list: "No change of any kind occurred with regard to the summer class for K-12 teachers; its participants received credit, and would today if the class was still offered" (RPF).

Finally, Daniels made the point that his criticism of Zinn, and his authorization of a scheme to have his book banned from use in Indiana public schools, cannot be construed as an attack on tenure, since tenure "does not confer immunity from criticism of shoddy work and it certainly gives no entitlement to have one's work taught to young schoolchildren in our public schools" (SAP). Nor can it be interpreted as inconsistent with academic freedom, since (in nearly identical language) "Academic freedom…does not immunize a person from criticism and certainly does not confer entitlement to have one's work inflicted upon our young people in the K-12 public school system" (SPD).[9]

Assessing Daniels's Claims and Arguments

Notice, first, that in the initial emails Daniels offers no evidence, argument, or reasoning of any kind in support of his harsh judgment of Zinn's work. Nor does he engage Zinn's text—no page numbers or specific claims or analyses are cited. This raises disturbing questions about the intellectual standards in play here. Note, for example, that we demand much more of our freshman students in the papers they write for our introductory courses. They must provide a rational defense of their conclusions in order to receive a good grade. One would think that as much or more would be required of one who would presume to determine unilaterally that a specific text should be removed from Indiana classrooms.

Similarly, what is the significance of the fact that none of his four email correspondents asked any critical questions or raised any concerns in response to Daniels's demands? Note that none asked for supporting evidence, or examples, or a detailed explanation of what was wrong with Zinn's book. (Are we to think that all of them had read it themselves?) None asked how or why, if the book were really that bad, it had become "the textbook of choice in high schools and colleges around the country." None asked why the judgment of Daniels, who is not a historian, should be assumed to be superior to that of history professors and other teachers who specialize in teaching history. Note, further, that these are rather obvious questions—the sort that any at least minimally rational person would be inclined to ask.

While some might defend Daniels on the grounds that his concern for education is admirable, it must nonetheless be pointed out that he pursues that interest in an autocratic, undemocratic way. He asks no questions of others who might disagree with him, makes no attempt to address their concerns, and engages in no public process of inquiry into the merits of using Zinn's text, but rather simply decides, completely on his own, that Indiana must "get rid of" it, and that his subordinates are to "disqualify" it.

It is worth noting, in this connection, the precise wording of the proposal that Daniels authorized when he said, "Go for it. Disqualify propaganda." David Shane proposed a plan "*quietly*" to do "a 'what's needed' list (subject matter knowledge plus results-focused pedagogy) & then '*survey*' each of the major institutions & see how it matches up. Would force to daylight a lot of the excrement" (emphasis added). But why would anyone with the slightest concern for democracy propose (or approve) undertaking such a project "quietly"? Shouldn't such an effort be carried out publicly, with input from teachers solicited, and different points of view given careful consideration? One suspects that the point of proceeding "quietly" is precisely to prevent those who disagree with the education views of Daniels and his team from having a chance to be heard. And what legitimate reason could there possibly be for putting the word "survey" in quotation marks? Is the implication that no genuine fact-finding effort would be undertaken, but rather that the word "survey" would be used simply to provide cover for an attempt to suppress the teaching of ideas that Daniels disliked?

Those familiar with Daniels's writings might also wonder how his actions in this case can be squared with the views he advocates in his book, *Keeping the Republic: Saving America by Trusting Americans* (KTR). There he decries the "steady decline in freedom" that he sees as resulting from the activities of government bureaucrats, who "try to regulate every aspect of our lives." Daniels speaks disdainfully of the claim of superior expertise that he finds to be implicit in their actions. Indeed, he sarcastically calls such bureaucrats "our Benevolent Betters," and argues at length—indeed, as the subtitle suggests, this is one of the major themes of his book—that we would be much freer, and much better off, if we trusted Americans to go about their business without such meddling (KTR 60–2, 72–4, 156, 214, 221).[10] Well then, why not leave history teachers alone and let them decide what to teach? Why should Daniels, by his own logic, not be condemned as a meddling, freedom-destroying "Benevolent Better"—one who arrogantly assumes that his judgment is superior to that of the good folks who teach history in Indiana, and who, even more arrogantly, attempts to impose that judgment unilaterally, by force, and without even bothering first to consult those professionals whose judgment he would overturn?

While Daniels has not, to my knowledge, offered any explanation of how his attempt to ban Zinn can be reconciled with his critique of "our Benevolent Betters," presumably he would base his defense on an appeal to his responsibility as governor to oversee public education.[11] But surely such responsibility does not entail that a governor should intervene at the micro-level, such as in choosing textbooks, any more than a CEO of a hospital should dictate to surgeons what surgical techniques they should use or the owner of a baseball team should tell the pitching coach how to teach pitching.

And such meddling is rendered all the more troubling when the meddler displays a defective grasp of the activity over which he insists on asserting his authority. Such is the case with Daniels's dubious claim, for which he offers no evidence, that the assigning of Zinn's work amounts to a "force-feeding" of his theories and conclusions, as if teachers and students were incapable of engaging Zinn's claims thoughtfully and critically. Indeed, the comparison of reading to eating betrays a serious misunderstanding of the nature of education. When a person eats something, the food produces effects in the body, but the eater plays no active role in this process beyond the act of eating itself. Once the food is in the body, the eater exerts no control over the results. But reading, in quite radical contrast, calls for constant interaction between the reader and the text. The reader's rationality is continually engaged, as he or she interprets the text, assesses its cogency, evaluates its significance, and, in general, considers how to respond to it. Reading is not like eating, and assigning a text is not at all the same thing as "force-feeding" it to one's student. No competent teacher encourages a passive approach to reading, in which the process of learning is analogous to digestion.

Similarly disturbing questions of competence are raised by Daniels's implicit claim to know, based solely on the title of an Indiana University course ("Social Movements in Modern America: Labor, Civil Rights, and Feminism") and on Scott Jenkins's incomplete, undetailed, one-sentence description of its reading list, that the course will be "crap," that "no student will be better taught because someone sat through this session," and that the seminar "should not be accepted for any credit by the state." Wouldn't one, at a bare minimum, need to know a few more details about the course contents, and about how it would be taught, to be in a position to make such sweeping judgments competently?

And matters only get worse for Daniels when we turn to his later statements, those that he issued following the disclosure of the emails and the ensuing criticism. First of all, how can it be seriously maintained that Daniels's emails "had nothing to do with higher education at all"? His initial email, in which he inquired as to how to "get rid of Zinn's book," so that it "is not in use anywhere in Indiana," mentioned both high schools and colleges, and drew no distinction between them. Then, the one class that was specifically discussed during his subsequent exchange with his subordinates was a course offered at Indiana University, not at a K-12 school. It was in connection with this *university* course that Daniels had instructed his colleagues to "Go for it. Disqualify propaganda." It is noteworthy, in this connection that, according to Associated Press reporter, Tom LoBianco, in Daniels's meeting with the press following the publication of his emails he "declined to speak with the AP. Neither he nor his spokesperson replied to questions about his statement's focus on K-12 classrooms despite the emails' references to classes taught at the state's public universities" (DDT).

Indeed, Daniels has offered very little by way of explanation of, or support for, his after-the-fact interpretation of his emails as having been concerned only with K-12 education. Rather, for the most part he has simply *asserted*, in effect asking us to take his word for it, that when he instructed state education officials in 2010 to make sure that Zinn's history text was "not in use anywhere" in the state, he was talking solely about middle school classrooms, rather than universities, that his "only concern in two e-mail questions years ago was what was being taught to middle school children in their formative lessons in American history," and that his "questions expressed no interest in higher education" (RPF).

Standing in the way of this interpretation is the simple fact that if Daniels had wanted to communicate that his concerns were confined to questions of what is taught at the middle school level, it would have been quite easy for him to communicate that limitation clearly. Instead, he quoted a claim that Zinn's book was "the textbook of choice in *high schools and colleges* around the country" (emphasis added); then, just two sentences later, asked whether it is "in use *anywhere in Indiana*" (emphasis added); and then, in the next sentence, asked how, if it is in use, we can "get rid of it." In the absence of any clarifying or qualifying statement saying otherwise, wouldn't any reasonable reader infer that Daniels's questions pertained to high school- and college-level education, at least as much as to any level that is not mentioned at all—such as that of middle school? Indeed, if Daniels were trying to communicate by these utterances that his concerns were confined to the middle school arena, wouldn't he have to be judged, at least in this instance, as having been extraordinarily inarticulate? Given that Daniels, for all his other faults, is certainly not inarticulate, does not this consideration speak against his after-the-fact explanation of his intent in the emails? Indeed, doesn't it strongly suggest that this explanation is a prime example of "revisionist history"?

And this problem is exacerbated by the fact that Daniels's explanation obviously conflicts with the entire remainder of the email exchange following his initial salvo, since that discussion was devoted, first, to a university course, and then to a review of university courses statewide. For at no time during that discussion did Daniels say anything like, "wait a minute—why are we talking about university courses? My only concern is about impressionable middle-schoolers. Let's get back on track!" Instead he said, specifically in reference to university courses, "Go for it. Disqualify propaganda."

Another puzzling feature of Daniels's after-the-fact

commentary on his initial emails is the utterly inappropriate tone he has adopted in his criticism of the original Associated Press article in which their contents were first disclosed. For Daniels's claims about the intended meaning of those emails are tenable only on the assumption that he had rather miserably failed to make his meaning clear during the initial email exchange. Accordingly, in attempting to set the record straight, he should have taken responsibility for the (alleged) misunderstanding and said something like, "I would like to correct the false impression created by the imprecise and misleading language of my emails." But instead, he began his response to the AP article this way: "I would like to respond to a muddled and misleading article that has been in the media this week. If the article were an accurate representation of my actions, I would be the first to agree with the many concerns I have heard" (SPD). Similarly, in interviews with reporters conducted at Purdue, Daniels called the AP report "unfair and erroneous" (DDT). If Daniels's claims about his intended meaning are true, then the report is, indeed, erroneous. But since the error would, on that assumption, have been entirely due to his own inarticulateness, it is hard to see how he could make a case that the report was unfair.

Similarly disturbing is a statement that the Purdue Board of Trustees issued in support of Daniels: "What we see [in the AP article] is a complete misrepresentation of President Daniels' views and concerns. The exchange had nothing to do with academic freedom or censorship. Rather, it had to do with concerns over what is being taught in Indiana's K-12 public schools.... The board rejects as totally misleading the original article and reaffirms its unanimous and complete support of President Daniels."[12] Naturally, the Board offered no explanation as to how its interpretation could be squared with the plain meaning of the words in Daniels's email communications. Nor did it address the obvious point that Daniels would have a clear motive, when offering his after-the-fact interpretation of the meaning of those words, to ward off criticism from the university constituency with which he must deal in his capacity as the president of Purdue University. For recall that his Zinn emails, written when he was governor of Indiana, rather than president of Purdue University, had not been intended for public consumption, but rather had been issued privately, and to his like-minded subordinates, with no expectation that they would ever be viewed by, and have to be defended to, anyone who did not share his political stance.

Like the Board of Trustees, Daniels has, for the most part, declined to explain his bizarre interpretation of the meaning of his initial emails, preferring instead simply to assert it on his authority as their author, and to imply that his critics are malicious, unfair, and incapable of reading. But to be fair, it should be pointed out that he has on two occasions attempted to explain, albeit tersely, why he called for action against a university course, and how that can be reconciled with his claim that his emails were exclusively concerned with K-12 (or, in some versions, just middle school, or in others, just eighth-grade) education. In remarks to *Inside Higher Ed,* Daniels "said that his concern about Zinn was appropriate because elementary and secondary school teachers were taking professional development courses at public universities that could have been teaching Zinn's work, and he did not want these teachers—and their students—exposed to 'falsifications' of history" (JAS). And he elsewhere asserted that the point of his emails was "only to inquire whether a book I (and legions of other, more expert commentators) consider highly misleading was in use in our elementary or secondary schools, *or whether the state should encourage and reward its teaching through professional career advantages it awards as 'professional development'*" (RPF, emphasis added). So now we have something of an explanation from Daniels as to how he can inquire about, and meddle in, university courses, and yet still maintain that such actions "ha[ve] nothing to do with higher education at all," that his questions "expressed no interest in higher education," and that his "only concern in two e-mail questions years ago was what was being taught to middle school children in their formative lessons in American history." The explanation, evidently, is that the university courses interested him, not for their own sake, but rather only insofar as they might ultimately affect middle school education. Elementary and secondary school teachers who are "exposed" in university courses to Zinn's "falsifications" of history might then pass on those falsifications to their students, especially if the teachers are encouraged and rewarded for taking such courses by receiving professional development credit. Therefore, by Daniels's unique logic (fully backed by the Purdue Board of Trustees), calling for the "getting rid of" or the "disqualification" of Zinn's text from university courses has nothing at all to do with those same university courses, because the *underlying reason* for such actions is unrelated to any concern about university education itself, but rather is based on the worry that the taking of such university courses might lead to bad results in middle school education.

But this argument obviously lacks cogency and serves only to create more problems for Daniels's position. First, it is fallacious to attempt to reduce intent or interest to ultimate goals, and to deny that these categories also apply to the instruments used to achieve those goals. If I were to torture you during an interrogation, with the intent of persuading you to reveal information that you would otherwise refuse to divulge, it would be absurd for me to claim that I had "no interest" in hurting you, since my motive in torturing you is not sadism, but rather is based on my ultimate goal of obtaining the information. Rather, the more accurate analysis would be that I am interested in hurting you, but that my interest is instrumental—I am interested in hurting you, but only as a means to a quite different end. Clearly, it is equally absurd for Daniels to claim that his questions and actions "expressed no interest in higher education." Rather, his attempt unilaterally to dictate changes to higher education obviously did express an interest in higher education, even if that interest was instrumental rather than ultimate.

Second, and in the event that this strikes the reader as quibbling or as verbal nit-picking, notice the enormously disturbing *practical* implications of Daniels's argument. For now Daniels's many reassuring statements that he will not interfere with teaching at the university level must be understood this way: "I will not interfere with teaching at the university level, unless such interference has the effect of improving the quality of middle school teaching, in which case it doesn't even count as interference at the university level, because such interference isn't the ultimate purpose of the action in question, and isn't based on any concern about university education." By the same logic, other comforting utterances would have to be similarly interpreted. For example, when several Purdue professors expressed the worry that Daniels's Zinn emails, when read in conjunction with some of his other statements, might imply that Daniels would seek to overturn the tenure system, he replied as follows: "I support the tenure system as a protection of academic freedom.... I have nothing to do with faculty tenure and promotion decisions and would never seek any role" (RPF). But what if an education professor, overwhelmingly qualified for tenure, and endorsed for tenure by all of the faculty committees involved in the tenure process, also happened to be an admirer of Zinn, and encouraged his or her students (future teachers in middle schools) to teach Zinn? If Daniels's argument about his Zinn emails were to be granted cogency, there would be nothing to stop him in such a case from interfering in the tenure process, denying tenure to the professor, and then claiming that his action expressed no interest in the tenure system, and did not constitute participation in it or interference with it, since the ultimate purpose of his action had nothing to do with tenure, or with anything else having to do with university education, but rather was ultimately based on concern about middle school education. And if the ultimate purpose/instrumental means distinction is indeed the key to his argument, then there is no need to assume that only concerns about middle school education would justify tampering with university education (and then claiming that the action had nothing to do with university education). The same "logic" would work for, say, firing a tenured professor who criticized a U.S. war effort. So long as such an action was based on concerns about national defense, it could be defended as having nothing whatsoever to do with university education. And no doubt the (Daniels-appointed) trustees would agree, and would reject any suggestion to the contrary as "misleading" and "unfair" — a complete "misrepresentation of President Daniels' views and concerns."

Finally, the explanation that Daniels has offered for his concern about middle school education completely, albeit unwittingly, undercuts his rationale for taking action against university courses that, in his view, ultimately harm middle school education. In one of the many explanations of his original emails that he has given after they were published, he claimed that his "only comment was, I didn't think [Zinn's book] belonged in an eighth-grade classroom, where there's one teacher, no critical thinking skills developed, I mean one book and young children, and what the teacher says is gospel." He then offered the assurance that, by contrast, "Anything that anybody wants to do on our campus is absolutely fine with me, because at a college campus there's more than one book, and ideas are freely debated, and the students have some level of — we hope — of critical thinking" (WAR).

Before moving on to my main point about this passage, notice that it completely misrepresents the content of his original emails. It is simply false to claim that in those emails his "only comment" was that Zinn's book did not belong in an eighth-grade classroom. He made no such comment there, and in fact never mentioned eighth-grade (or middle school more generally) education at all. Nor did he say anything about one book, one teacher, an absence of critical thinking skills, or the teacher's word being gospel. Moreover, if, in contrast to the actual facts, he had said something about these things, it would still be ludicrously false to say that such a statement constituted his "only comment" in the emails, since he clearly addressed several other matters. And since he must surely have known that he had made no such comment (let alone it having been his only one), it is difficult to see how this misstatement can reasonably be taken for an error rather than a deliberate lie.

Be that as it may, if Daniels truly believes what he says here about university classes, then, by his own logic, he clearly had no business interfering with a university course—even though that course was attended by middle school teachers who would return to teaching middle school after taking the course. The quick way to arrive at this conclusion is simply to draw out the implications of his statement that "Anything that anybody wants to do on our campus is absolutely fine with me." Well, the "Social Movements in America: Labor, Civil Rights, and Feminism" course at Indiana University, the one that featured Zinn on its reading list, was "something that somebody wanted to do [and did] on campus." Therefore, it should have been "fine" with Daniels.[13] Of course, a defender of Daniels could try to get cute and say that his trying to "get rid of" Zinn's book from the course, or "disqualifying" the course for credit, is perfectly compatible with his being "absolutely fine" with it. But then one would have to acknowledge that all of his reassuring utterances—about tenure, academic freedom, or what have you—are to be understood as not excluding such meddling.

But Daniels's inconsistency is more fully revealed by focusing on the specific reasons he has given for distinguishing between middle school and the university, such that his interference in the former is warranted whereas it is not in the latter. For notice that the students in the "Social Movements in America" course were not "young children," but rather adult teachers, presumably with well-developed critical thinking skills, and with no propensity to take what the teacher says as gospel. And Zinn's book was not the only one used in the course. So on what grounds, given his own stated principles, could Daniels possibly have been justified in interfering? Recall that Daniels had said that he did not want teachers of young students to be "exposed" to Zinn's [alleged] "falsifications" of history. But this contradicts his claim that such "exposure" is only problematic when those exposed are young children lacking in critical thinking skills. The adult teachers in the course in question should have been able to use their critical thinking skills so as to recognize, and to reject, any "falsifications" to which they were exposed — an exercise from which they presumably would have learned something of value (after all, given the popularity of Zinn's book, there would be value in coming to understand how other people see the world, even if that vision is defective), in addition to enjoying the benefit of exercising their critical thinking muscles. Thus, if he were to go by his own principles, Daniels should not have objected to the course, and should not have attempted to interfere with it in any way.

Similar problems attend Daniels's repeated claim that his actions had nothing to do with censorship, that he had "proposed absolutely no censorship of any person or viewpoint," and that "no one tried to 'censor' anyone's right to express any opinion they might hold." As with so many of his claims, he provided no explanation, or argument, in support of these assertions. For example, he did not tell us what he thinks the word "censorship" means, so that we might understand just what it is that he is denying when he denies that he proposed any censorship. But such an explanation or argument would seem necessary, given that his actions clearly do fit the dictionary definition of "censorship." According to *Merriam-Webster*, "censor," as a transitive verb, means "to examine books, movies, letters, etc., in order to remove things that are considered to be offensive, immoral, harmful to society, etc.," or "to examine in order to suppress or delete anything considered objectionable."[14] One need only convert this definition to the noun form in order to refute the contention that Daniels's actions "had nothing to do with censorship." Similarly, the Dictionary.com website defines a "censor" as "an official who examines books, plays, news reports, motion pictures, radio and television programs, letters, cablegrams, etc., for the purpose of suppressing parts deemed objectionable on moral, political, military, or other grounds."[15] Since Daniels attempted to "get rid of" and to "disqualify" Zinn's book, and did so because he deemed it objectionable, it is difficult to know what he could possibly mean by denying that he was acting as a "censor." One would think that he should have argued that censorship is sometimes justified, and is so in this case, as opposed to issuing the straightforwardly absurd claim that he was not attempting to engage in censorship.

While Daniels offered no explanation for his bizarre claim, I can think of two possibilities as to what he might have meant, though neither one, in my judgment, acquits him of the censorship charge. The first possibility is that he associates "censorship" with such extreme actions as burning books or imprisoning authors, so that he thinks that his milder actions do not rise to the level of "censorship." But such a position is refuted by the simple observation that there are *degrees* of censorship, since there are degrees of suppression. The fact that Daniels did not remove copies of Zinn's book from libraries and bookstores and burn them does not mean that he did not engage in censorship. For an authority to remove an item from a textbook, or a textbook from a class, because he or she objects to its content, fits the definition of censorship, even if the item or textbook in question remains available elsewhere.

Alternatively, the argument could be that Daniels cannot be accused of censoring anyone, for the simple reason that, ultimately, no action was taken—Zinn's book wasn't removed from any classroom, and credit wasn't denied to anyone who took a course with Zinn content. But such an argument is unimpressive, since Daniels did order these actions to be taken. The fact that his subordinates failed to follow through on the order does not acquit Daniels of having issued the order. This point takes on extra weight when we notice that Daniels claimed that he had "*proposed* absolutely no censorship of any person or viewpoint" (emphasis added), and that "no one *tried* to 'censor' anyone's right to express any opinion" (emphasis added). He clearly denied having *attempted* to censor—a claim that is left untouched by the attempt's having failed.

Incidentally, while, to my knowledge, no explanation has ever been offered as to why Daniels's team did not carry out his order to "disqualify" the "Social Movements in America" course or carry out a statewide review of university courses so as to "force to daylight a lot of excrement," we do have his explanation for his failure to remove Zinn's book from Indiana K-12 public schools: there was no need to do so, since the book was (allegedly) not in use anywhere in the state. But this explanation raises further questions about the competence of Daniels and his subordinates, since the conclusion that he and his team drew regarding the non-use of Zinn's book in Indiana K-12 classrooms is erroneous. I know this for two reasons. First, in the "Critical Thinking" course that I teach every year we do a brief unit on the evaluation of U.S. history textbooks. One of the readings we discuss argues that such textbooks exhibit a consistent bias in that they play up, and sometimes exaggerate, everything good and admirable in U.S. history, while playing down, if not omitting entirely, many significant events that show our nation's leaders in a negative light. When I ask the students whether they find this analysis to be accurate with respect to the history textbooks they read in high school, I find that about ten percent of the students from Indiana public high schools, year after year, say something like this: "no, it isn't, because in my history class we read Howard Zinn's *A People's History of the United States*." My experience is confirmed (and this is my second piece of evidence) by this nugget from the Zinn Education Project website: "Governor Daniels' advisers evidently found no evidence that Zinn's *A People's History of the United States* was in use in K-12 schools in Indiana. I guess they didn't look hard enough. There are more than 300 Indiana teachers registered at the Zinn Education Project to access people's history curriculum materials.... And these are only the teachers who have formally registered at the site."[16]

So Daniels's attempt to discourage people from reading Zinn did not succeed, and ultimately backfired. For not only were his orders that Zinn's text be "gotten rid of" and "disqualified" from use in Indiana classrooms never carried out, but the publicity generated by the exposure of his attack on Zinn only served to stimulate interest in Zinn's work. Indeed, in the wake of the controversy surrounding the publication of Daniels's emails, sales and library borrowings of *A People's History of the United States* soared. When Rob Burgess, of the *Kokomo Tribune* (Indiana), attempted to get a copy of the book from any nearby library (he tried Kokomo, Carmel, Fishers, and Noblesville), he found in each case that the book was checked out, and that there was a waiting list (a 91-day wait for the library in Fishers).[17] The South Bend, Indiana library system purchased 19 additional copies of Zinn's book to keep up with demand. "A few weeks ago, the St. Joseph County [Indiana] Public Library had one copy of Zinn's book. Based on demand, the county library purchased 19 additional print copies and four electronic copies. As of Monday, all those copies were checked out or on reserve, with 10 patrons on the waiting list."[18]

Nor do things get better for Daniels when we turn to his

repeated assertion that his actions "infringed on no one's academic freedom." For, once again, just as in the case with his claims about censorship, (1) his actions appear clearly to fit the dictionary definition of the relevant term, and (2) he has offered no alternative definition, leaving us somewhat in the dark as to what his denials mean.

A straightforward, uncontroversial definition of "academic freedom" is offered by the *Encyclopedia Britannica*:

> the freedom of teachers and students to teach, study, and pursue knowledge and research without unreasonable interference or restriction from law, institutional regulations, or public pressure. Its basic elements include the freedom of teachers to inquire into any subject that evokes their intellectual concern; to present their findings to their students, colleagues, and others; to publish their data and conclusions without control or censorship; and to teach in the manner they consider professionally appropriate. For students, the basic elements include the freedom to study subjects that concern them and to form conclusions for themselves and express their opinions.[19]

Nothing more need be said to refute the contention that Daniels's actions "had nothing to do with academic freedom."

As against this conclusion, Daniels offers two arguments. First, he asserts that "Academic freedom, a concept central to higher education, [is] not applicable to K-12 public education" (SAP). Therefore, since his actions (allegedly) "had nothing to do with higher education at all," but rather dealt exclusively with K-12 instruction, it follows that his actions could not possibly have infringed on anyone's academic freedom.

This argument is open to at least two objections. First, as I have argued extensively above, it simply isn't true that his actions steered clear of university education. His "Go for it. Disqualify propaganda" edict was issued in connection with a university course, not a middle school course, and authorized a plan to get rid of "crap" from university courses, not middle school courses.

Second, Daniels's claim that the concept of "academic freedom" is "not applicable to K-12 public education" is overstated. It is true that K-12 teachers have historically not been granted the same level of academic freedom that university professors enjoy. But it does not follow from this, nor is it true, that they have no academic freedom at all.[20] Moreover, there is an ongoing debate concerning the degree of academic freedom to which K-12 teachers are (or should be) entitled. It is not as if the concept of academic freedom were "inapplicable" to them in a way that, for example, a proposed right to shoes would be inapplicable to people who have no feet.

In "An Open Letter to Mitch Daniels," a response to the publication of his Zinn emails, signed by 92 members of the Purdue faculty and published on July 22, 2013, authors Susan Curtis (Professor of History and American Studies) and Kristina Bross (Associate Professor of English and American Studies) appeal to the importance of academic freedom at all academic levels, including that of K-12 education (in addition to making the point that Daniels's paternalistic concerns about exposure to wrong ideas is utterly out of place in the context of a university course for adult teachers):

[W]e note that in the original emails you were concerned in particular with a summer institute taught at Indiana University for high school teachers, not students. Surely you don't believe that fully accredited teachers need to be protected from Zinn, whatever you may believe about children being "force-fed" information that you find objectionable. We know better of our K-12 colleagues. As do all teachers, they need to read peer-reviewed scholarship from across the spectrum and be challenged with points of view that they may not hold; as we all do, they crave energetic, vibrant discussion with other professionals—just the kind of experience the program at Indiana University was designed to provide. And then, as all teachers should, they bring the insight and energy of such experiences back to their own classrooms.

We trust our colleagues to introduce young people to the facts of history, but also to the much more difficult, much more essential practices of critical thinking. We trust our K-12 colleagues to know how and when to present challenges to received knowledge and how to encourage their students to judge such challenges for themselves. And we trust them to decide how and when to use controversial scholarship such as Zinn's in their classrooms. This kind of academic freedom is essential to all levels of education, whether within a tenure system or not. And we promise you, this kind of challenging, stimulating approach will result in better, more engaging education of all Indiana students, from our five-year-old kindergartners, to members of Purdue's class of 2017, and beyond. (OLM)

It is noteworthy that Daniels, in his official reply to this letter, does not address any of the points made in the passage just quoted (RPF).

The American Historical Association also issued a statement condemning Daniels's actions, and did so in language that implicitly repudiated both his denial that K-12 teachers are entitled to any level of academic freedom and his more general attempt to justify his actions by appealing to a distinction between university and K-12 education. For example, the statement asserts: "The American Historical Association would consider any governor's action that interfered with an individual teacher's reading assignments to be inappropriate and a violation of academic freedom." Notice that the reference to "an individual teacher" does not specify that the teacher must teach at the college level. Similarly inclusive in its reference is the document's endorsement of the idea that "the open discussion of controversial books benefits students, historians, and the general public alike. Attempts to single out particular texts for suppression from *a school* or university curriculum have no place in a democratic society."[21]

Daniels's other argument for the conclusion that he has not abridged anyone's academic freedom runs as follows: "Academic freedom...does not immunize a person from criticism and certainly does not confer entitlement to have one's work inflicted upon our young people in the K-12 public school system" (SPD).

Here again, there are two problems. First, Daniels also attempted to prevent Zinn's work from being "inflicted" on adult teachers in university courses. But second, and more fundamentally, the argument is a red herring. No one on the other side has ever claimed that academic freedom "immunizes a person from criticism." Nor has anyone ever suggested that academic freedom (or, for that matter, having tenure—as Daniels has made the same argument in connection with that) "confers entitlement to have one's work" taught in any school. Daniels is attacking a straw man.

Let's take these last two points in turn. It is startling, as we will see below, how many of Daniels's defenders have tried to cast the controversy over his Zinn emails as being about whether or not he had the right to criticize Zinn. It has been repeatedly asserted that the issue boils down to leftists' alleged intolerance of criticism of one of their heroes. This is nonsense. The outrage directed against Daniels has been based not on his having criticized Zinn, but rather on his having attempted to make sure that Zinn's book "is not in use anywhere in Indiana." John K. Wilson, in making an argument that Daniels should be fired, draws the distinction clearly, and expresses, I think, the consensus view among Daniels's critics: "I believe that academic freedom protects everyone at a university, including college presidents. I believe Daniels should be free to express his incredibly stupid views about Zinn, without fear of any retaliation. But what Daniels did as governor went far beyond expression. He actively suppressed academic freedom" (MDF).[22]

Even more absurd is Daniels's suggestion that banning a book from a classroom does not violate academic freedom since academic freedom "does not confer entitlement" to have one's work taught in schools. From the standpoint of academic freedom, the problem with Daniels's attempt to "disqualify" Zinn's book from use in the Indiana University course on "Social Movements in America" is not that Zinn, by virtue of his status as a tenured professor, or as a person entitled to academic freedom, thereby has some sort of right to have his work taught. Indeed, Zinn, who was by then dead, is not even the person whose right to academic freedom was threatened by Daniels's actions. Rather, the rights in question are those of the professor who teaches the course (and who, in radical contrast to the governor, has proven expertise in its subject area) to select the course textbooks, and of the students who elect to take the course (university course syllabi are often published prior to the start of the class; and even when they are not, they are usually distributed on the first day of class, thus affording students the opportunity to drop the course if they don't find the reading list to be to their liking). The fallacy in Daniels's argument, then, is that it misidentifies the basis on which it is established that a particular book has a right to be taught in a particular class. Having tenure does not "confer an entitlement" to have one's work taught in the public schools. (No one had put forth the bizarre thesis that it does—Daniels was, once again, attacking a straw man.) But being chosen by a professor for assignment to his or her students does "confer such an entitlement," which Daniels tried to violate. It is as if he were to argue that he would be justified in taking my Martin guitar from me, since my status as a tenured professor does not confer the right to have such a guitar. Indeed, it does not, but that is not the issue. The guitar is mine, not because I have tenure, but because I legally purchased it. Similarly, Zinn's book belongs in the classroom because (and only to the extent that) teachers and students choose to study it. A politician's attempt to interfere with that choice is an assault on their academic freedom, just as much as his (hypothetical) taking of my guitar would be an instance of theft.

So Daniels's principal claims in defense of his Zinn emails—that they were exclusively concerned with K-12 education, that they had nothing to do with censorship, and that they in no way threatened anyone's academic freedom—stand exposed, not only as false, but as ludicrous, laughable, ridiculous, stupid. What, then, should we infer from the fact that the Board of Trustees uncritically, and without supplying any kind of explanation, evidence, or argument, unanimously affirmed all of these absurd claims?

First, as already noted, eight of the ten of them were appointed to their position as trustees, and the other two re-appointed, by Daniels, when he was governor. Second, Daniels took the job in spite of Indiana's "cooling off" rule that bars executive branch employees from seeking employment with organizations that do business with the state.[23] Third, Daniels's hiring appears to have violated Indiana's open meetings law. Though Purdue is a public university, the meeting of its Board of Trustees at which the trustees deliberated over the presidential hiring decision was held behind closed doors, with no public notification, at an undisclosed location in Chicago O'Hare International Airport. In response, a newspaper, the *Lafayette Journal and Courier*, filed a complaint. But, as AP reporter Tom LoBianco reports, the state's public access counselor ruled that "simply knowing the meeting would happen at the out-of-state location was open enough. When the *Indianapolis Star* went looking for records of the deliberations over Daniels's hiring,

Purdue wrote back that it had none, and even if it did, the public couldn't see them." The public access counselor who ruled that Purdue's secret, closed-door meeting at an undisclosed location fully satisfied the state's "open meetings" law, thus enabling the hiring of Mitch Daniels, had been appointed to that position by— you guessed it—Mitch Daniels.[24] In light of these considerations, I think it is fair to ask, is there anyone in the state of Indiana or on the Board of Trustees who is independent of him, and capable of holding him accountable for his actions?

In any case, let's move on to Daniels's case against Zinn. Certainly Daniels has provided plenty by way of name-calling and summary judgment. In referring to Zinn and/or his work, he has used such words and phrases as "terrible," "anti-American," "execrable," "anti-factual," "disinformation," "misstates American history on every page," "totally false," "crap," "fraud," "biased," and "purposely falsified," and claimed that Zinn's work is on a par with theories that have been decisively refuted and discredited (phrenology and Lysenkoism) and with a book (*The Protocols of the Elders of Zion*) that has been exposed as an anti-Semitic hoax. But what arguments does Daniels give in support of these harsh judgments? So far as I can see, he has offered only three. The first is an appeal to the authority of professional historians, as in his claim that Zinn "has been criticized all across the ideological spectrum," that "no one credible defended his versions of history," and that Daniels's own evaluation of Zinn reflects the "overwhelming judgment of historians." The second is that Zinn "admits" to being "a biased writer." The third is that Zinn's critique of "objectivity" allegedly undermines "the foundations of Purdue's entire research enterprise." Since a response to the latter two arguments requires a substantive engagement with Zinn's writings (something we never get from Daniels), we will have to put off considering those arguments until we have had a chance to discuss Zinn's historical and theoretical work in some detail. Accordingly, we will confine our attention here to the first argument.

The main generic problem with arguing by means of an appeal to authority is that such arguments are frustratingly indirect. Truth is determined by a reasoned examination of the relevant evidence. But here what we get is not a confrontation with the evidence itself, but rather a summary of what some other people have concluded about it. The appeal to authority therefore runs the risk of raising as many questions as it answers. Instead of asking whether the evidence truly supports a given conclusion, we are instead left to wonder whether or not the authorities consulted who have reached that conclusion have done so based on an adequate appraisal of that evidence. Our attention is thus directed away from the evidence that would confirm or disconfirm a claim, and focused instead on issues concerning the competence and honesty of the cited authorities.

Another generic problem with such appeals to authority is that, in the case of controversial matters about which there is no consensus, the appeal can easily be countered by an appeal to authorities on the other side. For example, as the letter signed by 92 Purdue faculty points out, Zinn's book upon publication received a largely favorable review in the *New York Times* from one of America's most eminent historians, Eric Foner, the DeWitt Clinton Professor of History at Columbia University, who is one of only two persons to have served as president of all three major professional organizations in the field of history (the Organization of American Historians, the American Historical Association, and the Society of American Historians), and is the recipient of two prestigious prizes: the Bancroft and the Pulitzer. As he received these awards and distinctions after praising Zinn, it can be inferred that his colleagues did not take that praise as indicating professional incompetence.[25] And Foner reasserted his appreciation for Zinn's work in two 2010 articles (ZCH; MIL). Two other historians, Martin Duberman (Distinguished Professor Emeritus of History at the CUNY Graduate Center, Bancroft Prize winner, and recipient of the American Historical Association's Lifetime Achievement Award) and Davis D. Joyce (Professor Emeritus of History at East Central University) have written admiring biographies of Zinn (DUB; JOY). Other experts who have praised Zinn's historical works include—but remember that, according to Daniels, "no one credible defended Zinn's versions of history"!—Ron Briley,[26] William H. Chafe,[27] Carl Cohen,[28] Robert Cohen,[29] Blanche Wiesen Cook,[30] Merle Curti,[31] Susan Curtis,[32] Kenneth C. Davis,[33] Peter Dreier,[34] Ellen DuBois,[35] Mark A. Graber,[36] James Green,[37] Jack P. Greene,[38] David Kennedy,[39] James Levin,[40] James W. Loewen,[41] Thaddeus Russell,[42] Robert C. Twombly,[43] Kelly Welch,[44] Henry West,[45] and Donald Wright,[46] to name just a few. A quick web search of articles on the Daniels–Zinn affair will turn up many other fully credentialed historians who have rushed to Zinn's defense. Additionally, Zinn's works have been cited in over 7000 scholarly articles. In the great majority of these articles, the primary point of the citation is to apply or otherwise make positive use of Zinn's findings, rather than to reject them.[47]

It should be noted, further, in the light of Daniels's comparison of Zinn's writings on history to phrenology, Lysenkoism, and *The Protocols of the Elders of Zion*, that readers who use any search engine to locate scholarly articles on these items will have difficulty finding any that evaluate them positively, or even in a neutral manner. To the contrary, when phrenology and Lysenkoism are discussed in scholarly literature, they are routinely dismissed as discredited pseudosciences, just as *The Protocols of the Elders of Zion* is uniformly referred to as a "hoax" or a "lie." By contrast, while Zinn has plenty of detractors, he also has many enthusiastic supporters; and there are literally hundreds (or, more likely, thousands) of scholars who cite his findings positively in the context of developing their own scholarly projects. Daniels's analogy is unsound.

The fact that Daniels's critique of Zinn consists of almost

nothing but quotations from other writers raises, once again, questions about his intellectual standards. We would expect our freshman students to do more, and to do better, in criticizing an author, than simply finding some quotes by a few experts who also are critical of that author. That's much too easy, and proves little—it can be easily done to almost any prominent author, including Daniels's favorites, such as the economists Milton Friedman and Friedrich Hayek. To illustrate this point, let's do it to Oscar Handlin, the Pulitzer Prize-winning Harvard University Professor of History—the author of the nastiest of the anti-Zinn comments that Daniels cited as "proof" that his concerns about Zinn were "well-founded." And since Handlin's harsh comments on Zinn that Daniels cited were all drawn from Handlin's review of one of Zinn's books, his *A People's History of the United States*, let's limit our inquiry to a couple of reviews, by experts, of just one of *his* books, *Truth in History*, a book published by Harvard University Press at roughly the same time (1979) as Zinn's book (1980).

Bruce Kuklick, Nichols Professor of American History at the University of Pennsylvania, and author of at least ten books in American history, reviewed Handlin's book in *Social Science History* (Vol. 5, No. 2 [Spring 1981], 238–9). One passage reads as follows: "I'm unimpressed. His ideas about logic, methodology, and the philosophy of history are unsophisticated; his ideas about quantification and the connection of history to the social sciences are not worth much time. He seems to be a fan of Charles Peirce but his repeated belief that Peirce and the other pragmatists adhered to a correspondence theory of truth is false" (239).

Paul K. Conkin, Distinguished Professor of History at Vanderbilt University, President of the Southern Historical Association, and award-winning author of several books in American history, reviewed Handlin's book in *History and Theory* (Vol. 19, No. 2 [February 1980], 224–37). In the first paragraph of his review he complains about his experience of "struggling through Oscar Handlin's inept, often naïve commentary on the history profession," and states that he is "sorry that this ill-focused and often angry book ever reached print" (224). Still on the first page, he informs the reader that Handlin "quickly falls into confusion. Rarely can he maintain a clear and coherent argument for more than one paragraph." Further, "For his purposes he needs an informed understanding of most other empirical disciplines, and in addition a proclivity for philo-sophical reasoning. He lacks both. His frequent references to other fields...are facile at best, completely mistaken at worst. He glibly refers to a wide array of experts in many fields..., but rarely does he understand the exact point of view of such experts. He displays no bent at all for philosophical complication, for the endless distinctions and qualifications needed to flesh out any clear and consistent position" (224). Still further, "Handlin consistently confuses words and concepts." "On numbers, Handlin offers nothing but confusion.... Throughout he confuses numbers with objects counted or measured" (225). "From this verbal confusion, I am hard put to know what Handlin is trying to tell us." "Handlin cannot carry through anything close to a convincing appraisal of Cold War historiography" (226). Conkin later says of one of Handlin's recommendations, "I cannot conceive of worse advice," (231) speaks of "Handlin's confused arguments about the uses of history," (232) and asserts that "his position is far-fetched and his fumbling defense of it only makes this obvious" (233). Finally, in the concluding paragraph of the review, Conklin refers to "the manifest confusions" that he finds "in almost every statement Handlin makes about history" (236).

While several other similarly negative comments on Handlin could be provided, it should be clearly stated that they would not reflect a consensus opinion on his work. To the contrary, Handlin has a great many admirers, as well as detractors, among his peers. In this respect he strongly resembles Howard Zinn, though one would never learn that from Mitch Daniels.

Indeed, just as Daniels's reliance on an argument from authority reflects negatively on his intellectual standards, so does his gross misrepresentation of Zinn's standing among professional historians reflect negatively on his moral standards. To list only experts who are harshly critical of Zinn, and not to mention that many others admire and recommend his work (and further, to assert, as Daniels did, that there are no such "credible" experts), is intellectually dishonest. The "Open Letter" signed by 92 Purdue faculty did not miss this point: "we...note that you do not quote the many positive reviews of [Zinn's] work—just the kind of biased presentation you accuse Zinn of making in his publications. For every negative comment that you note in your letter, you can find a positive one published in expert venues" (OLM). In Daniels's reply to this letter (RPF) he offers no rebuttal to this gently-phrased charge of intellectual dishonesty, and no explanation either for his failure to acknowledge the professional historians who admire Zinn or (what is even worse) his false claim that there are none.

He does offer something of a reply to the letter's claim that there are as many positive as negative comments on Zinn in professional books and journals: "I do respectfully disagree that Prof. Zinn's work is as widely accepted or as mainstream as you portray it. By his own avowal, it expresses his biases in what it includes and just as notably in what it omits. That is why it has been criticized all across the ideological spectrum." I would offer four points in response.

(1) Daniels's comment is non-responsive. The faculty did not deny that Zinn has been widely criticized. No one has claimed that he is uncontroversial. Rather, the faculty's assertion was that he is widely praised, and every bit as much as he is also, admittedly, widely criticized. This claim is obviously left completely untouched by the (reiterated) observation that he is widely criticized.

(2) It is significant that Daniels cites Zinn's bias, and specifi-

cally mentions his omissions, as the reason for the widespread criticism he has received. This is highly ironic, given that the letter, as quoted in the immediately preceding paragraph, accuses Daniels of precisely the same bias, and implicitly charges him with hypocrisy, in omitting to mention the praise that Zinn's work has garnered. Daniels (a) declines to answer the criticism (indeed, he completely ignores it), (b) repeats the behavior (that of giving a one-sided presentation of the critical reception of Zinn's work) that gave rise to the charge in the first place, and (c) accuses *Zinn* of objectionable bias.

(3) Daniels fails to explain how it can be that, if Zinn is indeed universally repudiated by professional historians, his book is nonetheless, as the quotation that Daniels sent to his subordinates in his initial email put it, "the textbook of choice in high schools and colleges around the country." After all, at the college and university level, textbooks for each course are generally chosen by the faculty who teach them. So the popularity of Zinn's book, at least at that level, must be due to the choices of professional historians. And in what sense is a book that has sold over two million copies not "mainstream"?

(4) In Daniels's RPF he fails to address the implications of his remarks with regard to the history faculty at his own university. The faculty "Open Letter" (OLM) co-written by a Purdue University Professor of History who specializes in American history, and signed by 16 Purdue history professors, explicitly rejects Daniels's hostile characterization of Zinn's work. Moreover, the letter points out that Daniels's "assessment of Zinn's work goes against the judgment of Purdue's own faculty members, many of whom do include his work in their syllabi or in their published research—not to mention historians across the nation and the world." Now, since Daniels is on record as saying that "no one credible defended Zinn's versions of history," does this mean that Daniels regards several of the history professors at his own university as "not credible"? He does not comment on

this issue.

But the errors and distortions in Daniels's representation of the critical reception of Zinn's work are not limited to his failure to acknowledge the many professional historians who praise and recommend Zinn's historical writings, or worse, his false insistence that there are no such historians. For in addition, he misrepresents the views of the historians whose criticisms of Zinn he does cite. Recall that when Daniels quotes historians who criticize Zinn, he does so in support of his claim that his own perspective on Zinn is in line with the "overwhelming judgment of historians," and that "no one need take my word that my concerns were well-founded." The implication is that the quoted historians judge Zinn as harshly as Daniels does. But while they do indeed criticize Zinn in harsh terms, none, with the possible exception of Handlin, approach the severity of Daniels. They, unlike Daniels, do not issue such extreme claims as that Zinn's work is "totally false," or that it "misstates American history on every page." Nor do they compare Zinn's work to anything like phrenology or Lysenkoism, thus fallaciously conflating something that is merely controversial (Zinn's approach to history) with ideas that have been conclusively refuted and are now unanimously rejected by the scholarly community. Even more significantly, they do not call him a "fraud," claim that he "purposely falsified" anything, or compare his work to *The Protocols of the Elders of Zion,* a work that has been exposed as a hoax. John K. Wilson makes the point clearly and accurately: "Like many historians who write for a popular audience, and who express strong opinions, Zinn had his detractors. But I know of no academic except Daniels who imagines that Zinn purposefully lied in his work" (MDF).

Once again, this raises disturbing questions about Daniels's moral standards. To accuse someone publicly of purposeful falsification, and to call him a fraud, all without producing a shred of evidence to support such charges is, perhaps, consistent with the *de facto* moral standards of the world of contemporary American electoral politics—the world from which Daniels came when he transitioned to a leadership role in academia. But it is not consistent with the prevailing standards at American universities.

Daniels's attempt to equate the opinions about Zinn of the professional historians he quotes with his own much more severe views also overlooks the fact that different criticisms of scholarly works, even when they are strongly worded, admit of many distinctions, both qualitative and quantitative. A harshly worded criticism might, for example, be based on the conviction that there is a flaw in the methodology used in the criticized work, or that some of its conclusions are not adequately supported by the cited data, or that it overlooks something important, or that there is another perspective on the relevant data that makes more sense, all things considered. It need not mean (unless it explicitly says so) that the criticized work is incompetent, or worthless, or fraudulent, or not worth reading or studying. Still less can one infer from such criticism that the critic thinks that it would be wrong for a teacher to assign the work in question to students. And it would be an even greater error to assume that the critic would consider it appropriate for a governor, or any other such official, to order that the book be banned, or removed from a classroom, or be the cause of denying credit for a course using the work.

And indeed, because Daniels made the mistake of including living historians, capable of commenting on his actions, among the Zinn critics he chose to quote, his appeal to their authority ultimately backfired. In an article entitled "The Historians Cited by Mitch Daniels Denounce Him," John K. Wilson explains and documents this:

In his statement defending his efforts to censor Zinn's book, Mitch Daniels argued, "Respected scholars and communicators of all ideologies agree that the work of Howard Zinn was irredeemably slanted and unsuited for teaching to school-children." I surveyed the living historians cited by Daniels, and got responses from three of them, who unanimously condemned Daniels.

Academe Blog posted Michael Kazin's response last night, in which Kazin wrote that Daniels "should be roundly condemned for his attempts to stop students from reading Zinn's big book and for calling Zinn a liar..." Kazin wrote about Zinn's book, "chapters of it can be quite useful if contrasted with alternative interpretations."

Sam Wineburg took to Twitter to respond to Daniels, writing: "Mitch Daniels uses my work to defend his shameless attempts to censor free speech. Shame!" Wineburg noted, "I have criticized Zinn but will defend to my death the right to teach him. Shame on Mitch Daniels." He explained, "Mr. Daniels, free societies openly teach ideas we disagree with. We do not censor objectionable speech. Study your Orwell." As Wineburg put it, "How could I possibly agree that 'banning Zinn' makes sense when I assign him in my own classes?"

Michael Kammen disagreed with Daniels' belief that Zinn "intentionally falsified" his work. While Kammen might not recommend the use of Zinn's book in schools today, it is "only because it was written 35 years ago and there are now more balanced and judicious treatments of the US survey." Kammen also rejected Daniels' view about banning Zinn's work from professional development classes for teachers: "I think that some teachers might need to know about its emphases because when Zinn wrote the US history textbooks omitted a great deal. Although it is not a great book, it remains a kind of historiographical landmark. Teachers should at least be aware of it." And Kammen emphatically opposed the idea of politicians deciding what books should be used in schools rather than historians and teachers: "Absolutely not!" (HCD)

Nor was Daniels's appeal to historical consensus even consistent with his own publicly expressed philosophy. For just as his attempt to meddle in the textbook decisions of history teachers contradicted his critique of the arrogance of the "Benevolent Betters," so does his appeal to the (alleged) consensus of historians contradict his rejection of appeals to consensus in connection with global warming. In his May 30, 2009 Commencement Address at the Rose-Hulman Institute of Technology, then-Governor Daniels complained that the public debate about global warming, "so far, has been dominated by 'experts' from the University of Hollywood and the P.C. Institute of Technology." He went on to urge the graduates to challenge scientific orthodoxy with regard to global warming. In support of his claim that such a challenge would require "courage," Daniels charged that "anyone raising a contrary viewpoint or even a challenging question [on this issue] is often subjected to vicious personal criticism. Any dissident voice is likely to be the target of a fatwa issued by one Ayatollah or another of the climate change theocracy, branding the dissenter as a 'denier' for refusing to bow down to the 'scientific consensus.'" Daniels then launched his broadside against appeals to consensus:

The late author and scientist Michael Crichton spoke witheringly of this pattern in a speech at Cal Tech. He said, "I regard consensus science as an extremely pernicious development that should be stopped cold in its tracks. Historically, the claim of consensus has been the first refuge of scoundrels; it is a way to avoid debate by claiming that the matter is already settled.... Let's be clear: The work of science has nothing whatever to do with consensus. Consensus is the business of politics. In science consensus is irrelevant. What is relevant is reproducible results. The greatest scientists in history are great precisely because they broke with the consensus." He's right, of course: Galileo was a denier. Darwin was a denier.

Einstein denied virtually everything men "knew" at the time.

Crichton concluded by saying "There is no such thing as consensus science. If it's consensus, it isn't science. If it's science, it isn't consensus. Period." Defending the scientific method, and reaching scientifically sound public decisions, will require credible people to speak up. When I say these things, that's just one more politician spouting off. If a Rose-Hulman grad says them, people will have to listen.[48]

But if appeals to consensus are illegitimate in science, why does Daniels think they are appropriate in history? He does not say. Is not evidence, rather than the opinion of experts, the ultimate arbiter in both disciplines? Daniels is silent on this question. And if Zinn goes against consensus views in history, why does Daniels not consider the possibility that he, like Galileo, Darwin, and Einstein, is "great precisely because [he] broke with the consensus"? He does not address this issue. In the absence of answers to these questions, Daniels appears to be guilty of a straightforward inconsistency:

He appeals to consensus in criticizing Zinn; but he ridicules an appeal to consensus in connection with global warming. It is difficult to see any principled basis for such a distinction. It is far more likely that, just as in the case of his critique of the "Benevolent Betters," he invokes lofty principles when doing so serves his political purposes, and readily jettisons them when they stand in his way. Once again, these are the intellectual and ethical standards of contemporary American electoral politics, rather than those of scholarly teaching and research in American universities.

Notice, further, that even if we confine our attention to the passage just quoted, Daniels sends a very mixed message on the issue of the legitimacy of appeals to authority. His main point is that only evidence ("reproducible results") matters, and that we need not respect anyone's opinion on the evidence—not even the consensus opinion of scientists on scientific questions. Surely it follows from this that in evaluating claims and arguments about global warming we should care only about the evidence supporting or undermining what is said, and precisely not the identity or credentials of the person saying it. But notice that in the very passage in which Daniels makes this point, he undercuts it twice. Recall, first, his complaint that the public debate about global warming "has been dominated by 'experts' from the University of Hollywood and the P.C. Institute of Technology." Though it is beside my present point, let me briefly point out that, to the limited extent that this claim is clear, it appears to be false, since mainstream scientists have played a larger role in the public debate about global warming than have Hollywood movie stars or others in the film business. Be that as it may, the complaint is inconsistent with his overall message. It would be an *ad hominem* fallacy to dismiss the reasoning of a Hollywood actor on global warming merely on the grounds that he or she is a movie star, rather than a scientist. The only issues should be: is the evidence presented by the movie star accurate and relevant, and are the arguments that he or she makes cogent? If these questions can be answered positively, then Daniels, by his own principles, has no grounds for complaint. And if the answers are negative, his complaint should be directed against the quality of the evidence and arguments presented, not against the (non-scientist) nature of the person providing the evidence and arguments—especially since Daniels goes out of his way to say that we should not respect a scientific consensus on this issue.

Even more amazing is the second instance in which Daniels undermines his main message. Recall that in his exhortation to the Rose-Hulman graduates to participate in the public debate over global warming, he speaks of the need for "credible people to speak up," before adding, "When I say these things, that's just one more politician spouting off. If a Rose-Hulman grad says them, people will have to listen." Notice that now the focus is completely off the evidence, and totally on the issue of who is speaking. Daniels's inconsistency—his complete inability to maintain his stated principles when they stand in the way of his political or personal interests—is once again on full display. When the overwhelming majority of climatologists and other scientists with relevant expertise on the issue go against Daniels (who aligns himself on this issue with the interests of big business and the Republican party), their opinion is to be rejected—you know, evidence is what counts; consensus has nothing to do with science; Galileo, Darwin, and Einstein were "deniers," etc., etc. But on the other hand, if experts, such as (some) Rose-Hulman gradates, were to agree with Daniels, they must be exhorted to participate in the public debate, not because they necessarily have new evidence or arguments to contribute (Daniels makes no such claim), but because people will pay attention to them and believe them—there is need for *"credible* people to speak up," and *"people will have to listen"* to Rose-Hulman graduates. Why are the tiny minority of scientists who agree (or might agree) with Daniels to be deemed "credible" and worthy of being listened to, while the overwhelming majority of scientists who disagree with him are not? Is there some principled reason for this? Daniels does not say. Indeed, here as elsewhere, and indeed typically, he seems not to notice the obvious problems and contradictions that emerge as soon as one thinks critically about his pronouncements for, say, 15 consecutive seconds. This is not the mark of a serious thinker.

Another negative mark is plagiarism, and Daniels appears to be guilty of that as well. On December 19, 2012 the Stanford University website published an article by David Plotnikoff, publicizing another article, by Stanford Professor, Sam Wineburg, on the work of Zinn. In Plotnikoff's article the following sentence appears: "Wineburg writes that a heavily filtered and weighted interpretation becomes dangerous when 'we are talking about how we educate the young, those who do not yet get the interpretive game.'"[49] Note that while Plotnikoff quotes Wineburg here, that quotation begins with the words, "we are talking about." The phrase "a heavily filtered and weighted interpretation," by contrast, is Plotnikoff's. It does not appear in Wineburg's article (WIN).

Now compare that sentence to this one, from the original "Statement from President Daniels" (available at RIL), issued in response to the controversy generated by the publication of his Zinn emails: "Stanford history education expert Sam Wineburg cautioned that exposing children to a heavily filtered and weighted interpretation such as Zinn's work is irresponsible when 'we are talking about how we educate the young, those who do not yet get the interpretive game.'" The phrase "a heavily filtered and weighted interpretation," which is neither common nor particularly felicitous, appears in both sentences, and is conjoined in the same way with the same quotation from Wineburg. And yet Daniels fails to cite Plotnikoff's article, and instead passes the sentence off as his own. Are we really to think that he had not seen Plotnikoff's piece, but had instead, independently of Plotnikoff, read Wineburg's eight-page article, which is full of negative comments on Zinn, chosen the same fragment of a sentence to quote from it, and invented the same clunky paraphrase to introduce that fragment?

Similarly, note the striking similarity between a passage from a 2010 article in *Reason* magazine by Michael C. Moynihan with a passage from the same Daniels document that was just quoted. The relevant section from Moynihan's article reads as follows:

Arthur M. Schlesinger Jr. once remarked that "I don't take him very seriously. He's a polemicist, not a historian." Last year, the liberal historian Sean Wilentz referred to the "balefully influential works of Howard Zinn." Reviewing *A People's History* in *The American Scholar*, Harvard University professor Oscar Handlin denounced "the deranged quality of his fairy tale, in which the incidents are made to fit the legend, no matter how intractable the evidence of American history." Socialist historian Michael Kazin judged Zinn's most famous work "bad history, albeit gilded with virtuous intentions." (MOY)

Here is the similar passage from Daniels (which, incidentally, is immediately followed by the plagiarized sentence on Wineburg, just discussed):

Arthur M. Schlesinger said, "I don't take him very seriously. He's a polemicist, not a historian." Socialist historian Michael Kazin judged Zinn's work as "bad history, albeit tilted with virtuous intentions" and said the book was more suited to a "conspiracy monger's website than to a work of scholarship." Reviewing the text in *The American Scholar*, Harvard University professor Oscar Handlin denounced "the deranged quality of his fairy tale, in which the incidents are made to fit the legend, no matter how intractable the evidence of American history."

How does Daniels reply to the plagiarism accusations? "Look, if there's anything I do, I write my own stuff. All of it. I always have." With regard, specifically, to Moynihan's *Reason* article, he insists, "I don't read *Reason Magazine*. I never saw what he wrote. Maybe we are just like-minded" (COL).[50] Here again, the question of moral and intellectual standards is raised. We would not accept this explanation from a freshman student. But we are asked to accept it from the president of a university.

Within a week of the publication of the "Statement from President Daniels," the document had been altered. The new version of the "Statement," which is still available, as of this writing (January 2017), at the Purdue University website, is considerably shorter. When asked for an explanation for the changes in his statement, Daniels told the *Lafayette Journal &* *Courier* that he had deleted the quotation from Wineburg because he (Wineburg) had objected to being included in the original version (COL). But this explanation is unconvincing, since (1) the Wineburg material accounts for only a fraction of the deletions; (2) complaints from quoted historians cannot explain the excision of Oscar Handlin's quotation, since Handlin, being dead, had not complained; and (3) a better explanation—one that would completely explain all of the deletions—is available: the new version removes the evidence on which the charge of plagiarism had been based.

The precise nature of the material that Daniels plagiarized— passages in which writers quote other writers who criticize Zinn—raises other disturbing questions. Despite Daniels's eagerness to "get rid of" and to "disqualify" Zinn's work, he shows no evidence of having read Zinn himself. In none of his several comments on Zinn has he ever cited specific claims or arguments of Zinn's, referred to specific passages in his writings, or presented original objections or arguments of his own. Instead, he relies exclusively on quotations from others who criticize Zinn. But the plagiarized passages suggest, further, that he probably has not even read the works of Zinn's critics that he quotes. It is not as if he has read a number of critical pieces on Zinn, and then put together his own list of quotations from their writings. Rather, he has taken the shortcut of finding other writers who have already done the (rather minimal, non-arduous work) of collecting hostile quotes on Zinn from a variety of critics. Thus, Daniels's knowledge of Zinn appears to be derived neither from primary sources (Zinn's own writings), nor secondary sources (critics who engage Zinn's own writings), but rather from tertiary sources (writers who summarize the work of others who respond critically to Zinn's work). We expect more from freshmen.

Chapter 2

Bias and Objectivity in History

One of Daniels's stated criticisms of Zinn is that he was "by his own admission a biased writer" (SAP). Another of his objections is that Zinn's critique of "objectivity" allegedly undermines "the foundations of Purdue's entire research enterprise" (RPF). Unlike most of Daniels's negative comments on Zinn, these have the virtue of addressing, however minimally, things that Zinn actually said. Responding to these criticisms is necessary, not only in order to complete our refutation of Daniels's critique of Zinn, but also to shed light on a variety of interesting and important issues having to do with the role of bias and objectivity in history, and in scholarship and teaching more generally.

A formidable obstacle to any attempt to answer Daniels's "biased writer" objection is that Daniels, consistent with his general scholarly standards, neither cites any passages in which Zinn "admits" to being a biased writer, nor offers any interpretation of what he takes such an admission to mean. Since *A People's History of the United States* is the one work of Zinn's that Daniels has specifically attacked, we might guess that the "admission" he has in mind is Zinn's statement, in that book, that it is "a biased account, one that leans in a certain direction" (APH 631). But what does Daniels take Zinn's bias to be? So far as I can see, the one bias he has attributed to him is anti-Americanism. (Recall that the opening sentence of his Zinn emails was "This terrible anti-American academic finally passed away" [EMA]).

Before moving on to address the substance of this charge of anti-Americanism, it is worth noting that, in issuing it, Daniels once again acts in opposition to one of his own stated principles. For one of the major themes of his book, *Keeping the Republic*, is that we desperately need a more civil public discourse. He decries "the politics of personalization" and the fact that seemingly "everyone these days has joined in the game of attack [and] demonization...of political differences" (KTR 169). He spends three pages (KTR 171–3) complaining about personal attacks perpetrated by "the Dobermans of the left" (KTR 173), before informing us that he has advised those on his side "not to attempt to match our opponents' invective, but rather to concede the field of hate speech to them, striking instead a contrast through a more temperate and positive politics that assumes the best in our fellow citizens" (KTR 173–4). How these sentiments are to be reconciled with his own conduct—that of gleefully announcing the (apparently long wished for) death of a political adversary, and pronouncing that adversary a "terrible anti-American"—is, of course, left unexplained. Nor is it clear how such behavior can be seen as consistent with his recommendation that we adopt a new commandment: "Speak no ill of another American" (KTR 180).

But Daniels's inconsistency is not confined to the realm of disagreements between his statements and his actions. Rather, as we have already observed in connection with his thoughts on expert opinion in science, he sometimes has great difficulty maintaining a coherent line of thought from one sentence to the next. For example, he declares that he doesn't like and doesn't use political labels, such as "conservative" or "liberal," because "labels often divide Americans into warring camps," and "this obscures the common threats we face and makes it more difficult to solve national problems" (KTR 2–3). While this argument against labeling people as "conservative" or "liberal" would, if sound, appear to cover the label "terrible anti-American" as well, that is not my present point. Rather, I wish to call attention to the fact that, right in the middle of making these points about the need not to "divide Americans into warring camps" by slapping simple-minded labels on them, Daniels comes out with this shot: A "liberal" today is "someone who seeks to subjugate individual liberty to state control" (KTR 2). Certainly there is nothing gratuitously divisive about that characterization!

Who Was Howard Zinn?

Did Zinn bring to his work an "anti-American" bias? In order to begin to answer this question, let's take a quick look at Zinn's life.[1]

Zinn was born in Brooklyn in 1922. His parents, factory workers with little formal education, were Jewish immigrants from Austria (his father, Eddie) and Russia (his mother, Jenny).

At the age of 20, eager to defeat fascism ("I saw the war as a noble crusade against racial superiority, militarism, fanatic nationalism, expansionism" [YCB 87]), Zinn volunteered to fight in World War II, and joined the U.S. Army Air Corps. He served as a bombardier from May 1943 until the end of the war, in late 1945, bombing targets in Germany, Czechoslovakia, Hungary, and Royan, France. He rose to the rank of lieutenant, and received an Air Medal, an award given to "U.S. military personnel who display heroism or perform an extraordinary achievement while onboard a plane flight."[2] (Incidentally, Mitch Daniels, that super patriot who blasts Zinn as anti-American, has no record of military service.)[3]

In 1944, during an 11-day furlough, he married Roslyn Shechter, an artist. They remained married for over 60 years, until her death in 2008. They had two children, a daughter, Myla, and a son, Jeff.

After the war, Zinn resumed his education, taking full advantage of the G.I. Bill. He graduated with a B.A. from New York University in 1951. He then moved on to graduate school at Columbia University, a prestigious Ivy League institution, earning an M.A. in history with a minor in economics (1952), and then a Ph.D. in history with a minor in political science (1958). His teachers at Columbia included several major historians of the period, including Jacques Barzun, Harry Carman, Henry Steele

Commager, David Donald, Richard Hofstadter, William Leuchtenburg, and Richard B. Morris.

While completing his doctoral dissertation he embarked on his career as a college professor, beginning at Spelman College, a liberal arts college in Atlanta, whose students were African-American women. He taught there, and served as chairman of the history and social science department, from 1956 until he was fired (for unspecified reasons, but presumably because of his many clashes with Spelman president Albert Manley, who disapproved of Zinn's political activism) at the end of the academic year in 1963. (Three other professors resigned their positions in protest over his firing. Zinn was invited back in 2005 to receive an honorary degree and to give the commencement address.) He landed on his feet, taking a job as a professor at Boston University in 1964, where he taught until his retirement in 1988.

Throughout his academic career, during his retirement, and continuing until his death (so much appreciated by Mitch Daniels) in 2010, he wrote and published prolifically, producing several notable books and scores of articles. His first book, *LaGuardia in Congress*, published in 1959, received an award from the American Historical Association. Over 50 years after its initial publication, it remains in print, and continues to be cited by contemporary historians.[4]

SNCC: The New Abolitionists, published in 1964, told the story of the Student Non-Violent Coordinating Committee, one of the most important organizations of the civil rights movement of the 1960s. In addition to doing traditional archival research, as he had done for his LaGuardia book, Zinn also interviewed the members of SNCC, and observed them in action. The book remains in print, and is widely regarded as an important scholarly resource on the history of the civil rights movement.[5]

Vietnam: The Logic of Withdrawal (VLW) was published in 1967. It is historically significant, in that it was the first book to call for an immediate U.S. withdrawal from Indochina. It quickly went through eight printings. A businessman bought over 600 copies and gave one to every U.S. senator and every member of Congress. Senator Wayne Morse of Oregon inserted part of it into the Congressional Record. It is still in print.[6]

Disobedience and Democracy: Nine Fallacies on Law and Order, which appeared in 1968, offers a point-by-point rebuttal to the arguments of then-Supreme Court justice Abe Fortas, who had written a short booklet entitled *Concerning Dissent and Civil Disobedience.* Zinn's book sold approximately 75,000 copies, and was much discussed and debated, as civil disobedience was at the time being widely practiced, both in the civil rights movement, and in protests against the Vietnam War. It is now considered a classic work on civil disobedience, and is often excerpted in anthologies on that subject. It is still in print.[7]

The Politics of History (POH), published in 1970, is notable as Zinn's major theoretical contribution to historiography and the philosophy of history. It is perhaps the work of Zinn's that is most relevant to Daniels's criticisms, since it contains Zinn's arguments about bias and objectivity in history. It remains in print.

The book that Mitch Daniels specifically attacked, *A People's History of the United States* (APH), which appeared in 1980, is, of course, by far Zinn's most famous and successful work. Though the publisher's expectations for it were quite modest, as indicated by its initial print run of a mere 4000 copies (NYT), it has now "sold upward of 2 million copies [over 2.6 million in North America alone as of 2015, according to Anthony Arnove's "Introduction" to the 2015 edition of APH, page xviii], making it the bestselling work of American history *in* American history. According to Hugh Van Dusen, [Zinn's] editor at HarperCollins, the book has increased its sales every year since its original publi-cation in 1980, a trend that has only continued since [Zinn's] death [in 2010]." Van Dusen remarks, "I have never heard of another book, from any publisher, fiction or nonfiction, on any subject, of which that can be said—and I have asked a lot of people at other publishers whether they have heard of such a book" (TIZ xxi). It is somewhat amusing to note that even Zinn's harshest right-wing critics, those who violently object to almost every other aspect of his life and work, cannot help but concede a grudging admiration for his achievement in the one arena that they seem to understand and to appreciate most—success in the marketplace. For example, in a stunningly vicious attack on Zinn, entitled "Professor of Contempt," published on the occasion of Zinn's death, Roger Kimball notes that the Amazon sales rank of Zinn's book "as of February 1, 2010, was 7. Seven." Kimball's envy is palpably on display when he goes on to comment, "That's a number most authors would climb over broken bottles to achieve 30 days after their books were published. Here it is 30 years on" (POC). Naturally, the book remains in print, with the most recent edition having appeared in 2015. It has been translated into Spanish, German, French, and at least 17 other languages.

Declarations of Independence: Cross-Examining American Ideology (DOI), published in 1990, marshals evidence from history in arguing against several beliefs that are so widely held by Americans that they can be characterized as "American ideology." For example, most Americans believe that the First Amendment guarantees our freedom of expression. Zinn devotes one chapter to debunking this by informing his readers about (1) the Alien and Sedition Acts of 1798, which made it a punishable offense to, for example, "publish…any…writings against…either house of the Congress of the U.S. or the President of the U.S., with intent to…bring either of them into contempt or disrepute"; (2) Supreme Court decisions in which the Court has interpreted the First Amendment as applying only to "prior restraint" (so that the government cannot stop one in advance from publishing an opinion it doesn't like), but not as precluding prosecution of the offending opinion after it has been published; (3) court decisions in which dubious appeals to "national security" have nonetheless resulted precisely in prior restraint—the government has been able successfully to prevent some material from being published in the first place; (4) the Espionage Act of 1917, which was used to imprison people who made anti-war speeches; (5) the Smith Act of 1940, which made it a crime to write or speak in such a way as to cause "insubordination or refusal of duty in the armed forces"; (6) court decisions upholding the supposed right of the government to prevent artists, writers, and scholars, who are not criminals but whose views the government doesn't like, from entering our country to speak, teach, engage in debate, or otherwise participate in an exchange of ideas; (7) Supreme Court decisions that have severely limited the First Amendment rights of U.S. military personnel; (8) Supreme Court decisions finding that the right to freedom of speech has to be "balanced" against the "police powers" of the states and municipalities; (9) the failure of the courts to follow precedents consistently, leaving citizens in the dark as to the nature and scope of their free speech rights; (10) the fact that citizens do not have an absolute right to "take this all the way to the Supreme Court," since no matter how egregious a lower court's decision depriving a citizen of his or her free speech rights may have been, the Court is under no obligation to hear an appeal of that decision (it only chooses to hear about one out of 80 appeals that are brought before it); (11) the fact that most citizens have neither the time nor money necessary to fight an unjust abridgement of their free speech rights in the courts, with the result that very few such abridgements are ever corrected; (12) the fact that many (though of course not all) police officers, mindful of the point noted at (11), willfully strip citizens of their free speech rights whenever doing so is in the interests of the police officers; (13) the fact that most people have little or no free speech rights on the job (such rights, in theory, protect individuals from persecution by the government, but not from being fired by their boss), with the result that many people who are highly competent at their jobs face the risk of losing their employment merely for articulating opinions that their boss does not like—even if they do this on their own time, and in their own name, without implicating their employer in their free speech act; (14) the numerous cases in which the FBI or CIA has spied on, infiltrated, harassed, and waged covert war against U.S. citizens who have peacefully and lawfully exercised their free speech rights on behalf of causes that these agencies did not like—such as civil rights for blacks and an end to the Vietnam War; (15) the fact that citizens are equal in their free speech rights only in the abstract; practically and concretely, the wealthy and powerful have the means to get their ideas across to a much greater extent than is true of the rest of us; (16) some of the many cases in which the U.S. news media, on whom we depend for information, have deferred to the government and declined to exercise their free speech rights to deliver vital information to U.S. citizens; and (17) some of the history of governmental secrecy and covert action— the point being that there can be no exchange of ideas, no free speech discussion, of that which is kept hidden. Other chapters adopt the same strategy, that of gathering together the relevant facts of history, in order to debunk such claims as that those who are poor are in that condition because they don't work hard enough; that when the U.S. intervenes in the affairs of other nations, it does so in order to promote democracy, freedom, and human rights; and that ordinary people, without wealth or power, can do nothing to ameliorate the great injustices of the world. The book is still in print, though in its newer edition it has been retitled *Passionate Declarations: Essays on War and Justice.*[8]

I'll mention Zinn's other books much more briefly. *The Southern Mystique*, published in 1964, offers an historical interpretation of the culture of the American south, where Zinn at that time lived and worked.[9] *Postwar America: 1945–1971* (PA) appeared in 1973. Similar in style and content to APH, which would come out seven years later, Zinn here presents an account of American history in the aftermath of World War II.[10] Zinn's autobiography, *You Can't Be Neutral on a Moving Train: A Personal History of Our Times* (YCB), appeared in 1994.[11] Beginning with *Failure to Quit: Reflections of an Optimistic Historian* (FTQ), published in 1993, several wide-ranging collections of Zinn's essays and/or interviews on history, politics, and education have appeared.[12] *The Future of History* (FOH) was published in 1999, followed by *Terrorism and War* (TAW) in 2002, *Artists in Times of War* (ATW) in 2003, *Howard Zinn on Democratic Education* (ODE) in 2005, *Original Zinn: Conversations on History and Politics* (OZ) in 2006, *A Power Governments Cannot Suppress* (PGC) in 2007, *The Historic Unfulfilled Promise* (HUP) in 2012, and *Some Truths Are Not Self-Evident* (KRE) in 2014. Eleven of the twelve books mentioned in this paragraph remain in print.[13]

Several anthologies of Zinn's writings, containing excerpts from his other books in addition to essays that had not been collected in earlier volumes, have also been published. These include *The Zinn Reader* (ZR),[14] originally published in 1997, *Howard Zinn on History* (OH)[15] in 2001, *Howard Zinn On War*[16] in 2001, *Howard Zinn on Race*[17] in 2011, and *The Indispensable Zinn* in 2012. There is even a volume, *Uncommon Sense from the Writings of Howard Zinn* (2009), that collects, and arranges by topic, a selection of short, aphoristic statements drawn from Zinn's many published writings.[18]

As a measure of Zinn's productivity as a writer, note that the extensive list of his writings presented above makes no mention of (1) books that he edited or co-edited, and to which he contributed both essays and introductory and other editorial material; (2) books that he co-authored; (3) shorter works that have been published as pamphlets; (4) variations on APH (for example, a children's version and a graphic novel version); and (5) countless scholarly articles, popular essays, book chapters, newspaper columns, reviews, and other writings, that have never been published in one of his own books.

Nor is this all. Zinn has also written three plays, each of which has been produced. His first play, *Emma*, about the famous anarchist writer, Emma Goldman, has been staged in New York, Boston, London, Edinburgh, and several cities in Japan (in translation).[19] It received a largely positive review from Walter Goodman in the *New York Times* (February 17, 1986): "The first act of *Emma*, Howard Zinn's play about Emma Goldman, is a small miracle. Here is a drama that holds down the heroics, polemics and didacticism to which works about heroes and heroines are prone. True, Emma is idealized; she is loving, honest, selfless, daring, but she is also human and believable." The Boston production ran for 8 months, making it the longest running play in that city for 1977. *Daughter of Venus*, a family drama about the nuclear disarmament movement first performed in 1984, has run in New York, Westport, Connecticut, and on Cape Cod.[20] A 2010 production received a favorable review from Louise Kennedy in the *Boston Globe* (June 9, 2010).[21] *Marx in Soho*, a one-man play written in 1999, is perhaps Zinn's most successful play.[22] It has been translated into at least six languages, and has been staged hundreds of times around the world. When it was performed in Greek in 2009, Zinn, at the age of 87, flew to Athens to see it (DUB 283). And the published version has been widely, and mostly favorably, reviewed.

Prolific as Zinn was as a writer, his record of productivity as a public speaker is equally impressive. As Zinn's 1960s books and essays on civil rights, the Vietnam War, civil disobedience, and other events of contemporary history began to establish him as a national figure (many of his articles were first published in *Harper's Magazine*, *The Nation*, *The New Republic*, and other publications that reached a nationwide—and not merely scholarly—readership), invitations to speak on these topics began to multiply. His great skill as a speaker—always clear, informative, thought-provoking, passionate, and, above all, warm and witty—caused the frequency of such invitations to increase, a process that was greatly accelerated by the spectacular success of APH.[23]

As his teaching schedule permitted, and even more so after his 1988 retirement, Zinn traveled extensively, both in the U.S. and abroad, speaking at high school and college graduation ceremonies, academic conferences, political rallies, and other venues. Duberman reports that even as Zinn was nearing the age of 70, he "continued to crisscross the country giving lectures, serving on panels, doing book signings. No matter where he went, he drew packed houses, with hundreds sometimes being turned away" (DUB 270). The intensity of his speaking schedule is revealed by the fact that in one month alone (October 1994—he was 72) he had 19 different speaking engagements (DUB 340 note 5), and that in November 2003 (he was 81) he spoke at seven teach-ins against the Iraq war, traveling from his home in the Boston area to such faraway places as Miami and California (DUB 303). Some sense of his achievement as a public speaker can be gleaned from the book *Howard Zinn Speaks: Collected Speeches 1963–2009* (HZS).

One might assume, given the extent of Zinn's activities as a writer and public speaker, that he would have had little time left over for his teaching duties. To the contrary, for a period of over 30 years, until his 1988 retirement, he devoted much of his time and energy to teaching. As I was a student of his at Boston University in the late 1970s, I can personally testify to his dedication. He was always in great demand as a teacher, and he readily agreed to accommodate that demand by teaching large classes. As a result, he usually taught over 400 students each semester. Ordinarily, at a large research university, such as Boston University, a professor with such a heavy teaching load would be given teaching assistants (typically graduate students) to take on all or most of the grading and to lead weekly discussion sessions that would supplement regular class sessions. But for most of his years at B.U. Zinn was denied teaching assistants. The reason is that he was an outspoken critic of the university's president, the petty, vindictive, and tyrannical

John Silber—and Silber delighted in punishing his adversaries. So he refused to allot funds to hire teaching assistants for Zinn. (Professors who refrained from crossing Silber had no difficulty in procuring teaching assistants.) So in his teaching Zinn was compelled to do all by himself work that would ordinarily be divided among at least two, but more typically three or four, different people. But he did it; and he did it with a smile.

While many teachers would be tempted, in such circumstances, to relieve their grading burden by using true-false or multiple-choice exams, as these can be graded mechanically, Zinn instead maintained high standards by requiring research projects and lengthy essays. Moreover, he invited students to come to his office to discuss their papers with him in detail. This required him to keep absurdly extensive office hours. And the line of students waiting outside his door to get his feedback and to pick his brain was always long. As one who went to his office often, I observed this at first hand.

I should point out that Zinn was not my mentor. My field was (and is) philosophy; he was a historian. My experience with his teaching was limited to taking two classes from him. There were many other students with whom he worked more closely. Nonetheless, I was astonished by the degree of interest he seemed to take in my work, and the care with which he analyzed and critiqued it.

In my experience, his great range as a scholar significantly enhanced his effectiveness as a teacher. For example, on the very first occasion in which I visited his office in order to discuss a paper I had written for him, he noticed that I was carrying a copy of Plato's *Republic*. After we had finished talking about my paper, he asked me what I thought about Plato. As our conversation unfolded I was amazed at his detailed knowledge of the *Republic*, and his ready command of that knowledge. I would make a critical argument about something Plato says in Book II of the *Republic*, and Zinn would counter with something like, "yes, but that overlooks the following distinction, which he makes in Book VII...." Since many of Zinn's critics accuse him of being a propagandist, I should also point out that all of the comments on Plato that he made during this conversation were directly responsive to my questions, or to points I was making, and all of them had the effect of deepening my grasp of Plato, and of helping me to strengthen the arguments I was developing (especially by calling to my attention considerations that I had overlooked). Once he had initiated the conversation, the entire remainder of its direction was determined by my concerns. I could not at the time, and still cannot in retrospect, detect any agenda on his part other than that of helping me. Moreover, now that I have read almost all of his published works (at the time I had read none of them), I can see in this conversation evidence that his intellectual curiosity—his reading, and learning, and thinking about things—extended far beyond the already wide domain of topics and figures that he addressed in his own projects. For, while he has written about Plato's *Crito* in connection with his work on civil disobedience, I know of no significant engagement with the *Republic* in his published writings.

On another occasion when I visited him at his office I was carrying a copy of the French philosopher Jean-Paul Sartre's *Critique de la raison dialectique*, which had not yet been translated into English. To my amazement, he initiated a conversation about that as well, and showed himself to be quite familiar with its contents. When I complimented him for having read the book, he "confessed" that he had read only parts of it, and that his knowledge had been derived in part from reviews and commentaries. In any case, since Zinn has never written anything substantial on the *Critique of Dialectical Reason* (though occasional scattered references to Sartre can be found in some of his works), this incident suggests, once again, that he was a scholar who read widely, and on a great variety of subjects, so that both his teaching and his scholarship rested on a strong foundation of knowledge.

In addition to this impressive knowledge base, and his extra-ordinary gift (acknowledged even by many of his harshest critics) for clear expression, perhaps the biggest factor leading to Zinn's success as a teacher was his relaxed, friendly, good-humored, unthreatening manner.[24] While he certainly offered a challenge to the beliefs of many of his students, which he accomplished by presenting ideas of deadly seriousness, he also did so with a light hand, and with plenty of wit and humor. He encouraged everyone, not only to participate in class discussions, but also to "challenge authority" by disagreeing with him. In my experience, those who did so were always treated with the utmost respect, and were never ridiculed, patronized, or scolded.[25] His classes, though rich in content, were fun, and my sense was that nearly everyone in them, no matter what their political orientation, not only learned a lot, but also had a good time in doing so.[26]

Several of Zinn's students have published their own accounts of his teaching. Alice Walker, the National Book Award- and Pulitzer Prize-winning author of *The Color Purple*, was a student of Zinn's at Spelman College. She calls him "the best teacher I ever had,"[27] adding, "Howard Zinn was magical as a teacher. Witty, irreverent, and wise, he loved what he was teaching and clearly wanted his students to love it also. We did" (AW). Zinn also mentions Walker in his memoir, recalling that she took a course in Russian history from him: "I tried to liven the history by having students read Gogol, Chekhov, Dostoevsky, Tolstoy. Their first written essays came in, and I read with wonderment the one by Alice Walker, on Dostoevsky and Tolstoy. Not only had I never read a paper by an undergraduate written with such critical intelligence, but I had rarely read a literary essay of such grace and style by anyone" (YCB 44). Walker recalls the same paper:

[I]nspired by [Zinn's] warm and brilliant ability to communicate ideas and conundrums and passions of the characters and complexities of Russian life in the 19th century, I flew back to my room after class and wrote my response to what I was learning about these writers and their stories that I adored. He was proud of my paper, and, in his enthusiastic fashion, waved it about. I learned later there were those among other professors at the school who thought that I could not possibly have written it. His rejoinder: "Why, there's nobody else in Atlanta who could have written it!" It would be hard not to love anyone who stood in one's corner like this. (AW)

At least one student who, by his own admission, wrote a paper that was not as good as Alice Walker's, nonetheless shares Walker's enthusiasm for Zinn's teaching. Roger Ochoa was a student of Zinn's at Boston University at the very end of his teaching career. He writes:

The unique combination of great self-confidence and greater humility made [Zinn] an enigma of sorts.... He would never point, but instead he leaned forward and raised his hand out in front of him, welcoming students into a safe haven for debate, dissent, and intellectual stimulation.... Even as a teacher, a role in which he assumed authority, he welcomed criticism, debate, and dissent...

[He] told us that...if we had an issue with our grade and wanted to sit down and talk about it with him, he would welcome it warmly. Taking Howard's advice, I decided to question authority, sit down with Professor Zinn, and challenge my C+. He sat calmly as I pleaded my case, and even more calmly pointed out the deficiencies in my argument. When all was said and done, he looked at me and asked, "Roger, do you think you deserve a better grade?" "No." "I would agree with you," he replied.

In my teaching career, I've looked to emphasize the humility that Howard instilled in me.... And along with the world's luckiest B-, I can say proudly that I walked away from Howard Zinn with qualities that I still treasure.[28]

Another of Zinn's Spelman students was Marian Wright (now Marian Wright Edelman). She would go on to Yale Law School, become the first black female lawyer in Mississippi, become founder and President of the Children's Defense Fund in Washington, D.C., write several books, and receive a MacArthur Fellowship ("genius grant") and the Presidential Medal of Freedom (the highest civilian award of the United States), among many other honors and distinctions. She reports:

I feel very lucky to have been [Howard Zinn's] student. He was a very creative, magical teacher. He taught us how to think for ourselves, to analyze, to question what we read, and speak truth to power. He was just engaging in every way.... [H]e was extraordinary.... [W]e students loved him. He was always accessible.... I also just appreciated his great respect for me as a young black girl from a little segregated town. [He] has...irrevocably shaped my life and I'm profoundly grateful....[29] Howie encouraged students to think outside the box and to question rather than accept conventional wisdom. He was a risk-taker. He lost no opportunity to challenge segregation in theaters, libraries, and restaurants, and encouraged us to do the same.... We called him Howie and felt him to be a confidant and friend as well as a teacher, contrary to the more formal and hierarchical traditions of many Black colleges. He stressed analysis over memorization; questioning, discussions, and essays rather than multiple choices and pat answers; and conveyed and affirmed my Daddy's belief and message that I could do and be anything and that life was about far more than bagging a Morehouse man for a husband.... He was passionate about justice and his belief in the ability of individuals to make a difference in the world. Not a word-mincer, he said what he believed and encouraged us as students to do the same.... Howie taught me to question and ponder what I read and heard and to examine and apply the lessons of history in the context of the daily political, social, and moral challenges all around us in the South like racial discrimination and income inequality.... He taught us to be neither victims nor passive observers of unjust treatment but active and proud claimants of our American birthright. Howie helped prepare me to discover my leadership potential. I was so blessed to have Howie Zinn as a teacher and lifelong friend and will miss him deeply.[30]

Betty Stevens (now Betty Stevens Walker), who would become the first Southern black woman to attend Harvard Law School, and who would go on to a long career as an attorney and professor, was student-body president at Spelman when Zinn was fired. In an open letter to the Spelman students, published in the campus newspaper, she responded to the news of his termination:

To list this man's contributions to this college and to the community at large would be unnecessary. You are all aware of them. They are many and impressive. There are few Dr. Zinns in the world. Spelman was fortunate to have one in her midst. As President of the student body, I articulate a need — the need to know why this professor who is nationally acclaimed as a scholar, who is an excellent professor, is no longer here to inspire (as he and he alone can do) the student to excel.[31]

Further testimony comes from David Colapinto, an attorney with the nationally recognized Washington, D.C. firm of Kohn, Kohn

& Colapinto. He writes:

> Looking back on the late 1970s and early 1980s at Boston University, it is easy to understand why Howard Zinn was "our favorite teacher." He was more than just a teacher and historian. He was probably the most popular mentor and faculty adviser on campus. Anyone who visited the Political Science department will remember the long line of students patiently waiting outside his office to discuss projects or seeking his advice or support. He was always accessible, optimistic, and encouraging.

Noting that he has been practicing law for more than 25 years with Stephen Kohn, another of Zinn's students, Colapinto adds, "Much of our effective advocacy for whistleblowers is due in no small part to Howard Zinn's teaching and influence" (DC).

Nadine Dolby, a professor in the College of Education at Purdue University, was a student of Zinn's at Boston University in the 1980s. She recalls him this way:

> He was a very funny man and warm man. Told jokes all the time. Very self-deprecating. And very humble. When it came to his students and students who disagreed with him—and a lot of students in our classes disagreed with him; it was the mid-'80s, Reagan and all that, a very conservative era—he didn't sit there and shut them down…He would lecture for a little while, maybe a guest speaker, and then it was an open forum for students to talk and challenge him. He enjoyed being challenged. It kept him fresh and it kept him on his toes and it kept him connected to the next generation. He always wanted to connect to young people.[32]

Dr. Stuart W. Shulman, a software inventor and political science professor, writes:

I took classes with Howard at BU in 1987 and 1988. He taught in a very large movie theater. It was always packed. People came from across the ideological spectrum to listen, rapt, to the greatest teacher I have ever known. People stood in the back row and sat in the aisles. Students felt free to take him on; he welcomed it. There was complete freedom of speech.

Shulman also relates an anecdote that perhaps sheds some light on Daniels's "anti-American" charge: "I asked him if he ever thought of moving to Canada. He told me about why he and Roz decided this was a country worth fighting for and that the victories over the years, slow and hard won, were on the books because we people spoke out, marched, got arrested, and practiced politics." Shulman concludes: "I loved that man. He changed me forever."[33]

Duberman reports that Zinn

had always been a greatly admired teacher. A colleague who sat in on several of his classes in the 1980s found no trace of the boredom that often emanates from those who've been teaching for a long time—and from their catatonic students. In his notes, the colleague emphasized Howard's "outgoing, tolerant and relaxed" style—"he has a way of teaching that is disarmingly open," welcoming interruption, disagreement, and controversy (DUB 258).... As a teacher, [he] was all but unanimously beloved and revered by his students—even, as a person, by some of the conservative detractors who would unexpectedly appear in his classes. He cared about them, and they knew it (DUB 316).

Not content merely to teach history and to write about it, Zinn, throughout his adult life, also helped to *make* history through his social activism.[34] For example, while teaching at Spelman College, he engaged in many acts intended to overcome segregation. In 1959 the Spelman Social Science Club, for which Zinn served as faculty advisor, orchestrated a nonviolent protest against the segregationist policies of the Atlanta library system. Black students began, with increasing frequency, to go to the library to attempt to check out books, often classic philosophical works devoted to issues of freedom, human rights, and justice. They were always turned away. Then, as the frequency of these requests continued to accelerate, and as Zinn made public his plan to assemble a group of plaintiffs to sue the library, the library board relented and gave up its segregationist policies.

Similarly, Zinn was not only a theoretician, but also a practitioner, of civil disobedience. One summer day in 1961 Zinn and his wife, Roz, entered Rich's Department Store, the largest in Atlanta. They bought sandwiches and coffee at the counter and then sat down at a table. Then, by prearrangement, two black students joined them, followed by the philosopher Henry West and his wife, Pat (a white couple), and more black students. The management at Rich's responded by turning off the lights and shutting down the lunch counter. But by the fall, after several other such acts of civil disobedience had taken place, Rich's ended its policy of segregation, and nearly two hundred other Atlanta restaurants did the same. Zinn and his African-American students and other friends challenged segregation often and wherever they found it—not only in restaurants, but also in courtrooms and in the Georgia state house while the legislature was in session—and did so by the simple act of congregating where law and/or policy demanded that they remain separated.

Later Zinn participated in nonviolent protests against the Vietnam War. As a result of such actions he was repeatedly arrested and occasionally briefly jailed. Once, when someone praised him for his courage in continually sticking his neck out in this way, he responded, "it's not courage to me.... I'm not going to be executed. I'm not even going to be given a long jail sentence. I may be thrown into jail for a day or two, and that has happened to me eight to nine times. I may be fired, I may get a salary decrease, but these are pitiful things compared to what happens to people in the world" (DUB 51).[35]

He also had to tolerate constant verbal abuse. Duberman recounts a typical episode. Zinn, along with a few others, picketed Leb's restaurant in Atlanta in protest of its segregation policy. "Pedestrians passed by the pickets, calling out the standard epithets: 'Nigger lover!' 'Commie!' 'White nigras!' One said to Howard with a somewhat confused anger, 'You look Italian. Why don't you go back to Khrushchev?'" (DUB 75). One of the most common epithets was the one that Daniels would later use: "anti-American."

Zinn also consistently supported the social activism of others, both by serving as faculty advisor, first at Spelman and then at Boston University, for nearly every student organization fighting for progressive social change, and by answering the call of activist groups across the country who asked him to come and speak at the teach-ins, rallies, and demonstrations that they organized.

Yet another way in which Zinn made history was by serving as an expert witness in important trials, including those of the Camden 28, the Baltimore 4, the Milwaukee 14, and the Winooski 44. At these and many other trials he provided expert testimony on the Vietnam War, on the history of U.S. foreign policy, on civil disobedience, and on the history of social movements. According to Duberman, he "was a highly effective court witness. Following his testimony, prosecution lawyers often waived their right to cross-examine him, and juries often acquitted the defendants" (DUB 152).

A good case in point is the trial of the Camden 28, a group that included four Catholic priests and a Protestant minister, who in 1971 raided a New Jersey draft board and destroyed draft records in protest of the Vietnam War. Though the facts of the case, if applied straightforwardly to the letter of the law, would have supported guilty verdicts, Zinn, testifying on the history of civil disobedience as an effective means for fighting gross injustices, made a case for jury nullification. The jury responded by acquitting all 28 defendants on all charges.

Another case in which Zinn's testimony was instrumental in winning improbable acquittals for the defendants was the trial of the Winooski 44, a group of peace activists who occupied the offices of Senator Robert Stafford in Winooski, Vermont to protest U.S. policy in El Salvador and Nicaragua. They were arrested and charged with unlawful trespass, and 26 of them were tried before a jury of their peers in November 1984.

The defense strategy was unusual. The defendants invoked the concept of "necessity" — the idea that an action that would otherwise be in violation of the law can be justified if it is urgently needed for the purpose of preventing a greater harm, which in this case was the Reagan administration's support for death squads in El Salvador and Contra terrorists in Nicaragua.

Zinn's testimony placed the defendants' actions in the context of American history:

By civil disobedience I mean the technical violation of law in order to try to bring to public attention some very powerful issue, some very fundamental principle. This is an approach which goes back to the American Revolutionary period, to the movements of that time when, as most everybody knows who has learned something about the American Revolution, the colonists in New England used a variety of tactics which were technically outside the law, but which the colonists believed fit in with what they called a higher law. When they went onto the property of stamp tax collectors and destroyed the stamps, when they violated property lines in various ways in order to bring the attention of people to the abuses of the British King and Parliament, they were appealing to fundamental principles of government which they then expressed in the

Declaration of Independence.

The Declaration of Independence was really the summing up of what is the relationship between people and government. The basic idea of the Declaration was that government derived its power from people. People set up governments. People set them up for certain purposes, and the purposes were to do something for people to guarantee life, liberty, and the pursuit of happiness. And that if such times arise in the history of a society where the government itself begins to act against the liberties of the people, then people have a right to assert these basic principles, to do things in defense of their rights, to disobey the government, to alter or abolish the government, as the Declaration of Independence put it. And therefore, by extension, to do those things which might not go so far as abolishing the government, but which would go so far as engaging in the technical violation of laws for these fundamental principles. That idea of social protest, of civil disobedience, was carried on into the movement against slavery.

Then, after describing several acts of civil disobedience that had been undertaken in American history—in connection with the anti-slavery abolitionist movement, the civil rights movement, and the movement against the Vietnam War, among others—Zinn continued:

[T]he organizations and activities that you're talking about today, relating to Central America, are in keeping with a very long American tradition. At certain critical moments in history there are people who are willing to technically violate the law in order to stand up for fundamental principles of life and liberty; that is central to the American tradition....

Democracy is not just voting. Democracy is not just writing letters to congressmen. Democracy in America has always

meant people getting together, meeting, petitioning, demonstrating, going out in the street; yes, sitting in, trespassing,
doing various acts of nonviolent, technical disobedience to
arouse large numbers of people.[36]

Despite the centrality of Zinn's testimony to the defendants'
"necessity" defense, the prosecuting attorney declined to
challenge him during cross-examination, asking him only one,
rather innocuous, question: "Isn't it true that sitting-in is only one
form of civil disobedience that can effect change" (NG 108)?

Jack McCullough, one of the attorneys for the defense, recalls
Zinn's involvement in the case:

When I met Dr. Zinn he was very gracious and willing to be of
assistance. His testimony was eloquent, and fleshed out the
themes of his academic career and the deeply American values
of political protest.... [R]epresenting the Vermonters standing
up for the people of El Salvador and Nicaragua in the face of
a hostile government, and hearing the Vermont jury
pronounce them not guilty, was one of the highlights of my
legal career, and working with Howard Zinn to present his
testimony was a great pleasure.... Dr. Zinn expressed some of
the most fundamental values of American democracy, and I
was proud to know him, however briefly.

McCullough's essay, written on the occasion of Zinn's death,
concludes with these words: "Howard Zinn died on January 27 at
the age of 87. He will be missed by all of us who value justice and
freedom."[37]

Perhaps the most famous trial at which he testified was that of
Daniel Ellsberg, the whistleblower who leaked the "Pentagon
Papers," the government's own history of the Vietnam War,
which had been written for the internal use of the war planners,
and which had been classified "top secret." At that trial Zinn

spoke to the jury for several hours about the history of the Vietnam War. Unlike Mitch Daniels, who claims (and, consistent with his nearly uniform practice, does so without citing any evidence in support of his position, let alone confronting and answering evidence speaking against it) that the Vietnam War was an instance in which "the United States [had] taken on the mission of defending freedom under threat" (KTR 211), Zinn on the stand cited chapter and verse from the Pentagon Papers, in pointing out (a) that the United States violated its pledge, given in exchange for Vietnamese help in World War II, to allow the Vietnamese to govern themselves; (b) that the White House ignored, and failed to reply to, 14 letters sent by Ho Chi Minh asking that the pledge be kept; (c) that Ngo Dinh Diem, the first president of South Vietnam, was a U.S. puppet, installed and propped up by the U.S., with little support among the people he governed; (d) that the United States, knowing that Diem would lose to Ho Chi Minh in any election to unify Vietnam, blocked the election, thus subverting democracy (such an election had been agreed to by the French, when they signed the peace treaty in Geneva that temporarily divided Vietnam into two governmental bodies, one in the north and one in the south); and, among other points, (e) that the U.S. war planners took no interest whatsoever in the rights or welfare of the Vietnamese people, but rather were exclusively concerned with U.S. geopolitical interests in the context of the Cold War, and with U.S. economic interests in the material goods of Indochina, such as rubber, tin, oil, and rice.

The prosecutor declined to cross-examine Zinn about the war, limiting his interrogation to a single question, designed merely to establish that Zinn and Ellsberg were friends. (The judge eventually dismissed the charges against Ellsberg and terminated the trial because of governmental misconduct and illegal evidence gathering.)[38]

For his many achievements as a scholar, writer, speaker, teacher, and activist, Zinn has received a number of prestigious awards. The Thomas Merton Center for Peace and Social Justice in Pittsburgh presents The Thomas Merton Award annually to "national and international individuals struggling for justice." The award is given to just one person per year. Zinn was the recipient in 1991.

In 1996 the Peace Abbey Foundation gave the Peace Abbey Courage of Conscience Award to Zinn "for leadership in the Peace Movement, for giving voice to the victims of oppression, and for his revealing book, *A People's History of the United States.*"

The Eugene V. Debs Foundation gives the Eugene V. Debs Award annually to an individual whose "work has been in the spirit of Debs and who has contributed to the advancement of the causes of industrial unionism, social justice, or world peace." Zinn received the award in 1998.

The Lannan Literary Awards, presented annually by the Lannan Foundation, are meant "to honor both established and emerging writers whose work is of exceptional quality." Zinn received the Lannan Literary Award for Nonfiction, and, along with it, a $75,000 cash prize, in 1998.

The Liberty Hill Foundation presents the Upton Sinclair Award each year to "those whose work illustrates an abiding commitment to social justice and equality." Zinn won the award in 1999.

The Otis Social Justice Award, presented by Wheaton College, "honors the women and men who bring members of the community closer to compassionate action." Zinn was the 2001 recipient.

In 2003 Zinn was awarded the *Prix des Amis du Monde diplomatique* for the French translation of APH, *Une histoire populaire des Etats-Unis.*

The Havens Center for Social Justice, housed at the University of Wisconsin in Madison, gave Zinn its 2006 Havens Center Award for Lifetime Contribution to Critical Scholarship, because of his "distinguished and extensive record of scholarly achievement in the critical tradition of social thought."

The Ridenhour Courage Prize is presented annually by The Nation Institute and the Fertel Foundation "to an individual in recognition of his or her courageous and life-long defense of the public interest and passionate commitment to social justice." Zinn was given the award, posthumously, in 2010, "for his determination to showcase the hidden heroes of social movements throughout history, his refusal to accept the history of only the powerful and victorious, his steadfast belief in the potential for a better world, his unflinching moral stance on fighting whatever he perceived was wrong in society, his fight to inspire students to believe that together they could make democracy come alive, and, in the words of his former student Alice Walker, 'his way with resistance.'"

In the light of Mitch Daniels's comparison of Zinn's work with certain other theories and texts, it is worth noting, once again, that no defender of Lysenkoism, phrenology, or *The Protocols of the Elders of Zion* has been winning any of these awards, or any comparable awards issued by organizations of any political stripe.

Returning to Daniels's charge that Zinn was a "terrible anti-American," I trust that the evidence presented above is sufficient to refute the "terrible" part. No matter what one might think of Zinn's politics, or his theories of history, it is an undeniable fact that he devoted his life to fighting racism and war, and working for greater economic equality, did so at great personal cost, and did so in spite of the fact that he was not himself a victim of the injustices he fought (he was white, a veteran in no danger of having to serve in war again, and not poor), which means, in short, that he devoted his life to others. There are many things that people like that can reasonably be called. "Terrible" is not one of them.[39]

Duberman documents many instances in which Zinn upheld his principles and fought for others, even when doing so went against his self-interest. To give just one example, at Boston University he argued against the idea that faculty members who are highly productive scholars should receive higher pay than those who produce little. His stance was based not only on his general preference for egalitarianism, but also on his belief that teaching "is what we are in the university for; otherwise we could be in a think tank somewhere. Research and publication are admirable and desirable, but have always been over-emphasized." What makes his advocacy for this position remarkable is that, as Duberman points out, Zinn "knew he was a good writer and a far more productive one than most faculty at BU" (DUB 246).

And the costs that Zinn incurred for his activism on behalf of others went far beyond the demands on his time, the occasional beatings and jailings he endured, and the incessant criticism he received from racists, militarists, political conservatives, some orthodox historians, and sundry university administrators. He was also subjected to illegal persecution on both of his professorial jobs. He was fired from Spelman, almost undoubtedly solely because of his activism, and because of his disagreements with the college's president, in spite of the fact that he was a full professor and presumably (the matter is in dispute) had tenure. (Zinn chose not to spend the necessary time and money fighting his dismissal in the courts, in part because he was immediately able to secure another faculty position at Boston University.)

At B.U. Zinn found himself the object of President John Silber's wrath, as Silber, even more than his colleague at Spelman, disliked Zinn's politics, activism, and public criticism of the school's administration. Silber was a petty tyrant who used his position to punish his critics in mean-spirited and childish ways. For example, as mentioned above, he denied Zinn teaching assistants routinely provided to other professors, even when Zinn's classes attracted four hundred students. Similarly, he persistently withheld pay raises for Zinn, even when, as was generally the case, the result of the university's official performance evaluation procedure was a recommendation that Zinn receive a merit-based pay raise.

For example, in 1974 Zinn's department recommended that he receive a $1,000 raise. The dean approved the recommendation, but Silber overrode it and reduced Zinn's raise to zero. Zinn signed his contract, but attached a note: "Considering my record of teaching and publication, this action is at first puzzling. [But] noting my strong criticism of the Silber administration in the past, and John Silber's tendency to go into tantrums when criticized, one is led to reasonably conclude that his veto of my salary raise is a petty act of revenge." Zinn went on to charge Silber "with flagrant disregard...for democratic process" with being "unable to deal with men and women who voice opinions that differ from" his or who object to his policies (with the result that his administration was staffed with "sycophants, panderers, and incompetents"), and with "misusing his authority by manipulating salary raises to punish critics." Noting that "this is a serious violation of ordinary standards of decency and fairness," he pointed out that it "should be remedied by the university community." What should the remedy be? "The corrective for abuse of presidential power is the same in the university as in the nation—removal from office" (DUB 192–3; JOY 86).

In 1979, Zinn's department recommended a $2400 raise for him. Silber's provost cut it in half. Then, before Zinn could register an objection to the provost's action, Silber cut the raise down to zero (DUB 220). In the academic year 1982–3 Zinn once again was recommended for a salary increase, this time by a series of committees. Silber overruled the committees, and denied him any raise at all. The American Association of University Professors (AAUP) investigated and concluded that "the administration improperly deprived Professor Zinn of an earned and deserved merit increase of $750" (DUB 245–6). By 1982, despite the fact that he taught more students than most professors, received highly favorable teaching evaluations, and published more than most of his colleagues, he was the lowest-paid full professor in his department, and among the 15 percent lowest-paid full professors at the university. When he retired in 1988, his salary was $41,000, a figure far below the average for full professors with nearly 25 years' experience at the university. It took the intervention of the AAUP for him finally to receive merit and equity back pay that had been wrongly denied him.[40]

Anti-Americanism

What about Daniels's accusation that Zinn was "anti-American"? As usual, we are handicapped by Daniels's failure, both in his initial emails in which he first made the charge, and in his subsequent statements after the emails were published, to explain just what he meant by it, or what evidence he thinks supports it. Presumably Daniels's use of this epithet is intended to refer to the fact that Zinn's writings on American history are far more critical of the actions of the American Founders, of U.S. presidents, and of other political, military, and business leaders, than is the case with standard textbooks on U.S. history; that Zinn highlights cases of American lying, treachery, aggression, brutality, and lawlessness; and, in short, that he does not present United States history as a glorious success story, an utterly unique triumph of freedom, democracy, goodness, and decency, marred only by a few regrettable, but understandable, lapses—mistakes that we have either already (virtuously) overcome or are even now in the process of overcoming.

But the claim that historical writing of the sort just described merits the label "anti-American" (or perhaps that it can only result from an anti-American bias on the part of its author, Zinn) is open to several powerful objections. First, such a position rests on an indefensibly restrictive identification of "America" as synonymous with the actions of the government, or of the rich and powerful, more generally. But "America" includes way more than that, and Zinn's writings show that he, as much as anyone, appreciates such things as the physical beauty of America's mountains, rivers, valleys, great plains, forests, and deserts; the wonderful richness of the English language; the outstanding record of creativity of America's writers, artists, and musicians; the impressive record of discovery and innovation of its scientists, scholars, technologists, and engineers; the honesty, industry, integrity, and friendliness of millions of its people; and, most especially, its inspiring historical record of struggle for moral progress, a record of ordinary Americans banding together in common cause, over and over again, to oppose injustice, and to make their country better—as in the movements to abolish slavery, to end racial discrimination, to establish equal rights for women, to bring about fairer wages and better working conditions for laborers, and to oppose unjust wars, among many others.[41]

Second, the charge of anti-American bias misidentifies the basis for Zinn's criticisms. If Bob bullies Tim, and Zinn calls Bob out for his bullying, this does not show that Zinn has an "anti-Bob" prejudice. Rather, a much more straightforward and plausible explanation for his criticism is that he is anti-bullying. Similarly, if the United States government takes action to prevent a people from governing themselves, perhaps by preventing or subverting an election, by violently overthrowing a democratically elected leader, and/or by installing a puppet dictator to rule a country against the wishes of its people (as has happened in Iran, Guatemala, Vietnam, and Chile, among other countries), criticism of the United States for doing so can be fully explained as resting on respect for the right of all people to self-determination; there is no need to invoke anti-American bias. To establish that Zinn's criticisms are based on such a bias, one would first need to show that in making them he appeals to indefensible principles, or that he applies defensible principles in inappropriate ways, or that he has his facts wrong, or that he commits logical errors of some sort, or, in general, that there is some specific flaw in his analysis. (After all, it makes no sense to posit a psychological deficiency to explain how it is that someone has arrived at a cogent, logical analysis.) But to show any of these things, one would have to engage Zinn's text, and to address his arguments in detail. This is something that Daniels has never done. He prefers the lazy "anti-American" shortcut.

Approaching this point from the standpoint of history education, consider the question of what students should learn from studying the American Revolution. One possible lesson is that we were the good guys, and that our enemies, in this case the British, were the bad guys. But students with a bit more curiosity, and perhaps a greater capacity for abstract thought, are likely to ask *why* it is that we were the good guys in this case, and the British the bad guys. A big part of the answer would seem to be that we Americans were seeking self-determination, the right to govern ourselves, while the British wanted us to remain a British colony, subject to British rule. This sets up a significant parting of the ways in the interpretation of political events. Those who think that the lesson to be learned from the story of the American Revolution is simply that "we are the good guys" are likely to think that we are *always* the good guys, even when we seek to deny others the right to self-determination, and attempt to turn their land into an American colony. This might explain why they would reject any strong criticism of an American policy—any claim that it is not merely unwise or mistaken, but rather fundamentally immoral—as "anti-American"—and thus obviously wrong. But those who think that the lessons to be learned from the story of the American Revolution are that colonialism is wrong, that people have a right to self-determination, and that self-interested attempts to usurp other people's right to self-determination are undemocratic and morally wrong, take a very different view of American actions in Iran in 1953, in Guatemala in 1954, or in Chile in 1973. These are the people who are called "anti-American" by the likes of Mitch Daniels.[42]

Third, Zinn has repeatedly pointed out that his criticisms of American elites often apply with equal or greater force to such elites in other countries. Nowhere does he state or imply that the powerful in America are more evil than the powerful elsewhere—quite the contrary (see, for example, VLW 5–6). Is it not plausible to maintain, for reasons well understood by Acton and Machiavelli (neither of whom were American), that those in power, whatever their nationality, tend to act for their own interests, at the expense of the interests of the less powerful, and that they are more than willing to lie, cheat, steal, and kill in doing so?

Lord Acton, a British historian and politician, who died in 1902, famously claimed that "power tends to corrupt," that "absolute power corrupts absolutely," and that "great men are almost always bad men."[43] If Acton is right, any accurate work of history, insofar as it focuses on the powerful and the "great," would be a description of bad people doing bad things, in which case it would appear that it is mainstream U.S. histories that exhibit a bias, a "patriotic" one, rather than that Zinn manifests an "anti-American" bias. And in his classic work *The Prince*, published in 1513, Italian political philosopher Niccolò Machiavelli argues that successful political leaders must become adept at breaking promises and treaties, disguising their true nature, violently crushing their political opponents, and lying and dissembling. In short, they must develop, and judiciously use, a talent for being "other than good."[44] So, once again, if Machiavelli (who is often called "the father of political science") is right, Zinn's account of American history is more accurate than the version found in more mainstream texts, so that it is the bias of the conventional historians, not that of Zinn, that must be explained.

Fourth, to reject a criticism of American actions as "anti-American" is to betray a misunderstanding of the basis on which actions and policies can be justified. Without having to commit oneself to one particular moral theory, it can nonetheless be said that some considerations are plausible candidates as justificatory principles, while others clearly are not. Thus, one can plausibly justify an action or policy by making a good case that it is fair, or honest, or kind, or respectful of people's rights, or conducive to the promotion of happiness, or something of that sort; but it makes no sense at all to claim justification for an action on the basis of the fact that it was done on Tuesday, or by someone named "Sam," or in Iowa, or that it leads to greater consumption of mango salsa, or that it can be described without using the word "purple." The problem, then, is that an attempt to justify an action or policy by claiming that it is "American," or to reject it on the basis of the idea that it is "anti-American," is to offer a justification that is more like those on the absurd second list of justifications than the plausible first list. Fundamental moral principles of the sort that can justify actions or policies are abstract and general, as are the most basic things that make life good (such as health, happiness, knowledge, friendship, and peace). Moreover, there is a kind of logic, a readily graspable necessity, to the connection between principles of this sort (such as "be kind," "be fair," "respect the rights of others," and so forth), the good things of life just mentioned, and the justification of actions. But there is no such necessary connection between, on the one hand, the history, traditions, and policies of any particular nation, and, on the other hand, morality and the good life. Any such connection is merely contingent. To be sure, it is logically possible for there to be a country whose policies have tended to be morally admirable. But such a connection is still contingent, in that it is readily imaginable that it could have been otherwise. While there is something absurd about the statement, "it was fair, honest, kind, respectful of people's rights, and conducive to happiness, and yet it was wrong and unjustified," there is no absurdity whatsoever attached to the statement, "it was the way things have always been done in America, it was in keeping with the American tradition, and it was the American policy (or French, or Nicaraguan, or Chinese, or what have you), and yet it was wrong and unjustified." In short, an action or policy isn't right because it is American; rather, America is good only to the extent that its actions and policies are right.[45] Thus, "anti-American" is never a good criticism, because it begs the question with respect to the issue of whether or not the American policy or action being criticized is, indeed, defensible.

To deny this, and to hold, instead, that whatever American policy happens to be, it is, by definition, right, simply because it is American, would be to adopt either the kind of simple-minded cultural relativism that conservatives like Mitch Daniels deplore, in my view rightly[46] (the idea that moral rightness varies from culture to culture, and is reducible, for each culture, simply to what that culture in fact believes and does), or a thuggish and irrational ethnocentrism according to which our ways set the standard for everyone else, simply because we are us. Further, such a stance brings with it the awkward consequence that statements praising America as a great nation would have to be understood as trivial tautologies, drained of significant meaning, and no longer compliments at all. For if whatever American policy happens to be, it is, by definition, right, simply because it is American, then it cannot be said that America has resisted the temptation to do wrong things, and has virtuously chosen instead to do what is right. Rather, anything it might have done, no matter how heinous it might appear based on other criteria, would have to be counted as right, simply by definition. It is no compliment to say that America was right to do X if America would, by definition, have been equally right to have done not-X. Finally, the idea that American policies and actions are, as such, automatically right, blocks any motivation to strive for moral progress. After all, why should we change when we are already perfect?

Consider, in this light, the ethic of "patriotism" that typically underlies criticisms of "anti-Americanism." According to this ethic, one is obliged to take pride in one's country, and to be devoted and loyal to it. But the appropriateness of pride depends upon the worthiness of the object of pride. Thus, it cannot be virtuous for pride in one's country to be uncritical or unqualified. There is no virtue in supporting immoral objectives or practices. Moreover, if pride is not constrained by the limits of the merits of its object, and if it is not accompanied by due respect for the rights and good qualities of others, it can easily descend into an ugly arrogance or conceit.

This problem is exacerbated when we move from considerations of "pride" to those of "devotion" and "loyalty," since we are now moving beyond the sphere of feeling into that of action. Each of us bears some responsibility for the actions of our government. But the exercise of this responsibility requires clear and accurate understanding, and these tend to be precluded by an *a priori* commitment to devotion and loyalty.

Zinn's position is that our primary loyalty should not be to a nation-state, or to political leaders, or to their specific policies, but rather to our fundamental political ideals, such as freedom, democracy, and human rights. But this entails (1) that our pride in and loyalty to our country should be contingent on the degree to which our country realizes these ideals; and (2) that there is no reason for our pride and loyalty to be directed specifically at our country, rather than at the ideals themselves, and at their instantiation anywhere.

Accordingly, Zinn often declares his allegiance to the principle, articulated in the Declaration of Independence, that everyone has an equal right to life, liberty, and the pursuit of happiness. But he also insists on interpreting "everyone" to include "men, women, and children all over the world, who have a right to life not to be taken away by their own government or by ours" (YCB 3). When their lives are taken away by our government, Zinn points it out. And when he does, people like Mitch Daniels call him "anti-American."

Bias

I have been arguing against Daniels's insinuation that Zinn had an anti-American bias. But perhaps he had some other bias. After all, as we have seen, Daniels has claimed that Zinn was "by his own admission a biased writer," and Zinn has said that APH is "a biased account, one that leans in a certain direction." Well then, what was Zinn's bias?

Before getting to that, however, I want to point out that Daniels's assertion that Zinn "admitted" to being a biased writer is, at best, highly misleading. Daniels is guilty of taking Zinn's statements about bias out of context, a rhetorical trick that is par for the course in the world from which Daniels came, that of U.S. electoral politics, but utterly outside the bounds of acceptable conduct according to the ethical standards of the world he now inhabits, that of U.S. higher education.

Daniels distorts the meaning of Zinn's statements about his bias in at least three ways. First, the word "admit," in the relevant sense, is very close in meaning to "concede" or "confess." One "admits" having done something wrong or poorly, or having made a mistake, or having done something else that casts oneself in a negative light. But Zinn does not present his statement of bias as an admission, and he does not do so in the context of saying that he has done something wrong.

Second, Zinn makes an argument that bias is absolutely unavoidable in historical writing, and that historians, as a consequence, should be wise and scrupulous in choosing their biases, honest with themselves in recognizing them, and candid to their readers in announcing them. This point connects with the one just made, in that one cannot be faulted for doing something when it is impossible to do otherwise—if all historians, necessarily and unavoidably, are biased, the statement that one has a bias oneself need not be conceptualized as an "admission." But Daniels ignores Zinn's argument on this issue, thus further encouraging people to assume, falsely, that Zinn's statements about his own bias amount to a confession of his inferiority relative to the more "patriotic" historians that Daniels admires.

Third, while the word "bias" usually has a negative connotation, and is frequently used to refer to an unfair prejudice, it can also be used in a more neutral fashion simply as denoting a leaning, a preference, or an inclination. The evaluation of a "bias" in this sense depends crucially on the quality of its object. While a bias in favor of something bad is itself bad, a bias in favor of something good—as in, for example, a bias in favor of honesty or nonviolence—can be good, especially when (to return to the point just made) it is not possible simply to avoid having a bias.[47]

To flesh out those examples, consider the thesis that lying and violence can occasionally be justified (as in lying to Nazis to prevent them from locating a potential victim, or in using violence to stop them from executing that victim), but that honesty and nonviolence are in principle much better than their opposites, so that lying and violence should be used only when absolutely necessary, as a last resort, when no other means are available to prevent even greater evils. On this view, debates between proponents of honesty and lying, or between advocates for nonviolence and violence, should not be approached from a standpoint of neutrality and impartiality. Rather, given the intrinsic badness of lying and violence, advocates for such actions should have to meet a burden that their adversaries need not. Honesty and nonviolence should be the "default" positions, to be adopted unless a very compelling case can be made for their abandonment in a specific instance. In short, there should be a "bias" in favor of honesty and nonviolence. Whether one agrees or disagrees with this analysis of these examples, or with the more general claim that some biases are good, there should be no confusion about the *meaning* of that claim, and it is very clear, in context, that when Zinn has said that he has a "bias," he is using the term to refer not to an unfair prejudice, but to a leaning or inclination that can, depending on its object, be good.[48] Daniels's failure to inform the reader as to Zinn's intended meaning in his use of the word "bias" thus joins his failure to address Zinn's arguments for the inevitability of bias, and his inappropriate use of the word "admits," as the third way in which he has distorted Zinn's meaning.

To get a more accurate sense of that meaning, one has only to read the opening pages (more specifically, the first 11) of APH. Zinn begins the book with a description of the greeting the Arawaks gave Columbus when he first arrived in what many Europeans came to call "the New World": "Arawak men and women, naked, tawny, and full of wonder, emerged from their villages onto the island's beaches and swam out to get a closer look at the strange big boat. When Columbus and his sailors came ashore, carrying swords, speaking oddly, the Arawaks ran to greet them, brought them food, water, gifts."

Zinn then quotes Columbus's initial thoughts on the Arawaks, as recorded in his log:

> They…brought us parrots and balls of cotton and spears and many other things, which they exchanged for the glass beads and hawks' bells. They willingly traded everything they owned…. They were well-built, with good bodies and handsome features…. They do not bear arms, and do not know them, for I showed them a sword, they took it by the edge and cut themselves out of ignorance. They have no iron. Their spears are made of cane…. They would make fine servants…. With fifty men we could subjugate them all and make them do whatever we want. (APH 1)

Another log entry informs us that Columbus immediately put that plan into action: "As soon as I arrived in the Indies, on the first Island which I found, I took some of the natives by force in order that they might learn and might give me information of whatever there is in these parts" (APH 2).

Zinn reports that some of the Arawaks wore tiny gold ornaments in their ears. This gave Columbus the idea that there must be a great abundance of gold on the Islands, and that he would be able to force the Arawaks to give it to him. In a report to Spanish royalty he promised that, if given support for a second voyage, he would bring back "as much gold as they need...and as many slaves as they ask.... Thus the eternal God, our Lord, gives victory to those who follow His way over apparent impossibilities" (APH 3–4).

On Columbus's second expedition he and his crew "went from island to island in the Caribbean, taking Indians as captives.... [T]hey...roamed the island in gangs looking for gold, taking women and children as slaves for sex and labor." In 1495 they "rounded up fifteen hundred Arawak men, women, and children, put them in pens guarded by Spaniards and dogs, then picked the five hundred best specimens to load onto ships. Of those five hundred, two hundred died en route. The rest arrived alive in Spain and were put up for sale...." Columbus later wrote: "Let us in the name of the Holy Trinity go on sending all the slaves that can be sold" (APH 4).

At the same time, in the province of Cicao on Haiti, Columbus and his men "ordered all persons fourteen years or older to collect a certain quantity of gold every three months. When they brought it, they were given copper tokens to hang around their necks. Indians found without a copper token had their hands cut off and bled to death," as a warning to the others, intended to motivate them to find gold and bring it to Columbus. But there was not much gold to be found, so the Arawaks "fled, were hunted down with dogs, and were killed" (APH 4).

The chief source of information on these matters is Bartolomé de las Casas, a Spanish priest who participated in the conquest of

Cuba, and for a time owned a plantation on which Indian slaves worked, but who later "gave that up and became a vehement critic of Spanish cruelty" (APH 5). He wrote a multivolume *History of the Indies,* from which Zinn quotes: "Endless testimonies...prove the mild and pacific temperament of the natives.... But our work was to exasperate, ravage, kill, mangle and destroy." The Spaniards "thought nothing of knifing Indians by tens and twenties and of cutting slices off them to test the sharpness of their blades." Las Casas tells how "two of these so-called Christians met two Indian boys one day, each carrying a parrot; they took the parrots and for fun beheaded the boys" (APH 6).

Many Arawak men were forced to work in mines. They were worked so hard that after 8 months of labor about a third of the men had died. By 1508, according to Las Casas, "there were 60,000 people living on this island, including the Indians; so that from 1494 to 1508, over three million people had perished from war, slavery, and the mines. Who in future generations will believe this? I myself writing it as a knowledgeable eyewitness can hardly believe it..." (APH 7).

It is at this point that Zinn begins both his critique of conventional, orthodox history, and his articulation (and explanation and defense) of his own alternative "bias":

> Thus began the history, five hundred years ago, of the European invasion of the Indian settlements in the Americas. That beginning, when you read Las Casas...is conquest, slavery, death. When we read the history books given to children in the United States, it all starts with heroic adventure—there is no bloodshed—and Columbus Day is a celebration. (APH 7)

Here Zinn is obviously criticizing children's U.S. history books for presenting an inaccurate, grossly distorted picture of

Columbus. But notice that the distortion is accomplished, not through the telling of falsehoods, but simply through omission. What the books say about Columbus is true. He was indeed a courageous sailor, who embarked on a bold and daring adventure of exploration and discovery. But he was also a mass murderer and enslaver of Indians. By leaving that part out entirely, it is possible to turn a ruthless killer into a hero to be celebrated.

Zinn next turns to works intended for older readers, and finds that they are only slightly better in this regard. He discusses the work of Samuel Eliot Morison, the Harvard historian, whom Zinn calls "the most distinguished writer on Columbus, the author of a multivolume biography." Zinn quotes a sentence from his 1954 book *Christopher Columbus, Mariner*, in which Morison comments on the enslavement and the killing: "The cruel policy initiated by Columbus and pursued by his successors resulted in complete genocide." Noting that this remark "is on one page, buried halfway into the telling of a grand romance," Zinn juxtaposes it with the book's last paragraph, in which Morison sums up his view of Columbus: "He had his faults and his defects, but they were largely the defects of the qualities that made him great—his indomitable will, his superb faith in God and in his own mission as the Christ-bearer to lands beyond the seas, his stubborn persistence despite neglect, poverty and discouragement. But there was no flaw, no dark side to the most outstanding and essential of all his qualities—his seamanship" (APH 8).

Note Morison's explicit value judgment here. While he acknowledges Columbus's cruelty, and concedes that Columbus's policy "resulted in complete genocide," he nonetheless concludes that his "most outstanding and essential" quality was "seamanship."[49] (Recall, at this point, that the reason Mitch Daniels gave for ordering his subordinates to "get rid of" and "disqualify" Zinn's book is that it is "anti-factual" and exemplifies "propaganda." "We must not falsely teach American history in our schools," he told the Associated Press. Well then, what about a history book that downplays genocide, and holds "seamanship" to be something of greater importance? Is that a more factual and less propagandistic approach to history than Zinn's? Daniels has not said. Nor has ever displayed the slightest awareness or understanding of the issue.)

Distortion can be accomplished through the complete omission of certain facts, as in the treatment of Columbus in books for young children, but it can also be achieved, as in Morison's case, by means of the subtler mechanism of one-sided emphasis. Zinn comments on this:

> One can lie outright about the past. Or one can omit facts which might lead to unacceptable conclusions. Morison does neither. He refuses to lie about Columbus. He does not omit the story of mass murder; indeed he describes it with the harshest word one can use: genocide.
>
> But he does something else—he mentions the truth quickly and goes on to other things more important to him. Outright lying or quiet omission takes the risk of discovery which, when made, might arouse the reader to rebel against the writer. To state the facts, however, and then to bury them in a mass of other information is to say to the reader with a certain infectious calm: yes, mass murder took place, but it's not that important—it should weigh very little in our final judgments; it should affect very little what we do in the world. (APH 8)

While Zinn is critical of Morison here, it is crucial to understand that he does not criticize him for the mere fact that he has emphasized some things and downplayed others. To the contrary, Zinn explicitly states that historians cannot avoid doing so, and that his argument is therefore not "against selection, simplification, emphasis, which are inevitable for...historians" (APH 8). A moment's reflection shows, I think, that he is right about this. If, for example, a historian were to attempt to relate absolutely every fact that there is about Columbus, the task could never be completed (because there are an infinite number of such facts), and the resulting text would be pointless and incoherent: "Columbus was a vertebrate and a mammal. His body temperature tended to sit at about 98.6 degrees Fahrenheit. He never traveled to Mars. He found it necessary to consume food in order to survive. He had only one nose, and was less than 4000 feet tall, which entails that he was also less than 5000, or 6000, or 7000, etc. He was not alive when dinosaurs roamed the earth; and by the time Barack Obama was elected President of the United States, he had been long dead. He traveled by boat, but not by automobile or airplane. He never saw Jackson Pollock's painting *Blue Poles*. He is not famous for contributions to theoretical physics; and, as far as we know, he was not a world champion at any sport or game. He never gave birth to children. There are no recordings of his speaking voice. He was a human being, and not an iguana. His existence, and the events of his life, shed no light whatsoever on the question of whether Michael Jordan or Wilt Chamberlain was the better basketball player. He drank water. He saw mountains and trees. He sometimes slept, etc., etc., etc." Clearly, to tell any kind of story, it is necessary to focus on what is in some way interesting or important, to leave out what is dull or obvious or irrelevant to the general thrust of the narrative, and to relate the included items to each other in such a way as to render the whole coherent and comprehensible. In short, all narrative writing, including historical accounts, must be selective. Such writing must include some things and omit others, emphasize some of the included points while downplaying others, and arrange the included material in such a way as to make one point or set of points, at the expense of others that might have been made.

Accordingly, it would appear obvious that historians should (1) give careful thought to the issue of selection, (2) be self-aware about their selection criteria, (3) make those criteria clear to the reader, and (4) be answerable to criticism, not only for making factual or logical errors, but also for making poor choices as to what they include, exclude, emphasize, and downplay. This last point, of course, is the basis for Zinn's criticism of Morison.

The failure to confront these issues, or worse, the failure even to recognize them, results in work reflecting a very clear and pronounced conservative bias—a bias in favor of traditional, conventional, "mainstream" views and perspectives. The reason is that while non-traditional, non-mainstream views are instantly recognized *as* views (as positions that are not merely neutral or factual, but rather expressions of one particular perspective among others), the opinionated or perspectival character of conventional views often goes unnoticed. If, when discussing meat, one highlights the suffering of cows, pigs, and chickens on modern factory farms, and the high environmental costs of modern meat production, one is perceived to have an ideological bias. But somehow no ideological bias is detected when a writer ignores these issues, and focuses instead on tasty meat dishes, and the fun of having friends and neighbors over for a barbecue. So while the idea that one can dispense with ideological or value-laden considerations when deciding what to include or exclude is an illusion, it is one that can be sustained only when the values in question are orthodox ones. Thus, the call for value-free, or neutral, or non-ideological history, in addition to being objectionable on theoretical grounds, must also be seen as itself biased in favor of conservatism.[50]

This explains why the obvious bias inherent in Morison's treatment of Columbus could go unnoticed for such a long time. Had Morison written a biography of Adolf Hitler in which he focused on Hitler's paintings (he produced hundreds of works, and aspired to be a professional artist), mentioned in passing that Hitler's "cruel policy" toward the Jews resulted in "near genocide," and concluded by saying that "there was no flaw, no dark side to the most outstanding and essential of all his qualities—his masterful neo-classical facility with architectural drawing," everyone would be rightly outraged. This did not happen when Morison treated another genocidist in parallel fashion, because his story about Columbus was an elaboration of the traditional, conventional story that we've all heard a hundred times. It therefore *seemed* factual, non-ideological, with no bias or axe to grind. (And in writing it, Morison, having presumably been trained to write non-ideological history, was only doing what he thought the principles of professionalism required.)

Given the perversity of the value-judgments implicit in Morison's traditionalist account, a perversity that is obvious once it is pointed out, and immediately apparent in the fictional parallel Hitler example, it is interesting to speculate as to how such a narrative could have ever become the dominant one in the first place. Notice that Columbus was not among the first persons to arrive in "the New World." The Arawaks were already there. Columbus's distinction in that regard was more limited—he was one of the first Europeans to arrive. His adventures, one would think, would therefore hold special interest (analogous to interest in Hitler as a painter) only for certain specialized or parochial audiences—nautical enthusiasts, for example, and Americans of European (and especially Italian) descent. But slavery and genocide are universal human concerns. So the fact that those concerns were subordinated in the traditional Columbus story to matters of far less human and moral significance, but greater parochially European import, suggests that the historians who first established the mainstream Columbus narrative were racists and European chauvinists, who cared little about slavery and genocide when the victims were merely the Arawaks, and who gave extra weight to certain achievements in world exploration precisely because they were accomplished by Europeans. Maintaining such morally obtuse value judgments, by means of choices of inclusion, exclusion, and emphasis, is not value-neutral and non-ideological; and overturning them is not an instance of injecting avoidable bias and ideology into a domain in which they would otherwise be absent.

Another problem with conventional, mainstream history, according to Zinn, is that it assumes that all readers of history have a "common interest" that "historians serve to the best of their ability." Zinn does not see this as intentional deception, however, because historians have "been trained in a society in which education and knowledge are put forward as technical problems of excellence and not as tools for contending social classes, races, nations." By contrast, Zinn argues that the inevitable distortions resulting from the historian's choices of emphasis and omission are "released into a world of contending interests, where any chosen emphasis supports (whether the historian means to or not) some kind of interest, whether economic or political or racial or national or sexual" (APH 8).

And these distortions in writings about past history are important, in part because they exert a powerful influence on our thoughts and actions today:

To emphasize the heroism of Columbus and his successors as navigators and discoverers, and to de-emphasize their genocide, is not a technical necessity but an ideological choice. It serves — unwittingly — to justify what was done. My point is not that we must, in telling history, accuse, judge, condemn Columbus *in absentia*. It is too late for that; it would be a useless scholarly exercise in morality. But the easy acceptance of atrocities as a deplorable but necessary price to pay for progress (Hiroshima and Vietnam, to save Western civilization; Kronstadt and Hungary, to save socialism; nuclear proliferation, to save us all) — that is still with us. One reason these atrocities are still with us is that we have learned to bury them in a mass of other facts, as radioactive wastes are buried in containers in the earth. We have learned to give them exactly the same proportion of attention that teachers and writers often give them in the most respectable of classrooms and textbooks. This learned sense of moral proportion, coming from the apparent objectivity of the scholar, is accepted more easily than when it comes from politicians at press conferences. It is therefore more deadly. (APH 9)

Zinn then offers a brief sketch of mainstream, conventional American history, followed by a programmatic statement of his own alternative approach:

The treatment of heroes (Columbus) and their victims (the Arawaks)—the quiet acceptance of conquest and murder in the name of progress—is only one aspect of a certain approach to history, in which the past is told from the point of view of governments, conquerors, diplomats, leaders. It is as if they, like Columbus, deserve universal acceptance, as if they—the Founding Fathers, Jackson, Lincoln, Wilson, Roosevelt, Kennedy, the leading members of Congress, the famous Justices of the Supreme Court—represent the nation as a whole...(APH 9).

My viewpoint, in telling the history of the United States, is different... [Mainstream] history...conceals fierce conflicts of interest (sometimes exploding, most often repressed) between conquerors and conquered, masters and slaves, capitalists and workers, dominators and dominated in race and sex. And in such a world of conflict, a world of victims and executioners, it is the job of thinking people, as Albert Camus suggested, not to be on the side of the executioners.

Thus, in that inevitable taking of sides which comes from selection and emphasis in history, I prefer to try to tell the story of the discovery of America from the viewpoint of the Arawaks, of the Constitution from the standpoint of the slaves, of Andrew Jackson as seen by the Cherokees, of the

Civil War as seen by the New York Irish, of the Mexican war as seen by the deserting soldiers of Scott's army, of the rise of industrialism as seen by the young women in the Lowell textile mills, of the Spanish-American war as seen by the Cubans, the conquest of the Philippines as seen by black soldiers on Luzon, the Gilded Age as seen by southern farmers, the First World War as seen by socialists, the Second World War as seen by pacifists, the New Deal as seen by blacks in Harlem, the postwar American empire as seen by peons in Latin America. And so on, to the limited extent that any one person, however he or she strains, can "see" history from the standpoint of others....

[T]his book will be skeptical of governments and their attempts, through politics and culture, to ensnare ordinary people in a giant web of nationhood pretending to a common interest.... [T]o think that history-writing must aim simply to recapitulate the failures that dominate the past is to make historians collaborators in an endless cycle of defeat. If history is to be creative, to anticipate a possible future without denying the past, it should, I believe, emphasize new possibilities by disclosing those hidden episodes of the past when, even if in brief flashes, people showed their ability to resist, to join together, occasionally to win. I am supposing, or perhaps only hoping, that our future may be found in the past's fugitive moments of compassion rather than in its solid centuries of warfare.

That, being as blunt as I can, is my approach to the history of the United States. (APH 10–11)

As I see it, Zinn's case for his alternative approach to U.S. history proceeds in two stages. First, as discussed above, he argues for the inevitability of selection, omission, and emphasis in historical writing. Choices of inclusion and exclusion are unavoidably value-laden (they reflect what the writer takes to be interesting and important), biased (they expose the writer's leaning in one direction or another), and ideological (they are released into a world of competing interests, some of which they end up supporting, even as they oppose others). Honest historians, therefore, cannot pretend that their work is neutral, and contains no value-laden choices, and must, if they are to be responsible, instead make such choices in a principled way, and be prepared to answer for them.

The second stage of Zinn's case, in my reconstruction, is the justification he offers in defense of his own principles of selection—principles that entail, for example, his giving greater emphasis to Columbus's acts of killing and enslaving the Arawaks than to his daring as a seaman and explorer. I think he offers at least four different, but connected, arguments in support of his principles. I will call these the moral argument, the "counterweight" argument, the causality argument, and the consequentialist argument.

The moral argument can be developed in several ways. One is to invoke Camus's dictum, as Zinn does in a passage quoted above, about executioners and their victims. To cover up atrocities committed by the executioners is an immoral act; to expose such atrocities, by contrast, is moral. Another way is to develop the distinction between universal values and more parochial ones. It is immoral to celebrate the enrichment of one particular culture (a parochial value) when that enrichment is brought about through genocidal campaigns, or through the enslavement of others—actions that violate universal moral principles. Yet another way is to employ the distinction between ultimate values and instrumental values. The justification for particular U.S. policies, laws, and actions is instrumental—they are not ends in themselves, but rather are justified only to the extent that they promote more basic values, such as life, liberty, and the pursuit of happiness (to borrow from the Declaration of Independence). Therefore, when U.S. laws, policies, and actions in fact serve, not to promote these values, but rather to deprive people of their life, liberty, and ability to pursue happiness, it is morally wrong to glorify those laws, policies, and actions (perhaps because they are American, or implemented or performed by American heroes, so that criticism of them would be "anti-American"), and to ignore or deemphasize the ways in which they offend against ultimate values.

The "counterweight" argument is based on the premise that Zinn's account of American history is very far from the only one available. His book is offered neither as the first nor the final word on its subject, but rather as a contribution to a discussion already in progress. Consequently, his choices with regard to the selection of material—what to include, what to omit, and what to emphasize—should be judged from a standpoint that takes due notice of the patterns of inclusion and omission in other texts. Thus, when Zinn states, toward the end of APH, that his history is "a biased account, one that leans in a certain direction," he immediately goes on to explain that he is "not troubled by that, because the mountain of history books under which we all stand leans so heavily in the other direction—so tremblingly respectful of states and statesmen and so disrespectful, by inattention, to people's movements—that we need some counterforce to avoid being crushed into submission" (APH 631).[51]

The causal argument is one that emerges gradually over the course of APH. Zinn attempts to demonstrate that significant social change, over and over again, with remarkable consistency, has been instigated by agitation from below, rather than bold and visionary action from the top. Presidents and other national holders of power have not caused change to happen through their own leadership. Rather, change has happened when those not in power—the "people" of Zinn's "People's History"[52]—have banded together to demand it.

To supplement the many examples of this phenomenon that Zinn presents, I'll illustrate it with a more contemporary case, that of the recent dramatic change in Americans' acceptance of same-sex marriage. While it is true that President Barack Obama eventually came out, on May 9, 2012, in support of the right of same-sex couples to marry (after having opposed that position for many years, when that was the more politically advantageous stance to take), and that the U.S. Supreme Court decided on June 26, 2015, by a 5–4 margin, that state laws banning same-sex marriage were unconstitutional, these "leaders" were definitely followers with respect to this fight. The massive change in American attitudes that facilitated these actions was accomplished largely through the work of artists, writers, and political activists. The president and the Supreme Court merely followed suit. Zinn's point, then, with regard to what I am calling his "causal" argument, is that if we want to understand what drives history, what causes significant moral progress, we must have a much larger focus on "the people," on agitation from below, than is found in mainstream history texts.

The consequentialist argument, as the name suggests, holds that mainstream, traditional history produces bad results, and that Zinn's alternative approach can bring better consequences. Traditional texts encourage the casual acceptance of atrocities as the cost of progress. They do this not by directly asserting the odious claim that we should tolerate atrocities—doing so would surely inspire resentment and resistance—but through the subtler mechanism of consistently playing up the glories of the progress while playing down the horrors of the accompanying atrocities (as in the case of Columbus). A history that deals with atrocities more frankly, and that gives them the attention they deserve, would presumably not produce the same effect.

Another bad consequence of mainstream history, according to Zinn, is that it encourages passivity and teaches us to rely on our great leaders—the ones who, in the traditional texts, drive history:

All those histories of this country centered on the Founding Fathers and the Presidents weigh oppressively on the capacity of the ordinary citizen to act. They suggest that in times of crisis we must look to someone to save us: in the Revolutionary crisis, the Founding Fathers; in the slavery crisis, Lincoln; in the Depression, Roosevelt; in the Vietnam–Watergate crisis, Carter. And that between occasional crises everything is all right, and it is sufficient for us to be restored to that normal state. They teach us that the supreme act of citizenship is to choose among saviors, by going into a voting booth every four years.... (APH 631)

Standard historical texts imply, more by their choices of selection (their emphases and omissions) than by their overt statements, that all significant history is made by kings, presidents, generals, business leaders, and the like; that the rest of us should feel lucky to be beneficiaries of their genius, industry, and generosity; that the world cannot be much better than it is now; that such improvements as are possible will have to be made very gradually; and that they will be made by great leaders—the rest of us will play a minimal role (voting, obediently doing our jobs, and reproducing). By contrast, Zinn's history, which emphasizes the role of ordinary people in generating positive social change, might be expected to produce the opposite effect on its readers—that of encouraging vigorous political activism.

As a final point on Zinn's defense of a certain "bias" on his part, notice that he does not in any way advocate, or attempt to justify, lying, carelessness about factual accuracy, the suppression of data that would undermine one's thesis, or the violation of any other classical scholarly norm, with the single exception of the norm calling for neutrality, or "objectivity," or freedom from bias—a norm that Zinn has attempted to expose as spurious. The "bias" that Zinn defends is restricted to the domain of selection—the decisions that all historians, in common with all other narrative writers, must make as to what to include, what to exclude, and what to emphasize. Within the bounds established by these decisions, Zinn, as much as any other scholar, insists on fairness, factual accuracy, and logical rigor in dealing with the material selected for discussion. His argument is that it is legitimate and defensible to place as much emphasis on Columbus's killing and enslaving of the Arawaks as more traditional texts place on his boldness as an explorer. But he offers no defense of lying about Columbus, or presenting facts about him out of context in order to make his conduct look worse than it really was, or suppressing facts that would support a more generous interpretation of his behavior, or anything like that.

Objectivity

Daniels's final criticism of Zinn is that he is discredited by his rejection of "objectivity": "One of many faculty members who wrote me supportive messages pointed out that Prof. Zinn's disdain for the idea of objective truth went far beyond American history. In his essay, 'The Uses of Scholarship,' Prof. Zinn criticized 'disinterested scholarship,' 'objective study' and the 'scientific method' across the disciplines, thus attacking the foundations of Purdue's entire research enterprise" (RPF).

Before moving on to the substance of this criticism, notice that it, in common with every one of Daniels's other negative comments on Zinn, fails to suggest that Daniels has even *read* Zinn, much less made any attempt to understand his work, or developed any original critical thoughts about it on his own. Instead, Daniels here, once again, simply accepts uncritically, and passes on to the public, a criticism formulated by someone else — in this case an unnamed faculty member. Still, by characterizing the faculty member's rebuke of Zinn as something that he or she "points out," rather than as something that he or she (to use more neutral language) merely "claimed," "asserted," "stated," "said," or the like, Daniels clearly endorses the criticism, and thus puts himself in the position of having to take responsibility for its deficiencies.

Next, notice that the criticism, as quoted, is hopelessly vague. What exactly is "objective truth," and what does it mean to have disdain for the very idea of it? Further, what is meant by such abstract and controversial concepts as "disinterested scholarship," "objective study," and the "scientific method"? Finally, what specific criticisms of these notions does Zinn (allegedly) make, and in what way do those criticisms constitute an "attack on the foundations of Purdue's entire research enterprise"? None of this is clear. No explanation is provided.

Competent scholars who have written about "objectivity" have, by contrast, generally acknowledged a need to clarify with some precision what they mean by the term, since, as Peter Novick points out in a book-length treatment of the issue, "'Historical objectivity' is not a single idea, but rather a sprawling collection of assumptions, attitudes, aspirations, and antipathies. At best it is what the philosopher W. B. Gallie has called an 'essentially contested concept,' like 'social justice' or 'leading a Christian life,' the exact meaning of which will always be in dispute" (NOV 1). Naturally, Zinn fully recognizes this as well. So when he states that he rejects "objectivity," as he does in many of his writings, speeches, and published interviews, he is usually careful to explain his meaning and to warn against possible misinterpretations of his intent. As he puts it in OTO, his statement that he does not desire objectivity "is troubling to some people. It needs explanation (after which it may still be troubling, but for clearer reasons)" (29).[53]

Fortunately, for once Daniels (or, more precisely, the unnamed faculty member he quotes) provides a reference to a specific essay of Zinn's, making it possible to determine what Zinn's claims, in context, actually mean. And that determination, in turn, facilitates an evaluation of the accuracy (or lack thereof) of the charge that Zinn rejects the idea of objective truth and the scientific method and attacks the foundations of Purdue's research enterprise.

While I find Zinn's discussion of these issues to be admirably clear, I also think it evident that many of his critics have misunderstood him. As we will see, most of these misunderstandings can be corrected simply by citing relevant passages from Zinn's writings that the critics in question overlook. However, in an attempt to make Zinn's meaning even more transparent, I will offer a distinction, firmly grounded in Zinn's own examples and clarifying remarks, but not rendered fully explicit in any of his texts, among three different conceptions of "objectivity": objectivity as accuracy, as neutrality, and as centrism. Clarifying the differences among these three different ideas, and analyzing Zinn's disagreements with mainstream historians with regard to two of them, will enable us to see (1) that Zinn rejects only some versions of "objectivity," but by no means all of them; (2) that in the best sense of "objectivity," Zinn's approach allows him to achieve much greater objectivity than is realized in more orthodox historical writings; and (3) that, contrary to Daniels's claim, Zinn does not attack "objective study" and the "scientific method," but rather attacks *arguments that appeal to* "objective study" and the "scientific method" *in making the case that scholars should refrain from addressing, and participating in debates about, controversial issues of contemporary interest,* a quite different matter.

Generically, the idea of "objectivity" has to do with carrying out activities such as thinking and writing (activities that are subjective in the sense that they are done by subjects—that is, by humans, who have feelings, attitudes, desires, and biases) in a manner that is maximally faithful to the external objects with which those activities deal. Accordingly, the first sense of "objectivity," and, I would argue, the primary one, is objectivity-as-accuracy. Objectivity, in this sense, is most likely to be achieved when one's conclusions are based on precise measurements, careful observations, and rigorously logical appraisals of relevant evidence—in short, on a maximally attentive and responsive engagement with the object being investigated. Objectivity is not attained when one's conclusions are based on tradition, or majority opinion, or faith, or what one wants to believe, or anything else that is rooted in something other than the discernible nature of the object itself.

Zinn endorses objectivity in this sense. He, as much as anyone, favors accuracy in measurements and in observations, logical rigor in thinking, evidentialism as the basis for drawing conclusions, and, for that matter, clarity and precision in communicating those conclusions. Mainstream historians also claim to favor this kind of objectivity. The problem, however, is that many of them wrongly believe that objectivity in this sense entails objectivity in the two additional senses to be discussed below, when in fact commitments to those kinds of "objectivity" either preclude entirely the achievement of objectivity in the primary sense of objectivity-as-accuracy, or else (and at the very least) greatly limit its scope and utility.

One of these additional senses of "objectivity" is objectivity-as-neutrality. To be "objective" in this sense one must refrain from taking sides on controversial issues; avoid ideological or political commitments; devote oneself to the discovery and presentation of facts, leaving value-judgments about those facts to others; and, in general, behave as a neutral, impartial, disinterested, evenhanded judge, not as an advocate or propagandist.

Objectivity in this sense might be both desirable and achievable in connection with certain tasks. Consider, for example, a line judge in tennis, whose job is to determine, simply by means of extremely focused and careful observation, where a tennis ball landed during the playing of a point—did it hit the line, or land inside it (in which case the shot is good), or did it land outside the line (in which case the shot is out, and the player who hit it loses the point). To do this job well there is no need for the line judge to make decisions as to what issues to address and which to ignore, or to consider what the criteria for such decisions should be, or to take into account any moral or political or ideological controversies (much less to participate in debates about them), or to construct any elaborate and possibly controversial arguments or interpretations. Indeed, the line judge would rarely need to engage in any reasoning at all—his or her conclusions would be based on elementary observation alone (rare exceptions would include drawing inferences about where a ball landed by noticing such things as the location of a mark on clay that appeared right after a ball struck it, or the fact that chalk from a line drawn on a grass surface was disturbed when a ball landed). The line judge should make his or her calls impartially, and should not be in a position to gain or lose anything based on the outcome of the match. Ideally the line judge should not care one way or the other who wins and who loses.

But the tasks of the historian are very different from those of the tennis line judge, and Zinn argues that objectivity-as-neutrality is neither possible nor desirable for historians. Zinn offers two main arguments in support of his "impossibility" thesis. First, historians, unlike tennis line judges, must make decisions about what to include, what to exclude, and what to emphasize. It is impossible to discuss everything that happened in the past, or even in some finite portion of it, and it would be a very poor narrative that assigned equal emphasis to every topic it did discuss. So historians must be selective and must make choices. These choices, in turn, are based on values—the historian's beliefs as to what is or is not especially interesting or important or illuminating. To return to the Columbus example, a historian might choose to emphasize Columbus's feats as a navigator and explorer, or emphasize his acts of torturing, enslaving, and murdering the Arawaks, or give roughly equal weight to "both sides" of Columbus, or offer a novel interpretation that focuses on some entirely different aspect of him, or ignore him entirely in favor of other topics. Zinn's point is that none of these options can reasonably be described as "neutral."[54]

Zinn's second argument is encapsulated in the phrase he chose for his autobiography: "you can't be neutral on a moving train." His point is that society is already moving in some directions rather than in others, with certain values being favored at the expense of others. In such a situation, the decision to refrain from taking sides does not constitute genuine neutrality, but rather acquiescence in the status quo. Moreover, in a manner that has no parallel in the work of a tennis line judge, the historian's decisions of inclusion, exclusion, and emphasis with regard to the treatment of topics seemingly quite remote from issues of contemporary controversy nonetheless contribute in a decidedly non-neutral way to our thinking about and our understanding of those current controversies. Recall in this connection Zinn's point that emphasizing Columbus's skill and daring as an explorer, while minimizing his acts of enslavement and murder, subtly communicates the message that large-scale violence against "others" — those who are not "us" — is of little importance, and is a perfectly acceptable price to pay for "progress." Emphasizing his treatment of the Arawaks communicates the opposite message. Neither message is lacking in relevance to contemporary conflicts, and neither is remotely "neutral."

As for Zinn's reasons for holding objectivity-as-neutrality to be undesirable, his main point is simply that the deliberate refusal to apply historical knowledge to the task of attempting to resolve controversial issues is a colossal waste of a precious resource. For example, in "The Uses of Scholarship," the essay that Daniels cites, Zinn points out that at the 1969 annual meeting of the Association of Asian Studies there were many sessions on "problems of the Ming Dynasty and a battery of similarly remote topics," but not a single session, of the dozens at the conference, dealing with the war that was then going on in Vietnam (UOS).[55] Experts on Asian history and Asian culture would presumably have knowledge that would be relevant to the evaluation of U.S.

policy in waging war in Vietnam. By constructing arguments on that controversial issue that would have been informed by such knowledge, these scholars could have made a valuable contribution to the debates that were then raging about it. But if scholars, because of a conviction that engagement with contemporary controversial issues is inconsistent with objectivity, and therefore constitutes "propaganda" rather than genuine scholarship, decline to contribute their expertise to ongoing debates, the gap will be filled by participants who lack specialized knowledge, and the debates will be impoverished as a result.

The idea that historians should refrain from taking sides on controversial issues, since their partisan bias might lead them to distort the facts to favor their chosen cause, has little to recommend it. For such a prohibition presumes that it is the scholar's initial bias that drives her appraisal of evidence, when it might often go the other way around—the scholar's careful, logical assessment of the relevant evidence determines her conclusion on the controversial issue at hand. Where that is the case, it is beneficial to the debate for the scholar's presentation of her reasons for supporting one side or the other to be made available for consideration by the public. This is not to deny that partisan bias will lead some scholars to produce fallacious arguments—but surely this problem is better addressed by encouraging other scholars to point out those fallacies, and to present counter-arguments of their own, than by laying down a ban on scholarly participation in arguments about contemporary controversial issues as inherently "propagandistic." That "cure" would be worse than the disease. If we are given both cogent and fallacious arguments, we can examine them critically, and ultimately accept the former and reject the latter. But if scholars are discouraged from contributing to the discussion at all, there are many cogent arguments that we will never even have a chance to consider. Are we so afraid of "bias," of not being "detached" or "disinterested," that we are willing to keep knowledge and intelligence away from the places where they are most sorely needed? Shall we let ignorance and special interests fill the void?

Objectivity-as-neutrality thus stands in tension with objectivity-as-accuracy. For these two conceptions, if taken as ideals by means of which we might regulate our conduct, issue quite different instructions in connection with our handling of important controversial issues. The ideal of objectivity-as-accuracy demands that we confront such urgent issues with the full resources of rationality—employing careful observations, precise measurements, controlled experiments, rigorous logical arguments, and constructive dialogue and debate with others, in an attempt to overcome illusions and confusions and arrive at the truth, the best answer, the solution that is most consistent with the way things really are, that is, with "objectivity." But objectivity-as-neutrality demands that scholars simply steer clear of such issues, insisting that entanglement in them is inherently unscholarly, and that taking sides on them marks the one who does so as "partisan," a "propagandist," and as "biased" and "not objective." Such a demand is defective theoretically, since it rests on the absurd (and usually tacit) assumption that a careful, rigorous, logical, and fair analysis will always lead to a neutral position, so that anyone who lands decidedly on one side or another of a controversy must automatically be assumed to be biased, and to have reasoned poorly or unfairly.[56] And it is defective practically because it deprives us of the full benefits of objectivity-as-accuracy in the domain of controversial issues.

Even greater problems attend the third conception of objectivity, which holds that objectivity entails a centrist position on controversial issues. According to the ubiquitous rhetoric of objectivity-as-centrism, genuine "objectivity" requires "balance" and "evenhandedness," an avoidance of the "bias" and "propaganda" of the left and right, and a commitment to "playing it right down the middle."

The first problem to be noted is that objectivity-as-centrism takes us away from the focus on evidence and rational argumentation that objectivity-as-accuracy emphasizes. The ethic of objectivity-as-accuracy is to follow the evidence wherever it leads, and to draw conclusions based exclusively on a rational appraisal of what that evidence indicates to be the case. But an *a priori* commitment to centrism clearly violates that ethic. While it is true that a rational appraisal of the relevant evidence might in any given case provide warrant for a centrist conclusion, in other cases it may not. When the evidence points toward a conclusion that falls at or near the left or right end of a given spectrum, there is no principled basis for insisting on nonetheless affirming a conclusion that lies at the center of that spectrum.

It is noteworthy, in this regard, that those who speak of the need to reject leftist and rightist bias rarely (if ever) acknowledge a need to reject centrist bias. Indeed, one suspects that such thinkers may regard the concept of "centrist bias" as unintelligible. But if those on the left or right are to be condemned when they affirm their leftist or rightist conclusions in defiance of the evidence, or when they twist that evidence so that it conforms to their pre-conceived leftist or rightist conclusions, there is no principled reason for withholding such condemnation from centrists who ignore or twist evidence so as to support their pre-fabricated *centrist* conclusions.

Many centrists seem to think that the question of whether or not someone has an objectionable bias swings entirely free from the question of whether or to what extent a rational appraisal of the relevant evidence would support that person's position, so that leftist, rightist, or in any other way anti-consensus or non-mainstream views *as such* are to be condemned as *inherently* "biased," while centrist, or consensus, or mainstream views are held to be "objective" *in principle*. And because this confused and meritless view is widespread, a good case can be made that centrist bias is a far more pervasive phenomenon than is either leftist or rightest bias. What is worse, it creates more obstacles to fruitful public discourse. The reason is that those who hold "extreme" or unorthodox views generally recognize that their claims will be met with skepticism, and they accordingly tend to make an effort to support them with evidence and arguments. But those with more mainstream views often recognize no need to defend them, with the result that they are perpetuated, not by reason, but by the inertia of constant repetition, by psychological factors inclining people to believe what others believe, and by the unprincipled, non-evidence-based rejection of alternate views as "biased" and "not objective." In this way objectivity-as-centrism facilitates a kind of lazy criticism that floats free of evidence and stands as an obstacle to the intelligent consideration of controversial issues. Those who defend leftist or rightist views, or positions that in some other way can be regarded as non-mainstream, can be summarily dismissed as "biased," not on the basis of logical blunders or other flaws in their handling of evidence, but simply on the basis of their conclusions.

Support for objectivity-as-centrism may flow, in part, from a confusion about what is implied by entirely legitimate concerns about "balance" and "evenhandedness." Balance and evenhandedness are fine ideals when it comes to the handling of evidence, but not for the evaluation of conclusions. For example, one should not employ double standards when evaluating one's own conduct and that of others, or the conduct of one's friends and one's enemies, or ideas one is inclined to favor and those one is inclined to reject. Rather, a single, consistent standard should be used throughout. Similarly, one should not look only for evidence that supports one's favored position, while ignoring evidence that undermines it. Instead, one should attempt to gather all evidence that is relevant to the issue in question. But once evidence has been both gathered and evaluated in a balanced, evenhanded way, the conclusions one draws should be dictated by that evidence. There should be no expectation or requirement that *conclusions* should turn out to be "balanced" and "evenhanded." For, once again, the evidence may show that one widespread view is demonstrably false, while another is probably true; that one proposal is wise and another foolish; and that one person is cruel and dishonest, and displays few positive personal characteristics, while another is kind, honest, and generous, and exhibits only the most trivial of character flaws. To reject a conclusion that falls strongly on one side of a controversial issue, or to dismiss a characterization of a person as "character assassination" or "hagiography" (because it is either strongly negative or strongly positive, rather than "balanced"), without first considering whether the conclusion or characterization is justified by a scrupulous appraisal of the relevant evidence constitutes lazy criticism, as well as a (usually unwitting) rejection of objectivity-as-accuracy. Similarly, it is not "objective" (in the sense of accuracy) to present "evenhandedly" the story of a bully beating up his victim, so that the point of view of the bully and that of his victim are treated with equal sympathy.

Bias cannot be accurately determined by looking at conclusions alone, without reference to the evidence that supports or undermines them. Suppose that a referee in basketball calls 29 fouls on one team, but only three on another. While that may be because the referee is biased (or incompetent for some other reason), alternatively it may be because the one team in fact committed 29 fouls, while the other committed only three. Indeed, if one knows only the number of fouls called on each team, but not the evidence on the basis of which the fouls were called, one cannot rule out the possibility that the referee was biased in the opposite direction. Perhaps a less biased, more fair, more accurate referee, given exactly the same conduct on the part of the players, would have called 57 fouls (rather than just 29) on the one team, and only one (rather than three) on the other.

While these points, once they are articulated, may appear

obvious, the fact remains that very many, and perhaps most, of the critics who accuse Howard Zinn of "bias" fail to support their criticism by citing errors in his handling of evidence or flaws in his arguments. Instead, they seem to think it sufficient merely to cite some of his conclusions.

Yet another problem with the idea that objectivity requires one to "play it right down the middle" and arrive at a centrist conclusion is that there are multiple spectra of opinion. Should one affirm ideas that lie in the center of the spectrum of "mainstream" American political opinion? But what if the center of that spectrum is located at a great distance from the center of the spectrum of world opinion, or the center of the spectrum of opinion of certified experts on the issue in question? While Americans who push the objectivity-as-centrism line usually seem to think of "the center" as residing in the middle of the spectrum of mainstream American political opinion, one might well suppose that it would be better to consult the spectrum of world opinion, as this would eliminate parochial bias, or the spectrum of expert opinion, because the opinions within it would presumably be founded on a stronger base of knowledge. For that matter, why should we favor a spectrum of current opinion over a spectrum of opinion from the past or future? If one rejects the spectrum of past opinion on the grounds that we have made progress over time, so that the spectrum of present opinion is superior to that of past opinion (for example, support for slavery is no longer part of the spectrum of mainstream American political opinion, as it was in the late 1700s and early 1800s), then shouldn't we also assume (or at least hope) that future opinion will be superior to present opinion? And if so, why would we want to locate ourselves at the center of present opinion? Who would want to be merely average, when he or she could be far ahead of the curve? Perhaps if we forget entirely about where our views lie on any particular spectrum of opinion, and instead try to align them with the evidence, we will end up with views that are decidedly better, closer to the truth, more in line with objectivity-as-accuracy, than are views at the center of any current spectrum of opinion. In this way, we might make genuine progress. Objectivity-as-centrism, by contrast, because of its evidence-free bias in favor of current mainstream thinking, stands as an obstacle to the task of replacing such thinking with ideas that would more accurately reflect objective reality.

While some who think that objectivity commits them to a centrist position are willing to say so explicitly, there are also many who act as if they believe in objectivity-as-centrism, but who say that objectivity requires neutrality. I am referring to those who claim that historians and other scholars should in their scholarly work refrain from advocating any particular position on moral or political issues, but who themselves nonetheless issue scholarly writings that are shot through with endorsements of mainstream, conventional, centrist, and "patriotic" moral and political positions. The explanation, apparently, is that the value-laden positions in question are so widely shared, so uncontroversial, within the intellectual circles that these scholars inhabit, that the scholars fail to recognize them as such. Like the air these scholars breathe, their moral and political opinions, while a constant presence in their environment, have become invisible to them. Moral and political values that are shared, and never challenged, by anyone within the group that "matters," tend not to be recognized as values at all. Scholars who do challenge these consensus values, and who instead promote and defend an alternative set of values, are then seen, not as scholars with a different point of view, to be taken seriously and dealt with on the basis of a critical evaluation of their evidence and arguments, but rather simply as partisans, as propagandists, as people who deserve to be summarily rejected since they have injected their personal values into a domain that (allegedly) had been objective and value-free.[57]

To put the point another way, many who claim allegiance to

125

the principle of objectivity-as-neutrality in fact only attempt to remain neutral with regard to disagreements within respectable, mainstream circles. Values that are uniformly held within such circles can be explicitly endorsed, even as the endorsers vehemently deny that they endorse any values at all. No attempt is made to support these value judgments with evidence or arguments of any kind, much less defend them against criticisms. Rather, the value judgments go unacknowledged, and presumably unrecognized. Conversely, value judgments that oppose the consensus, mainstream values of these scholars are rejected straightaway, not on any reasoned basis, but simply because they are values, and are therefore not part of any legitimate scholarship. Once again, if one opposes the *status quo*, it is clear that one is taking a stand. But if one simply reaffirms current practices and ways of thinking, that is often seen as being "objective," in the sense of not taking a stand. In this way, a rhetorical commitment to objectivity-as-neutrality emerges at the level of conduct as a commitment to objectivity-as-centrism (or, more precisely, objectivity-as-endorsement of mainstream, consensus values). Such a version of "objectivity" is obviously utterly inconsistent with objectivity-as-accuracy, and is hopelessly biased in favor of *status quo* thinking. As Zinn puts it, this is "a spurious objectivity disguising conservatism" in the historical profession (CW 35).

We are now in a position to appreciate the jaw-dropping depths of Mitch Daniels's intellectual dishonesty in asserting, without any kind of explanation or qualification, that Zinn simply rejected objectivity disdainfully, and that in doing so he "attack[ed] the foundations of Purdue's entire research enterprise." For a start, note that in "The Uses of Scholarship," the very essay that Daniels cites in making this ridiculous charge, Zinn says this: "If to be objective is to be scrupulously careful about reporting accurately what one sees, then of course this is laudable" (UOS; ZR 504; OH 183; KFP 10).[58] If a freshman student, in an essay for a college class, were to criticize a writer for rejecting "objectivity," the student would be obliged, at least if he or she wanted to get a grade better than, say, C-, to explain with a fair degree of precision what such a criticism meant, and, in particular, what sense of "objectivity" was at issue. The failure to address this issue would be especially egregious if (1) the student ignored clear statements, in the very essay that the student cited, in which the writer being criticized explained his meaning, and (2) that explanation established that the writer did not reject objectivity in its primary sense of objectivity-as-accuracy. Daniels utterly fails to reach this "freshman C-" standard, but instead operates at the moral and intellectual level of American political campaign television attack ads.

The point of Zinn's essay is not to reject accuracy, careful observation, precision, logical rigor, or anything else that might plausibly be said to undermine "Purdue's entire research enterprise." His point, rather, is that all of these tools of good scholarship should be brought to bear on pressing social problems, even if scholarly engagement with such problems might require scholars to take sides on controversial issues. Recall the precise language of Daniels's criticism: "In his essay, 'The Uses of Scholarship,' Prof. Zinn criticized 'disinterested scholarship,' 'objective study' and the 'scientific method' across the disciplines, thus attacking the foundations of Purdue's entire research enterprise." But what Zinn actually says in that essay, in the one passage that uses the language that Daniels quotes, is something quite different. The context in which the passage occurs is one in which Zinn is developing the argument just mentioned—that historians and other scholars should devote more of their scholarly energy to addressing current social problems. He then makes the point that many scholars are attracted to this idea— they would like to help, to use their skills to make a positive contribution to society beyond that of contributing incrementally to the growth of knowledge about subjects of concern mostly to other specialists—but there is a problem. It is in naming this problem that Zinn uses language that Daniels quotes in order to indict him: "Still we are troubled, because the new urgency to use our heads for good purposes gets tangled in a cluster of beliefs so stuck, fungus-like, to the scholar, that even the most activist of us cannot cleanly extricate ourselves. These beliefs are roughly expressed by the phrases 'disinterested scholarship,' 'dispassionate learning,' 'objective study,' 'scientific method'—all adding up to the fear that using our intelligence to further our moral ends is somehow improper" (UOS; ZR 502–3; OH 181; KFP 8). The next several pages of Zinn's essay are then devoted, not, as Daniels claims, to attacking "objective study" and "scientific method," but rather to attacking the claim that allegiance to these ideals precludes "using our intelligence to further our moral ends." If this constitutes an "attack [on] the foundations of Purdue's entire research enterprise," does this mean that Purdue is committed to the idea that we should *not* use our intelligence to further our moral ends?[59] In any case, and in summary, Zinn does not attack "objectivity" (if this is understood in its primary sense as objectivity-as-accuracy) or the scientific method;[60] rather he attacks the claim that a *commitment* to these scholarly ideals requires scholars to remain neutral on urgent matters that are currently controversial, or that an appeal to "objectivity" is sufficient, all by itself, without any consideration of evidence or arguments, to warrant the adoption of a "proper," conventional, mainstream, "patriotic" stance on political issues.

To put the point another way, there is a difference between (1) attacking "objective study" and the "scientific method," and (2) attacking arguments that *appeal to* "objective study" and the "scientific method" *in making the case that scholars should refrain from addressing controversial issues of contemporary interest*. Is this distinction too subtle for Daniels? Or did Daniels deliberately distort Zinn's point, by omitting the context of his references to "objective study" and "the scientific method"? Or did he pass on someone else's ignorant libel without even bothering to check whether it was fair or accurate? Is there another possibility?

Daniels's criticism is also defective in that it implies that Zinn was attempting to justify lax intellectual standards, when in fact his argument moves in the opposite direction. Daniels invites his readers to think that the point of Zinn's "attack on objectivity" was to justify (or rationalize) his desire to free himself from scholarly norms so that he might, in the guise of scholarship, engage in propaganda on behalf of his preferred political positions. But Zinn does not call for any weakening of rigorous intellectual standards.

Note, first, that in calling on historians and other scholars to engage controversial contemporary issues, as in his complaint that in a conference of Asian studies scholars held during the Vietnam War no sessions were devoted to that topic, there is no suggestion that in doing so they should leave their intellectual standards behind. To the contrary, the whole point of Zinn's call for such engaged scholarship is that we desperately need to take advantage of all of the benefits of careful, logical, data-based, rational inquiry so that we can make progress toward solving pressing problems. Those whose approach to contemporary controversial issues is that of sloppy subjective propagandizing that cannot withstand logical scrutiny will find their arguments exposed as such by means of criticism by others. There is nothing in Zinn's argument for increased scholarly attention to present-day controversies to suggest that he thinks that such attention should be accompanied by laxity in intellectual standards. Thus, his call for greater scholarly attention to contemporary problems, far from constituting an attack on scholarly norms, is instead an argument for their wider use and application.

Second, Zinn calls for increased intellectual rigor with regard to the crucial issue of selection—which issues and facts to include, which to emphasize, and which to omit. Many scholars fail to give this issue serious and careful thought. Instead, they simply choose to include, emphasize, and omit the same things that their teachers did, and that other professionals in their field do. They passively internalize the same values. The result is an uncritical perpetuation of those values, as in the case, to return to an earlier example, of American historians who for many generations gave us Columbus as explorer and discoverer, but not Columbus as murderer, torturer, and enslaver of the Arawaks. If scholars were to give this issue of selection more sustained critical attention, as Zinn advocates, the result would be a strengthening, not a weakening, of intellectual standards. A greater variety of perspectives on different subjects would emerge, as in two views on Columbus, rather than just one. This would facilitate the engagement of our critical faculties in comparing and evaluating these different perspectives, so that no one perspective—not even the mainstream, traditional, consensus one—would be sustained by default, without having to stand up to rational, evidence-based scrutiny.

Third, Zinn calls on scholars to adopt, in a very conscious and clear-minded way, certain values in their work, and argues that doing so will aid them in their efforts to achieve a high level of accuracy. The first premise in this argument is that the necessity of selection precludes value neutrality. Historians must choose what to include, exclude, and emphasize, and these choices are based on their values—their sense of what is important, relevant, and interesting. Zinn argues that the values guiding such selection decisions should be universal (things that are good for everyone), rather than parochial (things that are good only for one nation, class, race, sex, culture, etc., but not for others), and ultimate (things that are good for their own sake), rather than instrumental (things that are good only as a means for bringing about things that are good for their own sake).

A concern for universal values is more conducive to objectivity than is a concern for parochial values, since unanimity in subjective responses to an objective reality is more likely to indicate an accurate assessment of that reality than is a response that tends to vary depending on the subjectivity of the responder. If Americans differ from Africans, the rich differ from the poor, men differ from women, the old differ from the young, and so forth, in their reaction to some objective reality, it seems likely that their differing evaluations of that reality will be colored by, or reflect some bias arising from, their different subjectivities. But if everyone, no matter what his or her race, sex, ethnicity, nationality, economic status, and so on, agrees that, for example, "love is preferable to hate, peace to war, brotherhood to enmity, joy to sorrow, health to sickness, nourishment to hunger, life to death (HPE 23)," it seems likely that these judgments are indeed accurate, and do not reflect distortions stemming from any kind of subjective bias.

Accordingly, Zinn writes, in the essay to which Daniels refers, that "The university and its scholars (teachers, students, researchers) should unashamedly declare that their interest is in eliminating war, poverty, race and national hatred, governmental restrictions on individual freedom, and in fostering a spirit of cooperation and concern in the generation growing up. They should *not* serve the interests of particular nations or parties or religions or political dogmas" (UOS; ZR 504; OH 183; KFP 10).[61] While Zinn's reason for advocating this is primarily moral, his proposal also carries the advantage, for the reason just mentioned, of enhancing the scholar's ability to achieve objectivity-as-accuracy. In that light, it is ironic, as Zinn notes, that "scholars have often served narrow governmental, military, or business interests, and yet withheld support from larger, transcendental values, on the ground that they needed to maintain neutrality" (UOS; ZR 504; OH 183; KFP 10). That irony is only enhanced by the observation, to be documented and discussed below, that many of Zinn's critics, who condemn his explicit opposition to war and racism as biased and contrary to scholarly norms of objectivity, nonetheless in their own "scholarly" work evidently think it perfectly consistent with such norms to promote the economic model of their own country, the interests and policies of their own government, and above all, their country's military objectives, even when these are opposed by tens of millions of people around the world. Even more impressively, they seem able to do this without even noticing the apparent contradiction, and without betraying so much as the slightest awareness of the issues their conduct raises, or the most minimal understanding of the arguments that could be leveled (and are by Zinn, among others) against that conduct.

The reason why adherence to ultimate values is more conducive to the achievement of objectivity-as-accuracy than is allegiance to instrumental values is that the assessment of instrumental values is much more strongly tied to the assessment of empirical matters of fact than is the assessment of ultimate values. For example, and to return to Zinn's list, while it is hard to imagine any factual discovery, any empirical observation, that would throw doubt on the thesis that peace is (in itself, all else equal) better than war, that joy is better than sorrow, that health is better than sickness, and that life is better than death, the question of means, the instrumental question of which action, or policy, or social arrangement is best able to *bring us* peace rather than war, joy rather than sorrow, and so forth, is, in quite radical contrast, a thoroughly empirical matter, one in which observations and other factual discoveries are perfectly capable of showing our judgments to be wrong. Thus, while someone who is committed only to ultimate values (such as that health is better than sickness) need not fear that any assessment of facts will show his or her commitment to be unwise, that is not the case for one who is committed to instrumental values (such as that some particular kind of health care system is the most efficient way to promote health and combat sickness).[62] Consequently, it is only the scholar who is committed to a particular instrument for achieving health, and precisely not the scholar whose only allegiance is to the value of health itself, who has a motive (whether conscious or unconscious) to spin or twist the facts so that they line up in support of his or her value choices. Similarly, once we recognize that particular American laws, policies, traditions, and actions are not ends in themselves, that is, not ultimate values, but rather things that should be evaluated only as instruments, that is, in terms of their ability to support such ultimate values as "life, liberty, and the pursuit of happiness," then we see that those who face the greatest danger of succumbing to a reality-distorting bias are not radical critics like Zinn, who prioritize ultimate values over instrumental values, and who on that basis criticize the United States for engaging in actions that violate its ideals, but rather those "patriots" who either confuse or conflate ultimate and instrumental values, so that their ultimate allegiance is to American policies and traditions.[63] Once again, while no observation is likely to show that it is a mistake to value life, liberty, and the pursuit of happiness, it is easy to think of observations that could undermine the claim that a particular American policy *promotes* life, liberty, and the pursuit of happiness, or that American policies do this best, or that the United States is "unique" and "exceptional" in doing so, because we are, after all, the greatest nation on earth, with the best health care system, the best economic system, the best political system, the best education system, the greatest commitment to human rights, the most generous people, and blah, blah, blah. When observations can undermine commitments, there is a motive to distort the observations. When observations are powerless to undermine commitments, there is no such motive.

Zinn puts the point this way:

At the bottom of the [scholar's] fear of engagement [with current problems], it seems to me, is a confusion between ultimate values and instrumental ones. To start historical inquiry with frank adherence to a small set of ultimate values—that war, poverty, race hatred…should be abolished; that mankind constitutes a single species; that affection and cooperation should replace violence and hostility—such a set of commitments places no pressure on its advocates to tamper with the truth.[64] The claim of Hume and his successors among the logical positivists, that no *should* can be proved by what *is*, has its useful side, for neither can the moral absolute be disproved by any factual discovery. (HPE 20)

This point enables us to understand one of the ways in which Zinn's approach, in this case that of commitment to ultimate values, allows him to achieve greater objectivity-as-accuracy than is achieved by those of his critics (and there are many of them) who claim to bring no value commitments into their scholarly work, but who in fact are ultimately committed to values that are merely instrumental (usually those associated either with patriotism or conformity to mainstream, conventional thinking).

Moreover, Zinn is careful to explain, and even to emphasize (though Daniels and other critics typically ignore the point), that his call for a scholarly commitment to ultimate, universal values is confined to the domain of selection—the issue of choosing among different projects to undertake, different problems to address, different aspects of those problems on which to focus, different questions to ask, and so forth—and precisely not to the domain of determining what the answers are to the questions one has chosen to ask. While evidence emerges as such only in the context of answering a specific question, or testing a certain theory, or exploring a well-defined subject domain, or something of that sort, the answers to the questions the scholar poses, once the value-laden decisions of selective focusing have been made, should be determined by a rational and accurate assessment of the relevant evidence, rather than by further consulting the scholar's values.

Zinn himself makes this point by observing, first (as already quoted above) that: "If to be objective is to be scrupulously careful about reporting accurately what one sees, then of course this is laudable." He then continues:

> But accuracy is only a prerequisite. Whether a metalsmith uses reliable measuring instruments is a prerequisite for doing good work, but does not answer the crucial question: will he now forge a sword or a plowshare with his instruments? That the metalsmith has determined in advance that he prefers a plowshare does not require him to distort his measurements. That the scholar has decided he prefers peace to war does not require him to distort his facts.[65]
>
> Too many scholars abjure a starting set of values, because they fail to make the proper distinction between an ultimate set of values and the instruments needed to obtain them. The values may well be subjective (derived from human needs); but the instruments must be objective (accurate). Our values should determine the *questions* we ask in scholarly inquiry, but not the answers. (UOS; ZR 504; OH 183–4; KFP 10)

Or again, Zinn insists that his argument "does not call for tampering with the facts.... My point is not to approach historical data with preconceived answers, but with preconceived questions. I assume accuracy is a prerequisite, but that history is not praiseworthy for having merely achieved that" (IFE 2).[66]

While Zinn emphasizes the need for, and the legitimacy of, selection in historical research and writing, he makes it clear that omissions are to be justified only by considerations having to do with the degree to which a given datum is or is not interesting, or important, or relevant—especially to the ultimate, universal values discussed above. He repeatedly states that he does not condone omitting information that runs counter to one's thesis. If evidence in a certain domain, or with respect to a certain question, is worthy of inclusion, then so is the corresponding counter-evidence. He specifically condemns as unethical the strategic use of omissions so as to make one side of an argument look stronger than it really is. For example, in the passage just quoted, in which he states that his argument "does not call for tampering with facts," he goes on to list "concealment," along with "distortion" and "invention," as one of the ways in which such tampering might be accomplished (IFE 2). Similarly, in a 1995 speech, in which he states, once again, that he considers objectivity to be neither possible nor desirable, he qualifies that claim in this way: "unless objectivity mean[s] telling the truth as you [see] it, not lying, not distorting, not omitting information, and *not omitting arguments because they don't conform to some idea that you have*" (REE 94, emphasis added). Elsewhere he clarifies the meaning of his rejection of "objectivity" by noting that it does "not mean looking only for facts to reinforce the beliefs I already [hold]. It [does] not mean ignoring data that would change or complicate my understanding of society" (DOI 48). And in a 1988 interview, after first making the point that "We're faced with an infinite number of facts—an infinite amount of information—and the historian...*selects* out of that what he/she considers important," he immediately adds, "Of course you have an obligation not to hide things that are embarrassing to you, or embarrassing to people who employ you, or embarrassing to the nation you belong to, or embarrassing to some set of ideas you uphold" (OHM).[67]

Finally, while Zinn does call on scholars to address contemporary problems, and to use their knowledge and skill in an attempt to solve them, even if that means taking sides on controversial issues, he also repeatedly stresses (1) that he intends his call to be non-coercive, (2) that he respects and indeed values approaches other than the sort he is encouraging, and (3) that the issue is merely one of proportion—there should be much more historical and other scholarship that is directly relevant to contemporary concerns than is currently the case. For example, he tells us that he "does not argue for a uniform approach—mine or anyone's—to the writing of history, and certainly not for the banning of any kind of historical work, bland or controversial, pernicious or humane, whether written for pleasure or profit or social objectives." Rather, his "aim is, by encouragement and example, to stimulate a higher proportion of socially-relevant, value-motivated, action-inducing historical work" (IFE 2). Similarly, in the essay Daniels cites, Zinn asks: "Am I trying to obliterate all scholarship except the immediately relevant?" His answer: "No—it is a matter of proportion."[68] It is in this context that he remarks: "It was not wrong for the Association of Asian Studies at its 1969 meeting to discuss some problems of the Ming dynasty and a battery of similarly remote topics." His objection, however, is to the fact that "*no* session of the dozens at the meeting dealt with Vietnam" (UOS; ZR 502; OH 180; KFP 7–8). And as for his appreciation for more traditional historical works that are not addressed to contemporary social justice issues, note his comment that his criticism is not directed "against those few histories which are works of art, which make no claim to illuminate a social problem, but instead capture the mood, the color, the reality of an age, an incident, or an individual, conveying pleasure and the warmth of genuine emotion. This needs no justification, for it is, after all, the ultimate purpose of social change to enlarge human happiness" (HPE 19). Indeed, Zinn's main point is not to denigrate scholarship that is addressed to remote topics, but rather to refute fallacious arguments that wrongly persuade scholars that the taking of sides on controversial contemporary issues is propagandistic and unscientific, and that *only* work that maintains its "neutrality" by avoiding such topics entirely can be truly "scholarly."

As we have seen, in many of his writings, including "The Uses of Scholarship," the essay that Mitch Daniels singles out for criticism, Zinn anticipates objections to his critique of objectivity, and attempts to clarify his views further by responding to those objections. These responses are featured prominently and discussed clearly and in detail in Zinn's work, so that any minimally competent discussion of his views on this issue would need to come to terms with them. Indeed, it would be astonishingly incompetent and irresponsible for a critic to present as his or her own decisive objections to Zinn criticisms that he himself had already articulated, and to which he had responded, without the critic so much as mentioning, much less answering, those responses. To fail to meet such an elementary standard of rational discussion and scholarly fairness would be unacceptable in the work of a college freshman in an introductory class. And yet, to my amazement, while I have found several works by professional scholars—college professors, professional historians, many of whom work and teach at prestigious institutions—which indict him with criticisms that he had already anticipated and to which he had replied (a point to be discussed and documented in the next chapter), I have yet to find a single critical essay on Zinn that addresses, or even acknowledges, those replies.

Of course it is possible that Zinn's arguments are unsound, his conclusions untrue, and his recommendations unwise. But to show that, it would be necessary to discuss what he actually says.[69] Before condemning him for "admitting" that he is biased, or dismissing him as a "propagandist" because he rejects "objectivity," one would first have to (1) take up the question of what he means by "bias" and "objectivity," (2) address his arguments that bias is unavoidable (even by his critics and by more orthodox historians) and that "objectivity," in one of its senses, is both unachievable (even by his critics and by more orthodox historians) and undesirable, (3) acknowledge that he, no less than his critics, condemns "bias" (in the sense of an unfair and irrational prejudice) and affirms "objectivity" (in the sense of accuracy), (4) come to terms with his argument that the role of values in scholarship is confined to issues of selection and the posing of questions, and precisely not to the assessment of evidence or to the determination of answers, (5) address his distinctions among universal, parochial, ultimate, and instrumental values, and refute his argument that his approach, based on those distinctions, is a better one for the achievement of objectivity-as-accuracy than is that of more traditional, conventional, mainstream, or "patriotic" historians, (6) refute his argument that his approach upholds every classic scholarly norm, with the single exception of the one that calls for objectivity-as-neutrality—a norm that he has criticized as spurious, (7) acknowledge that his call for scholars to engage, and to take sides on, urgent contemporary problems is not a call for the abandonment of logic, reason, the careful assessment of evidence, or anything of that sort, but rather a plea for the wider use and application of these and other tools of scholarly rigor—specifically in domains that had been declared out of bounds for scholars, due to concerns, which in Zinn's view are misplaced, that legitimate scholarly norms demand either neutrality or evidence-free centrism, and (8) acknowledge that he does not reject and attempt to abolish more traditional or conservative approaches to history, but rather tries merely to make a case for the legitimacy of his own approach, and to encourage a higher percentage of historical work that is addressed to contemporary controversies.

It is also possible that Zinn, in spite of his stated support for the ideals of scholarly accuracy and honesty, in fact does sloppy work and gets facts wrong, or draws incorrect conclusions from the evidence he discusses, or covers up evidence that goes against his preferred views. But to show this it is necessary, once again, to deal with the details of his texts, to show specifically which of his conclusions are wrong and why. And this, in turn, requires attention to the evidence that is relevant to those conclusions, and a demonstration of the ways in which Zinn has mishandled that evidence—either by ignoring it, misstating it, analyzing it incorrectly, or drawing the wrong conclusions from it due to some or another specific logical mistake.

However, as we will see in the next chapter, Zinn's critics tend to address very few (and in many cases none at all) of these issues. Instead, they, like Mitch Daniels, tend to limit themselves to three moves: (1) name-calling ("biased," "propagandist," "not a historian"); (2) taking his quotations about bias and objectivity out of context and presenting them as "admissions" that he feels free to be a dishonest propagandist whose work is unconstrained by concerns of fidelity to evidence or logical rigor; and (3) dismissing him as a radical extremist on the basis of citing some of his conclusions that go against a mainstream consensus, but doing so without considering the evidence and arguments he gives in support of those conclusions.

Chapter 3

Zinn's Critics

In this chapter I will attempt to refute the standard objections to Zinn, especially those harsh criticisms, circulating widely in right-wing circles, that are intended to show that he is incompetent, or a charlatan, rather than an honest scholar with whom one might merely disagree. These are the criticisms that might persuade some to believe that Mitch Daniels acted reasonably and responsibly when he attempted to ban Zinn's work from Indiana classrooms.

While I cannot possibly address every one of Zinn's critics, I will respond to the criticisms of (a) every critic that Daniels personally named and quoted, both in his initial comments on the controversy caused by the publication of his anti-Zinn emails and in the list of additional quotations that he advertised on his Purdue webpage as being available "on request"; (b) every substantial article that I could find by an academic figure who defended Daniels's actions with respect to Zinn; (c) the pieces of Zinn criticism that are most frequently cited by those who have written in support of Daniels; (d) a few other especially lengthy and harshly critical essays; and (e) some other pieces that either contain arguments not found in other works or else present some of the standard criticisms especially clearly. I have generally not responded to those many critics who have given Zinn a mixed review, or who have offered only such criticisms as one would make against a respected scholarly colleague—for these are the kinds of criticisms that all scholars receive, and they are not of the sort that could provide any support for Daniels's public comments on Zinn or for his actions in attempting to disqualify Zinn's work from being taught for credit in Indiana schools. But I will attempt to show that the opinion that Zinn is worthy of

141

contempt, that he is either incompetent or dishonest, and that the teaching of his work in schools would therefore be an outrage, rests on arguments that are, uniformly, not merely wrong, but rather ludicrous, crudely fallacious, themselves either incompetent or dishonest, or, at the very least, utterly lacking in evidentiary support. The fact that they are presented, in some cases, by distinguished professors of history, that they circulate widely, and that they are readily believed, tells us, I fear, something very disturbing about contemporary intellectual standards.

Sam Wineburg

Wineburg, one of the authorities that Daniels cited in support of his extreme anti-Zinn views, is the Director of the Stanford History Education Group. A specialist in history education, he is a Professor of History at Stanford University, in addition to holding the title of Margaret Jacks Professor of Education at that same prestigious institution.

Wineburg's major work on Zinn, and the one from which Daniels quotes, is "Undue Certainty: Where Howard Zinn's *A People's History* Falls Short," an eight-page essay published in the Winter 2012–13 issue of *American Educator* (WIN). At first, Wineburg strikes a moderate tone, claiming that he is not particularly critical of the "substance" of Zinn's book: "My own view is that Howard Zinn has the same right as any author to choose one interpretation over another, to select which topics to include or ignore" (WIN 28). Wineburg goes on to explain that while he agrees with some of Zinn's conclusions and disagrees with others, the issue of where his "proclivities align with or depart from Zinn's is beside the point" of his critique:

> I am less concerned here with what Zinn says than his warrant for saying it, less interested in the words that meet the eye than with the book's interpretive circuitry that doesn't. Largely invisible to the casual reader are the moves and

strategies Zinn uses to tie evidence to conclusion, to convince readers that his interpretations are right. More is at stake in naming and making explicit these moves than an exercise in rhetoric. For when students encounter Zinn's *A People's History*, they…are exposed to and absorb an entire way of asking questions about the past and a way of using evidence to advance historical argument. For many students, *A People's History* will be the first full-length history book they read, and for some, it will be the only one. [W]hat does *A People's History* teach these young people about what it means to *think historically?*…To examine in detail the book's moves and strategies, what I refer to as its *interpretive circuitry*, I train my sights on a key chapter, one of the most pivotal and controversial in the book. Chapter 16, "A People's War?," covers the period from the mid-1930s to the beginning of the Cold War. Unlike chapters in which Zinn introduces readers to hidden aspects of American history—such as the Flour Riot of 1837—the stakes here are much higher. This is not the first time we've heard about Pearl Harbor or the Holocaust or the decision to drop the atomic bomb. But Zinn's goal is to turn everything we know—or think we do—on its head. (WIN 28)

The first example of Zinn's handling of evidence that Wineburg considers has to do with Zinn's alleged conclusion that "'*widespread* indifference, even hostility,' typified African Americans' stance toward the war" (WIN 28, citing the 2003 edition of Zinn's *A People's History of the United States*, 418–19, Wineburg's emphasis added). Wineburg's complaint is (a) that Zinn bases his conclusion on insufficient evidence, and (b) that he ignores counterevidence. On the first point, Wineburg writes: "Zinn hangs his claim on three pieces of evidence: (1) a quote from a black journalist that "the Negro…is angry, resentful, and utterly apathetic about the war"; (2) a quote from a student at a black college who told his teacher that "the Army jim-crows us.

The Navy lets us serve only as messmen. The Red Cross refuses our blood. Employers and labor unions shut us out. Lynchings continue"; and (3) a poem called the "Draftee's Prayer," published in the black press: "Dear Lord, today / I go to war: / To fight, to die, / Tell me what for? / Dear Lord, I'll fight, / I do not fear, / Germans or Japs; / My fears are here. / America!" (Wineburg 28, citing APH 418–19).

With regard to the omission of counterevidence, Wineburg points to two pieces of data, both drawn from the same source (Lawrence Wittner's *Rebels Against War*)[1] as that from which Zinn took his three pieces of evidence: (1) a statement by Horace Mann Bond, a black college president, indignantly denying that "a Negro in the United States is indifferent to the outcome of a great national struggle," and (2) statistics showing that blacks were greatly underrepresented among those granted "conscientious objector" status for World War II (WIN 29).

Let's begin our critical discussion by considering the way in which Zinn establishes a context for discussing this issue, together with Wineburg's representation of Zinn's contextualizing. The chapter of Zinn's book in question (Chapter 16) is entitled "A People's War?," and on its first page (APH 407) Zinn does indeed ask whether World War II was a people's war. Immediately after posing this question, the first two sentences of his reply read as follows: "By certain evidence, it was the most popular war the United States had ever fought. Never had a greater proportion of the country participated in a war: 18 million served in the armed forces, 10 million overseas; 25 million workers gave of their pay envelope regularly for war bonds" (APH 407). Wineburg introduces his discussion of this issue this way: "Consider the question of whether World War II was 'a people's war.' On one level, as Zinn has to admit, it was. Thousands suited up in uniform, and millions handed over hard-earned dollars to buy war bonds" (WIN 28). One who has read only Wineburg, and not Zinn, might guess from this, especially given Wineburg's repeated claim that Zinn omits evidence that runs counter to his claims, that it is only Wineburg, and not Zinn, who cites the evidence in question. That is, such a reader might assume that Zinn merely "admits" what the evidence implies, not that he presents that evidence himself.

To show that I am not being picky and pedantic about this, consider how Zinn's and Wineburg's parallel discussions unfold. Zinn ends the paragraph from which I quoted above by posing another question: "Was there an undercurrent of reluctance; were there unpublicized signs of resistance?" (APH 407) But Wineburg's paraphrase, clearly presented as such, reads this way: "Was there, in fact, widespread resentment and resistance to the war that was hidden from the masses?" (WIN 28) An "*undercurrent* of *reluctance*" becomes "*widespread resentment*"; "*signs of* resistance" becomes "*widespread* resistance." True, as we have seen from one of the quotations cited above, Zinn did a few pages later go on to use the word "widespread" in connection with lack of enthusiasm for the war by black Americans. But even here, Wineburg subtly distorts what Zinn says. Zinn's sentence reads as follows: "There seemed to be widespread indifference, even hostility, on the part of the Negro community to the war despite the attempts of Negro newspapers and Negro leaders to mobilize black sentiment" (APH 419). Wineburg's paraphrase: "Zinn claims that an attitude of '*widespread* indifference, even hostility,' typified African Americans' stance toward the war." Here Wineburg distorts Zinn's meaning in at least three ways: (1) Wineburg leaves out Zinn's introductory "seemed to be" locution, a phrase by means of which Zinn qualifies what follows as uncertain. This is an important omission, since it makes Zinn seem more dogmatic than he really was (and one of the main burdens of Wineburg's essay is to convict Zinn of dogmatism, as his title, "Undue Certainty," suggests). Indeed, Wineburg's seemingly harmless deletion of Zinn's "seemed to be" must be judged egregious, given what he goes on to claim: that, whereas most historians frequently use "qualifying language to signal the soft underbelly of historical certainty...a search in *A People's History* for qualifiers mostly comes up empty" (WIN 32); and that Zinn's approach "detests equivocation and extinguishes *perhaps, maybe, might*," and the like (WIN 34). That these two claims are false, as I will argue subsequently, is not my present point. Rather, it is that anyone who wants to accuse someone else of being allergic to qualifying language must not edit out of quotations from that person such phrases as "seemed to be."

(2) Wineburg converts Zinn's more modest claim that indifference and hostility were (we'll waive the "seemed to be" issue for the moment) *widespread* among the black community, to the much stronger claim that indifference and hostility *typified* (a word not used by Zinn) the stance of that community. "Widespread" means "found or distributed over a large area or number of people." So, for example, while to say that poverty is widespread in America is definitely to say that there is a lot of it, and it is found in many places, it certainly carries no implication that *most* Americans are poor. But to say that poverty "typifies" Americans is to say that most Americans are poor—indeed, it is to make a stronger claim even than that. For "typify" is a verb meaning "to embody the essential or salient characteristics of," while its related adjective, "typical," means "having the distinctive qualities of a particular type of person or thing." So if Zinn had said what Wineburg claims he did, he would have been asserting that most black Americans were indifferent to or hostile toward the war, indeed, that such attitudes embodied the essential or salient characteristics of the response to the war by the American black community. By contrast, Zinn's actual claim was much more modest. It was merely that such attitudes were (well, actually, "seemed to be"—but we're letting that go) found among a large number (though a number that might come nowhere close to constituting a majority) of black Americans, and in many parts of the country. These distortions are crucial,

because they go directly to the issue that most concerns Wineburg, that of Zinn's handling of evidence. While the evidence that Zinn cites may well be, as Wineburg charges, inadequate for supporting the claim that Wineburg puts in his mouth (that an attitude of indifference, even hostility, "typified" African Americans' stance toward the war), perhaps it fares better when it is put in support of Zinn's actual thesis (that such attitudes were merely "widespread" among African Americans).

(3) In another passage Wineburg distorts Zinn's thesis even further. Wineburg, in connection with the black press having referred to the "Double V," meaning victory over fascism in Europe and victory over racism at home, attributes to Zinn the claim that "black Americans restricted their support to a single V: the victory over racism" (WIN 28). Note that Wineburg inserts no qualifier here. He claims that Zinn "asserts" not that "*many* black Americans restricted their support to a single V: the victory over racism," or that *most* of them did so, but rather, simply that "*black Americans*" did so. But Zinn says no such thing. A search reveals that the phrases "double V," "single V," "victory over fascism," and "victory over racism" do not appear in Zinn's text. They are introduced as part of Wineburg's alleged paraphrase of what Zinn says about the attitudes of black Americans toward the war. Immediately after issuing his (false) claim that Zinn "asserts that black Americans restricted their support to a single V: the victory over racism," he offers this explanation: "As for the second V, victory on the battlefields of Europe and Asia, Zinn claims that an attitude of '*widespread* indifference, even hostility,' typified African Americans' stance toward the war." And that is followed immediately with: "Zinn hangs his claim on three pieces of evidence..." We have encountered this before. So not only does Wineburg incorrectly think that "there seemed to be widespread indifference, even hostility, on the part of the Negro community to the war" can be accurately paraphrased as "an attitude of '*widespread* indifference, even hostility,' typified African

Americans' stance toward the war" (with the "seemed to be" qualifier dropped, and the word "typified" added—so that a significant minority of black Americans can be converted to a huge majority of them), but we now see that he also thinks it can be accurately paraphrased in such a way as to entail that black Americans (all of them, without exception) cared nothing about a victory over fascism in Europe, because "black Americans restricted their support to a single V: the victory over racism." In this way Wineburg converts Zinn's hedged ("seemed to be") statement about the beliefs and attitudes of *many* black Americans both into an insufficiently qualified and inadequately documented statement about *most* black Americans (that is, about beliefs and attitudes that "typified" African Americans' stance) and, finally, into a wildly dogmatic claim about *all* black Americans. Ironically, it is *Wineburg* who, apparently with a straight face, uses such words and phrases as "slippery" and "plays fast and loose" when discussing *Zinn's* work!

Wineburg omits Zinn's reference to "the attempts of Negro newspapers and Negro leaders to mobilize black sentiment." Such an omission is important because (a) it stands as an example of Zinn's citing evidence of black support for the war—presumably black leaders and black newspaper editorialists would not be attempting to mobilize support for the war if they did not support it themselves, and (b) it may partially explain why he did not cite the specific example of a black leader (a college president) speaking in favor of the war—an omission for which Wineburg faults Zinn.

Wineburg also fails to mention that, immediately following Zinn's presentation of evidence in support of his claim about widespread indifference and hostility, he includes, in addition, a piece of counterevidence: "There was no organized Negro opposition to the war" (APH 419). (And, in light of the fact that the broader context in which this issue was raised was a discussion of the question of whether or not World War II was genuinely "A People's War," and given Wineburg's accusation that Zinn fails to present evidence that runs counter to his favored conclusions, it should be noted that the quotation just cited continues as follows: "In fact, there was little organized opposition from any source" [APH 419]. Moreover, on page 421 of APH we read: "Public opinion polls show large majorities of soldiers favoring the draft for the postwar period.")

Nor do these omissions and distortions constitute the only failings in Wineburg's discussion of Zinn's claim about the attitudes of black Americans regarding World War II. Amazingly, he also follows the pattern of almost every critic of Zinn's allegedly bad scholarship in that he commits clear, demonstrable, unscholarly factual errors in the course of his own brief discussion of Zinn. (I know of no Zinn critic who does not commit many times more demonstrable errors per page than Zinn himself does.) Recall that Wineburg says, in connection with Zinn's claim about black indifference to and hostility toward World War II, that "Zinn hangs his claim on three pieces of evidence." There is nothing subtle, unclear, or ambiguous about this statement. Adding to its admirable clarity, Wineburg lists the three pieces of evidence, and cites the page number where they can be found in Zinn's text. And yet, Wineburg's claim is flatly wrong, and wrong in a way (as is true of all of his mistakes) that slights Zinn and (illegitimately) lends support to Wineburg's own thesis. For on the very page that Wineburg cites, Zinn provides, not three pieces of evidence, but five—with the two omitted pieces being of the same (admittedly anecdotal) type and character as the three included ones. Let's recall Wineburg's list of three: (1) a quote from a black journalist that "the Negro...is angry, resentful, and utterly apathetic about the war"; (2) a quote from a student at a black college who told his teacher that "the Army jim-crows us. The Navy lets us serve only as messmen. The Red Cross refuses our blood. Employers and labor unions shut us out. Lynchings continue"; and (3) a poem called the "Draftee's

Prayer," published in the black press: "Dear Lord, today / I go to war: / To fight, to die, / Tell me what for? / Dear Lord, I'll fight, / I do not fear, / Germans or Japs; / My fears are here. / America!" But, ignored by Wineburg, we find, between items (1) and (2) from his list, the following: "A black army officer, home on furlough, told friends in Harlem he had been in hundreds of bull sessions with Negro soldiers and found no interest in the war." Even more significantly, Wineburg omits another piece of evidence that is presented immediately following item (2) from his list. To give the full context, I will quote the full version of item (2), as it is presented in Zinn's text, with the quotation continuing to include the evidence that Wineburg leaves out (indeed, the evidence that he explicitly denies, falsely, even exists in Zinn's book): "A student at a Negro college told his teacher: 'The Army jim-crows us. The Navy lets us serve only as messmen. The Red Cross refuses our blood. Employers and labor unions shut us out. Lynchings continue. We are disenfranchised, jim-crowed, spat upon. What more could Hitler do than that?' [Then, the piece of evidence that Wineburg misses]: "NAACP leader Walter White repeated this to a black audience of several thousand people in the Midwest, thinking they would disapprove, but instead, as he recalled: 'To my surprise and dismay the audience burst into such applause that it took me some thirty or forty seconds to quiet it'" (APH 419).

To grasp the full extent of Wineburg's blunder here, consider some other ways that he might have handled the two missing pieces of evidence. He could have simply passed them over in silence, contenting himself with pointing out what he takes to be some flaw or flaws in Zinn's other three pieces of evidence, without stating or implying that these three exhaust Zinn's evidentiary contribution to the issue at hand. Alternatively, he might have offered some kind of argument or explanation as to why he is unwilling to count the rejected two pieces of evidence as genuinely independent items, distinct from the three items that he does acknowledge. But he does neither of these things. Rather, while citing a page in Zinn's writings in which Zinn presents what appear to be five distinct evidentiary items, Wineburg, without offering any explanation for the discrepancy whatsoever, baldly asserts that Zinn provides only three pieces of evidence, and then proceeds to condemn him for this evidentiary deficiency.

As if this were not appalling enough, notice that the two evidentiary items that Wineburg excludes are stronger than the three he acknowledges, because the excluded two report on the attitudes of many (hundreds of bull sessions, audience of several thousand), while the included three each reflect the voices of single individuals (a black journalist, a soldier, a poet). So Wineburg illegitimately makes Zinn's case weaker not only by excluding 40 percent of his evidence, but also by cherry picking that evidence in such a way as to leave standing only his weakest examples.

With regard to Wineburg's criticism of Zinn's failure to include, as counterevidence to his thesis, the fact that blacks were underrepresented in the class of conscientious objectors to World War II, it seems to me that Zinn's omission is defensible on the grounds that this datum is of little evidentiary value. The reason is that the fact that few blacks became conscientious objectors might be plausibly explained by a great number of factors that are fully consistent with an attitude of indifference to, or hostility towards, the war among black Americans. For one thing, as Charles Bogle and Fred Mazelis point out, "Conscientious objectors, including pacifists and those who claimed religious motives, came overwhelmingly from middle class layers of the population. At that time, the great majority of the black population would have barely known of the conscientious objection option."[2] Pete Dolack identifies several other likely factors:

Professor Wineburg...complains that the number of conscientious objectors was not only low, but that Black C.O.s were proportionally fewer than White C.O.s. He simply uses the raw numbers in these categories without making any attempt to analyze them, an irony when a primary accusation against *People's History* is that it is too simplistic. I am not an expert on World War II and am in no position to issue judgments, but a reasonable analysis would take into account the fact that Blacks consistently faced much harsher punishments than Whites, perhaps dampening the willingness to act on ambivalences toward the war. We might also consider the racism that would have made it more difficult for a Black objector to be granted C.O. status by White decision-makers.

Any analysis would surely have to contend with the fact that, as *People's History* does but Professor Wineburg does not, the World War I-era espionage act criminalizing dissent was still on the books and the Smith Act passed in 1940 made criticism of the war effort illegal. These acts, while applied ruthlessly against Left critics of the wars, likely would have come down especially hard on African-Americans who publicly objected and wielded as racist object lessons. Would this not have an effect?[3]

Similarly, Alison Kysia points out that: "There is no direct correlation between draft refusal and support for war; many draftees may not want to fight but nevertheless report for duty due to a variety of reasons. Wineburg does not inform the reader about the complex and expensive process of being certified as a conscientious objector. Nor does Wineburg acknowledge the emotional, financial, and political repercussions of a black man resisting the draft or publicly challenging the morality of the war while living in the Jim Crow United States" (KYS).

Before proceeding further, let's pause to note that Wineburg's announced intention is to examine the "interpretive circuitry" of

Zinn's book, that is, "the moves and strategies," "largely invisible to the casual reader," that "Zinn uses to tie evidence to conclusion, to convince readers that his interpretations are right." But now we have exposed something of Wineburg's own "interpretive circuitry," and it is clear that it stands in need of substantial repair. For as we have seen, in making his critique, Wineburg (1) omits multiple instances in which Zinn presents evidence running counter to his own thesis, even as he accuses Zinn of omitting such evidence; (2) paraphrases Zinn inaccurately in multiple ways, so that Zinn's claims about *many* are illegitimately transformed into claims about *most*, and then into claims about *all*; (3) edits out of a Zinn quotation the qualifying phrase, "seemed to be"—an unethical deletion, given (a) that the main point of Wineburg's article, entitled "Undue Certainty," is to convict Zinn of dogmatism, and (b) that one of the main pieces of evidence that he cites in support of this charge is Zinn's (alleged) aversion to such qualifying phrases; (4) accuses him of "hanging" a claim on just three pieces of evidence, when in fact Zinn cites five—with the other two appearing on the same page, and being of the same type, as the three that Wineburg is willing to acknowledge; and (5) criticizes Zinn for omitting a piece of counterevidence, even though (a) a good case can be made that the piece in question is of dubious relevance, and (b) Wineburg fails to inform the reader of any of the grounds for challenging its relevance. What are the intellectual standards in play here? Note finally that, excluding the bibliography and the index, Zinn's text runs to 688 pages, and contains hundreds of claims about United States history, many of which are controversial—and Wineburg was free to pick whatever examples he wanted in his attempt to prove that Zinn is a bad scholar, that there is something wrong with his "interpretive circuitry," that he handles evidence badly, and that his text shouldn't be used in classrooms. Indeed, if Zinn's work were as bad as Wineburg claims it is, there should be many—perhaps dozens or even hundreds—of examples of bad scholarship that a Stanford University historian would be able to call to the attention of the non-expert reader. And yet, we find that, even when Wineburg is free to choose his own example, he cannot make his case against Zinn without the aid of grotesque omissions, distortions, and factual errors. What does that suggest about the status of Zinn's scholarship (and of Wineburg's)?

Next, Wineburg criticizes Zinn for the sorts of questions he asks in his book. Wineburg's point seems to be that Zinn's questions reveal his dogmatism, his "undue certainty." Wineburg offers the opinion that: "At their best, questions signal the unfinished nature of historical knowledge, the way its fragments can never be wholly put together." But, he complains, "For Zinn, questions are not shoulder-shrugging admissions of the historian's epistemological quandary so much as devices that shock readers into considering the past anew" (WIN 29).

The problem here, I would argue, is that Wineburg's premise about the role of questions in history is arbitrary and unconvincing. To be sure, where crucial evidence is lacking, or hopelessly conflicting, or for any reason insufficient for the drawing of a firm conclusion, this "epistemological quandary" should be admitted, not denied or covered up; and the posing of questions, especially when they remain open and unanswered, is one good way of handling this. But it hardly follows from this that "signaling the unfinished nature of historical knowledge" is the only legitimate, or in all cases "the best," use of questions in history. "Did human beings and dinosaurs live at the same time, or did human beings only come into existence after the dinosaurs had become extinct?" is a question of natural history. The evidence, I submit, permits of a definitive answer. Does that make it a bad question? If so, why? Perhaps Wineburg's reason (though he doesn't say this—he offers no explanation) is that questions that have clear-cut answers have limited educational value (he is, after all, an education professor). But in response it should be pointed out that Zinn's questions (some of which will be quoted shortly) are not presented as specially marked exercises for the students, but rather are simply sprinkled throughout his narrative. So, to return to my example, whereas one could write, as a declarative sentence, that "human beings only came into existence after all the dinosaurs had become extinct," Zinn occasionally chooses instead the rhetorical device of asking a question (in this case, something like, "Did human beings and dinosaurs live at the same time, or did human beings only come into existence after the dinosaurs had become extinct?"), followed by a presentation of evidence necessary (and frequently sufficient) for answering it. If the objection is to dogmatism, why is the posing of a question, followed by answering it (or by implying an answer through the presentation of evidence) more dogmatic than simply announcing one's conclusion in a declarative sentence? This would seem to be a rather superficial rhetorical issue, raising no substantive episte- mological concerns. And if the objection is pedagogical (perhaps on the grounds that in order for a question to have educational value, the answer to it should not be obvious—it should be an open question, one about which there is room for debate and reasonable disagreement), there is also a ready reply. The posing of questions for which the evidence provides a clear and convincing answer can still have educational value because (a) the questions can help the student to focus on and to assess criti- cally the relevant evidence—the student will take in that evidence not as a string of random facts, but as clues to the answering of the question posed; and (b) because there are non- evidentiary reasons why some questions are controversial, and their answers are not perceived to be obvious, even though the evidence concerning them, once it is laid out, is conclusive—and these are precisely the sorts of questions that Zinn tends to ask. For a major theme of Zinn's book is to debunk myths about American history that are in wide circulation in American culture, including in mainstream history textbooks.

To see this, let's return to Wineburg's discussion. He offers a couple of short lists of Zinn's questions, followed in each case by his own brief commentary:

(Zinn's questions):
- Would America's behavior during the Second World War "be in keeping with a 'people's war'?"
- Would the Allies' victory deliver a "blow to imperialism, racism, totalitarianism, [and] militarism," and "represent something significantly different" from their Axis foes?
- Would America's wartime policies "respect the rights of ordinary people everywhere to life, liberty, and the pursuit of happiness?"
- "Would postwar America, in its policies at home and overseas, exemplify the values for which the war was supposed to have been fought?" (WIN 29, citing APH 408) (Wineburg's commentary): "No, no, no, and no. When questions aren't rattled off as yes-no binaries, they're delivered in a stark either-or, a rhetorical turn almost never encountered in professional historical writing" (WIN 29).

(Zinn):
- "Did the behavior of the United States show that her war aims were humanitarian, *or* centered on power and profit?" (WIN 29–30, citing APH 412, emphasis added)
- "Was she fighting the war to end the control by some nations over others *or* to make sure the controlling nations were friends of the United States?" (WIN 30, citing APH 412, emphasis added)
- With the defeat of the Axis, were fascism's "essential elements—militarism, racism, imperialism—now gone? *Or* were they absorbed into the already poisoned bones of the victors?" (WIN 30, citing APH 424, emphasis added)
(Wineburg): "Facing the abyss of indeterminacy and multiple causality, most historians would flee the narrow

straits of 'either-or' for the calmer port of 'both-and.' Not Zinn. Whether phrased as yes-no or either-or, his questions always have a single right answer" (WIN 30).

By way of reply, (1) Notice that Wineburg says nothing material about any of the issues raised by these questions. He makes no attempt to *argue* that Zinn's answers to any of these questions are wrong. This makes the precise nature of his objection difficult to determine. Perhaps, given his remarks about "the unfinished nature of historical knowledge," about the need to acknowledge "the historian's epistemological quandary," and about "the abyss of indeterminacy and multiple causality," he thinks that there are no clear answers to these questions, and that Zinn is being dogmatic to suggest otherwise. But unless Wineburg is a complete historical skeptic, and thinks that we cannot achieve any real knowledge of the past, he would have to address the particulars of these specific claims if he is to make the charge of dogmatism ("undue certainty") stick. Perhaps, given his complaints about "yes-no binaries" and about "the narrow straits of 'either-or,'" his criticism of Zinn is that his answers are too simplistic: the answers to the first four should not be "yes" or "no," but rather something messy and complicated, such as "in this sense, and to this degree, yes, but in that sense, or to that degree, no"; and the answers to the last three should be "both-and." But unless he wants to take the ridiculous position that the answer to every "yes-no" question is messy and complicated (including "did dinosaurs and human beings live simultaneously?") and that the answer to every "either-or" question is "both-and" (including "did Lyndon Johnson win the 1964 U.S. presidential election, or was it Barry Goldwater?"), then there is no escaping the need to address the material substance of these questions and Zinn's answers. And if some "yes-no" and "either-or" questions do admit of clear, definitive answers (even though some of them do not), it is not clear why all of them should be rejected as illicit (though some of them indeed should be).

(2) Notice, and it is remarkable that Wineburg seems to miss this entirely, that the Zinn questions he quotes have the educational virtue of focusing the reader on issues and evidence that are both vitally important to the understanding of the past and typically ignored in traditional textbooks and in mainstream American culture. Consider two examples: "Would America's wartime policies 'respect the rights of ordinary people everywhere to life, liberty, and the pursuit of happiness?'" That is hardly a trivial question, and yet it certainly is not posed in mainstream, traditional history textbooks. And Zinn's negative answer, which goes against what would be the default "patriotic" assumption, is clearly, in light of the relevant evidence (for example, racial segregation in the U.S. military and the dropping of bombs on civilian populations), the correct one. If Wineburg thinks that the evidence warrants a more complicated and messy answer, let's hear the argument. The same goes for the other "yes-no" questions. Or again, "With the defeat of the Axis, were fascism's essential elements—militarism, racism, imperialism—now gone? *Or* were they absorbed into the already poisoned bones of the victors?" Surely this is a vital question, and, just as surely, one that is omitted from traditional history textbooks. With regard to the answer, not only does the historical record make it abundantly clear (again, in opposition both to mainstream history texts and to default patriotic assumptions) that militarism, racism, and imperialism have characterized the post-war activities of the victors, but, also at least in this case, the "both-and" answer that Wineburg seems to favor is precluded, since the alternatives on offer are mutually exclusive. If the "either" part is affirmed (militarism, racism, and imperialism are now gone), then it would be impossible for the "or" part to be true (these evils live on in the activities of the victors); and vice versa.

Wineburg is on stronger ground with regard to the other two

"either-or" questions, since it is both logically possible, and materially plausible, that "both-and" answers to them could be correct. But here too Zinn is asking important, neglected questions, and helping readers to focus on the evidence necessary for answering them. And indeed, as the book unfolds, he makes a strong case that the "or" answer to both of them is correct. Briefly, the evidence he marshals, both in the chapter on World War II and in the discussions in later chapters of subsequent U.S. foreign policy, shows that while the U.S. does sometimes act in ways that are consistent with the pursuit of humanitarian goals, all of these actions appear also to be aimed at increasing power and profit. While this is consistent with a "both-and" answer, the problem is that (a) there are plenty of cases in which the U.S. has pursued power and profit at the expense of humanitarian concerns, and (b) very few in which it has pursued humanitarian concerns at the expense of power and profit. Similarly, while there are historical cases in which the U.S. has acted for the purpose of ending one nation's control over others, it is impossible to conclude that respect for the principle of self-determination plays a significant role in U.S. foreign policy, since (a) there are numerous cases in which the U.S. has fought against a people's struggle for self-determination and for control of those people by itself or its allies, and (b) there are very few if any cases in which the U.S. has renounced its control over another nation, or fought against such control by one of its allies, so as to facilitate the self-determination of the nation in question (see, for example, APH 408–10). If Wineburg disagrees, let's see the argument.

A few more points are in order with regard to Wineburg's general attack on undue certainty and his call for epistemological modesty (recall his insistence on "the unfinished nature of historical knowledge," his references to "the historian's epistemological quandary" and to "the abyss of indeterminacy and multiple causality," his opposition to questions that yield simple "yes-no" or "either-or" answers, and so forth; such rhetoric is to be found throughout his essay). First, as I have already argued, such a cautious stance is not always defensible, because, while it is true that the available evidence concerning a given issue is often inadequate for yielding a clear, definitive answer, on the other hand sometimes it is more than sufficient. Second, notice that the "sometimes yes, sometimes no" position on this issue that I am defending is, ironically, more nuanced, more context-sensitive, more tolerant of complexity, than is Wineburg's seemingly blanket condemnation of "the narrow straits of 'either-or'" (30) and of "history as truth" (34). Third, there is something self-referentially inconsistent about such uniform epistemological modesty. If it is as hard to know about the past as Wineburg claims it is, and if unqualified assertions of truth are as unprincipled as he says they are, then how can he know all the things he claims to know, and say all the things he says, in his essay? How does he *know* that history's "fragments can never be wholly put together" (29), that the use of "stark either-or" questions is "a rhetorical turn almost never encountered in professional historical writing" (29), that "the Nazis' aims went far beyond forcing a Polish surrender; their explicit goal was to terrorize" (30), that Zinn's book "relegate[s] students" to the role of "absorbers—not analysts—of information" (32), and that his history "invites a slide into intellectual fascism"? For someone who adopts such a posture of epistemological modesty, Wineburg seems to know a lot of things, and to have no scruple about issuing strong, frequently unqualified, claims about them! Fourth, and most important, while (to say it once again) a judicious, discriminating, principled skepticism (as opposed to the rhetorically indiscriminate and universal but in fact self-referentially inconsistent kind) is essential and necessary, an uncritical and unwarranted skepticism in the face of genuinely adequate evidence is disastrous, not only from a logical point of view, but from a practical one as well. I am old enough to remember that some "sophisticates" responded to the civil rights movement—the drive to bring about integration and equal rights and dignity for black Americans—with talk of "complexity," "respect for different points of view," "who is to say?," and the like. Howard Zinn saw racism and segregation for what they were, and fought them.

But many of the sloppy errors that litter Wineburg's essay can be exposed much more easily, without much need for philosophical argumentation. Consider the following passage:

> [Zinn] approvingly cites Simone Weil, the French philosopher and social activist. At a time when the *Einsatzgruppen* were herding Polish Jews into the forest and mowing them down before open pits, Weil compared the difference between Nazi fascism and the democratic principles of England and the United States to a mask hiding the true character of both. Once we see through this mask, Weil argued, we will understand that the enemy is not "the one facing us across the frontier or the battlelines, which is not so much our enemy as our brothers' enemy," but the "Apparatus," the one "that calls itself our protector and makes us its slaves." Zinn adds that the real struggle of World War II was not between nations, but rather that the "real war was inside each nation." (30, citing APH 420)

Now let's compare that to the relevant passage in APH, the one that Wineburg cites:

> A few voices continued to insist that the real war was inside each nation: Dwight Macdonald's wartime magazine *Politics* presented, in early 1945, an article by the French worker-philosopher Simone Weil:
>
> > Whether the mask is labeled Fascism, Democracy, or

Dictatorship of the Proletariat, our great adversary remains the Apparatus—the bureaucracy, the police, the military. Not the one facing us across the frontier or the battle lines, which is not so much our enemy as our brothers' enemy, but the one that calls itself our protector and makes us its slaves. No matter what the circumstances, the worst betrayal will always be to subordinate ourselves to this Apparatus, and to trample underfoot, in Its service, all human values in ourselves and in others. (420)

Notice, first, that Wineburg makes a false statement when he says that "Zinn adds that the real struggle of World War II was not between nations, but rather that the 'real war was inside each nation.'" Zinn does not "add" this to Weil's statement. The words "the real war was inside each nation" are clearly used to *introduce* the quotation from Weil (not to *add* to it), and they are offered as a *summary* of her main point. Contrary to Wineburg's claim, Zinn does not present these words as the expression of his own position, but rather as an exposition of the views of someone else. Many books and essays contain both statements that represent the views of the author and others, usually (as in this case) clearly marked as such, that represent views that the author wishes to make available to the reader even though the views in question are not the author's own. Wineburg's mistake is that of conflating a writer's own views with views that are not his or her own, but which he or she includes for purposes of information, discussion, and/or criticism.

Wineburg also errs when he claims that Zinn quotes Weil "approvingly." While it is possible that Zinn did agree with Weil, he neither states nor implies that he does. Moreover, a look at the context in which the Weil quote appears shows that Zinn, in that particular part of his text, was not addressing issues related to the truth, reasonableness, or defensibility (or their opposites) of Weil's position. Rather, the issue in play when the Weil quotation appears is that of gauging popular support for and opposition to American involvement in World War II.

To see this, let's look at the context. The paragraph preceding the one in which Weil is quoted begins this way: "Only one organized socialist group opposed the war unequivocally. This was the Socialist Workers Party." The paragraph concludes by telling of the criminal convictions, and subsequent prison sentences, that 18 members of this party received as a consequence of their anti-war advocacy (APH 420). Then comes the Weil paragraph quoted above ("A few voices continued to insist..."). After the Weil quote has concluded, the next paragraph begins this way: "Still, the vast bulk of the American population was mobilized, in the army, and in civilian life, to fight the war, and the atmosphere of war enveloped more and more Americans. Public opinion polls show large majorities of soldiers favoring the draft for the postwar period" (APH 421). So the role that the Weil quotation plays in Zinn's text is to serve as an example, like that of the Socialist Workers Party from the immediately preceding paragraph, of those who did not share the more dominant attitude of enthusiasm for the war. The next paragraph is obviously also addressed to the question of attitudes toward the war, with the turn toward a discussion of a different attitude than that which had just been discussed being marked by the word "still." Zinn offers no analysis of the merits of Weil's quotation here, or, for that matter, elsewhere in his book. Rather, the function it plays in Zinn's text is to document and to illustrate a minority attitude. Wineburg's claim that Zinn quotes Weil "approvingly" is inaccurate.

Finally, I would argue that Wineburg's gloss of Weil's statement distorts her meaning, and that this distortion is facilitated by his eliding some crucial passages from the quotation as it is found in Zinn's text. Notice that Weil's statement, unlike Wineburg's paraphrase of it, neither mentions specific countries nor discusses differences between fascism and "democratic principles." While Wineburg seems to want to pin on Weil (and, by extension, on Zinn, by means of having him "add" things that he didn't add, and having him "approve" of things that he didn't approve) the claim that there are no significant differences between Nazi Germany, on the one hand, and the U.S. and England, on the other, I think that a more faithful reading of her statement (and certainly a more charitable one) reveals that it is not about the ways in which these entities differ, but rather about what they have in common. And what is it that they have in common? As I read her, Weil points to three things: (1) In each case we find "the bureaucracy, the police, [and] the military." (Wineburg quotes her term for this, "the Apparatus," but does not include in his quotation her explanation of what the term means.) (2) In each case "the Apparatus," defined as such, "calls itself our protector and makes us its slaves." (3) In each case the Apparatus uses both coercion ("makes us its slaves") and the inculcation of fear, coupled with the promise of protection, in order to persuade its citizens to (and this is another key passage missing from Wineburg's quotation and paraphrase) "subordinate ourselves to this Apparatus, and to trample underfoot, in Its service, all human values in ourselves and in others." Perhaps what misleads Wineburg into thinking that Weil is comparing fascism to "democratic principles," and failing to find the former to be worse than the latter, is that she says that "our great adversary" is not what is "facing us across the frontier or the battlelines," but rather "the Apparatus" in our own society. I speculate (Wineburg does not lay out his reasoning clearly here) that Wineburg thinks that this means that Weil (and Zinn) think that the American society, culture, and political system of that time was no better than that of Nazi Germany. (Wineburg even exaggerates Weil's position by attributing to her the view that "the enemy is *not* 'the one facing us across the frontier or the battlelines,'" [30, emphasis added], when she in fact says [and Wineburg even quotes it] that it "is *not so much* our enemy as our brothers' enemy" [Zinn 420, emphasis added]. Similarly, Weil does not call the Apparatus "our adversary," but rather "our *great* adversary," which implies that there can be lesser adversaries.) But I think it is more plausible that Weil's reason for thinking that our greatest adversary is the Apparatus in our own society, as opposed to any foreign enemy, is not based on an assessment of the relative merits of the two societies, but rather on an assessment of the requirements of moral responsibility. We are responsible for our own actions much more so than we are for the actions of others. Similarly, we are more responsible for the actions of our own nation than we are for the actions of other nations. We are a part of our own nation. We have an opportunity to participate in decisions about its policies. We are typically more knowledgeable about it than we are about other nations. We are usually in a better position to influence it than we are to influence other nations. And our nation exerts more influence on us than other nations do. For all of these reasons, and others like them, our first responsibility is to behave ethically, to "uphold human values," in our own conduct—and this requires us to resist our own nation's attempts to force or persuade us to act otherwise. Our second responsibility is to participate in political deliberations and struggles within our own nation in an attempt to move it in the direction of moral conduct. These responsibilities take precedence over any responsibility to intervene against the immoral conduct of foreign nations. That responsibility falls more prominently on the citizens of those nations in question (the meaning, it seems to me, of Weil's "our brothers' enemy" locution). This interpretation is suggested by the final sentence of Weil's quotation, which is not included in Wineburg's presentation: "No matter what the circumstances, *the worst betrayal* will always be to subordinate ourselves to this Apparatus, and to trample underfoot, in Its service, all human values in ourselves and in others" (Zinn 420, emphasis added). That is a statement about what moral responsibility, universally, requires; it is not a declaration that democracy is as bad as or worse than fascism. And if Zinn seems to be as indignant about Jim Crow as about the Nazi Holocaust (a complaint that Wineburg lodges on page 33), it is not because he is so morally obtuse as to think that legally enforced racial segregation is, on the scale of evils, equal to genocide, but rather because Jim Crow is what *we* did.[4] On his view, achieving a moral plane higher than that of the Nazis is an insufficient goal, and its achievement is no cause for celebration.

In a section entitled "A Slippery Timeline," Wineburg goes so far as to accuse Zinn of intellectual dishonesty. He quotes Zinn: "At the start of World War II German planes dropped bombs on Rotterdam in Holland, Coventry in England, and elsewhere. Roosevelt had described these as 'inhuman barbarism that has profoundly shocked the conscience of humanity.' These German bombings [of Rotterdam and Coventry] were very small compared with the British and American bombings of German cities" (WIN 30, quoting APH 421). Wineburg then points out that Zinn, in making this comparison, cites "some of the most devastating Allied bombing campaigns, including the most notorious, the firebombing of Dresden" (30). Wineburg immediately concedes that "In a technical sense, Zinn is on solid ground": the Allied bombing campaigns were indeed far more lethal than those of the Germans. What, then, is the problem?

Wineburg explains: "In order to make this point, Zinn plays fast and loose with historical context. He achieves his desired effect in two stages. First, he begins his claim with the phrase 'at the start of World War II,' but the Dresden raid occurred five years later, in February 1945, when all bets were off and long-standing distinctions between military targets ('strategic bombing') and civilian targets ('saturation bombing') had been rendered irrelevant... Zinn's point only derives its force by violating chronology and sequence" (30). Before moving on to the second of Wineburg's "two stages," two comments are in order. First, while Wineburg does not say this (and even may, with his talk of "playing fast and loose," be read as implicitly denying it), Zinn does, in fact, provide a date for the Dresden bombing, and does so on the very page (APH 421) from which Wineburg has been quoting: "The climax of this terror bombing was the bombing of Dresden in early 1945." Note also that by calling this "the climax," Zinn is indicating that there has been a progression, and specifically an escalation, in the historical unfolding of these bombing campaigns, that such a progression takes time, and that the Dresden bombing, "the climax," comes near the end. Zinn does not hide or disguise from the reader the temporal distance between the German and Allied bombing missions that he is comparing.

Second, why is this temporal distance, this issue of "chronology and sequence" supposed to be crucially relevant to Zinn's point, so that his (alleged) failure to mark it adequately constitutes objectionable "slipperiness"? Zinn's point is that if the bombing of civilians constitutes "inhuman barbarism" that "shocks the conscience of humanity" when the Germans do it, then the same should hold true when the Allies do it on a much larger scale. It is not obvious why the issue of *when* these actions took place should make any difference. Wineburg's explanation, as we have seen, is that the Allied bombings in question, unlike their German counterparts, took place when "all bets were off and long-standing distinctions between military targets ('strategic bombing') and civilian targets ('saturation bombing') had been rendered irrelevant." But how can such a claim be defended? The significance of the distinction between military and civilian targets is moral. Many civilians—for example, young children—are innocent. They take no part in the hostilities of war. They do not attack or threaten to attack anyone. (Indeed, Franklin Roosevelt, in the same communication that Zinn and Wineburg quote, in which he refers to the bombing of civilians as "inhuman barbarism," points out that, unless such campaigns are stopped, "hundreds of thousands of innocent human beings who are not

even remotely participating in hostilities, will lose their lives.")
To kill innocent civilians deliberately is, therefore, murder. To do
so for the motive of attempting to influence the policies of the
government in which such innocents happen to live is terrorism.
How can historical events of any kind nullify such moral
judgments as that the deliberate killing of innocent people is
wrong, or render the distinctions underlying them irrelevant? To
violate a moral imperative is not to destroy its legitimacy, but
rather to stand convicted of having violated it. So what can
Wineburg mean? My best guess (once again, he doesn't spell out
his reasoning) is that he thinks that the foundation for the moral
prohibition against killing the innocent is contractual: We will
agree not to target your civilians if you will agree not to kill ours.
(This interpretation of Wineburg is based on his use of the rather
imprecise idiomatic expression "all bets were off," which can
mean "an agreement that was decided on before is no longer
valid.") But contractualism of this sort is a hopeless theory when
it comes to explaining the wrongness of murder (the killing of
innocents). If you murder my family, my complaint is with you,
not your family. If you have killed my parents, or spouse, or
children, and your parents, spouse, and children in no way
participated in or had knowledge of your actions, I obviously
have no right to kill them.

So Wineburg's first complaint, on analysis, evaporates into
thin air. Far from deceiving his readers about the temporal
distance separating the events he is comparing, Zinn explicitly
informs them of this, in spite of the fact that, contra Wineburg,
such temporal distance is of dubious relevance to his point.

Now we turn to the second of Wineburg's "two stages": "A
closer look at [Zinn's] claim shows a second mechanism at work,
one even more slippery than this chronological bait and switch.
The claim ultimately derives its power from a single source: the
expected ignorance of the reader. People familiar with the
chronology of World War II immediately sense a disjuncture

between the phrase 'at the start of World War II' and the date of the Coventry raid" (30). Here Zinn is open to legitimate criticism, in that his "at the start of World War II" locution is needlessly imprecise. But it seems to me that Zinn is *merely* imprecise here, rather than incorrect. The Rotterdam and Coventry bombings that Zinn placed "at the start of World War II" both took place in 1940. World War II began in September 1939. While there is room for reasonable disagreement on this point, it hardly seems a major transgression to refer to events occurring in the eighth and fourteenth months of a war lasting six years (it ended in September 1945) as having occurred "at the start" of that war. And it is outrageous, in my judgment, for Wineburg to refer to "the *expected* ignorance of the reader (emphasis added)," which implies that Zinn was attempting deliberately to deceive. Perhaps Wineburg believes this because he, unlike Zinn, thinks that Nazi atrocities justify, or at least mitigate, Allied atrocities. That hypothesis would also explain why Wineburg devotes the next three paragraphs of his essay to a discussion of the Nazi bombing of Warsaw on September 25, 1939, pointing out both that Zinn fails to mention it and that it killed 40,000 Poles (many more than were killed in Rotterdam or Coventry, the two German bombing missions that he does cite—though the inclusion of these killings still leaves the number of civilians killed by German bombs well short of the number killed in Allied bombing campaigns). But Zinn's book is a history of the United States, not a history of World War II, and his point about bombing civilian targets is that if it is an atrocity when the Nazis do it (even on the relatively small scale of Rotterdam and Coventry), then so is it an atrocity when the Allies do it. The fact that the Nazis did it first, and earlier, and on a larger scale than was the case in the instances Zinn mentioned, is irrelevant to this point, for the reasons explained above. And surely Wineburg cannot seriously be suggesting that Zinn is some sort of apologist for the Nazis, eager to minimize the scale of their crimes. For at the very outset of his chapter on World War II, Zinn declares unequivocally: "It was a war against an enemy of unspeakable evil. Hitler's Germany was extending totalitarianism, racism, militarism, and overt aggressive warfare beyond what an already cynical world had experienced" (APH 407). So Zinn's omission of the Nazi bombing of Warsaw from his narrative is not deceptive or manipulative, because (a) his focus is on American history, as opposed to German history, or the history of World War II, and (b) because the inclusion of this detail of the war would not affect, either positively or negatively, the point he is making—that, by targeting and killing civilians in their bombing campaigns, the Allies committed the same atrocity, the same act of "inhuman barbarism," that they had rightly condemned when the conduct was carried out by the Nazis. This point is not nullified or diminished by any of the facts about the Nazi bombing of Warsaw.

Moreover, Wineburg seems not to be considering the educational value of Zinn's focus here. When our country has committed crimes and atrocities, should our main educational point, the one we want our students to remember, think about, and learn from, be, "hey, we're not so bad—look, we can point to some others who are even worse—and they did it first—they started it!"? Or should it instead be that we can, and must, behave differently, and that we should take responsibility for doing what we can to see that our nation meets its moral responsibilities? Here, once again, Kysia shows herself to be a perceptive reader of Zinn: "Zinn is not asking us to excuse Hitler or the Nazis. He is not asking us to ignore genocide. He is asking us to think about our own nation's history and the ways we create and support terrorism, racism, and militarism. He is asking us to reject the moral posturing that afflicts war histories in power-centric history textbooks. These are vitally important perspectives we need to encourage students of history to consider" (KYS).

Wineburg also takes Zinn to task for his treatment of the decision by the United States to drop two atomic bombs on Japan.

Whereas traditional, patriotic history textbooks justify the use of the bomb as having been necessary to end the war, shortening it by months, if not years, and thereby saving more lives that would have been lost in the prolonged fighting than were lost as a result of the use of the bombs, Zinn, by contrast, argues that Japan was already primed for surrender prior to the dropping of the bombs, and would have done so had the allies been willing to grant one minor concession—allowing Emperor Hirohito to remain as a figurehead.

Wineburg faults Zinn for relying too heavily on just two, rather old, sources: Gar Alperovitz's *Atomic Diplomacy* (1967) and Martin Sherwin's *A World Destroyed* (1975), for failing to incorporate the fruits of newer scholarship into later revisions of his book, and, most of all, for making counterfactual historical claims with insufficient modesty (this is the charge of dogmatism, once again).

To underscore this last point, Wineburg quotes three other historians who have speculated about what might have happened had the U.S. refrained from using the bomb, and notes that their discussions are laden with such words as "may," "might," "perhaps," and the like, and with admissions that the evidence precludes certainty, so that "we will never know." Wineburg then comments as follows: "The counterfactuals' qualifiers and second-guesses convey the modesty one is obliged to adopt when conjuring up a past that did not occur. But when Zinn plies the counterfactual, he seems to know something no one else knows—including historians who've given their professional lives to the topic: 'If only the Americans had not insisted on unconditional surrender—that is, if they were willing to accept one condition to the surrender, that the Emperor, a holy figure to the Japanese, remain in place—the Japanese would have agreed to stop the war.' Not might have, not may have, not could have. But 'would have agreed to stop the war.' Not only is Zinn certain about the history that's happened. He's certain about the history that didn't" (WIN 31–2, citing Zinn 423).

While I agree with Wineburg that it would have been better for Zinn to have used more cautious language, I don't think that his failure to do so carries the significance that Wineburg attributes to it. The reason is that the failure to qualify one's assertions with such phrases as "may," "might," "perhaps," "maybe," "seems," and the like does not mean that one is claiming certainty for the utterance that is unencumbered by such utterances. If someone asks me for directions, and I say, "go north on this street, then take a left at the second stoplight—it will be on your right," no one would assume that my direct, unqualified, language implied that my directions came with a guarantee of infallibility. Most reasonable people, I would wager, are aware that almost all of our beliefs and claims are open to some degree of doubt, some much more so than others. But language would become extremely tedious if people felt an obligation to qualify every claim with a declaration of their awareness of its fallibility. So the decision of whether or not to issue a modest qualifier is a judgment call, depending on such factors as the importance of the issue and the degree of confidence (or lack thereof) that one has in the truth of his or her statement. Where exactly the line should be drawn is far from clear, but it is well understood that the line at which one must issue a fallibility qualifier lies well south of the line of absolute certainty. Note, in this connection, that Wineburg issues many criticisms of Zinn that are not accompanied by any cautious qualifiers. When Wineburg says that "Zinn is certain about the history that's happened," and "about the history that didn't," is Wineburg really certain of *that*? Toward the end of his essay, in a passage to be discussed in more detail below, he says that Zinn's approach to history "is dangerous because it invites a slide into intellectual fascism…It seeks to stamp out the democratic insight that people of good will can see the same thing and come to different conclusions. It imputes the basest of motives to those who view the world from a different perch...Such a history atrophies our tolerance for complexity. It makes us allergic to exceptions to the rule. Worst of all, it depletes the moral courage we need to revise our beliefs in the face of new evidence. It ensures, ultimately, that tomorrow we will think exactly as we thought yesterday—and the day before, and the day before that." These are very strong claims, and many knowledgeable "people of good will" (to use Wineburg's phrase) would, I strongly suspect, find them highly dubious. And yet, Wineburg does not qualify a single one of these claims with a "maybe" or a "might" or a "perhaps" or a "seems." Does that mean he is certain of them? And would that not be "Undue Certainty" on his part?

But there is another point to be made in defense of Zinn's discussion of the American dropping of atomic bombs on Japan, and it addresses both Wineburg's complaint about Zinn's limited sourcing and his criticism of the boldness of Zinn's counterfactual claim. For among the items on this issue listed in Zinn's bibliography is one that Wineburg's summary of Zinn's discussion omits, even though Zinn quotes it in the body of his text, and despite the fact that it is the one that is most directly relevant to his counterfactual claim. The text in question is: United States Strategic Bombing Survey, *Japan's Struggle to End the War* (Washington: Government Printing Office, 1946). Here is what Zinn says about it in APH (422):

The United States Strategic Bombing Survey, set up by the War Department in 1944 to study the results of aerial attacks in the war, interviewed hundreds of Japanese civilian and military leaders after Japan surrendered, and reported just after the war:

Based on a detailed investigation of all the facts and supported by the testimony of the surviving Japanese leaders involved, it is the Survey's opinion that certainly prior to 31 December 1945, and in all probability prior to 1 November 1945, Japan would have surrendered even if the atomic bombs had not been dropped, even if Russia had not entered the war, and even if no invasion had been planned or contemplated.

Notice that Wineburg, in criticizing Zinn for inadequate sourcing and for allegedly claiming to know with certainty that Japan would have surrendered in 1945 even without the dropping of the atomic bomb, somehow fails to mention his quoting from a U.S. government study that explicitly supports Zinn's conclusions as to what would have happened. And this U.S. government study qualifies its claim, not, as Wineburg would prefer, with "perhaps" or "might" or "maybe"—but with "certainly."

As further evidence of Zinn's dogmatism, and, more specifically, of Wineburg's contention that "it seems that once [Zinn] made up his mind, nothing...could shake it" (32), Wineburg offers this: "On occasions when Zinn was asked if a quarter century of new historical scholarship had shed light on his original formulations, he seemed mostly unfazed. Consider his response to questions about the espionage trial of Julius and Ethel Rosenberg."

Note that, although Wineburg says that there were "occasions" (plural) in which this happens, he cites only one instance. Wouldn't it be better to cite several others, not only to bolster his case, but also as a caution against being undone by the "indeterminacy and multiple causality" of history, and by the "unruly fibers of evidence that stubbornly jut out from any interpretive frame" (really? All of them? All the time? With regard to every question?)? But no. Although Wineburg chastises Zinn for "hanging [a] claim on three pieces of evidence" (as you recall, there were really five, but that is not to the present point)—and this, in a section entitled "Anecdotes as Evidence" (28), the point of which is to criticize Zinn for using anecdotes as evidence, Wineburg supports his claim, not by giving us anecdotes, but rather by giving us *an* (as in one, singular) anecdote. Here is his discussion of it:

> *A People's History* devotes nearly two and a half pages to the case, casting doubt on the legitimacy of the Rosenbergs' convictions as well as that of their accomplice, Morton Sobell. Sobell escaped the electric chair but served 19 years in Alcatraz and other federal prisons, maintaining innocence the entire time. However, in September 2008, Sobell, age 91, admitted to a *New York Times* reporter that he had indeed been a Russian spy, implicating his fellow defendant Julius Rosenberg as well. Three days later, in the wake of Sobell's admission, the Rosenbergs' two sons also concluded with regret that their father had been a spy. Yet, when the same *New York Times* reporter contacted Zinn for a reaction, he was only "mildly surprised," adding, "To me it didn't matter whether they were guilty or not. The most important thing was they did not get a fair trial in the atmosphere of cold war hysteria." (WIN 32)

This anecdote does not support Wineburg's claims. The reason is that in Zinn's discussion of the Rosenberg case (APH 432–5) he neither asserts nor even implies that the Rosenbergs were innocent. Rather, he merely argues that their trial was unfair and that their conviction was, therefore, illegitimate.[5] The context in which the discussion occurs is that of McCarthyism and the persecution of real and alleged communists, of which criminal prosecutions were one important manifestation. And a prime example of that particular manifestation was the Rosenberg trial. Zinn makes no attempt to settle the question of the Rosenbergs' factual guilt or innocence. His discussion of their case is offered only as an illustration of a wider and more general historical phenomenon. Not a single one of the many aspects of the trial that he discusses in any way establishes, or even strongly implies, that the Rosenbergs were innocent. But all of them cast doubt on the legitimacy of their trial.

Wineburg does not challenge, or even discuss, any of the specific points that Zinn makes about the Rosenberg case. So Wineburg's one and only example of Zinn's alleged tendency to refuse to change his mind even when he is specifically asked whether "a quarter century of new historical scholarship had shed light on his original formulations," turns out to be a case in which the new information cited did not contradict anything he wrote.

Moreover, since Wineburg is the one attempting to make this case against Zinn, and since he gives only one example, and it is the one he selected, a reasonable person might conclude that he knows of no other examples that would lend greater help to his argument.

Finally, given that Wineburg seems to believe, erroneously, that Zinn had argued in APH that the Rosenbergs were innocent, his presentation of what Sobell told the *New York Times* in 2008 contains a crucial material omission: While Sobell did indeed implicate Julius Rosenberg, he maintained that Ethel had taken no part in her husband's espionage activities. (His version of events is corroborated by David Greenglass, Ethel Rosenberg's brother and the key prosecution witness, who has recanted his testimony about his sister's having typed notes containing U.S. nuclear secrets. In 2001 he stated that he gave false testimony to protect himself and his wife, Ruth.)[6] If Zinn's point really had been to exonerate the Rosenbergs, then the subsequent testimony indicating that Zinn was right about Ethel would be just as relevant as that indicating that Zinn was wrong about Julius. But Wineburg cites only the latter, saying nothing about the former. Indeed, Wineburg errs when he refers to Sobell as "their" (that is, *both* Rosenbergs's) accomplice, and, consistent with the scholarly standards on display throughout his article, seems not to have noticed that, according to the quotation that he himself chose from the *New York Times*, Sobell implicated, not both Rosenbergs, but rather "his fellow defendant Julius Rosenberg."

Continuing to press his allegation that Zinn's book is dogmatic and exhibits "undue certainty," Wineburg also claims, as briefly mentioned above, that "A search in *A People's History* for qualifiers mostly comes up empty" (32), and that Zinn's approach to history "detests equivocation and extinguishes *perhaps, maybe, might,* and the most execrable of them all, *on the other hand.* For the truth has no hands" (34). (Wineburg seems to be especially proud of that last locution—he titles the final section of his essay, "A History with No Hands.")

Well then, are Wineburg's claims true? The first one is vague. What does he mean by "mostly comes up empty"? So let's move on to the second one, which appears to be merely an elaboration of the first. Does Zinn's text "extinguish" the word "perhaps"? To the contrary, a search reveals that the word appears in the 2003 edition of his book a total of 101 times, not counting instances in which the word appears in quotations from other writers. Zinn uses this "extinguished" word on pages 2, 5, 11, 16 (twice), 17, 18 (three times), 21, 22, 29 (twice), 32, 36 (twice), 37, 47, 49 (twice), 60, 67, 77, 81, 99, 110, 112, 114, 120, 138, 141, 162, 172 (three times), 174, 185, 188, 208 (twice), 233, 236, 238, 242, 249, 268, 273, 281, 289, 294, 326, 331, 340, 354, 357 (twice), 360, 366, 372, 387, 395 (three times), 404, 422 (twice), 426, 427, 428, 443 (twice), 449, 459, 463, 484, 486, 501, 506, 510, 511, 514, 517, 519, 557, 564 (twice), 567, 585, 591, 594, 596, 597 (three times), 598, 619, 636, 638, 648, 655, and 679.

What about "seem," "seems," and "seemed"? Excluding the use of these words in quotations from others, Zinn himself uses these words 130 times. They can be found on pages 5, 14, 15, 19, 35, 40 (three times), 47, 50, 53, 54, 60, 61, 65, 66, 68, 70 (twice), 72, 79, 80, 83, 86 (twice), 90, 95, 99, 100 (three times), 103, 104, 106,

109, 136, 142, 150, 160, 164, 198, 219, 228, 235, 264, 273, 295, 301, 303, 346, 353 (twice), 359 (twice), 374, 382 (twice), 395, 402 (twice), 409, 410, 411, 414, 418, 419, 422, 424, 425, 426, 428, 434, 440, 441 (twice), 442 (twice), 450, 453, 459, 463, 474, 476, 479, 492, 499, 504 (twice), 506, 510, 512, 523, 524, 536, 541, 546, 548, 553, 554, 555 (twice), 559, 561, 562, 564, 565 (twice), 575, 576, 579, 582, 584, 585, 594, 595, 596 (twice), 597, 599, 610, 611, 612, 613, 621, 638 (three times), 676, and 679 (twice).

How did Wineburg get this so wrong? One thought that occurred to me was that, since he chose in his essay to focus in detail on only one chapter of Zinn's book (Chapter 16: "A People's War?"), perhaps the problem is that this particular chapter had a dogmatic tone, characterized by an absence of modest qualifiers, and that Wineburg carelessly and unscrupulously generalized from that one chapter to the rest of the book. But Chapter 16 qualifies statements with "seem," "seems," or "seemed" 17 times—a total that exceeds that of any other chapter. Zinn uses these words in that chapter roughly once every other page. If we add in his use of "perhaps," the frequency jumps up to roughly twice every three pages. But even that is not accurate, since Zinn uses several other modest qualifiers in addition to these. The charge that he "extinguishes" such qualifiers is demonstrably a ludicrous falsehood.

What about "on the other hand"? (Recall that Wineburg claims that Zinn "detests" such phrases, and finds this one "the most execrable of all," because, don't you know, for a dogmatist like Zinn, "the truth has no hands"—and so he produces "A History with No Hands.") It is true that Zinn does not use this particular phrase frequently—only 15 times in A People's History, not counting its use in a quotation from another writer. But the idea that there is another "hand," that is, another side to things— evidence that points in a direction other than, and often opposite to, what Zinn has been saying, is expressed often in his text. It is just that Zinn doesn't usually mark this with the phrase "on the

other hand," preferring "still," "yet," "and yet," "though,"
"although," "nevertheless," "but," and several other words and
phrases. Sometimes he simply begins a new sentence or
paragraph by laying out counterevidence to what he has been
saying or arguing, without indicating this with any special word
or phrase.

Here are three random examples of Zinn acknowledging
"other hands": (1) On pages 90–1 Zinn summarizes the
arguments of historian Charles Beard's book *An Economic
Interpretation of the Constitution.* Beard points out that the authors
of the Constitution were rich men, that the Constitutional
Convention did not include any representation of slaves, indentured servants, women, or men without property, and that the
Constitution favored the interests of wealthy men over those of
any other group. For this reason, Beard argued, wealthy men
favored ratification of the Constitution. But while Zinn presents
Beard sympathetically (and we know from some of Zinn's other
writings that he tends to agree with Beard), he nonetheless
immediately goes on to say this: "Not everyone at the
Philadelphia Convention fitted Beard's scheme. Elbridge Gerry of
Massachusetts was a holder of landed property, and yet he
opposed the ratification of the Constitution. Similarly, Luther
Martin of Maryland, whose ancestors had obtained large tracts of
land in New Jersey, opposed ratification" (91). (2) On page 237
Zinn discusses the butchery of the Civil War: "The Civil War was
one of the first instances in the world of modern warfare: deadly
artillery shells, Gatling guns, bayonet charges—combining the
indiscriminate killing of mechanized war with hand-to-hand
combat. The nightmare scenes could not adequately be described
except in a novel like Stephen Crane's *The Red Badge of Courage.* In
one charge before Petersburg, Virginia, a regiment of 850 Maine
soldiers lost 632 men in half an hour. It was a vast butchery,
623,000 dead on both sides, and 471,000 wounded, over a million
dead and wounded in a country whose population was 30

million. No wonder that desertions grew among southern soldiers as the war went on. As for the Union army, by the end of the war, 200,000 had deserted." But then Zinn provides "the other hand": "Still, 600,000 had volunteered for the Confederacy in 1861, and many in the Union army were volunteers." (3) On page 569, after discussing ways in which the U.S. had exploited poorer nations economically, Zinn comments, "And yet the United States cultivated a reputation for being generous with its riches. Indeed, it had frequently given aid to disaster victims." Contrary to Wineburg's claim, passages like these abound in Zinn's work.[7]

On the last two pages of his essay Wineburg's own "undue certainty," which I have already noted above, is put on constant, though apparently unselfconscious, display. Consider, for example, what he says about Zinn's alleged "Undue Popularity" (to quote another of Wineburg's section headings). The popularity of APH is indeed remarkable (a 30-plus-year-old book, with an initial print run of just 4000 copies, it has now sold over 2.6 million copies, and remains a perennial bestseller). As a result, several commentators have advanced hypotheses to explain its success. Wineburg quotes historian Michael Kazin, who suggests that the book's popularity is due to its offering "a certain consolation" to the American left, which has otherwise not fared well since 1980. But Wineburg knows better: "Kazin often hits the mark, but on this score he's way off. Zinn remains popular not because he is timely but precisely because he's not. *A People's History* speaks directly to our inner Holden Caulfield. Our heroes are shameless frauds, our parents and teachers conniving liars, our textbooks propagandistic slop. Long before we could Google accounts of a politician's latest indiscretion, Zinn offered a national 'gotcha.' *They're all phonies* is a message that never goes out of style" (WIN 33). Note that there is no "perhaps," "maybe," "might," or "on the other hand" to be found here. I would have thought that the question of why a particular book catches on and attracts a wide readership would, in most cases (including this one), be difficult to determine and impossible to prove. Accordingly, I would also have thought that it would be appropriate for any attempt to answer it, especially when offered by someone with no particular expertise in this area, to be issued with some modesty.

Notice also that Wineburg severely caricatures Zinn here. His book is full of heroes, such as Frederick Douglass, Mark Twain, Helen Keller, and Martin Luther King, Jr., who are celebrated, and not depicted as "shameless frauds." Many of those who are treated more critically by Zinn than they are in traditional textbooks are revealed by him to be complex, multi-sided persons, with both admirable and deplorable characteristics, rather than simply dismissed as "frauds" or "phonies." Nor does Zinn say or imply that our parents and teachers are "conniving liars." I take it that Wineburg's point is that an implication of what Zinn says about American history is that what our parents and teachers have been telling us about this is wrong. But if Zinn were to address that point (which he doesn't in APH), I suspect that he would say that such parents and teachers are more likely victims—they, too, have been fed the "propagandist slop" (Wineburg's one palpable hit here)—than "conniving liars." Here, as elsewhere, the critics of Zinn who accuse him of presenting a one-sided, reductionistic, caricature of American history, are themselves guilty of painting Zinn in precisely such cartoonish terms.

One also wonders what warrant Wineburg could have for positing such a condescending explanation for Zinn's success. After all, Wineburg speaks of Zinn's "undeniable charisma," achieved, in part, by his having "lived an admirable life, never veering from the things he believed in" (33). Moreover, he concedes that *A People's History* "is written by a skilled stylist," adding that "Zinn's muscular presence makes for brisk reading compared with the turgid prose" of most textbooks (32). Finally, he also admits that, at least on a topical level, it is "undoubtedly true" that Zinn's text provides "a corrective to the narrative of progress dispensed by the state" (27). One wonders why these factors might not be sufficient to explain the book's success, rendering it unnecessary for Wineburg to offer instead a gratuitously insulting comparison of Zinn's admiring readers to immature teenagers who enjoy the spectacle of seeing their parents and teachers being taken down a peg.[8]

And just as Wineburg's assertions about the causes of Zinn's success are shaky (indeed, I think it is fair to say that he "hangs" them on just—let's see—*zero* pieces of evidence), his claims about the effects of Zinn's text on students must be judged equally speculative. Let's quickly review those claims. Wineburg says that APH relegates students to the role of "absorbers—not analysts—of information" (32), and that the strategy of pairing Zinn's book with a conservative, "patriotic" American history text, so that the students might compare, contrast, and draw their own conclusions, would yield the disappointing result that instead of "encouraging" students "to think," it would only "teach" them "how to jeer" (33). And then we have the words, most of them already quoted above, with which Wineburg concludes his essay:

A history of unalloyed certainties is dangerous because it invites a slide into intellectual fascism. History as truth, issued from the left or from the right, abhors shades of gray. It seeks to stamp out the democratic insight that people of good will can see the same thing and come to different conclusions. It imputes the basest of motives to those who view the world from a different perch. It detests equivocation and extinguishes *perhaps, maybe, might,* and the most execrable of them all, *on the other hand.* For the truth has no hands.

Such a history atrophies our tolerance for complexity. It makes us allergic to exceptions to the rule. Worst of all, it depletes the moral courage we need to revise our beliefs in the face of new evidence. It ensures, ultimately, that tomorrow we will think exactly as we thought yesterday—and the day before, and the day before that.

Is that what we want for our students? (WIN 34)

I have already pointed out both that Wineburg is wrong to claim that Zinn avoids words like "perhaps," and that it is Wineburg, by ironic contrast, who "extinguishes" them from his presentation, especially at its (just quoted) climax, and who thereby, according to his own criteria, exhibits the same "undue certainty" that he (falsely, in my view) ascribes to Zinn. But several other problems should also be noted.

(1) What does Wineburg mean by "history as truth"? He does not say, but his discussion suggests three possibilities. First, he may mean dogmatic history—history that takes itself to be certain and infallible. (This reading is consonant with the fact that the sentence immediately preceding the one beginning with the undefined "history as truth" locution refers to "a history of unalloyed certainties.") If so, "history as truth" is an unfortunate phrase, since the standard of "truth" is lower than the standard of certainty or infallibility. (If that were not the case, all empirical judgments—that is, judgments that depend for their verification or falsification on observation of the data of experience, as opposed to being strictly demonstrable, in the manner of mathematical or logical proofs—would have to be denied the status of "truth.") But more importantly, as I have argued, Wineburg fails to make a good case for his charge that Zinn either asserts or implies any claim to certainty or infallibility.

Second, Wineburg might be referring to non-centrist history. On that interpretation, the point of his "issued from the left or right" phrase would be to suggest that his objection to Zinn's leftism is not based on Zinn's failure to be right-wing, but rather from his failure to occupy a middle-of-the-road position. If this is what Wineburg means, then he is trading on the widespread, but fallacious, view that centrist positions, at least generally or typically, if not always, are superior to (because more "balanced," more nuanced, less doctrinaire, less "ideological") than leftist or rightist positions. But, as argued extensively in the previous chapter's discussion of "objectivity," the question of which position is best (or wisest, or most likely to be true) can only be settled, in any given case, by consulting the relevant evidence; there is no reason to assume that the truth will always, or even typically, be found near the center of any particular spectrum of opinion.

Third, and I think most probably, Wineburg intends both of these meanings. On this interpretation, Wineburg is assuming that non-centrist positions are, in principle, dogmatic, so that in condemning "history as truth" he is condemning both non-centrism in history and historical dogmatism at the same time. Notice in this connection that he says that "History as truth, issued from the left or from the right, abhors shades of gray," but he says nothing about "history as truth, issued from the center." But why can there not be dogmatic, unnuanced, approaches to history that are issued from a position that is centrist relative to some spectrum? Are there not indeed many people who quite dogmatically, and with great certainty, reject both left-wing and right-wing positions? One often hears talk of the need to ward off bias or propaganda from "both the left and the right." But if there is, then there is also a need to ward off bias or propaganda from the center. And this is not merely an academic point. In many circles, in the real world, pointing out that a position is "moderate" or centrist is irrationally conflated with demonstrating that it is reasonable and probably correct. No evidence need be produced or argument given. Similarly, to show that a position is leftist or rightist is often taken, on a similarly non-evidentialist basis, as a decisive refutation. Some people think that the military effort of the United States in Vietnam was a noble endeavor, one of which Americans should be proud.

Howard Zinn thought that the war was an abomination, a war crime, an illegal, immoral, murderous act of aggression. Still others hold that the war was fought for a complex mixture of admirable and base motives, and that it was, at worst, a mistake, in the sense that its costs outweighed its benefits. But there is no basis for concluding, *a priori*, that this third, middle-of-the-road, position must be the best, or wisest, or most rational one, or that it, suitably qualified with lots of iterations of "perhaps," "maybe," "might," and "on the other hand," must be the best one to present to students in history textbooks. It is entirely possible, and not remotely offensive to any sound principle of logic, that a careful examination of the relevant evidence would reveal that every single argument that has ever been advanced in support of the American war in Vietnam rests on a demonstrable falsehood, and that the only reason anyone might feel otherwise is that the entire culture in which he or she lives has been saturated with patriotic propaganda and lies. If a logical and scrupulous investigation of the relevant evidence were to show that, what, as a consequence, would it be best to teach children about the war in history classes? It seems to me that Wineburg's stance renders him ill-equipped to answer such a question.

(2) What warrant is there for the claim that Zinn's approach to history "seeks to stamp out the democratic insight that people of good will can see the same thing and come to different conclusions," or that "it imputes the basest of motives to those who view the world from a different perch"? I don't recall that Zinn ever either states or implies that people of good will cannot disagree with him, or that those who reject his view of history do so for "the basest of motives." Wineburg certainly does not cite any such passages. To the very limited extent that Zinn does address this issue, his explanation is quite different. Recall that in the first chapter of APH Zinn discusses the idea that there are an infinite number of facts about the past, so that any historical narrative must be highly selective. He suggests, further, that the

pattern of omission, inclusion, and emphasis that one finds in most American history textbooks does not vary widely, but rather maintains a remarkable consistency. For example, such textbooks, at least prior to the publication of Zinn's text, tended to emphasize the heroic aspects of Columbus, highlighting his exploits as a daring sailor and explorer, and very much downplaying, if not omitting entirely, his acts of torturing, mutilating, enslaving, and murdering Native Americans. So the explanation for the failure of most Americans to agree with Zinn's portrayal of Columbus need not entail any denial of their good will, or any imputation to them of motives any baser than that of tending to believe what one is taught in school, especially when it is reinforced in standard textbooks and by the concurring opinion of most other people in one's culture. While it is true that Zinn argues for, and marshals evidence in support of, several conclusions about American history, I fail to see how these activities imply anything negative about the motives of his readers, or that they insult or disrespect those readers in any other way. The presence of argument in a work does entail that the author anticipates readers who will not initially share his or her conclusions (for if the readers already agreed, there would be no need for argument), but it need not entail any particular view, let alone a negative one, as to *why* they might disagree. And honest (non-deceptive) argumentation is non-coercive. If anything, it expresses respect for readers by appealing to their reason (in weighing and considering the arguments given) and to their freedom (to give or to withhold assent). This is well understood in the sciences, in philosophy, and perhaps in other fields as well. When a scientist or a philosopher thinks that she has figured out what the truth is on some difficult or controversial question, making her reasoning available to others is regarded (favorably) as a contribution to a conversation, not (negatively) as an insult to those who do not already agree with her. But in history and journalism the idea has taken hold in some circles that "objectivity" demands that one merely "report the facts," and avoid drawing any conclusions. Since facts have to be reasoned to, and selected, this conception of objectivity is senseless. The result, in practice, is that bland, centrist, non-boat-rocking views are favored (and mistakenly seen as not being views at all), as are conventional choices of selection, omission, and emphasis (which, again, are not recognized as such). By contrast, non-mainstream, iconoclastic views are dismissed as "ideological," "propagandistic," "non-objective," and, apparently, as evidencing contempt for those who do not agree with them.

(3) One problem with Wineburg's speculations about the educational effects of Zinn's text is that they are based solely on a consideration of the book's alleged defects, ignoring its more positive features. Wineburg's insistence that APH will harm students rests on his critique of that book as simplistic, dogmatic, and one-sided (no "on the other hand"). But because his analysis considers only these (alleged) characteristics, and fails to take into account features that might be expected to yield more positive educational outcomes, that analysis shows *itself* to be simplistic, dogmatic, and one-sided. There is certainly no "on the other hand" here.

What might a more complete analysis reveal? First, by nearly all accounts, including those of Zinn's critics, APH is clearer, and written in a more agreeable style, than other standard American history texts. Second, Zinn's text, because of his definite point of view and strong authorial presence, exhibits a coherence and consistency of tone that greatly enhances its readability. In this respect it differs markedly from the competitor texts, many of which are written by committee. These texts typically strive to be "objective" and inoffensive, with the result that they largely consist of masses of facts piled promiscuously on top of one another, in such a way as to make no point, tell no story, and hold no one's interest. Clear, well-written books with a consistent point of view are more likely to be read than are bland, play-it-safe, compendiums of unthreatening facts. Third, Zinn's book pays substantial, and largely positive, attention to people who are often slighted in traditional texts: women, blacks, other racial and ethnic minorities, laborers, artists, writers, musicians, and political radicals. Students who are members of these groups, or are children of parents who are, may well as a result take a greater interest in APH than they would in a book that excludes, marginalizes, or denigrates them. Fourth, Zinn's book offers an understanding of American society that runs counter to the dominant narrative that one encounters relentlessly throughout the culture. Accordingly, it seems likely that it would challenge some readers (principally those who have accepted the dominant narrative) and inspire others (primarily those who have been marginalized by that narrative, or who, for some other reason, have regarded it with suspicion). All of these factors seem likely to result in Zinn's book being read, analyzed, pondered, discussed, quarreled with, and argued about much more than is the case with traditional texts.

And the danger of students becoming victims of indoctrination, of being seduced into accepting Zinn's worldview uncritically, is mitigated by several factors. First, Zinn's text, in radical contrast to its competitors, announces that it expresses one point of view among others, and openly proclaims its biases and its principles of inclusion, exclusion, and emphasis. Second, Zinn's book pushes against the worldview that is dominant in American society; and that worldview can be counted on to continue to assert itself throughout the culture, offering a constant challenge to Zinn's account. Third, American students typically take a course in American history multiple times. I had it in elementary school, junior high school (or middle school, if you prefer), and high school, before taking more specialized courses in American history in college. It is highly unlikely that a student will be repeatedly assigned Zinn in all of these courses, and not be exposed to more traditional American history textbooks. Fourth, many teachers who use Zinn (probably most, and perhaps nearly all—I speculate because I know of no study of this issue, so the evidence I have is anecdotal) assign at least one other text for students to study alongside his. Zinn presents his book as a counterweight to standard histories, and I suspect that most teachers teach it that way, and use it to foster critical thinking, discussion, and debate.   ,

So it would appear that even if one were to grant, for the sake of argument, that Zinn's text suffers from some of the deficiencies that Wineburg attributes to it, a more complete assessment of its features shows both that it has positive attributes that are likely to yield good educational results that other textbooks are unlikely to achieve, and that the bad educational consequences of its use that Wineburg speculatively attributes to it are likely to be greatly mitigated by the book's candid modesty, and by the wider educational and societal background against which it is used.

(4) But the biggest problem with Wineburg's argument that Zinn's text has baleful educational consequences is precisely that it is speculative, and needlessly so. Zinn's book has been taught in American history classes for over 30 years. The question of its educational effects is empirical. But Wineburg ignores all of the evidence. He shows no interest in investigating the question of what happens to students who study Zinn. This is the main point of New York University history professor Robert Cohen's critique of Wineburg, entitled "When Assessing Zinn, Listen to the Voices of Teachers and Students" (WAZ):

> [Wineburg] drew his conclusion about Zinn's lack of educational value without talking to a single teacher or gathering other primary source data about how they teach *A People's History* in their U.S. history classes or on how students see their learning experience when they read *A People's History*. There is actually a wealth of data on both teacher and student responses to Zinn's *People's History* and Wineburg missed it

all. Some of this data takes the form of correspondence that high school teachers and students sent to Zinn, dating back to the publication of *A People's History* in 1980 through Zinn's death in 2010. This correspondence is housed in the Howard Zinn papers at NYU's Tamiment Library, and virtually none of it confirms any of Wineburg's conclusions about Zinn's book stifling independent historical thought and debate...

The most complete set of letters students sent to Zinn after they read (parts of) *A People's History* come from those in the classes of Bill Patterson, an innovative history teacher who taught in public high schools in two conservative communities in Oregon during the 1980s and 1990s. Patterson asked his students to send Zinn their thoughts, criticisms, and questions about *A People's History,* and over the years more than a hundred did so.... The reason Patterson continued over two decades to have his students read select Zinn chapters as a counter to the textbook and then write to Zinn was because he found that it promoted critical thinking skills and fostered lively debate. Instead of sleepy sessions in which students covered only a traditional textbook, the contrast between Zinn and the textbook "provoked spirited (sometimes rowdy) discussions in class," which sparked student interest in history, an interest Patterson used to push students "to investigate various topics, form conclusions, and articulate how they came to those conclusions." Students who disagreed with Zinn's radical take on history, no less than those who agreed with him, tended to find these sessions intellectually stimulating since Zinn's writing was so accessible and his ideas so new to them. As Patterson told Zinn, "over the course of the school year, no matter if a student 'loved' you or 'hated' you, they all looked forward to what you had to say on a topic."

The student letters to Zinn confirm Patterson's assessment.... Seeing how different Zinn's history was from their textbooks led them, haltingly at first and in diverse ways and varied levels of sophistication, to begin thinking about historical methodology, and to question the relationship between evidence, bias, and historical conclusions. It was for most the first time they realized that historical truth was contested, historical narratives selectively constructed. As one of Patterson's students wrote Zinn: "Your writings are very educational. They help us to think about a side of history that we usually aren't exposed to. Until I read one of your writings I never even stopped to think about the fact that our History [text] books were only giving us one viewpoint...I didn't realize that there were so many controversial happenings to be written about." The students were making their first moves towards recognizing that history was more than a simple trivia game involving remembering names and dates, that history was a critical discipline.

Patterson's students were...divided about Zinn. Some admired Zinn's radical view of the American past, while others were either strongly critical or ambivalent about it.... Different as the pro- and anti-Zinn responses might seem, and however divergent they may have been politically, there was actually something many of the best pro and con letters shared: a concern with evidence, and a new and developing ability to use evidence to test the conclusions historians drew. The anti-Zinn students were using evidence from their textbook and other sources to question Zinn's conclusions while Zinn's admirers were employing evidence from *A People's History* to challenge the historical conclusions of their textbook. And some were even questioning *both* Zinn and the textbook. This is quite an achievement, when one considers that these students of Patterson were so young, just juniors in high school. One can see...in [these] letters...the development of genuine historical thought, critical interrogation of texts, and an attempt to glean historical truth out of competing interpretations.

Additional testimony on the effects of Zinn's text in the classroom can be found at the Zinn Education Project website.[9] Here are three samples: (1) Shannon White, Indiana Public Schools, High School Government and Economics Teacher: "I use Howard Zinn's *A People's History of the United States*...in my high school social studies classes because it offers a new and different perspective without the feel of a traditional textbook, which helps my students hone their evaluation skills and learn to synthesize information while discussing and interacting with the content...I use Zinn in the classroom because I want to give a voice to those that have been silenced and marginalized in traditional history textbooks; those are the voices that my students identify with the most. Identifying with history helps my students remember, learn from, and engage with it." (Note that, according to the "investigative" work of the crack team in Mitch Daniels's governor's office, Zinn's book was "not being used anywhere in Indiana"!)

(2) Ralph J. Coffey, South Bronx, New York, U.S. A.P. History teacher, Cardinal Hayes High School: "*A People's History of the United States* is one book that makes my students think. They are shocked by it, moved by it, question it, challenge it and are motivated to find out more of our history because of it."

(3) Josh Weissberg, New York, New York, 7th-Grade Social Studies Teacher: "Now, whenever I pull out the textbook, they groan. And if we do happen to read a textbook account of something, they always want to know what other historians have said or found about the event."

Finally, historian Eric Foner, author of a review of APH in the *New York Times* in 1980, commented 30 years later: "I have long been struck by how many excellent students of history first had their passion for the past sparked by reading Howard Zinn" (ZCH 212).

Granted, the evidence provided by Cohen, the teachers quoted at the Zinn Education Project website, and Foner, is anecdotal. But it is both plausible and highly suggestive. And, in radical contrast to Wineburg's claims, it is not *armchair speculation* as to what the educational effects of Zinn *must be*, but rather *data* on what those effects have *actually been*.

While "Undue Certainty" remains Wineburg's most extensive discussion of Zinn, he weighed in again when Mitch Daniels quoted him in the context of defending his (Daniels's) attempt to ban Zinn from Indiana classrooms. Wineburg forthrightly condemned Daniels's action, and defended the right of teachers to assign Zinn, pointing out that he had done so himself. And when 92 Purdue professors wrote an open letter to Daniels expressing their concerns over his action, Wineburg decided once more to jump into the fray, this time criticizing the professors and renewing his attack on Zinn (in an op-ed piece, "In Indiana, history meets politics," published in the *Los Angeles Times*):

"Had the letter confined itself to a defense of academic freedom, I would have applauded.

But it didn't. The letter went on to endorse Zinn's scholarship. And in doing so, it took liberties with the facts."[10]

How so? What liberties did it take? Here is Wineburg's first example: "For every negative comment about 'A People's History of the United States,' the faculty letter to Daniels claimed, 'you can find a positive one published in expert venues.'" How does Wineburg show this to be incorrect? "Really? Of the two leading history journals, neither the *American Historical Review* nor the *Journal of American History* saw fit to review the book when it came out. And the work has been criticized by historians from across the political spectrum." Wineburg then proceeds to cite Oscar Handlin and Michael Kazin as examples of historians who have criticized Zinn. That's it.

Let's review. The Purdue faculty letter says that there are as many positive comments on Zinn's book published in expert venues as negative comments. Had Wineburg pointed out that the letter failed to document this claim, he would have been on sound ground. (Perhaps the letter's assertion was based on nothing more scientific than the impression of the Purdue historians who regularly read scholarly history journals.) But in asserting that the letter "took liberties with the facts," Wineburg is making a stronger charge. To make it stick, he would obviously have to undertake, or cite, a systematic study of Zinn citations in scholarly publications. Instead he "hangs" his accusation on just two pieces of evidence. The first is utterly irrelevant to his point. The non-existent reviews of Zinn's book in the two journals Wineburg mentions obviously contain no comments at all on Zinn's work, whether positive or negative. The second piece of evidence would be relevant indeed if the letter had claimed that there was a positive scholarly consensus about the quality of Zinn's work. But the claim that the letter actually did make is not even remotely undermined by Wineburg's point that several historians (though here he only cites two) have criticized Zinn, for that claim is not that Zinn is without critics, but rather that criticism of Zinn is balanced by scholarly praise for his work. So Wineburg, at this point, is zero-for-one.

Incidentally, for whatever it is worth, Zinn's biographer, Martin Duberman (Distinguished Professor Emeritus of History at the CUNY Graduate Center, and recipient of the American Historical Association's 2007 Lifetime Achievement Award) informs us that "*A People's History* was widely reviewed" (DUB 336, note 8). His assessment of the book's reception in the scholarly community is closer to that of the Purdue faculty than to that of Wineburg: "When *A People's History* was published, early in 1980, the reception was mixed. Some well-known historians gave the book a drubbing in various journals, though the majority of fellow scholars, critical to varying degrees, admired the undertaking and recognized it as a game changer" (DUB 235). Or again: "Within the historical profession, [Zinn] has nearly as many detractors as admirers" (316).

Here is Wineburg's second example of the letter's "taking

liberties with the facts": "The Purdue faculty claimed in its letter to Daniels that 'most experts in the field of U.S. history do not take issue with Howard Zinn's facts, even when they do take issue with his conclusions.'"

How does Wineburg refute that one? "But Zinn got important facts wrong. In successive editions, from the original 1980 imprint to the 2006 'Modern Classics' edition, Zinn quoted a cable supposedly sent by Japanese Foreign Minister Shigenori Togo in 1945 to his ambassador to Moscow. 'Unconditional surrender is the only obstacle to peace,' the cable was supposed to have said. Zinn concluded from those words that Japan would have been willing to surrender if the U.S. would have agreed that its emperor could remain in place. Yet no cable with these words exists: not in the Japanese archives, the American archives or anywhere else."

Once again, Wineburg would have been correct had he simply made the observation that the letter fails to document or in any other way justify its claim. But to insist, as he does, that the letter takes liberties with the facts, obligates him to show that the claim is false. And this he manifestly fails to do. For one thing, he says nothing at all about what "most experts" think on this issue. But we can waive that, because the important issue is whether or not Zinn gets his facts wrong, not whether experts *think* he does. And here Wineburg "hangs" his claim on just one piece of evidence. If Wineburg is right in what he says here, then he has shown that Zinn got *one* important fact wrong. But that, by itself, is surely not very damning. It is doubtful that any 688-page book on American history is entirely free of factual errors. Surely the issue is one of degree: does Zinn achieve a high degree of factual accuracy, relative to the difficulties inherent in such an ambitious project as writing a 688-page history of the United States, and in comparison to the achievement in this regard of other historians? (In light of the discussion above, I am uncertain that Zinn's 688-page text contains more factual errors than does Wineburg's eight-page critique of it.) Since a positive answer to that question would be fully compatible with the presence of one error of the sort that Wineburg cites, he, by resting his case with that one example, fails to establish his point.

Moreover, while I have no expertise on this issue, I will note, for the record, that not everyone agrees with Wineburg that Zinn is in error on this point.[11] But, even if Wineburg is indeed right about the non-existence of the Togo cable, it is hard to see this as an especially egregious error. On Wineburg's own account (WIN 34, note 31) Zinn's mistake was to rely on the work of Martin Sherwin, a highly-regarded, Pulitzer Prize-winning historian who (again, on Wineburg's interpretation) made the original mistake of confusing a paraphrase of an American reaction to a Japanese intercept with an actual cable from Togo. Moreover, if the Togo cable is indeed a "chimera," as Wineburg claims, it is "a chimera with astonishing longevity" (these are Wineburg's words) that has taken in, and continues to take in, a great number of scholars—a fact that can be readily verified by conducting a Google search on this issue. So, at best, Wineburg has shown that Zinn made one factual error—one that a number of other competent scholars also made, and one that he made by relying on the work of another highly credible historian—not exactly a smoking gun for establishing the thesis that Zinn is careless with factual accuracy. Wineburg is now zero-for-two.

It should be noted that Wineburg also introduces a factual error of his own into the discussion at this point, when he asserts that "Zinn concluded from those words [the ones in the alleged Togo cable] that Japan would have been willing to surrender if the U.S. would have agreed that its emperor could remain in place." Zinn's text simply does not support that interpretation. On page 422 of APH Zinn cites two other pieces of evidence in support of his conclusion about Japan's willingness to surrender: a quotation from *New York Times* military analyst Hanson Baldwin and, more importantly, a study conducted by the United

States Strategic Bombing Survey, conducted shortly after the end of the war, in which hundreds of Japanese civilian and military leaders were interviewed. The Togo cable is mentioned only on the subsequent page, and it is introduced, not, as Wineburg seems to think, to show that Japan was ready to surrender, but rather to address the different, and logically posterior, question of whether American leaders *knew* that Japan was ready to surrender. So, at best (for Wineburg), the scorecard now reads: one error for Zinn (in a 688-page book), and one error for Wineburg (in a short op-ed newspaper column accusing Zinn of making factual errors, and chastising Purdue professors for "taking liberties with the facts").

Here is Wineburg's third example: "The Purdue faculty dismissed criticisms of Zinn's scholarship by Handlin and presidential historian Arthur M. Schlesinger Jr. as coming from the 'consensus school of U.S. history.' But their dismissal ignored the searing criticisms of historians with impeccable leftist credentials, such as Kazin and Princeton historian Sean Wilentz."

How is this supposed to stand as an example of taking liberties with the facts? The letter neither asserts nor implies that the *only* critics of Zinn are historians from the consensus school. Nor does the letter purport to address every critic of Zinn, except by means of the general comments, already discussed, that Zinn has as many scholarly admirers as critics, and that the critics do not generally challenge the accuracy of the facts he cites. Wineburg is correct in stating that the letter offers an explanation of the criticisms of Handlin and Schlesinger as flowing from their allegiance to the consensus school, and that this point is inapplicable to Kazin and Wilentz, who are not directly discussed. But none of that amounts, even to the slightest degree, to "taking liberties with the facts." Wineburg is now zero-for-three.

Here is Wineburg's fourth example: "The letter quotes Columbia University's Eric Foner as saying that Zinn should be

'required reading.' But Foner wrote those words referring specifically to Zinn's chapter on Vietnam. In the same review, Foner
also concluded that Zinn's 'history from the bottom up, though
necessary as a corrective, is as limited in its own way as history
from the top down.' Hardly a ringing endorsement."

Wineburg finally scores. It is true, as he points out, that the
letter attributes to Foner's review the claim that Zinn's book
should be "required reading," when in fact Foner had said that
only about Zinn's chapter on the Vietnam war. The letter is wrong
on this point, and Wineburg is right to call attention to the error.
But this one, rather small, mistake is the only one he has successfully identified, and that is hardly sufficient to support his thesis
that the letter "takes liberties with the facts," or to justify his
conclusion: "What bothers me most about the whole flap—about
Daniels' emails and about the Purdue faculty's reaction to them—
is the way nuance was sacrificed to politics. We've come to expect
politicians under fire to engage in spin. But when academics
respond in kind, they reduce education to a game of politics. The
loser in this game is truth and the students we are supposed to
teach about the value of pursuing it."

Moreover, Wineburg's discussion of the Foner issue has its
own deficiencies that are worth noting. For one thing, if, as he
implies, it is objectionable for the letter to omit Foner's critical
remark on Zinn's book, then so is it objectionable for Wineburg to
omit something highly relevant that the letter includes—Foner's
words of praise for Zinn, uttered in 2010, 30 years after the publication of his original review of APH: "Over the years I have been
struck by how many excellent students of history had their
interest in studying the past sparked by reading Howard Zinn.
That's the highest compliment one can offer to a historian."
Moreover, while Wineburg is correct in his comment that the
Foner quote that he (Wineburg) provides is "hardly a ringing
endorsement," it should be pointed out that it is also hardly a
damning criticism. Foner's point is not that Zinn has done

something wrong, or done anything poorly, and still less that he has gotten his facts wrong, or made logical blunders, or anything like that. Rather, the criticism amounts to the mere pointing out of the inherent limitations of Zinn's project—to provide a corrective, or a counterweight, to the traditional "patriotic," top-down American historical narrative. I take it that Foner's point is that we ultimately need a history that is free both from the distortions of the traditional texts, and the distortions of emphasis and selection that are necessarily attendant to the project of correcting something that has gone wrong. Notice, in that regard, that while Foner cites the "limitations" of Zinn's approach, he nonetheless hails his book as "necessary as a corrective."

Though I think, and have tried to demonstrate, that Wineburg's case against the intellectual integrity of the Purdue professors completely falls apart on analysis, perhaps this just demonstrates the soundness of Wineburg's strictures about "the historian's epistemological quandary," the "unfinished nature of historical knowledge, the way its fragments can never be wholly put together," the "indeterminacy and multiple causality" of history, and the "unruly fibers of evidence that stubbornly jut out from any interpretive frame." Maybe we are dealing with incredibly difficult questions here, so that the important thing is to be modest and tentative in making claims about them. We must not extinguish "perhaps," "maybe," "might," or, above all, "on the other hand"—for we must not write "history with no hands." But no. Here, as elsewhere (such as in connection with issues of factual accuracy, the careful handling of evidence, basic fairness, and intellectual honesty) Wineburg ignores the demands that he imperiously attempts to impose on others. A search of his article condemning the Purdue faculty's letter shows that it never uses "maybe," "might," "seem," "seems," "seemed," or "on the other hand." But it must be admitted that Wineburg does use "perhaps" once. He tells us that Mitch Daniels's attempt to ban Zinn's book was "perhaps clumsy."

In any case, we have certainly made some discoveries about the "interpretive circuitry" in Wineburg's own work—that is, "the moves and strategies, largely invisible to the casual reader, that he uses to tie evidence to conclusion, to convince readers that his interpretations are right."

David Greenberg

Greenberg is a Professor of History and of Journalism and Media Studies at Rutgers University. His article, "Agit-Prof: Howard Zinn's influential mutilations of American history," published in the March 25, 2013 issue of *The New Republic*, claims that "Zinn's famous book [APH] is...a pretty lousy piece of work" (GRE 45). I have found that those who claim, in Internet discussions, that Zinn is a terrible historian, and that Mitch Daniels was therefore justified in his attempts to rid Indiana classrooms of his book, frequently defend their opinion by citing Greenberg's article.

On the first page of his essay Greenberg informs us that as a teenager he had been "enamored" of Zinn, and had "thrilled" to his "deflation of what he presented as the myths of standard-issue history" (GRE 44). Recalling his 16-year-old self, Greenberg continues, "Mischievously—subversively—*A People's History* whispered that everything I had learned in school was a sugar-coated fairy tale, if not a deliberate lie. Now I knew" (GRE 45).

Predictably, however, Greenberg cites his teenage views only to contrast them with his current mature perspective as a history professor, thus implying that those who admire Zinn do so because of the naivety, historical ignorance, and lack of sophistication that they share in common with typical American teenagers.

This is how he attempts to make that case: "Do you know that the Declaration of Independence charged King George with fomenting slave rebellions and attacks from 'merciless Indian Savages'? That James Polk started a war with Mexico as a pretext for annexing California? That Eugene Debs was jailed for calling

World War I a war of conquest and plunder? Perhaps you do, if you are moderately well-read in American history. And if you are very well-read, you also know that these statements themselves are problematic simplifications" (44–5).

Greenberg's rhetoric is open to at least two objections. First, these are caricatures of what Zinn says on these topics. For example, with regard to Debs, Zinn makes it clear that he was convicted of violating the Espionage Act, which made it a crime to obstruct the recruitment of young men into military service (APH 367–8). Thus, even on Zinn's account, Debs was not jailed as a result of the mere fact that he had called World War I a war of conquest and plunder. Rather, the government had to make the case that these and other words of Debs's had the "natural and intended effect" of obstructing recruiting.

But more importantly, Greenberg never gets around to explaining in what ways these claims (let alone, the non-caricatured versions as Zinn actually presented them) are "problematic simplifications." Since most of Greenberg's readers are presumably not "very well-read" in American history (few people are), they probably will not know the un-problematic, un-simplified truths about these matters. Why not enlighten them? Greenberg chooses not to, and in this he follows the pattern of almost all of Zinn's critics—heavy charges are asserted, but they are supported by no documentation, no evidence, and no argument. (This shows what kind of readers Greenberg is aiming to address—those who don't demand evidence, and are willing, instead, simply to bow to his authority as a history professor.)

Next, Greenberg asserts that "The orthodox version of the American past that Howard Zinn spent his life debunking was by the 1980s no longer quite as hegemonic as Zinn made out" (45). Here again, one can note a couple of objections. First, the reference to "the 1980s" is imprecise, and in other ways problematic. Greenberg is attempting to undermine the argument that APH provided a useful corrective to the one-sided nature of existing history textbooks. To the extent that this "orthodox version" was no longer dominant when Zinn wrote, such an argument cannot be sustained, and Zinn's own biases in terms of selection and emphasis are harder to justify. But Zinn wrote his book in the 1970s, and it was published in 1980. So the crucial issue is not the state of history textbooks, vaguely, "in the 1980s," but rather, more precisely, in 1980. If the change took place later in the decade, it may well be that this occurred in part because of Zinn's influence (as Greenberg subsequently [45] concedes).

Second, the evidence that Greenberg cites in support of his claim that the orthodox version of American history was no longer hegemonic is scanty. It consists of two items: (a) an anecdote about the way in which his own high school history teacher taught Columbus (this at a date that Greenberg does not specify), and (b) a quotation from historian Jon Wiener, published in the *Journal of American History*, to the effect that radical history was institutionalized in the early 1970s. But Greenberg himself points out that the "goring of sacred cows" that the radical historians accomplished was something that was known by professional historians, as opposed to being contained in textbooks that reach students. Indeed, he also allows that "in the popular books and public ceremonies of the 1980s, you could still find a whitewashed tale of the nation's past, as you can today; and many cities around the country shielded their charges from such heresies" (45). So Greenberg has not provided much of a defense of his claims. He cites no review of high school history textbooks that were widely used in 1980 to demonstrate that Zinn's debunking efforts were by then no longer necessary. I suspect that is because any such review would clearly establish the opposite.

Another of Greenberg's strategies, undertaken repeatedly in his essay, is to assert or imply that Zinn makes perverse moral judgments. For example, he tells us that "After reading John

Hersey's *Hiroshima*, Zinn decided that the dropping of the atomic bomb on Japan was an indefensible atrocity. While not endorsing a moral equivalence between fascism and liberalism, Zinn found the flaws of the latter, not the former, gnawing at him—an unusual position, to say the least, in the time of the Holocaust" (46)

Note, first, that Greenberg's explanation of Zinn's opposition to the use of the atomic bomb against Japan grossly oversimplifies Zinn's thought—a failing that runs throughout his essay. As discussed in connection with Wineburg above, Zinn's opposition was based, in part, on evidence that Japan was already prepared to surrender, and would have done so even without the use of the bomb, a point that undermines the argument that the bomb saved lives by shortening the war.

And while Greenberg is not wrong to assert, in his final sentence here, that Zinn's position was "unusual," the implied criticism is unwarranted. For, consistent with the superficiality of Greenberg's entire essay, he does not even mention, much less mount an argument against, Zinn's reason for feeling this way. A conscientious person tends to be bothered much more by his or her own moral failings than by those of others, even if the latter are worse. I am responsible for, and can do something about, my own transgressions. I am not responsible for, and often can do nothing about, those of others. This explains why Zinn is more bothered by—why they "gnaw at him" more—the crimes of his own country. He considers himself to be partially responsible for them, and feels an obligation to try to correct them. That is why the shame and anger he felt about racism in the U.S. military when he served in World War II, not to mention the obvious hypocrisy (in a war, supposedly being fought in part to combat racism, white and black platoons were segregated, with the black soldiers getting the worst of it—for example, having to wait until all of the white soldiers had finished eating before entering the mess hall), was qualitatively different from the feelings he had in reaction to the Holocaust, which was obviously, in his mind no less than that of anyone else, much worse.[12] This is a point that Zinn's critics consistently overlook. As a result, Zinn's focus on the crimes of his own state is wrongly interpreted as a perverse anti-Americanism. Greenberg misses this, in part because of his ignorance of Zinn's work (to be documented immediately below), and in part because of his lack of interest in ideas, principles, and arguments—as manifested in his tendency to condemn Zinn simply by paraphrasing (often inaccurately) his attitudes and conclusions, without bothering to inquire into, let alone respond to, the principles, arguments, and evidence underlying them.

And if Greenberg's criticisms are unsound with respect to the actual record of Zinn's writing and speaking, he can always make his case stronger by misrepresenting that record—and he does not fail to employ this strategy: "[Zinn] relentlessly criticized American policy and seems to have stayed silent about the Soviet Union" (46).

Note, first of all, the extreme oddity of Greenberg's "*seems* to have stayed silent" phrase. On what was this "seeming" based? Why resort to "seeming" here? What kind of scholar does this? What kind of scholar writes sentences like that? Why not do a little research, check out Zinn's writings—perhaps even actually *read* them, and *find out* whether or not he stayed silent? Had Greenberg done so (that is, had he risen to the level of scholarly standards that we demand of freshmen), he would have found, for example, the following:

> The Soviet Union…has been brutal in its treatment of its own citizens, murdering peasants in large numbers during the process of collectivization; imprisoning, torturing, and executing those it considered dissidents, whether ordinary people, intellectuals, artists, or distinguished leaders of the 1917 Revolution. The term *police state* fits it very well…. It has imitated the imperialist powers in invading other countries—

Hungary, Czechoslovakia, and Afghanistan, killing thousands
of people. (DOI 268)

"Seems to have stayed silent"? How lucky the students of
Rutgers are to be instructed by such a careful, honest, and
competent scholar!

The depths of Greenberg's recklessness and irresponsibility in
falsely claiming that Zinn (whose scholarship he, of all people,
calls "lousy") "seems to have stayed silent about the Soviet
Union," is underscored by four further observations. First, the
passage just quoted would have been easy to find if Greenberg
had undertaken even the most modest research project of
searching for statements by Zinn on the Soviet Union. For the
quoted passage appears, not as an aside buried in a piece that
would seem to have nothing to do with that subject, but rather in
an essay called "Communism and Anti-communism." Surely that
title is a clue that the essay might contain some of Zinn's thoughts
about the Soviet Union. So had Greenberg wanted to check
whether his claim that Zinn "seems to have stayed silent on the
Soviet Union" was correct, he would only have had to check the
"Table of Contents" pages of Zinn's major books in order to find
this highly promising chapter.

Second, since Greenberg apparently thinks himself qualified
to pronounce APH "a pretty lousy piece of work," surely he
should have read it. But had he done so, he would have found in
it such statements of Zinn's as that "In the early nineties, the false
socialism of the Soviet system had failed" (APH 638); that the
Soviet Union, far from being a dictatorship of the proletariat,
"had turned out to be [a] dictatorship *over* the proletariat" (APH
591); that it was "inefficient and oppressive" (APH 658); that it
was a "dictatorship" that had "betrayed socialism" (APH 635);
and that Stalin "killed peasants for industrial progress in the
Soviet Union" (APH 17).

Third, since Greenberg's essay purports to be a review of

Duberman's biography of Zinn, he should have read it. But had he done so, he would have found this: "'Millions,' Howard wrote, 'were killed in the Soviet Union to 'build socialism' but the result was totalitarian state control" (DUB 270).

Fourth, such passages are far from unique in Zinn's writings. Rather, and in opposition to Greenberg's ridiculous and irresponsible utterance, one can cite numerous passages in which Zinn did not "stay silent" about the Soviet Union:

(1) "The belief, fostered in the Soviet Union, that 'socialism' required a ruthless policy of farm collectivization, as well as the control of dissent, brought about the deaths of countless peasants and large numbers of political prisoners" (DOI 1).

(2) "When Khrushchev gave his astounding speech in 1956 acknowledging Stalin's crimes (which involved, though Khrushchev did not stress this, the complicity of so many other members of the Soviet hierarchy), he was affirming what [Arthur] Koestler and other critics of the Soviet Union had been saying for a long time. When Soviet troops invaded Hungary and then Czechoslovakia to crush rebellions, it was clear to me that the Soviet Union was violating...a universal principle...of international solidarity (DOI 50).

(3) "It has been a century of atrocities: the death camps of Hitler, *the slave camps of Stalin,* and the devastation of Southeast Asia by the United States" (DOI 65, emphasis added).

(4) The Soviet Union was an "oppressive regime"[13] and an "ugly dictatorship" (ZR 223).

(5) "As for the motives of Stalin and the Soviet Union—it is absurd even to ask if they were fighting [in World War II] against the police state, against dictatorship. Yes, against *German* dictatorship, the Nazi police state, but not their

own. Before, during, and after the war against Fascism, the fascism of the gulag persisted, and expanded."[14]

More briefly, one can note Zinn's calling the Soviet Union a "police state" (OZ 157), his claim that the Soviet Union's foreign policy was based, contrary to its claims of lofty moral purpose, merely on concern for its own national power (PA, 21), his assertion that a "rigid devotion to Stalin...led to fabrication of history in the Soviet Union about the purges and other things" (HPE 22), his insistence that "the Soviet Union, with its claim to be a socialist state, was a fraud" (YCB 178), his claim that the Soviet invasion of Finland was "a brutal act of aggression against a tiny country" (YCB 171), his reference to "the horrors of Stalinism"[15] and to the "monstrous tyranny created by Stalin,"[16] his claim that the Soviet Union, "before Gorbachev's *glasnost* policies opened things up," was a "totalitarian country" in which there was "no freedom of speech, no freedom of the press" (DOI 217), and his statement that "Millions were killed in the Soviet Union to 'build socialism'" (DOI 280), in addition to his lengthier critiques touching on several of these and other issues.[17]

As bad as this error of Greenberg's is, it only gets worse when it is magnified by his followers. One blogger writes: "I appreciate Greenberg's approach to revisionism such as Zinn's: he calls out Zinn's willingness to castigate the USA's actions and ideologies while ignoring or minimizing other nations' cruelties—his silences on the brutalities of Soviet Russia, and so on."[18] Here Greenberg's incorrect "seems to have stayed silent" morphs into the more definitive, and thus more incorrect, "his silences"—and with a nebulous but suggestive "and so on" tacked on for good measure. In this way myths are created, inflated, and disseminated.[19]

Further errors, distortions, and logical lapses ensue when Greenberg turns his attention to Zinn's persecution at the hands of John Silber, who became Boston University's president in 1971

(Zinn was by then a professor there):

> John Silber, swaggering in from Texas, had a vendetta against
> the left…. Heedless of due process, intolerant of dissent, Silber
> imposed his will on the faculty and students…. And Zinn
> became Silber's archenemy, subject to capricious punishments
> and unwarranted invective. Duberman [Zinn's biographer]
> reports that when Zinn received an offer to teach in Paris and
> secured Herbert Marcuse [a world famous philosopher] to
> teach in his stead, Silber vetoed what should have been a
> routine leave of absence. Silber also denied Zinn promotions
> and raises for years. In 1982, with help from the AAUP, he
> won an appeal to gain his long-withheld back pay.
>
> That Zinn deserved sympathy for his victimization by
> Silber, however, does not mean that his own ideas or pursuits
> were admirable. (47)

So far, so good. But then, after a two-paragraph discussion of the
alleged defects of Zinn's "ideas and pursuits," Greenberg offers
this stunning conclusion: "Duberman makes it easy to see why
Zinn earned Silber's contempt" (47). Note that Greenberg had
already quite adequately explained the *cause* of Silber's contempt
("vendetta against the left," "intolerant of dissent"). But now he
is asserting that Zinn *earned* that contempt. How does Greenberg
make a case for that? He makes just two points: (1) "At B.U., Zinn
regularly and cavalierly denounced prevailing academic
standards, arguing that the university should teach 'relevant'
subjects and forego what he described as the 'endless academic
discussion' of 'trivial or esoteric inquiry' that goes 'nowhere into
the real world'" (47); and (2) "Zinn [was]…a lazy, conventional
theorist, with an undeveloped political philosophy," who failed
to develop a "'creative, original' [political] philosophy" (47).
Greenberg then offers the judgment that this second "shortcoming cannot be…easily excused, given Zinn's ambitions, any

more than we can excuse Zinn's trite calls for politically useful history." Immediately following this sentence, we are told that "Duberman makes it easy to see why Zinn earned Silber's contempt" (47).

Where does Greenberg go wrong? (1) He offers no evidence in support of his claim that "At B.U., Zinn regularly and cavalierly denounced prevailing academic standards, arguing that the university should teach 'relevant' subjects and forego what he described as the 'endless academic discussion' of 'trivial or esoteric inquiry' that goes 'nowhere into the real world.'" Presumably Greenberg thinks that his source is Duberman's biography of Zinn, of which Greenberg's article is ostensibly a review. But Duberman does not say anything that supports Greenberg's claim. The quotations that Greenberg lists here ("relevant," "endless academic discussion," "trivial or esoteric inquiry," goes "nowhere into the real world") are all to be found on, and thus were presumably taken from, page 158 of Duberman's book. But Duberman is not there discussing Zinn's behavior at Boston University. Rather, he is summarizing Zinn's article, "The Case for Radical Change" (also published, with minor changes, as "The Uses of Scholarship" and as the first chapter, entitled "Knowledge as a Form of Power," of his *The Politics of History*). Greenberg's claim that this is one of the two things that Zinn did to "earn" Silber's contempt owes any plausibility it may possess to Greenberg's insinuation that Zinn made a nuisance of himself at his university, "regularly" hectoring his colleagues for producing "trivial" scholarship that failed to meet his standards of "relevance." Indeed, that would have been annoying. But there is no evidence that Zinn did that. Instead, he *wrote an article*, in which he merely *argued* for *greater attention* in scholarly work to the criterion of contemporary relevance. The article was a non-coercive appeal to reason. Anyone wishing to avoid Zinn's views on this topic could have accomplished it by not reading him. Anyone wishing not to be persuaded by his arguments could have accomplished this by refuting them logically. Zinn's article might have "earned" him spirited disagreement on the part of some of his readers. It is far from clear that it should have "earned" him anyone's contempt.

(2) Greenberg's summary of Zinn's views on relevant, politically useful history caricatures his position. First of all, Zinn's main point has to do with the selection of subject matter, which seems a rather different issue than any concern about "prevailing academic standards," whatever Greenberg might mean by that phrase. To say that scholars should devote more attention than they presently do to pressing social concerns is not to say that they should diminish their concern for factual accuracy and logical rigor—a point that Zinn makes repeatedly.

Second, it is a demonstrable falsehood that Zinn calls for scholars to "forego" work that lacks present social or political relevance: "Am I trying to obliterate all scholarship except the immediately relevant? No, it is a matter of proportion... It was not wrong for the Association of Asian Studies at its last annual meeting to discuss some problems of the Ming Dynasty and a battery of similarly remote topics, but *no* session of the dozens at the meeting dealt with Vietnam" (UOS; ZR 502; OH 180; KFP 7–8).[20] Zinn makes clear over and over again that the issue is one of proportion. He does not call for an end to other kinds of scholarly endeavors, but rather merely encourages an increase in scholarly engagement with current social problems. His reference to "trivial or esoteric inquiry," and "endless academic discussion" that goes "nowhere into the real world" (UOS; ZR 502; OH 180–1; KFP 8) is clearly presented in this context. His point is not to call for the banning, or even the discouraging, of such work, but rather to encourage scholars to expend more of their energy in a different direction. He also attempts to show, by means of rational arguments, that many of their reasons for refraining from doing so rest on fallacies and confusions. (Moreover, it should be pointed out that Zinn does not accuse scholars of deliberately engaging in "endless academic discussion" that goes "nowhere into the real world." Rather, he says that this "can" be the result when social scientists invent "catch-phrases," "schemes," "models," and "systems.")

Third, Zinn repeatedly states (though one cannot learn this from Greenberg) that his stance with regard to much non-immediately relevant historical work is one of genuine appreciation that goes well beyond an attitude of mere tolerance. For example: "I am not directing my criticism against those few histories which are works of art, which make no claim to illuminate a social problem, but instead capture the mood, the color, the reality of an age, an incident, or an individual, conveying pleasure and the warmth of genuine emotion. This needs no justification, for it is, after all, the ultimate purpose of social change to enlarge human happiness" (HPE 19).

Fourth, Greenberg errs when he states that "Zinn never seems to have grasped that scholarship differs from more perishable forms of writing precisely in that it begins in a freedom to explore topics that may appear remote from today's pressing concerns but that can still change our understanding of the world" (47). To the contrary, Zinn readily acknowledges that scholarship engaging "topics that may appear remote from today's pressing concerns" can nonetheless "still change our understanding of the world." Indeed, he offers the example of "the mathematician, whose formulas have no knowable immediate use," and the scientist who works "on data which open toward infinity in their possible future uses" (HPE 19). But he rejects the claim that esoteric historical research ("the historian working on a dead battle or an obscure figure") always or even typically has these qualities of openness and transitivity. Such investigations, unlike the "pure research" of the mathematician or theoretical scientist, are too localized and specific to be applicable to a variety of cases, or to open up new avenues of research. Perhaps Zinn is wrong on this point, but it is hard to make the case that he has failed to think about, or to "grasp," the point at issue.

Fifth, it is ironic that Greenberg would invoke "freedom" in arguing against what he takes to be Zinn's position, since Zinn, too, calls for freedom, and does so in connection with the same domain—that of choosing which topic to investigate. Greenberg's reference to "a freedom to explore topics that may appear remote from today's pressing concerns" subtly implies that there is pressure on scholars to stick to subjects of clear contemporary relevance, so that there is a need for, and a great value in, establishing a "freedom" to resist such pressure and be able to work on other issues of one's own choosing. But Zinn's argument, unaddressed by Greenberg, is that this reverses the actual situation. In the real world, scholars who work on esoteric subjects bearing no obvious consequences for our present conduct are rewarded for their efforts, while scholars who use their special expertise and scholarly energies to contribute to public discussions of pressing social issues are, quite irrespective of the quality of their work and the cogency of their arguments, condemned as "propagandists," admonished to be "objective" and "neutral," encouraged to carry on "disinterested scholarship," and subjected to ignorant, irresponsible, lazy, and uncomprehending criticisms by the likes of Greenberg. Granting, as Zinn does, that scholars should be free to pursue projects of no obvious immediate social relevance, and further, that such work can be quite valuable, would Greenberg concede that scholars should also be free to pursue projects that *are* of obvious immediate social relevance, and that this work, too, if it is well done, can be valuable? He does not say, though that is precisely the point at issue in assessing Zinn's argument.

Sixth, what could Greenberg possibly mean by his charge that there is something "cavalier" about Zinn's discussion of these issues? "Cavalier" means "showing a lack of proper concern; offhand." Its synonyms include "indifferent," "casual," "dismissive," and "unconcerned." To the contrary, Zinn presents several dozen pages of careful argumentation, draws a number of subtle distinctions (all of which are ignored by Greenberg—for example, between ultimate values and instrumental values, between preconceived questions and preconceived answers, between the issue of criteria for the selection of problems and the issue of accuracy in dealing with those problems, and so forth), attempts to answer a number of objections to his stance (organizing these under the headings "disinterested scholarship," "objectivity," "disciplinary specialization," "science and neutrality," and "rationality and emotionalism"—see UOS; ZR 503–6; OH 181–6; POH 9–13), and displays an almost fanatical concern for clarity and the avoidance of possible misunderstandings. Greenberg, by contrast, provides nothing to support his "cavalier" insult. Indeed, if anything here is genuinely cavalier, it is Greenberg's dismissive, uncomprehending, error-riddled characterization of Zinn's position.

In short, because he is apparently unaware of Zinn's actual views, Greenberg, like many other of Zinn's critics, utterly fails to address them. While he attacks the straw-Zinn, the phantom who calls for scholars to "forego" work that lacks present social or political relevance, he has nothing to say about Howard Zinn, the person who merely urges that a greater portion of scholarly work be devoted to issues of pressing social concern. The pseudo-Zinn of Greenberg's imagination is someone who, to return to an earlier example, might want the Association of Asian Studies at its annual meeting in 1969 or 1970 to devote *all* of its sessions to the Vietnam war, and *none* to the Ming Dynasty. Greenberg has nothing to say about the real Zinn, who argues merely that *some* attention at this meeting be paid to the Vietnam war, and not *all* of it devoted to the Ming Dynasty and other subjects similarly distant from urgent present concerns. Were Greenberg to confront Zinn's actual convictions, he would find himself in the following dilemma. He would either have to defend the thesis that historians must avoid all subjects of present social or political concern, and that the presenters at the Association of Asian Studies conference were therefore completely right to make no contribution whatsoever to the debate over Vietnam (and that Zinn's complaint about their failure to discuss Vietnam was unreasonable), or else admit that the first of his two cited reasons for concluding that Zinn's behavior "earned" Silber's contempt stands exposed as completely lacking in merit.

But Greenberg offers very little by way of reasoned *argument* against Zinn's call for historical work on issues of contemporary social and political relevance, and what he does provide quickly collapses under modest scrutiny. Endorsing what he takes to be Duberman's rejection of Zinn's views on this topic, Greenberg writes: "Relevance is an uncertain guide to those embarked on a long, tortuous path of scholarship. And the question of which topics are 'trivial or esoteric,' Duberman notes, is hardly self-evident" (47). Greenberg then briefly illustrates his point by offering one example of a topic that New Left historians took to be significant, but which "the academic gatekeepers of the early 1960s would surely have deemed inconsequential or arcane": "Was the class consciousness of workers forged on or off the shop floor?" With that, Greenberg moves immediately to his conclusion, already quoted, that "Zinn never seems to have grasped that scholarship differs from more perishable forms of writing precisely in that it begins in a freedom to explore topics that may appear remote from today's pressing concerns but that can still change our understanding of the world."

Since Greenberg cites Duberman here, perhaps we can flesh out Greenberg's argument a bit by quoting Duberman on this issue: "Who decides which topics are 'trivial or esoteric'? Even if a consensus could be reached on what is or is not 'important,' that determination can, and almost certainly will, change through time." Duberman then lists women's studies and gay studies as examples of areas of inquiry that once were derided as trivial, but now are widely recognized as having made valuable intellectual contributions (DUB 159). Putting these points together, we get something like this:

1. It is not self-evident what is or is not "relevant and important," as opposed to "trivial or esoteric."
2. It is unclear who should decide what is or is not "relevant and important," as opposed to "trivial or esoteric."
3. Even if a consensus could be reached on these matters, that determination would almost certainly change over time.
   Therefore, 4. "Relevance is an uncertain guide" to the task of scholarship.
   Therefore, scholars need not concern themselves about the issue of relevance, but rather should fully embrace the "freedom to explore topics that may appear remote from today's pressing concerns."

Is this a sound argument? To see that it is not, consider what this reasoning would say about calls for scholars to conduct themselves ethically and to seek truth:

1. It is not self-evident what is or is not "ethical."
2. It is unclear who should decide what is or is not "ethical."
3. Even if a consensus could be reached on this matter, that determination would almost certainly change over time. (It is easy to cite examples of ethical disagreement, and of changes over time as to what is widely believed to be ethical.)
   Therefore, 4. Ethics is an uncertain guide to the task of scholarship.
   Therefore, scholars need not concern themselves about conducting themselves ethically, but rather should fully embrace the freedom to conduct their investigations without being burdened by such constraints.

Or again:

1. It is not self-evident what is or is not "true."
2. It is unclear who should decide what is or is not "true."
3. Even if a consensus could be reached on this matter, that determination would almost certainly change over time. (It is easy to cite examples of disagreements about what is true, and of changes over time as to what is widely believed to be true.)

Therefore, 4. Truth is an uncertain guide to the task of scholarship.

Therefore, scholars need not concern themselves with the question of truth, but rather should fully embrace the freedom to conduct their investigations without being burdened by worries over whether their findings are "true," rather than "false."

What has gone wrong here? The Greenberg–Duberman argument rests on at least four false assumptions. The first, and most important, of these is the belief that the only standards we are obliged to consult in regulating our conduct are those that yield clear, obvious, and uncontroversial applications. But that can't be right. Surely we should try to be honest and kind, for example, even if it is not always clear, in every circumstance, what the ideals of honesty and kindness concretely demand. Similarly, a host of imperatives that nearly every scholar would recognize as valid (do not draw conclusions that are not adequately supported by the evidence; do not overlook or exclude important evidence that goes against your conclusion; do not misrepresent the views of those you are criticizing, etc.) rests on concepts with fuzzy and controversial borders. (Just how much evidence is "adequate"? Which counterevidence is "important"?)

A second false assumption is that standards with fuzzy and controversial *borders* are thereby fuzzy and controversial *absolutely* and *unqualifiedly*, ignoring the fact that such standards often have a clear and uncontroversial core. Thus, while scholars may well disagree in some cases about the ethical principles underlying their scholarly activity, those principles would appear to be clear enough to rule out plagiarism, the falsification of data, and the suppression of evidence undermining one's thesis. It is unclear, then, why the same cannot be said about Zinn's proposed principles of relevance and importance. While there undoubtedly will be great controversy about the application of these principles in some cases, surely everyone can agree that, for example, an ongoing war is relevant and important. Zinn's point, then, is that some scholarly energy should be expended so that findings that bear on such issues as those concerning the wisdom, legality, and likely outcome of the war should be uncovered and presented to the public.

A third false assumption is that the infamous "Who's to say?" question somehow undermines the standard with reference to which that question is asked. The answer to the question as to "who's to say" what is relevant (or important, or true, or ethical) is, I would suggest, (a) everyone, (b) no one, and (c) everyone. Let me explain. (a) Everyone has an obligation to speak truly and to live ethically, and every scholar has a duty to respect evidence, to report it honestly, and to treat one's intellectual adversaries fairly. Moreover, in carrying out these obligations, everyone should think for himself or herself as to what these duties entail. Everyone should carefully consider what it means, given his or her situation and occupation, what his or her moral and intellectual duties are in the abstract, and what they amount to concretely. In that sense, everyone is "to say," and indeed has an obligation to say, what is true and what is right. One reason why we have these obligations is that (b) there is not, and in principle cannot be, an authority whose pronouncements could establish what is true or what is morally right. The reason is that these are not the sorts of things that *can* be established by authority or fiat.

Saying that the earth is flat cannot make it so, no matter who says it, or how many say it. Rather, this is to be determined by evidence. In principle, and as a regulative ideal, what is true or right is whatever is favored by a careful, logical, rational, exhaustive assessment of the relevant evidence. In that sense, no one, or at least no one in particular, is "to say" what is true or right. However, (c) as we think about these matters for ourselves, each of us is also answerable to others who may find our position to be defective from an evidentiary and/or logical standpoint. Our views are open to correction based on the criticisms and counter-arguments that others (anyone and everyone) might advance against our tentative conclusions.

Finally, the fourth false assumption is that changes of opinion concerning the application of some standard undermine the legitimacy of that standard. But isn't it more plausible to conclude, at least in many cases, that the change is due more to an *improvement* in our knowledge of the standard and its application (a good thing, surely) than in some inherent unreliability in the standard itself? Recall that Duberman seems to suggest that the fact that women's studies and gay studies were once dismissed as trivial should give us reason to reject relevance and importance as criteria in the evaluation of scholarly work. But wouldn't it be more reasonable to say that we have made progress—there has been an improvement—in our sense of what is and is not important? To be sure, this example would have great cautionary value against any proposal to ban or even to strongly discourage scholarly work that might appear trivial. But, as already mentioned (and as Duberman [158], but not Greenberg, acknowledges), Zinn is not proposing that. His point is not that apparently "trivial" research should be disallowed, but rather that scholarly work that bears on clearly important but controversial contemporary issues be welcomed and encouraged (or at least tolerated), rather than summarily and uncritically dismissed as "propaganda." To be clear, Zinn's point is obviously not that such work should be granted immunity from criticism, but rather merely that such criticism should be based on the merits of the work (Are its factual claims correct? Are its arguments logical? Has it omitted important data?), rather than rejected as "unscholarly" solely on the basis of its taking a stand on a controversial social or political issue. Moreover, to recall a point made in connection with the second false assumption noted above, not all beliefs about truth or ethics or importance have undergone significant change, or seem likely to change. (Here we have the solid core/fuzzy boundaries distinction again.) While there has been, and undoubtedly will continue to be in the future, many changes of opinion with regard to, say, the ethical responsibilities of scholars, I think it is safe to say that there will not be a large shift of opinion overthrowing the consensus against plagiarism or the deliberate falsification of data. Similarly, when it comes to the issue of "importance," I doubt that a consensus will ever emerge according to which concerns about genocide are to be regarded as trivial.

(3) Even if we were to overlook Greenberg's gross distortions of Zinn's position on relevant scholarship, and assume, for the sake of argument, that he has presented Zinn accurately, this still would not justify Silber's holding Zinn in contempt. When administrators evaluate professors for purposes of consideration for raises and promotions, this should be done on the basis of the quality of their work (primarily their teaching and scholarship), not by their views on the value of what other professors do. I think Greenberg's claim that research into topics "that may appear remote from today's pressing concerns" can nonetheless "change our understanding of the world" and be quite valuable is correct. As against Greenberg, I think that Zinn thought so too (see above), but even if he didn't, so what? To argue that non-presentist, not-obviously-of-immediate-relevance scholarship and teaching can be valuable (as Greenberg has done), is not to show that *only* such work can be valuable (which he has not

done). So if Zinn did good work that is not of the sort that Greenberg is defending, that should be all that matters—not his (alleged) belief that more of his colleagues should have done likewise. But if Greenberg's claim is indeed that *only* the non-presentist, apolitical stuff is valuable, he has said nothing in its support.

(4) As for the second charge, by what standard was Zinn—the author of over 20 books, three plays, and scores of articles; the tireless political activist; the teacher of over 400 students each semester, who kept ridiculously extensive office hours; the globe-trotting national and international speaker; the expert witness in many famous trials, etc., etc.—*lazy*?

And in what way was he *conventional*? That is not explained at all. (Does *The New Republic* not have any editors? Did no one there have any curiosity as to what that claim might have meant? Upon looking into it, I find that Greenberg himself has served as managing editor and acting editor of *The New Republic*. Perhaps that explains it.)

And how many people, including professors of history or political science, or, for that matter, my field, philosophy, ever develop a "creative, original political philosophy"? In the entire history of the world, surely the number of people who have done this does not reach three digits. Are there even 50 original political philosophies in circulation? Are there 20? Zinn, like just about everybody else, made use of political philosophies created by others. Moreover, though Greenberg doesn't say it explicitly, he implies (correctly, in my view) that Zinn's borrowings were eclectic. He was not a doctrinaire Marxist, or anarchist, or democratic socialist, or liberal, or libertarian, but rather a person who tried to make use of good ideas wherever he found them, and to apply them wherever they seemed most helpful (in the sense of promoting his basic values—peace, justice, freedom, and so forth). While I regard such eclecticism as virtuous (and it is refreshing that Greenberg implicitly attributes such a stance to him, since many Zinn critics claim—with no evidence, but rather simply because it makes it easier to slam him—that he was, straightforwardly, a "Marxist" or "communist" or, even more unscrupulously, a "Stalinist"), Greenberg implies that it is lazy, muddled, confused. But why? And what exactly are "Zinn's ambitions," such that his failure to develop a "creative, original" political philosophy is so damning—something that makes him so deserving (he "earned" it, you'll recall) of Silber's contempt? Certainly John Silber did not develop a "creative, original" political philosophy, even though his field, in contrast to Zinn's, was philosophy. (Silber's scholarly activities, which were quantitatively utterly dwarfed by Zinn's, were mainly addressed to the explication of the difficult philosophical thought of the great German philosopher, Immanuel Kant. That was a worthy endeavor indeed, but it was not by a long shot the creation of an original political philosophy.)

And how plausible is it that Silber's disdain for Zinn had anything whatsoever to do with the fact that he did not develop an original political philosophy? Not only are the other reasons, cited above, more than sufficient, but we also know that Silber favored people whose intellectual creativity paled in comparison to Zinn's. For example, a Silber sycophant, Jon Westling, became Silber's provost, and later Silber's successor as president, at Boston University, in spite of the fact that the highest degree he earned was a B.A., and his C.V. lists no scholarly publications.[21] And if David Greenberg has ever produced a "creative, original" political philosophy, it has escaped my attention.

But if Greenberg's entire essay exhibits astonishing depths of ignorance, error, illogic, unfairness, and general incompetence, one can still pinpoint its breathtaking nadir:

The fatal flaw of Zinn's historical work is the shallowness, indeed the fallaciousness, of his critique of scholarly detachment. Zinn rests satisfied with what strikes him as the scandalous revelation that claims of objectivity often mask ideological predilections. Imagine! And on the basis of this sophomoric insight, he renounces the ideals of objectivity and empirical responsibility, and makes the dubious leap to the notion that a historian need only lay his ideological cards on the table and tell whatever history he chooses. He aligns himself with the famous line from the British historian James Anthony Froude, who asked rhetorically if history "was like a child's box of letters, with which we can spell any word we please. We have only to pick out such letters as we want, arrange them as we like, and say nothing about those which do not suit our purpose." Froude made this observation in the middle of the nineteenth century. (48–9)

Where to begin? (1) Greenberg offers no citation from Zinn in support of this "interpretation" of his views. It could not have been otherwise. No text of Zinn's defends a position anything like the one that Greenberg here attributes to him.

(2) While Greenberg refers to "the ideal of objectivity," he makes no attempt to explain what that is, or what he thinks Zinn meant by it. But as I documented extensively in the immediately preceding chapter, Zinn's rejection of objectivity was a rejection of (a) neutrality—the idea that scholars must refrain from taking a stand on controversial political issues—and (b) unmerited centrism—the idea that centrist or "mainstream" ideas are automatically right, irrespective of evidence. Most importantly, Zinn endlessly clarified that it was not a rejection of (c) accuracy, logical rigor, fidelity to evidence, or anything else of that sort.

(3) Zinn does not renounce "empirical responsibility." That is a demonstrable falsehood. Greenberg cites no passage in Zinn's writings that would support such a ridiculous libel, for the obvious reason that no such passages exist. Over and over again in Zinn's many published statements in which he announces his rejection of "objectivity" he also carefully explains that such

rejection is not to be construed as a refusal of the demands of accuracy—the duty to record faithfully the data of experience and observation. For example, precisely in the context of explaining what is, and is not, meant by his rejection of "objectivity," Zinn underscores his commitment to "scrupulous honesty in reporting on the past" (DOI 49) and states that "If to be objective is to be scrupulously careful about reporting accurately what one sees, then of course this is laudable" (UOS; ZR 499–508; OH 183; KFP 10).[22]

(4) Zinn does not say that an ideologically honest and forthcoming historian (or anyone else, for that matter) is entitled to "tell whatever history he chooses." Radically to the contrary, as documented in the preceding chapter he insists on several constraints—including factual accuracy, logical rigor, respect for (and skill in handling) evidence, the absence of material omissions (the suppressing of evidence undermining one's thesis), and judiciousness and consistency in decisions over matters of selection (what to include, exclude, emphasize, and deemphasize).

(5) He does not align himself with Froude—this is another demonstrable falsehood. While Zinn does argue that much traditional historical writing rests on principles of inclusion, omission, and emphasis that are never stated or defended, and that the legitimacy of historical scholarship that rests on (some) different principles of selection should be respected and welcomed, his is not an "anything goes" position. He, no less than any other historian, rejects historical writing that is inaccurate, illogical, or lacking in evidential support. And he repeatedly goes out of his way to say that his rejection of objectivity does not entail a right to omit evidence that would speak against one's own theories, or values, or political preferences. For example, he explains that his rejection of "objectivity" does "not mean looking only for facts to reinforce the beliefs I already [hold]. It [does] not mean ignoring data that would change or complicate my understanding of

society" (DOI 48). Similarly, immediately after stressing the inevitability of selection in historical writing, he immediately adds, "Of course you have an obligation not to hide things that are embarrassing to you, or embarrassing to people who employ you, or embarrassing to the nation you belong to, or embarrassing to some set of ideas you uphold" (OHM).[23] It is a ridiculous error, unworthy of a C- freshman student, to attribute to Zinn the view that he is entitled to "say nothing about those [facts] which do not suit [his] purpose."

When Greenberg speaks of Zinn's supposed "sophomoric insight," he seems to be saying that the idea in question is true, but trite and obvious, and incapable of lending adequate support to Zinn's approach to history. But Greenberg's characterization of Zinn, here as elsewhere, fails to rise to the level of sophomoric insight. It is demonstrably false—and false in ways that should have been obvious to any scholar who bothered to do his or her homework.[24]

In an attempt to shore up his critique of what he takes to be Zinn's position, Greenberg, like Mitch Daniels, points out that even some leftist historians of the 1960s shared that critique, agreeing "with their stodgy forebears that the intellectual had to hew to the highest standards of rigor." As Greenberg tells it, these historians aimed to "revise entrenched beliefs that gave rise to the social conditions that, as a political matter, they decried," but tried to accomplish this "by the strength of their scholarship." "[Eugene] Genovese, most vociferously, flatly rejected the siren song of 'relevant' history: he, too, hoped at the time for a socialist future, but he believed that it was best served by history that was true to the evidence, valid in its interpretations, and competent in its execution" (GRE 49).

Notice Greenberg's question-begging false dilemma here: One can have "relevant" history, or one can have history that achieves "the highest standards of rigor," and that is "true to the evidence, valid in its interpretations, and competent in its execution." Why can one not have both—a history that, in its choice of subject matter, questions, and issues, is guided by present political concerns, but which in its pursuit of answers to the questions raised "hews to the highest standards of rigor"? Cannot medical researchers, for example, be strongly guided in their research by considerations of utility (thus choosing to work on, say, cancer, rather than a less serious medical issue [without, of course, condemning or interfering with those who choose to work on cures for male baldness]), and by such values as the conviction that health is good and disease bad, without these concerns getting in the way of the accuracy and objectivity of their research? (As we have seen, this is Zinn's own example. But Greenberg, consistent with his scholarly standards, question-beggingly ignores it, and shows no awareness of it.)

Comically, immediately after his assertion of this false dilemma, and his making of the unwarranted claim that the New Left "activists" who, like Zinn, were opposed by Genovese, were thereby bad scholars, Greenberg tells the story of "a donnybrook at the meeting of the American Historical Association in 1969, at which Jesse Lemisch, a leading activist, ran for association president on an insurgent plank, prompting the cantankerous Genovese—still very much a radical—to bellow from the floor that Lemisch and his allies were 'totalitarians.' Lemisch's insurrection sputtered..."(49). Why is this comical? Because Greenberg has his facts wrong. The insurgent activist running for the association's presidency was not Jesse Lemisch, but Staughton Lynd. Admittedly, this is a trivial mistake, but it continues the following disturbing pattern: None of the harsh critics of Zinn—those who, like Greenberg, say that his work as a historian was "lousy," and that his scholarly contributions were "meager" (49)—can get through a short essay on his alleged incompetence without committing sloppy, demonstrable factual errors.

What, one wonders, is Greenberg's problem? Is it

dishonesty—perhaps he is deliberately deceiving his readers about the nature of Zinn's work? Or is it laziness and irresponsibility—maybe he simply can't be bothered to check out Zinn's writings, and bases his criticisms on second- and third-hand caricatures? Or perhaps he simply has poor reading comprehension skills.

Let's briefly explore this last possibility. Staughton Lynd, in a critical article on Greenberg's essay, accuses him, among other failings, of getting his facts wrong with respect to Zinn's firing by Spelman College and his subsequent hiring by Boston University.[25] In Greenberg's response to Lynd and two other critics of his article he offers few concessions (though he does admit that he confused Lynd with Lemisch, and points out that he corrected the error in the online version).[26] But here is his complete response to the specific criticism of Lynd's just mentioned: "My account of Zinn's termination from Spelman, and most other matters, follows Martin Duberman's footnoted book."

Lynd is correct in stating that Greenberg gets the details of Zinn's termination from Spelman wrong. Notice that Greenberg, in his reply, does not explicitly deny this, but rather shifts the responsibility for this to Duberman, whom he claims to have "followed." But Greenberg has not followed Duberman accurately. For example, Greenberg writes that "In 1963, [Spelman president Albert] Manley fired Zinn, ostensibly on scholarly grounds" (46). This struck me as so obviously incorrect, when I first read it, that I found myself wondering whether I might be confused about the meaning of the word "ostensibly." So I looked it up. It means, as I had thought, "apparently or purportedly, but perhaps not actually," or "outwardly appearing as such; professed." So no, that's not the problem. Rather, the problem is that there is nothing in Duberman's account of Manley's firing of Zinn that would suggest that the grounds were "ostensibly" scholarly. Duberman quotes the letter of termination: "You are relieved of all duties with the College after June 30, 1963. The College's check for your termination pay is enclosed" (DUB 77). Duberman quotes Zinn's assertion, from a letter he wrote to the Spelman Board of Trustees, that the dismissal had been done with "no warning, no reason given, no explanation" to which Duberman adds his own comment that this charge of Zinn's "was entirely accurate" (DUB 80). Duberman reports, further, that when Zinn wrote to Manley asking for an explanation for his termination, Manley's reply was to say that "it is not necessary for the college to give reasons when it is decided not to renew the contract of a teacher" (DUB 84). When others made inquiries, Manley's uniform response, according to Duberman, was to say that he'd "never made it a practice to discuss internal matters with those who were outside of the immediate situation" (DUB 84). So how does Greenberg get from Duberman's account the idea that Zinn was fired "ostensibly" on scholarly grounds? Returning to the definition of "ostensibly," we can observe that Manley most assuredly did not "purport" or "profess" to have fired Zinn on scholarly grounds. So does Greenberg mean that the firing would have "outwardly appeared" to have been done for reasons of Zinn's scholarship? That seems highly unlikely. Greenberg's own account of the Manley–Zinn dynamic, in this case accurately reflecting Duberman's narrative, has it that Manley was strict and autocratic, and that he "frowned on his students' activism and Zinn's encouragement of it" (46). Duberman's description of Zinn's Spelman years is replete with tales of clashes between Manley and Zinn over the latter's political activism. By contrast, it contains only one account of Manley expressing dissatisfaction with Zinn's scholarship—and with that occurring only after Zinn had been fired, and issued defensibly in direct response to an AAUP statement mentioning Zinn's "national reputation as a teacher and a scholar." (Duberman added that in making this criticism of Zinn's scholarship "Manley was being disingenuous"

[DUB 85].) No one reading Duberman's book attentively could come away from it with the impression that Manley's firing of Zinn had the outward appearance of having been done for reasons of concern about Zinn's scholarly achievements. Indeed, historian Michael Kammen, in a review of Duberman's book, reports that Zinn was fired "for insubordination," adding that "Essentially, he was thrown out for civil rights activism" (IH). Zinn was not fired "ostensibly on scholarly grounds." Greenberg's statement that he was is incorrect, as is his claim that such a statement accurately follows Duberman's account.

Greenberg's assertion that "Zinn mistakenly believed that he had tenure—how such an extraordinary confusion came to pass is not fully explained" (46) is similarly unfaithful to the source it is allegedly following. Why does Greenberg think that Zinn's belief was mistaken? Duberman reports that the AAUP investigated the issue and notified both Manley and Zinn that "according to Spelman's own regulations, [Zinn's] promotion to a full professorship in 1959 had automatically carried with it the presumption of tenure" (DUB 85). The closest that Duberman ever comes to Greenberg's reading is when he says that the issue was "clouded" by the fact that Spelman's "Policies and Rules" did not explicitly address the question of the tenure status of someone who had, as was the case with Zinn, been promoted early, rather than after the customary six years of service (Zinn had been promoted after just three years) (DUB 80–1). As I read it, Duberman's presentation of this tenure controversy has it that the issue is somewhat fuzzy, but that Zinn was probably right. There is no warrant in it whatsoever for the conclusion that Zinn was simply "mistaken," as Greenberg says. And indeed, "how such an extraordinary confusion came to pass is not fully explained."

In Greenberg's response to his three critics he complains about their "shrill" tone and lack of generosity. By contrast, he insists that he had "tried hard to ensure" that his "review was moderate in its tone and fair to Zinn." His critics had been "so predisposed to construe [his] review as an attack on Zinn" that they had failed to "see how much praise I afford *A People's History*." To support his claim that he had praised Zinn's book, he cites his opening anecdote, which I have discussed above, in which he tells us how much he had admired Zinn's work as a teenager. Commenting on this passage, he writes, in his response to his critics, "like many young readers, I was drawn to *A People's History*—and that's a point in its favor, as I said."

This is more nonsense. There is nothing moderate in the tone of Greenberg's article. His subtitle is "Howard Zinn's influential mutilations of American history." He calls APH "a pretty lousy piece of work" (45), calls Zinn's scholarly contributions "meager" (49), says that clear-eyed scrutiny of Zinn's thinking causes a "damning portrait to emerge" (47), claims that Zinn's thoughts on scholarship are "jejune" (47), calls Zinn a "lazy, conventional theorist" (47), says of his alleged shortcomings, including his allegedly "trite" calls for politically useful history, that they "cannot be so easily excused" (47), and claims that his "historical work" suffers from a "fatal flaw" (48)—that of a "shallow" and "fallacious" critique that rests on a "sophomoric insight" (48).

Such language is by no means moderate. So Greenberg's claim that the tone of his article is moderate could only be true if his strongly-worded criticisms were balanced by roughly equally strongly-worded praise. But, despite Greenberg's explicit claim to the contrary in his reply to his critics, his original article contains almost no significant praise of Zinn, strongly-worded or otherwise. Greenberg's only positive words about Zinn are mild, and are to be found in brief asides—he was "handsome in profile, gentle in manner" (44), his dissertation was "creditable" and is "still occasionally cited by scholars" (46), APH was commercially successful (47–8), and so forth—but there is nothing in Greenberg's text that comes close to balancing the severe statements quoted in the previous paragraph.

And as for Greenberg's opening anecdote about his youthful enthusiasm for APH, it simply isn't true that Greenberg "said" in his review that this was "a point in its favor." To the contrary, it is clear that the point of this anecdote is that Greenberg's initially positive assessment of Zinn was entirely due to Greenberg's youthful naivety and historical ignorance. Indeed, even in his reply to his critics he makes the point that "Like many such [young] readers, with time and learning I came to see the book's severe problems." Similarly, in a more recent article Greenberg is quoted as saying of APH that "It's very simplistic and appeals to the high school mind."[27] And if Greenberg's three critics failed to "see how much praise I afford *A People's History*," I can only say that, having read his article carefully, and more than once, I am guilty of the same failing—and I'm willing to bet that if you read it, you will be, too.[28]

Even more ridiculous is Greenberg's claim to have "tried hard to ensure" that his review was "fair to Zinn." For example, no one with the slightest concern for fairness could say, without offering a word of explanation, argument, or response to the readily available mountains of counter-evidence, that Zinn "seems to have stayed silent about the Soviet Union," when in fact, as documented above, in Zinn's frequently-issued denunciations of the Soviet Union he consistently characterized it as "ruthless," "oppressive," "brutal," "murderous," a "dictatorship," a "police state," and an example of "fascism," and criticized its "aggression," its "atrocities," and its "monstrous tyranny."

Similarly, it is ironic that Greenberg, who claims (inaccurately in every case) that Zinn "never seems to have grasped" (47) or "never seemed aware of" (49) this or that point (much as he *seems* to have stayed silent on the Soviet Union), himself utterly fails to understand one of the most basic principles of fairness in scholarly criticism: that when a writer has anticipated a criticism and has already, prior to the writings of the critics, offered an explanation or argument as to why that criticism is unsound, it is unfair simply to assert the criticism without responding to the writer's explanation or argument. While the critics obviously are not obliged to concede that their objection is unsound and that the writer's argument against it is cogent, surely they are obliged not to ignore that argument. Rather, if they think their objection still holds, they need not only to present that objection clearly, but also to explain why the writer's response to it is unconvincing. For replying to anticipated objections is one of the ways in which many writers, Zinn included, make their meaning clear. To attack a writer's position without taking such clarifications into account is to attack a straw man. In addition to its unfairness, such a strategy also constitutes a total failure of scholarship—a failure to take up the discussion at the point of its development, and consequently a failure to advance the discussion.

In this light, let's note that Greenberg, given his criticisms of Zinn, should have acquainted himself with Zinn's many statements that his rejection of "objectivity" was not to be understood as entailing any diminishing of the historian's fidelity to the principle of "scrupulous honesty in reporting on the past" (DOI 49), and that "If to be objective is to be scrupulously careful about reporting accurately what one sees, then of course this is laudable" (UOS; ZR 499–508; OH 183; KFP 10). Or, if it is too much to ask of Greenberg that he take notice of Zinn's writings before condemning them, we might at least expect him to have read Duberman's biography, the book he is supposed to have been reviewing. Had he done so, he would have found this: "[Zinn] did insist (and in this regard he has often been misunderstood) that objectivity—scrupulous accuracy when researching and reporting data—must remain the historian's goal" (DUB 159); and this: "[Zinn] insisted on 'scrupulous honesty' in reporting on the past" (DUB 167); and this: Zinn was "insistent on accuracy in his historical scholarship" (DUB 263). Now, had Greenberg wished to be fair to Zinn in criticizing his views on objectivity, he would have been obliged to say something like this: "Although Zinn claims that his rejection of objectivity is consistent with a robust commitment to honesty and accuracy, that claim is undermined by the following argument...." Or this: "Although Zinn claims that his rejection of objectivity is consistent with a robust commitment to honesty and accuracy, in his own practice he routinely violates that commitment, as the following evidence shows...." And then, of course, he would have had to make a good, logical, evidence-based case for these claims. Instead, Greenberg handles this issue by blithely asserting that Zinn simply "renounces the ideals of objectivity and empirical responsibility."

Similarly, given his criticisms of Zinn, Greenberg should have taken a glance at Zinn's many statements that, in spite of the inevitability of selection in historical writing, "Of course you have an obligation not to hide things that are embarrassing to you, or embarrassing to people who employ you, or embarrassing to the nation you belong to, or embarrassing to some set of ideas you uphold" (OHM), or that his rejection of "objectivity" does "not mean looking only for facts to reinforce the beliefs I already [hold]. It [does] not mean ignoring data that would change or complicate my understanding of society" (DOI 48). We might especially expect Greenberg to have noticed the latter statement, since it is quoted on page 167 of Duberman's book, the book of which Greenberg's essay purports to be a review. Anyone trying to be fair to Zinn in criticizing him on this issue would then have had a responsibility to say something like this: "Although Zinn claims that his insistence on the inevitability of selection in historical writing is consistent with a robust commitment to seek and then to disclose evidence that contradicts or complicates the case one wishes to make, that claim is undermined by the following argument...." Or this: "Although Zinn claims that his insistence on the inevitability of selection in historical writing is consistent with a robust commitment to seek and then to disclose evidence that contradicts or complicates the case one wishes to make, in his own practice he routinely violates that commitment, as the following evidence shows...." And then, of course, he would have had to make a good, logical, evidence-based case for these claims. Instead, Greenberg handles this issue by blithely asserting that Zinn simply "aligns himself" with the view that he is entitled to "arrange [historical facts and data] as we like, and say nothing about those which do not suit our purpose."

Or, to make the point one last time, given his criticisms of Zinn, Greenberg should have noticed a consistent pattern in the way Zinn qualifies his call for historical work that is relevant to present-day political concerns: "Am I trying to obliterate all scholarship except the immediately relevant? No, it is a matter of proportion" (UOS; ZR 502; OH 180; KFP 7–8); and "[I do] not argue for a uniform approach—mine or anyone's—to the writing of history, and certainly not for the banning of any kind of historical work, bland or controversial, pernicious or humane, whether written for pleasure or profit or social objectives. [My] aim is, by encouragement and example, to stimulate a higher proportion of socially relevant, value-motivated, action-inducing historical work" (IFE 2). Once again, since it is obviously too much to ask of Greenberg that he actually read the author he is slamming, it should be noted that the first of these two quotations appears also on page 158 of Duberman, the book that Greenberg has the temerity to claim to be reviewing. Accordingly, a fair criticism should have gone something like this: "Although Zinn claims that he is merely calling for a greater proportion of historical work to be geared to present-day political concerns, and is not contending that historical work with a different focus is in any way illegitimate, the logic of his argument commits him to the stronger claim that all historical writing should strive for contemporary relevance, as the following argument shows...." Or this: "Although Zinn claims that he is merely calling for a greater proportion of historical work to be geared to present-day political concerns, and is not contending that historical work with a different focus is in any way illegitimate, in his actual practice he routinely bashes any historian whose work does not conform to his strictures about relevance, as illustrated by the following examples...." And then, of course, he would have had to make a good, logical, evidence-based case for these claims. Instead, Greenberg handles this issue by blithely asserting that Zinn calls for scholars to "forego" work that lacks present social or political relevance, and that "Zinn never seems to have grasped" that other kinds of historical writing can also be legitimate and valuable.

Greenberg's critique of Zinn reminds me of nothing so much as the work of those creationists who think they can score points against evolutionary theory by pointing out that monkeys don't give birth to humans, that there are no "crocoducks," and that apes somehow continue to exist in spite of the fact that we supposedly evolved from them. To paraphrase Richard Dawkins, one wants to say to the likes of Greenberg, "It would be so nice if those who oppose [Howard Zinn] would take a tiny bit of trouble to learn the merest rudiments of what it is that they are opposing."[29]

Indeed, Greenberg's critique of Zinn, from start to finish, is untrue and unfair. The irony of his essay is that almost all of the insults that he aims at Zinn instead apply, with perfect justice, to his own essay. While he refers to "Howard Zinn's influential mutilations of American history," it is instead his essay that mutilates the writings of Howard Zinn. His description of APH as "a pretty lousy piece of work" applies aptly to his essay. He calls Zinn's scholarly contributions "meager"—a word that accurately summarizes the extent of his contribution to the scholarly study of Zinn. The same can be said for the rest of his rhetoric: "damning portrait," "jejune," "lazy" (he can't even be bothered to check his claims against Zinn's texts), "cannot be so easily excused" (see the immediately preceding point), "trite," "cavalier," "how such an extraordinary confusion came to pass is not fully explained," "fatal flaw" (in Greenberg's case, that of not having the slightest idea what he's talking about), "shallow," "fallacious," and "sophomoric." Actually, the last adjective is too generous. Greenberg's effort fails to reach the standards we demand of freshmen.

David J. Bobb

According to his author biography posted at Amazon.com, "David J. Bobb, Ph.D., is president of the Bill of Rights Institute. Formerly he was the founding director of two national centers for Hillsdale College, the Washington, D.C.-based Allan P. Kirby, Jr. Center for Constitutional Studies and Citizenship, and the Hoogland Center for Teacher Excellence."[30]

Bobb's article, "Howard Zinn and the Art of Anti-Americanism," appeared in *The Wall Street Journal* on August 12, 2013.[31] Bobb writes:

> In Indiana, then-Gov. Mitch Daniels...sent emails to his staff wondering if [Zinn's] "execrable" books were being force-fed to Hoosier students. The recent revelation of these emails provoked an angry backlash. High-school teachers within Zinn's vast network of admirers blogged their disapproval of the governor's heresy, and leading professional organizations of historians denounced the supposed threat to academic freedom. At Purdue University, where Mr. Daniels now serves as president, 90 faculty members hailed Zinn as a strong scholarly voice for the powerless and cast the former governor as an enemy of free thought.

Note, first of all, that like the great majority of Daniels's defenders, Bobb does not inform his readers that Daniels ordered Zinn's text to be "banned," "disqualified," "gotten rid of." Instead, he tells us that Daniels merely "wondered" whether

Zinn's books were being used in Indiana, and that he called them "execrable." This omission of one of the most elementary facts of the case, and one that is absolutely crucial to its rational assessment, must be attributed either to incompetence (at best) or dishonesty (at worst, and, unfortunately, much more likely) on Bobb's part. It is this omission that facilitates Bobb's insinuation that Daniels's critics were intolerant and unreasonable when they denounced Daniels's "heresy," and "cast" him as an enemy of free thought. The point is an elementary one. Those who merely call a book names ("execrable"), and "wonder" whether it is being used in classrooms, do not by those actions threaten academic freedom or establish themselves as enemies of free thought. The same cannot be said of those who try to ban books from classrooms.

Bobb: "[Zinn's] story line appealed to young and old alike, with the unshaded good-guy, bad-guy narrative capturing youthful imaginations, and his spirited takedown of 'the Man' reminding middle-aged hippies of happier days."

Comment: This is typical of the patronizing tone, the relentless caricaturing of Zinn's text, and the *ad hominem* attacks directed against Zinn and his admirers, that run throughout Bobb's short essay.

Bobb: "Zinn's arguments tend to divide, not unite, embitter rather than heal. The patron saint of Occupy Wall Street, Zinn left behind a legacy of prepackaged answers for every problem...."

Comment: No evidence is offered for either claim. The former ("tend to divide") is empirical, but Bobb cites no study or research in its support. The latter ("prepackaged answers") is a demonstrable falsehood. Zinn repeatedly denies that he has answers, and calls for experimentation, and the bold use of imagination in thinking up new solutions.[32]

Bobb refers to "the lack of hard evidence in three-plus decades that using 'A People's History' produces positive classroom results."

Comments: (1) For how many texts is there "hard evidence" of the sort to which Bobb refers? (2) While it may not satisfy Bobb's (unspecified) definition of "hard evidence," Robert Cohen, Professor of Social Studies and Steinhardt Affiliated Professor in the History Department at New York University, tells us, in an article that pre-dates Bobb's, that "there is actually a wealth of data on both teacher and student responses to Zinn's People's History," and that this evidence indicates that "*A People's History of the United States* has been a useful, and in some ways a uniquely valuable book" in the classroom. "Zinn engages students, angers and inspires them, prods them to think critically about how historical evidence is used and historical conclusions reached" (WAZ). Naturally, Bobb ignores Cohen's article, and also the evidence, which is summarized in that article, for a conclusion that runs counter to Bobb's entirely evidence-free claim.

Mary Grabar

On her website Grabar identifies herself as a "conservative professor, writer, speaker," who received a Ph.D. in English from the University of Georgia in 2002, and who has taught college English since 1993.[33] She is now a resident fellow at the Alexander Hamilton Institute for the Study of Western Civilization in Clinton, New York.[34]

Grabar begins her defense of Mitch Daniels this way: "Miffed by the fact that a layperson, like former Indiana governor and current president of Purdue University, would dare question any history book a history professor or education professor chooses... a bunch of professors are organizing a 'read-in' of Zinn's bestseller *A People's History of the United States* at Purdue University..."[35]

Note, first of all, that here we have another example of a defense of Daniels that proceeds by distorting what he did. Grabar does not tell us that Daniels ordered his subordinates to "get rid of" and "disqualify" Zinn's book. Instead, she tells us that he had merely "questioned" the use of Zinn. The absurdity of this characterization of his actions is further heightened by her use of the word "dare"—for she does not inform her readers that Daniels's actions were done privately and covertly, in emails to a few persons in his inner circle, rather than openly and publicly (which would have put him in a position of having to answer criticisms of his actions).

She continues: "Purdue philosophy professor Jerry Davitch, former student of Zinn, gave what appears to be a teach-in on Zinn and argued that Daniels's objections amounted to 'censorship.'"

Grabar "documents" this claim by providing a link to a newspaper article.[36] Anyone who consults that article will immediately notice that Jerry's last name is "Davich," not Davitch—an admittedly trivial error. But Grabar's competence is more seriously called into question by the fact, which the newspaper article makes abundantly clear to anyone who can read at the fourth-grade level, that the Purdue philosophy professor and former student of Zinn's who gave a talk on the Daniels–Zinn controversy was I, David Detmer, and not Jerry Davich, who is, instead, the newspaper columnist who wrote about it. Nor is this all. Grabar then goes on to compound this error by referring to (so help me, you can't make this stuff up) "Jerry Detmer, the former Zinn student and currently Purdue philosophy professor," showing that her facility with English grammar matches her flair for reading comprehension and factual accuracy.

More substantively, I did not argue (and neither did Jerry Davich, Jerry "Davitch," or "Jerry Detmer") that Daniels's "objections" to Zinn's book amounted to censorship, but rather that his orders to "get rid of it," "disqualify it," "make sure it is not being used for credit anywhere in the state" amounted to censorship. This is not a subtle distinction.

Grabar is also the author of a more substantial essay on Zinn, "The 'Bad History' of Howard Zinn and the Brainwashing of America." In this work Grabar presents Zinn, not merely as someone whose interpretation of history differs from hers and whose politics she dislikes, but as a participant in a sinister plot to "brainwash" America's youth. The essay abounds in sentences like this one: "As a history professor, [Zinn] targeted young and vulnerable populations" (GRA 3). Even more ominously, she informs us that one of Zinn's essays "draws on a deep well of familiarity with the works of Karl Marx" (GRA 3), and that in another one (or perhaps the same one—the imprecise citation she provides leaves the matter unclear) "Zinn displays his familiarity with the writings of Karl Marx" (GRA 24).

Nor does Grabar let pass the opportunity to make ignorant and/or unscrupulous use of Zinn's statements about objectivity: "Zinn cleverly distanced himself from the truth, proclaiming, in a fashion that has become common for academics, 'Objectivity is impossible, and it is undesirable'" (GRA 3). Naturally, Grabar says nothing about what "objectivity" means in this context; fails to explain just how Zinn's position allows him to "distance himself from the truth"; addresses none of Zinn's many statements in which he clarifies what his denial of objectivity entails, and specifically blocks misunderstandings like Grabar's; and declines to provide the source of the Zinn quotation she uses, thus inhibiting readers' ability to access the context of Zinn's remark, and his clarification of its meaning, for themselves. Similarly, she tells us that Zinn "cleverly disavows any loyalty to objectivity, and thus preempts criticism" (GRA 7). Once again, there is no citation, no clarification of Zinn's meaning, and no explanation as to how and why Zinn's rejection of "objectivity" is supposed to be able to disable criticism. Grabar's point is refuted by the simple observation, extensively documented above in the previous chapter and in this one, that Zinn's rejection of "objectivity" is not a rejection of the supreme historian's value—

accuracy. Zinn, by his own principles, is every bit as vulnerable as anyone else to criticism for any failings in that area, or, for that matter, in the areas of logical rigor and fairness in the handling of evidence.

While Grabar attempts to make a case against Zinn in this regard, her presentation is unsuccessful. She claims that Zinn's work contains "outright lies about events in American history" (GRA 3), but fails to name them. She assures us that Daniel Flynn pointed out "several key historical lies" (GRA 7), but once again, while she cites Flynn's article (which I will discuss below), she declines to list these "lies" herself. (To be clear, she does not succeed in naming any errors of fact in Zinn's historical works, let alone the more difficult task of documenting that the claims in question are, indeed, wrong, or the even more demanding task of showing that they are "lies"—that is, intentional deceptions, rather than mere mistakes.) The bulk of her essay consists, instead, of (a) citing other people who criticize Zinn (Eugene Genovese, David Horowitz, and Michael Kazin, in addition to Flynn—all of whom I will address below), (b) quoting Zinn statements that she finds politically outrageous (but without in any way showing that they are factually incorrect), and (c) complaining about his choices of emphasis and omission.

As examples of (b), she lists, as evidence in support of her claim that Zinn's "presentation of historical facts...should make any serious historian or educator outraged" (GRA 18), such items as the following (each presented without further specific discussion, argument, or any kind of documentation of error on Zinn's part):

> "[In colonial America] conflicts existed between 'slave and free, servant and master, tenant and landlord, poor and rich'" (GRA 18).
>
> "During the 'Roaring Twenties' 'most of the wealth was in the hands of a few people at the top of society's pyramid'"

(GRA 19).

"The invasion of Afghanistan led to civilian deaths, and 'Critics of the bombing felt that terrorism was rooted in deep complaints' like the stationing of troops in Saudi Arabia, the trade embargo on Iraq, and U.S. support of 'Israel in its occupation of land claimed by Palestinian Muslims'" (GRA 21).

A photo of Harvey Milk is accompanied by this caption: "Harvey Milk was the first openly gay elected official in the United States. Milk was elected to the San Francisco Board of Supervisors in 1977. He and Mayor George Moscone were murdered in 1978 by a conservative city supervisor, Dan White" (GRA 22).

"[S]anctions against Iraq..., according to the U.N. reports[,] killed as many as a half million children" (GRA 23).

As an example of (c), Grabar complains that Zinn "throws doubts on the legitimacy of President Bush's term by devoting an inordinate amount of space to the 2000 election" (GRA 20). Note that Grabar does not claim that Zinn makes factual errors in his discussion of this issue, that he makes unsound arguments with respect to it, or that he fails to make a good case for the illegitimacy of the 2000 election.

For another example, this one developed at greater length, Grabar faults Zinn for allegedly neglecting James Madison's arguments against the kind of "pure democracy" that she claims Zinn advocates (GRA 9–11). She cites, in particular, Madison's *Federalist Paper 10*, and scolds Zinn for "deny[ing] that such works as the *Federalist Papers* ever existed" (GRA 10). However, when we turn to Zinn's text, we find a discussion of precisely this issue. It begins this way: "In *Federalist Paper # 10*, James Madison argued that representative government was needed to maintain peace in a society ridden by factional disputes" (APH 96). Four quotations from this document, accompanied by commentary, immediately ensue (APH 96–7). This, in turn, is followed by a consideration of the views of Alexander Hamilton on the same issue, together with quotations from, and discussion of, other *Federalist Papers*, including *Federalist Paper # 63* (APH 97–8).[37]

With equally impressive logical consistency and scholarly rigor, she issues the bizarre claim that "Zinn never acknowledges his intellectual forebears" (GRA 10), only to complain on the very next page that (so help me), "he cites only like-minded" historians, such as "Charles Beard, Eric and Philip Foner, Herbert Aptheker, and I. F. Stone." Later she mentions that he cites Eugene Debs, Clarence Darrow, Mother Jones, Emma Goldman (15), W. E. B. Du Bois (17), Edward Bellamy (19), Frederick Douglass, Susan B. Anthony, Langston Hughes (23), Herbert Marcuse, and Simone de Beauvoir (24), among others, in support of his own political ideas.

Returning to reality, we find, with regard specifically to American historians, that Zinn in APH draws on the work of such figures as Gar Alperovitz, Bernard Bailyn, Richard Barnet, Carl Becker, Barton Bernstein, Basil Davidson, Robert Fogel, John Hope Franklin, Lloyd Gardner, Herbert Gutman, Alonzo Hamby, Richard Hofstadter, Francis Jennings, Gabriel Kolko, Walter LaFeber, Lawrence Levine, David Montgomery, Edmund Morgan, Gary Nash, Arnold Offner, Nell Painter, Bruce Russett, Arthur Schlesinger, Jr., Page Smith, and Kenneth Stampp, among many others. So not only do Grabar's two criticisms contradict one another—so that we know, *a priori*, that they cannot both be true—but, as it turns out, each of them is also false on its own. Zinn most certainly does "acknowledge his intellectual forebears," and they are not all "like-minded," but rather constitute an ideologically diverse lot.

Grabar's other criticisms are equally sweeping and inaccurate. For example, instead of saying something along the lines of, "Zinn's narrative emphasizes American misconduct and unfairly downplays America's positive contributions to the world" (which would be a restrained and plausible criticism),[38] Grabar flatly (and preposterously) asserts that Zinn "condemns every aspect of the United States" (GRA 3). Here a familiar pattern exhibited by Zinn's many harsh critics is once again put on full display: those who accuse Zinn of caricaturing United States history, of presenting it in a distorted, one-sided, simplistic way, lacking in subtlety and nuance, themselves caricature *his* work, and present *it* in a manner far more distorted, one-sided, simplistic, and free of subtlety and nuance, than is true of anything he has ever written.

Other criticisms fail because of errors in logic. For example, Grabar accuses Zinn of tricking students into accepting his version of history as the only alternative to taking the side of "rich oppressors." Her argument in support of this claim runs as follows: "There is no recourse in a third way, either, for, remember, 'there is no such thing as a pure fact.' The young student is left with only one choice: whose side are you on? The oppressed or the oppressor? Zinn's side or the side of the traditional textbook writer or teacher?" (GRA 21)

But how is Zinn's claim that "there is no such thing as a pure fact" supposed to entail that there are only two options, traditional history or Zinn's alternative? To address this, we need first to understand what Zinn's claim means. It can be found (though Grabar, who neglects to provide a citation, does not tell us this) in the "Afterword" to APH, and reads as follows: "[T]here is no such thing as a pure fact, innocent of interpretation. Behind every fact presented to the world—by a teacher, a writer, anyone—is a judgment. The judgment that has been made is that this fact is important, and that other facts, omitted, are not important" (684). When asked, in a 2008 interview, to elaborate on this, Zinn replied: "Every presentation of history, indeed of any phenomena, must inevitably be a selection out of an infinite amount of data."[39]

So now we are in a position to see that Grabar's argument is a simple *non sequitur*. Zinn's "no pure fact" doctrine has to do simply with the necessity of selection, as opposed to the issue of the number of options available to one in making that selection. And when Zinn does comment on the latter issue, it is clear that he rejects Grabar's "only two options" interpretation, as his reference to "an infinite amount of data" strongly suggests that there would be quite a few different ways of making a selection out of the great mass of historical material. Nothing that Zinn says, here or elsewhere, even remotely suggests that there are only two interpretations of history, such that one must either side with him or with "rich oppressors."

Nor is this all. As if her mischaracterizations of Zinn's texts and fallacious criticisms of his views were not enough, Grabar also litters her essay with irrelevant and unfounded personal attacks against him. For example, she claims that Zinn "attempted to pass himself off as a hero to the downtrodden proletariat of America" (GRA 3), but fails to cite any passage from his writings or speeches in which he does so, and neglects to provide any other kind of evidence in support of her charge. Here she parts company with other harsh critics of Zinn's politics or scholarship, most of whom concede that he was an affable, self-effacing person, not given to self-aggrandizement. For example, Michael Kazin, who is not at all shy about calling APH "bad history," "quite unworthy of [its] fame and influence," nonetheless credits Zinn for being one celebrity "who appears to lack the egomaniacal trappings of the breed" (KAZ). And Michael C. Moynihan agrees, arguing that Zinn is "an exceptionally bad historian," and yet, at the same time, "a man of great modesty" (MOY).

Even more bizarre is Grabar's equally evidence-free accusation that Zinn "is especially careful to convince his reader that only *he* has the correct version" of American history (GRA 3). To the contrary, Zinn is unusual among historians in that he repeatedly argues that the necessity of selection makes it impossible for any one historical narrative to establish itself as final or definitive (see, for example, APH 7–11), even going so far as to point out (as his critics often gleefully remind us) that his is "a biased account," offered neither as the first nor last word on American history, but rather as a "counterforce" against more orthodox interpretations (APH 631).

In one case Grabar stoops to the use of innuendo, as she informs her readers that Zinn "was fired from a black women's college in 1963 for insubordination to a black president" (GRA 3). What, one wonders, was the point of her gratuitous reference to Albert Manley's race if not to imply that Zinn was at least a mild racist and a hypocrite to boot—someone who pretended to be for blacks in the civil rights movement, but who, as a white man, could not tolerate taking orders from a black man? Grabar's insinuation is undermined by such observations as that (a) Zinn was even more insubordinate to the other university president under whom he served, John Silber of Boston University, a white man; (b) a major theme of Zinn's philosophy is that excessive obedience to law or to powerful authorities is dangerous—individuals should instead try to do what is morally right, even when that stands at odds with what the authorities demand (see, in particular Zinn's *Disobedience and Democracy*)—a general point having nothing in particular to do with race; and (c) the specific way in which Zinn was insubordinate to Manley had to do with his refusal to quit participating with his black students in marches, sit-ins, and other actions in support of equal rights for those same black students and other African-Americans.

In addition to everything else, Grabar's essay is larded with careless grammatical and typographical errors. She tells us that Zinn was "better known for implementing his activist view of education," but fails to provide a second term to complete this comparative judgment (GRA 3). She complains that "the public by large" is too willing to accept people like Zinn as legitimate scholars (GRA 7). She refers to "the idea of all men being 'created equal' black men" (GRA 9). And she frustrates readers who would like to know which edition of APH she is citing and discussing, as she identifies it as the edition published in the year "200" (GRA 8, note 18).

It must be admitted, however, that these are fairly trivial errors, amounting to no more than a mere nuisance. The same cannot be said, unfortunately, about the transgressions against logic, factual accuracy, and basic fairness that permeate her work.

Eugene D. Genovese

Genovese (1930–2012) was a professor of history who taught at several institutions, including Brooklyn's Polytechnic Institute, Rutgers University, and the University of Rochester. He is one of the figures included on a document, entitled "Criticism of Howard Zinn and his work crosses ideological lines," that names a handful of Zinn's critics and exhibits some of their anti-Zinn quotations. This is the document that Mitch Daniels advertised on his Purdue University website as available on request. The complete Genovese entry in this document reads as follows: "Eugene D. Genovese, a historian who evolved from Marxist to American conservatism has said that even when he was a Marxist, he viewed Zinn's work as 'incoherent left-wing sloganizing.'"

Unfortunately, the document provides no citation indicating the source of this passage, making it difficult for the reader to put this pithy comment in its context, or to see whether Genovese has provided any clarifying explanation as to its meaning, or any evidence or argument in support of its accuracy.

A Google search suggests that the source is not a published writing of Genovese's, but rather a personal communication to Mary Grabar. Grabar tells us that Genovese had declined an invitation to review APH when it was first published in 1980, on the grounds that it was not worth reviewing. The next sentence in her essay contains the quotation that Daniels cited: "Genovese's assessment of the book, as he told me recently: 'incoherent left-wing sloganizing'" (GRA 5).

Since we do not have Genovese's arguments (if any) in support of his judgment, we are not in a position to assess them. Thus, in our consideration of the Genovese quotation we will not be able to go beyond Daniels's use of it—that is, as a simple appeal to authority.

In addition to the generic limitations of reasoning by appeal to authority, discussed in Chapter One above, at least three problems with this particular specimen should be noted. First, the argument implied by Daniels's "even when he was a Marxist" locution is defective. Daniels appears to be suggesting that while harsh criticisms of Zinn by political conservatives might be attributable to bias, if even a fellow leftist slams him the criticism is probably just. But people on the same side of the left/right fence rip each other on a regular basis.

For example, consider the recent feud between two major figures in contemporary American conservative journalism and commentary, George Will and Bill O'Reilly. Will's *Washington Post* review of *Killing Reagan*, a book co-authored by O'Reilly, is entitled "Bill O'Reilly Makes a Mess of History."[40] It begins with these words: "Were the lungs the seat of wisdom, Fox News host Bill O'Reilly would be wise, but they are not and he is not." When Will then mentions O'Reilly's bestselling history books, he is careful to put the word "history" inside quotation marks. As Will continues his examination of O'Reilly's work, he makes copious use of such words and phrases as "slipshod" and "multitude of errors" before asserting, in the review's final sentence, that "O'Reilly's vast carelessness pollutes history and debases the historian's craft." O'Reilly responded by calling Will "a hack" to his face, among other insults.[41]

More to the point, Genovese in particular, "even when he was a Marxist," (a) notoriously attacked other leftist historians, and (b) did so in ways that did not reflect well on his fairness or acumen. For example, with regard to (a), Duberman refers to a speech that Genovese delivered at the 1969 convention of the American Historical Association as a "rage against the left in general" (DUB 162), and tells us that Genovese trashed a book by Staughton Lynd in a review, calling it "a travesty of history" (DUB 161). With regard to (b), Duberman's treatment of Genovese's critique of Zinn's call for historical work attuned to contemporary political problems ends with the claim, which my own research confirms, that Genovese's criticisms "distorted Howard's subtle discussion of these issues." Even more disturbingly, Duberman asserts that "Genovese seemed unperturbed, or unaware, of [this] fact" (DUB 163).

Historian Peter Novick, in *That Noble Dream: The "Objectivity Question" and the American Historical Profession*, paints a similar picture of the Marxist Genovese, confirming both that he attacked leftist historians in general, and not just Zinn in particular (NOV 432–9), and that he made something of a fool of himself in doing so. For example, Novick tells of Genovese's opposition to a resolution, sponsored by Staughton Lynd and others, calling on the American Historical Association to express opposition to the Vietnam War. While a principled opposition to the involvement of scholarly organizations in the taking of political sides on controversial issues is not in itself unreasonable, Novick provides evidence that:

Genovese's fantasies were paranoid. He predicted that if the antiwar resolution passed, there would be a purge of the AHA, since all members who dissented would be forced to leave the organization. (This phenomenon was not observed at universities like Harvard where the faculty had passed an antiwar resolution, or in other academic associations which had done likewise, nor, for that matter, in the AHA, when, a few years later, it quietly followed suit.) Genovese, in language so extreme that he alienated many of his closest supporters, labeled the Lynd group "totalitarians," and in an at-the-top-of-his-lungs conclusion to a speech at the business meeting, urged the association to "put them down, put them down hard, and put them down once and for all." (435)[42]

Second, returning to the language of the quoted anti-Zinn comment of Genovese's, its bizarre nature makes it surprising that Grabar and Daniels would be so eager to cite it in support of their position. For the one compliment that almost all of Zinn's critics, even those whose criticisms are especially harsh, are willing to pay him is that his writing is exceptionally clear. Indeed, Zinn's critics often point out with consternation that Zinn's lucid writing is pernicious, because it attracts readers and makes it easier for them to grasp his (from the critics' point of view) false and dangerous views. So why on earth would Genovese choose, of all possible insults he might have hurled at Zinn, the wildly implausible judgment that he was "incoherent"? "Incoherent" means "expressed in an incomprehensible or confusing way; unclear." It is safe to say that this description does not apply to the works of Zinn.

It might be added that there are many ways in which a given piece of writing might be unclear. It might use a forbiddingly arcane vocabulary; it might employ complex and convoluted syntax; it might use terms that are overly vague and lacking in specificity; and so forth. But the particular kind of unclear writing that tends to be called "incoherent" is writing that is jumbled, fragmentary, contradictory, lacking in a clear theme, so that its parts do not fit together smoothly. To my knowledge, Genovese is the only critic (other than those, like Daniels and Grabar, who quote him uncritically) who accuses Zinn of that kind of failing. The standard charge moves radically in the opposite direction—that Zinn's narrative is much too coherent, in the sense that it fails to acknowledge the nuances, the counterevidence, the messy complications, that would stand as obstacles to his seamless narrative. In other words, critics accuse Zinn of telling a story that is too neat and clear—the rich and powerful have motives that are greedy and base; they exploit the less powerful ruthlessly; the only progress comes when the people rise up and struggle against such oppression; and so forth. To criticize Zinn for lack of coherence is comparable to criticizing Woody Allen for making films that give audiences nothing but gun fights, car chases, and spectacular explosions. Anyone who would cite such a ridiculous criticism in making a case against Allen's films would be someone who is willing to grasp at anything, no matter how patently absurd, that supports his or her case. The same is true of those who would cite Genovese's "incoherent" charge against Zinn, at least if they do so without offering some kind of explanation of what they think the basis is for a claim that is so implausible on its face.

Finally, even setting the "incoherent" issue aside, it is absurdly reductionistic to characterize APH as "left-wing sloganizing." Here again a critic of Zinn exhibits the all-too-familiar pattern of committing the very sin that he (falsely) attributes to Zinn. A slogan is "a motto associated with a political party or movement or other group." Synonyms of "slogan" include "catchphrase," "jingle," "byword," and "motto." APH contains descriptions of historical events, arguments about their meaning or interpretation, and some discussion of principles of historiography. But readers would be hard-pressed, I think, to find many "slogans" or "catchphrases" in it, and neither Genovese, nor Grabar, nor Daniels cite any. Thus, while critics accuse Zinn of reducing American history to something crude, simplistic, and lacking in nuance (America's foreign policy is evil; the rich and powerful exploit the poor; and so forth), here, as elsewhere, it is Zinn's critics who reduce his work to a crude, simplistic caricature. "Left-wing sloganizing" is itself a mere slogan, oblivious to subtlety and complication, and contemptuous of evidence.

Robert Paquette

Paquette is Publius Virgilius Rogers Professor of American History at Hamilton College and co-founder of the Alexander Hamilton Institute for the Study of Western Civilization. His two-part examination of the Daniels–Zinn controversy begins this way:

> A few weeks ago, Tom LoBianco, a muckraking, self-promoting reporter on Indiana politics for the Associated Press, broke a story about Mitch Daniels' alleged attempt, while governor of Indiana, to censor political opponents. LoBianco, it appears from online sources, has been trying to dig up dirt on Daniels for some time. A Freedom-of-Information-Act request by AP supplied LoBianco with extra-virgin cooking oil, which, upon close inspection, yields more splatter than sizzle. He turned up emails that show Daniels, as governor, raising concerns with Indiana's Superintendent of Public Instruction about the widespread use for the study of American history in Indiana's high schools of Howard Zinn's propagandistic masterwork, "A People's History of the United States" (1980). (PA1)

Note, first of all, that Paquette's discussion of Daniels's alleged censorship of Zinn exhibits the same spectacular intellectual dishonesty that we find in the work of so many other of Daniels's defenders—that of simply leaving out the evidence of Daniels's attempted censorship. Recall that Daniels, speaking about the use of Zinn's APH in Indiana classrooms, had told his subordinates to "get rid of it," disqualify it," "make sure it is not being used for credit anywhere in the state." Paquette never informs his readers of this, and instead says merely that Daniels "raised concerns" about the use of Zinn's text, criticized it, and looked at it "with a curious eye" (PA2).

Let's pause to consider the depths of Paquette's incompetence and/or deceitfulness in attempting to make his case in this way.

(1) While a discussion of any modestly detailed or complicated issue will necessarily omit some information, for reasons discussed at length above, it is reasonable to evaluate those omissions by the criteria of relevance, importance, and fairness. Admittedly, there are gray areas here. In a short essay assessing the merits of "X" and "not-X," there may not be room for a consideration of every possible subordinate issue, or every scrap of evidence pertaining to the main issue, making it therefore a defensible decision to leave some pieces of evidence out of the discussion. But surely these excluded items should be those of marginal relevance and minimal importance to the major issue at hand. Thus, when making an argument for "not-X," it would certainly be wrong to exclude from the discussion the single strongest piece of evidence for "X." Arguments that ignore the strongest counterevidence are pointless, because they can prove anything (and therefore nothing). One can "prove" that Babe Ruth was not a good home run hitter if one excludes from the discussion the fact that he hit over 700 home runs.

Moreover, such arguments are unfair. One "defeats" one's intellectual adversaries by illegitimately stripping them of their best ammunition. This is one of the reasons why Zinn was careful to insist, when making his case for the necessity of selection, that such necessity could not justify "looking only for facts to reinforce the beliefs I already [hold]," or "ignoring data that would change or complicate my [thesis]" (DOI 48), and that "Of course you have an obligation not to hide things that are embarrassing to you, or embarrassing to people who employ you, or embarrassing to the nation you belong to, or embarrassing to some set of ideas you uphold" (OHM). Any intelligent ten-year-old, and certainly any average high school freshman student, would well understand that when a governor has instructed his subordinates to "get rid of" a certain text, to "disqualify it," and to "make sure it is not being used for credit anywhere in the state," one cannot simply assert that the charge of "censorship" is unfounded without at least addressing this *prima facie* evidence to the contrary. Indeed, I challenge the reader to come up with any justification for Paquette's excising this information from his discussion, or any non-nefarious theory of his motivation for doing so.

(2) Paquette cannot possibly plead ignorance, since the LoBianco article to which he refers quotes Daniels's "get rid of it," "disqualify it," "make sure it is not being used for credit anywhere in the state" language (LOB), and cites Daniels's original emails, which the AP published along with LoBianco's article (EMA).

(3) Paquette is guilty of an inconsistency, since the standards he invokes in order to criticize Zinn are precisely the standards that he himself violates, much more flagrantly than Zinn ever did, by excluding the most important piece of evidence that would challenge his "no censorship" thesis. For Paquette's critique of Zinn essentially boils down to the claim that Zinn's approach to history was crude, methodologically and substantively one-sided, insensitive to subtlety and nuance, and intolerant of counterevidence.

Paquette's own approach to history, he confidently assures us, is quite different. As a prelude to his discussion of this point, Paquette relates an anecdote about the physicist Edward Witten, who allegedly switched his major as an undergraduate from history to theoretical physics because he thought the latter subject was the easier of the two. And indeed, when Paquette goes on to discuss "the discipline and practice of history," he emphasizes "the complexity and the difficulty of unlocking its mysteries through honest reconstructions." "Good history," he explains, "requires immersion in relevant sources of myriad types...." Such "Painstaking gathering of information leads serious historians to delicate, nuanced, and qualified assessments, configured by using time-tested standards and methods appropriate to the discipline, so as to yield meaningful patterns with explanatory power.... Good historians, when not blinded by ideology, have presented in Shakespearean richness an imperfect world of flawed beings whose behavior often brings out unintended, ironic, or contradictory consequences" (PA2).

But when we turn from Paquette's rhetoric and look instead at his behavior we find that, far from "immersing" himself in "relevant sources of myriad types," and "painstakingly gathering information," he evidently cannot be bothered to address in his own scholarship even the most important, and the most directly relevant, evidence, even when that evidence is extremely brief and, in every sense, completely accessible—that is, both readily available and easy to understand. Next, notice that, since the evidence that he excludes is precisely that which contradicts his thesis, we might expect that the inclusion of such evidence would complicate his case, perhaps resulting in one of those "delicate, nuanced, and qualified assessments" that he so much prizes. As things stand, however, readers would be hard pressed to find any such "delicate, nuanced, and qualified assessments" of anything in Paquette's entire two-part essay—and certainly none when he is commenting on Zinn or LoBianco.

(4) Paquette's central omission must be judged especially egregious given his decision as to what he evidently thought was more worthy of inclusion: an utterly irrelevant personal attack on Tom LoBianco. Recall that in the opening paragraph of his essay he calls LoBianco a "self-promoting reporter," and one who, "it appears from online sources, has been trying to dig up dirt on Daniels for some time." In the next paragraph he says of the "firestorm in academic circles" that ensued with regard to the Daniels emails that it is one that "LoBianco, no doubt, intentionally tried to conflagrate" (PA1). What makes this a textbook example of the *ad hominem* fallacy is that LoBianco's motives have no bearing on the question of whether or not his writing on this issue was accurate and fair. Suppose, just for the sake of

argument, that all of Paquette's claims about his motives are true—he looked for and found Daniels's emails because he wanted to make a name for himself, and because he disliked Daniels and wanted to bring him down, and because he thought it would be fun to stir up a fight among academics. None of that shows that anything he wrote was in any way wrong. Upon finding the emails, perhaps he calculated that a fair, accurate account of them, free of distortions or embellishments, would achieve all of his goals. He may even have considered that a slanted, unfair rendering would undermine those goals by bringing about a lessening of his own credibility, and with it, the credibility of his story. Or, more straightforwardly, he may in his reporting have struggled, because of his professional ethics, to overcome any such personal bias—and may have done so successfully.

The central point is quite simple: either LoBianco's motives (whatever those might have been) caused to him to write an inaccurate, misleading, unfair, or otherwise defective article, or they did not. If they did not, then it is obviously wrong to try to malign his article by impugning his motives. And if they did, then what needs to be done is to point out what he got wrong— what are his factual errors, his logical lapses, his unfair material omissions, his distortions of language, or whatever it might be. Find the errors and you've earned the right to speculate about the motives that might have led to them. But this is not what Paquette does. He does not point to a single factual error in LoBianco's article. He does not mention a single mistake in logic. He does not identify a single material omission. All he does is present LoBianco's (alleged) motives and then proceed to assure the reader, without providing a single specific citation, or explanation, or shred of evidence to support such claims, that LoBianco's article "upon close inspection, yields more splatter than sizzle," and that it provided "rather meager kindling" for the academic firestorm that followed (PA1).

In fairness to LoBianco, I hasten to remind the reader that I granted Paquette's claims about his motives only for the sake of argument. Paquette provides no evidence whatsoever in support of those claims. The closest he comes is his statement that LoBianco, "it appears from online sources, has been trying to dig up dirt on Daniels for some time." What kind of scholar says something like that? Paquette neglects to tell us what these online sources are, or what they say, or how, exactly, they make it "appear" that LoBianco has been trying to dig up dirt. What would we think of a statement like that if we found it in a paper submitted for class credit by a freshman — and, to be clear, I mean a *high school* freshman?

Naturally, when someone has something negative about Zinn to report, Paquette handles the issue of the reporter's bias and motives rather differently. Thus, when he tells us of Mary Grabar's interview with Eugene Genovese, in which Genovese (as discussed above) dismissed APH as "incoherent left-wing sloganizing," Paquette offers no speculation as to her possible desire to "dig up dirt" on Zinn, makes no mention of any bias against Zinn on her part (the existence of which might be suggested by her subsequent claim that "As a history professor, [Zinn] targeted young and vulnerable populations" for the purpose of "brainwashing" them — see above), and does not alert the reader to the fact that she, in radical contrast to LoBianco, litters her essays with factual inaccuracies and logical blunders.[43] Instead, he identifies her simply as "an intrepid, against-the-grain English professor" (PA1).

As further evidence that Paquette completely dispenses with critical standards of logic, evidence, and reason when it comes to assessing criticisms of Zinn, note that he joins Daniels and Grabar in explicitly endorsing Genovese's characterization of Zinn's APH as "incoherent left-wing sloganizing" (PA1). Without rehashing my entire argument against that absurd comment (see the discussion of Genovese above), I would simply recall the point that "incoherent" means "expressed in an incomprehensible or confusing way; unclear." But Paquette, in the second part of his two-part essay, uses the phrase "lucid prose" to describe Zinn's writing in APH. Indeed, in this regard he compares APH favorably to "most standard-issue texts from commercial publishers," which, he further asserts, "could serve as either a useful door stop or a cure for insomnia" (PA2). Now "lucid" means "expressed clearly; easy to understand." Its synonyms include "clear," "intelligible," "comprehensible," "under-standable," "coherent," and "articulate." Paquette, of course, provides no explanation as to how a "lucid" text can be fairly described as "incoherent." Nor does he show the slightest sign of recognizing the contradiction. For if anything is "clear," it is that "lucid" and "incoherent" are antonyms. So if anything is genuinely "incoherent," it is Paquette's claim that Zinn's text is both clear and unclear, comprehensible and incomprehensible, lucid and incoherent.

Paquette's inconsistent use of language makes another appearance in the very first sentence of "Part 2" of his two-part essay: "The flagellation of Purdue's President Mitch Daniels continues in the press over his criticism, while serving as governor of Indiana, of the widespread use in the state's high schools of Howard Zinn's 'execrable text' *A People's History of the United States*." For now, let's set aside Paquette's unscrupulous inaccuracy, discussed above, in saying that Daniels's unfavorable press coverage was directed against his "criticism" of Zinn, or of the teaching of Zinn, when in fact most of it focused on his attempt to ban and disqualify Zinn's text. (And let's also move past his error, committed both here and at the beginning of his first essay on this topic, of claiming that Daniels in his emails had criticized "the widespread use in the state's high schools" of Zinn's book, when in fact Daniels had criticized Zinn in the context of asking *whether* his book was being used in the state's high schools, and had subsequently concluded, inaccurately, that it was not. While this is a trivial mistake, it constitutes another example of the utter failure of the Zinnophobes to discuss anything related to Zinn for even a page or two without making factual errors.) My current point is rather that Paquette is clearly using an illogical and unfair double standard when he uses the word "flagellation" to describe journalists' objections to Daniels, but the much more restrained term, "criticism," to describe Daniels's objections to Zinn. "Flagellation" means "flogging" or "beating." One "flogs" with a whip or stick. The word is associated with torture, or with ancient and medieval forms of punishment that are too barbaric to be used in modern times. In choosing the word "flagellation" Paquette attempts to persuade the reader, not by means of logic or evidence or reasoning of any kind, but rather merely by exploiting the connotations of his chosen term, that the published objections to Daniels were excessively harsh—indeed, that they were brutal, savage, and vicious. The word "criticism," by contrast, in the relevant sense means "the expression of disapproval of someone or something based on perceived faults or mistakes." The term is neutral, rather than negative, in its connotation—some criticisms are sound and just, others not. The word itself does not directly suggest that the latter possibility is more likely to obtain than the former.

To see that Paquette, in his word choice, is holding Daniels and his critics to quite different standards, we need only recall what Daniels actually said about Zinn. As documented in Chapter One, he called him a "terrible anti-American academic" and "a fraud," claimed that he "purposely falsified American history," and expressed satisfaction that he had "finally passed away." He called APH "a truly execrable, anti-factual piece of disinformation that misstates American history on every page," "a totally false version of our history," "crap," and "propaganda" that "represents a falsified version of history" and has "no more place in Indiana history classrooms than phrenology or Lysenkoism would in our biology classes or the 'Protocols of the

Elders of Zion' in world history courses." That, according to Paquette, is mere "criticism." Some journalists, but by no means all, said that Daniels's actions amounted to censorship, and that it was improper for a governor to attempt to dictate which history texts are used in his state's classrooms. That, according to Paquette, is "flagellation."

When Paquette himself speaks of Zinn, he proves to be every bit the equal of Daniels at the art of hyperbolic denunciation. Paquette closes the first installment of his two-part essay by calling APH "the most influential libel against the history of America's common people ever written." Unlike Daniels, however, he promises that in the sequel he will "explain why."

But he fails to do so. He does not show, or even claim to show, that Zinn got any particular facts wrong, or committed any logical blunders, or made any other kind of gross error. Nor does Paquette provide detailed analyses of passages in APH to demonstrate that they are defective in some other, perhaps more subtle, way. Instead, for the most part he contents himself with (1) telling his readers that history is difficult and complicated, that there are many conflicting strands to it, and that competent historians, accordingly, must proceed with great caution, and will typically end up telling a nuanced, many-sided story; and (2) simply asserting, without in any way demonstrating it, or supporting it with any kind of evidence or argument, that Zinn's work is crude, doctrinaire, propagandistic, and utterly lacking in appropriate sophistication—the kind that leads to the delicate, qualified assessment of historical events and individuals that is the distinguishing characteristic of a genuine scholar of history.

He also uses the tactic, so common among Zinn's critics, of telling his readers that a mountain of anti-Zinn evidence exists, but neither providing that evidence to them, nor telling them how to find it themselves, nor even informing them of the nature of that evidence. Paquette makes this move in the context of complaining that APH was used in his son's high school

Advanced Placement course in American history: "In a meeting with the superintendent of schools, I asked why it was being used in the AP course. I provided him with a folder at least an inch thick with information from prominent scholars, right, left, and center, of the execrableness of Zinn's text" (PA2). Since Paquette doesn't identify this "information," I am obviously in no position to evaluate it. But his tactic does call for five comments.

(1) If the "information" in question were truly powerful, surely it would be in Paquette's interest to present some of it. Given the brevity of his two-part essay, he could be forgiven for selecting just a few pieces of evidence, which could be the cherry-picked strongest ones. What would a reasonable person infer from the fact that he chooses not to, opting instead to ask his readers simply to take his word that he has in his possession a thick file of anti-Zinn data?

(2) As I have documented above, and will document below, an astonishingly high percentage of the anti-Zinn "information from prominent scholars, right, left, and center" is pure nonsense—recall "hangs his claim on just three pieces of evidence"; extinguishes "perhaps"; "seems to have stayed silent about the Soviet Union"; "renounces empirical responsibility"; "denies that such works as the *Federalist Papers* ever existed"; etc., etc., with plenty more to come.

(3) Paquette's refusal to make this "information" available to his readers stands in stark contradiction to his rhetorical insistence on high scholarly standards. Good scholars do not ask their readers to take their word for what the evidence shows, whether that evidence consists of a scientific experiment, a historical document, a logical reconstruction of a philosophical argument, or what have you. Rather, scholars are required either to "show their work," or, at the very least, provide information as to how their readers can obtain access to the evidence themselves (scientists must publish their protocol, so that other scientists can replicate their experiments; humanists must cite their sources, so

that other scholars can check them).

(4) Paquette's characterization of academic history—in particular, his insistence that "serious historians" tend to arrive at "delicate, nuanced, and qualified assessments," and his judgment that "good historians" do not typically describe terrible people doing despicable things, but rather depict "an imperfect world of flawed beings whose behavior often brings out unintended, ironic, or contradictory consequences"—makes all the more objectionable his failure to observe prevailing scholarly norms by disclosing his evidence. For recall that the hidden evidence is supposed to establish "the execrableness of Zinn's text." "Execrable" means "extremely bad" or "of very poor quality." Its synonyms include "appalling," "atrocious," "egregious," "awful," "dreadful," "terrible," "deplorable," "reprehensible," "abhorrent," "loathsome," "odious," "vile," "abysmal," "godawful," "rotten," "lousy," "detestable," and "abominable." That hardly sounds like a "delicate, nuanced, and qualified assessment" of the work of a (merely) flawed author. Consequently, those who would be persuaded by Paquette's account of what "serious" and "good" history is like should be skeptical of Paquette's judgment of Zinn and his work, and should be unwilling to accept it blindly without having had the chance to judge the evidence for themselves.

(5) Paquette's hypocrisy in this regard is further underscored by the fact that he offers no examples from APH in which Zinn's assessments are insufficiently "delicate, nuanced, and qualified," or in which he judges with excessive harshness the actions of people who are merely "imperfect" and "flawed." Still less does Paquette provide the sort of detailed textual and evidentiary analysis needed to show that in cases where Zinn's assessments are harsh and lacking in nuance, those judgments are indeed inaccurate and unjustified. Rather, Paquette seems to think that in order to show that a historian is bad and unserious, it is sufficient to show that he or she makes harsh, indelicate, unqualified

judgments that are lacking in nuance. Thus, by his own standards, in calling APH "execrable" and "libelous," Paquette convicts himself.

The closest Paquette comes to offering a specific example of Zinn's alleged lack of nuance is to imply (though, of course, he neither quotes nor cites anything that Zinn says on the issue) that Zinn judges slave owners too harshly, failing to take into account historical context and inappropriately applying contemporary moral standards to people who lived in earlier times:

> An assessment in a classroom of, say, the history of slavery—the peculiar institution—by a professional historian should take into consideration the fact that the institution was not peculiar at all in the sense of being uncommon, and that it had existed from time immemorial on all habitable continents. In fact, at one time or another, all the world's great religions had stamped slavery with their authoritative approval...One cannot expect people of the past to act according to standards that their intellectual and moral horizon could not possibly have had. Yet Zinn relishes the sentencing of those in power by inappropriate or impossible standards, informed by his preferred anti-capitalist ideology. (PA2)

In addition to its absence of documentation and specificity, this passage is open to at least four objections. (1) Paquette misrepresents the logic of Zinn's moral and political thinking. Zinn's standards are not "informed by his anti-capitalist ideology." That gets it backward. It is more accurate to say that his critique of capitalism is informed by his moral standards.

Recall from the discussion in the previous chapter that Zinn draws a sharp distinction between ultimate values (things that are good for their own sake) and instrumental values (things that are good only as a means to an end—that of bringing about the ultimate values). The great significance of this distinction for

Zinn's historiography lies in his observation that commitment to the former is fully consistent with the highest standards of scholarly accuracy, honesty, and rigor, while commitment to the latter compromises those scholarly norms, and is thus to be avoided. The reason is that while no observation (no factual discovery, nothing empirical) can possibly show that such ultimate values as those enumerated in the Declaration of Independence (life, liberty, and the pursuit of happiness—examples cited by Zinn) are not good, by contrast the goodness of instrumental values, such as specific economic and political arrangements intended to *bring about* life, liberty, and the pursuit of happiness, can be assessed in no other way. We must look to experience to determine which actions, procedures, and institutions facilitate such ultimate values and which do not. Thus, while scholars whose commitments are restricted to ultimate values need not fear that their commitment will tempt them, even unconsciously, to fudge the facts so as to support their preferred values, those who are committed to specific instrumental values—a political party, a particular economic system, a singular approach to educating the young, and so forth—run the risk that such a commitment will create a bias in them, whether conscious or unconscious, compromising their ability to recognize fully and to acknowledge frankly factual discoveries showing that the policies that they favor are ineffective or counterproductive. Accordingly, while Zinn urges scholars to take on in their work an interest in "eliminating war, poverty, race and national hatred, governmental restrictions on individual freedom, and in fostering a spirit of cooperation and concern in the generation growing up," he quickly adds that they "should *not* serve the interests of particular nations or parties or religions or political dogmas" (UOS; ZR 504; OH 183; KFP 10). Similarly, he urges historians to start their "inquiry with frank adherence to a small set of ultimate values—that war, poverty, race hatred…, should be abolished; that mankind constitutes a single species; that affection and cooperation should replace violence and hostility" (HPE 20), but is also careful to caution that history should not be used "as a buttress to any particular party, nation, or ideology" (CW 51).

So for Zinn, neither capitalism nor anti-capitalism is fundamental. The value of capitalism, on his view, is instrumental. It should be judged in accordance with its tendency either to promote or to hinder such ultimate values as life, liberty, the pursuit of happiness, peace, economic security, health, knowledge, and so forth. While Paquette is not wrong to describe Zinn's views as "anti-capitalist," since Zinn's assessment of capitalism on this score is predominantly negative, it is not absolutely or unqualifiedly so. For example, Zinn has on more than one occasion acknowledged that capitalism has "developed the economy in an enormously impressive way," increasing "geometrically the number of goods available" (see DUB 158). (This is yet another example of the presence in Zinn's thought of the subtlety and nuance, the complexity and many-sidedness of judgment, that Paquette theoretically prizes as a characteristic of "good" and "serious" historians. Though Paquette denies that these qualities can be found in Zinn's works, in fact their rich abundance in his writings contrasts starkly with their total absence in Paquette's two-part essay on Zinn.) A "good" and "serious" scholar, conscientiously adhering to prevailing scholarly norms, would recognize an obligation, prior to charging Zinn with basing his standards on an anti-capitalist ideology, to acknowledge, and to refute, his explicit argument to the contrary. Paquette, by contrast, fails to discuss Zinn's argument. Nor does he address the distinction on which it is based, that between ultimate and instrumental values. Indeed, he shows no awareness of this distinction, in spite of the fact that it constitutes a major theme of POH, Zinn's most significant historiographical work.

(2) Paquette's claim that Zinn's standards are rooted in his

anti-capitalist views is rendered all the more implausible when we consider some of the actual examples in APH of Zinn's "sentencing of those in power" for their moral transgressions. Three of the most frequently discussed kinds of such transgressions in APH are (a) acts of aggression in which one country invades another, (b) acts aimed at denying the people of a country a right to self-determination—for example, by violently overthrowing their democratically elected leader, and (c) acts of killing innocent non-combatants indiscriminately—for example, by dropping bombs on heavily-populated civilian centers. Would Paquette want to claim that there is something specifically capitalist about such actions? Is it his view that only anti-capitalists would oppose them? And if so, does this mean that he considers such acts to be justified, since the only people who object to them are those who harbor an unjustified anti-capitalist bias?

In any case, the fact that Zinn objects to such actions is much more straightforwardly explained by his commitment to the ultimate values of life, liberty, and the pursuit of happiness. The cogency of this analysis is further underscored by the fact that Zinn has repeatedly criticized the Soviet Union for precisely these same actions, as documented above.

(3) Moreover, Paquette's claim that "Zinn relishes the sentencing of those in power by inappropriate or impossible standards" is open to a more direct challenge. While APH certainly does pay more attention to the misdeeds of the powerful than is customary in traditional, mainstream history texts, Zinn generally does not add to his descriptions of these actions a denunciation of the individuals who perpetrated them. In the opening chapter of APH he explains why: "My point is not to grieve for the victims and denounce the executioners. Those tears, that anger, cast into the past, deplete our moral energy for the present" (10). Or again, after criticizing histories that "emphasize the heroism of Columbus and his successors as

navigators and discoverers, and...de-emphasize their genocide," in part on the grounds that such an approach "serves—unwittingly—to justify what was done," Zinn offers a more expansive explanation for his lack of interest in vilification:

> My point is not that we must, in telling history, accuse, judge, condemn Columbus *in absentia*. It is too late for that; it would be a useless scholarly exercise in morality. But the easy acceptance of atrocities as a deplorable but necessary price to pay for progress (Hiroshima and Vietnam, to save Western civilization; Kronstadt and Hungary, to save socialism;[44] nuclear proliferation, to save us all)—that is still with us. One reason these atrocities are still with us is that we have learned to bury them in a mass of other facts, as radioactive wastes are buried in containers in the earth. We have learned to give them exactly the same proportion of attention that teachers and writers often give them in the most respectable of classrooms and textbooks. This learned sense of moral proportion, coming from the apparent objectivity of the scholar, is accepted more easily than when it comes from politicians at press conferences. It is therefore more deadly. (9)[45]

Since Paquette charges Zinn with passing "sentence" on the powerful for their misdeeds, minimal standards of good scholarship would demand that he at least address this explicit statement by Zinn of his refusal to do so. A "good" and "serious" scholar would acknowledge that his or her interpretation of what Zinn is doing differs from Zinn's own self-interpretation, and would feel obliged to offer some sort of textual, evidence-based argument that the author (Zinn) has misrepresented his own text. Simply to assert, without argument, that the author says "X," when he explicitly states that he is saying "not-X," will obviously never do. And such an assertion must be judged even more egregious if the critic fails even to mention the author's "not-X" declaration. But then again, Paquette's abject failure to meet minimal scholarly standards in this regard may be due to his lack of awareness of Zinn's "not-X" statement. For to learn of it, he would have had to read all the way to page 9 in Zinn's book.[46]

And just as Paquette uncritically assumes that Zinn "relishes the sentencing of those in power," so does he imagine that Zinn regards the victims of oppression as necessarily virtuous. Thus, he fantasizes that he scores a point against Zinn with the following utterance: "let it be said, by a great historian, if not by Zinn, 'the experience of oppression does not inevitably transform fallible men and women into saints...'" (PA2).

The problem for Paquette is that Zinn makes this point himself in APH. After pointing out that "In the long run, the oppressor is also a victim" (and note that Zinn here expresses some sympathy for the oppressors, and thus gives us yet another of those "delicate, nuanced, and qualified assessments" that Paquette so much prizes, even as he denies that they can be found in Zinn's work), he goes on to add that "In the short run (and so far, human history has consisted only of short runs), the victims, themselves desperate and tainted with the culture that oppresses them, turn on other victims.... I will try not to overlook the cruelties that victims inflict on one another as they are jammed together in the boxcars of the system. I don't want to romanticize them. But I do remember (in rough paraphrase) a statement I once read: 'The cry of the poor is not always just, but if you don't listen to it, you will never know what justice is'" (10). It is worth noting that Zinn wrote that in 1980. The quotation by "a great historian," which Paquette offers as a corrective to what he mistakenly regards as Zinn's view, was published in 1997.[47]

(4) Paquette's claim that Zinn anachronistically holds the powerful to standards that are "inappropriate or impossible," since one cannot fairly "expect people of the past to act according to standards that their intellectual and moral horizon could not possibly have had," is open to at least two objections.

First, the great majority of cases of misconduct by the powerful that Zinn describes involve behaviors—such as military aggression, the deliberate killing of civilians, and assassinations of democratically elected leaders—that were widely recognized at the time to be morally objectionable. Indeed, the fact that the perpetrators of such actions well understood that accurate knowledge of the deeds in question would have resulted in widespread condemnation of them explains why the perpetrators tended, when possible, to do them in secret, and to deny having done them at all, or, when this was not possible, to provide elaborate propaganda intended to make the actions appear justifiable. Paquette's example of slavery, an institution that was once legal and widely defended, but which was subsequently outlawed and almost universally condemned, is in this respect unusual. Paquette's use of it supposedly to show that there is a problem, broadly and generally, with Zinn's way of holding people to moral standards, is therefore defective to the extent that slavery is an atypical example, unrepresentative of the more typical cases in which Zinn holds the powerful to moral standards.

Second, even in the case of slavery, and other kinds of conduct that resemble it in that they are now seen as odious but were at the time widely accepted as legitimate and proper, there was always also at the time a robust campaign against the practices in question by reformers who considered them to be immoral. So, while slave owners may have had the law, official decrees by various churches, and a good percentage of public opinion on their side, many of them (and especially the wealthy and powerful figures discussed by Zinn, who tended to be well educated and highly literate) were nonetheless well aware of the arguments of the abolitionist movement, and perfectly capable of grasping their force and significance. Would Paquette want to claim that such arguments were beyond "the intellectual and moral horizon" of such slave owners as, say, George Washington and Thomas Jefferson?

Naturally, just as is the case with every one of Paquette's other criticisms, Zinn anticipated it and answered it before Paquette wrote his essay. For example, in a 1991 speech he addressed his audience as follows:

> [W]ho are we to point the finger at Columbus and what happened there? This was, after all, the fifteenth century. You may have heard that argument before. You will hear that argument made lots of times. What right do we in the twentieth century have to judge the fifteenth century? Or to put it another way, in the fifteenth century people killed one another, exploited one another, treated other people as if they were nonhuman, violently conquered one another. So we mustn't judge. How lucky we are to be living in this time....
>
> But there are values, aren't there, that transcend centuries, that are applicable to the fifteenth, sixteenth, seventeenth, eighteenth, nineteenth and twentieth centuries? There are values of human life, of concern for human beings, which are not limited to one historical period. Greek playwrights in the fifth century BC cried out against war in the same way that people in the twentieth century cry out against war. People at that time made war and visited atrocities against people, as the Athenians did against the inhabitants of Melos, just the way people do in our time. So it's absurd, it seems to me, to talk about this as being an ahistorical criticism, as being anachronistic to look back at that time....
>
> [O]ne of the proofs of the fact that there are transcendental values is simply that there are people in all times who protest against what is going on. It isn't as if they were the conquerors of the fifteenth century and they're the protestors of the twentieth century. They were the protestors of the fifteenth and sixteenth centuries. There were the resisters, of course they were the Indians themselves, who resisted and protested,

the victims themselves. But there were also Spaniards who protested against what was going on. Bartolomé de Las Casas, the chief of them, who spent forty years in this hemisphere and went back and forth to Spain, taking up the cause of the Indians and crying out against things that he had seen with his own eyes.[48] Even those who argued against Las Casas—there was another priest named Sepulveda who argued for the right to enslave and kill Indians on the grounds they were barbaric and uncivilized and unchristian and deserved what they got. But in all ages there are people who are on the side of the powerful and people who take up the cause of the victims. (LOC 80–1)

Paquette, for his part, takes up the cause of the powerful. When considering the actions of powerful genocidists, like Columbus, Paquette is quick to call for "delicate, nuanced, and qualified assessments," to emphasize that ours is "an imperfect world of flawed beings whose behavior often brings about unintended, ironic, or contradictory consequences," and to insist that one should not judge people of the past by "inappropriate or impossible standards"—standards "that their intellectual and moral horizon could not possibly have had." But when considering the actions of Howard Zinn, whose "crime" was not genocide, but rather the act of calling attention to genocidal actions that his colleagues in the historical profession had largely ignored, Paquette offers no such sympathy or understanding—just a string of insults.

Nor can Paquette be bothered to pay Zinn the professional courtesy of consulting his writings for the purpose of learning about, and then responding to, his numerous anticipatory refutations of the objections that Paquette would go on to publish after Zinn was safely dead. For example, Paquette takes no notice of Zinn's arguments, like those just quoted, against the criticism that his standards in evaluating Columbus are anachronistic, in spite of the fact that Zinn published them 20 years prior to the appearance of Paquette's two-part essay on Zinn.[49]

Perhaps the following fact illustrates Paquette's point about the "ironic" aspects of the actions of "flawed beings." Paquette is a co-founder of The Alexander Hamilton Institute for the Study of Western Civilization. The organization's charter states that it "aspires to create an educational environment of the highest standards in which evidence and argument prevail over ideology and cant."[50]

David Horowitz

Horowitz, a well-known conservative writer and activist, is the author of *The Professors: The 101 Most Dangerous Academics in America* (TP). The heart of the book consists of a series of profiles, averaging about three-to-four pages in length, of the "dangerous academics" mentioned in the book's subtitle. The very last profile that the reader encounters, because Horowitz presents them in alphabetical order, is that of Howard Zinn.

The first point to note about the book is that it is jam-packed, to a truly astonishing degree, with clear, obvious, uncontroversial factual errors, as I will document below. Granted, many of these are inconsequential. Still, it is ironic that one who would presume to judge the competence of college professors would be so careless about putting his own incompetence on full display. Moreover, the consistency with which Horowitz gets elementary facts wrong, and the staggering variety of ways in which he does so, ultimately dazzles the reader. His is a kind of rare and wondrous virtuosity. One finds oneself repeatedly thinking, "no!—he didn't get that one wrong too, did he? How *does* he *do* that?"

As a case in point, the subtitle of his book is incorrect. When one adds up the book's profiles of the "dangerous academics," they total 100, not 101. Horowitz offers something of an explanation for this, but it does not help his case. In his "Introduction" he refers to "the 101 portraits in this volume" (TP xxiii), but attaches to this an endnote that reads as follows: "One hundred and two, if one includes Ward Churchill and Cornel West" (TP 381, note 26). There are two problems with this explanation. First, it fails to address the fact that the book's central chapter, entitled "One Hundred and One Professors," contains profiles of only 100 professors. So that chapter title is in error. Second, Ward Churchill is discussed in the "Introduction," but not formally profiled in the same manner as those included in the chapter just mentioned. Cornel West, who is also denied a formal profile, is treated in a short chapter following the one containing those portraits. So if they are excluded, because they are treated differently than the others, then the total of "dangerous academics" presented is 100, not 101, and the book's subtitle is wrong. But if they are included, then the total is 102, not 101, so the subtitle is still wrong. So on any interpretation, and even taking into account Horowitz's explanation, Horowitz has committed a factual error in the very subtitle of his book. And the title of one of his chapters is in error. And his explanation of all of this is also in error! Here, displayed in its full glory, is Horowitz's rare and exotic talent.

While anyone familiar with Horowitz's career would expect his book, given its title, to consist of an extended complaint about the existence of professors with political views that differ from his, Horowitz explicitly denies that his text is motivated by such narrowly partisan concerns: "This book is not intended as a text about left-wing bias in the university and does not propose that this bias is necessarily a problem. Every individual, whether conservative or liberal, has a perspective and therefore a bias. Professors have every right to interpret the subjects they teach according to their individual points of view. This is the essence of academic freedom" (TP xxvi). So far, so good. What, then, is the problem? Horowitz explains:

But [professors] also have professional obligations as teachers, whose purpose is the instruction and education of students, not to impose their biases on students as though they were scientific facts. The professorial task is to teach students how to think, not to tell them what to think. In short, it is the responsibility of professors to be professional—and therefore "academic"—in their classrooms, and therefore not to require students to agree with them on matters which are controversial....

As teachers they are expected to make their students aware of the controversies surrounding the evidence, including the significant challenges to their own interpretations....

Their teaching must not seek the arbitrary imposition of personal opinions and prejudices on students, enforced through the power of the grading process and the authority of the institutions they represent. (TP xxvi–xxvii)

Well, that's clear enough. Horowitz's objection is not to leftist professors, but rather to professors, whatever their political orientation, who teach dogmatically, who do not respect their students' right to think for themselves, who fail to inform students about objections and alternatives to their own preferred views, and who abuse their power and authority by insisting that their students agree with those views. Let's see how well he documents that those he identifies as "dangerous professors" are indeed guilty of these transgressions.

Toward that end, consider Horowitz's portrait of Professor Anatole Anton of San Francisco State University. This is the fifth profile in his "One Hundred and One Professors" chapter, and the first one that I read. I was looking for what Horowitz had to say about professors in my field, philosophy, and Anton was the first philosopher in the series. This short profile (TP 11–12) consists of just three paragraphs. The first simply identifies Anton by giving his title (professor), field (philosophy), and institution (San Francisco State University). We are told that he had formerly been chair of the department, that he "writes and researches on political philosophy, the philosophy of social science, and Hegel and Marx," and that he is the general editor of the San Francisco State University *Series in Philosophy*.

The second paragraph informs us that Anton is co-coordinator of the Radical Philosophy Association. We are told that this group believes "that fundamental change requires broad social upheavals but also opposition to intellectual support for exploitative and dehumanizing social structures, [including] capitalism, racism, sexism, homophobia, disability discrimination, environmental ruin, and all other forms of domination," that it opposes U.S. economic and military aid to Israel, and that it has taken a strong stand against the Afghanistan and Iraq wars, among other positions.

The third paragraph tells us that on September 27, 2004 Anton emailed to his colleagues some remarks by the acclaimed novelist E. L. Doctorow on then-President George W. Bush, in which Doctorow accuses Bush of being unfeeling, of not suffering when 21-year-olds die, of regretting nothing, and being unable to mourn.

That's it. The profile contains not one word about Professor Anton's teaching, about his classroom demeanor, about how he relates to his students. For that matter, there is nothing about his scholarship beyond a single sentence, quoted above, describing in broad terms the subject areas in which he works. He is condemned as one of the country's 101 most dangerous professors solely on the strength of the alleged political views of an association with which he is affiliated, and his having sent the Doctorow piece to his colleagues.

Recall that in his "Introduction" Horowitz claims that he does not object to professors having left-wing views, provided that they do not in their teaching inflict those views on their students in a dogmatic, authoritarian, intolerant way. But in his profile of

Anton he provides evidence only that Anton has left-wing views. We learn nothing whatsoever about his teaching.[51] Nor is this an aberration. Horowitz's profile of Zinn (TP 358–64) also says nothing about his behavior in the classroom, but instead focuses on a critique of APH (to be discussed below). Indeed, 52 of Horowitz's 100 profiles deal exclusively with the professor's activities outside of the classroom and contain no information about the professor's in-class performance.[52]

Jacob Laksin defends Horowitz on this score by arguing that Horowitz's critique of his professorial targets was from the outset never intended to be limited to their teaching. He attempts to make this case by offering the following quotation from the "Introduction" to TP:

> When viewed as a whole, the 101 portraits in this volume reveal several disturbing patterns of university life.... These include (1) promotion far beyond academic achievement...; (2) teaching subjects outside one's professional qualifications and expertise for the purpose of political propaganda...; (3) making racist and ethnically disparaging remarks in public without eliciting reaction by university administrations, as long as those remarks are directed at unprotected groups, e.g., Armenians, whites, Christians, and Jews...; (4) the overt introduction of political agendas into the classroom and the abandonment of any pretense of academic discipline or scholarly inquiry... (LAK, quoting TP xxiii)

Summarizing this point, Laksin emphasizes that "*The Professors* makes four distinct critiques, two of which focus on in-class conduct and two of which do not. In other words, half the critique is about activities that violate academic standards that are not confined to in-class presentations." So apparently the reason why it is acceptable for Horowitz to exclude information about in-class performance from 52 of his profiles is that in those

52 cases Horowitz's criticism is not directed against their teaching, but rather against their either having been "promoted far beyond their academic achievement" or their having made "racist and ethnically disparaging remarks in public" — the two "activities that violate academic standards that are not confined to in-class presentations."

But clearly this doesn't help. For Horowitz says not a word about Anton's qualifications to have achieved professorial rank — nothing to suggest that his academic achievements are insufficient to justify his having been promoted to such a position. Horowitz offers no critique of his scholarly writings, for example. Nor does he claim that Anton has ever made racist or ethnically disparaging remarks. So, once again, all we are left with is the fact that Anton has political views, as manifested in his membership in the Radical Philosophical Association and his decision to share with colleagues some remarks that were critical of George W. Bush, that clash with those of Horowitz. This, and this alone, makes him one of the "101 most dangerous academics in America."

Noticing this pattern, which recurs throughout Horowitz's book, an organization called "Free Exchange on Campus," in a report entitled "Facts Count," charges that "Mr. Horowitz chiefly condemns professors for expressing their personal political views outside of the classroom" (FC). (In the case of Anton, the expression of personal political views outside of the classroom took the form of sending to his colleagues an email containing Doctorow's critical remarks on Bush.)

But to this, Laksin has a ready reply:

This is false. *The Professors* in fact says exactly the opposite, and in so many words: "This book is not intended as a text about leftwing bias in the university and does not propose that a leftwing perspective on academic faculties is a problem in itself. Every individual, whether conservative or liberal, has a perspective and therefore a bias. Professors have every right to interpret the subjects they teach according to their individual points of view. That is the essence of academic freedom." Since these sentences appear in the introduction to the text and have been repeated by the author many times since publication, it is clear that this is not an honest error but a calculated distortion of the intentions of both author and book.

But to *that*, I have a ready reply. While a critic is indeed obliged to take seriously and to address a writer's self-interpretation, especially when it contradicts an objection that the critic wishes to press (something that almost all of Zinn's critics fail to do, incidentally, as I have documented extensively above), the critic is not obliged to accept the writer's self-interpretation when the evidence renders it untenable. Accordingly, I conclude that the "Facts Count" criticism under discussion is cogent, and neither "an honest error" nor "a calculated distortion." The situation is rather as if Horowitz had said in his "Introduction," "let me be clear, I have no objection to someone's having red hair," but then, in the body of his text, without providing any other evidence in support of his contention, had repeatedly said, "Here's someone who is a terrible, dangerous professor—he has red hair." Note in this connection that Horowitz often includes in his profiles of the "dangerous academics" the observation, offered without further comment, that the profiled person did not support the war in Afghanistan and/or the war in Iraq. How is that supposed to be relevant?

With regard to Anton specifically, the "Facts Count" document offers the following comment: "Mr. Horowitz does not provide a single footnote in his chapter on Anatole Anton and nothing in this chapter addresses Professor Anton's research or teaching" (FC). Laksin's complete reply to this criticism reads as follows:

Here is how Professor Anton is introduced in *The Professors*: Professor Anton is co-coordinator of the Radical Philosophy Association, an anti-capitalist group of Marxist professors who "believe that fundamental change requires broad social upheavals but also opposition to intellectual support for exploitative and dehumanizing social structures, [including] capitalism, racism, sexism, homophobia, disability discrimination, environmental ruin, and all other forms of domination." Note that the Radical Philosophy Association presents itself as a professional association of philosophers and that Anatole Anton is an official of this organization. If this isn't evidence of a confusion between scholarship and activism, what is?

By way of reply I would note, first, that while scholarship and activism are not the same thing, it does not follow, and nor is it true, that activism cannot be informed by scholarship. To establish that second-hand smoke is harmful, that capital punishment is not a uniquely effective crime deterrent, or that certain educational practices are counterproductive, one needs good, sound scholarship. To change policies so as to protect non-smokers from the dangers of unwanted second-hand smoke, to abolish the death penalty, to alter educational practices, one needs activism. So, to address Laksin's question, if someone were to list under "scholarship" on a curriculum vita his or her activities in agitating for changes in social policy, that would count as "evidence of a confusion between scholarship and activism." But belonging to a scholarly organization devoted to the study of social problems—devoted, that is, to the attempt to develop a greater understanding of such problems, and of the best and most effective ways of ameliorating them—evidences no such confusion.

Perhaps the mistake underlying Laksin's reasoning here is the conviction, expressed in another book, co-authored by Horowitz and Laksin, that "An open academic inquiry would not be 'for' or 'against' anything."[53] While it is true that scholarly research and scientific investigation should be open to following the evidence wherever it leads, that doesn't mean that one must start from scratch, absolutely from ground zero, every time one undertakes a research project. If one has drawn some conclusions from previous studies, one might then undertake a new project based on accepting those conclusions, at least tentatively, as true. It is as if Horowitz wants biologists, in each one of their projects, to be trying to figure out whether evolutionary theory is sound, rather than undertaking projects in which they make use of evolutionary theory to try to shed light on some specific problem. Similarly, why should not scholars who have concluded that, say, racism or capitalism is a bad thing, undertake projects based on that premise? To be sure, Horowitz would think that the anticapitalist premise is wrong, but that is a material disagreement, not a principled objection to any scholarship that is based on an assumption. Would Horowitz reject as a confusion of scholarship with activism a scholarly project in which a researcher attempts to use free-market economic theory to solve some pressing social problem? Would there be a problem if like-minded free-market enthusiasts were to form a scholarly society, so as to share ideas in conferences and through a journal? What about people like Professor Walter Williams of George Mason University? He writes a syndicated column in which he regularly sings the praises of free-market capitalism and denigrates other economic approaches, systems, or theories. If his teaching also follows this pattern, does this mean that he is a political propagandist who has abandoned any pretense of scholarly inquiry? Or, consistent with Horowitz's own methods, are his writings alone enough to convict him of being a propagandist rather than a scholar, no matter what he does in the classroom?

Indeed, the absurdity of the unqualified, unnuanced premise that Horowitz and Laksin advance is revealed by the context in which they advance it—that of objecting to a conference devoted to the topic of combating criminal injustice. As John K. Wilson points out in his review of the book, the authors invoke the principle that "An open academic inquiry would not be 'for' or 'against' anything" precisely in order to advance the absurd claim that (in Wilson's words) "it is improper for any professor to be against the wrongful conviction of innocent people and to hold a conference that seeks action against wrongful convictions" (REV).

Would it be wrong, on Horowitz's view, for a professor to conduct research on ways to minimize racism in society? After all, such a project would be built on the assumption that racism is a bad thing, and Horowitz seems to think that genuine scholarship can never be based on value assumptions. Everything must, at all times, be open. So perhaps the scholar must first undertake some kind of inquiry to determine whether or not racism is bad. But wait, isn't that a somewhat political question? So perhaps this can't be investigated at all. Are chemistry professors wrong to instruct their students to handle the chemicals safely, or even, God help us, to show them how to do so, so as not to cause a fire or an explosion, or is this wrong because it assumes, before the inquiry has even begun, that safety is good, and that uncontrolled fires and explosions are bad? And I suppose that medical researchers, to return to one of Zinn's examples, discussed above, should not assume that health is better than sickness; nor should such value commitments guide their research. (Note that Horowitz ignores all of Zinn's arguments on this score, and shows no awareness of them.)

Moreover, while Horowitz seems not to understand the point, some disciplines, by their very nature, are concerned with political questions. It is not unscholarly for professors in those disciplines to address such questions in their scholarly work. For example, in my field, philosophy, two of the largest sub-fields are ethics and political philosophy. So what sense does it make to say that scholars should not address political questions?

Is it Horowitz's desire that political questions should only be thought about and debated by people who are not scholars? Why? Does he think that economists, historians, psychologists, sociologists, criminologists, and the like who, in the context of their professional scholarly work, make discoveries about what the world is like that would, if intelligently applied to current political problems, help us to make advances in dealing with those problems more knowledgeably, intelligently, effectively, and, by widely-shared standards, more fairly and justly, should nonetheless scrupulously refrain from pursuing such applications (or perhaps even the original research underlying it), so as to avoid the taint of politics? If there is currently a proposal in the political arena to attempt this or that strategy in dealing with some social issue, should a historian, who has, more than anyone else in the world, conducted detailed studies of the use of the strategy in question at various times and in different places, scrupulously avoid making any kind of comment about what that research might show about the advisability of the present proposal? Does Horowitz think that, in the political sphere, ignorance is better than knowledge?

Coming at it from another direction, what kind of participation in politics would Horowitz's strictures allow for academics? Presumably he would agree that they should, like other citizens, be allowed to vote. But isn't discussion and debate also an important part of the political process? Horowitz seems to think that any time an academic engages in political discussion or debate, even outside of the classroom (on the evidence of his profiles) he or she has crossed the line, become a propagandist, dispensed with scholarly standards, and so forth. And the same holds to an even greater degree if the scholar actually engages in scholarly research in an attempt to discover politically relevant knowledge, or to determine how existing knowledge might profitably be applied to human problems that have a political dimension.

And why does the taking of political stands imply an abandonment of scholarly standards? Could one not adopt, and advocate, a political position precisely on the basis of the fact that it is supported by one's scholarly standards—it is the one that is warranted by a careful and logical appraisal of the relevant evidence and arguments on the issue in question? Or is it his view that only political views that are very much like his are reasonable and responsive to such norms, in which case his case boils down to the fact that there are many professors whose politics he thinks are wrong?

Notice, furthermore, that Horowitz's argument in TP makes many value-laden assumptions—that promotion far beyond achievement is bad; that teaching outside one's professional qualifications and expertise for the purpose of political propaganda is bad; that making racist remarks is bad; that the overt introduction of political agendas into the classroom is bad. So does this mean that his own project is profoundly unscholarly? For that matter, the author bio of Horowitz that appears on the dust jacket of TP says that he is "a lifelong civil rights activist." By his own strictures, doesn't that mean that he is not a scholar?

Moving on, I wanted to see if Horowitz had anything more substantive to say about someone in my field. I was especially interested in trying to find a case in which he addressed the *teaching* of philosophy. His profile of Lewis Gordon fit the bill. Horowitz went online and found a syllabus! And it is for a course on existentialism—a subject that I also teach regularly, and about which I have published extensively.

This is what Horowitz has to say about Gordon's syllabus: "Absurdly for a course about existentialism—which was exclusively the creation of European thinkers from Kierkegaard to Sartre—but wholly in keeping with Professor Gordon's Afrocentrist prejudices, his course is not limited to what he calls the 'Western perspective' but includes 'contributions from Africana and Eastern thought,' including the work of such obscurities as 'Nishtani' and 'Jones'" (TP 200).

Where to begin? I suppose the first point to be made in reply is that "existentialism" does not name anything very precise. It is, rather, a rough-and-ready term, like so many others used to name broad currents in intellectual or cultural history (think of "romanticism," "the baroque style," or "the Enlightenment"). So, there is nothing "absurd" about making a case for the importance of some hitherto unrecognized figures as important members of a rough, imprecisely defined general tendency or movement. While it is true that existentialism has traditionally been thought of as a primarily European philosophical movement, it hardly follows, and nor is it true, that no one outside Europe has contributed to it. While impressionism in painting first arose in France, would it be "absurd" to include in a university course on impressionism some of the American impressionists alongside Monet, Renoir, Degas, and the rest? Philosophers in many other parts of the world read the European existentialists, responded to their work, and developed some of their insights in new directions. One of these philosophers was Keiji Nishitani, who studied with Heidegger in Germany in the late 1930s.

Next, one is obliged, once again, to point out Horowitz's sloppy scholarship and appalling ignorance. Nishitani (not "Nishtani," as Horowitz incorrectly spells it) is not an "obscurity," but one of the major Japanese philosophers of the twentieth century. (Nishitani's name is spelled correctly on Professor Gordon's syllabus.)[54] And how, one wonders, is the inclusion of this important *Japanese* philosopher supposed to be "in keeping with Professor Gordon's [alleged] *Afro*-centrist prejudices"?

Things do not get better for Horowitz when he turns to the evaluation of a philosopher's scholarship. In his attack on Professor Cornel West (who is not profiled in Horowitz's list of the 100 worst professors, but who is discussed extensively in a subsequent chapter), Horowitz quotes Leon Wieseltier's claim that West's books "are almost completely worthless." Horowitz immediately indicates his agreement with Wieseltier, adding that his judgment is "amply justified by the texts themselves" (TP 366). A person with a modicum of modesty and a sense of fairness would hesitate to form such a harsh judgment, let alone utter it and put it in print, without a thorough acquaintance with, and firm grasp of, the relevant evidence, in this case, Professor West's books. So let's take a look at what Horowitz has to say about one of these books. Horowitz tells us that in 1989 West "published *The Evasion of Philosophy*, a reworking of his PhD thesis. It consisted of summaries of the ideas of leading pragmatist philosophers along with a scolding by Professor West when they did not share his 'progressive politics.' This constituted the 'evasion' of the title" (TP 367-8).

What does this tell us about Horowitz's familiarity with West's book? Well, for starters, he's got the title wrong. The correct title is *The American Evasion of Philosophy*. And he's wrong about the meaning of "evasion" in the title. As West makes abundantly clear (for example, on page 5 of his book),[55] what the American pragmatists evaded, on West's interpretation, is "epistemology-centered philosophy," that is, an approach to philosophy in which questions about the nature of knowledge, and about how knowledge can be achieved, is thought to be central to the philosophical enterprise. On West's interpretation, the American pragmatists oriented philosophy more toward social and cultural criticism — a move of which West approves. So Horowitz is wrong about West's title, wrong about the meaning of the "evasion" referred to in the title, and wrong about West's attitude toward that evasion. Horowitz says nothing else about this book, and offers no such "detailed analysis" of any of West's other books. On this firm ground he publishes his opinion that West's books are "almost completely worthless."

In addition to his obvious incompetence and recklessness,

Horowitz also puts his hypocrisy on display here. Elsewhere in TP he repeatedly rails against those who make pronouncements about matters outside of their areas of expertise: "Hired as experts in scholarly disciplines and fields of knowledge, professors are granted tenure in order to protect the integrity of their academic inquiry, not their right to leak into the classroom their uninformed prejudices on subjects which are outside their fields of expertise" (TP xxvi). Or again, recall that one of his four fundamental criticisms of some of the "dangerous academics" in his book is that they teach "subjects outside [their] professional qualifications and expertise" (TP xxiii). Well, Horowitz, in radical contrast to Cornel West (who has a Ph.D. in philosophy from Princeton), certainly has no professional credentials or demonstrated expertise in philosophy. Why, then, according to his own strictures, does he feel qualified to dismiss as "almost completely worthless" the interpretations that West presents in his book of the philosophies of (among others) Charles Sanders Peirce, William James, John Dewey, and Richard Rorty?

Perhaps a defender of Horowitz will reply that he does not pretend to be an academic, and thus should not be held to the same standards that he applies to professors. Well, according to John K. Wilson, Horowitz was recently "invited to speak at his fiftieth reunion at Columbia University, and he complained that his books 'are more effectively banned in its classrooms than were the books of Marxists fifty years ago, during the height of the McCarthy era'" (REV). And Scott McLemee reports that Horowitz's book *Left Illusions: An Intellectual Odyssey* contains a preface noting bitterly that no dissertations had yet been based on a study of his career.[56] So if Horowitz's works are not taken seriously as contributions to scholarship, Horowitz evidently thinks that they should be.

Similarly inconsistent and unprincipled is Horowitz's handling of the Lawrence Summers controversy. Horowitz informs us that Stephan Thernstrom, whom he identifies as "one of Harvard's handful of conservatives," had in 2005 defended Harvard's then-president, Lawrence Summers, who was under fire from several members of the Harvard faculty for having said, in a faculty symposium on women in science, that one possible reason why there were not more women in positions of prominence in the sciences is that there may be a "different availability of aptitude at the high end." When this caused an uproar, Thernstrom rose to Summers' defense with the following words: "[I]t is amazing to me that many of us here no longer seem to understand that the expression of controversial ideas and the freedom to debate them is at the heart of any greater institution of higher learning. The whole point of tenure, as I understand it, is to protect professors from the thought police. But now they are not just outside, on some congressional or state legislative committee. They are inside too in our midst" (TP 371). Horowitz makes it abundantly clear that he agrees with Thernstrom, as he expresses dismay that Summers' opponents would attempt to "silence one side of a scientific debate," states that "it is hard to imagine a more anti-intellectual position" than the one they took, and heartily endorses both the cogency and the applicability to this case of Thernstrom's further claim that "the life-blood of [academic life] is free inquiry and unfettered debate" (TP 371). But how is all of this to be squared with Horowitz's incessant complaints about academics who express controversial opinions about matters "outside of their professional qualifications and expertise"? And, in the light of Thernstrom's reference to "the whole point of tenure," how is it to be squared with Horowitz's explicit claim that tenure protects only "the integrity of [professors'] academic inquiry" in the "scholarly disciplines and fields of knowledge" in which they have been "hired as experts," and precisely does not protect their right to spew "their uninformed prejudices on subjects which are outside their fields of expertise"? In case this point is not clear, perhaps I should add that Summers' field of academic expertise was economics—

training that presumably would not qualify him as an authority on the "different availability of aptitude at the high end" of men and women for scientific work.

Incidentally, Thernstrom must be judged guilty of the same inconsistency, since he, in concert with his wife, Professor Abigail Thernstrom, gives Horowitz's book his full endorsement. The Thernstroms' blurb, printed on the book's back cover, not only calls Horowitz's argument "a scathing critique," but also informs us that Horowitz's critics "will be hard-pressed to answer his charges." That's undoubtedly why I'm struggling so hard to find any flaws.

In any case, one should not exaggerate Horowitz's inconsistency. He is very consistent, for example, when it comes to misstating the facts about every subject he touches. Thus, since he had occasion to mention Stephan Thernstrom in passing (he appears on just one page of Horowitz's book), he could not resist the temptation to misinform his readers about him. According to Horowitz, years before the Summers controversy Thernstrom "had been driven from his classroom for expressing views that were politically incorrect" (TP 371). While that story circulated widely way back in 1991, it has since been thoroughly and conclusively debunked. In fact, while some students had alleged that Thernstrom had made racially insensitive statements in his classroom, no formal complaint was lodged against him, and no disciplinary action was taken. The university publicly defended his academic freedom. He chose, of his own accord, to stop teaching the course in question rather than risk being again accused of racial insensitivity. No one asked, let alone demanded, that he stop teaching the course—not even the students who had complained.[57]

The completely fraudulent nature of Horowitz's entire enterprise in TP is perhaps best illustrated by his profile of the famed linguist, Noam Chomsky of the Massachusetts Institute of Technology. Recalling Laksin's point that "*The Professors* makes four distinct critiques, two of which focus on in-class conduct and two of which do not," the first point to be noted is that Horowitz's five-page portrait of Chomsky (TP 84–8) says nothing whatsoever about his teaching, so it contains nothing to support either of the two criticisms that have to do with in-class conduct. Nor does Horowitz suggest that Chomsky has ever made "racist and ethnically disparaging remarks in public." The only remaining possibility is that Chomsky was "promoted far beyond [his] academic achievement."

Let's pursue that one. Chomsky is, by all accounts, one of the most renowned scholars in the world. He is arguably the single most influential figure in the history of the discipline of linguistics. Moreover, many other leading figures in linguistics were once students of his. Even Horowitz acknowledges that, at least according to the *Chicago Tribune*, he is "the most cited living author" and "ranks just below Plato and Sigmund Freud among the most cited authors of all time" (TP 84).

The Wikipedia entry on Chomsky accurately describes his influence across a wide range of scholarly disciplines:

Linguist John Lyons remarked that within a few decades of publication, Chomskyan linguistics had become "the most dynamic and influential" school of thought in the field. His work in automata theory has become well known in computer science and he is much cited within the field of computational linguistics. By the 1970s, his work had also come to exert a considerable influence on philosophy. Chomskyan models have been used as a theoretical basis in various fields of study; the Chomsky hierarchy is often taught in fundamental computer science courses as it confers insight into the various types of formal languages, and this hierarchy has also generated interest among mathematicians, particularly combinatorialists. Some arguments in evolutionary psychology are derived from his research results. Nim Chimpsky, a chimpanzee who was the subject of a study in animal language acquisition at Columbia University, was named after Chomsky in reference to his view of language acquisition as a uniquely human ability.

The 1984 Nobel Prize laureate in Medicine and Physiology, Niels Kaj Jerne, used Chomsky's generative model to explain the human immune system, equating "components of a generative grammar...with various features of protein structures." The title of Jerne's Stockholm Nobel Lecture was "The Generative Grammar of the Immune System."

Chomsky has been a highly influential academic figure throughout his career, and was cited within the Arts and Humanities Citation Index more often than any other living scholar from 1980 to 1992. His linguistic work has influenced a wide range of domains, including artificial intelligence, cognitive science, computer science, logic, mathematics, music theory and analysis, psychology, and immunology. He has been described as "arguably the most important intellectual alive," and academia regards him as a paradigm shifter who "contributed substantially to a major methodological shift in the human sciences, turning away from the prevailing empiricism of the middle of the twentieth century." In a 2005 poll that asked readers of *Foreign Policy* and *Prospect* magazines to vote for "the top five public intellectuals" in the world, Chomsky ranked first.[58]

And the same article contains a section entitled "Academic achievements, awards, and honors." One cannot but be astonished by the sheer number and variety of the items listed there, and equally by their prestigious character. It is doubtful that a comparable list could be compiled for any other living academic. Clearly, Horowitz would only make himself look ridiculous were he to suggest that Chomsky's academic promotions have outstripped his academic achievements. Wisely, he does not do so.

So what is left? In addition to Chomsky's influential technical work in linguistics, he is also the author of numerous works on American foreign policy and other politically charged subjects. The point of view that he defends in these works differs, to put it mildly, from that of David Horowitz. But since both Horowitz and his defender, Laksin, deny that Horowitz's complaint is directed simply against left-wing views, I suppose the charge (even though it is not one of the four formally recognized by Laksin as being part of Horowitz's thesis) must be the same as the one raised against Anton—that Chomsky, by writing books that take sides on political issues, is guilty of blurring the distinction between scholarship and activism.

But the problem with this criticism, in addition to those already elaborated above in connection with Anton, is that Chomsky's political writings constitute a kind of amazing hobby on his part. His academic promotions have been based on his scholarly contributions and teaching in the field of linguistics. His political writings and speeches stand outside of, and in addition to, that body of work. So Horowitz has no leg to stand on. He offers no criticism of Chomsky's teaching, or of his massive contributions in his scholarly field. Chomsky joins Horowitz's list of "the most dangerous academics" solely because he has a secondary career of defending political positions that Horowitz rejects.

In addition to that, Horowitz's profile of Chomsky is larded with factual errors. (Were this not the case, we would have strong *prima facie* evidence that the essay must have been written by someone else.) According to Horowitz, Chomsky "is promoted by rock groups such as Rage Against the Machine and Pearl Jam at their concerts the way the Beatles once promoted the Guru Maharaji, solemnly reading excerpts from his work in between sets and urging their followers to read him too" (TP 84–5). The Beatles' history is well chronicled, and those familiar with it will immediately recognize two errors here. First, Horowitz is confusing the Guru Maharaji with Maharishi Mahesh Yogi. The Beatles had no involvement at all with the former, the one that Horowitz maintained they promoted. He was born in 1957 and was unknown until the 1970s, by which time the Beatles had disbanded. Second, the Beatles' brief involvement with the latter figure (meeting him in late 1967, and studying with him in India in early 1968) happened only after the Beatles had, quite famously, stopped giving concerts (the last one took place in San Francisco in August 1966). There never were Beatles concerts in which the works of the Maharishi were read, or in which the audiences were encouraged to read them. Adding to the unintentional hilarity of this utterly gratuitous error-laden sentence is that it occurs just two sentences following one in which Horowitz alludes to Chomsky's allegedly "cavalier relationship with the factual record" (TP 84).

And as if that weren't funny (and simultaneously disturbing) enough, two sentences after his blundering sentence about the Beatles, Horowitz says this: "at the climactic moment in the Academy Award-winning *Good Will Hunting*, the genius-janitor, played by Matt Damon, vanquishes the incorrect thinking of a group of sophomoric college students with a fiery speech quoting Chomsky on the illicit nature of American power" (TP 85). In fact, no such scene appears in the film. Chomsky is mentioned once in the film, but not by Matt Damon's character, not as part of a fiery speech, not addressed to a group of students, and not at the climactic moment in the film. Rather, one of Chomsky's books is briefly mentioned (but not quoted or discussed) by a psychiatrist (played by Robin Williams) in a private conversation with Damon's character.[59]

Turning to more consequential errors, Horowitz attributes to Chomsky the view that "Whatever evil exists in the world, the United States is to blame," calling this thesis "the principal theme of what may be loosely termed his intellectual *oeuvre*" (TP 86). This claim of Horowitz's is so preposterous on its face that any intelligent reader, even if he or she had never read Chomsky, would probably (and appropriately) greet it with skepticism. Does Horowitz really expect anyone to believe that Chomsky blames the U.S. for every hurricane, flood, drought, plague of locusts, and fire that exists in the world? Does he think that Chomsky attributes the Ebola virus to nefarious deeds by the U.S.? Or, if by "evil" Horowitz means to include only human actions, does he really mean to attribute to Chomsky the view that every act of cruelty or deception enacted anywhere in the world—a large child bullying a smaller one in Sweden, a business owner setting fire to his store in a case of insurance fraud in England, a teenage gang leader murdering a rival gang leader in India—is properly to be blamed on the United States?

In any case, it is easy to demonstrate that Horowitz's claim is false. First, many of Chomsky's books and articles (and what exactly Horowitz is trying to imply by his "what may be loosely termed his intellectual *oeuvre*" phrase escapes me completely) are on the subject of linguistics, his primary academic field. These works bear such titles as *Syntactic Structures, Aspects of the Theory of Syntax, Cartesian Linguistics, Topics in the Theory of Generative Grammar, The Sound Pattern of English, Language and Mind, The Logical Structure of Linguistic Theory, Reflections on Language, Morphophonemics of Modern Hebrew, Rules and Representations, Language and the Study of Mind, Modular Approaches to the Study of the Mind, Language in a Psychological Setting, Language and Problems of Knowledge, Language and Thought, The Minimalist Program, On Language, New Horizons in the Study of Language and Mind,* and *The Science of Language,* among many others. Since these works say little if anything about the issue of who is or is not responsible for the world's evils, it is manifestly not the case that their "principal theme" is a thesis about this issue. And, since these linguistic works account for a major chunk of Chomsky's output, their existence falsifies Horowitz's unqualified claim about what is supposedly the principal theme of his work.

Of course, a more generous interpretation is that Horowitz's formulation is meant to apply only to Chomsky's political works (a plausible interpretation in light of the sloppiness that characterizes Horowitz's writing). But here, too, a decisive refutation is easy to construct. Perhaps the most straightforward way to do so is to cite an analytic tool that Chomsky, together with his co-author, Edward S. Herman, develop in their two-volume work, *The Political Economy of Human Rights*, that of a three-fold distinction among "constructive," "benign," and "nefarious" bloodbaths.[60] As Chomsky defines these terms, "constructive bloodbaths" are those that advance the interests of U.S. power; "benign bloodbaths" neither advance nor hinder such interests; and "nefarious bloodbaths" are those that can be blamed (often accurately) on official U.S. enemies. Chomsky's main point about this three-fold distinction is to claim that mainstream U.S. media and political figures treat these different kinds of bloodbaths quite differently. Constructive bloodbaths are largely welcomed, benign bloodbaths ignored, and nefarious bloodbaths passionately condemned. For our purposes, the main point to be made about this analysis is that it refutes Horowitz's claim. If Chomsky really claimed that the United States were responsible for all of the world's evils, this three-fold distinction would collapse—for two of his three categories refer to evils perpetrated by others. Benign bloodbaths are typically carried out by others and against others, while nefarious bloodbaths are generally carried out by U.S. enemies against either the U.S. or its allies. Only constructive bloodbaths, which are perpetrated either by the U.S. or its allies, fit the pattern that, according to Horowitz, Chomsky ascribes to every bloodbath.

Instead of issuing the ludicrously false claim that the principal theme of Chomsky's work is the assertion that the United States is responsible for all the world's evils, Horowitz could have said something like this: "A major theme of Chomsky's political writings is that the United States is, or so he alleges, responsible for many of the world's evils"; or "Chomsky's attribution of responsibility to the United States for many of the world's evils is extensive and unrelenting, and places him firmly outside of mainstream U.S. political thought." These statements move in the direction of what Horowitz says, but unlike his utterance, they have the characteristic of being true, fair, and restrained— attributes that are utterly lacking in Horowitz's discussion of Chomsky. If that seems unduly harsh, consider this. If Chomsky's writings really are so egregious as to merit his being placed on a list of the most dangerous professors in the country, why is it that Horowitz cannot make that case without exaggerating and distorting Chomsky's work at every turn?

As another example of such distortion, consider this statement: "Professor Chomsky sees the 9/11 attack on the World Trade Center as a turning point in history when the guns that were historically trained on the Third World by imperialist powers like America, have been turned around. And that is a good thing, because in Professor Chomsky's eyes unless American 'hegemony' is destroyed, the world faces a grim future" (TP 88). The reader will not be shocked to learn that Horowitz provides no citation or any other kind of documentation in support of this claim. In fact, in his book on the 9/11 attack Chomsky writes that "nothing can justify crimes such as those of September 11."[61] Horowitz also attributes to Chomsky the view that "on September 11, 2001 the U.S. got what it deserved." Naturally, he provides no citation in support of this fabrication.

Sloppy scholarship abounds. Curious to learn the source of one quotation from Chomsky included in Horowitz's profile, I checked the relevant endnote (note 181, on page 392). Surprisingly, the citation was not to one of Chomsky's own writings. Rather, Horowitz cites an article on Chomsky, by Keith Windschuttle. Upon reading that article, I note that the quotation from Chomsky does indeed appear there, but with no citation giving its source. So, in the end, Horowitz quotes Chomsky without even indirectly telling the reader where (if anywhere) in Chomsky's writings it can be found. Moreover, elsewhere in his essay Windschuttle incorrectly attributes to Chomsky language that appears only in a petition he signed—exactly the same mistake (and with regard to the same words) that Horowitz would go on to make (TP 87), leaving one to wonder whether Horowitz had ever even read the two relevant primary documents (a petition that Chomsky signed but was not written by him and an essay on free speech that he did write), having perhaps instead gotten this information second-hand from Windschuttle. Such suspicions are further fueled by the fact that Windschuttle runs together in one sentence a quotation (containing the phrase "apolitical liberal") that is by Chomsky with another one (containing the phrase "extensive historical research") that is not, exactly as Horowitz would go on to do. (While both Windschuttle and Horowitz are guilty of falsely claiming that both quotations are by Chomsky, only Horowitz compounds this error by falsely claiming that they are from the same essay.) But then again, the final endnote for Horowitz's profile of Chomsky (note 184, on page 392) tells us that this profile was "[a]dapted from Peter Collier's Introduction to *The Anti-Chomsky Reader,*" a book that Collier edited with David Horowitz. Since the Windschuttle essay cited in note 181, page 392, of TP turns out to be a review of that very book, perhaps it is Windschuttle who picked up these errors originally from Collier before passing them on, like a venereal disease, to Horowitz, who, in turn, attempts to pass them on to his readers.

The final profile appearing in TP's main chapter is that of Howard Zinn (358–64). Consistent with his practice in the majority of his portraits, Horowitz says nothing at all about Zinn's performance in the classroom. Nor does he accuse Zinn of "making racist and ethnically disparaging remarks." Nor, finally, does he provide any evidence whatsoever that Zinn had been "promoted far beyond [his] academic achievement," for Zinn's profile confines almost all of its attention to APH, which had been published only after Zinn had already been promoted to full professor. So, once again, Horowitz fails to prove, or even to *attempt* to prove, that any of the "four distinct critiques" that supposedly constitute his indictment of the contemporary American professoriate are even to the slightest degree applicable to him.

For the most part Horowitz's critique of APH confines itself to claims and moves that others have made, and that have been discussed above. For example, he quotes Zinn as saying that his history is "a biased account" (TP 358–9) and that "Objectivity is impossible" (TP 361), but, quite predictably, makes no attempt to explain, or in any way take account of, what Zinn means by these statements. Rather, he leaves the reader with the impression that Zinn is confessing his sins, as opposed to making an argument about history to which any serious critic of his would be obliged to respond. In criticizing Zinn's "admission" of bias, Horowitz seems to have forgotten his own admission that "Every individual, whether conservative or liberal, has a perspective and therefore a bias," so that the obligation of teachers and scholars is not to be unbiased, but rather to refrain from presenting "their biases as though they were scientific facts" (TP xxvi). Not even Horowitz could possibly accuse Zinn of doing that!

Horowitz does advance one entirely original criticism, however. It has to do with Zinn's decision to begin his history of the United States with a chapter on Columbus:

Zinn begins his narrative not with the settling of North America, or the creation of the United States as one might expect, but with a long chapter on Columbus's "genocide" against the native inhabitants, an event—which even if it had happened as Zinn describes it—was an act committed by agents of the Spanish empire more than a century before the English settled North America and nearly three centuries before the creation of the United States, which is also geographically well-removed from the scene of the crime. It is Zinn's unintended way of announcing the tendentiousness of his entire project, which is really not a "history" of the American people, but an indictment of white people and the capitalist system. (TP 359)

Notice that Horowitz's argument assumes that Zinn's decision to discuss Columbus in a history of the United States is an unusual one. Otherwise it would not be the case that "one might expect" a historian to start with a later event, and Zinn's decision would not constitute evidence of "tendentiousness" on his part.

But Zinn's decision is in this regard not unusual at all. It is entirely orthodox. James W. Loewen surveys 18 mainstream, widely-used American history textbooks and analyzes what they say about several standard topics in American history.[62] His first chapter on a particular historical event is, like Zinn's, devoted to Columbus (LMT 31–69). There he informs us that every one of the 18 textbooks he surveyed includes a discussion of Columbus—so much so that "The one date that every schoolchild remembers is 1492" (LMT 32). So while it may be technically true that "one might expect" the writer of a history of the United States to skip Columbus, the only "one" who would do so would be one who shared Horowitz's evident ignorance of the contents of standard U.S. history texts. Zinn's inclusion of Columbus does not in any way indicate the "tendentiousness of his entire project," but Horowitz's bizarre *claim* that it does might with greater plausibility be said to reveal the tendentiousness of *his*.

Another prominent feature of Horowitz's profile is its inclusion of several decontextualized quotations from Zinn. Curious to see how these statements fit into the contexts in which they had originally appeared, I consulted Horowitz's endnotes.

Over and over again Horowitz cites not Zinn's book but secondary sources (TP 419, endnotes 854–62). Turning to these secondary sources, one does indeed find the quotations that Horowitz reproduces but, once again, no information as to where one might find them in Zinn's writings! What possible justification could Horowitz have for this? Why does he not read and cite Zinn directly? Why does he not tell the reader on which page he or she might find each quotation as it appears, so that the accuracy of the quotation, and its surrounding context, might be checked?

This excessive reliance on secondary sources for quotations from the profiled professors is a problem that pervades TP, evidencing the utter lack of seriousness of Horowitz's project. Since many of these secondary sources, like those quoting Zinn, fail to provide citations for their quotations, the reader cannot easily find them. More importantly, this betrays Horowitz's lack of interest in determining whether or not the quotations are accurate, or whether they have been fairly or unfairly removed from their original context. It shows his lack of interest in the arguments and evidence that the profiled professors use to support the conclusions found in the selected quotations. It shows his lack of interest in the ways in which those conclusions might, elsewhere in their original texts, be qualified, clarified, and/or explained. This is why no competent scholar—absolutely none—tries to indict other scholars with quotations drawn from secondary sources.

Horowitz rarely provides evidence or detailed argument to show that the things that Zinn says in the decontextualized quotations from him, drawn from secondary sources, are incorrect, evidently hoping instead that the mere fact of their deviation from the mainstream, generally-accepted version of events will be sufficient to persuade the reader that Zinn is an unhinged extremist. On the rare occasions when Horowitz does offer something of substance, things tend to go badly. For example, he criticizes Zinn for having said that the Sandinistas of Nicaragua (Horowitz calls them "the Marxist dictators of Nicaragua") were "'welcomed' by the people." As evidence for the falsity of Zinn's claim, Horowitz informs us that the opposition Contras "triumphed when free elections were held as a result of U.S. pressure." Similarly, Horowitz rebuts Zinn's description of the Contras as "a terrorist group" by insisting that "In fact, the Contras were the largest peasant army in Latin America's modern history" (TP 361).

While it is true that the Contra-backed candidate prevailed in the 1990 election, Horowitz conveniently leaves out of his account the election of 1984, in which the Sandinista candidate, Daniel Ortega, won. Over 450 international observers, representing delegations from nations, scholarly societies, religious groups, and human rights organizations, monitored the election. They reported that they were allowed to move freely about the country, to talk to anyone with whom they wished to speak, and to observe every aspect of the electoral process, including the casting and counting of votes. The consensus of these observers was that the election, while not entirely free of problems and irregularities (things such as the Sandinistas abusing their incumbency by occasionally using a government truck to transport supporters to a rally), qualified as free and fair. Indeed, it was judged to be far superior in fairness and legitimacy to any previous election in Nicaragua or in the region generally, and to compare favorably to U.S. elections, which also always contain some irregularities. (The international observers concluded that abuses were minor and few, and in no way cast doubt on the legitimacy of the outcome.) Significantly, the Sandinista government set in place a proportional representation system, rather than a U.S.-style winner-take-all system, for elections to the legislature. This afforded their opponents greater representation (36.5% of the seats) in the National Assembly than they otherwise would have had. All six of the presidential candidates defeated by Ortega were also granted seats.[63] This is not how dictators behave. Nor do dictators peacefully abandon office when they are defeated in an election, as Ortega did in 1990.

While it perhaps occurred too late to be included in Horowitz's book (published in 2006), it must have been a great disappointment to him that the Sandinistas won the election of 2006, returning Daniel Ortega to power as President.

Horowitz's denial that the Contras were terrorists coincides with U.S. propaganda but flies in the face of the findings of human rights monitoring organizations. For example, a 1989 study by Human Rights Watch concluded that "[The] contras were major and systematic violators of the most basic standards of the laws of armed conflict, including by launching indiscriminate attacks on civilians, selectively murdering non-combatants, and mistreating prisoners."[64] And Americas Watch, in a 1992 report, concluded that the Contras were guilty of targeting health care clinics and health care workers for assassination; kidnapping, torturing, and executing civilians, including children; raping women; seizing civilian property; and burning civilian houses in captured towns.[65] In an affidavit to the World Court, Edgar Chamorro, a former colonel with the Contras, testified that "The CIA did not discourage such tactics.... We were told that the only way to defeat the Sandinistas was to use the tactics the agency [the CIA] attributed to Communist insurgencies elsewhere: kill, kidnap, rob and torture.... Many civilians were killed in cold blood. Many others were tortured, mutilated, raped, robbed, or otherwise abused.... When I agreed to join...I had hoped that it would be an organization of Nicaraguans.... It turned out to be an instrument of the U.S. government."[66] Zinn quotes some of this testimony (APH 585). Horowitz ignores it, along with every other item in the mountainous pile of evidence that proves conclusively that the Contras were terrorists.

Horowitz, that notorious stickler for factual accuracy, tells us that "Professor Zinn's text abounds in factual inaccuracies."

Given Horowitz's eagerness to trash Zinn, one would expect him to go on to provide a long list of Zinn's factual errors. Instead, he says only this: "George Washington, for example, was not 'the richest American' at the time of the revolution, nor did unemployment grow during the Reagan years" (TP 363). After providing these two examples, Horowitz abruptly drops the subject (what?—were there no errors in Zinn's account of the events taking place during the administrations of John Adams, Thomas Jefferson, James Madison, and so forth, all the way up through the Jimmy Carter years?), proceeding instead, in the very next sentence, to criticize Zinn's choices of what topics to include in or exclude from his narrative (a very different matter).

Oh well, let's look at his two examples. But before doing so, it might be instructive to consider Horowitz's behavior when he is confronted with his own propensity for factual errors. In an email interview with Scott Jaschik, he says that the only mistakes he had seen in his work were "trivial and normal to a book of this size and do not affect in the slightest the argument I have made."[67] One of his mistakes was identified by the historian Eric Foner, one of Horowitz's "101 most dangerous academics." In an email to reporter Alec Magnet, Foner reported that "Mr. Horowitz's 'chapter' on me is full of errors, beginning with the long quote with which he opens, which was written by someone else, not me. This is a fair example of the reliability of his work."[68] When the "Facts Count" report included a mention of this error, Horowitz responded (as quoted in Laksin) as follows: "The article is correct about the error. The question is how did it happen and how does it affect the validity of the profile of Foner in my book. As I pointed out in the introduction to *The Professors*, the 101 profiles were the work of thirty researchers. In these circumstances, juxtaposing a quote—which is clearly what happened—is not too difficult a possibility to imagine. The Foner quote and the [erroneous] quote appeared in sequence on a page in the *London Review of Books* which was referenced in *The*

Professors, and during the many revisions of the manuscript that's how the error was made." Horowitz then supplies the correct quotation and asserts that it serves the purposes of his critique of Foner just as well, and perhaps better, than the erroneous quotation did. He then concludes: "In other words, the error in my book is an inconsequential one and does not affect the accuracy of its portrait of Professor Foner. Readers can judge themselves whether this is a reason for dismissing my work as Foner advises. And they can judge his honesty by the same measure."

Horowitz took a similar tack when, during a hearing in Pennsylvania on his proposed "Academic Bill of Rights," he had to admit, as Scott Jaschik reports, "that he had no evidence to back up two of the stories he has told multiple times to back up his charges that political bias is rampant in higher education. In an interview after the hearing, Horowitz said that his acknowledgements were inconsequential, and he complained about 'nit picking' by his critics." One of these stories, which he had repeated several times, claimed that "a biology professor at Pennsylvania State University used a class session just before the 2004 election to show the Michael Moore documentary *Fahrenheit 9/11.*" But Horowitz acknowledged at the hearing

> that he didn't have any proof that this took place.
>
> In a phone interview, Horowitz said that he had heard about the alleged incident from a legislative staffer and that there was no evidence to back up the claim. He added, however, that "everybody who is familiar with universities knows that there is a widespread practice of professors venting about foreign policy even when their classes aren't about foreign policy" and that the lack of evidence on Penn State doesn't mean there isn't a problem.
>
> "These are nit picking, irrelevant attacks," he said.
>
> Others think that it's quite relevant that Horowitz couldn't

back up the example, especially since there have been previous incidents in which his claims about professors have been debunked.

"So much of what he has said previously has been exposed to be lies or distortions that it makes any of his examples questionable," said Jamie Horwitz, a spokesman for the American Federation of Teachers....

The other example Horowitz was forced to back down on Tuesday is from the opposite end of the political spectrum. He has several times cited the example of a student in California who supports abortion rights and who said that he was punished with a low grade by a professor who opposed abortion. Asked about this example, Horowitz said that he had no evidence to back up the student's claim.

In the interview, he said that he didn't have the resources to look into all the complaints that he publicizes. "I can't investigate every story," he said....

Even if these examples aren't correct, he said, they represent the reality of academic life. "Is there anybody out there who will say that professors don't attack Bush in biology classrooms?" he said. Horowitz characterized the debate over his retractions as a diversionary tactic by his critics. "First they say that there is no problem [with political bias]. Then they say I'm a McCarthyite. Then they say I'm spreading false rumors. Everyone who is in public life and makes commentaries makes mistakes."[69]

To comment on these statements, in reverse order, it should be noted, first, that while it may be true that "everyone who is in public life and makes commentaries makes mistakes," it is not true that everyone, or hardly anyone besides Horowitz, makes these *kinds* of mistakes—attempting to pass legislation based on unverified and untrue stories; publicly labeling someone one of the "101 most dangerous academics in America" based on a quotation from someone else that he falsely attributed to him; publicly saying that another scholar's books are "almost completely worthless" based on a comically error-laden characterization of just one of them; and so on, and so forth.

Second, a failure to produce a single example of a pattern of conduct that one claims to be common cannot be overcome by claiming that "everybody knows" that things like that are going on. It isn't hard to imagine what Horowitz would have said had Howard Zinn advanced such a pathetic face-saving rationalization for an error of his.

Third, with regard to Horowitz's explanation that he "can't investigate every story" and doesn't have the resources to look into all the complaints that he publicizes, the obvious response is that he should not publicize such cases. Again, imagine Horowitz's response if Zinn were to "explain" a false or unsubstantiated statement of his by pleading that he hadn't had the time or resources to verify it before publishing it.

Fourth, as to the quotation wrongly attributed to Foner, while it is one thing for Horowitz to explain that this was a mistake rather than a deliberate fabrication (and given Horowitz's obvious sloppiness and incompetence I'm inclined to take his word on that), surely a minimally decent person would recognize a need to apologize for the mistake, to at least say something like, "I regret the error." Horowitz does not do so.

Fifth, this mistake is directly attributable to Horowitz's absurd practice, in which he engages repeatedly in TP, of presuming to pass judgment on a scholar based solely on decontextualized quotations drawn from secondary sources. To understand a quotation, and thus to be in a position to evaluate it fairly, one needs to know how it fits into the larger work in which it appears. The material preceding and following the quoted words often clarifies the author's intent, explains the meaning of ambiguous or technical terms, modifies a thesis that might be stated more boldly in the quoted passage, answers anticipated objections, or, in myriad other ways, helps the reader to achieve a more accurate grasp of the meaning of the quoted passage. Moreover, the practice of consulting the source in which a quotation originally appeared, and of situating the quotation within that context, should also make it more difficult to confuse one author with another. Whereas it might be easy to mix up different quotations by different authors when these are ripped from the connective tissue that enhances their coherence and instead presented adjacent to one another in a work by someone else, an effort to grasp the meaning of the quotations by situating them within the context of their authors' work should preclude such confusion. The attempt to find the non-Foner quotation in Foner's work will fail, as will the attempt to make sense of it in the light of the other things that Foner says. It is precisely Horowitz's lack of interest in achieving an in-depth understanding of his opponents' work that allows him to make such mistakes. For his purposes, one terse, decontextualized, left-wing "unpatriotic" quotation is interchangeable with another.

Sixth, it is Horowitz's name—and Horowitz's alone—that appears on the cover of his book. It is his responsibility, not that of the thirty "researchers" assisting him, to make sure that his book's nasty accusations are based on accurate information. But there is something in Horowitz's pitiable attempt to cast blame on his research assistants that renders it especially pathetic in this case. Each profile in TP ends with a citation crediting someone for the "research" on that profile. For example, the research credit for the essay on Matthew Evangelista is awarded to Jacob Laksin (TP 159), whom we have encountered before. But who is credited for the "research" for the profile of Eric Foner? The answer: David Horowitz (TP 179).

Finally, with regard to Horowitz's general comment on how his errors are to be evaluated, he clearly is saying that factual errors should not be considered important if (a) they are few in number, relative to the size of the work in which they appear, and

(b) they do not significantly affect the overall argument being made in that work. Let's see whether he remains consistent, and applies those same standards to the factual errors of those he criticizes, such as Howard Zinn, as any honest, ethically principled person would do, or whether he will jettison those standards whenever it suits his ideological agenda to do so.

Returning now to Zinn's alleged factual errors, recall that the first one had to do with George Washington's wealth, more specifically Zinn's claim that he was "the richest American" at the time of the revolution. Is this indeed an error? The evidence appears to be uncertain. Zinn's source for this claim is the book *Out of Our Past*, by Carl Degler, a Pulitzer Prize-winning Stanford University history professor, so highly regarded by his peers that he was elected President of both the American Historical Association and the Organization of American Historians.[70] Richard Brookhiser, an author, senior editor of the conservative magazine *National Review*, and former speechwriter for George H.W. Bush, also concurs that Washington was "America's richest man."[71] But Andrew G. Gardner, while conceding that some consider Washington to be the richest American of all time, lists him as just the second-richest colonial American (and just the fifty-ninth richest American of all time, though he does rank him as the richest U.S. president).[72] Other writers decline to assign Washington a specific ranking, though all agree he was fantastically wealthy, both at the time of the revolution and subsequently. So if Zinn missed with this one, he did not miss by much.

Moreover, if Horowitz were to apply his principles consistently, he would have to agree that this error (if, indeed, it is one) does not merit criticism. For one thing, it is one of only two errors that Horowitz identifies in Zinn's 688-page text. More importantly, it does not undermine the point he was making when he made the (possibly) erroneous claim—which was simply that most of the leaders of the American revolution were wealthy (APH 85). Obviously it makes no difference to the assessment of the cogency of this point whether Washington was at the time the single wealthiest American, or whether he was, instead, merely the second, or third, or hundredth.

With regard to Zinn's second alleged factual error, having to do with unemployment under Reagan, I think it would be fairer and more accurate to say that Zinn's claim is unclear and imprecise than that it is simply wrong. Unemployment rates can be measured in several ways. One is the "snapshot" method, which is to determine how many people are unemployed right now. But another method, and perhaps a more meaningful one if one wishes to know how many people have been negatively affected by unemployment, is to ask how many people have been unemployed during some more extended period of time. Suppose, for example, that one person has been employed at a given job from January through June, but then loses that job and is unemployed for the rest of the year. Suppose, further, that the person who then takes over the job in question is someone who had been unemployed from January through June. By the snapshot method, no matter what time of year the survey is conducted, just one of these two is unemployed. But if the question is how many of these two have been unemployed for a significant period of time during the past year, the answer is two, not one. It may be that this is the measure to which Zinn was referring, because his one sentence in which he elaborates on his claim that "unemployment grew in the Reagan years" is this (and it immediately follows the sentence just quoted): "In the year 1982, 30 million people were unemployed all or part of the year" (APH 578).

Another ambiguity in Zinn's claim is this. He might be referring to the change in the unemployment rate from when Reagan first took office to when he left office, at the end of his second term. If that is what he meant, then Zinn is, indeed, wrong. The snapshot unemployment rate was 7.5% when he took office, and 5.4% when he left. But the unemployment rate fluctuated widely during Reagan's time in office (it rose as high as 10.8% at one point), as it does during most administrations. Thus, another approach is to ask what the average unemployment rate was during a given administration. Did it go down, relative to the average of the preceding administration, or did it go up? By that measure, Zinn's claim is correct. The average unemployment rate during the Reagan years was 7.54%, an increase from Carter's 6.54% average.[73]

In any case, given his own lackluster performance with regard to factual accuracy, and his failure to criticize conservatives for their factual errors, it is evident that Horowitz's real complaint, despite his protestations to the contrary, is that there are professors who have political views of which he disapproves. Indeed, the utter lack of seriousness of Horowitz's entire project is indicated by the fact that none of his profiled "dangerous" professors are right-wingers. But in fairness to him, he does offer an explanation for this: "I don't know of any conservatives who use the classroom for political agendas."[74] Yes, absolutely. Who could possibly find that explanation unconvincing?[75]

Michael Kazin

Kazin is a Professor of History at Georgetown University and co-editor of *Dissent* magazine. He is one of the figures cited on the list of Zinn critics that Mitch Daniels made available to interested parties on request. He is represented on that list as follows:

"*A People's History* is bad history, albeit gilded with virtuous intentions. Zinn reduces the past to a Manichean fable and makes no serious attempt to address the biggest question a leftist can ask about U.S. history: why have most Americans accepted the legitimacy of the capitalist republic in which they live? His failure is grounded in a premise better suited to a conspiracy-monger's Web site than to a work of scholarship." Michael Kazin, socialist historian.

Let's address these criticisms in order. "Manichean" is a derogatory term for a simplistic philosophy according to which the world is divided, in a clear, uncomplicated way, between good and evil. Kazin's point is that history is messy, and that flesh-and-blood historical actors have complex, often contradictory motives. As he sees it, Zinn implicitly denies this complexity, presenting history as a struggle between cartoonish, single-minded good guys and bad guys. To illustrate this claim, Kazin offers this criticism of Zinn's treatment of World War II: "Zinn thins the meaning of the biggest war in history down to its meanest components: profits for military industries, racism toward the Japanese, and the senseless destruction of enemy cities—from Dresden to Hiroshima.... [T]he idea that Franklin Roosevelt and his aides were motivated both by realpolitik and by an abhorrence of fascism seems not to occur to him" (KAZ).

This criticism is open to several objections. First, it simply isn't true that it "seemed not to occur to Zinn" that "Franklin Roosevelt and his aides were motivated both by realpolitik and by an abhorrence of fascism." When a writer explicitly names a thesis, and mounts an argument against it, that means that the thesis has indeed "occurred to" him or her. And a good portion of Chapter 16 of APH, and especially pages 408–10, are directed against the thesis that Kazin names. (The main thrust of Zinn's argument is that, while many of the actions of the United States, before, during, and after World War II, were fully consistent both with realpolitik and an abhorrence of fascism, there are also a great many that are consistent only with the first and not the second—and few, if any, in which the former interest was sacrificed for the sake of the latter.)

Second, Kazin, like so many others of Zinn's critics, systematically ignores (and denies) the complexities and nuances that are present in his text. For example, in the passage just cited, Zinn refers to the Roosevelt administration as "a government whose main interest was not stopping Fascism but advancing the imperial interests of the United States" (APH 410). Notice that in referring to a "main interest" Zinn is clearly acknowledging the possibility of having more than one interest. (Once again, this is not a possibility that "seemed not to occur to him.") Or again, he says of Roosevelt that his "priority in policy (whatever [his] personal compassion for victims of persecution) was not minority rights, but national power" (APH 410). So of course Zinn recognizes that Roosevelt may have abhorred fascism, and may have had compassion for its victims. But it does not follow from this that his policies would necessarily be dictated by those attitudes. This distinction between Roosevelt's personal feelings and his priority in policy is illustrative of a degree of subtlety in Zinn's discussion of this issue that is entirely lacking in Kazin's critique of that discussion.[76] Here Kazin exhibits a common pattern—a critic accuses Zinn of producing a crude, simplistic caricature of American history; but in making that case, it becomes clear that it is itself based on a crude, simplistic caricature of Zinn's work.[77]

Third, while Kazin is obviously right to hold that many issues in history are complicated and messy, so that the truth about them is far from clear, and there is plenty of room for reasonable debate and disagreement with respect to them (and no place whatsoever for certainty), it should also be pointed out that not everything is like that. In some cases, the evidence points overwhelmingly in one direction. That is the case, or so it seems to me, with many of Zinn's claims that critics find objectionable (for example, that the wealthy and the poor often have quite different interests; that the rich and powerful tend to act to promote their own interests, rather than those of the poor or powerless, or those of the nation or the world in general; that U.S. foreign policy is not guided by concerns about human rights; that the U.S. is by far the most militarily aggressive nation in the world; that it kills far more innocent civilians than does any other country; and that it is a rogue, outlaw nation that routinely violates international law and its own treaty commitments). But if these are indeed evident truths, why do historians reject them (or, at least, insist on qualifying and "complicating" them)?

The answer, I suspect, has to do with the ideological nature of the discipline of history, in comparison, say, to mathematics, or geology, or meteorology. While no one has any motive, in general, to fudge the truth about numbers, or rocks, or clouds, or the behavior of gasses, that is not at all the case when it comes to the behavior of U.S. presidents and other national leaders. So all of us, from childhood on, are relentlessly subjected to patriotic propaganda, from teachers, textbooks, the corporate media, and the general culture. How else to explain the fact that Columbus Day is a national holiday? To give just one example of the repression of official U.S. misconduct in mainstream U.S. culture, Edward S. Herman and Noam Chomsky report that "Of 522 articles in the *New York Times*, the *Washington Post*, the *Los Angeles Times*, *Newsweek*, and *Time* during the 1990s that mentioned Agent Orange and Vietnam together, the vast majority focused on the harm done to U.S. service personnel; only nine articles acknowledged the targeting of food crops…; only eleven discussed in any detail the impact on Vietnamese and the Vietnamese environment; only three characterized the use of Agent Orange as a 'chemical weapon' or 'chemical warfare;' and in only two articles was it suggested that its use might constitute a war crime" (MC xxxi–xxxii). It is in this ideological environment that the vast majority of Americans form their ideas about U.S. history.[78]

Then, on top of this, the issue of personal interest as a factor in the choice of career must be considered. Those who choose to pursue a career as a scholar tend to be those who are deeply interested in, indeed, fascinated by, the subject matter of their academic specialty. Mathematicians love numbers; astronomers love planets and stars; ichthyologists love fish; and so on. Historians love history. And history, as it has traditionally been written and taught, emphasizes the exploits of the powerful, and interprets those exploits benignly. Now, professors of American history will obviously tend to be much too well informed about the details of historical events to be able to gulp down the ubiquitous patriotic propaganda uncritically. But at the same time, it seems to me likely that, through the process of career self-selection, they will tend to be people who at least initially had been inclined to respond positively to the great heroes of traditional historical accounts—the Founding Fathers, the presidents on Mount Rushmore, the famous Supreme Court justices, and so forth. To find history interesting, at least as it is presented when one is young, one must be fascinated by questions of why this president made this decision, and that president made that one— where at least some of these decisions are taken to be both wise and well motivated. Someone temperamentally and ideologically well prepared to recognize dark and ugly truths about the whole lot of them would likely not be the sort of person who would find the subject matter sufficiently attractive as to want to pursue it professionally.[79] So the typical professional historian, I speculate, is too knowledgeable to accept an uncritically triumphalist account of American history, but also at the same time temperamentally and ideologically predisposed to reject an account that is as harshly critical of U.S. elites as is Zinn's. What is the solution? To see American history as complex, many-sided, and even paradoxical—perhaps, at least in some respects, such as those concerning the motives of U.S. foreign policy, much more so than it really is. Reinforcing this "complexity bias" is the expectation that scholars, in general, should traffic in "complicated" theories, inaccessible to untrained lay persons, and that, in the ideological disciplines, "objectivity" demands a balanced, many-sided position. But notice that these are non-epistemic, non-evidentiary reasons to hold a position. They are, in short, factors that produce and sustain a "bias" against views like Zinn's, irrespective of the evidence.[80]

Finally, let me point out that, while it is generally true that people tend to oversimplify things much more often than they overcomplicate them, it is not as if the latter never happens. Nor is it true that the more complicated theory is always the better theory. There is a principle, widely accepted in both philosophy and in science, called Occam's razor, or the principle of parsimony. It states that of two competing hypotheses which equally well explain a set of facts or data, one should prefer, all else equal, the simpler hypothesis, the more straightforward one, the one requiring fewer assumptions (especially extravagant ones). So if the facts of U.S. foreign policy are equally well explained by these hypotheses: (a) the U.S. cares very little about human rights, international law, treaty obligations, civilian deaths, honesty, or morality in its foreign policy actions; or (b) the U.S. cares about these things deeply, in fact more so than any other nation does, because we are better, more moral, more lawful, more decent, more honest, than anyone else—but our 397,468 deviations from these principles have been caused by these 493 different factors in different cases—parsimony would suggest that the simpler hypothesis (a) should be adopted.[81] Zinn argues for (a). His critics, Kazin included, ignore those arguments and content themselves with reporting (in overly simplified terms) his conclusions, and then pointing out their relative lack of complexity, sophistication, and balance.

Let's move on to Kazin's second criticism—that Zinn "makes no serious attempt to address the biggest question a leftist can ask about U.S. history: why have most Americans accepted the legitimacy of the capitalist republic in which they live?" Zinn, in a brief (less than one page long) response to Kazin's article, published in *Dissent*'s "Letters" section, essentially concedes the point, offering as an explanation that he did not see it as part of his project to deal with "theoretical" questions of that sort in his history, however interesting and important they might be. In an even briefer (just one modest paragraph) reply to Zinn's letter, Kazin addresses Zinn's explanation by asking a rhetorical question: "Shouldn't a 'people's history' concern itself with what most Americans actually thought?"[82]

Well, let's consider what a text on American history might be expected to cover. Surely it would tell us about important events, that is (a) what people did. We have a good deal of evidence about what happened, what took place, what actions people took, and any chronicle of history will deal primarily with that. While we do not have quite the same access to (b) what people thought, we do have some evidence on this. We have the books, articles, letters, diaries, and speeches of many individuals who are regarded in traditional textbooks as major historical figures, and also those of many artists, poets, labor organizers, activists, and others who are elevated to prominence in APH. Indeed, APH, fully in keeping with Kazin's charge that it should "concern itself with what most Americans actually thought," devotes a great deal of its coverage, and far more so than is the case with more traditional texts, to this topic. Zinn's book is studded with quotations from Americans of all walks of life. Moreover, he frequently takes up the topic of public opinion on important events in American history as they are unfolding (recall, for example, the discussion, analyzed in the section on Wineburg above, about American attitudes toward World War II). But the question of (b) *what* people thought, is very different from the question of (c) *why* they thought it, and it is remarkable that Kazin, in his brief reply to Zinn, conflates the two. In replying to Zinn's admission that he had not said much about (c), Kazin's response was to insist that he should have addressed (b)—which in fact he had done, and which Kazin had not originally even claimed that he had not done. It is noteworthy that while people generally know (b) what they think, and are able to communicate this content to us in their own words, the question (c) of why they have the thoughts and attitudes that they do is far less accessible, both to them and to us. Undoubtedly biological, psychological, socio-logical, and economic factors all play a role—but in a way that is murky and controversial, calling for a good deal of theorizing. Perhaps this is why American history textbooks generally avoid the topic. Accordingly, I ask the reader a rhetorical question of my own. Have you ever encountered, aside from Kazin's critique of Zinn, a criticism of an American history text for failing to discuss adequately the attitudes of ordinary Americans regarding capitalism? That Mitch Daniels would include in his press release a quotation containing this particular criticism of Zinn strongly suggests, once again (as in the case of his Genovese quotation, discussed above), that he is simply casting about for any critical remarks he can find, not particularly caring whether they are accurate or make much sense. Or are we really to think that Daniels is himself troubled by Zinn's failure to address the question of the causes of ordinary Americans' attitudes about capitalism, such that had Zinn made a brilliant and thorough contribution to that topic Daniels would have taken a more favorable view of his book?

But having said this, Stuart Easterling makes a strong case that in APH Zinn actually did (his modest denial to the contrary notwithstanding) analyze the question of why so many Americans have accepted the legitimacy of the capitalist republic in which they live, and did so far more persuasively than Kazin did in his critical essay on Zinn. Before getting to Zinn's answer, Easterling comments that "anyone who has lived, worked, organized among or been in the camp of oppressed people knows that they have a range of common sense answers to this question. Zinn—having been born into an immigrant Jewish working-class family, worked in blue-collar jobs during the Depression, and been a soldier, a teacher, and an activist—was exposed to this question countless times in his life. In short, Zinn likely understands consent far better than the historians who criticize him" (EAS).

As for Zinn's answer, Easterling tells us that:

He emphasizes a range of factors, including the effects of the ideology of the oppressor (in the news media, for example), the use of violence and repression by the oppressor, forcing the oppressed to compete for scarce resources, the oppressor's control of the main available political alternatives (that is, Democrats and Republicans), and the oppressor's knack for "dispersing [their] controls" and giving the oppressed "small rewards" for maintaining the organizations and institutions that help perpetuate oppression.

It turns out that these, taken together, can be powerful mechanisms to help produce consent. Every chapter in *A People's History* talks both about how the oppressed struggle against their oppressors, and also the ways the oppressors use these various means to try to counter these struggles, or keep them from emerging or re-emerging.[83]

The final criticism mentioned in the Kazin quotation that began this section is that Zinn is a conspiracy theorist, someone whose ideas are "better suited to a conspiracy-monger's Web site than to a work of scholarship." Immediately after making this claim Kazin attempts to support it by citing three quotations from APH (I have labeled them and added the page numbers for them, which Kazin fails to provide):

(a) According to Zinn, "99 percent" of Americans share a "commonality" that is profoundly at odds with the interests of their rulers. And knowledge of that awesome fact is "exactly what the governments of the United States, and the wealthy elite allied to them—from the Founding Fathers to now—have tried their best to prevent." (632)

(b) [Zinn] describes the American Revolution as a clever device to defeat "potential rebellions and create a consensus of popular support for the rule of a new, privileged leadership." (59)

(c) His Civil War was another elaborate confidence game. Soldiers who fought to preserve the Union got duped by "an aura of moral crusade" against slavery that "worked effectively to dim class resentments against the rich and powerful, and turn much of the anger against 'the enemy.'" (237)

In his response to Kazin, Zinn rejects the charge that he is a conspiracy theorist:

That's not in my book. In dealing with the American Revolution I write: "... by the 1760's this local leadership [that is, the colonial elite] saw the possibility of directing much of the rebellious energy against England and her local officials. It was not a conscious conspiracy, but an accumulation of tactical responses" (59). At another point in the book I talk not about conspiracy but about "the natural selection of accidents" (LET 357).

Who is right? In order to answer this question, let's begin by noting that a conspiracy is "a secret plan by a group to do something unlawful or harmful." Synonyms for "conspiracy" include "ploy," "scheme," "machination," "trick," "ruse," and "subterfuge."

Next, notice that while none of these terms appears in any of the three quotations that Kazin cites, Zinn does use the word "conspiracy" in one of the passages that he quotes—and does so precisely in order to deny that a particular group of actions undertaken by several individuals at roughly the same time had resulted from a conspiracy. The words in the cited passages that come somewhat close in meaning to "conspiracy" or its synonyms listed above, namely, "clever device" and "duped," come from Kazin's paraphrases of Zinn, rather than from Zinn himself.

Moreover, in the case of the latter two of the three quotations that Kazin presents, he omits material preceding the quoted words that would, if they were to be included, speak against his "conspiracy theory" interpretation. Putting some of Zinn's words back in, we get:

(b) They [the Founding Fathers] found that by creating a nation, a symbol, a legal unity called the United States, they could take over land, profits, and political power from favorites of the British Empire. In the process, they could hold back a number of potential rebellions and create a consensus of popular support for the rule of a new, privileged leadership. (59)

(c) 600,000 had volunteered for the Confederacy in 1861, and many in the Union army were volunteers. The psychology of patriotism, the lure of adventure, the aura of moral crusade created by political leaders, worked effectively to dim class resentments against the rich and powerful, and turn much of the anger against "the enemy." (237)

The language in (b) suggests that the effect of "holding back a number of potential rebellions and creating a consensus of popular support for the rule of a new, privileged leadership" was not one that was consciously sought, but rather something that was "found," that is, discovered, "in the process" of doing something else—creating a new nation. And the context of (c) is not that of discussing the motives, or tactics, or strategies of "political leaders," but rather that of explaining why so many young non-rich men volunteered to fight in the Civil War. Only one of the three factors cited ("the aura of moral crusade," but not "the psychology of patriotism" or "the lure of adventure") is attributed to the actions of political leaders. Moreover, we are not told that the one that they did create was brought about for that purpose. Nor, finally, are we told that it was brought about by planned, coordinated action.

In Zinn's response to Kazin on this point, quoted above, he explains, albeit extremely briefly, that the mere fact that a number of individuals behave in a similar manner does not imply that they are involved in a conspiracy. The fact of their shared interests is often perfectly adequate to explain their behavior. For example, those who own for-profit businesses have an economic interest in keeping labor costs down. Consequently, they tend overwhelmingly to oppose any proposal to raise the federal minimum wage. They need not get together in secret for the purpose of deliberating about what common stand to take on this issue. Instead, each owner simply pursues his or her own interest, and the result is a series of actions against such a proposal, an "accumulation of tactical responses," that might have the outward appearance of having been planned and coordinated, even though it was not.

Zinn's reference to "the natural selection of accidents," a term borrowed from evolutionary theory, helps him to make a different anti-conspiracy theory point. Whereas the "accumu-lation of tactical responses" concept explains how the appearance of planned collective purposive action might really be the result of the uncoordinated purposive actions of several individuals who share an interest in common, the "natural selection of accidents" concept explains how certain seemingly intended effects can be brought about and perpetuated without having been intended at all. The basic point is that actions typically have multiple effects, some directly intended, others not even antici-pated. When the unanticipated consequences are bad, from the standpoint of those who brought them about, then those individuals will tend to change their conduct in an effort to bring about whatever good effects they were originally trying to cause but without the bad side effects. But if the unanticipated conse-quences are good, this "reinforces" the conduct in question. In this way, some "accidents" (unintended consequences of actions) are favored, while others are eliminated.

Consider, for example, the way in which, when political ideas are discussed on commercial television, the time constraints of the medium favor mainstream, consensus opinions. The reason is that whereas one need not provide background, context, evidence, arguments, or responses to objections when one is mouthing platitudes that are widely accepted, all of these things are required in great abundance if one is to make a case for a radical view that challenges conventional wisdom. As a result, the mainstream idea can be stated in the extremely brief amount of time allotted each speaker, while the radical idea cannot. Similarly, while the incessant commercial interruptions will undermine the coherence of the radical's necessarily long, involved presentation of strange (and initially implausible) ideas, the familiarity and widespread acceptance of the mainstream thinker's ideas eliminates the need for detailed argument, and guarantees that interruptions will not hinder the audience's comprehension. Now, while both the insistence on brevity (done to cater to the short attention span of a large segment of the audience, who can turn to another channel with a flick of the remote) and the constant intrusion of commercials (the source of the program's income) are consciously enacted policies, brought about for clearly intended economic reasons, it seems unlikely that the reinforcement of mainstream views against radical criticisms that would undermine them was even one of the anticipated, let alone intended, effects of such policies. And it is also possible that many network executives and producers of such shows have never even realized that this is one of the effects of those policies. But since it is, from their point of view, a good effect, the fact that it is brought about (whether this is noticed or not) gives them no motive to change the policies. But on the other hand, if, for some strange reason, these policies had the opposite effect, for example that of facilitating the presentation of criticisms of capitalism, one could bet that the result would be a sustained effort to moderate those policies in such a way as to eliminate, or at least ameliorate, that effect. In this way, television executives maintain policies that reinforce certain views and undermine others, and do so, in a sense, in part for that reason, even if they are completely unaware of the connection between those policies and that effect. This is an example of "the natural selection of accidents."

Thus, since (1) there are no passages in APH which explicitly invoke conspiracy as an explanation of events (and Kazin provides none), (2) Zinn himself denies that he regards the events and structures that he describes as having resulted from conspiracy, (3) he points out passages in APH in which he rejects conspiracy theories in favor of other kinds of explanations, and (4) he explains some of the mechanisms by which actions bearing the outward appearance of being planned and coordinated for a specific effect can occur without any such planning and coordination, I conclude that Kazin's "conspiracy theorist" criticism should be rejected.

As a final point on this issue, it should be noted that the rejection of conspiracy as an explanation for historical events is a persistent theme in Zinn's work, both in APH and in works preceding and succeeding it (and, as I can personally testify, in his teaching, as I recall discussions in his classes at Boston University in the 1970s on "the natural selection of accidents"). Thus, in his reply to Kazin, Zinn could easily have provided many more quotations from APH than he did (given the brevity of his letter, and of Kazin's reply to it, I suspect that he was operating within tight space limitations). For example, he could have quoted this:

> The two-party system came into its own in this time. To give people a choice between two different parties and allow them, in a period of rebellion, to choose the slightly more democratic

one was an ingenious mode of control. *Like so much in the American system, it was not devilishly contrived by some master plotters*; it developed naturally out of the needs of the situation. (APH 217, emphasis added)

Or this:

The severe depression that began in 1893 strengthened an idea developing within the political and financial elite of the country: that overseas markets for American goods might relieve the problem of underconsumption at home and prevent the economic crises that in the 1890s brought class war.

And would not a foreign adventure deflect some of the rebellious energy that went into strikes and protest movements toward an external enemy? Would it not unite people with government, with the armed forces, instead of against them? *This was probably not a conscious plan among most of the elite* — but a natural development from the twin drives of capitalism and nationalism. (APH 297, emphasis added)

To show that this was also his view long before the publication of APH, he could have quoted this:

There is the Establishment of political power and corporate wealth, whose interest is that the universities produce people who will fit into existing niches in the social structure rather than try to change the structure.... There is the interest of the educational bureaucracy in maintaining itself: its endowment, its buildings, its positions (both honorific and material), its steady growth along orthodox lines. These larger interests are internalized in the motivations of the scholar: promotion, tenure, higher salaries, prestige — all of which are best secured by innovating in prescribed directions.

All of these interests operate, *not through any conspiratorial decision* but through the mechanism of a well-oiled system, just as the irrationality of the economic system operates not through any devilish plot but through the mechanism of the profit motive and the market, and as the same kinds of political decisions reproduce themselves in Congress year after year.

No one *intends* exactly what happens. (UOS; ZR 503; OH 182; POH 9 [emphasis added])

Or this:

[S]hall we look beyond blame? In that case, we might see a similarity in behavior among the privileged (and their followers) in all times, all countries: the willingness to kill for a great principle—the word "principle" a euphemism for keeping the fruits of the earth divided according to present rules. Then, *we might see that the killing is not the result of an elitist conspiracy, but of a social structure larger than the consciousness of any of its parts.*[84]

And to show that this remained his view well after APH, he could have cited this (published before Kazin published his criticism):

The dominance of [ideas that constitute an American ideology] *is not the product of a conspiratorial group that has devilishly plotted to implant on society a particular point of view.* Nor is it an accident, an innocent result of people thinking freely. There is a process of natural...selection, in which certain orthodox ideas are encouraged, financed, and pushed forward by the most powerful mechanisms of our culture. These ideas are preferred because they are safe; they don't threaten established wealth or power.[85]

Or this (also published before Kazin published his criticism):

> *You don't have to conspire to have bad history,* inadequate history, history from the top down. All you have to do is play it safe, and that's the rule. I guess it's the American rule, generally, for professionals. Play it safe. And so historians, most of them, play it safe. They don't want to say anything which might raise an eyebrow anywhere. The same is true of heads of departments and administrators at colleges and universities. So we get a lot of safe history.[86]

Or this:

> I had to...ask myself, "How come none of this [the Lawrence textile strike of 1912, the Colorado coal strike of 1913–14, and the Ludlow massacre] was told to me? How come the name Mother Jones never appeared in any of my history books or courses? How come Emma Goldman never appeared in any of my courses? None of this."
>
> So I wanted to teach and write about that which I thought had been neglected. I began to think there was a reason for neglecting that. *Again, not a reason that seven people gathered in a room to plan, but a reason that comes out of the normal workings of a society, of an economic and social and political system in which power and wealth are concentrated at the top.* (REE 107, emphasis added)[87]

One more point about Daniels's use of Kazin should be mentioned. Recall that Daniels goes out of his way to refer to Kazin as a "socialist historian," that he titles his document listing anti-Zinn quotations, "Criticism of Howard Zinn and his work crosses ideological lines," and that he does these things in order to support his repeatedly made point that even Zinn's fellow leftists reject his historical scholarship. In response, let me reiterate a point made in the discussion of Genovese above—that people on the same side of the left/right divide often nonetheless disagree with one another passionately on significant political issues. Well, Kazin and Zinn clearly disagree in their attitudes toward the Democratic Party. Whereas Zinn tends to think that neither one of the two major political parties can be counted on to promote the interests of "the 99 percent" when these conflict with the interests of the rich and powerful, so that major political change has to be initiated instead by non-elites, from below,[88] Kazin criticizes Zinn for failing to realize that "Short of revolution, a strategic alliance with one element of 'the Establishment' is the only way social movements ever make lasting changes in law and public policy." In a similar vein, Kazin ridicules Zinn's support for Ralph Nader's presidential bid in 2000. Kazin, presumably, was backing Al Gore.[89]

I do not point this out for the purpose of suggesting that Kazin's criticisms of Zinn's history are ultimately attributable to this political difference. For one thing, I don't know that to be true. For another, such a move would be an instance of the *ad hominem* fallacy. Kazin's arguments must be taken seriously and assessed on their merits, in terms of evidence and logic, which I have tried to do above and below. Rather, I point it out solely to refute Daniels's fallacious appeal to authority. His claim that Kazin's criticism of Zinn must be cogent, since he shares Zinn's politics, falters, in part, precisely because he does *not* share Zinn's politics.

Returning to Kazin's criticisms, he offers two others to which Zinn responds in his letter. The first is that APH neglects the topic of religion. Zinn does not dispute the charge, and acknowledges, further, that religion is "obviously an important part of American culture." By way of explanation, Zinn mentions only that he had never intended to write a comprehensive history, but had chosen, instead, to concentrate on facts and events that are "not usually reported." Still, Kazin's criticism is a reasonable one. He has identified a significant lacuna in Zinn's text.

The other criticism of his to which Zinn responds is that APH is a "cynical," "fatalistic" work, "a painful narrative about ordinary folks who keep struggling to achieve equality, democracy, and a tolerant society, yet somehow are always defeated." Clearly, Kazin exaggerates. While it is true that Zinn's text describes many losing struggles, and several others in which the victory is small, or compromised, or short-lived, it also chronicles a number of important enduring victories that are neglected in most mainstream textbooks. While it might reasonably be assumed that some readers, those who are more impressed by Zinn's accounts of the former than by his descriptions of the latter, would find the book depressing, theirs may well be a minority response. In Zinn's reply to Kazin on this issue he points out that his book "is full of stories about encouraging victories, and resistance, and heroic people who struggled for justice and against war." Further, he cites "the huge amount of mail I receive," and reports that "The overwhelming reaction of readers is that they feel inspired by the book, motivated to become active" (LET). The evidence of APH's astonishing record of continuously accelerating sales, not to mention the limitless demand for Zinn as a speaker while he was alive, would seem to support that judgment.

Perhaps Kazin's nastiest criticism concerns Zinn's handling of the terrorist attacks of September 11, 2001:

> The latest edition of the book includes a few paragraphs about the attacks of September 11, and they demonstrate how poorly Zinn's view of the past equips him to analyze the present. "It was an unprecedented assault against enormous symbols of American wealth and power," he writes. The nineteen hijackers "were willing to die in order to deliver a deadly blow against what they clearly saw as their enemy, a superpower that had thought itself invulnerable." Zinn then

quickly moves on to condemn the United States for killing innocent people in Afghanistan.

Is this an example of how to express the "commonality" of the great majority of U.S. citizens, who believed that the gruesome strike against America's evil empire was aimed at them? Zinn's flat, dualistic view of how U.S. power has been used throughout history omits what is obvious to the most casual observer: al-Qaeda's religious fanaticism and the potential danger it poses to anyone that Osama bin Laden and his disciples deem an enemy of Islam. Surely one can hate imperialism without ignoring the odiousness of killers who mouth the same sentiment.

It is disappointing, but not surprising, to encounter a criticism of this sort. Anyone who claimed that the 9/11 attacks were motivated by grievances against U.S. foreign policy or who opposed a retaliatory military attack on Afghanistan has been subjected to denunciations of this sort. Kazin's is more restrained than most—at least he doesn't claim that Zinn "justified" the attacks.

But was Zinn really so oblivious to the odiousness of the 9/11 killers? In APH he writes, "As Americans all over the country watched, horrified, they saw on their television screens the towers collapse in an inferno of concrete and metal, burying thousands of workers and hundreds of firemen and policemen who had gone to their rescue" (678). Granted, Zinn did not add to this description an explicit statement to the effect that "this was an odious act," but any reader who had understood anything of the 677 pages preceding this passage could not have failed to discern what Zinn's evaluation would be of a violent act that killed thousands of innocent persons, including first responders engaged in the heroic act of entering burning buildings in an attempt to save others. Moreover, in another book, *Terrorism and War*, which appeared two years prior to the publication of Kazin's critique, Zinn expressed his condemnation more explicitly, referring to what happened on September 11 as an "awful thing," and a "horrible act," and declaring that it was "motivated by a murderous fanatical feeling" (TAW 15–16). He subsequently called it "a terrorist act, inexcusable by any moral code."[90]

Next, is Kazin right in saying that the attacks were "aimed at the great majority of American citizens," whom the terrorists regarded as "enemies of Islam"? The claim is ambiguous in a couple of different ways. First, if to say that the attacks were aimed at ordinary American citizens means that they were the ones who were directly targeted, then, yes, the claim is obviously true, and Zinn nowhere denies it. But if it means that the motivation for the attack was anger at the majority of American citizens, as opposed to anger at the foreign policy decisions of American leaders, then Zinn disagrees. Similarly, if being an "enemy of Islam" is interpreted in terms of official military and political actions in the Middle East, then Zinn agrees that the attacks were motivated by rage against those who the terrorists regarded as the enemies of Islam. But he denies that the events of September 11 were motivated by opposition to domestic U.S. policies—such as granting certain rights and freedoms to women and gays, for example—that are inconsistent with the terrorists' understanding of Islam.

In radical contrast to Kazin, Zinn offers evidence, including historical evidence, in support of his position, instead of uncritically endorsing "what is obvious to the most casual observer":

It seems clear from their own statements that what bothers the people who want to strike at the United States is not what we do internally and how much freedom we have, but what we do externally. What angers them are the troops we've stationed in Saudi Arabia, the enormous economic and military support we give Israel, our maintenance of sanctions against Iraq, which have devastated the country and hurt so many people. They have made it very clear what troubles them.

These issues come up again and again. The journalist Robert Fisk interviewed Osama bin Laden twice for the *Independent* in London. And even while bin Laden invokes religious symbolism and Islam, it is clear from these interviews that bin Laden is infuriated over the military presence of U.S. troops in Saudi Arabia and our policies in Israel and Iraq.

I think there is a simple test of what concerns bin Laden, whether it is our democracy and internal freedom or whether it's our foreign policy. And that simple test is: What side was Osama bin Laden on before 1990? That is, before the United States stationed troops in Saudi Arabia, made war against Iraq, and began its sanctions against Iraq. We were just as democratic and libertarian internally before 1990 as we are today. But Osama bin Laden was not offended by that. He was on our side—and we were on his side—in the fight to take control of the government in Afghanistan. The turning point for Osama bin Laden is very clear. It has nothing to do with democracy and liberty. It has to do with U.S. foreign policy. And that turning point comes in 1990 and 1991. (TAW 12–13)

Before going further, let me point out that to say that the terrorists may have been motivated in their actions by legitimate grievances against U.S. policies, as Zinn here implies, is not to come within a billion miles of saying that those actions were justified.[91] The reason is that a just cause is merely a *necessary* condition for a justified act of violence, not a *sufficient* condition. Suppose that you like to go around the neighborhood slashing tires for kicks. One day you slash mine. While I now have a legitimate grievance against you, it hardly follows that just any action I might take in response would be justified. For example, suppose my response were to murder your family, all of your friends and their families, and many of your neighbors. Such a response would obviously be wrong, because (a) the suffering it would cause would be excessive, and disproportionate to that caused by the original offense of your slashing my tire; (b) that suffering would be unnecessary in that there would (presumably) be a peaceful way of rectifying the original injustice (that is, by calling the police to have you arrested and prosecuted, and suing you in civil court); and, most importantly, (c) because such an action would result in the deaths of innocent people who took no part in your original transgression. Such considerations, and especially (c), show why the September 11 terror attacks were unjustified.

But they also show why the bombing of Afghanistan was unjustified. It resulted, predictably, in the killing of thousands of Afghan civilians who had played no role in the terror attacks. What horrified many Americans about those attacks was the fact that innocent *Americans* were killed. What horrified Howard Zinn was the fact that innocent *people* were killed. The former reaction, coupled with a desire for revenge, led to support for the bombing of Afghanistan. The latter led to opposition to it. Kazin offers no argument, indeed, no explanation of any kind, as to what exactly was wrong with Zinn's reaction. Kazin mentions the issue of "killing innocent people in Afghanistan," but then drops the subject without offering a word of commentary about it, as if it carried no moral weight whatsoever, and then immediately proceeds to condemn Zinn's stance summarily, as if it were self-evidently absurd to think that U.S. policy should be based, even in part, on anything so insignificant as concern for the lives of innocent civilians in Afghanistan.

And in APH Zinn offers another historically based argument against bombing Afghanistan, namely, that such a response to terrorism simply doesn't work:

It should have been obvious to Bush and his advisors that terrorism could not be defeated by force. The historical evidence was easily available. The British had reacted to terrorist acts by the Irish Republican Army with army action again and again, only to face even more terrorism. The Israelis, for decades, had responded to Palestinian terrorism with military strikes, which only resulted in more Palestinian bombings. Bill Clinton, after the attack on U.S. embassies in Tanzania and Kenya in 1998, had bombed Afghanistan and the Sudan. Clearly, looking at September 11, this had not stopped terrorism. (APH 678)

Once again, Kazin offers no objection to, or comment of any kind on, this argument. So, while Zinn offers two arguments, firmly rooted in the lessons of history (one on the motivation behind the terrorist attacks of September 11, the other on the inefficacy of military force as a response to terrorism), Kazin ignores both arguments, offers no counter-lessons from history of his own, and, based on nothing more substantial than conventional thinking ("what is obvious to the most casual observer"), complains of "how poorly Zinn's view of the past equips him to analyze the present."

An additional oddity concerning the harshness of Kazin's critique—bluntly calling APH "bad history," in addition to the other insults chronicled above—is that it contrasts so starkly with Kazin's tone in a review of DOI, published 13 years prior to his attack on APH, in spite of the fact that Zinn makes many of the same arguments in DOI as he does in APH, and that Kazin offers many of the same criticisms of it, albeit worded much more gently.

He begins his review of DOI by remarking that "Howard Zinn writes the type of history scholars are supposed to disdain" (MKR 1034). But Kazin makes clear that he does not disdain it, as he warns us not to "devalue his achievement," calls his book "a flawed success," praises Zinn's "clear style and compassionate voice," and, most importantly, states that DOI is "a work that should be taught" (MKR 1034–5). I see no reason why he could not have said the same about APH.

In any case, as a final criticism, Kazin, in an interview on the Occupy movement, claims that Zinn was "much more simplistic and reductionist than Marx. Marx understood that capitalism was improving living standards, for example."[92] The problem, of course, is that Kazin provides no evidence whatsoever in support of his absurd implication that Zinn did not share that understanding. To the contrary, as I documented above, in the discussion of Paquette, Zinn acknowledged that capitalism has "developed the economy in an enormously impressive way," increasing "geometrically the number of goods available." Indeed, one wonders how Kazin's claim can be squared with this statement of Zinn's: "It is true that the profit motive, in the history of capitalist development, has stimulated great industrial progress. Karl Marx, even when he looked forward to the disappearance of capitalism, acknowledged that it had brought the greatest increase in the productive forces of society, that it was a 'progressive' stage in history. And it produced many useful, worthwhile things."[93] To say that Zinn was too "simplistic and reductionist" to understand such ideas is a laughable falsehood. One can only imagine on what warrant Kazin thinks he can make such a claim.

Daniel J. Flynn

Flynn is represented on Daniels's list of Zinn critics as follows:

> "Readers of *A People's History of the United States* learn very little about history...the book is perhaps best thought of as a massive Rorschach Test, with the author's familiar reaction to every major event in American history proving that his is a captive mind long closed by ideology. If you've read Karl Marx, there's no reason to read Howard Zinn."
>
> —Daniel J. Flynn, conservative author and commentator.

Let's take these criticisms one at a time. Flynn provides no evidence whatsoever in support of his claim that readers of APH "learn very little about history." His substantive criticisms of APH, to be discussed below, collectively amount to the charge that Zinn got a small number of facts wrong, left out a few important events, interpreted others incorrectly, and, by means of selective omissions, gave a distorted account of the Pequot War of 1634–8. Such an indictment, even if it could be sustained, would hardly be adequate to show that a lucidly written 688-page book, devoted exclusively to the subject of American history and emphasizing material normally excluded from mainstream American history texts, presents the reader with "very little" to learn about that subject. Moreover, the claim is empirical, and Flynn ignores all of the empirical evidence (discussed in the previous chapter and in the treatments of Wineburg and Bobb above in this one) that strongly contradicts it. Finally, the first chapter of APH alone convincingly refutes Flynn's assertion. Prior to the publication of APH, very few Americans knew anything about Columbus's activities as a murderer and enslaver of Indians. Many readers have commented on how startled they had been to learn of these matters from Zinn's account, the accuracy of which Flynn declines to challenge.

Flynn's "Rorschach Test" analogy makes even less sense. A Rorschach Test is a psychological test in which subjects are asked to give their interpretations of vague or ambiguous inkblot shapes. The vagueness of the shapes is an important element of the test, since clearer shapes would tend to produce more uniform responses. The idea is that the less objectively determinate the image, the more its interpretation depends on the subjectivity of the observer—so that, in theory, differences in interpretation reveal differences in personality, or perhaps in psychological functioning. But Zinn's text, by all accounts (except that of Genovese), is remarkably clear. It does not give rise to wildly different interpretations. While I have criticized the interpretations offered by some of Zinn's critics, my complaint is that they tend to caricature his work—to play up some elements while ignoring others, removing many of the complexities of his text, with the result that his work is distorted, and presented in a crude, simplified, exaggerated form. But these distortions always stay within fairly well-defined bounds. It is not as if some readers see the book as an allegory about sexual politics, while others construe it as a satire, and still others interpret it as a conservative defense of "patriotic," triumphalist history. So what sense is there in Flynn's claim that the book is "perhaps best thought of as a massive Rorschach Test"? Additionally, Flynn's analogy unwittingly undercuts the main thrust of his essay (FLY), which is to claim that APH is a terrible book. For if it is really to be thought of as a Rorschach Test, then Flynn's negative reaction to it would have to be seen as revealing more about him than about it.

Flynn's complaint about the alleged uniformity of Zinn's "reaction to every major event in American history," while exaggerated, is considerably less absurd, as a case can be made that Zinn's explanations of major historical events are less varied than those found in more traditional American history texts. Zinn attempts to show in APH that those wielding power in the U.S. tend both to act out of self-interest and to present those actions as having been motivated by national interest, or by general benevolence, or by allegiance to lofty principles. Since these self-serving explanations vary, and since mainstream texts tend to give them credence, the result is that the interpretations of historical events in those texts perhaps do indeed vary more widely than do Zinn's. But Zinn gives *arguments*, based on *historical evidence*, in support of his interpretations. If those arguments are sound, then there is no need to posit a cognitive deficiency on his part, as in the *ad hominem* charge that his is "a captive mind long closed by ideology," in order to explain his (arguably) more uniform responses to historical events. Thus, in order to make his case, Flynn must provide an adequate response to those arguments—one that focuses on the degree to which competing interpretations agree with the evidence. But he does not do so. While he does charge Zinn with a few factual errors and material omissions, his approach to this is scattershot, rather than systematic or comprehensive, and lacks the crucial comparative component: Are more mainstream accounts freer of such errors and omissions than is Zinn's? Flynn makes no serious attempt to show this. Are Zinn's arguments against the distortions of other historians (such as Samuel Eliot Morison's on Columbus, discussed in the previous chapter) unsound? Flynn doesn't say.

Finally, Flynn returns to absurdity with his claim that one who has read Karl Marx has "no reason to read Howard Zinn." For starters, the first edition of APH was published in 1980, and the last revision includes coverage of events all the way into the early twenty-first century. Marx died in 1883. He said nothing about events happening after that date. Secondly, Marx was not American, but German, and not a historian, but rather a philosopher, economist, and sociologist. He was not a chronicler of events in American history. Very little of the information in APH can also be found in the works of Karl Marx.

Perhaps what Flynn meant, although he failed to say it, is that someone who was already well versed in the events of American history, and who had also grasped Marx's ideas well enough to understand how Marx would have interpreted those events, would have no need to read Zinn, since Zinn's interpretations are straightforwardly Marxist.

One problem with that criticism is that a major strength of APH is its inclusion of interesting and important events that are neglected in most American history texts. Thus, most readers, even if they are quite knowledgeable about American history, and even setting aside Zinn's interpretations, can learn a great deal from his text just in terms of becoming acquainted with basic information about events of which they had previously been unaware. Accordingly, on this interpretation Flynn's criticism boils down to the charge that a small handful of extremely knowledgeable readers may derive little benefit from APH, since they are already familiar with the subjects it discusses—a criticism that applies equally well or better to most works of nonfiction.

Another problem with this criticism is that in APH Zinn does not merely describe historical events and interpret them. He also gives *arguments* in support of those interpretations, usually in the form of citing other historical events so as to show that the one currently under discussion fits a certain wider pattern—a pattern that is inconsistent with the interpretation offered by more conventional historians. Accordingly, one reason why a reader already well versed both in American history and in Marx might still want to read APH would be to see whether, or to what extent, the case Zinn makes for an alternative understanding of American history is a persuasive one.

The most important point, however, and the one that goes to the heart of Flynn's complaint, is that Zinn's interpretations go well beyond orthodox Marxism. While Zinn was obviously influenced by Marx, and made use of some of his ideas, no one who has read both Zinn and Marx carefully could possibly conclude, as Flynn does, that Zinn is simply a Marxist ideologue, with "a captive mind long closed by ideology." A number of other currents in political thought—anarchist, syndicalist, non-Marxian socialist, and liberal (both of the classical and the modern-day variety)—have strongly influenced his thinking. Moreover, there are also elements within all of these traditions— and even more so within the popular understanding of them (for example, that Marxists are Stalinists, that socialists are advocates for totalitarian dictatorships, that anarchists are bomb-throwers, etc.)—that Zinn rejects. For this reason, he also rejects labels, telling Davis D. Joyce (one of his biographers): "I don't want to be labeled as a Marxist, although some of Marx's ideas I embrace heartily." On the other hand, he goes on to say that he "doesn't mind" such labels ("Marxist," "socialist," "anarchist," "liberal"), "so long as I can, 'guilty with an explanation, your honor'...explain them."[94]

Such eclecticism has been a constant throughout Zinn's intellectual career. In a 1969 essay on the New Left he urges that "A new radicalism should be anti-ideological" (ZR 624; OH 83) and that the new radicals should make good use of their "advantage over Marx of having an extra century of history to study" (ZR 626; OH 86). Moreover, as a specific criticism of Marxism, Zinn comments that "Surely we don't have...confidence in inevitabilities these days—we've had too many surprises in this century," and approvingly cites French philosopher Simone de Beauvoir's claim that "there is no inevitable proletarian uprising" (NR 628; OH 89). Similarly, he criticizes Marxism for offering little guidance to the question of how to change society, adding that "The traditional Marxian idea of a revolution taking place because of a breakdown in the capitalist mechanism and an organized, class-conscious proletariat taking over, is hardly tenable today" (NR 630; OH 92). And in a 1988 article, entitled "'Je Ne Suis Pas un Marxiste,'" Zinn offers gentle contempt for "any born-again Marxist who argues that every word in Volumes One, Two, and Three of *Das Kapital*, and especially in the *Grundrisse*, is unquestionably true" (FTQ 146; OH 74–5; ZR 575), and remarks that "Marx was often wrong, often dogmatic, often a 'Marxist'" (FTQ 148; OH 77; ZR 577). Finally, in his 1999 play, *Marx in Soho*, Zinn has Marx say, upon his return to contemporary times, "I was wrong in 1848, thinking capitalism was on its way out.... Nothing is certain. That is now clear. I was too damned certain. Now I know—anything can happen" (MIS 44, 46).

Accordingly, Zinn's interpretations of historical events often differ from those that an orthodox Marxist might offer. For example, there is no hint of historical determinism in APH—no sense that specific happenings inevitably had to transpire as they did and could not have unfolded differently. Although one of Zinn's chapters is entitled "The Coming Revolt of the Guards," he immediately assures the reader, in the very first sentence of the chapter, that its title "is not a prediction, but a hope" (APH 631). Similarly, Zinn does not suggest that the explanation of human actions is to be found entirely in economic, sociological, and political forces, leaving historical actors with no real choice to do other than what they in fact did.[95] (As documented during the discussion of Wineburg above, Zinn often gives an "on the other hand," in which, for example, someone distinguishes himself by deliberately choosing to act against his own economic or political interest.) Perhaps most importantly, the many distinct political concerns that animate Zinn's narrative are much broader and more varied than those arising out of a Marxist critique of capitalism. And for that matter, he clearly recognizes that the different social networks that have arisen to take part in different social "movements" (against slavery, against war, for environmental protection, for the rights of workers, or blacks, or women or gays, etc.) are too nuanced to be reducible to the blunt instruments of the Marxist analysis of "class."[96] So Flynn's claim that one who has read Marx has no reason to read Zinn is false—and false on multiple grounds.

Turning now to Flynn's criticisms that are not cited by Daniels, I begin by pointing out that I have already addressed several of them, since they appear, almost verbatim, in Horowitz's profile of Zinn in TP (Horowitz credits Flynn for "research" in connection with that profile [TP 364]). For example, Flynn chastises Zinn for maintaining that "The authoritarian Nicaraguan Sandinistas were 'welcomed' by their own people, while the opposition Contras, who backed the candidate that triumphed when free elections were finally held, were a 'terrorist group' that 'seemed to have no popular support inside Nicaragua.'" For the refutation of that objection, I refer the reader to the discussion of Horowitz above. The same holds for the issue of George Washington's wealth and of the unemployment rate during the Reagan presidency, both of which are also addressed there.

Like Horowitz, and so many other of Zinn's critics, Flynn does not overlook the technique of quoting, in truncated form, some of Zinn's theoretical pronouncements about history (such as his rejection of "objectivity," his statement that his version of history is "a biased account," and his claim that "there is no such thing as a pure fact") while withholding from his readers Zinn's explanations as to their meanings. (The meanings of the first two items are discussed extensively in the previous chapter; the third one in the treatment of Grabar above.) And like these other critics, he invites his readers to misunderstand these ideas, and to do so in a way that discredits Zinn. For example, he cites Zinn's statement that "there is no such thing as a pure fact" as proof that Zinn "finds fault with...facts themselves," when in fact his point is merely that facts do not select themselves, so that an author's decision to include any given fact and to exclude others constitutes a judgment as to what is or is not interesting or important or relevant. Once this is explained, Zinn's point turns out to be a harmless, even banal, truism. But Flynn suggests that it might serve "to rationalize intellectual dishonesty." While I am critical of this move of Flynn's, at least I cannot accuse him of a lack of familiarity with the phenomenon of "intellectual dishonesty."

As a case in point, consider this remark of Flynn's: "Through Zinn's looking-glass, Maoist China, site of history's bloodiest state-sponsored killings, transforms into 'the closest thing, in the long history of that ancient country, to a people's government, independent of outside control'.... Castro's Cuba, readers learn, 'had no bloody record of suppression.'" While Flynn, in the second paragraph of his article, accuses Zinn of "convenient omissions," it is he who, blatantly and outrageously, makes use of such omissions in order to make these criticisms of Zinn's statements about China and Cuba.

With regard to China, note, first, that Zinn's point was about the new government's independence, not its human rights record. Second, and more importantly, Flynn's insinuation that "Zinn's looking-glass" prevented him from recognizing Maoist China's "bloody state-sponsored killings" is not only false but an obvious lie. I say this because one place in which Zinn acknowledges it is on the very page (APH 657)—indeed, in the very same passage—that Flynn quotes. Flynn simply elides the passage that refutes his claim. For when Zinn says that Castro's Cuba "had no bloody record of suppression," the next four words, all cut from Flynn's quotation, are (so help me, brace yourself) "as did communist China." Indeed, the context in which Zinn makes this remark is precisely to criticize the U.S. for its hypocrisy in citing a concern for human rights as the reason for its harsh dealings with Cuba even as it simultaneously conferred "most favored nation" status on China, which had "massacred protesting students in Beijing in 1991" (APH 657), and, in general, compiled "a bloody record of suppression."[97] Note, in this connection, that Flynn's article, ostensibly on Howard Zinn, is entitled "Master of Deceit"!

And with regard to Cuba, Flynn, eager to make his readers believe that "Zinn's looking-glass" blinded him to Cuba's record of repression, conveniently omits what comes right before Zinn's claim that Cuba "had no bloody record of suppression." That sentence begins this way: "Cuba had imprisoned critics of the regime" (APH 657).

I invite the reader to pause briefly to reflect on Flynn's achievement here. To appreciate it fully, let's restore Zinn's sentence so that it can be read in full: "Cuba had imprisoned critics of the regime, but had no bloody record of suppression as did communist China or other governments in the world that received U.S. aid" (APH 657). Flynn, who calls Zinn a "Master of Deceit" and accuses him of "convenient omissions," and who states that Zinn's "looking-glass" causes him to overlook repressive acts by the governments of China and Cuba, removes from one of the two sentences he quotes in support of such allegations his clear statement that "Cuba had imprisoned critics of the regime" and that China, indeed, "*communist* China," had a "bloody record of suppression." I would have thought that it took the talents of a David Horowitz to pull off something like that! Perhaps it is no coincidence that Flynn's article appears on one of Horowitz's websites.

Next, Flynn complains that "The recently released updated edition [of APH] continues to be plagued with inaccuracies and poor judgment. The added sections on the Clinton years, the 2000 election, and 9/11 bear little resemblance to the reality his current readers have lived through." How does Flynn document this charge? He offers three examples. Let's take them up in turn.

Here is Flynn's first example:

> In an effort to bolster his arguments against putting criminals in jail, aggressive law enforcement tactics, and President Clinton's crime bill, Zinn contends that in spite of all this "violent crime continues to increase." It doesn't. Like much of Zinn's rhetoric, if you believe the opposite of what he says in this instance you would be correct. According to a Department of Justice report released in September of 2002, the violent crime rate has been cut in half since 1993.

In response, I will say, first, that, as is the case with so many of Flynn's quotations from Zinn, if you believe that he altered it in this instance, and did so to help him make an illegitimate anti-Zinn point, you would be correct. The relevant passage in APH reads as follows: "as criminologist Todd Clear wrote in the *New York Times* ('Tougher Is Dumber') about the new crime bill, harsher sentencing since 1973 had added 1 million people to the prison population, giving the United States the highest rate of incarceration in the world, and yet violent crime continued to increase" (647).

Notice that Flynn misquotes Zinn by changing his tense. Whereas Zinn had said that violent crime "continued" (past tense) to increase, Flynn changes this to the present tense, without indicating (with square brackets or by any other method) that he is doing so, thus twisting Zinn's words to say that violent crime "continues" to increase. Second, Flynn doesn't inform his readers that Zinn is here reporting what is said in an article by a criminologist, even though Zinn names the criminologist, gives the title of the article, and tells the reader in which publication it can be found. This is significant because, as Zinn implies and as the cited article makes abundantly clear, that article, though written "about the new crime bill," was published before its passage, as a contribution to the debate over whether it should be passed. It was not an analysis, published 20 years after the bill's passage, about its effects, but rather an examination of the effects of the previous 20 years of similar "get tough" approaches to crime. Clear's article, published on December 4, 1993 (Clinton's crime bill would not be passed until the following year), claimed that

> Since 1973, as a result of a vast nationwide increase in criminal sentences, imprisonment has risen more than fourfold; we have added a million citizens to the prison and jail population. More than 1 in 40 males 14 to 34 years old are locked up. No other nation has had so much growth.
>
> If such toughness had much to do with crime, you'd think we'd have seen some results by now. But surveys of victims show that overall crime has decreased only 6 percent since 1973; violent crimes are up 24 percent. The National Research Council of the National Academy of Sciences recently concluded that a tripling of time served by violent offenders since 1975 had "apparently very little" impact on violent crime.[98]

So Clear's point, accurately described (and with the appropriate tense) by Zinn, had to do with an increase in the rate of violent crime from 1973 to 1993. That claim is not refuted by a Department of Justice report about a decrease in violent crime from 1993 to September 2002. So Flynn's first example is a swing and a miss.

Here is his second example:

According to Zinn, it was Mumia Abu-Jamal's "race and radicalism," as well as his "persistent criticism of the Philadelphia police," that landed him on death row in the early 1980s. Nothing about Abu-Jamal's gun being found at the scene; nothing about the testimony of numerous witnesses pointing to him as the triggerman; nothing about additional witnesses reporting a confession by Abu-Jamal—it was Abu-Jamal's dissenting voice that caused a jury of twelve to unanimously sentence him to death.

If Zinn were claiming that Abu-Jamal is innocent, or if he were pretending to offer a significant, detailed analysis of his case, Flynn would definitely have a point. These would be unforgivable omissions. But Zinn does neither. Zinn's entire discussion of Abu-Jamal in APH consists of just two sentences. The first says nothing about his case, but merely informs the reader about a work stoppage undertaken by a labor union in protest over his incarceration and death sentence. The other sentence, the one from which Flynn quotes, reads as follows: "Jamal was a respected black journalist who had been tried and sentenced under circumstances that suggested his race and his radicalism, as well as his persistent criticism of the Philadelphia police, were the reasons he now sat on death row" (APH 668). That's it. Zinn says nothing else about Abu-Jamal in APH.

Zinn's point is not that an innocent person was convicted, but rather that a person legally entitled to the presumption of innocence and to a fair trial was denied these because of his race and his politics. In a 1997 speech he makes this clear and elaborates his position on Abu-Jamal more than he does in APH:

> He's black, he's radical, he's poor. Is he going to get a fair trial? Again, it's not known for sure guilt or innocence. One thing you do know for sure, so long as those factors are dominant, and those factors are dominant in a society which is filled with...hostility to Blacks and hostility to radicals, and so long as the justice system is dominated by money, then the question of whether you actually did this or did not do this becomes secondary to these other factors. (CSZ 128–9)

Though Flynn neglects to inform his readers of the fact, human rights organizations around the world have come to the same conclusion. For example, Amnesty International, while "tak[ing] no position on the guilt or innocence of Mumia Abu-Jamal," nonetheless states in its extensive report on the case: "After many years of monitoring Mumia Abu-Jamal's case and a thorough study of original documents, including the entire trial transcript, the organization has concluded that the proceedings used to convict and sentence Mumia Abu-Jamal to death were in violation of minimum international standards that govern fair trial procedures and the use of the death penalty," in part because "political statements attributed to him as a teenager were improperly used by the prosecution in its efforts to obtain a death sentence against him."[99]

In fleshing out this charge, the Amnesty International report highlights many additional issues, including the bias of the judge, Albert F. Sabo, the inadequacy of Abu-Jamal's legal representation at trial, and the unrepresentative nature of the jury.

Next, recall that in rejecting Zinn's claim that Abu-Jamal's death sentence was attributable to "his race and his radicalism," Flynn implies that a better explanation can be found in three pieces of evidence that are missing from Zinn's (one-sentence) discussion: Abu-Jamal's gun found at the scene, the testimony of numerous witnesses pointing to him as the triggerman, and additional witnesses reporting a confession by Abu-Jamal. But has Flynn omitted anything important in connection with these three items? Drawing once again on the Amnesty International report, here is a partial list of his omissions, organized around each of them.

1. The gun

A. "The police failed to conduct tests to ascertain whether the weapon had been fired in the immediate past. The test is relatively simple: smell the gun for the odour of gun powder, which should be detectable for approximately five hours after the gun was fired."

B. "Compounding this error, the police also failed to conduct chemical tests on Abu-Jamal's hands to find out if he had fired a gun recently."

C. Nor did they examine or test his clothing for this purpose.

D. The bullet in Abu-Jamal's body (he, too, had been shot) was determined to have taken a downward path in traveling through his body, suggesting that he had been shot from above (possibly by a standing person while he was in a prone position). This is inconsistent with the prosecution's theory of the relevant events.

E. "There were...inconsistencies in the original findings concerning the bullet removed from Faulkner's body [Faulkner was the police officer allegedly shot by Abu-Jamal]. The Medical Examiner first wrote in his notes that the bullet was '.44 cal.' (Abu-Jamal's gun was a .38 calibre weapon and could not possibly have fired such a bullet). This discrepancy, which was never made known to the jury, was later explained by the Medical Examiner as 'part of the paper work but not an official finding.' At trial, the

Medical Examiner testified that the bullet was consistent with those fired by Abu-Jamal's gun but that tests were inconclusive as to whether it actually came from his firearm. The court accepted the medical examiner as a ballistics expert. However, during the 1995 hearing, Judge Sabo contended that the medical examiner was 'not a ballistics expert' and that his original findings that the bullet was a .44 calibre were a 'mere lay guess.'"

2. Witnesses to the shooting: Three witnesses testified that they saw Abu-Jamal shoot the police officer.

A. General: "Based on a comparison of their statements given to the police immediately after the shooting, their testimony during pretrial hearings and their testimony at the trial, the key witnesses did substantively alter their descriptions of what they saw, in ways that supported the prosecution's version of events."

B. Cynthia White: She "was a prostitute working in the area on the night in question. At the trial she testified that she had seen Mumia Abu-Jamal run up to Officer Faulkner, shoot him in the back, and then stand over him firing at his head.

"Prior to the trial, White had given four written statements and one tape-recorded statement to the police. In one interview she estimated the height of the person who shot Faulkner to be shorter than five feet eight inches. Abu-Jamal is six feet one inch tall. In her first court appearance at a pretrial hearing, she testified that Abu-Jamal held the gun in his left hand. Three days later she testified that she was unsure which hand he held the gun in. At trial she denied knowing which hand the gun was in. During her trial testimony, she claimed that the diagram she originally drew of the incident was incorrect and that her placement of the actors prior to Abu-Jamal's appearance was inaccurate.

"There is evidence to show that Cynthia White received preferential treatment from the prosecution and police. At the time of the trial, she was serving an 18-month prison sentence for prostitution in Massachusetts. She had 38 previous arrests for prostitution in Philadelphia; three of those charges were still pending at the time of trial. She was arrested twice within days of the shooting incident (12 and 17 December). According to Abu-Jamal's current defence attorneys, there are no records of White ever being prosecuted for those arrests.

"In 1987, a detective involved in the prosecution of Abu-Jamal testified in support of bail for White at a court hearing concerning charges of robbery, aggravated assault and possession of illegal weapons. Despite the judge pointing out that White had failed to appear in court on 17 different occasions and that she had 'page after page' of arrests and convictions, the prosecution consented to the request that she be allowed to sign her own bail and the judge released her. According to information received by Amnesty International, White failed to appear in court on the charges and the authorities have since been unable to locate her. At an appeal hearings in 1997, the prosecution claimed Cynthia White was deceased and produced a 1992 death certificate in the name of Cynthia Williams, claiming that the fingerprints of the dead woman and White matched. However, an examination of the fingerprint records of White and Williams showed no match and the evidence that White is now dead is far from conclusive.

"A second prostitute, Veronica Jones, witnessed the killing and testified for the defence. She claimed she had been offered inducements by the police to testify that she saw Abu-Jamal kill Faulkner, stating that 'they [the police] were trying to get me to say something the other girl [White] said. I couldn't do that.' Jones went on to testify that 'they [the police] told us we could work the area [as prostitutes] if we tell them [that Abu-Jamal was the shooter].'

"However, Judge Sabo had the jury removed for this testimony and then ruled that Jones' statements were inadmissible evidence. The jury were thus left unaware of the allegations that police officers were offering inducements in return for testimony against Abu-Jamal....

"In a sworn affidavit, Jones described her meeting with...plain clothes police officers: 'They told me that if I would testify against Jamal and identify Jamal as the shooter I wouldn't have to worry about my pending felony charges...The detectives threatened me by reminding me that I faced a long prison sentence—fifteen years...I knew that if I did anything to help the Jamal defense I would face years in prison'....

"In January 1997, another former prostitute who worked in the area of the crime scene in 1981, came forward. In a sworn affidavit, Pamela Jenkins stated that she knew Cynthia White, who had told her she was afraid of the police and that the police were trying to get her to say something about the shooting of Faulkner and had threatened her life. Jenkins was the lover and informant of Philadelphia police officer Tom Ryan. In her statement, Jenkins claimed that Ryan 'wanted me to perjure myself and say that I had seen Jamal shoot the police officer.' In 1996, Tom Ryan and five other officers from the same district went to prison after being convicted of charges of planting evidence, stealing money from suspects and making false reports. Their convictions resulted in the release of numerous prisoners implicated by the officers. Jenkins was a principal prosecution witness at the trials of the officers."

C. Robert Chobert: He was a cab driver who "had just let a passenger out of his cab and was parked when he viewed the incident." He was "approximately 50 feet from the shooting."

At the time of the trial Chobert was on probation for "the arson of a school." Moreover, on the night of the killing "Chobert had been driving his cab with a suspended drivers' license.... [I]t was still suspended at the time of the trial, and...the police had never sought to charge him for this offence."

D. Mark Scanlan: "In one of his original statements to the police, Scanlan stated several times that he did not know whether Abu-Jamal or his brother shot Faulkner: 'I don't know who had the gun. I don't know who fired it.' He also misidentified Abu-Jamal as the driver of the vehicle stopped by Officer Faulkner and was approximately 120 feet from the scene. A diagram that Scanlan drew for police indicated that Abu-Jamal and Faulkner were facing each other when the first shot was fired, contrary to the prosecution's theory that the police officer was initially shot in the back. At trial, Scanlan admitted that he had been drinking on the night in question and that 'There was confusion when all three of them were in front of the car.'"

3. Abu-Jamal's alleged confession: "During the trial, the jury heard testimony from hospital security guard Priscilla Durham and police officer Gary Bell. According to both witnesses, when about to receive treatment for his bullet wound at the hospital, Mumia Abu-Jamal stated: 'I shot the motherfucker, and I hope the motherfucker dies.'

"During an appeal court hearing in 1995, a third witness, police officer Gary Wakshul, also claimed to have heard the statement. However, Officer Wakshul, who was in the police vehicle that took Mumia Abu-Jamal to the hospital, had written in his report that 'we stayed with the male at Jefferson [hospital] until we were relieved. During this time, the negro male made no comments.'

"None of the many other police officers in and around the hospital treatment room at that time claimed to have heard the statement, which Abu-Jamal allegedly shouted. Doctors who treated Abu-Jamal at the hospital stated in their testimony that they were with him from the moment he arrived, that he was 'weak...on the verge of fainting,' and that they did not hear him make any statement that could be interpreted as a confession.

"None of the three witnesses to the alleged confession reported what they had claimed to have heard until February 1982, more than two months after the shooting.... Officer Wakshul claimed that his delay in reporting the confession was due to 'emotional trauma' caused by the murder of Officer Faulkner. The two other witnesses stated that they did not believe the outburst was significant enough to report to the police....

"Gary Wakshul, the officer who noted in his report that 'during this time, the male negro made no statements,' did not testify at the trial. When the defence lawyer attempted to call him as a witness, it transpired that he was on holiday, despite a notation on a police investigation report that Wakshul was not permitted to be on leave at the time of the trial. The defence requested that Officer Wakshul's whereabouts be established or that the trial be temporarily halted to enable them to locate him. That request was denied by Judge Sabo....

"The jury was never informed of the existence of Officer Wakshul's written report of his custody of Mumia Abu-Jamal which clearly contradicts the claim that the suspect 'confessed' to killing Officer Faulkner. Therefore, the jury was left with little reason to doubt the testimony of the two witnesses who claimed to have heard the confession. "The likelihood of two police officers and a security guard forgetting or neglecting to report the confession of a suspect in the killing of another police officer for more than two months strains credulity. Priscilla Durham's claim that she believed Mumia Abu-Jamal's 'confession' was...not important enough to notify the police is scarcely credible.

"In a conversation with an Amnesty International researcher, one of Mumia Abu-Jamal's current legal team stated that a number of the jurors have told defence investigators that they had taken into consideration Abu-Jamal's 'confession,' not just in deciding his guilt but also in sentencing him to death, since the statement portrayed him as aggressive and callous. However, the jurors refused to make any public statements to this effect. The concern remains that a possibly fabricated 'confession' may have been a major contributing factor in the jury sentencing Mumia Abu-Jamal to death."

Flynn says nothing about any of this. In 2001 a federal appellate court vacated Abu-Jamal's death sentence, and prosecutors announced that they would no longer seek the death penalty for him. Though Flynn's essay was written in 2003, he doesn't tell his readers about that, either.

Here is his third example: "Predictably, Zinn draws a moral equivalence between America and the 9/11 terrorists. He writes, 'It seemed that the United States was reacting to the horrors perpetrated by the terrorists against innocent people in New York by killing other innocent people in Afghanistan.'"

In reply I would add the following to the comments I made in the discussion of Kazin above about Zinn's reaction to 9/11: Zinn neither says nor implies here that the actions of the 9/11 terrorists and those of the United States in response are "morally equivalent." The point is an elementary one. To say of two events that they are similar, or even identical, in one morally relevant aspect is not to say that they are equivalent in every morally relevant aspect, or that they are, all things considered, morally equivalent. Zinn makes quite clear the respect in which he finds the two events to be similar—both were instances of killing innocent people, and of doing so on a large scale. But this is not to deny that they might differ in other morally relevant respects, such as the number of people killed by each party, or the issue of whether or not the innocent people killed in either case were directly targeted (as opposed to being killed by indiscriminate bombing campaigns, with their deaths having been merely foreseen, rather than directly intended).

In this connection, note that two things might differ from one another in ways that are relevant to some issue, and yet those differences might fail to reach a critical threshold that would justify their being evaluated differently or treated differently. For example, two students might differ significantly in their performance on an exam, and this difference might be relevant to, or even totally determinative of, the question of what grade they should receive. Nonetheless, even if one student scores ten times as many points as another, it could be that both would deserve to receive the same grade—as when a score of 60 points out of one hundred is required to receive a passing grade, and one student earns a score of 40 points (and receives a failing grade) while another earns just four points (and gets the same grade). Similarly, two actions that involve the large-scale killing of innocent people (whether deliberately or as the inevitable and perfectly foreseeable consequence of other actions—that is, as "collateral damage") may both, for that very reason, be indefensible, in spite of their differences in other morally significant aspects.

To make the point another way, consider the example of crime. No two acts of vandalism, or theft, or assault, or kidnapping, or murder are identical. Moreover, the differences between one and another act constituting the same crime are often morally significant, and sometimes in such a way or to such a degree as to justify a different response to these different acts—for example, by assigning to their perpetrators different punishments. So to say of two acts that they are both instances of "theft" or "murder" is not at all the same thing as saying that they are "morally equivalent." But the morally significant differences among different acts of, for example, murder, are rarely, if ever, of such a nature as to elevate one of them all the way into the realm of the morally permissible (at least if we exclude such wild scenarios as traveling back in time to murder Adolf Hitler in his crib). Zinn has made it abundantly clear in his many writings on the subject that he finds actions that will inevitably result in the wholesale slaughter of innocent civilians to be unjustifiable. On that basis, he condemns both the September 11 terrorist attacks and the U.S. bombing campaign in Afghanistan. While one might disagree with his moral judgment, the mere fact that he condemns both actions, and does so for the same reason, does not entail that he regards them as "morally equivalent."

I would point out, next, that the rhetoric of "moral equivalence" in mainstream American political discourse is almost always used as a device to immunize American conduct against principled criticism. When our enemies kill innocent people, assassinate foreign leaders, engage in torture, prop up corrupt authoritarian puppet regimes, crack down on political dissent, violate international laws, break treaty agreements, or interfere in foreign elections, they are roundly criticized. But when the United States engages in behavior that can accurately be described as falling under one of these categories, anyone who, as a basis for objecting to such conduct, cites U.S. criticism of its enemies for doing what it is now also doing, is condemned for naively ascribing "moral equivalence" to the two actions.

And the technique for showing that the two cases are morally dissimilar is almost always the same. When "we" do something that would normally, out of context, be regarded as wrong, the solution is to supply the necessary context (and a moral motive). If we support a ruthless dictator, it is because the alternative in that country would be even worse; if we kill innocent civilians, it is a regrettable side-effect of legitimate acts of self-defense on our part; if we curtail our citizens' civil liberties, it is because the events of September 2001 "changed everything." But if our enemies do any of these things, anyone who attempts to explain or contextualize their actions, to find a motive for them other than madness, fanatical hatred, or pure naked malevolence— anyone who points out, for example, that Castro's acts of political repression in Cuba must be understood against a backdrop of a U.S. sponsored invasion of his country, eight admitted attempts by the U.S. to assassinate him, several successful U.S. acts of poisoning Cuban livestock and destroying Cuban crops, among other instances of sabotage—is accused either of hopeless naivety (he or she is a "dupe" of enemy propaganda), or of "justifying" the enemy's evil action. Reflection on this point reveals, I think, that while Zinn is often accused of Manichaeism, that charge is more accurately leveled against mainstream U.S. political discourse, with its doctrine of "American exceptionalism," its refusal to acknowledge that the U.S. ever does anything immoral (as opposed to occasionally doing harm by mistake), its insistence that U.S. foreign policy is always driven by altruism and concern for human rights, and its relentless demonizing of all of its enemies.

So much for Flynn's three examples. Let's review. He claims that the sections of APH dealing with events of the 1990s and the new century are "plagued with inaccuracies and poor judgment," that these sections "bear little resemblance to the reality his current readers have lived through," and that "much" of the time, "if you believe the opposite of what he says…you would be correct." If those charges were true, it would be easy to submit a long list of false claims, illogical arguments, and absurd judgments, all drawn from the relevant sections of Zinn's text. But Flynn provides just three examples—crime rate, Mumia, and "moral equivalence"—and none of them withstand modest critical scrutiny. He is the one who chose those examples. Presumably, he thought they were his strongest ones, those that would best help him make that case. If he thought he had better examples, surely he would have used them.

When Flynn next turns to Zinn's treatment of earlier events in U.S. history the result is distortion, as Flynn consistently removes all complications and nuances from Zinn's text and reduces it to a Manichean caricature. For example, according to Flynn, "Zinn suggests that America, not Japan, was to blame for Pearl Harbor." But when we look at what Zinn actually says, a much messier picture emerges. While he does point out that the United States had initiated economic sanctions against Japan, and that these "were widely recognized in Washington as carrying grave risks of war" (APH 411, quoting Yale University political science professor Bruce Russett [from his book *No Clear and Present Danger*]), he also (a) calls the Japanese bombing of Pearl Harbor "an immoral act," (b) dismisses as "wild accusations" that are "without evidence" the claim that Roosevelt "knew about Pearl Harbor and didn't tell, or that he deliberately provoked the Pearl Harbor raid," and, most importantly, (c) endorses Russett's conclusion that "Japan's strike against the American naval base climaxed a long series of mutually antagonistic acts" (APH 410–11). That's rather different from claiming, flatly, that "America, not Japan, was to blame."

In order to make his next criticism of Zinn, Flynn finds it necessary to contradict (without acknowledging it) one of the main theses of his article. Recall Flynn's complaint that Zinn's "familiar reaction to every major event in American history" proves "that his is a captive mind long closed by ideology," and that "If you've read Karl Marx, there's no reason to read Howard

Zinn." Elsewhere Flynn elaborates this point, making it crystal clear: "The single-bullet theory of history offered by Marx—'The history of all hitherto existing societies is the history of class struggle'—is relied upon by Zinn to explain all of American history. Economics determines everything." Or again, Flynn attributes to Zinn a "rigid worldview," a "one-size-fits-all explanation of history," according to which "every major figure or event...[is] motivated by economic interests."

But almost immediately after saying this, Flynn abruptly changes course and announces that "Zinn's Marxism extends beyond economic concerns. If classical Marxism can be boiled down to 'worker=good, entrepreneur=bad,' cultural Marxism's primitive grunt might be translated into 'minorities, good; white guys, bad.'"

Note, first, the obvious contradiction. One cannot charge Zinn with the view that "Economics determines everything," so that "every major figure or event...[is] motivated by economic interests," and, with a straight face, simultaneously concede that his theoretical framework "extends beyond economic concerns." Flynn tries to cover up this contradiction by using the same term, "Marxism," to refer to both of the theoretical concerns that he attributes to Zinn. But there is nothing in the works of Marx that even remotely corresponds to this "minorities, good; white guys, bad" nonsense. Calling it "Marxism," albeit qualified with the adjective "cultural," is nothing but a desperate attempt on Flynn's part to cover up his implicit admission that he is wrong to accuse Zinn of reducing everything to economics, and equally wrong to say that there is nothing in Zinn's theorizing beyond what can be found in the works of Marx. Moreover, setting the issue of Marxism aside, there is no getting around the fact that Flynn, in one and the same article, attributes to Zinn both the view that economics—and economics alone—explains and determines everything, and the thesis that some things are explained by something else—something cultural and racial, but not economic.

Flynn could have avoided this problem simply by modifying his initial criticism of Zinn as a rigid ideologue. Rather than accuse him of holding that "Economics determines everything," he could have said, much more plausibly, something like this: "Zinn's explanations of historical events tend to overstate the importance of economic interests, at the expense of other factors." This more modest claim, being perfectly compatible with the idea that Zinn might have analyzed some events differently, would have left Flynn free to criticize those non-economic analyses of Zinn's on their merits without undermining the major premise of his own critique in the process. But Flynn is evidently so determined to paint Zinn as a simplistic, unyielding, one-dimensional, doctrinaire Marxist, that he would rather contradict himself than give up this caricature.

Moving on to the substance of Flynn's new charge, how does he make the case that Zinn analyzes history through a "minorities, good; white guys, bad" lens? He offers just one example: Zinn's handling of the Pequot War of 1634–8.

It is interesting that Flynn would pick this particular historical event on which to stake his claim that Zinn's history exhibits a "white guys, bad" bias, since it is one in which the "white guys," by Flynn's own admission, did indeed behave badly. In what Flynn himself calls "the war's most significant event," the English settlers set fire to the Pequot compound, killing about 600 of the Pequots, including, in Flynn's words, "untold numbers of women and children." Nor was this in any sense an accident. Zinn quotes colonial historian Francis Jennings's account of this event (from his book *The Invasion of America: Indians, Colonialism, and the Cant of Conquest*): Captain John Mason "proposed to avoid attacking Pequot warriors, which would have overtaxed his unseasoned, unreliable troops. Battle, as such, was not his purpose. Battle is only one of the ways to destroy an enemy's will to fight. Massacre can accomplish the same end with less risk, and Mason had determined that massacre would be his objective" (APH 15). Though Zinn does not use the term, this act—that of deliberately targeting innocent noncombatants in order to "destroy an enemy's will to fight"—perfectly fits the definition of "terrorism," much as the actions of the 9/11 hijackers do. Accordingly, and to his credit, Flynn concedes that an accurate description of "the truth" about this event would be sufficient "to discredit the white settlers."

What, then, is Flynn's complaint? It is that Zinn, not being satisfied with the unvarnished truth, "cannot resist the temptation of piling on" by telling a one-sided story. More specifically, Flynn accuses Zinn of depicting the Pequots as a peaceful people, when in fact, according to Flynn, they were aggressive and belligerent, frequently instigating violent conflicts both with the English settlers and with other Indian tribes. Similarly, he charges Zinn with downplaying Pequot "massacres," "atrocities," and, in general, "Pequot violence against whites," while playing up comparable behavior by the whites against the Pequots. As a result of these unscrupulous manipulations, "The reader is left," according to Flynn, "unsupplied with...facts that might give context to the brutal assault on Fort Mystic [the Pequot compound]."

Before taking up the details of Flynn's criticism, notice what is implied by the fact that he provides this specific example—and only this one—as evidence of Zinn's alleged anti-white bias. If such bias does indeed characterize Zinn's work, as Flynn claims, then it should be possible to cite numerous instances of its occurrence in his text. Or, if, perhaps for reasons of space, only one example is to be given, one would expect it to be an especially clear and egregious one. But Flynn, who is obviously free to pick his own example, and who would presumably be motivated to pick the one that would best help him to make his case, picks an example in which Zinn's transgression is merely to have failed to provide information adequately contextualizing an unjustified act of terrorism on the part of whites against Indian noncombatants.

Notice, also, that implicit in Flynn's criticism is the admission that (a) it is sometimes necessary to provide "context" if we are to understand morally odious acts—even massacres, terrorist attacks, acts in which innocent women and children are deliberately murdered, and (b) that providing that context, seeking that understanding, recognizing that the acts in question might have been motivated by legitimate grievances—these are not at all the same thing as justifying those actions. But it is significant that neither Flynn nor any others of Zinn's critics recognize these obvious truths when it comes to the misdeeds of America's official enemies. Anyone who attempts to itemize the grievances that may have motivated the 9/11 terrorist attacks, or who mentions illegal U.S. acts of aggression against Castro's Cuba as part of the context necessary for understanding his acts of repression directed against political dissidents, is straightaway accused of justifying those actions, and is called names—"dupe," "apologist," "anti-American," and so forth.

In any case, when we turn to the details of Flynn's indictment, his case very quickly unravels. First, Zinn neither denies nor fails to mention Pequot violence against the whites. Rather, as Flynn concedes, Zinn explicitly acknowledges that "Massacres took place on both sides" (APH 14).

Second, Flynn complains that "For reasons not hard to deduce, the author details only the atrocities committed by one side: the Puritans. Pequot atrocities are brushed aside. Graphic descriptions of Puritan violence are highlighted." If Zinn's account of the Pequot War were lengthy and detailed, and if it included descriptions of a great number of acts of violence carried out by the Puritans against the Pequots, then Flynn's complaint would be entirely understandable. But in fact Zinn's account of the Pequot War is less than two pages long (APH 14–15), and it describes only one specific instance of Puritan violence—the event that even Flynn admits was "the war's most significant event."

Third, Zinn does mention a specific act of Indian-on-white violence. Flynn reports it as follows: "Also briefly mentioned is the killing of John Oldham, which Zinn justifies by labeling the murder victim a 'trader, Indian-kidnapper, and troublemaker.'" This is a blunder on Flynn's part. Oldham is not mentioned in APH. The murder victim in question is John Stone, not John Oldham. In the paragraph immediately after his reference to the murder Zinn quotes the governor of the Massachusetts Bay Colony, John Winthrop, who wrote of an expedition originating from Boston that was "to go to the Pequods to demand the murderers of Captain Stone and other English" (APH 14). And in the definitive scholarly study of the Pequot War, historian Alfred A. Cave states that "It is a matter of record that the English assaulted the Pequots after the failure of efforts to persuade them to apprehend and surrender to Puritan justice those Indians believed to be responsible for the deaths of Captain John Stone and other Englishmen" (CAV 1). Thus, while Flynn complains of Zinn's propensity for factual error, we have now identified two clear, unambiguous, straightforward factual errors in his own presentation, as this confusion of Stone with Oldham joins his confusion, identified above, of the 1993–2002 crime rate with that of the 1973–1993 period. Given the brevity of his essay, there is no doubt that Flynn commits more such factual errors per page than Zinn does.

Fourth, while Flynn objects to Zinn's description of Stone (well, Flynn thinks it's Oldham, but let that pass) as a "trader, Indian-kidnapper, and troublemaker," Cave's characterization makes Zinn's look generous. Cave calls Stone "a disreputable trader" (40), "a smuggler and sometime privateer of unsavory reputation" (59), and "a drunkard, lecher, braggart, bully, and blasphemer" (72). More importantly, he confirms the "Indian-kidnapper" charge: "Stone had abducted two Indians near the mouth of the Connecticut River.... Stone forced his captives to guide him upriver. After Stone's ship anchored for the night, the captain (Stone) and two of his men took their Indian prisoners ashore, 'their hands still bound,' and made camp. An Indian rescue party, tracking Stone, waited until dark, then attacked, killing the captain and his men while they slept and freeing the prisoners" (59).

Fifth, on what possible grounds can Flynn claim that Zinn "*justifies*" the killing of Stone (whom he thinks is Oldham) by labeling him a "trader, Indian-kidnapper, and troublemaker"? Zinn certainly never *says* that the murder was justified. Why could not Zinn's reference to Indian-kidnapping be seen as an attempt to contextualize his murder, and to render it understandable, rather than to justify it, much as Flynn calls for the inclusion of descriptions of Pequot violence against the Puritans, not in order to justify the Puritan massacre of Pequot children, but merely to make it comprehensible? Could it be that it is Flynn, rather than Zinn, who harbors a bias based on race, such that he only insists that atrocities carried out by whites be contextualized, with such contextualization being conflated with justification when the perpetrators of violence are non-whites?

Sixth, though Flynn errs by confusing John Stone with John Oldham, perhaps his mistake is motivated by the idea that Zinn should have mentioned the killing of Oldham, as another instance of Pequot violence against the white settlers. But Cave, while acknowledging that "Some writers blame the Pequots" for his death (105), spends four pages (105–8) debunking that claim, concluding that Oldham was killed, instead, by members of another tribe, the Narragansett.

Finally, and most importantly, though Cave mentions neither Zinn nor Flynn (the latter's essay appeared only after Cave's book had been published), his entire book thoroughly demolishes Flynn's characterization of the Pequot War and presents an account of it that much more closely resembles that of Zinn. The following passages summarize, and give the flavor, of Cave's findings:

> The historiography of the Pequot War is often more polemical than substantive. Puritan apologists justified their savagery by demonizing the victims. Contemporary chroniclers and later historians sympathetic to the Puritans painted a portrait of the Pequots as a "cruell, barbarous and bloudy" people. That portrait reflected a long-standing stereotype of the New World "savage" as irrational, unpredictable, malicious, treacherous, and inhumane.... Puritan writers declared that the Pequots were "the Devil's instruments" and charged them with masterminding a plot to exterminate all Christians in New England. The Puritans and their later apologists asserted that the English colonists had no choice but to strike first. They also argued that, given the savagery of their adversary, they were under no obligation to respect the rules of civilized warfare. In his chronicle of the war, Captain John Underhill proclaimed that God himself demanded that the Pequots suffer "the most terrible death that may be" in punishment for their sins. "Sometimes," he wrote, "the scripture declareth that women and children must perish with their parents.... We had sufficient light from the Word of God for our proceedings."...
>
> [T]he Puritan explanations of the war will not stand close scrutiny. Their allegation that the Pequots threatened the security of Puritan New England cannot be confirmed. A close reexamination of the Puritans' own testimony suggests that it was without any foundation whatsoever. In their justifications of the war, Puritan writers advanced interpretations of Pequot character and intentions based on prejudice and supposition rather than hard evidence. Nonetheless, with very few exceptions, writers for three centuries uncritically echoed Puritan fantasies about Pequot malevolence.... (2–3)

[T]he documentary evidence and ethnohistorical data available to us not only do not support the Puritans' more extreme allegations that Pequots plotted the extermination of all Christians in New England but also discredit the commonly accepted assumption that the Pequots were obstacles to English expansion in the Connecticut River valley. Instead, the record indicates that they actively sought European trading partners... *There is no evidence that the Pequots were guilty of any acts of violence against English settlers in Connecticut prior to John Endicott's initiation of hostilities. The Pequots neither desired nor anticipated war with the Puritans. The origins of the Pequot War are to be found in the actions of the Massachusetts Bay Colony....* (7–8, emphasis added)

In their justification of the war against the Pequots, Puritan mythmakers invoked old images of treacherous savages and told tales of diabolical plots. It is now clear that their portrayals of the Pequot bear little resemblance to reality. The Puritans transformed their adversary into a symbol of savagery. Rumors of Pequot conspiracy, although flimsy in substance and of dubious origin, reinforced expectations about savage behavior and justified preemptive slaughter and dispossession.... The images [Puritan apologists] framed of their adversary have been remarkably persistent but now should be recognized as the products of wartime propaganda. (177–8)

Thus, while Flynn accuses Zinn of providing a distorted account of the Pequot War, leaving the impression that it was a case of unprovoked aggression on the part of the whites, Cave's research indicates that this impression would in fact be the correct one. So, to sum up our findings with regard to Flynn's criticism of Zinn's work as exhibiting an anti-white bias, it turns out that this accusation (1) contradicts a major tenet of Flynn's general critique of Zinn; (2) is supported by just one example; with that example being one in which Zinn (allegedly) (3) merely fails to contextualize adequately a white-on-Indian atrocity; even though (4) he does acknowledge Pequot "massacres." And Flynn's demand for further anti-Pequot concessions (5) undermines his criticism of Zinn's handling of the 9/11 terrorist attacks; (6) rests in part on a factual error, and, most importantly, (7) makes sense only if we accept an outdated and discredited theory of the War's origins— a theory that had been debunked in the major scholarly study of the Pequot War, which was published seven years prior to the appearance of Flynn's article, but which Flynn neither refutes, nor responds to, nor even acknowledges or mentions. I conclude that Flynn has failed to make his case.

He is on firmer ground when he criticizes Zinn for leaving out entirely certain important events and figures of American history:

> Washington's Farewell Address, Lincoln's Gettysburg Address, and Reagan's speech at the Brandenburg Gate all fail to merit a mention. Nowhere do we learn that Americans were first in flight, first to fly across the Atlantic, and first to walk on the moon. Alexander Graham Bell, Jonas Salk, and the Wright Brothers are entirely absent. Instead, the reader is treated to the exploits of Speckled Snake, Joan Baez, and the Berrigan brothers.... D-Day's Normandy invasion, Gettysburg, and other important military battles are left out. In their place, we get several pages on the My Lai massacre and colorful descriptions of U.S. bombs falling on hotels, air-raid shelters, and markets during the Gulf War of the early 1990s.
>
> How do students learn about U.S. history with all these omissions? They don't.

Flynn is entirely correct to imply that the exclusion of these persons and events is a weakness of Zinn's text, in the sense that, all else equal, a book of American history that included these interesting and significant topics would be better than one that did not. However, all else is not equal, and several points can be made in Zinn's defense.

First, in my judgment Flynn's complaints about Zinn's *inclusions* (what we get [supposedly] *in place of* these omissions) is without merit. We are not "treated to the exploits" of Speckled Snake or Joan Baez. All we are told about Speckled Snake is that he was "A Creek man more than a hundred years old." We are given this information as introductory matter preceding a quotation from him on his reaction to Andrew Jackson's policy of Indian removal. The introductory sentence and the quotation, combined, take up less than half a page (135). Is it Flynn's view that students should not receive even a brief exposure to the perspective of Indians with regard to this important historical event?

Joan Baez is given less than one full sentence of coverage. She is lumped together with Bob Dylan in a sentence briefly describing the emergence of popular protest music in the 1960s (537). And while we do learn something of the "exploits" of the Berrigan brothers, they receive just two brief mentions (488–9, 601–2).

Further, it is not true that "we get several pages on the My Lai massacre," but rather about one-and-one-half pages (478–9), a defensible allotment of space for this important historical occurrence.

The topic of civilian casualties from U.S. bombing during the Gulf War of the early 1990s receives about two-and-one-half pages of coverage (from the final line of 596 to the middle of 599). Several considerations support this level of attention:

1. A major part of the U.S. propaganda campaign aimed at generating support for the war on the part of the American people was the assurance, which turned out to be false, that the use of "smart bombs" would keep civilian

casualties to a minimum. As Zinn points out, "The American public was overwhelmed with television photos of 'smart bombs' and confident statements that laser bombs were being guided with perfect precision to military targets. The major networks presented all of these claims without question or criticism.

This confidence in 'smart bombs' sparing civilians may have contributed to a shift in public opinion, from being equally divided on going to war, to perhaps 85 percent support for the invasion....

In fact, the public was being deceived about how 'smart' the bombs being dropped on Iraqi towns were. After talking with former intelligence and Air Force officers, a correspondent for the Boston *Globe* reported that perhaps 40 percent of the laser-guided bombs dropped in Operation Desert Storm missed their targets.... Reuters reported that the air raids on Iraq first used laser-guided bombs, but within a few weeks turned to B-52s, which carried conventional bombs, meaning more indiscriminate bombing" (APH 596–7).

2. Civilian casualties were extensive, a fact which the U.S. government callously treated as uninteresting and irrelevant. Zinn: "John Lehman, Secretary of the Navy under President Reagan, estimated there had been thousands of civilian casualties. The Pentagon officially had no figure on this. A senior Pentagon official told the *Globe*, 'To tell you the truth, we're not really focusing on this question'" (APH 597).

3. The U.S. government imposed censorship, and attempted to hide the level of U.S. killing of noncombatants. Zinn: "American reporters were kept from seeing the war close-up, and their dispatches were subject to censorship....
"After the war, fifteen Washington news bureau chiefs complained in a joint statement that the Pentagon

exercised 'virtual total control...over the American press' during the Gulf War" (APH 597–8).

4. The U.S. government repeatedly lied. When civilian sites were hit, the government falsely claimed that its bombs had struck military targets. Zinn cites an example: "In mid-February, U.S. planes dropped bombs on an air raid shelter in Baghdad at four in the morning, killing 400 to 500 people. An Associated Press reporter who was one of few allowed to go to the site said: 'Most of the recovered bodies were charred and mutilated beyond recognition. Some clearly were children.' The Pentagon claimed it was a military target, but the AP reporter on the scene said: 'No evidence of any military presence could be seen inside the wreckage.' Other reporters who inspected the site agreed" (APH 598).

5. Much of the U.S. media failed to act independently of the government, but rather acted as its spokespersons and apologists. Zinn offers an example: "[L]eading television news commentators behaved as if they were working for the United States government. For instance, CBS correspondent Dan Rather, perhaps the most widely seen of the TV newsmen, reported from Saudi Arabia on a film showing a laser bomb (this one dropped by British aircraft in support of the American war) hitting a marketplace and killing civilians. Rather's only comment was: "We can be sure that Saddam Hussein will make propaganda of these casualties" (APH 598).

6. U.S. actions included atrocities that brought no legitimate military benefit. Zinn: "With victory certain and the Iraqi army in full flight, U.S. planes kept bombing the retreating soldiers who clogged the highway out of Kuwait City. A reporter called the scene 'a blazing hell...a gruesome testament.... To the east and west across the sand lay the bodies of those fleeing'" (APH 598).

7. Secondary effects of the U.S. bombing campaign devastated the Iraqi civilian population. Zinn reports: "The
human consequences of the war became shockingly clear
after its end, when it was revealed that the bombings of
Iraq had caused starvation, disease, and the deaths of tens
of thousands of children. A U.N. team visiting Iraq
immediately after the war reported that 'the recent conflict
has wrought near-apocalyptic results upon the infra-
structure.... Most means of modern life support have been
destroyed or rendered tenuous....'

"A Harvard medical team reporting in May said that child
mortality had risen steeply, and that 55,000 more children
died in the first four months of the year (the war lasted
from January 15 to February 28 [1991]) than in a comparable period the year before.

"The director of a pediatric hospital in Baghdad told a *New
York Times* reporter that on the first night of the bombing
campaign the electricity was knocked out: 'Mothers
grabbed their children out of incubators, took intravenous
tubes out of their arms. Others were removed from oxygen
tents and they ran to the basement, where there was no
heat. I lost more than 40 prematures in the first 12 hours of
the bombing'" (APH 598–9).

Would Flynn really want to argue that these matters are trivial,
uninteresting, unworthy of attention? Would it not be important
for students to have this information so that they might make use
of it in the future when, as citizens, they must decide whether to
give or withhold their support for another military adventure? A
negative answer would appear to make sense only if one thinks
that U.S. citizens should, automatically and uncritically, support
their government's decision whenever it chooses to go to war and
to drop bombs, and if, furthermore, one regards the lives of Iraqis
(or at least non-Americans, or perhaps non-whites) to be of little

value. Sadly, Flynn's reference to Zinn's "colorful descriptions of U.S. bombs falling on hotels, air-raid shelters, and markets during the Gulf War" is suggestive of such an attitude. "Colorful," in the relevant sense, means "full of interest; lively and exciting." Its synonyms include "vivid," "dramatic," "graphic," and "evocative." Flynn's language thus subtly implies that the wholesale killing of Iraqi civilians is not inherently "full of interest" or "dramatic," so that it can only become so when it is spiced up with "colorful" language. Perhaps I am being unfairly picky here, but it is hard to imagine Flynn referring to descriptions of American civilian deaths from the September 11 terrorist acts as "colorful."

Turning now to the issue of APH's omission of important historical events and figures (the Gettysburg address, the invasion of Normandy, the Wright brothers, etc.), several points are in order.

First, no textbook includes every significant topic in American history. There are simply too many of them. Nor would there be time even in a year-long course, let alone one lasting just one semester, for students to study everything of importance. Accordingly, all textbooks are selective. One could compile a list, for any one of them, of key events and people that it excludes.

Second, to the extent that a textbook does attempt exhaustive coverage, it thereby becomes overly long, and students do not have time to read all of it. If students have time to read only, say, 60 percent of a textbook, the effect, from the standpoint of their learning, is the same as if the remaining 40 percent of the book's content had been omitted.

It is worth noting, in this regard, that APH, at 688 pages of text (excluding Bibliography and Index), is considerably shorter than standard American history textbooks. James Loewen reports: "American history textbooks are full of information—overly full. These books are huge. The specimens in my original collection of a dozen of the most popular textbooks averaged...888 pages in length. To my astonishment, during the last twelve years they grew even larger. In 2006 I surveyed six new books.... These...average 1,150 pages" (LMT 3). And even this understates the size of these volumes, since most of them have pages that are, to use Loewen's phrase, "enormous"—both wider and taller than all but the biggest of oversized volumes (LMT 4).

Third, the particular way in which these gigantic books cram in information greatly diminishes their readability. The reason is that many of the facts they include are not there because they add clarity and coherence to the author's narrative—quite the opposite. Rather, "The books are huge so that no publisher will lose an adoption because a book has left out a detail of concern to a particular geographical area or group" (LMT 5). APH, in part because it boldly ignores this economic consideration, vastly exceeds all of its competitors in readability.

To come at this another way, when traditional textbooks are used, "None of the facts is remembered, because they are presented as one damn thing after another. While textbook authors tend to include most of the trees and all too many twigs, they neglect to give readers even a glimpse of what they might find memorable: the forests" (LMT 6–7). In order to render the forests visible, it may be necessary to remove some of the trees— even some of the important trees.

Or again, another critic complains that with mainstream textbooks "Students are snowed by an avalanche of facts ladled out one after another in a monotonous style devoid of what English teachers call 'voice' or 'tone'.... Names that even profes- sional historians would not always be able to identify—for example, of some of the failed early nineteenth-century vice- presidential candidates—pile up one after another as details concerning the election of 1816, the election of 1820, the election of 1824...are described."[100] Zinn's more selective approach enables him to overcome this problem. Not even Zinn's harshest critics have ever claimed that his writing lacked "voice" or "tone."

Fourth, including fewer topics allows an author to go into greater detail on the topics that are included. Given that there is no time to cover every significant historical event in a single class, and given the difficulty of producing a coherent narrative when one has to jump around so as to include every conceivable relevant fact, it seems likely that students would learn far more from a lucid, coherent, selective text (like Zinn's) that goes into a smaller number of topics in greater detail than from a book that is more complete in its coverage of topics, but provides less information about each one of them.

Fifth, Flynn's criticism overlooks the fact that teachers often assign only some sections of APH, as a supplement to another textbook. Zinn's work is used to provide an alternate perspective on selected topics, or to introduce students to events and figures not included in the main course textbook. (Recall in this connection Zinn's explicit statements to the effect that he intends APH to serve as a "counterweight" to more orthodox histories.)

Sixth, the force of Flynn's criticism is mitigated by a consideration of the limitations of introductory courses. No one can possibly learn more than a small fraction of what an American should know about American history merely from taking one class (or, for that matter, from reading one book). Accordingly, the goal of such a class should not be for the students to acquire knowledge of all of the important details. Instead, the course should enable them to learn about an intelligent selection of them, illustrating main themes and principles; should help them to acquire skill at assessing historical evidence, so that they can think about history, and draw conclusions about it, on their own; and, perhaps most importantly, should ignite their interest in history, so that they will continue to read about it, study it, and think about it continually for the rest of their lives. If that analysis is sound, the exclusion from a textbook of some undeniably important events and persons that are included in other texts, is not necessarily a cause for concern.

While I am not a historian, I know something about this from my experience as a philosophy professor. In an introductory philosophy course it is not possible to introduce students to everyone who has made a significant, or even an absolutely crucial, contribution to philosophical thought. For the list of such figures, even if one confined oneself to western philosophy, would have to include Plato, Aristotle, Augustine, Aquinas, Machiavelli, Bacon, Descartes, Spinoza, Leibniz, Hobbes, Locke, Berkeley, Hume, Rousseau, Kant, Hegel, Kierkegaard, Nietzsche, Mill, Peirce, James, Dewey, Husserl, Heidegger, Sartre, Russell, Wittgenstein, and Rawls, among several others. No one could possibly teach all of these thinkers in one introductory course. While there are some huge textbooks that include them all, the purpose of doing so is to accommodate the different selections that different teachers might want to make. Accordingly, some perfectly fine textbooks simply leave some of these figures out. It is not a decisive objection to such a text that it leaves out, say, Spinoza, Berkeley, Kierkegaard, Peirce, and Rawls. The same principle applies, it seems to me, to the omissions in APH that Flynn identifies.

Having said that, let me concede, once again, that the omissions that Flynn mentions do indeed, taken in isolation, by themselves, all else equal, constitute a weakness of APH, justifiable only if they (or exclusions like them) facilitate coherence and readability or confer other comparable advantages, and do not stand as obstacles to meeting the goals (discussed above) of an introductory course on American history. But Flynn grossly overplays his hand when he asks, rhetorically, "How do students learn about U.S. history with all these omissions?" — and then tersely answers: "They don't." The counter-argument is a simple one: Generally speaking a text's omissions only block the learning of the excluded material. They leave the way fully clear for students to learn the included material. The exclusions would prevent the learning of the included material only if somehow the excluded material held the key to the proper interpretation of the excluded material, or if the omitted information distorted the meaning of the included information, rendering it misleading. But it is far from clear how, say, the exclusion of Jonas Salk stands as an obstacle to the understanding of World War II, or any other topic discussed in APH; and the same point holds for Zinn's other omissions. Certainly Flynn does not even make an attempt to explain how Zinn's exclusions prevent students from learning about anything that his 688-page text includes.

Moreover, and to repeat a point I have made more than once above, the question of what students learn from studying Zinn is empirical. A good deal of such empirical evidence is available; and Flynn fails to address any of it. It establishes conclusively that, at the very least, the answer to the question of what students learn from studying APH is not: "nothing." To the contrary, it strongly suggests that Zinn's text, more so than any of its competitors, is likely to be read, pondered, discussed, and debated. That's how students learn.

Turning now to a section entitled "Uncooperative Facts," Flynn returns to the theme of Zinn's alleged propensity for factual error. He offers three examples, two of which (George Washington's wealth and the unemployment rate under Reagan) we have already discussed (in the section on Horowitz above). Here is the remaining example:

"When the Scottsboro case unfolded in the 1930s in Alabama," Zinn writes, "it was the Communist party that had become associated with the defense of these young black men imprisoned, in the early years of the Depression, by southern injustice." Perhaps the Party had become "associated" with the defense of the Scottsboro Boys, but in reality the Communists merely used the embattled youngsters. Richard Gid Powers points out in *Not Without Honor* that the

Communists had raised $250,000 for the Scottsboro Boys' defense, but had put up a scant $12,000 for two appeals. At the time, a black columnist quoted a candid Party official who stated, "we don't give a damn about the Scottsboro boys. If they burn it doesn't make any difference. We are only interested in one thing, how we can use the Scottsboro case to bring the Communist movement to the people and win them over to Communism."

The first point to be noted is that Flynn doesn't even try to assert that Zinn gets any facts wrong here. He only mentions one claim that Zinn makes—that the Communist party had become associated with the defense of the Scottsboro Boys—and he concedes that Zinn's claim is "perhaps" true (which it certainly and uncontroversially is). So his complaint is merely that Zinn omitted two pieces of evidence that (allegedly) show that the Communists had ulterior motives and were "using" the Scottsboro Boys.

This is a definite case of bait-and-switch. The section of Flynn's article in which this example appears begins as follows: "History is too complicated to find a perfect fit within any theory. For the true believer, this inconvenience can be overcome. When fact and theory clash, the ideologue chooses theory. To the true believer, ideology is truth. Time and again, *A People's History of the United States* opts to mold the facts to fit the theory." And at the conclusion of Flynn's presentation of three examples, including the one just quoted, that are supposed to illustrate and document this claim, we get this: "These are but a few of Howard Zinn's errors." But if there really were so many errors, why does Flynn not submit a long list of them? Why is it that, even when he presents only three, one of them turns out to be an example in which there is not even a suggestion that Zinn has gotten any facts wrong—we merely get the much different charge, which can be leveled against almost any piece of nonfiction writing, that something important has been left out?

But is it even true that Zinn omitted this issue? The passage in APH that immediately follows the one quoted above about the Communists' association with the Scottsboro Boys' case reads as follows: "The party was accused by liberals and the NAACP of exploiting the issue for its own purposes, and there was a half-truth in it, but black people were realistic about the difficulty of having white allies who were pure in motive. The other half of the truth was that black Communists in the South had earned the admiration of blacks by their organizing work against enormous obstacles" (APH 447). So, Flynn, who accuses Zinn of omitting the issue of the Communists' impure motives in this case, himself omits from his quotation from Zinn the sentence in which he addresses that very issue. And he omits it in spite of the fact that it appears immediately after the passage that he does quote. Remember, the title of Flynn's article, ostensibly about Howard Zinn, is "Master of Deceit."

This omission of Flynn's provokes one to wonder whether he might have left out anything else on this issue that might undermine his thesis. For after all, "when fact and theory clash, the ideologue chooses theory," and "opts to mold the facts to fit the theory." Well, it seems to me that in his zeal to criticize the Communists, so that he can, in turn, slam Zinn for (allegedly) failing to include relevant anti-Communist information, Flynn omits information that complicates his thesis. For one thing, he fails to mention that the Communist Party was hardly unique in taking its own interests into account when deciding which people or causes to champion. In fact, a major factor leading to the involvement of the Communists in the case was the decision of another organization, for self-interested reasons, initially to decline to lend its support. Law professor Douglas O. Linder explains:

The NAACP (National Association for the Advancement of

Colored People), which might have been expected to rush to the defense of the Scottsboro Boys, did not. Rape was a politically explosive charge in the South, and the NAACP was concerned about damage to its effectiveness that might result if it turned out some or all of the Boys were guilty. Instead, it was the Communist Party that moved aggressively to make the Scottsboro case their own. The Party saw the case as providing a great recruiting tool among southern blacks and northern liberals. The Communist Party, through its legal arm, the International Labor Defense (ILD), pronounced the case against the Boys a "murderous frame-up" and began efforts, ultimately successful, to be named as their attorneys. (LIN)

Next, while Linder agrees with both Flynn and Zinn that the motives of the Communists were impure, only Flynn goes so far as to say that their interests were exclusively selfish, and that they simply "used" the defendants for their own purposes. Might Flynn have omitted information that would have undermined that interpretation? Yes, he did. Linder reports that:

The ILD selected two attorneys to represent the Scottsboro Boys in the retrials. The ILD quieted skeptics who saw the organization caring more about the benefits it could derive from the case than the Boys' welfare by asking Samuel Leibowitz to serve as the lead defense attorney. Leibowitz was a New York criminal attorney who had secured an astonishing record of seventy-seven acquittals and one hung jury in seventy-eight murder trials. Liebowitz was often described as "the next Clarence Darrow." Liebowitz was a mainline Democrat with no connections with or sympathies toward the Communist Party. (LIN)

If the Communists truly were unconcerned about the fate of the Scottsboro Boys, and took their case solely because it would make the Party look good for having done so, thus aiding the Party's recruitment efforts, would they really have gone to the trouble and expense of securing the services of such an acclaimed and accomplished criminal defense attorney? Flynn says nothing about this.

So, to sum up, this supposed example of Zinn's tendency to commit factual errors turns out (1) not to contain any factual errors at all, but rather only an (alleged) omission; (2) not even to contain that omission, since the topic allegedly omitted is in fact present in Zinn's text, but merely omitted in Flynn's quotation from it, so that we are left simply with a difference of opinion between Flynn and Zinn as to the evaluation of that topic; and (3) to expose Flynn's tendency to omit evidence contrary to his theses, since he leaves out not only the relevant portion of the Zinn text that he quotes (as just noted), but also the evidence supporting Zinn's interpretation over his of that (supposedly but not really) omitted topic.

Thinking that he has exposed Zinn as a serial mis-stater of facts, Flynn then remarks:

> By now one might be thinking: On what evidence does Zinn base his varied proclamations? One can only guess. Despite its scholarly pretensions, the book contains not a single source citation. While a student in Professor Zinn's classes at Boston University or Spelman College might have received an "F" for turning in a paper without documentation, Zinn's footnote-free book is standard reading in scores of college courses across the country.

Here Flynn makes two false claims. While it is true that APH is "footnote-free," it is false, indeed ludicrously false, to say that it is "without documentation," or that it "contains not a single source citation." APH contains a 20-page bibliography (689–708), with the entries organized to correspond with the chapters of

Zinn's text. Then, all throughout the body of that text, Zinn documents facts and quotations by giving brief (just author and title) mentions of works for which the full information is provided in the bibliography. A college student who turned in a paper using such a documentation system would not receive an "F" for doing so (unless the instructor happened to give instructions insisting on a different citation system). But a student who littered his or her paper with demonstrable falsehoods along the lines of Flynn's claim that APH is "without documentation" and "contains not a single source citation" very well might receive, and richly deserve, that grade.

Oscar Handlin

Handlin (1915–2011), a Pulitzer Prize-winning Harvard University historian, is the author of a scathing review of APH, published in *The American Scholar* (HAN). He is represented on Daniels's list of Zinn critics by means of an ungrammatical (sentence-fragment) quotation from his review, as follows: "'The deranged quality of his fairy tale, in which the incidents are made to fit the legend, no matter how intractable the evidence of American history.' —Book review in *The American Scholar*, Harvard University professor Oscar Handlin."

Handlin's first criticism reads as follows:

[Zinn] ascribes the topsy-turvy quality of his description to its perspective — the Constitution viewed by the slaves, Andrew Jackson by the Cherokees, the Civil War by the New York Irish, the Spanish-American War by Cubans, the New Deal by Harlem blacks, and the recent American empire by Latin-American peons. Alas, he can produce little proof that the people he names, from slaves to peons, saw matters as he does. Hence the deranged quality of his fairy tale, in which the incidents are made to fit the legend, no matter how intractable the evidence of American history. (HAN 546, 548)

In reply I note, first, that it is only by means of selective quotation that Handlin is able to insinuate that Zinn, arrogantly and naively, claims to know exactly how "slaves," "peons," and the rest viewed the major events of American history. For when we turn to the relevant passage in APH we find that Zinn's programmatic statement about chronicling history from the standpoint of various constituencies that have been marginalized in more traditional works both begins and ends with modest qualifiers. He begins by saying "I prefer to *try* to tell the story of the discovery of America from the viewpoint of the Arawaks," and ends, after a long list of examples of historical events paired with perspectives from which he will try to view them, with the candid admission that he expects to succeed only "to the limited extent that any one person, however he or she strains, can 'see' history from the standpoint of others" (APH 10, emphasis added).

Second, Zinn never claims "that the people he names, from slaves to peons, saw matters as he does." The issue, rather, is whether he has accurately described how *they* saw matters—a quite different thing.

Third, Handlin's charge that Zinn "can produce little proof" that his interpretations of the views of others are correct is true only if "proof" is taken to mean a strict, conclusive, demonstration—a standard that is appropriate in mathematics and formal logic, but utterly alien to the discipline of history or any other kind of empirical inquiry. Thus, while Zinn perhaps does not provide much "proof," he certainly does present a good deal of *evidence*. He quotes from the writings and oral statements of those whose views he attempts to represent; he cites opinion polls; he documents and describes actions, where these are indicative of attitudes. (Recall, for example, the issue of Zinn's analysis of the attitudes of African-Americans toward World War II, discussed during the treatment of Wineburg, above.) And Handlin, for his part, offers neither proof nor even evidence that Zinn's handling of this material is deficient in any way. Here, as

379

elsewhere, his attack consists of bald assertion, unaccompanied by reasoned argument or by any other kind of independent corroboration.

Fourth, by falsely attributing to Zinn the assertion that "the people he names saw matters as he does," and by claiming that in his work "the incidents are made to fit the legend," Handlin invites the reader to assume that Zinn represents the groups he mentions as monoliths, united in their thinking. But he does not do so. Rather, as in the just-mentioned example of African-American views of World War II, Zinn consistently points out that there are disagreements within every community on almost every issue. Moreover, he acknowledges (and often highlights) this diversity, not only among the historically disenfranchised groups that he is most interested in representing, but also among the dominant groups that sometimes oppress them. Thus, Zinn gives us not only Columbus, the Spanish murderer and enslaver of Indians, but also Bartolomé de las Casas, the Spanish chronicler and harsh critic of such cruel and immoral conduct. Here, as elsewhere, Zinn achieves a vastly greater degree of subtlety and sophistication than Handlin attributes to him, or than Handlin himself, at least in this crude polemic, is able to attain.

Fifth, consider the meaning of Handlin's claim that in Zinn's narrative "the incidents are made to fit the legend, *no matter how intractable the evidence of American history.*" "Intractable" means "difficult to manage, deal with, or change to an acceptable condition." Its synonyms include "stubborn," "obstinate," "inflexible," "unbending," "unyielding," "uncompromising," "unaccommodating," and "uncooperative." Thus, Handlin is saying that Zinn's interpretations clash with the evidence, which will not accommodate them. But this conclusion, clearly marked as such by Handlin's use of the word "hence," is drawn directly from a much milder premise that does not even remotely support it—that Zinn merely "can produce little proof" in support of his representations. From the premise, "X does not follow from Y," one cannot validly derive the conclusion, "X is inconsistent with Y." But Handlin, displaying the lack of logical competence that permeates his review, implies that it does.

In his next paragraph Handlin says in connection with Zinn's handling of his scholarly sources that "many" are "used uncritically (Jennings, Williams)," while others are "ravaged for material torn out of context (Young, Pike)" (HAN 548). But Handlin undertakes not even the slightest effort to explain or document such charges. He does not mention any specific claim drawn from Jennings or Williams that Zinn should have rejected but instead wrongly passes on to his readers as a reliable fact or interpretation. Still less does he explain why such claims are false, or provide any evidence in support of his contention that they are. Similarly, Handlin does not tell us just how Zinn misrepresents material from Young or Pike by taking it out of context. Such a demonstration is easy to carry out, as I have done repeatedly above. Often all that is required is to quote some material that the appropriator (in this case Zinn) fails to quote—material, perhaps occurring just before or after the quoted words—that would cast their meaning in a different light. But Handlin does not do this, and thus, in effect, boldly asks us simply to take his word for it.

Similarly, he tells us that "Any careful reader will perceive that Zinn is a stranger to evidence bearing upon the peoples about whom he purports to write. But only critics who know the sources will recognize the complex array of devices that pervert his pages" (HAN 548). Unfortunately, here again Handlin only gives us these harsh conclusions, and completely forgoes the opportunity to demonstrate their accuracy. Instead, he asks us to accept his assurance that "any careful reader" will agree with him (and with it the logical corollary that any reader who disagrees with him must be a careless one), and that those who "know the sources" (presumably experts, professional historians like him), but "only" they, will grasp the multifarious methods of

Zinn's unscrupulous madness. Once again, however, and much to the frustration of "any careful reader," Handlin refuses to document, demonstrate, or explain any of the "complex array" of Zinn's "devices" of "perversion," in spite of the fact that such a demonstration would, presumably, prove both enlightening and entertaining to his readers, and would benefit him by establishing to them that his harsh rhetoric can be backed up with substance. But instead, Handlin continues with his strategy of asking us simply to take his word for it, to bow before his authority uncritically. It is difficult to think of a benign interpretation of his motives in choosing to do so.

The unfairness of Handlin's evidence-free but accusation-heavy method, and its gross deficiency from the standpoint of intellectual and scholarly standards, is only exacerbated by the ferocity of his rhetoric. When claiming that a scholarly colleague has made a mistake—has gotten a fact wrong, or made an unsound argument—one is obliged to back up the charge with evidence. And this obligation intensifies in direct proportion to the severity of the charge. To suggest that someone might have committed an error, one needs modest documentation; to convict someone of murder, one needs proof beyond a reasonable doubt. Handlin calls Zinn's history a "deranged fairy tale." "Deranged" means "mad, insane, demented." "Fairy tale" means either "a children's story about magical and imaginary beings and lands" or "a fabricated story, especially one intended to deceive." Any real scholar—indeed, any decent human being—would recognize a moral and intellectual duty to back up a charge like that with mountains of evidence. Asking readers to accept it on authority, as something that anyone who "knows the sources" would recognize, would, once again, be utterly unthinkable to any scholar of at least minimum competence and integrity. But Handlin, the Pulitzer Prize-winning Carl H. Pforzheimer University Professor at Harvard University, apparently thinks that such strictures do not apply to him.

Handlin's tactic of appealing to his own authority brings with it the additional disadvantage of exposing him to legitimate (that is, non-fallacious) *ad hominem* arguments. Ordinarily it is illogical to attempt to refute a person's argument by attacking him personally, or by attributing to him a motive to lie, or by suggesting that his station in life renders him incapable of grasping the truth about some issue, or by in any other way citing something about him personally at the expense of attending to his premises and to the nature of their connection to his conclusion. If Joe makes an argument about, say, global warming, we cannot refute him by pointing out that he is a notorious liar, or that he has no credentials in the field of climatology, or that he would have a personal motive, based on his position in the energy industry, to look at this issue one way rather than another. For one thing, his argument might very well turn out to be sound, in spite of our suspicions to the contrary based on these personal considerations. After all, as the cliché has it, even a stopped clock is right twice a day. But more importantly, such speculations about Joe, and their possible connection to his conclusion, are unnecessary. All we have to do, in assessing his argument, is to check his premises so as to see whether or not they are true, and, if they are, to determine whether his conclusion follows from them (or, if it is an inductive argument, to evaluate the degree of strength that his premises supply to his conclusion). But in an argument that takes the form of an appeal to authority, this is not possible. If Joe says, "trust me on this issue, I'm an expert," he is giving us no premises to check and no reasoning to evaluate. He offers us nothing but himself in support of his conclusion. Therefore, that is all we have to evaluate. If the argument is simply "trust me," it is very relevant indeed to know whether the "me" in question is trustworthy.

With that in mind, I think it is fair to point out two facts about Handlin that are pertinent to the evaluation of his (argument-free and evidence-free) anti-Zinn claims. First, Handlin was a strong proponent of the Vietnam War[101] and a supporter of Richard Nixon.[102] Needless to say, his attitude toward Zinn's politics would not have been one of sympathy, but rather virulent antipathy. It is therefore plausible to speculate that his extreme dislike of Zinn's politics might render him incapable of assessing Zinn's scholarship rationally—which also might explain why he so quickly resorts to insults, and uses them as a substitute for a rational and critical engagement with Zinn's arguments, on which he seems incapable of focusing.

Second, Handlin has shown that he has a tendency to engage in preposterously overheated rhetoric when dealing with historians whose politics he despises. Most notoriously, his review of *The Contours of American History* by William Appleman Williams begins this way: "In evaluating this book, one cannot exclude the possibility that it was intended as an elaborate hoax."[103] The second paragraph informs us that "Scattered through the volume are uproariously funny passages," that "the discussion of Poe...must surely have been designed as a satire," and that "It takes a rereading of Poe's story to appreciate the extent of the perversion" (743). Later we are told that despite the fact that "large sections are altogether farcical," we must nonetheless "conclude that Professor Williams was deadly in earnest in writing this book," leaving the reviewer with the burden of explaining how it could be such a "total disaster," with a "pervasive wrongheadedness that distorts every page." "Professor Williams," Handlin assures us, "simply does not understand that words cannot be used arbitrarily but must be fixed to concepts that will convey meaning." As a result, Williams's book is "altogether incoherent" (744).

Williams would go on to be elected president of the Organization of American Historians. Perhaps this helps to contextualize Handlin's word choices in his review of Zinn.

In the next paragraph of Handlin's review of APH, which has often been quoted by other Zinn critics, he asserts that APH "pays only casual regard to factual accuracy"—a charge that he attempts to flesh out by offering a list of Zinn's alleged factual errors. Once again, however, he offers no documentation or argument in support of his claim that he is right on these matters and Zinn wrong. In many cases the claims in question are somewhat complex, and must be assessed in the light of evidence. It is not as if Handlin were claiming that, according to Zinn, Wichita is the capital of Kansas, Benjamin Franklin is a former U.S. president, and George W. Bush's favorite pastime is to read Plato in the original Greek.

Here is Handlin's list, just as he presents it, but with the addition of numbers in parentheses to mark each item so as to facilitate discussion of each one:

(1) It simply is not true that "what Columbus did to the Arawaks of the Bahamas, Cortez did to the Aztecs of Mexico, Pizarro to the Incas of Peru, and the English settlers of Virginia and Massachusetts to the Powhatans and the Pequots." (2) It simply is not true that the farmers of the Chesapeake colonies in the seventeenth and early eighteenth centuries avidly desired the importation of black slaves, or (3) that the gap between rich and poor widened in the eighteenth-century colonies. (4) Zinn gulps down as literally true the proven hoax of Polly Baker and (5) the improbable Plough Jogger, and (6) he repeats uncritically the old charge that President Lincoln altered his views to suit his audience. (7) The Geneva assembly of 1954 did not agree on elections in a unified Vietnam; that was simply the hope expressed by the British chairman when the parties concerned could not agree. (8) The United States did not back Batista in 1959; it had ended aid to Cuba and washed its hands of him well before then. (9) "Tet" was not evidence of the unpopularity of the Saigon government, but a resounding rejection of the northern invaders. (HAN 548)

With regard to (1), Handlin's use of the word "simply" is troubling. Zinn knows as well as anyone that no two historical events are identical, so when he says that "what Columbus did to the Arawaks of the Bahamas, Cortez did to the Aztecs of Mexico, Pizarro to the Incas of Peru, and the English settlers of Virginia and Massachusetts to the Powhatans and the Pequots," he obviously does not mean that what each of these parties did was exactly the same as what each of the others did. Rather, his statement must be understood as referring to sameness or identity on a general level, that is, at a certain level of abstraction.[104] There is nothing strange about such a way of talking. If two people both vote for the same candidate, or enroll in the same class, or order the same dessert, it is not uncommon to say that they "did the same thing," even if, for example, they voted at different times of day, or took the class for different reasons, or used different methods in communicating to the server their dessert orders (one by naming the item ordered, the other by pointing at it on the dessert tray). Zinn's meaning, rather transparently, is that what each of these parties did to the people to whom they did it is to steal from them, physically attack them, and, in great numbers, kill them. He details and documents this, for Columbus and the Arawaks, on pages 1–7 of APH, citing Las Casas's *History of the Indies*; for Cortez and the Aztecs and Pizarro and the Incas, on pages 11–12, citing the Spaniards' own accounts; for the English settlers and the Powhatans and the Pequots, on pages 12–17, citing Edmund Morgan's *American Slavery, American Freedom*, Francis Jennings' *The Invasion of America*, William Bradford's *History of the Plymouth Plantation*, and Virgil Vogel's *This Land Was Ours*, among other sources.

When we turn to Handlin, however, the situation is very different. To support his claim that what Zinn says about this is "simply not true," Handlin provides no documentation and no argumentation—indeed, no evidence of any kind. Nor, for that matter, does he even offer an explanation as to what, exactly, he thinks Zinn gets wrong. Does Handlin think that none of these explorers ever killed any Indians? Or merely that some of them did not? Or that they did, but in different ways, or for different reasons, so that it was not "the same thing"? He "simply" doesn't tell us.

The same problems plague (2) and (3). Zinn makes his case, with extensive documentation, in the second chapter of APH (especially on pages 24–6 and 29–30—with respect to the desire of seventeenth and early eighteenth century Chesapeake farmers for black slaves), and in the third chapter (especially on pages 47–52—for the widening wealth gap in the eighteenth-century colonies). The positions he takes on these matters are quite orthodox. For example, one mainstream textbook features a section entitled "The colonies of the Chesapeake region— Virginia, Maryland, and North Carolina—developed agricultural economies which relied on slave labor." It contains the following "Key Points" summary: (a) "The Chesapeake colonies developed similar agricultural systems, initially based on tobacco, and later diversified to include cotton and indigo." (b) "Tobacco required intensive labor for cultivation, and the declining availability of white indentured servants made Chesapeake planters turn towards slave labor." (c) "The introduction of large-scale cheap labor, via slavery, allowed an increase in tobacco exports which generated significant wealth for whites in the region." (d) "The presence of slaves created an economic gap between wealthy and poor Chesapeake farmers, with the wealthy elites dominating the social and political life."[105]

Handlin's positions on these matters, by contrast, fly in the face of common sense. Zinn reports that there were about 6000 slaves in Virginia in 1700, and about 170,000 by 1763 (APH 32). How does Handlin suppose that they got there if their owners did not "desire their importation"? Does he think that the ownership of slaves was somehow imposed on the farmers against their will, with their attitude toward both the institution of slavery and the great wealth that it created for them being one of resentful tolerance? Or is his objection a hair-splitting one— perhaps that the farmers did desire slaves, but not "avidly"? Because Handlin tells us neither the nature of his disagreement nor its evidentiary basis, we have no way of knowing. Once again, his statement that Zinn's claim "simply isn't true" itself simply isn't helpful.

Nor does Handlin explain why he rejects the data showing widening income inequality in the eighteenth century. It is easy to see why the introduction of slavery would increase such inequality. African slaves were expensive, but generated huge profits for their owners. As a result rich farmers who could afford many slaves became richer, enhancing their competitive advantage over poor farmers who could afford few or any slaves. And the slaves themselves, of course, were the poorest of the poor. So as more of them entered the colonies, and created more and more wealth for their owners, the gap between themselves and their owners continually widened. On what basis does Handlin deny this? He doesn't tell us. What evidence does he provide to show that it "simply isn't true"? None. And yet, it is a remarkable and revelatory phenomenon that dozens of articles and Internet postings cite Handlin's "it simply isn't true" claims as "proof" of Zinn's incompetence—in spite of the fact that (a) Handlin doesn't explain, and nor is it clear, what his claims mean; (b) he provides no evidence in support of them; (c) he fails to back them with arguments; (d) he does not explain what is wrong with the data and arguments that Zinn and others give in favor of the claims that he rejects; (e) he cites no other historians who agree with him; (f) his positions stand in opposition, not only to APH, but also to what is stated in traditional, mainstream textbooks; and (g) some of his claims, as just mentioned, defy common sense.

With (4) Handlin finally scores. It is true that in the original edition of APH Zinn quotes from Polly Baker's speech without indicating that both Baker and her speech were fictional creations. However, he corrected this error, so that subsequent editions include this statement: "The speech was Benjamin Franklin's ironic invention" (APH 107).

But with regard to (5), it appears that Handlin is the one in error. James A. McCue, author of *The Legend of Plough-Jogger*, explains that "Jedediah Peck, alias Plough-Jogger, was a real person. He lived an amazing life in amazing times (1748–1821)."[106] As usual, Handlin provides no explanation as to why he judges the existence of Plough-Jogger to be "improbable," and supplies no evidence or argument in support of his assertion that Zinn is wrong on this point.

This same failing applies to (6), in which Handlin chastises Zinn for "repeat[ing] uncritically the old charge that President Lincoln altered his views to suit his audience." An old charge it may be, but that does not make it a false charge, and Handlin gives us no reason to think that it is. Zinn makes his case as follows:

In his 1858 campaign in Illinois for the Senate against Stephen Douglas, Lincoln spoke differently depending on the views of his listeners (and also perhaps depending on how close it was to the election). Speaking in northern Illinois in July (in Chicago), he said:

Let us discard all this quibbling about this man and the other man, this race and that race and the other race being inferior, and therefore they must be placed in an inferior position. Let us discard all these things, and unite as one people throughout this land, until we shall once more stand up declaring that all men are created equal.

Two months later in Charleston, in southern Illinois, Lincoln told his audience:

I will say, then, that I am not, nor ever have been, in favor of bringing about in any way the social and political equality of the white and black races (applause); that I am not, nor ever have been, in favor of making voters or jurors of negroes, nor of qualifying them to hold office, nor to intermarry with white people....

And inasmuch as they cannot so live, while they do remain together there must be the position of superior and inferior, and I as much as any other man am in favor of having the superior position assigned to the white race. (APH 188)

Lincoln issued his anti-racist remarks (those from the first quotation above) on July 10, 1858, in response to Stephen Douglas's assertion that the United States government was "made by the white man, for the benefit of the white man, to be administered by white men."[107] Douglas, in turn, was appalled by Lincoln's response, and "indignantly turned this back on Lincoln, proclaiming 'this Chicago doctrine of Lincoln's— declaring that the negro and the white man are made equal by the Declaration of Independence and by Divine Providence—is a monstrous heresy.'"[108]

The second quotation comes from one of the famous "Lincoln–Douglas debates," more specifically the fourth debate, held in Charleston, Illinois on September 18, 1858.[109] Lincoln spoke first, with the quoted passage occurring right at the beginning of his presentation, in reply, he tells us, to an inquiry he had received earlier that day as to whether he really was "in favor of producing a perfect equality between the negroes and white people." Zinn has not (of course) fabricated either quotation; nor has he taken either one out of context. What, then, could be the basis for Handlin's complaint?

Because of his irresponsibility we can only speculate, but it could be that he is persuaded by the defense that Lincoln himself offers against the charge that he had said different things about slavery to different audiences. In the fifth Lincoln–Douglas debate, held in Galesburg, Illinois on October 7, 1858, Lincoln states that his different speeches on slavery

> have been before the public for a considerable time, and if they have any inconsistency in them, if there is any conflict in them, the public have been unable to detect it. When the Judge [Douglas] says, in speaking on this subject, that I make speeches of one sort for the people of the northern end of the State, and of a different sort for the southern people, he assumes that I do not understand that my speeches will be put in print and read north and south. I knew all the while that the speech that I made at Chicago, and the one I made at Jonesboro and the one at Charleston, would all be put in print and all the reading and intelligent men in the community would see them and know all about my opinions. And I have not supposed, and do not now suppose, that there is any conflict whatever between them. But the Judge will have it that if we do not confess that there is a sort of inequality between the white and black races, which justifies us in making them slaves, we must, then, insist that there is a degree of equality that requires us to make them our wives.[110]

The problem with Lincoln's argument is that in his Chicago speech his claim was not merely that racial inequalities between whites and blacks were insufficient to justify slavery. It was, rather, that we should "discard" distinctions of racial superiority and inferiority entirely.

Lincoln also claims in that same debate that in all of his speeches he has insisted that "the inferior races are our equals" in only one respect, that of "their right to 'life, liberty and the pursuit of happiness,' as proclaimed in that old Declaration," with their inferiority in other respects precluding the achievement of "perfect social and political equality" between the races. He further asserts that since this distinction is [allegedly] to be found in all of his speeches, there is no inconsistency among them, but only a pseudo-inconsistency generated by illegitimately juxtaposing "they are our equals" passages with "they are inferior" passages, but without including the material explaining that the races are equal and unequal with respect to entirely different things—equal in certain fundamental rights; unequal in natural abilities. As proof, Lincoln suggests that "by taking two parts of the same speech, he [Douglas, and we might add, by parallel reasoning, Zinn] could have got up as much of a conflict as the one he has found."

But unfortunately, the texts of Lincoln's speeches will not sustain this self-interpretation. While it is true that in many of his speeches he makes the point that refusing to enslave blacks does not entail an obligation to marry them, he often does so without reference to racial superiority or inferiority. For example, in the Chicago speech he makes the point this way:

> I protest, now and forever, against that counterfeit logic which presumes that because I do not want a negro woman for a slave, I do necessarily want her for a wife. [Laughter and cheers.] My understanding is that I need not have her for either, but as God made us separate, we can leave one another alone and do one another much good thereby. There are white men enough to marry all the white women, and enough black men to marry all the black women, and in God's name let them be so married.

And in that speech he takes no pains to clarify that his soaring egalitarian rhetoric ("Let us discard all this quibbling about this man and the other man, this race and that race and the other race being inferior...[and] stand up declaring that all men are created equal") is meant to have only the most modest application; nor is there anything in that speech corresponding to the thunderous racism of the Charleston statement ("there must be the position of superior and inferior, and I as much as any other man am in favor of having the superior position assigned to the white race"). Lincoln's claim that one could generate as much conflict by comparing different parts of his Chicago speech as one could by juxtaposing that speech with his performance at Charleston will not survive a reading of the two documents.

Most admirers of Lincoln who address this issue concede that the charge of politically motivated inconsistency is sound. For example, one writer, determined to "stamp out" the "ridiculous myth" that Lincoln was a racist, nonetheless admits that "when he was addressing racist audiences during his senate campaign, he ramped up the racism in his own comments, assuring people he would never want to see blacks living equally with whites, and that the U.S. was a nation by and for whites alone."[111] And historian Brooks D. Simpson, who partially accepts Lincoln's own argument rebutting Douglas's charge of inconsistency ("Lincoln distinguished between different sorts of equality—Douglas did not"), still grudgingly acknowledges that "Lincoln did vary in his emphasis according to his audience."[112]

I conclude that the weight of evidence favors Zinn on this issue, rather than Handlin. And Handlin's case is not helped by his failure, once again, to provide any evidence or argument whatsoever in support of his claim, or to respond to the documentation that Zinn presents in support of his.

Handlin's (7) presents us with a complicated case. The relevant passage in APH reads as follows: "An international assemblage at Geneva presided over the peace agreement between the French and the Vietminh. It was agreed that the French would temporarily withdraw into the southern part of Vietnam, that the Vietminh would remain in the north, and that an election would take place in two years in a unified Vietnam to enable the Vietnamese to choose their own government" (472).

Handlin's objection, as we have seen, consists of the claim that "The Geneva assembly of 1954 did not agree on elections in a unified Vietnam; that was simply the hope expressed by the British chairman when the parties concerned could not agree." Who is right?

The Geneva Conference produced two significant documents: a cease-fire agreement, dated July 20, 1954, and "The Final Declaration of the Geneva Conference," dated July 21, 1954.[113] Both call for an election to unify Vietnam, allowing the Vietnamese to choose their own government, exactly as Zinn says. The one and only point in Handlin's favor is that only two parties signed the first document (the Democratic Republic of Vietnam [or "Viet Minh"] and the French State of Vietnam—the two groups that had been fighting each other for nearly a decade), and no one signed the second. Most important, from Handlin's point of view, is that neither the United States nor its client, the State of Vietnam (later the "Republic of Vietnam"), was a signatory.[114]

In spite of this point, however, a good case can be made that Zinn's claims are correct and Handlin's criticism is unwarranted. For one thing, as just mentioned, the cease-fire agreement did indeed call for elections to unify Vietnam, and was indeed signed by both of the combatants of that time. (And this, most assuredly, did take place in Geneva in 1954.) If this is the agreement to which Zinn's mention of "the peace agreement between the French and the Vietminh" is intended to refer, his statements about it are accurate.

But even if Zinn's statement is taken to be about "The Final Declaration of the Geneva Conference," as Handlin's reference to a statement by "the British chairman" implies, there is a good deal to be said for it—and little to be said for Handlin's error-laden rebuttal. To begin with the latter point, Handlin, who is clearly talking about "The Final Declaration," erroneously states that the United States was "not a party in 1954." In fact, the participants were: Cambodia, the Democratic Republic of Vietnam, France, Laos, China, the State of Vietnam, the Soviet Union, Great Britain, and the United States (VAA 74).

Moreover, it is an overstatement to say of the Declaration in general, or of the call for elections in particular, that it "simply" articulated "the hope" of "the British chairman." Rather, it "expressed the official consensus of these participants" (VAA 74), albeit with objections and reservations by particular parties noted for the record. A transcript of a session at the close of the Geneva Conference makes this clear. The chairman, British Foreign Minister Anthony Eden, explaining the purpose of "The Final Declaration," begins his remarks by noting that "agreement has now been reached on certain documents," and that "it is proposed that this Conference should take note of these agreements." He subsequently refers to a draft of the "Declaration," and asks all of the representatives to "express themselves upon" it (VAA 77). When they do so, five of the parties (France, Laos, China, the Soviet Union, and Great Britain) express their complete agreement with the document (VAA 77–8). Cambodia and the Democratic Republic of Vietnam raise a concern having to do with relations between their two nations, but voice no objection to anything else (VAA 78). Thus, seven of the nine parties give their support to the provision calling for elections to unify Vietnam. And while the U.S. delegate, Walter Bedell Smith, states that his government "is not prepared to join in a Declaration by the Conference such as submitted," he goes on to offer, on behalf of the United States, a "unilateral declaration of its position in these matters": "In connection with the statement in the Declaration concerning free elections in Vietnam, my government wishes to make clear its position...as follows: In the case of nations now divided against their will, we shall continue to seek unity through free elections, supervised by the United Nations to ensure they are conducted fairly" (VAA 78–9). Perhaps even more significantly, Smith pledges that the United States will "refrain from the threat of or the use of force to disturb" the Geneva agreements (VAA 78). Thus, while it is true, as Handlin says, that the United States "did not support" the Final Declaration, it is not true that it withheld support for free elections to unify Vietnam.

This point is the crucial one in terms of the critique of U.S. behavior that Zinn goes on to develop in APH:

The United States moved quickly to prevent the unification and to establish South Vietnam as an American sphere. It set up in Saigon as head of the government a former Vietnamese official named Ngo Dinh Diem, who had recently been living in New Jersey, and encouraged him not to hold the scheduled elections for unification. A memo in early 1954 of the Joint Chiefs of Staff said that intelligence estimates showed "a settlement based on free elections would be attended by almost certain loss of the Associated States [Laos, Cambodia, and Vietnam—the three parts of Indochina created by the Geneva Conference] to Communist control." Diem again and again blocked the elections requested by the Vietminh, and with American money and arms his government became more and more firmly established. As the *Pentagon Papers* put it [recall that this work is a classified history of the Vietnam War written by the Pentagon's own historians for secret internal use]: "South Viet Nam was essentially the creation of the United States." (472)

There is little doubt that Zinn is right about the U.S. motive for trying (successfully) to block free elections in Vietnam—it knew that its side would lose. President Dwight D. Eisenhower candidly admits this in his memoirs: "I have never talked or corresponded with a person knowledgeable in Indochinese affairs who did not agree that had elections been held as of the time of the fighting, possibly 80 per cent of the population would have voted for the Communist Ho Chi Minh as their leader."[115] And an April 1955 U.S. Department of Defense report concluded that if an election were to be held in Vietnam under international supervision, "there is no reason to doubt" that the Viet Minh "would win easily" (as quoted in TVR 75). So the U.S. war effort in Vietnam, which had been sold to the American people as a fight for freedom and democracy, was in fact a violent campaign, carried out in violation of an explicit pledge, for the purpose of blocking a people from freely choosing their own leader. Despite what Handlin says, Zinn is right about this, not wrong.

With regard to (8), Handlin is also wrong in attributing to Zinn the claim that the United States had backed Cuban dictator Fulgencio Batista "in 1959." After all, as Zinn himself points out, "The Batista government fell apart on New Year's Day 1959" (APH 439), and "Castro took over Havana on January 8, 1959" (ZRH 432). Nonetheless, Handlin complains that when Zinn speaks of the revolution of 1959, in which Batista was overthrown, he refers to Batista as "the American-backed dictator," without acknowledging that the United States (allegedly) "had ended aid to Cuba and washed its hands of him well before then."

What justification is there for Zinn's asserting, without qualifying it by date, that Batista was "American-backed"? First, Batista relied on U.S. support for all but about a month of his nearly seven-year rule. This aid—economic, military, and diplomatic—began shortly after he took power in a coup, on March 10, 1952, and did not end until December 11, 1958, when U.S. Ambassador Earl Smith visited Batista personally to inform him that he would no longer be receiving U.S. support.[116] Second, revolutions take time—they do not occur in a day. Thus, while Batista did not flee Cuba until January 1, 1959, Zinn correctly points out that U.S support "continued until it was clear Batista was finished" (ZRH 432). It is not as if the U.S. pulled its aid, say, five years before the revolution, and with that revolutionary movement having begun only well after the Washington government had ceased its involvement. If it had happened that way, then it would indeed have been misleading for Zinn to speak of the overthrow of an "American-backed" dictator. But if, as is in fact the case, the U.S. backed Batista until it was obvious that he was already defeated and would be ousted imminently, this means that he was "American-backed" to the end, even if he would technically remain in office for the whopping total of 21 additional days.

The only point that might be cited in favor of Handlin's assertion that the U.S. "had ended aid to Cuba and washed its hands of him well before [the 1959 revolution]" is that the U.S. had stopped arms delivery to Batista in March 1958. Zinn himself brings this up (ZRH 432), citing Arthur M. Schlesinger, Jr.'s *A Thousand Days*. However, as Schlesinger explains, (a) the U.S. continued its "military mission" in Cuba, and thus continued to provide armed support for the Batista regime, well past that date even though it ceased to supply him with new armaments; and (b) this was a compromise measure—some in the U.S. State Department wanted to continue backing Batista in full, while others wanted to terminate U.S. aid entirely—adopted in response to the realization that Batista's dictatorship was already by that date doomed.[117] So, in sum, U.S. aid to Batista, including military support, continued until very shortly before he was overthrown, and ceased only when his ouster was perceived to be both inevitable and imminent. The man who was deposed in the 1959 revolution was, indeed, "an American-backed dictator"; and the claim that the U.S. "had ended aid to Cuba and washed its hands of him well before then" is false. Once again, Zinn is right and Handlin is wrong.

HRZ contains one more comment worth discussing. In addition to his main point, the one about the timing of the revolution relative to that of the U.S.'s withdrawal of support, Handlin also suggests that the phrase "American-backed" unfairly overstates the extent of U.S. aid to Batista. He does so by saying that "the United States had...recognized Batista, as did Cubans of all shades of political opinion including Marxists" (HRZ 432). This attempt to equate the U.S. stance or attitude toward Batista with that of Marxist Cubans is absurd. While the latter may indeed have "recognized" Batista, in the sense of acknowledging that he had, as a brute matter of fact, taken power and was now in charge, that is fully consistent with their also opposing and despising him; and, in any case, "recognizing" him is very different from praising him, defending him against criticism, and supplying him with weapons, as the U.S. did. Sketching a few details of Batista's relations with the U.S., on the one hand, and with his political opponents in Cuba, on the other, should help both to clarify this point and to underscore the justice of Zinn's characterization of Batista as "an American-backed dictator."

Note first that, as Zinn points out, "U.S. business interests...dominated the Cuban economy" (APH 439). John F. Kennedy, in a 1960 speech, provides some of the details: "At the beginning of 1959 United States companies owned about 40 percent of the Cuban sugar lands—almost all the cattle ranches—90 percent of the mines and mineral concessions—80 percent of the utilities—practically all the oil industry—and supplied two-thirds of Cuba's imports" (JFK). And Earl Smith, who had been U.S. Ambassador to Cuba during the later part of Batista's reign, testified to the U.S. Senate in 1960 that, "the United States, until the advent of Castro, was so overwhelmingly influential in Cuba that...the American Ambassador was the second most important man in Cuba; sometimes even more important than the President."[118]

The effects of such economic domination on the Cuban people were anything but benign. Batista's venality and greed, combined with his willingness to sacrifice the interests of the Cuban people to those of his wealthy American benefactors, naturally provoked resistance. As historian Arthur Schlesinger, Jr., who analyzed Batista's Cuba in his capacity as a Special Assistant to President John Kennedy, explains:

> The character of the Batista regime in Cuba made a violent popular reaction almost inevitable. The rapacity of the leadership, the corruption of the government, the brutality of the police, the regime's indifference to the needs of the people for education, medical care, housing, for social justice and economic opportunity—all these...constituted an open invitation to revolution.[119]

As the anti-Batista resistance gained strength, the United States stepped in to help Batista fight it, supplying him with planes, ships, tanks, and napalm, which he promptly used against his domestic opposition (BAT). In an effort to acquire information about Castro's army, Batista's secret police used torture, often against innocent people, as an interrogation technique. Those suspected of having joined the insurgency were publicly executed as a warning against others who might be considering joining. In order to get the message across to those who had not personally witnessed the executions, Batista ordered that the corpses of those executed be left hanging from lamp posts or dumped in the streets (BAT). The result, as Kennedy points out in the speech just cited, is that:

> Fulgencio Batista murdered 20,000 Cubans in seven years...and he turned Democratic Cuba into a complete police state—destroying every individual liberty. Yet our aid to his regime, and the ineptness of our policies, enabled Batista to invoke the name of the United States in support of his reign of terror. [Eisenhower] administration spokesmen publicly praised Batista—hailed him as a staunch ally and a good friend—at a time when Batista was murdering thousands,

destroying the last vestiges of freedom, and stealing hundreds of millions of dollars from the Cuban people.... (JFK)

So, yes, Batista was "an American-backed dictator," and the accuracy of Zinn's characterization of him as such is unassailable. Zinn's discussion of Batista in APH provides students with information on a topic that is ignored in many conventional United States history texts—the tendency of the United States government to support murderous dictators who are willing, for a price, to support U.S. business and political interests at the expense of the interests of the people they are supposedly governing. Handlin, a more traditional and "patriotic" historian, does not like this, and, as we have seen, accuses Zinn of producing a "deranged fairy tale, in which the incidents are made to fit the legend, no matter how intractable the evidence of American history." But, as the present example illustrates, in the few instances in which Handlin actually offers an explanation as to what, exactly, Zinn got wrong, the "errors" are, at best (from Handlin's point of view), minor and technical, and do not upset Zinn's main point in the slightest. Thus, while I have argued that Zinn's entire statement about Batista is completely true and fair, let's suppose that I am wrong about that, and that Handlin's point about the U.S. having withdrawn its support from Batista prior to the completion of the revolution is a salient one. In that case, Zinn's error in his discussion of the 1959 Cuban revolution would have been merely that of describing Batista as "the American-backed dictator," when it should have been something like, "the dictator who had until recently, and for nearly the entirety of his murderous reign, been backed by the United States." Obviously this would not have altered the main point of his discussion—the "anti-American," "unpatriotic," but entirely true and obviously important one that the likes of Handlin and Mitch Daniels so much despise. So even if Handlin were right, and Zinn wrong, on this one small detail, that would not show Zinn's account of

Batista and his relations with the U.S. to be a "deranged fairy tale, in which the incidents are made to fit the legend, no matter how intractable the evidence of American history." But sadly, that description perfectly fits Handlin's critique of Zinn.

And the same point applies to the previous example—the one about the Geneva conference and the Vietnam War. The essential point that Zinn makes is that the United States, despite its claim that the war was being fought for freedom and democracy, was actually blocking elections that would unify the country—and was doing so because it knew that its preferred candidate would lose, even (or especially) if the elections were free and fair, and faithfully monitored by the United Nations and other neutral parties. Recall that Handlin's criticism is that the United States had never signed the document calling for such an election, even though its ambassador to the Geneva conference, while explicitly refusing to sign the document, did nevertheless "unilaterally" declare that the United States would support the election. On this small distinction, rendered even more minor by the consideration that Zinn's main point had to do with the hypocrisy on the part of the United States in publicly claiming to support freedom, democracy, and self-determination for the Vietnamese people while in fact violently preventing them from electing their own preferred leader, Handlin would have us believe that Zinn is unscrupulously twisting the truth so as to enable his "fairy tale" to evade "the intractable evidence of American history." That's pathetic.

That brings us to (9), the last item on Handlin's list, which addresses Zinn's treatment of the "Tet Offensive," a significant event in the Vietnam War. Impressively, Handlin packs into his two sentences of commentary on this matter (one in his initial review and one in his response to Zinn's letter replying to that review [I am not counting one additional sentence from the latter document that merely quotes Zinn]) six distinct errors of fact or logic:

(a) In his review Handlin clearly implies that Zinn had denied, or at least failed to acknowledge, that the Tet Offensive had resulted in a military defeat for the forces that had launched it, and a victory for the United States and its client, the government of South Vietnam. For Handlin's entire comment at (9), which is clearly intended as a refutation of Zinn—it is an item in a list allegedly documenting his "casual regard to factual accuracy"—reads as follows: "'Tet' was not evidence of the unpopularity of the Saigon government, but a resounding rejection of the northern invaders." And again, in his response to Zinn's reply, he states, as if it were a telling point against Zinn, that "the offensive was not a success" (HRZ). But when we turn to look at what Zinn had written in APH to provoke this response, we find his clear statement that "The offensive was beaten back" (480).

(b) Handlin seems to think that the mere fact of this military victory is sufficient to refute Zinn's argument that the Tet Offensive demonstrated the unpopularity of the Saigon government and the popularity of the National Liberation Front (NLF; also called "Viet Cong"). It doesn't. For one thing, the Saigon government had the U.S. military on its side. Thus, to the precise extent that the "Tet" victory is attributable to U.S. firepower it is not an achievement of the government of South Vietnam. Second, since the soldiers fighting for that government were conscripts, their efforts do not constitute evidence of support for it.[120] Third, and perhaps most importantly, military victories and defeats are not all-or-nothing affairs. Disturbing weaknesses in the victors might be exposed even in their victory; startling strengths in the defeated forces might be revealed even in their defeat. The details of Zinn's account, coupled with his explicit statement that the U.S.–South Vietnamese forces ultimately prevailed, clearly establish that his claim about the unpopularity of the Saigon government is to be understood in this light:

The unpopularity of the Saigon government explains the success of the National Liberation Front in infiltrating Saigon and other government-held towns in early 1968, without the people there warning the government. The NLF thus launched a surprise offensive (it was the time of "Tet," their New Year holiday) that carried them into the heart of Saigon, immobilized Tan San Nhut airfield, even occupied the American Embassy briefly. The offensive was beaten back, but it demonstrated that all the enormous firepower delivered on Vietnam by the United States had not destroyed the NLF, its morale, its popular support, its will to fight. It caused a reassessment in the American government, more doubts among the American people. (APH 480)

Two other points about this issue should be noted. First, Handlin fails to respond to Zinn's argument. As we have seen, he thinks that he can refute it simply by pointing out that the anti-Saigon military forces were ultimately unsuccessful militarily; but Zinn never claims otherwise, so Handlin's "refutation" consists solely of the rejection of an assertion that was not in any sense a premise of Zinn's argument.

Second, while one might suspect that Zinn is engaging in special pleading here by attempting to turn a defeat into a sign of strength for the losers, and a victory into a sign of weakness for the winners (perhaps we finally have an example of Zinn's horrible tendency to make "the incidents fit the legend, no matter how intractable the evidence of American history"), it turns out that his interpretation of this issue is entirely orthodox. Part One of TVR, entitled "Textbook Synthesis," summarizes the consensus account of the Vietnam War as it is presented in 28 mainstream American history textbooks.[121] Unlike Handlin, the textbook authors show themselves able to grasp the elementary point that those who eventually lose can still demonstrate surprising strength before losing—for example, by achieving partial control of 26 provincial capitals in South Vietnam (out of 30 that were attacked), thus forcing the American and South Vietnamese armies to pay "a heavy price to regain a portion of the lost territory." Further, the textbooks assert, in complete agreement with Zinn, that the Tet Offensive showed "that 'the other war'—the effort of the Saigon government to win the allegiance of the Vietnamese people—was still far from won." Moreover, this event "stunned the administration and refuted completely its optimistic statements," making the Tet Offensive a "turning point in the war."[122] Indeed, as Daniel Ellsberg, the famous leaker of the Pentagon Papers points out, "The scale and coordination of Tet, almost simultaneous attacks in nearly every province in South Vietnam as well as in Saigon itself," was regarded as "astonishing" at the time, and exerted an "immense impact...on public consciousness and the attitude of Congress" (ELL 199). For that reason, General William Westmoreland and the chairman of the Joint Chiefs of Staff, General Earle Wheeler, privately admitted that, despite their public statements to the contrary, the Tet Offensive was, in the final analysis, not a U.S. victory.[123]

(c) Handlin's description of the defeated forces as "the northern invaders" flies in the face of the facts. While forces of the North Vietnamese Army did participate in the Offensive, they did so in tandem with NLF fighters from South Vietnam. In fact, so much did the NLF dominate the effort that, while some descriptions of the Tet Offensive in history textbooks or in scholarly studies say that it was carried out by a coalition of NLF and North Vietnamese forces, many others omit the North Vietnamese entirely, and refer to the event as an attack undertaken by the NLF. The idea that the Offensive was launched by "northern invaders" appears to be an invention of Handlin's, for which he provides no evidence.

(d) Handlin's bizarre "northern invaders" line begs the question against Zinn. Recall that Zinn had argued that the Tet offensive "demonstrated that all the enormous firepower delivered on Vietnam by the United States had not destroyed the NLF, its morale, its popular support, its will to fight." But that claim only makes sense if the fighters confronting "the enormous firepower" of the United States had been the NLF, rather than Handlin's "northern invaders." Thus, Handlin was under an obligation to defend his claim, since it is essential to his argument against Zinn. But he fails to do so, and simply asserts his "northern invaders" thesis, as if it were uncontroversial.

(e) Handlin's response to Zinn's letter replying to Handlin's original review (HRZ) is, in fact, non-responsive. Recall that in his review Handlin had challenged Zinn's claim that the Saigon government was unpopular. In Zinn's reply (ZRH), he quotes (with a documentary citation) from a memorandum in the Pentagon Papers in which the Pentagon officials criticize "the Saigon leadership" for showing "no signs of a willingness—let alone an ability—to attract the necessary loyalty or support of the people" (432). Bizarrely, Handlin replies that such criticism is "irrelevant to the fact that the offensive was not a success and that the NLF evoked no signs of popular support" (432). But this statement of Handlin's is utterly irrelevant to the point Zinn was making in quoting the Pentagon officials. That point was that the South Vietnamese government was unpopular, not that the Tet Offensive had been a military success, or that the NLF was popular. (Zinn makes the latter point elsewhere, of course, but this was not what was at issue here.) Note that, although this is contrary to historical fact, it would have been perfectly possible, from the standpoint of logic, for both the Saigon government and the NLF to have been unpopular. So pointing out the (alleged) unpopularity of the NLF does nothing to undermine Zinn's claim that the South Vietnamese government was unpopular. It is Handlin, rather than Zinn, who is guilty of an irrelevancy here.

(f) Handlin's assertion that "the NLF evoked no signs of popular support" is pulled out of thin air, and is objectionable on at least two other grounds. First, it makes no sense in light of Handlin's equally bizarre claim, already discussed, that the perpetrators of the Tet Offensive were "northern invaders." For if that were the case, "the fact that the offensive was not a success" would tell us something negative only about the northern invaders. It wouldn't show, as Handlin now suddenly insists, that "the NLF evoked no signs of popular support."

Second, in denying the popularity of the NLF Handlin simply ignores—completely fails to address, let alone refute—all of the evidence and arguments that Zinn presents in support of the opposite conclusion. For, in addition to his argument based on the Tet Offensive, discussed above, he also presents such information as the following:

> In 1960, the National Liberation Front was formed in the South. It united the various strands of opposition to the regime; its strength came from South Vietnamese peasants, who saw it as a way of changing their daily lives. A U.S. government analyst named Douglas Pike, in his book *Viet Cong*, based on interviews with rebels and captured documents, tried to give a realistic assessment of what the United States faced:
>
>> In the 2561 villages of South Vietnam, the National Liberation Front created a host of nation-wide socio-political organizations in a country where mass organizations...were virtually nonexistent.... *Aside from the NLF there had never been a truly mass-based political party in South Vietnam....*
>
> *Pike estimated that the NLF membership by early 1962 stood at around 300,000. The Pentagon Papers* said of this period: "*Only the Viet Cong had any real support and influence on a broad base in the countryside*" (APH 473, emphasis added)....
>
> Most of the South Vietnam countryside was now [June

1963] controlled by local villagers organized by the NLF (APH
474)....

Again and again, American leaders expressed their bewil-
derment at the popularity of the NLF. (APH 475)

Handlin ignores these claims, and the quotations and citations
that Zinn provides in their support. Instead, he blithely asserts
that "the NLF evoked no signs of popular support." But sadly, it
is Handlin's critique of Zinn, here and elsewhere, that evokes
"only casual regard to factual accuracy," or, for that matter, to
logical rigor, general scholarly standards, or basic fairness.

Immediately after completing his list of Zinn's nine "factual
errors," Handlin continues his bumbling attack as follows: "Since
Zinn does not comprehend the simple meaning of words, he
labels John Adams an aristocrat and Theodore Parker a racist..."
(548). Very well then, let's attend to "the simple meaning of
words." "Aristocrat" has several meanings, but the context in
which Zinn calls Adams an aristocrat suggests that he is using the
word in this sense: "an advocate of an aristocratic form of
government," where the relevant sense of "aristocracy" is
"government by those considered to be the best or most able
people in the state." This definition fits what Zinn says about
Adams:

[Thomas Paine's pamphlet, *Common Sense,*] caused some
tremors in aristocrats like John Adams, who were with the
patriot cause but wanted to make sure it didn't go too far in
the direction of democracy. Paine had denounced the so-called
balanced government of Lords and Commons as a deception,
and called for single-chamber representative bodies where the
people could be represented. Adams denounced Paine's plan
as "so democratical, without any restraint or even an attempt
at any equilibrium or counter-poise, that it must produce
confusion and every evil work." Popular assemblies needed to

be checked, Adams thought, because they were "productive of hasty results and absurd judgments." (APH 70)

So Handlin's charge that Zinn doesn't know what the word "aristocrat" means is in error. To show that Zinn's claim about Adams is wrong, Handlin would have to show that he has not accurately characterized Adams's views on government. But he doesn't do this, any more than he explains just how he thinks Zinn has misunderstood the meaning of "aristocrat." Rather, consistent with his practice throughout most of his critique, here we have assertion—and nasty, condescending assertion at that— accompanied by neither explanation nor argument. What kind of intellectual standards are these?

"Racist" is another word that has a meaning. A "racist," at least in one sense of that term, is "a person who believes in racism, the doctrine that one's own racial group is superior and has the right to dominate others or that a particular racial group is inferior to the others." So on what basis does Zinn call Theodore Parker a racist?

> The Reverend Theodore Parker, Unitarian minister in Boston, combined eloquent criticism of the war [against Mexico] with contempt for the Mexican people, whom he called "a wretched people; wretched in their origin, history, and character," who must eventually give way as the Indians did. Yes, the United States should expand, he said, but not by war, rather by the power of her ideas, the pressure of her commerce, by "the steady advance of a superior race, with superior ideas and a better civilization...by being better than Mexico, wiser, humaner, more free and manly." (APH 156–7)

Why, exactly, is this not racism? Handlin does not say.

Handlin's other examples of Zinn's supposed failure to comprehend the meaning of words fare no better. The paragraph on this topic, which begins with the cases of Adams and Parker, just discussed, continues with these alleged examples: "[Zinn] turns free trade into imperialism. Talk of liberty and country Zinn considers a rhetorical device to conceal rule by the rich few, and the Revolution of 1776 he describes as just the creation of a legal entity to take over land, profits, and power. Woman, in status, was 'akin to a house slave'" (548).

For each of these examples three objections should be noted. First, in every case Handlin grossly oversimplifies Zinn's position, reducing it to a caricature. Second, he offers no argument to show that Zinn's claims, whether understood in the simplistic manner in which Handlin represents them or in the much more nuanced form in which Zinn articulates them, are incorrect. Third, he doesn't offer any support at all for his wildly implausible contention that his disagreements with Zinn on these matters have anything to do with anyone's failure to understand the meanings of words.

To illustrate this, let's take up this last example, the one about the status of women. Here is the relevant passage in APH:

The biological uniqueness of women, like skin color and facial characteristics for Negroes, became a basis for treating them as inferiors.... It seems that their physical characteristics became a convenience for men, who could use, exploit, and cherish someone who was at the same time servant, sex mate, companion, and bearer-teacher-warden of his children.

Societies based on private property and competition, in which monogamous families became practical units for work and socialization, found it especially useful to establish this special status of women, something akin to a house slave in the matter of intimacy and oppression, and yet requiring, because of that intimacy, and long-term connection with children, a special patronization, which on occasion, especially in the face of a show of strength, could slip over into treatment as an equal. (103)

First, let's note the distortions. Handlin preserves the "akin to a house slave" part, but jettisons the "in the matter of intimacy and oppression" qualification, as well as the part about "a special patronization" that can on occasion "slip over into treatment as an equal." In this way, he eliminates the subtleties and nuances of Zinn's position, reducing it to something simple and crude. Second, which part of this does Handlin think is incorrect, and why? Third, what evidence is there that any of this passage from Zinn evidences a failure to understand "the simple meaning of words"? Handlin doesn't tell us.

Another of Handlin's criticisms is that APH "conveniently omits whatever does not fit its overriding thesis." For example, Handlin attributes to Zinn the claim that "American aggression continued after Vietnam, rearranged but pursuing the same vile military and economic goals." Handlin then concludes this comment with a zinger: "Not a word about the Soviet Union, of course" (548).

In his reply to Handlin, Zinn supplies three quotations from APH in which he criticizes the Soviet Union (for example, accusing it of "atrocities"), and asks, rhetorically, "Not a word" (ZRH 431–2)?[124] Handlin, in his response to Zinn's letter, neither defends, nor retracts, nor apologizes for his utterly baseless and demonstrably false charge. Instead, consistent with his ethical standards, he simply ignores Zinn's demonstration of his error on this point.

Yet another Handlin accusation is that Zinn is incapable of understanding "the men and women...who helped shape American society and its institutions," because "by his account, only one motive moved them: greed.... Hence, the blank incomprehensibility of those who acted contrary to their interests." To understand such individuals "would have called for an examination of intellectual and social forces beyond Zinn's ken" (HAN

550).

This charge, to borrow one of Handlin's phrases, "is pure invention" (550). Opening APH at random, in an attempt to find one of the numerous passages that refute this wild claim, I found the following in two seconds: "the motion picture industry, *wanting to preserve principle as well as profit*, set up a classification system (R for Restricted, X for prohibited to children)" (537, emphasis added).

Here Handlin follows the pattern of so many other of Zinn's critics, that of committing the very sins that he (falsely) attributes to Zinn. Handlin is criticizing Zinn's (alleged) reductionism in oversimplifying human motivation, but he can make this case only by oversimplifying Zinn's text, reducing it to a crude caricature. Had Handlin made a more restrained criticism—say, that Zinn's analyses overemphasize greed as an explanation for the actions of the rich and powerful, and sometimes fail to recognize the important role played by other motives—he might have been able to make his case. But by claiming that Zinn is a dolt who can't even understand individuals whose motives are complex and irreducible to personal greed, he shows himself to be the one who is unable to grasp the modest complexities and nuances of Zinn's lucid text.

It is at this point, immediately following its accusation that Zinn libels America's leaders by (supposedly) claiming that they are motivated solely by greed, that Handlin's broadside against Zinn reaches its unintentionally hilarious climax:

It would be a mistake…to regard Zinn as merely anti-American. Brendan Behan once observed that whoever hated America hated mankind, and hatred of humanity is the dominant tone of Zinn's book. No other modern country receives a favorable mention. He speaks well of the Russian and Chinese revolutions, but not of the states they created. He lavishes indiscriminate condemnation upon all the works of man—that is, upon civilization, a word he usually encloses in quotation marks. (Handlin 550)

Let's take these charges in turn. Is Zinn's book anti-American? Perhaps a case for that can be made if "America" is understood to refer exclusively to those who wield power (political, military, and business leaders)—though even then the charge is overstated (since it rests on a simplistic reading that overlooks Zinn's praise for some such leaders, and his treatment of several others as merely flawed, rather than as nakedly evil). But the charge collapses completely as soon as it is pointed out that "America" also includes (a) the domestic victims of misconduct by America's "leaders," (b) those who have struggled valiantly in efforts to combat and to overturn acts and structures of oppression and injustice, and (c) millions of other people—including teachers, farmers, artists, scientists, and doctors, to name but a few—who have made positive (nonviolent, nonoppressive) contributions to humanity. These are people with whom Zinn's book expresses sympathy and, often, profound respect and admiration. It seems that Handlin, like many other mainstream American historians, identifies so strongly with the likes of Columbus and the American Founding Fathers, that when Zinn calls attention to Columbus's treatment of the Arawaks, or the Founders' ownership of slaves, he can only understand this as an expression of hatred for his heroes. He seems genuinely unable to grasp the idea that Zinn's focusing on such issues might be rooted in respect for the Arawaks and the African slaves, and in concern that we learn from history that all people should be treated with respect in the future.

The idea that Zinn hates humanity is equally absurd.[125] For starters, one of the main things for which Zinn criticizes America's leaders is their frequently exploitative, violent, and/or criminal treatment of non-Americans—overthrowing their elected leaders, dropping bombs on them, imposing on them (and then propping up) brutal dictators who torture and kill them, and so forth. Once again, Handlin fails to perceive that such concerns are not rooted in hatred for America's leaders, and still less in hatred of humanity—supposedly "the dominant tone" of his book—but in respect for the rights of the victims of such actions.

Handlin's inability to comprehend this elementary point perhaps also explains his otherwise bizarre criticism of Zinn for failing to admire the governments of China or the Soviet Union. Given that Handlin shares Zinn's disapproval of these regimes (though how he knows about Zinn's attitude on this is a mystery, since, as discussed above, he elsewhere claims not to have noticed his critical statements about the Soviet Union in APH), one might have expected him to applaud, even if only grudgingly, this one aspect of Zinn's work. But his logic appears to have gone something like this: Since Zinn hates "America" (defined, of course, in terms of its rich and powerful), it must be because he is loyal to China or the Soviet Union. But if he hates "them" (defined in terms of *their* rich and powerful), too, it can only be because he hates humanity (for to grasp that someone might be genuinely concerned about the rights of poor children overseas, and to the extent of thinking that their welfare should not be subordinated to the political and economic interests of American elites would, to borrow Handlin's own words, "have called for an examination of intellectual and social [principles] beyond [Handlin's] ken").

Further support for the conclusion that Handlin confuses countries with their governments is that the supposition that he does so explains his otherwise inexplicable endorsement of an obvious *non sequitur*: that anyone who hates America hates mankind. Handlin's reasoning appears to run as follows:

1. The American government is better than any other government.

2. Zinn hates the American government.
3. Whoever hates the best thing in a given category also hates the lesser items in that category.
   Therefore, 4. Zinn hates all governments.
5. There is nothing to humanity but governments.
   Therefore, Zinn hates humanity.

Zinn, too, notices Handlin's conflation of "humanity" with "governments." His letter replying to Handlin's review concludes with these words:

> Behind [all of Handlin's distortions], I suspect, is a fundamental difference in our viewpoints which drives Handlin to fury. I am not merely "anti-American"; my book's "dominant tone" is "hatred of humanity." His evidence? "No other modern country receives a favorable mention. He speaks well of the Russian and Chinese revolutions, but not of the states they created." Handlin's logic: Humanity consists of states; Zinn does not speak well of any state; therefore Zinn hates humanity. I do speak well of lots of people, and of many movements of dissent and protest; indeed, that's what most of the book is about. But it is *states* Handlin cares about. And I seem to think there is a humanity beyond states, indeed, that states have generally acted against humanity.
>
> Well, that's worth an argument, but not a fit. (ZRH 432)

Handlin's response to this letter does not contain a reply to this point.

Lest anyone think that Zinn and I are wrong to attribute to Handlin a confusion of humanity with states, consider the sentence from his original review immediately following his point that Zinn does not speak well of the Russian and Chinese states. It begins this way: "He lavishes indiscriminate condemnation upon all the works of man...." The category "the works of man" surely includes novels, short stories, poems, plays, movies, songs, symphonies, paintings, drawings, sculptures, buildings, bridges—and so on endlessly. Zinn—a playwright, married to an artist, father of a theater director—loved the arts, a point that comes across clearly in almost all of his books, including APH (wherein he quotes and praises Mark Twain, Arthur Miller, and Langston Hughes, among countless others).[126] To the extent that the absurd claim that Zinn indiscriminately condemns "all the works of man" makes any sense at all, it can only do so on the supposition that states, that is, governments, are the only things that Handlin recognizes as "works of man."

Finally, let's restore the last part of the sentence just discussed, so as to facilitate a consideration of the part following the dash, which we have not yet addressed: "He lavishes indiscriminate condemnation upon all the works of man—that is, upon civilization, a word he usually encloses in quotation marks." Well, is that true? Does Zinn, indeed, "usually" (which, in case Handlin doesn't know, means "more than half of the time" or "in most cases") indicate his contempt for "civilization" by placing that word within quotation marks?

Here, at last, we have a hard, quantitative, verifiable (or falsifiable) claim, easily checked with the aid of an engine (readily available on my computer) that can search for words within a text. Surely a check of this claim will reveal that Handlin, the Pulitzer Prize-winning Carl H. Pforzheimer University Professor at Harvard University, is a careful, responsible, and trustworthy scholar, who can be relied upon to make accurate claims, fully warranted by the most scrupulous assessment of the relevant evidence. As it turns out, however, Zinn uses the word "civilization" 20 times in *A People's History* (not counting the appearance of the word in quotations from the sayings and writings of others). He encloses it in quotation marks twice. Two out of 20 comes out to 10% of the time—which is a far cry from "usually."[127] But remember, it is Howard Zinn who "pays only casual regard to factual accuracy."

"frankly speaking"

A contributor to an Internet discussion of the Daniels–Zinn controversy, "frankly speaking," offers a criticism of Zinn that we have not yet encountered: "Zinn basically saw American democracy and capitalistic economy as a sham while he made a good living tucked in the loving bosom [of] its higher education institutions. Like most prospering socialists and communists of his day, he preferred not to live in the radical socialist experiment states, the sort of state he idealized in writing. He never leveled vicious criticism on the Soviet Union or China...."[128]

The charge, I take it, is that Zinn's critique of the United States is undermined by his decision to live there. In reply, at least four points are in order.

First, Zinn did not "idealize the radical socialist experiment states." Like most who make this charge, "frankly speaking" neglects to quote a single passage from Zinn's writings or speeches in which he does so. There is, I would suggest, an obvious reason for this.

Second, as we have seen, it is also not true that Zinn "never leveled vicious criticism on the Soviet Union or China," unless it does not count as "vicious criticism" to call the Soviet Union "ruthless," "oppressive," "brutal," "murderous," a "dictatorship," a "police state," an example of "fascism," that is guilty of "aggression," "atrocities," and "monstrous tyranny," or to refer to China's "bloody record of suppression" (for documentation, see the discussions of Greenberg and Flynn above).

Third, Zinn was an American. Why should he be expected to abandon the country of his birth, the country where his family, friends, and loved ones lived, the one whose language and culture he best understood? Why should he be expected to live elsewhere, especially since, contrary to the delusions of "frankly speaking," he was not an admirer of China or the Soviet Union?

True, he may have admired the governments of Denmark or Sweden or Finland more, but (I presume) he did not know the languages, among other hardships such a move would have caused him to endure. Why should he not, instead, stay in the country of his birth and try to improve it, not just by criticism, but also by bold, courageous direct action, such as, for example, fighting segregation in the south? Moreover, there is more to a country than the actions of its government, as Zinn tirelessly pointed out. He obviously loved many of those things, and had no desire to abandon them.

Finally, with regard to the "made a good living" charge, consider the testimony of Ann M. Little, Associate Professor of History at Colorado State University, who responded directly to "frankly speaking":

You are wrong that he "made a good living" at Boston University. The president of the uni in the 1980s and 1990s, John Silber, was ideologically at war with Zinn, and he and his minions prevented Zinn ever from getting any merit increases since before he even published "A People's History."

How do I know? I worked in the summer of 1987 in the Office of Faculty Actions, and it was my job to Xerox tenure & promotion files and to mail out faculty contracts. I remember opening Zinn's returned contract and seeing that he had signed it but had also included a note to the effect that "I see once again you refuse to pay me any more money, but I don't care!"

The princely sum he made in the 1987–88 academic year? $41,000! For a full professor, a WWII vet, a Civil Rights stalwart, and someone who was among the few faculty willing to take a stand against John Silber. As a college sophomore interested in going into higher ed myself, that sure made an impression. It's a miracle I decided to go to grad school anyway.

I would add that Zinn certainly was aware that his chosen path—publishing radical ideas, criticizing the university president and other administrative bosses, speaking at teach-ins and anti-war rallies, engaging in acts of civil disobedience, and supporting his students when their rights were violated by university officials—would lead to reprisals, and would cost him financially. The odds of getting ahead in academia are far better if one toes the line, sucks up to the administration, and refrains from making waves. But Zinn, whether you agree with his conscience or not, followed it.

It is ironic that APH did finally provide him a good income. But that could not have been his motive in writing it, as neither he, nor anyone else, anticipated that it would sell as it did—the initial print run, recall, was 4000 copies. If Zinn had thought that his book had a chance to sell over two million copies he would have turned down the contract his publisher offered him and sought instead a publisher who would do a much larger print run, and who would put advertising muscle behind it.

Notice also a strange implication that follows from "frankly speaking's" charge that it would be wrong for a well-paid American historian to criticize America. If the praise of America by historians is to be meaningful, shouldn't it be based on America's merits, as determined by a careful and fair examination of the historical record? But "frankly speaking" seems to imply that a positive evaluation is owed as a debt of gratitude for the American system's having provided the historian with a good salary.

Michael Kammen

Kammen (1936–2013), a Pulitzer Prize-winning professor of American cultural history at Cornell University, is the author of a review of APH in the *Washington Post*.[129] He is represented on Daniels's list of Zinn critics by means of a quotation from that review:

"I wish that I could pronounce Zinn's book a great success, but it is not. It is a synthesis of the radical and revisionist historiography of the past decade.... Not only does the book read like a scissors and paste-pot job, but even less attractive, so much attention to historians, historiography and historical polemic leaves precious little space for the substance of history.... We do deserve a people's history; but not a simpleminded history, too often of fools, knaves and Robin Hoods. We need a judicious people's history because the people are entitled to have their history whole; not just those parts that will anger or embarrass them." Michael Kammen, in reviewing Zinn's book in the Washington Post.

Kammen's critique of Zinn, though severe, is qualitatively different from the others we have considered. While he objects to some of Zinn's decisions of inclusion and exclusion, and, primarily on that basis, judges his work to be "simpleminded" (his harshest insult) and lacking in "balance," there is no suggestion that he finds Zinn's work to be grossly incompetent. For example, he judges Zinn's "gravest error of commission" to be, not some appalling factual error or logical lapse, but rather merely the inclusion of too many quotations from historians, with the result that such an intensive focus on "historians, historiography and historical polemic" leaves "precious little space for the *substance* of history." To illustrate this point, he complains that historian Philip Foner "is cited nine times while Thomas Jefferson is mentioned only eight."

The example is absurd. The references to Jefferson are not mere "mentions." Jefferson's actions are treated in APH as significant events in American history, and his ideas are subjected to careful analysis. The references to Foner, in quite radical contrast, are merely documentary citations. Foner's name appears in the body of Zinn's text only because APH uses an internal documentation system (authors and works mentioned in the text, with full bibliographical information appearing in the bibliography) rather than footnotes or endnotes. Many of the references to Foner amount to little more than "according to Foner...," or "Foner says...," followed by information about some event in American history. For example, the first mention of Foner reads as follows: "There were demonstrations of Irish workers in New York, Boston, and Lowell against the annexation of Texas, Philip Foner reports" (APH 159). Here is the second: "During those years, trade unions were forming. (Philip Foner's *History of the Labor Movement in the U.S.* tells the story in rich detail)" (APH 223). And the fourth: "The centennial year of 1876—one hundred years after the Declaration of Independence—brought forth a number of new declarations (reproduced by Philip Foner in *We the Other People*)" (APH 244). Obviously these are not cases in which the focus is on historians or historiography, at the expense of "the substance of history." And the same is true of the more sustained references to Foner. They are documentary; they serve the dual purpose of giving credit to work from which Zinn has drawn and alerting readers to a resource that they might consult for further information. But they do not get in the way of a substantive discussion of historical events, as the following example, the third citation of Foner in APH, illustrates:

Strikes were called in the textile mills of Fall River, Massachusetts. In the anthracite coal district of Pennsylvania, there was the "long strike," where Irish members of a society called the Ancient Order of Hibernians were accused of acts of violence, mostly on the testimony of a detective planted among the miners. These were the "Molly Maguires." They were tried and found guilty. Philip Foner believes, after a study of the evidence, that they were framed because they were labor organizers. He quotes the sympathetic *Irish World*, which called them "intelligent men whose direction gave strength to the resistance of the miners to the inhuman

reduction of their wages." And he points to the *Miners'
Journal*, put out by the coal mine owners, which referred to the
executed men this way: "What did they do? Whenever prices
of labor did not suit them they organized and proclaimed a
strike." (APH 243–4)

Thus, in evaluating Kammen's critique of Zinn, it is important to
note (1) that this Jefferson–Foner example, which, as I have just
tried to show, will not withstand scrutiny, is Kammen's
handpicked bit of evidence intended to show that Zinn pays too
much attention to historians and historiography, with the result
that he does not leave enough space for the substance of history;
and (2) that this alleged shortcoming—the one that this dubious
example fails to establish—constitutes what Kammen calls
"Zinn's gravest error of commission."

Kammen is on sounder ground when he complains of Zinn's
"sins of omission." About half of Kammen's one-page review is
devoted to pointing out important material that APH either
ignores or discusses only briefly. For example, Kammen notes
that, in spite of its obvious importance to American history, Zinn
says very little about religion (a criticism that we have encountered before). Similarly, he castigates Zinn for neglecting philosophers, and also inventors and their inventions—including the
introduction into American life of radio and television. And he
cites particular individuals who are neglected—including
songwriter Stephen Foster, artist Charles Sheeler, philosopher
John Dewey, and jurist Hugo Black, among several others.

While Kammen is undoubtedly correct in holding that each of
these omissions, if considered in isolation, constitutes a weakness
in Zinn's text, in the sense that, all else equal, it would be better
for such material to be made available to the reader, the problem
(as noted in my reply to Flynn above) is that the inclusion of
every important figure and event would result in a gigantic,
unwieldy, unreadable book. Also, since Zinn's text is intended to

serve as a counterweight to standard, mainstream histories, it necessarily pays attention to a number of people and topics that tend to be excluded in such volumes. Were he also to discuss everything that the rival texts include, the result would be a book that addresses more subjects than are treated in those (often over 1000-page-long) behemoths. And while comprehensiveness of treatment is indeed a virtue in a textbook, it stands in tension with other virtues that might reasonably be judged more important. A more coherent text, and thus one that yields greater understanding on the part of its readers, might be produced by dealing with fewer events in greater detail than by discussing many events in lesser detail. An interesting, coherent, readable book, issued from a definite point of view, very well might, in spite of its exclusion of some worthwhile topics, have the compensating virtue of stimulating interest (or even excitement) in its subject matter (in this case, American history), thus inspiring its readers to pursue that subject further by reading other books, by other authors, covering a somewhat different range of subjects, and doing so from different perspectives.

In any case, Kammen's criticism of Zinn's omissions can be faulted for its failure to confront the problem of the inevitability of selection. A more responsible critique would (a) address Zinn's arguments for the necessity of selection (they are stated clearly in the first chapter of APH, and are discussed in detail in the previous chapter of the present volume), (b) assess the cogency of his stated criteria of selection (also presented in APH, and much more extensively in POH, and considered at length in the previous chapter of this book), and (c) evaluate how closely his actual decisions of inclusion, exclusion, and emphasis in APH conform to the principles of selection that he defends. If Zinn's criteria are indefensible, let's hear the objections to them, as well as a statement and defense of better criteria. And if Zinn deviates from his criteria, perhaps in order to make an unprincipled partisan political point, let's see a demonstration of that.

Criticisms of this sort, if they could be sustained, would be powerful. But Kammen, in line with other Zinn critics, ignores Zinn's criteria, as well as the arguments he provides in their support. Instead, he insists that "the people are entitled to have their history *whole*," and, on that basis, chastises Zinn for failing "to give us truly total history."

But that is an impossible demand, one that no work of American history could ever satisfy. To show this, let's start with Kammen's criticism of Zinn for failing to include in his history the artist Charles Sheeler. Now, while Sheeler was indeed an important and outstanding artist, one well worth knowing about, there are many other American artists who, by virtue of their fame, influence, or talent, or by the fact that the content of their work tells us something significant about their times or about the American experience more generally, could make a comparable claim to be worthy of inclusion. If an American history text can be criticized for leaving out Charles Sheeler, then so can it be criticized for neglecting John Singleton Copley, or Winslow Homer, or Ben Shahn, or Jacob Lawrence, or James Abbott McNeill Whistler, or Thomas Eakins, or Willem de Kooning, or John Singer Sargent, or Grant Wood, or Thomas Cole, or Frederick Edwin Church, or Albert Bierstadt, or George Inness, or Georgia O'Keeffe, or Arthur Dove, or Charles Burchfield, or Andrew Wyeth, or Arshile Gorky, or Albert Pinkham Ryder, or Edward Hopper, or Thomas Hart Benton, or John Steuart Curry, or John Marin, or Stuart Davis, or Robert Motherwell, or Clyfford Still, or Jackson Pollock, or Franz Kline, or Mark Rothko, or Roy Lichtenstein, or Jasper Johns, or Robert Rauschenberg, or Andy Warhol, or Helen Frankenthaler, among many others. And this is to mention only painters. There are also many sculptors who are as important to the American story as is Sheeler, just as there are architects, photographers, and film directors; and poets, novelists, and playwrights; and composers, musicians, and dancers; and magicians and stand-up comics; and scientists, engineers, and inventors; and philosophers and historians; and labor leaders and human rights activists; and doctors and lawyers and teachers; and on, and on, and on—and all of this is on top of the explorers, presidents, Supreme Court justices, and military and business leaders, who dominate traditional history textbooks. And this is to mention only *people*. Think, also, of all of the different kinds of *events* that would, ideally, be worthy of inclusion. Then add on to that significant *changes* in American life that come on gradually, rather than being tied to specific events— demographic changes; changes in America's economic systems, and educational systems, and political systems; changes in attitudes and corresponding changes in behavior—in connection with gender, sex, race, work, childhood and child-rearing, punishment, marriage, death, and a host of other issues; changes brought about by technological innovations—photography, audio recording, telephone, automobile, radio, motion pictures, airplane, television, computers, Internet. Then consider the almost limitless number of significant things that could be said *about* each of these individuals, events, and changes—the history of each, the consequences of each, the connections among different items, and so forth. Next, think of the different *interpretations of*, or *theories about*, these items, and of the *evidence* that it might be necessary to discuss in order to establish one interpretation or theory over another. One could, I dare say, write a multi-volume 50,000-page history of the United States, every sentence of which would be on something interesting, relevant, and important—and still be vulnerable to the sort of criticism of "sins of omission" that Kammen raises against Zinn. There would still, inevitably and unavoidably, be regrettable omissions. The demand for "truly total history" is unrealistic and irresponsible, as is any criticism of specific omissions that is based on such a preposterous demand.

The conclusion of Kammen's review suggests that he himself may recognize this, as he raises the possibility that a call for total history may be a case of "asking for the moon." But if that is the case, he continues, "then we will cheerfully settle for balanced history. Ours has encompassed grandeur as well as tragedy, magnanimity as well as muddle, honor as well as shame. Like Walt Whitman, we must embrace it all." On that note, Kammen's review ends.

Three comments are in order, by way of reply. First, there is plenty of "grandeur," "magnanimity," and "honor" to be found in Zinn's text. One suspects that critics who state or imply anything to the contrary are so shocked by the material in APH that casts the heroes of traditional American history texts in a negative light that they don't even notice (a) that some positive material about those heroes—some grandeur, magnanimity, and honor—remains, and (b) that the book is full of new heroes, excluded from other texts—workers, women, minorities, activists, radicals—who are depicted positively.

Second, Kammen's call for "balance," which includes a complaint that Zinn features only those parts of American history that "will anger or embarrass" the American people, suggests that he primarily identifies "America" with the "great white men" who are celebrated in mainstream American history texts and in traditional American history courses, and assumes that the American people do so as well. But the history of the reception of APH has proven Kammen wrong. It is a polarizing book—much hated, to be sure, but also much loved, as its astonishing sales figures would appear to confirm. There are those who are angered or embarrassed by Zinn's text, but others who are consoled and inspired by it. The different reactions tend to depend primarily on whether the reader in question identifies more with Columbus or with the Arawaks; with the Founding Fathers or with their slaves; the business giants or those who work for them; the American military or those who are bombed by it; and so on. While some are outraged by criticism directed against their heroes, others think, "at last—someone is saying that I am important, that the lives of people like me matter, and that crimes committed against people like me should be recorded as part of history, and not swept under the rug, or excused, merely because they were carried out by great men in pursuit of progress!" Many such readers are also inspired by the large cast of new heroes that Zinn introduces—not just warriors, but also war resisters and anti-war activists; not just captains of industry who accumulate great wealth, but also labor leaders who fight to attain a greater share of that wealth for the workers who create it; not just the political leaders who change America for the better by passing needed legislation, but also the writers, artists, and activists who help to bring about the popular demand that makes the passing of such legislation possible.

Finally, as I argued in the previous chapter, an objectionable lack of balance cannot simply be read off from the results of an inquiry. A conclusion that tilts heavily in one direction or another, rather than coming out roughly "even," might be fully warranted by the relevant evidence. Some things, events, people, or states of affairs truly are wonderful or excellent; others are horrible. The proper question, it seems to me, is whether Zinn is using appropriate criteria in distinguishing the wonderful, the horrible, and the in-between, and, if so, whether he is applying those criteria consistently and fairly. His decision to emphasize Columbus's acts of murdering and enslaving Indians, rather than his exploits as a sailor and explorer, is a principled one. Are those principles reasonable, and properly applied? If so, there should be no objection that the result looks "unbalanced." *Reality* is unbalanced. Considerations of accuracy demand that it be described accordingly.

So, in conclusion, I wish that I could pronounce Kammen's review of Zinn's book a great success, but it is not. It is undone, primarily, by his failure to deal with Zinn's philosophical arguments about selection, and by his naivety in thinking that Zinn's work should be judged in terms of either an impossible demand for a "truly total history" or an unprincipled, non-evidentiary, and therefore philosophically indefensible, insistence on "balance."

It is puzzling to me that the distinguished historians, like Kammen, who criticize Zinn, seem, in spite of their intelligence, learning, and impressive professional accomplishments (Handlin and Kammen, recall, are Pulitzer Prize-winners, as is Arthur Schlesinger, Jr.—see the discussion below), to be, universally, either unwilling or unable to cope with his arguments about selection, objectivity, bias, balance, and similar matters. Perhaps it is because Zinn's arguments, and the issues they address, are philosophical, rather than strictly historical, in nature. Historian Peter Novick, author of a 648-page book subtitled "The 'Objectivity Question' and the American Historical Profession," also notes (though not in connection with evaluating the critical reception of Zinn) that historians tend not to deal with these issues competently:

On one level what is at stake in the objectivity question is a philosophical issue: a technical problem in epistemology. Very few historians have any philosophical training, or even inclination.... Though all historians have had views on the objectivity question, these views have rarely been fully articulated; even more rarely have they been the fruit of systematic thought. The historical profession does not monitor the philosophical rigor of what historians have had to say on the question, and *no historian suffers professionally as a result of demonstrated philosophical incompetence.* All of which is to say that historians' reflections on objectivity, unlike their substantive historical work, have none of those positive attributes which privilege it as "rational" (NOV 11, emphasis added).... [W]hat historians do worst, or at least badly, [is] reflecting on epistemology (NOV 15).

In any case, Kammen's harsh view of Zinn seems to have softened over time. In a 2012 review he calls Duberman's biography of Zinn—a work which, while far from uncritical, evaluates APH much more favorably than Kammen had done in his 1980 review—"splendid," and "biography at its best," and makes a case that Zinn was "sufficiently significant to warrant a full-scale biography." To be sure, Kammen continues to suggest that APH is flawed, but he says so in much gentler terms, acknowledges (as he had not done in 1980) the book's strengths (including, most notably, that "teachers liked assigning it"), and fills his review with praise for Zinn as a person, noting his courage, the justness of his causes, his seriousness as a teacher, his skill as a public speaker, even his "sunny disposition" and "warm smile" (IH).

More importantly, as documented in Chapter One above, Kammen, like Wineburg and Kazin, when informed of Mitch Daniels's attempt to ban the teaching of APH in Indiana, forthrightly denounced it, and expressed displeasure at having his name invoked by Daniels in support of that nefarious effort.

The Editors of the *National Review*

Like nearly all of Mitch Daniels's defenders, the editors conflate orders to "ban," "disqualify," and "get rid of" a text, with mere criticism of it. Their editorial begins this way: "Mitch Daniels…is under attack because as governor of Indiana he objected to the use of Howard Zinn's *A People's History of the United States* in public-school curricula."[130] But if Daniels had merely said, "hey, I object—I don't think it's a good idea," that would be very different from ordering disqualification, and the criticism he would have received would have been of a correspondingly different character.

The editorial continues: "In recently published e-mails, the plainspoken Governor Daniels described Zinn's work as 'anti-American' and 'crap,' which, when expressed in sufficiently polite language, is the professional consensus." What evidence do the editors provide in support of this claim? They give us three hostile quotations, two of which (from Arthur Schlesinger and Oscar Handlin) are borrowed from Daniels's own presentation. The third is from Roger Kimball, who is not a historian. (Handlin is dealt with above; Schlesinger and Kimball will be discussed below.) Naturally, the editors ignore (and implicitly deny the existence of) the many historians who praise Zinn (see Chapter One above).

Next, the editors claim that "The book is full of errors and deliberate distortions, as Handlin noted in *The American Scholar*...." The editors then proceed to list a few alleged examples, all of which are taken directly from Handlin, and all of which are, of course, accepted and passed along uncritically.

Then comes the obligatory mention of the fact that "Zinn himself described *A People's History* as 'a biased account,'" followed by an equally obligatory misrepresentation of the nature of that bias, and a refusal to cite what he actually says on this score.

For the most part, as the discussion to this point would suggest, the editors are content simply to repeat the criticisms of Zinn that others have made, no matter how defective such criticisms may be. Thus, when they get around to complaining about Zinn's omissions, every item but one is taken directly from Flynn's list (which is discussed above). But the fresh example that the editors add is a doozy. They claim that in APH "The thought of Joan Baez receives more prominent attention than does that of Alexander Hamilton." However, if facts matter, Alexander Hamilton is mentioned in the book 15 times. He is quoted on pages 77, 96, and 98, and his political philosophy is discussed on pages 95–8 and 101. Joan Baez is mentioned in one sentence. Here it is: "Bob Dylan and Joan Baez, singing not only protest songs, but songs reflecting the new abandon, the new culture, became popular idols" (APH 537). That's it. The editors' ridiculous claim that Zinn's book pays more attention to the thought of Joan Baez than to that of Alexander Hamilton is quoted endlessly in other anti-Zinn articles, in spite of the fact that it is a demonstrable falsehood.

The editors continue: "Liberals can be relied upon to object to the teaching of the Christian creation story as an alternative to evolution in a science class on the very reasonable basis that whatever Genesis is, it is not high-school biology. Similarly, whatever *A People's History* is, it is not history." The analogy is unsound. It is easy to explain why the creation story in the book of Genesis is not science. Unlike every modern physical science, including biology, it is not based on observation or experiment; there is no way to test it; and it relies on supernatural causation. There is no comparable list of fundamental differences between Zinn's work and other books that are universally regarded as works of history. In any case, the editors offer neither explanation nor argument in support of their dubious analogy.

And the same objection holds for the following evidence-free charge: "If there were a course in the use of dishonest rhetorical devices, then Zinn's oeuvre could occupy a prominent place in that course prospectus." Naturally, the editors fail to name, let alone document, a single one of Zinn's alleged "dishonest rhetorical devices." By contrast, I can name, and have documented above, several such devices in the editors' brief editorial: conflating the distinction between censorship and mere criticism; suppressing evidence that would undermine one's thesis (as in historians who support Zinn, and Zinn's explanation of what he means by calling APH "a biased account"); telling lies (Hamilton and Baez); and constructing absurd analogies. Perhaps there is room for the *National Review* editorial on that course syllabus.

The editorial concludes with these words: "Governor Daniels's illiterate critics notwithstanding, it was not an act of censorship—there was no talk of banning publication of the bestselling book, only of declining to use it in school curricula.

From kindergarten through graduate school, American education is a sewer of left-wing ideology, and Zinn's work is an especially ripe excretion. Governor Daniels's office was right to bring attention to it—shoring up the integrity of public institutions is part of what governors are there for."

Comments: (1) "Illiterate?" As discussed in Chapter One above, "censorship" has to do with the official suppression of ideas. There are *degrees* of censorship, because there are degrees of suppression. For a governor to prevent teachers from using a certain book in their classes would fit the definition of "censorship," even if the book in question were still available in bookstores and libraries.

(2) "Declining" is not the same thing as ordering a ban and a disqualification. Daniels did not "decline" to use Zinn's text. He tried to stop others from using it, and ordered that credit be withheld from courses that did use it.

(3) No evidence is offered in favor of the "sewer of left-wing ideology" claim.

(4) Daniels did not "bring attention" to Zinn. That is another demonstrable falsehood—one that shows that the editors either are lying or (more charitably) just don't know what they are talking about, and lack a basic understanding of the facts of the case. Tom LoBianco, the reporter for the Associated Press who uncovered and published Daniels's emails, is the one who "brought attention" to Zinn. Daniels had tried to act covertly. He did not publish his emails; they were intended to be private.

(5) Finally, quite apart from the merits of the substantive issue of the suitability of APH for classroom use, the editors undertake no serious effort to deal with the major issue of process: should governors, rather than history teachers, be the ones to decide—unilaterally, with no discussion or debate—which history textbooks should be used? Some conservatives do grasp this point. John Leo articulates it succinctly: "A call for balance in the curriculum should have been made in the open, with input

432

expected from all sides. Daniels's behind-the-scenes effort was, in effect, a call to censor an opponent's ideas. He should apologize."[131]

Rich Lowry

Lowry is the editor of the *National Review*. As such, he bears some responsibility for the editorial just discussed. But he is also the author of an article, "Daniels vs. Zinn,"[132] published under his own name the day after that editorial appeared. His main contribution to the debate is condescension: "*A People's History* is a book for high-school students not yet through their Holden Caulfield phase.... If it is a revelation to you that we treated Native Americans poorly, and if you believe the Founding Fathers were a bunch of phonies, Zinn's volume will strike you with the power of a thunderclap. And one day, maybe, you will grow up."

His more serious point is indicated by the subtitle of his article: "Historians on the left would rather shout 'censorship' than maintain standards." As Lowry sees it, it is obvious that Zinn's work is, as Daniels describes it, "crap," and that the critics of Daniels's attempt to remove it from Indiana classrooms—more specifically, Michael Kazin, the American Historical Association, and the 92 Purdue professors who signed an open letter protesting his actions—"are willing to look the other way at Zinn's transgressions against his own academic discipline; for them, defending a fellow man of the Left and shouting 'censorship' are more important and congenial pursuits than maintaining standards." His article concludes with these words: "The sin of Mitch Daniels, it turns out, is to take history more seriously than they do."

How does Lowry support these claims? Let's start with the case he makes for the poor quality of Zinn's work:

[T]he low estimation that Daniels has for Zinn's work is

shared by a swath of distinguished historians. It's not that they disagree with Zinn or believe he's too controversial. They think his work is, to borrow the word Daniels used in another e-mail, "crap." As Michael Moynihan pointed out in *Reason* magazine, much of the incoming fire comes from Zinn's more intellectually credible comrades on the left. Sean Wilentz describes Zinn's work as "balefully influential." Arthur M. Schlesinger Jr. called him "a polemicist, not a historian." *The New Republic* recently ran a review of a biography of Zinn under the headline "Agit-Prof." Even...Michael Kazin believes Zinn "essentially reduced the past to a Manichean fable."

Notice, first, that Lowry presents no evidence that he has ever read Zinn, or even that he has read the *critics* of Zinn. All he offers are extremely short quotations, all culled from a single article by someone else (Moynihan), who had collected those quotations. So, as is the case with Daniels (who, according to Lowry's fantasy, "takes history more seriously than" does the American Historical Association), Lowry gives us no reason to believe that he has better than a third-hand knowledge of Zinn's work.

Second, the quoted opinions, though harsh, are less severe than those of Daniels. One could believe that Zinn's influence has been "baleful," that he was "a polemicist" and an "Agit-Prof," and that his history was "Manichean," without going so far as to think that his work was "crap," or that it "misstates American history on every page." So, while Lowry does indeed show that there are historians who think quite poorly of Zinn, he does not succeed in showing that they "share" Daniels's estimation.

Third, Lowry ignores the fact that many other historians praise Zinn. It is not the case that there is a consensus opinion among historians about Zinn. Rather, as documented in Chapter One above, he is a controversial figure. Similarly, while Milton Friedman is certainly a celebrated and influential economist, there are plenty of economists who consider his influence "baleful," and who regard him as a "polemicist." What would Lowry think of a governor who would declare Friedman's work to be "crap," order his subordinates to "ban" and "disqualify" it, and justify those actions by quoting economists who judged Friedman's work harshly?

Fourth, Lowry accepts the opinions he quotes uncritically. He makes no attempt to assess whether or not the arguments these historians make to support their anti-Zinn judgments are cogent. I have done so for Kazin and Greenberg (the author of the "Agit-Prof" article) above, and will do so for Moynihan, Wilentz, and Schlesinger below.

Next, let's consider Lowry's handling of the censorship issue. To his credit, Lowry does not go the route of many of Daniels's defenders, that of pretending that Daniels had done nothing more than criticize Zinn, or ask questions about him—actions that raise no concern about censorship. Nor does he emulate Roger Kimball (see the discussion below) in offering a dubious definition of "censorship," such that Daniels's actions would not qualify. But at the same time, Lowry seems reluctant to concede that Daniels's critics might have been motivated by such an important and honorable a principle as opposition to censorship, preferring to cast them as opportunists who merely "*shout* censorship" in order to "defend a fellow man of the Left." How, then, does he dismiss legitimate concerns about censorship?

The answer is: by means of innuendo and name-calling. Instead of *asserting* that Daniels's actions did not constitute censorship (or attempted censorship), and then giving arguments in support of such a claim, Lowry simply uses ridicule to *imply* that the perception by Daniels's critics of censorship on his part reflects poorly on the character of the critics, rather than on the quality of Daniels's actions. Thus, Lowry tells us that the publication of Daniels's emails resulted in "hysterics" and "much heavy breathing among the sorts of people for whom lacking perspective is a professional obligation. For them, Daniels might as well be a book-burning fireman out of Ray Bradbury's *Fahrenheit 451*." (Note that none of Daniels's critics had accused him of book burning, or had suggested that what he did in attempting to ban a book from being used in a classroom was equivalent to book burning.) In the same vein, when Daniels's critics express concern about the importance of academic inquiry, Lowry calls it "caterwauling"; and, as already noted, he dismisses their statements disapproving of censorship as "shouting." Lowry offers no arguments or evidence, preferring instead to let his slanted and insulting language do all of the work.

And what evidence does Lowry offer in support of his claim that both the American Historical Association and the entire list of 92 Purdue professors who protested Daniels's actions are leftists, let alone that their motivation in criticizing Daniels was to "defend a fellow man of the Left"? None.

So, in sum, Lowry offers little evidence to back up his claim that a concern for high intellectual, scholarly, and academic standards would support the banning of Zinn from the classroom, with opposition to such banning requiring a significantly lesser concern for such standards, or a tolerance for much looser standards—so that concerns about standards could be more easily trumped by (excessive) worries about censorship, or by an unprincipled desire to defend a fellow Leftist.

But, as against Lowry, I have tried to show throughout this work that an interest in maintaining high standards speaks entirely against Zinn's harsh critics, all of whom prove themselves absurdly error-prone and logically challenged. In fact, that statement is far too generous to these critics. High standards of intellectual rigor are not needed in order to expose the utter bankruptcy of their case. Modest standards—the kind we demand of college freshmen—are more than sufficient to do the job. The standards I have in mind are, simply, that criticisms must be backed up with evidence; that quotations, and factual claims, must be accurate; that quotations must not be distorted by being taken out of context; that an author's explanation of the meanings of ambiguous or modestly technical terms, such as "bias" or "objectivity," must be taken into account; that evidence that contradicts the claim one is trying to make must not be overlooked; and that blatant logical fallacies must be avoided. When these norms are observed, the case that Zinn is incompetent, or a fraud, or that his work is "crap," completely collapses (though, of course, he is, like every other competent scholar, vulnerable to many reasonable criticisms of a far less severe nature). Accordingly, many critics of Daniels and defenders of Zinn take those positions not *in spite* of a proper concern for intellectual standards, but rather precisely *because* of it.

Near the end of his essay, Lowry makes some additional comments about Zinn that demand a response: "The caterwauling in the Daniels controversy about the importance of academic inquiry is particularly rich, given that Zinn didn't believe in it. He had no use for objectivity and made history a venture in rummaging through the historical record to find whatever was most politically useful, without caring much about strict factual accuracy.... He joined his propagandistic purpose to a moral obtuseness that refused to distinguish between the United States and its enemies, including Nazi Germany."

First, Lowry produces no quotation from Zinn (nor would it have been possible for him to do so, since there is none) in which he expresses disbelief in, or in any other way disparages, the importance of academic inquiry. Lowry tries to suggest that such an attitude follows from his rejection of "objectivity," but, as we have seen in Chapter Two above, it does not.

Second, Lowry offers no evidence that Zinn "didn't care much about strict factual accuracy." As documented in Chapter Two above, Zinn repeatedly emphasizes that he fully embraces the demand for factual accuracy, and that his rejection of "objectivity," which he, unlike Lowry, carefully defines, in no way entails any lessening of the importance of that scholarly norm. Nor does Lowry provide any examples of Zinn's failure to conform to that norm in his historical writing. Who behaves this way? What kind of person publicly accuses a scholar of carelessness about factual accuracy without backing up that claim with evidence? Is this the sort of behavior Lowry has in mind when he refers to "maintaining standards"?

But what about Lowry's more specific charge? Did Zinn really "refuse to distinguish between the United States and its enemies, including Nazi Germany," as Lowry claims? He offers no citation, or any other kind of evidence, in support of this ridiculous accusation. I, on the other hand, have already cited Zinn's statement that "We didn't match the Holocaust—that's a unique event in World War II," his explicit denial that "we are just like the Nazis," and his affirmation that "we are different" (see, also, the discussion of Wineburg above).

And, lest we forget, as editor of the *National Review*, Lowry is also responsible for the statement, in its editorial, that in APH "The thought of Joan Baez receives more prominent attention than does that of Alexander Hamilton."

There is one thing that can be said for Rich Lowry: he is something of an authority on the phenomenon of "not caring much about strict factual accuracy."

Roger Kimball

Kimball, an art critic, author, political and social commentator, editor, and publisher, argues that "The most effective form of censorship is also the quietest. It operates not by actively proscribing speech but by rendering certain topics *hors de combat*, literally undiscussable. It does this by propagating an atmosphere of revulsion and taboo."[133] This statement appears in an essay that was written prior—and just four months prior, at that—to the publication of Daniels's emails on Zinn. But when

Kimball subsequently addresses the Daniels–Zinn controversy, he changes his tune considerably. In defending Daniels, he denies that what Daniels did, or tried to do, amounted to censorship: "Note well, Daniels doesn't say Zinn's book oughtn't to be allowed to be published. He doesn't want to *censor* the book. He merely says it shouldn't be taught as history" (KIM). So in order to make the case that Daniels is not guilty of attempted censorship, Kimball has to define "censorship" so narrowly that the act of ordering that a given textbook not be used in schools fails to qualify. But in the earlier article, in a different context, the mere act of criticizing and ridiculing an opinion, of "propagating an atmosphere of revulsion and taboo," is sufficient, even though nothing is forcibly banned, removed, or disqualified, let alone prevented from being published.[134] (Kimball's prime example of "censorship," incidentally, is "the conspiracy of silence that has surrounded the subject of the President's [that is, Barack Obama's] place of birth.")

Here is Kimball on academic freedom: "The very limitation of academic freedom is part of its strength. By excluding the political, it makes room for the pursuit of truth" (KIM). I cannot improve on John K. Wilson's reply: "This is the ultimate Orwellian claim: a political act by a politician seeking to ban a political viewpoint he dislikes is, according to Kimball and his ideological friends, an effort to defend academic freedom from political intrusions" (DOD).

Kimball also claims that "Public universities should not be breeding grounds for any ideology, Left or Right" (KIM). But what about centrist ideologies? Here we have the familiar conflation of objectivity with centrism, and of leftism or rightism with ideology. What is needed is an approach that draws conclusions, be they left, right, or center, based on a rigorous and logical examination of the relevant evidence. One way to facilitate that is to allow all voices, left, right, and center, to make their case at the university.

Kimball quotes Daniels as saying, in his initial email, that Zinn's book "misstates American history on every page." A reasonable person who agreed with Daniels's general line would, if pressed, admit that such a claim was hyperbolic, and obviously not literally true. But Kimball's comment is this: "That's exactly right" (KIM). So it should be possible to list at least 688 misstatements in Zinn's 688-page book. The number that Kimball points out, however, is zero. This shows that the audience for his work consists of people who make no demand for evidence. (Kimball does provide in this article a link to an earlier article of his on Zinn, but it, too, fails to offer any original examples of Zinn's factual errors; rather, Kimball there quotes Handlin's litany, without expressing any concern over the issue of whether or not Handlin's list is accurate. The earlier Kimball article is addressed below.)

Like many other defenders of Daniels, Kimball argues that "academic freedom" demands that people like Zinn should be "shown the door" *at the university level* (KIM). Because his work, according to Kimball, is political, ideological, and propagandistic, it is inconsistent with academic freedom for it to be taught at colleges and universities. But Kimball, and other defenders of Daniels who take this line, fail to observe that Daniels, in response to the controversy that followed the publication of his emails, has repeatedly insisted (falsely, but that is not my present point) that he had only been talking about K-12 instruction, and that, as a vigorous defender of academic freedom, he would not stand in the way of any faculty member at Purdue who chose to teach Zinn. Moreover, he has also stated, more than once, that if Zinn were a tenured professor at Purdue, Daniels would leave him alone and allow him to teach and to publish what he wanted. So Kimball's defense of Daniels's position is not, in fact, a defense of Daniels's position.

Kimball, like Horowitz, seems to think that academic freedom, the pursuit of truth, and the academic life in general, must rigorously exclude anything political. One can see the point of that if the subject being studied is, say, the behavior of gasses. But what about economics, history, political science, and philosophy? Political considerations, and value-considerations more generally, comprise a substantial part of their subject matter. Shouldn't these issues be studied, rationally considered, and openly debated, rather than (as if this were even possible) bracketed? And what forum for such study and rational discussion and debate could be better than the university—where scholars and students in pursuit of truth are gathered together precisely for the purpose of learning (as opposed to being in a position where one's pursuit of truth is constrained by pressure to reach conclusions that will please an employer or corporate sponsor)?

Note also the moving train problem. To the extent that political issues are set aside and not considered, then the existing political arrangements will continue unchallenged. So apoliticism amounts to political conservatism. Also, the very idea that there are apolitical inquiries in these areas depends upon the failure to perceive the currently operating political assumptions as being such—they are invisible, like the air we breathe.

Kimball and his ilk think, or pretend to think, that there is some clear and obvious distinction between ideas that should be excluded, that is, rejected out of hand as improper, on the grounds that they are "ideologies" and/or "propaganda," and ideas that are wholly free of such taint. Kimball and others state with great confidence that Zinn is an "ideologue" and a "propagandist," but they fail to explain what that means, or why they, themselves, are not ideologues and propagandists. If Zinn's emphasis on Columbus's acts of murdering and enslaving Indians makes him an "ideologue" and a "propagandist," does that mean that a historian like Samuel Eliot Morison, who deemphasizes those acts and instead focuses on Columbus's achievements as an explorer and navigator, is not an ideologue and propagandist? If not, why not? And if so, should he, too, be "shown the door"? And who should decide such matters—a governor?

Generally speaking, attempts to dismiss someone as an "ideologue" or a "propagandist" are irresponsible and intellectually lazy. If someone's ideas are wrong, it should be shown, with evidence and rational argument, that they are wrong. Slapping a label on them proves nothing. This strategy is used as a way of avoiding confrontation with views one doesn't like, but which may well be correct, requiring, if one wishes to be rational, a revision in one's own cherished views.

Here's a minor point. Kimball says that the effect on him of the publication of Daniels's initial anti-Zinn emails "was to increase" his "already high esteem for the man," since the emails (allegedly) reveal Daniels to be "someone who can spot a Communist fraud at 100 paces" (KIM). But even if it were true, which it is not, that Zinn is "a Communist fraud," it wouldn't follow that Daniels's labeling him as such would demonstrate any special acumen on his part. Rather, he might simply have been parroting the David Horowitz/Daniel Flynn right-wing playbook line on Zinn. He need not have ever read a word of Zinn in order to do that. So, on second thought, maybe there is something to Kimball's "100 paces" line. I see no evidence that Daniels has ever come closer than 100 paces to any Howard Zinn text.

In an earlier essay, a vicious smear written in response to Zinn's death and entitled "Professor of Contempt" (POC), Kimball writes: "Zinn's biography tells us that he was the author of 'more than 20 books.' But only one matters: *A People's History of the United States.*" The reference to "Zinn's biography" as the source for the information about his books (and note, by the way, that it is an imprecise reference—is he referring to the Joyce biography, the Duberman biography, the Zinn autobiography, or something else?) suggests that Kimball is not familiar with them.

(His comments about APH suggest that he probably has not read that, either—but let that pass.) So on what basis does he claim that the others—a prize-winning book on LaGuardia's congressional career; the major work on SNCC, a significant player in the American civil rights movement; the first book to argue for U.S. withdrawal from Vietnam; a groundbreaking extended essay on civil disobedience; and so forth—"don't matter" (whatever that means)? He doesn't say.

But he does explain why he thinks APH matters: "*A People's History* is *the* textbook of choice in high schools and colleges across the country." I note in passing that Daniels uses exactly this language in his initial email, citing, not Kimball, but rather, "the obits and commentaries." But in fact, only Kimball made that claim (as any Internet search will reveal). It seems likely that Daniels acquired almost all of his "knowledge" of Zinn from Kimball, Flynn, and Horowitz. He reproduces their mistakes, and adds very little that is not already contained in their work.

In any case, Kimball thinks he knows *why* APH is so popular: "Given a choice between a book that portrayed America honestly—as an extraordinary success story—and a book that portrayed the history of America as a litany of depredations and failures, which do you suppose your average graduate of a teachers college, your average member of the National Education Association, would choose? To ask the question is to answer it."

But does Kimball really think that the only way to "portray American history honestly" is to portray it "as an extraordinary success story"? So everybody who disagrees with Kimball about American history is not merely wrong, but dishonest?

Does he not recognize the overwhelming "patriotic" bias that pervades traditional American history texts? Most other nations' (and I say "most" merely as a caution—I know of no exceptions) textbooks attempt to glorify the home nation. Does Kimball think that America is the exception here (another example of "American exceptionalism")? Is there not something to be said for those who are willing to resist such bias, and to attempt to evaluate their own nation by the same standards that we routinely apply to other countries?

Moreover, based on admittedly anecdotal evidence, my sense is that most teachers who assign Zinn's book do not use it as the sole text in a history class. Rather, they use it to give their students a different perspective than that of the traditional text that the class also uses—with the result that students are asked to engage both books critically, rather than simply "gulping down" one or the other. So Kimball is setting up a false dilemma here. Often it is not a case of Zinn *or* the kind of text Kimball favors; but rather both texts are used.

Finally, while Kimball will, of course, reject this suggestion out of hand, the state of affairs that he bemoans—namely, that it is precisely scholars, teachers, educators, who tend to favor Zinn—might go more to Zinn's credit than to the teachers' discredit. History teachers and professors might know a bit more than Kimball does about both American history and education, and it might be this knowledge that undergirds their selection of Zinn's text. Note also that the university is one of the few places where serious ideas are regularly discussed but in which the discussants are not completely under the thumb of corporate values and corporate pressure (unlike the situation in electoral politics and journalism). This would explain why scholars are sometimes able to get much closer to the truth than journalists and politicians are able to do. That accrues to Zinn's credit.

And speaking of credit, Kimball's next paragraph begins this way: "To his credit—well, it's not really to his credit, since he offers the admission only to disarm criticism, but Zinn is entirely candid about the ideological nature of his opus. All history, he says, involves a choice of perspectives. Maybe so. Are we therefore to assume all perspectives are equally valuable? Zinn employs this relativist's sleight of hand…"

No, he doesn't. Kimball does not (and cannot) quote any

passage from Zinn in which he says anything like the relativist thesis that all perspectives are equally valuable. Nor does anything Zinn says even remotely imply anything like that. Zinn's point about perspectives includes the following three claims, none of which come within a billion miles of relativism: (1) Since all historical writing must, necessarily, involve selection—one can't say everything, so one has to choose what to include, what to exclude, what to emphasize, and what to de-emphasize—it follows that all historical writing expresses a choice of perspective. Unless the decisions about inclusion, exclusion, and emphasis are utterly random, they will be based on criteria and values of some sort, which influence beliefs about what is and is not important. But if these criteria and values are not recognized as such, but rather are adopted uncritically, passively (or even unconsciously), it is harder to correct their biases, distortions, and limitations. Therefore, unlike the great bulk of traditional, mainstream history, which pretends to be "objective," and which makes no acknowledgement of its perspective or value assumptions, Zinn will attempt to identify and make clear to the reader his own. (2) When there is a great imbalance in the representation of different perspectives in the literature, there is positive value in seeking out under-represented perspectives. How can this point be so hard to understand? Suppose there has been a particular dispute between a given employer and his employees. Suppose, further, that 100 accounts of this dispute have been written, and that all 100 have uncritically adopted the values and point of view of the employer, and not that of the employees. In that situation, there is something to be learned from an account of the event that is based on the values and point of view of the employees. This is not relativism. This is not the claim that "all perspectives are equally valid." Is the rule, in a criminal courtroom, that both the prosecution and the defense are to be heard from, a relativist rule, one that assumes that all perspectives are equally valid? Of course not. One has to evaluate the arguments of both the prosecution and the defense critically. Perhaps a rigorous and logical evaluation of the evidence will show that one side has the truth, and the other does not. But one needs to examine all of the relevant evidence in order to make that determination. This is a procedure designed to improve the chances of arriving at the objective truth. It is at the opposite end of the spectrum from relativism. The same goes for history. The concern for including in historical accounts perspectives that have been overlooked or denied is a necessary part of a concern for truth. (3) The dominant perspective, because it is based on narrow, parochial, and/or instrumental values (the patriotic celebration of "our great nation" [narrow and parochial] and its specific leaders and institutions [instrumental—their value should be recognized as being based on their ability to bring about ultimate values—peace, justice, fairness, happiness, etc.], rather than on the universal and ultimate values just named), makes it more likely to be biased, limited, untruthful, non-objective, than would a perspective based on the universal and ultimate values—the ones Zinn himself embraces.

Also, with regard to Kimball's "he only did it to disarm criticism" charge: (1) How could Kimball possibly know Zinn's motive? Is he a mind reader? He cites no evidence in support of this claim. (2) The desire to avoid criticism—is that a plausible motive to ascribe to a man who chose to spend his entire life doing things that attract criticism—civil disobedience on behalf of blacks; anti-war activism; publishing unpopular dissident views, etc.? (3) On the other hand, even Zinn's critics tend to concede that he wrote clearly. Might not his "admission" have been written for that purpose—to clarify his intentions, thus aiding the reader in understanding his writing? (4) The "admission," far from blocking criticism, has, predictably, facilitated lazy criticism: "he admits that he's biased, so let's reject him on that basis, without bothering with the details of his texts."

Kimball continues: "If 'all history is ideological' (it isn't really), then why not make your choice based on what appeals to your political sympathies, truth be damned?" Of course, Zinn never says or implies anything like that, either. Zinn's methodology is offered as an attempt to make history more truthful, not less. As discussed extensively in the previous chapter, Zinn's argument for reform has to do with issues of selection. He fully supports existing scholarly norms with respect to factual accuracy and fairness in the handling of evidence.

Also, what does Kimball mean by "ideological" here (since that's his formulation, not Zinn's—I did a web search for "Zinn all history is ideological," and found nothing but websites containing, or quoting from, Kimball's essay)? And what is his argument for the conclusion that "it isn't really"? He doesn't define his terms or defend his claims with arguments. He writes for people who don't care about such things. There are no intellectual standards here.

Kimball continues: "[W]hat Zinn offers us is not a corrective, but a distortion. It is as if someone said to you, 'Would you like to see Versailles?' and then took you on a tour of a broken shed on the outskirts of the palace grounds. 'You see, pretty shabby, isn't it?'"

Look at what this implies about what is and isn't important. Genocide of Native Americans, slavery, racism, the bombing and torturing of innocent people—these are insignificant, compared to what really matters. They are minor details—the "broken shed" that only a hater, an ideologue, a propagandist would consider important. By contrast, Columbus's intrepid sailing, exploring, and conquering—that's what is important, and it is magnificent and beautiful. It is Versailles.

Kimball continues:

The one indisputably valuable thing about *A People's History of the United States* is the way it illustrates a melancholy fact about the place of reasoned argument in human affairs. In brief, it occupies a lamentably attenuated place. Placed in opposition to a wish driven by the Zeitgeist (that's German for "what the *New York Times* preaches"), reasoned argument doesn't stand a chance. Item: Soon after *A People's History of the United States* was published, the historian Oscar Handlin wrote a devastating review of the book for *The American Scholar* (which was still a respectable magazine).

"It simply is not true," Mr. Handlin noted,

that "what Columbus did to the Arawaks of the Bahamas, Cortez did to the Aztecs of Mexico, Pizarro to the Incas of Peru, and the English settlers of Virginia and Massachusetts to the Powhatans and the Pequots." It simply is not true that the farmers of the Chesapeake colonies in the seventeenth and early eighteenth centuries avidly desired the importation of black slaves, or that the gap between rich and poor widened in the eighteenth-century colonies. Zinn gulps down as literally true the proven hoax of Polly Baker and the improbable Plough Jogger, and he repeats uncritically the old charge that President Lincoln altered his views to suit his audience. The Geneva assembly of 1954 did not agree on elections in a unified Vietnam; that was simply the hope expressed by the British chairman when the parties concerned could not agree. The United States did not back Batista in 1959; it had ended aid to Cuba and washed its hands of him well before then. "Tet" was not evidence of the unpopularity of the Saigon government, but a resounding rejection of the northern invaders.

And on and on. In any normal world, Zinn would have stolen away in the middle of the night, fled to a mountain fastness in Peru, and taken up llama ranching. In this world, however, he went on to fame and fortune.

Oscar Handlin left Zinn's "deranged...fairy tale" in tatters.

But it is the work of Roger Kimball, not that of Howard Zinn, that shows the "lamentably attenuated place of reasoned argument in human affairs." It is Kimball who, in a normal world, would have to steal away in the middle of the night. The fact that Kimball has readers, people who think he has something of value to contribute to an intelligent discussion of something—there is nihilism, the decline of our culture. Kimball offers no evidence of his own, quotes Handlin uncritically (reproducing his errors— see the discussion of Handlin above), misrepresents Zinn, ignores his arguments, and contradicts himself, shifting in an Orwellian fashion from one view to another, not for any principled reason, but simply so as to be able to defend his political prejudices (see his unacknowledged about-face on censorship, above).

Kimball then proceeds to reach a new low: "During his disreputable tenure as a professor at Boston University, Howard Zinn did everything in his power to subvert the university...partly by short-circuiting with malicious levity the high seriousness of a liberal-arts education. He would, for example, pass around his classes a bag containing bits of paper imprinted with the letters 'A' or 'B.' Whichever token a student picked denominated his grade, no matter what work he did or didn't do."

Notice that Kimball offers no evidence, or citation, in support of this libelous claim. I took two courses from Howard Zinn. He didn't do this, or anything like it, in either class. Moreover, while I heard dozens of "Zinn stories" from other students who had taken his classes when I was an undergraduate at Boston University, I never heard anything like this.

Kimball continues: "The point? It wasn't merely grade inflation. More insidiously, it was an expression of contempt for the entire enterprise of which he was a privileged beneficiary. Contempt, in fact, was Howard Zinn's leading characteristic."

Is that why Zinn worked tirelessly to fight against racism and segregation in the South when he taught at a college for black women? Was it because of contempt that he sat in with them at segregated lunch counters and went to jail as part of his fight to win for his students some dignity, justice, and equality before the law? Moreover, anyone who has ever met Howard Zinn knows of his love of the arts—of movies, theater, music, literature. Is that consistent with a personality that is dominated by contempt? And anyone who has ever taken a class from him has been able to observe, quite plainly, his enjoyment of teaching, his love of discussing important ideas, and his placing a high value on the friendly give and take of argument and debate about them. It is a ludicrous falsehood to say that he had "contempt for the entire enterprise." Someone who would say that is someone who would say anything, utterly unconstrained by considerations of evidence, or truth, or fairness. (In that connection it is worth noting that Kimball wrote his essay for the *National Review*, the publication responsible for the demonstrably absurd claim that APH pays more attention to the ideas of Joan Baez than to those of Alexander Hamilton.)

Near the end of his essay Kimball approvingly quotes Oscar Handlin's claim (discussed in the treatment of Handlin above) that Zinn hates not only America but also all humanity, indeed, that he "lavishes indiscriminate condemnation upon all the works of man—that is, upon civilization, a word he usually encloses in quotation marks." Thus, Kimball "gulps down as literally true" (to use Handlin's phrase) Handlin's laughably, and provably, false claim that Zinn "usually encloses in quotation marks" the word "civilization."

Kimball closes his article with the following words: "Howard Zinn has left us. But his repellent ideas—and even more, the contemptuous nihilism that stands behind and fires those ideas— live on." Kimball is right about one thing. "Contemptuous nihilism" lives on. It can be found in the works of Roger Kimball.

Jill Lepore

Lepore is the David Woods Kemper '41 Professor of American History at Harvard University. She is the author of an extraordinarily patronizing short essay on "Zinn's History,"[135] published on the occasion of Zinn's death. The point of this two-paragraph discussion is that APH is like *The Catcher in the Rye* in that it is a good book for smart 14-year-olds to read—it "gets them thinking" and "gives them something to argue about" and helps them to overcome the innocence of childhood—but it has nothing to offer to a person of greater sophistication and maturity. According to Lepore,

> Zinn wanted to write a people's history because he believed that a national history serves only to justify the existence of the nation, which means, mainly, that it lies, and if it ever tells the truth, it tells it too fast, racing past atrocity to dwell on glory. Zinn's history did the reverse. Instead of lionizing Andrew Jackson, he mourned the Cherokee. The problem is that, analytically, upending isn't an advance; it's more of the same, only upside-down. By sophomore year, the young whippersnappers have figured that out, too, which can be heartbreaking to watch....[136]

This is total nonsense. The question of whether or not a given "upending" constitutes an advance cannot be determined "analytically." The issue is material, not formal. Here is one way to grasp the distinction. No human being can shoot a score of 17 or 18 on a regulation size 18-hole golf course. But the reasons are different for these two cases. It is logically impossible to score a 17, since the rules of golf stipulate that a golfer must take at least one shot on each hole. The best score one could possibly achieve on any hole is "one." Therefore, a perfect score (one that not even an omnipotent being could better) is 18. So here the issue is formal and analytical—like the issue in knowing that "p and not-p" is necessarily false, and that "p or not-p" is necessarily true. But in order to know that no human being can shoot an 18, formal logic will not suffice. Rather, one needs knowledge about what the world is like—knowledge about how long some golf holes are; knowledge about human physiology (which tells us how far a human being could hit a golf ball); specific knowledge about the history of golf; and general knowledge about human fallibility. We know that no one will ever shoot an 18 in the same way that we know that no human will ever run one mile in four seconds. This knowledge is not analytical (based on pure logic— the analysis of concepts and the logical relations among them), but rather material (based on empirical knowledge of what the world happens to be like, even if there is no logical barrier to its having been otherwise).

Now, returning to Lepore's example of a supposedly analytical truth, in some cases an upending gets us closer to the truth; in other cases it takes us further away from it; in still others it does neither. Suppose that a given major league baseball pitcher had a win-loss record of 18–7 in 1963, but, for some reason, the record books record it as 7–18. "Upending" that would deliver the truth. Conversely, if the record books had recorded his record as 18–7, upending that would move us from truth to falsity. Whereas if no such pitcher really existed, but for some reason the record books erroneously listed him as having done so, and as having compiled a record of 13–12, upending that, so that his record would be changed to 12–13, would only move us from one falsehood to another, which would seem to qualify neither as an advance nor as its opposite. The same reasoning applies when the issue is not truth and falsehood, but rather, as better fits the Zinn case, the issue of emphasis. If for some reason history books tended to discuss Adolf Hitler primarily as a landscape painter, and mentioned his genocidal activities only in passing, the "upending" of that account would, most assuredly, be an advance. "Instead of lionizing Andrew

Jackson, [Zinn] mourned the Cherokee"—this, says Lepore, "isn't an advance." Why not? Was Jackson not responsible for the forced march of the Cherokees to Oklahoma? Was that not genocidal?

It is frightening to think that, no doubt under the influence of her expert guidance, Lepore's students "figure out" an "analytic truth" that is in fact neither analytic nor true.

Michael C. Moynihan

Moynihan is the cultural news editor for *The Daily Beast* and *Newsweek*. He was formerly a senior editor of *Reason*, the magazine in which his article calling Zinn "an exceptionally bad historian" appears (MOY).

How does Moynihan defend that harsh judgment? He starts with an appeal to authority, writing that "Much of the criticism of Zinn has come from dissenters on the left," before proceeding to quote, as cases in point, anti-Zinn remarks from Arthur Schlesinger, Jr., Sean Wilentz, Oscar Handlin, and Michael Kazin. (I have addressed Handlin and Kazin above; Schlesinger and Wilentz will be dealt with below.) It is revelatory of Moynihan's political orientation that he refers to Handlin, a supporter of Richard Nixon and a rabid hawk on the Vietnam War, as a "dissenter on the left."

Moynihan continues: "Just how poor is Zinn's history? After hearing of his death, I opened one of his books to a random page (*Failure to Quit*, 118) and was informed that there was 'no evidence' that Muammar Qaddafi's Libya was behind the 1986 bombing of La Belle Discotheque in Berlin. Whatever one thinks of the Reagan administration's response, it is flat wrong, bordering on dishonest, to argue that the plot wasn't master-minded in Tripoli."

Just how poor is this criticism? Notice that Zinn does not, in the passage Moynihan quotes or elsewhere, "argue that the plot wasn't masterminded in Tripoli." His claim is much more modest—merely that there was "no evidence" that Qaddafi was the mastermind. The distinction between saying "X didn't do it" and "there is no evidence that X did do it" is not even remotely subtle, making one wonder how Moynihan manages to miss it. In any case, the very thing that Moynihan calls "flat wrong, bordering on dishonest" for Zinn to have done, turns out to be something that he clearly did not do. Indeed, it is "flat wrong, bordering on dishonest" for Moynihan to have accused him of having done it. And yet, this is Moynihan's handpicked example, chosen to prove "just how poor" Zinn's history is.

Then there is also the issue of the date of Zinn's statement relative to the emergence of evidence in the case. The article that Moynihan quotes, "Terrorism Over Tripoli," was written in 1986. The collection in which it appears, FTQ, was published in 1993. But the one and only piece of evidence that Moynihan puts forth in order to refute Zinn's comment on the Berlin bombing is an article by the BBC (he provides a hyperlink to it in the online version of his article) published in 2001.[137] That article points out that the investigation of the case "went cold until the 1990 reunification of Germany and the subsequent opening up of the East's secret service archives." And the evidence of Libya's involvement in the bombing that the article presents is all drawn from a four-year trial that concluded in 2001.

Next, it is noteworthy that Moynihan's two paraphrases of Zinn's quotation subtly distort its meaning in another way. That quotation is quite specifically about Khadafi as an individual, rather than about the Libyan government. It is specifically in reference to the claim that "Khadafi was behind the discotheque bombing" that Zinn says "there is no evidence for this." But Moynihan's paraphrase, in addition to illegitimately converting a statement about an absence of evidence for X into a positive argument for not-X, also changes a statement about Khadafi into statements about "Qaddafi's Libya" and about a plot "masterminded in Tripoli." The distinction is important because it is at least theoretically possible that a plot could have been master-minded in Tripoli, and by some element of the government of "Qaddafi's Libya," without Khadafi himself having been involved. And this possibility takes on added significance in the light of the result of the trial referenced in the article that Moynihan cites. For the final sentence of that article—the one and only source that Moynihan gives in order to show how wildly off base was Zinn's statement that "there is no evidence" that "Khadafi was behind the discotheque bombing"—reads as follows: "[T]he prosecution was unable to prove that Colonel Gaddafi was behind the attack—a failure which the court blamed on the 'limited willingness' of the German and US governments to share intelligence."

Moynihan continues: "Nor is it correct to write that the American government, which funded the Afghan *mujahadeen* in the 1980s, 'train[ed] Osama bin Laden,' a myth conclusively debunked by *Washington Post* correspondent Steve Coll in his Pulitzer Prize-winning book *Ghost Wars*."

Here there are at least five problems. First, in contrast to the previous example, this time Moynihan provides no citation as to where this alleged quotation from Zinn might be found. Bin Laden is mentioned on two pages of APH, but neither page says anything about the American government having trained him. Since Moynihan's other citation of Zinn's work is to FTQ, I checked it, too, but the search came up empty. FTQ is not indexed, so I might have missed it. But on the other hand, it was published in 1993, well before the September 11, 2001 terrorist attacks, making a discussion of bin Laden in that work improbable. The most likely source would seem to be TAW, published in 2002 in direct response to that historical event. But while TAW's index lists six entries on bin Laden, none contains the quotation in question or anything like it. Several Internet searches—each a variation on "Howard Zinn American government trained bin Laden"—also proved fruitless, turning up nothing but Moynihan's article, quotations from it, or sources in which the search terms appear far apart from one another. So, while I cannot conclude that the quotation is a fabrication, since I have not exhaustively searched every possible source, I do think it is fair to note that Moynihan's failure to document his quotation has left me in a position from which I cannot evaluate it fairly. The quotation, as Moynihan presents it, consists of just one word plus one name: "train[ed] Osama bin Laden." The rest is given only in Moynihan's paraphrase, the accuracy of which I am left unable to assess. Since, as we have seen, he is fully capable of providing paraphrases that are inaccurate in multiple ways, there is no telling what liberties he might have taken in the present case. We don't know what came before and after the quoted words. We don't know the general context. We don't know what qualifications (if any) Zinn may have made, or what evidence or argument (if any) he may have cited in support of his alleged claim. This is no way to show "how poor is Zinn's history."

Second, Moynihan's assertion that Steve Coll's *Ghost Wars* "conclusively debunked" the widely held view that the U.S. had trained bin Laden is preposterous. Coll's claim is much more modest—namely, that in his research he uncovered no evidence in support of such a view. His discussion of this issue in *Ghost Wars* concludes with these words: "If the CIA did have contact with bin Laden during the 1980s and subsequently covered it up, it has so far done an excellent job" (GW 87). And in a question and answer session following the release of his book, Coll, in response to a question as to whether there is "any truth" to the "accusations from the left" that "the CIA [has] fund[ed] and train[ed] bin Laden," says only that he "did not discover any evidence of direct contact between CIA officers and bin Laden during the 1980s" (BLL). So, once again, Moynihan shows himself unable to distinguish between "I know of no evidence of X" and "X is false." But even that understates the error. In Moynihan's rendition, "I know of no evidence of X" somehow morphs into a "conclusive debunking" of X.

Third, Moynihan's conversion of "no evidence for" into "conclusive debunking of" is rendered even stranger when one takes into account that the basis for Coll's "no evidence for" conclusion appears to be the CIA itself:

> CIA archives contain no record of any direct contact between a CIA officer and bin Laden during the 1980s. CIA officers delivering sworn testimony before Congress in 2002 asserted there were no such contacts, and so did multiple CIA officers and U.S. officials in interviews. The CIA became aware of bin Laden's work with Afghan rebels in Pakistan and Afghanistan later in the 1980s but did not meet with him even then, according to these record searches and interviews. (GW 87)

It is immediately after this passage that Coll states his conclusion that: "If the CIA did have contact with bin Laden during the 1980s and subsequently covered it up, it has so far done an excellent job."

Fourth, Moynihan ignores evidence of CIA support for bin Laden. For example, political scientist and former CIA consultant Chalmers Johnson claims that such evidence is

> on the public record. The CIA supported bin Laden from at least 1984, including building in 1986 the training complex and weapons storage tunnels around the Afghan city of Khost, where bin Laden trained many of the 35,000 "Arab Afghans." They constituted a sort of Islamic Abraham Lincoln Brigade of young volunteers from around the world to become *mujahedeen* and fight on the side of the Afghans against the Soviet Union. Bin Laden's Khost complex was the one that Clinton hit in 1998 with cruise missiles; for once the CIA knew where the target was, since it had built it.

It is true that the CIA used a formal cutout to make deliveries of money and weapons to the "freedom fighters." It did so to maintain a facade of deniability with the Soviet Union. All US money was funneled through Pakistan's Inter-Services Intelligence (ISI) agency, which had taken the lead since 1982 in recruiting radical Muslims from around the world to come to Pakistan, receive training and fight on the Afghan side.

In Peshawar, Osama bin Laden, the well-connected, rich young Saudi (he was born around 1957), became close friends with Prince Turki bin Faisal, the head of the Istakhbarat, the Saudi Intelligence Service, and Lieut. Gen. Hameed Gul, head of the ISI, all of whom were joined in a common cause with the CIA to defeat the Soviet Union. It is barely conceivable that Milton Bearden, the CIA official in charge of this "covert" operation, never shook hands with Osama bin Laden, but it is simply not true that they did not have a relationship. Moreover, two genuine authorities, Abdel Moneim Said of the Al-Ahram Center for Political and Strategic Studies in Cairo, and Hazhir Teimourian, the prominent BBC and *London Times* analyst of Iranian Kurdish ancestry, claim that bin Laden received training directly from the CIA.[138]

Similarly, former British Foreign Secretary Robin Cook asserts that

Bin Laden was…a product of a monumental miscalculation by western security agencies. Throughout the 80s he was armed by the CIA and funded by the Saudis to wage jihad against the Russian occupation of Afghanistan. Al-Qaida, literally "the database," was originally the computer file of the thousands of mujahideen who were recruited and trained with help from the CIA to defeat the Russians. Inexplicably, and with disastrous consequences, it never appears to have occurred to Washington that once Russia was out of the way, Bin Laden's organisation would turn its attention to the west.[139]

Fifth, even if one were to assume, for the sake of argument, that Zinn is in error on this point, the error would not be of such a nature as to provide evidence that he is "an exceptionally bad historian." The reason is simply that there are degrees of wrongness. If the U.S. had consistently labeled bin Laden a terrorist, and had opposed him from the beginning, then it would indeed have been a gross mistake to say that the CIA had funded and trained him. But everyone concedes that the truth is nothing like that. Rather, those who insist that the U.S. did not fund or train bin Laden nonetheless admit (1) that bin Laden did receive such support from the Saudi and Pakistani intelligence agencies, (2) that the CIA collaborated with those intelligence agencies in coordinating the anti-Soviet effort in Afghanistan, in which bin Laden took part, and (3) that the U.S. knew of bin Laden's anti-Soviet terrorist activities at that time, and approved of them. For example, while Coll, Moynihan's preferred source on these issues, does say that "bin Laden's direct contacts were with Saudi intelligence and to some extent Pakistani intelligence, not with the Americans," he also concedes that in the 1980s bin Laden and the U.S. "were working more or less in common cause against the Soviets," and that "The CIA was certainly aware of bin Laden's activities, beginning in the mid-to late-1980s, and they generally looked favorably on what he was doing at that time" (BLL). He also reports that the three intelligence agencies "compartmented" their work, "even though all three collaborated with one another through formal liaisons" (GW 86). So, at the very least, the U.S. funded those who trained bin Laden, and monitored and approved the result. If it is an error at all to summarize those facts with the phrase "the American government trained bin Laden," it is not a very big error. (And remember, it is not even *that* if the evidence cited by Chalmers is correct.) Note also that this is Moynihan's second handpicked example intended to show "how poor is Zinn's history." If it were really so poor, wouldn't it be possible to find stronger examples?

Moynihan next turns his attention to Zinn's omissions. He faults Zinn for leaving "unmentioned" Castro's acts of imprisoning and executing political opponents. But the factual basis for this criticism is only half right, as Zinn duly notes that "Cuba had imprisoned critics of the regime" (APH 657). Similarly, Moynihan objects to the fact that Zinn makes "no mention of the Khmer Rouge or Pol Pot," even though many works on *American* history share with APH this failure to discuss the government of Cambodia. (All but one of APH's references to Cambodia have to do with the war in Vietnam, which pre-dated the Khmer Rouge's taking power in Cambodia. The one exception is the Mayaguez Incident, which took place during the first month of its reign, the subsequent genocidal character of which is not particularly relevant to that event.) Moynihan presents no other examples of Zinn's objectionable omissions.

But with regard to the Mayaguez Incident, Moynihan calls Zinn's discussion of it "misleading," on the grounds that "it is untrue, as Zinn claims, that President Gerald Ford knew Cambodia had released its American captives in 1975 but still allowed a small Marine invasion simply to show American muscle after the Vietnam humiliation."

Moynihan's criticism is based on a complete butchery of what Zinn actually says about this event in APH: "The men had been detained on a Monday morning. *On Wednesday evening the Cambodians released them* — putting them on a fishing boat headed for the American fleet. *That afternoon, knowing the seamen had been taken off Tang Island, Ford nevertheless ordered a marine assault* on Tang Island" (552, emphasis added). Notice that, contrary to what Moynihan claims, Zinn does not say that "Ford knew Cambodia had released its American captives" when he ordered a marine invasion, but rather that he knew only that the Americans "had been taken off Tang Island." Moreover, Zinn neither says nor implies that these are the same thing, but rather distinguishes them temporally—he clearly states that Ford ordered the marine assault in the afternoon but that the marines were not released until that evening. So, given the axiom that one cannot know what isn't true, Zinn is obviously not saying that Ford knew, when he ordered the marine invasion, that the Americans had already been released.

On the other hand, Zinn does point out that the Ford administration, in choosing to launch a military attack on the Cambodians, disregarded evidence that the Americans were likely *to be* released imminently, and did so precisely because, as Moynihan summarizes it (accurately, this time), it wanted "to show American muscle after the Vietnam humiliation." But this claim is true, and Zinn provides ample documentation for it in APH (552–4).[140]

So, to sum up: The "untrue" claim that Moynihan attributes to Zinn is complex, comprising (a) the assertion that "President Gerald Ford knew Cambodia had released its American captives in 1975 but still allowed a small Marine invasion," and (b) that Ford did so "simply to show American muscle after the Vietnam humiliation." But Zinn did not assert (a), so Moynihan's attribution of error to him on this point is itself erroneous, and further, is based on his own inaccurate paraphrase of Zinn; and Zinn's affirmation of (b) is accurate. So nothing remains of Moynihan's criticism on this issue.

Moynihan's next complaint is that "*A People's History* is full of praise for supposedly forgotten truth-tellers like 'Dalton Trumbo and Pete Seeger, and W.E.B. Du Bois and Paul Robeson,' all apologists for Stalinism."

Naturally, this one is another demonstrable falsehood. How "full of praise" for these people is APH?

Let's start with Seeger, the much-celebrated (Kennedy Center Honoree,[141] recipient of the National Medal of Arts,[142] winner of a Lifetime Achievement Grammy Award [GLA], inductee into both the Songwriters Hall of Fame[143] and the Rock and Roll Hall of Fame[144]) musician and political activist. APH gives him *one sentence*. The context is a description of cultural changes taking place in the United States in the 1960s. The paragraph in which Seeger is mentioned begins with this sentence: "There was a new popular music of protest." Then comes the one sentence on Seeger: "Pete Seeger had been singing protest songs since the forties, but now he came into his own, his audiences much larger" (APH 537). The remainder of the short paragraph immediately drops Seeger in order to say a few words about three other singers: Bob Dylan, Joan Baez, and Malvina Reynolds. That's it. There is no suggestion that Seeger was a "forgotten" figure. Nor is he specifically lauded as a "truth-teller." Certainly no specific truths that he might have told are mentioned. And such praise as is offered is quite mild and wholly factual—that he had become more popular and was reaching larger audiences.

What about Robeson? Clearly there is much that could be said about this astonishingly versatile person, whose high level of achievement in academics (Phi Beta Kappa, and valedictorian, at Rutgers University, before going on to earn a law degree at Columbia University [USP]), athletics (an All-American in football for two seasons, a member of the College Football Hall of Fame,[145] a professional career in the National Football League after college), acting (a member of the American Theater Hall of Fame,[146] honored with a star on the Hollywood Walk of Fame[147]), singing (recipient of a Lifetime Achievement Grammy Award [GLA]), and activism (official recognition from the United Nations General Assembly for his efforts in the international campaign against apartheid in South Africa[148]), won him worldwide fame and admiration. But APH mentions him in only two sentences, both in the same paragraph, with neither being solely devoted to him. The context is a discussion of prominent African-Americans who either joined the Communist party or publicly sympathized with it in the 1930s and 1940s. The first sentence in which Robeson appears merely places him in a list of four such individuals, describes him as a "singer and actor," and characterizes him as "nationally renowned." The other sentence explains that the reason why black Americans, including Robeson, tended, in comparison to their white counterparts, to take a more favorable attitude toward communists, is that blacks in a largely racist society could not afford to reject any of the very few people who were willing to fight on their side for justice and equal rights (APH 448). That's it—there is nothing about Robeson being a "truth-teller" or a "forgotten" figure, no mention of any particular truths that he might have told, and no praise beyond the mild, and entirely accurate, observation that he was "nationally renowned."

What about Trumbo, the highly accomplished Hollywood screenwriter, who twice received the Academy Award for his screenplays (*Roman Holiday* in 1953 and *The Brave One* in 1956)?[149] There is a good story to be told about him: He wrote those and several other screenplays clandestinely, crediting them either to pseudonymous or "front" writers, as he was one of a group of writers who were at the time subject to the American film industry's policy of "blacklisting" individuals suspected of being communists or communist sympathizers. But in APH Trumbo receives only two mentions, and they do not address his screenplays or his travails as a blacklisted writer. The first mention occurs in the midst of a paragraph about American anti-war literature published in the aftermath of World War I. Without going into much detail about each work, Zinn lists Ernest Hemingway's *A Farewell to Arms*, Irwin Shaw's play, *Bury the Dead*, and Ford Madox Ford's *No More Parades*. Between the citations of Shaw and Ford, we have this sentence about Trumbo: "And a Hollywood screenwriter named Dalton Trumbo would write a powerful and chilling antiwar novel about a torso and brain left alive on the battlefield of World War I, *Johnny Got His Gun*" (APH 374).

The context of the other reference to Trumbo is a discussion of

Vietnam War veteran Ron Kovic, author of a famous memoir, *Born on the Fourth of July*. Zinn reports that on one occasion, while attending an anti-war demonstration, Kovic "heard actor Donald Sutherland read from the post-World War I novel by Dalton Trumbo, *Johnny Got His Gun*, about a soldier whose limbs and face were shot away by gunfire, a thinking torso who invented a way of communicating with the outside world and then beat out a message so powerful it could not be heard without trembling." Zinn then quotes Kovic's reaction: "Sutherland began to read the passage and something I will never forget swept over me. It was as if someone was speaking for everything I ever went through in the hospital.... I began to shake and I remember there were tears in my eyes" (APH 496–7). So, once again, we have no claim that Trumbo is a forgotten person, and no passing on of any specific truths that he might have told, though there is, this time, genuine, albeit brief, praise ("powerful and chilling," in Zinn's words, which are confirmed by those of Kovic). Thus, while Zinn's treatment of Trumbo praises him, it is not true, given its extreme terseness, that it is "full of praise" for him.

That leaves Du Bois, the distinguished historian, social scientist, prolific author, and civil rights leader, who has been repeatedly honored by the United States government (for example, the site of the house where he grew up has been designated a National Historic Landmark,[150] and the United States Postal Service has twice issued a postage stamp featuring his portrait [USP]). Du Bois turns out to be, of the four individuals Moynihan names, the only who receives several mentions in APH (23, 175, 185–6, 192–3, 210, 328–9, 348–9, 363–4, 448, 686). But even here it must be noted that APH contains very little information *about* Du Bois. Instead, most of the references in APH to Du Bois are quotations from his works on various aspects of United States history. When Zinn quotes Du Bois on slavery, on John Brown, on the Civil War, on reconstruction, and on the exclusion of blacks from the trade union movement, the focus is squarely on those topics, not on Du Bois. Thus, for the most part, when Du Bois's name appears in Zinn's text, it is only as a source citation.

What little discussion *of* Du Bois as exists in APH occurs well after the appearance of quotations from him on subjects that pre-dated his birth. Zinn tells us that Du Bois was born in Massachusetts; that he was the first black to receive a Ph.D. degree from Harvard University (in 1895); that he "was a Socialist sympathizer, although only briefly a party member"; that he spearheaded the "Niagara Movement," which began with a conference, held near Niagara Falls, of black leaders throughout the country; and that he helped found the National Association for the Advancement of Colored People, serving as its only black officer and as the editor of its periodical, *The Crisis* (APH 348–9). (Du Bois also appears in the same two sentences, discussed four paragraphs ago, in which Robeson is mentioned. Du Bois, described simply as a "writer and scholar," is listed there, along with Robeson and two other figures, as examples of black Americans who had supported the Communist party in the 1930s and 1940s [APH 448].) That's it.

It is true that Zinn praises Du Bois, calling his *The Souls of Black Folk* a "poetic, powerful book" (APH 348), and his "The African Roots of War" a "remarkably perceptive article on the nature of the First World War" (APH 363), and twice using the locution "Du Bois saw..." (as opposed to something neutral, along the lines of "Du Bois claimed" or "Du Bois said"), thus implying that Du Bois's assertions were not only correct but insightful (APH 363). But that's the extent of it. There are no more words of praise for Du Bois in APH.

Let's review. Moynihan claims that "*A People's History* is full of praise for supposedly forgotten truth-tellers like 'Dalton Trumbo and Pete Seeger, and W.E.B. Du Bois and Paul Robeson,' all apologists for Stalinism." The word "full" has many related meanings, but the one that seems closest to Moynihan's intent is "having a great deal or many, as in 'a book full of errors.'" But, as we have seen, APH does not praise Robeson at all (he is barely mentioned), says nothing about Seeger (in the one sentence on him) that could be construed as praise beyond noting his popularity, offers only the briefest words of praise for one of Trumbo's books, and praises Du Bois just four times (each amounting to just one sentence or less), in addition to praising him implicitly by quoting him several times. That's not a great deal of praise, given that APH is almost seven hundred pages long. True, Moynihan's use of the word "like" implies that these four individuals are mere examples—there are supposedly many others who have gone unmentioned. But notice that Moynihan is the one who has chosen these examples. Presumably, he would have picked the ones that best support his case. So his claim falls completely flat. As is the case with so many of Zinn's critics, Moynihan's intended audience apparently consists entirely of credulous readers—those who are ready to swallow his implausible claims without undertaking the quite modest effort needed to check them for accuracy (in this case, all that is required is about five minutes' worth of work—consulting the index of APH to find the small number of references to the four mentioned figures, and then reading the relevant passages).

Notice, also, that Moynihan offers no explanation whatsoever as to what, specifically, is wrong with anything that Zinn says about Trumbo, Seeger, Du Bois, or Robeson. Is Moynihan's description of them as "apologists for Stalinism" supposed to be sufficient to show that they cannot possibly merit any positive mention in a work of American history? But wouldn't that be as reductive and Manichean as a hypothetical criticism of a traditional American history text for being "full of praise for George Washington, Thomas Jefferson, James Madison, James Monroe, and Andrew Jackson, all racists and slave-owners"? In any case, Moynihan fails to discuss anything that APH says about the four individuals he names. Are any of Zinn's claims about them false? Does he say anything about them that is illogical, or unwarranted, or defective in any specific way? Moynihan does not say, preferring instead to dismiss the four, simplistically, as "apologists for Stalinism," and to claim, quite falsely, that Zinn's book is "full of praise for them." What are the intellectual standards in play here?

Next, Moynihan informs us that in APH "There is no accounting of communism's crimes." Apparently, such statements as that Stalin "killed peasants for industrial progress in the Soviet Union" (APH 17), that "Cuba had imprisoned critics of the regime," and that China "had massacred protesting students in Beijing in 1991 and put dissenters in prison" and had a "bloody record of suppression" (APH 657), don't count.

Continuing on at this same level of intellectual rigor and scholarly sophistication, Moynihan writes: "Despite conclusive evidence from Russian archives, Zinn suggests the atom spies Morton Sobell and Julius Rosenberg were railroaded with 'weak' evidence and their subsequent trials were simply to show 'what lay at the end of the line for those the government decided were traitors.'" The main problem with this criticism is that it fails to observe a distinction between the following, quite different, questions: (1) Did Sobell and Rosenberg get a fair trial?; and (2) Were they guilty? The evidence from Russian archives to which Moynihan refers only addresses question (2), not question (1). But it is question (1) with which APH is exclusively concerned. APH argues that the trial was unfair (432–5); it does not argue that the defendants were innocent. The Russian archives evidence, therefore, is irrelevant to the claims of APH, and Moynihan's use of the word "despite" makes no sense.

Moynihan's failure to grasp this point is difficult to understand, since it is highlighted in one of the two articles on the case to which the online version of his article provides a link. Though that article's main point is that we now have compelling evidence of the guilt of Sobell and Julius (though not Ethel) Rosenberg, it also notes "that the government is not supposed to frame a guilty man," and quotes the observation of Robert Meeropol, one of Rosenberg's sons, who, while painfully conceding that the new evidence had brought to an end his hope that his father might be innocent, also remarked, "it's not the end of understanding what happened to due process."[151] One wonders what Moynihan might have thought these two quotations meant.

Despite the extreme brevity of Moynihan's discussion of this issue (that of Zinn on the Rosenberg case), he nonetheless manages to litter it with careless errors. (1) Moynihan misspells Sobell's name. (2) He quotes Zinn as saying that the evidence presented at trial against Sobell and Julius Rosenberg was "weak," but in fact Zinn uses that word exclusively, and specifically, in connection with Sobell (APH 434). (3) Moynihan attributes to Zinn the claim that the trial was "simply to show 'what lay at the end of the line for those the government decided were traitors,'" but in fact Zinn says that about the *execution* of the Rosenbergs, not the trial (APH 435). The point is not a subtle one. It would be one thing to say that the Rosenbergs should not be tried, and quite another to say that, if convicted, the proper sentence should not be death. (4) The word "simply" in Moynihan's assertion that, according to Zinn, the trial (well, really it was the execution, but let that pass) was "simply to show 'what lay at the end of the line for those the government decided were traitors,'" is a pure fabrication. There is nothing in Zinn's text corresponding to this paraphrase. To say that an execution "was a demonstration to the people of the country…of what lay at the end of the line for those the government decided were traitors" is not to say that it is "simply" (or "only" or "solely" or "purely") that, and Zinn says nothing to imply that he holds such a simplistic view.

Moynihan's essay then reaches a kind of crescendo of recklessness and irresponsibility, as he packs several falsehoods and half-truths into one sentence: "Zinn abjured footnotes (there are a number of quotes in *A People's History* that I couldn't verify), his books consist of clip jobs, interviews, and recycled material from *A People's History*, and he was more likely to be found protesting on Boston Common than holding office hours at Boston University."

Let's take these one at a time. Many of Zinn's books contain footnotes. He does not, as a general rule, "abjure" them. While it is true that APH does not contain footnotes, it does (as discussed above) make use of a documentation system. APH contains a 20-page bibliography, organized by chapter, in which full bibliographical information can be found for texts that are mentioned (by author and title) in the body of the text. Moynihan elects not to inform his readers of this fact. Nor does he identify any of the quotes from APH that he has been unable to verify. As I have, for the purposes of this book, checked dozens of Zinn's quotations, I am confident that, were Moynihan to list the ones that stumped him, it would tell us far more about his research skills than it would about Zinn's scholarly methods. In any case, it is ironic that Moynihan would make this complaint, since he himself provides a citation for only one of the many quotations in his article (though he does provide hyperlinks to some of them in the online version), and, as noted above, I was unable to find the source for one of his quotations from Zinn. So, according to my experience, for what it is worth, there are more undocumented, untraceable quotations in Moynihan's short article than there are in Zinn's 688-page book.

Next, the claim that Zinn's "books consist of clip jobs, interviews, and recycled material from *A People's History*" is, at best, a half-truth. *Some* of his books collect previously published articles; *some* of them consist of interviews; and *some* of them present material from APH in a different form (such as a children's version and a graphic version). But such descriptions do not apply to *La Guardia in Congress*, or *SNCC: The New Abolitionists*, or *Disobedience and Democracy*, or *Postwar America*, or his plays, or his autobiography, among others. Still other books, including *The*

Southern Mystique, Vietnam: The Logic of Withdrawal, The Politics of History, and *Declarations of Independence* incorporate some previously published material (usually re-worked and expanded) into a larger work consisting substantially of new writing. So, once again, Moynihan oversimplifies, in this case by falsely attributing to all of Zinn's books what is true of only a few of them. I would also add that it is a sign of Zinn's success as a writer that there is a demand for books consisting of interviews with him, or which collect his previously published short pieces. It is unclear why the existence of such books should count as a mark against him.

Lastly, we have the startling assertion that Zinn "was more likely to be found protesting on Boston Common than holding office hours at Boston University." Merely to call this "false" would be to give it far more credit than it deserves. It is, rather, a grotesque anti-truth, fully equivalent to calling "up" "down," or "night" "day." One might as well accuse Usain Bolt of being slow, or Shaquille O'Neal of being short. Indeed, one might equally well lament Donald Trump's poverty, while praising his tact and humility, or complain about Kanye West's shyness and lack of ego. As discussed in the previous chapter, Zinn taught over 400 students per semester at Boston University—an unusually high number, especially in the light of the fact that he did not have teaching assistants. In order to accommodate their needs, he kept astonishingly extensive office hours. As his student I observed this at first hand, and it was widely discussed at the Boston University campus. (Recall the testimony of David Colapinto, quoted in the previous chapter: "Anyone who visited the Political Science department will remember the long line of students patiently waiting outside [Zinn's] office to discuss projects or seeking his advice or support" [DC].) True, Zinn did more than his share of protesting on Boston Common—something that he did, perhaps, two or three times a year. But he held office hours on a daily basis. Anyone who would accuse Zinn of any kind of deficiency in connection with office hours—and note that

Moynihan provides no citation, or any other kind of evidence in support of his charge—is someone who will say anything, someone who is deeply indifferent to evidence and utterly contemptuous of truth.

Amazingly, it is immediately after issuing this abject falsehood that Moynihan suddenly announces: "But it is clear that those who have praised [Zinn's] work do so because they appreciate his conclusions, while ignoring his shoddy methodology." He then begins a new paragraph, as follows: "This helps explain why few of his acolytes mention the effusive blurbs Zinn provided for David Ray Griffin's two books of 9/11 conspiracy theories, *Debunking 9/11* and *The New Pearl Harbor*...."

Where to begin? First, there is no need for a special explanation as to why "few of Zinn's acolytes," whoever they might be thought to be, discuss the blurbs he wrote for two books by David Ray Griffin. In general, when people discuss a writer, they discuss the writer's own works, not the short blurbs he or she may have written to promote someone else's books. I suspect that it would be difficult to find extensive discussion of the blurb writing of anyone who is himself or herself also the author of significant books.

Second, what is the logic of the specific explanation that Moynihan offers? How is the (alleged) fact that Zinn's admirers base their admiration on his conclusions, rather than on his methodology, supposed to explain their (alleged) reluctance to discuss his Griffin blurbs? That sounds like a complete *non sequitur*. If they liked his methodology better than his conclusions, does that mean that they would want to discuss the Griffin blurbs? Why? Moynihan says that "this helps explain...," but he offers no explanation as to *how* it helps explain.

Third, Zinn's blurbs are not remotely "effusive." "Effusive" praise would be praise that is "unrestrained," "gushing," "extravagant," or "lavish." But Zinn's praise falls short of endorsing any of Griffin's conclusions. Instead, much more modestly, Zinn merely credits Griffin with having raised some good questions, and thereby having made a case for further investigation. Zinn's blurb for *The New Pearl Harbor* reads as follows: "David Ray Griffin has done admirable and painstaking research in reviewing the mysteries surrounding the 9-11 attacks. It is the most persuasive argument I have seen for further investigation of the Bush administration's relationship to that historic and troubling event."[152] And for *Debunking 9/11 Debunking*: "Considering how the 9/11 tragedy has been used by the Bush administration to propel us into immoral wars again and again, I believe that David Ray Griffin's provocative questions about 9/11 deserve to be investigated and addressed."[153]

Fourth, since Moynihan's obvious intent is to link Zinn up with wild 9/11 conspiracy theories, it should be pointed out that, not only does he never endorse such theories in any of his writings or talks, but also that, except for in his Griffin blurbs, he doesn't even pursue the much milder, and thoroughly mainstream, call for a further investigation of the 9/11 attacks.

Finally, even though Moynihan's discussion of these matters takes up only a fraction of one sentence, he naturally manages to introduce an error into it. Griffin has no book entitled *"Debunking 9/11."* The correct title is *"Debunking 9/11 Debunking."*

On the other hand, Moynihan does make a cogent point when he criticizes Zinn for using the work of David Irving in connection with his discussion of the bombing of Dresden in World War II. Zinn puts the death toll from that event at "more than 100,000" (APH 421), a figure that may have been derived from Irving's 1965 book, *The Destruction of Dresden*, which is listed in Zinn's bibliography. While Irving's work was once considered authoritative, and his casualty estimates approvingly cited by mainstream historians, he has since been discredited, and more recent works on the bombing of Dresden have tended to fix the number of casualties at a much lower level—roughly in the 20,000–25,000 range. It was wrong of Zinn not to revise his treatment of the Dresden bombing in light of more recent scholarship, and to fail to remove the mendacious Irving from his bibliography. And Moynihan was right to call him on it.

Unfortunately, Moynihan's brief brush with accuracy would prove short-lived, as he immediately goes on to accuse Zinn of having "defended injustice in the name of socialism, communism, and, in the case of Imperial Japan, anti-Americanism." He offers no explanation as to what he might mean by this accusation. What specific injustices has Zinn supposedly defended? What arguments did he use in doing so? Moynihan simply doesn't tell us. I cannot recall Zinn's ever having uttered a single kind word about "Imperial Japan." Is Zinn's argument that the U.S. should not have dropped nuclear bombs on Hiroshima and Nagasaki supposed to count as a "defense of injustice," and of "Imperial Japan"? And is the rationale for such a defense supposed to be "anti-Americanism," rather than, say, a respect for the right of Japanese civilians not to be incinerated? Is Zinn's argument that the people of Vietnam should have the right to self-determination, and the right not to be bombed by the U.S. if they should exercise that right in a way that the U.S. does not like, a "defense of injustice," undertaken "in the name of communism," and/or of "anti-Americanism"? And what does Moynihan think that the locution "in the name of" means? Zinn has certainly never argued that actions that would otherwise be indefensible can be justified if they somehow promote "socialism" or "communism" or, most laughably, "anti-Americanism."

Moynihan's essay ends with these words: "Call him [Zinn] what you will—activist, dissident, left-wing muckraker. Just don't call him a historian." But the motley collection of half-truths, quarter-truths, falsehoods, inaccurate paraphrases, unexplained and undefended absurdities, and *non sequiturs* that Moynihan has assembled to support this conclusion is plainly not up to the job. It is an ironic indication of the Orwellian times in which we live that this sustained exercise in inaccuracy and illogic appears in a publication called, of all things, *Reason*.

Arthur M. Schlesinger, Jr.

Schlesinger (1917–2007), a Pulitzer Prize-winning Harvard University historian, is represented on Daniels's list of quotations by Zinn critics as follows: "'I don't take him very seriously. He's a polemicist, not a historian.' — Arthur M. Schlesinger Jr."

The first problem with this quotation is that its source is unknown. An extensive search, which uncovered dozens of articles that include this quotation from Schlesinger, failed to turn up any publication of it prior to its appearance in the Associated Press obituary of Zinn. The relevant passage reads: "Arthur M. Schlesinger Jr. once said: 'I know he regards me as a dangerous reactionary. And I don't take him very seriously. He's a polemicist, not a historian.'" Note that this does not tell us where Schlesinger (allegedly) said this, or in what context. We don't know what (if anything) preceded those words, or what (if anything) followed them. We don't know what kind of explanation (if any) Schlesinger might have given for his remark, or what kind of argument (if any) he might have made in its support. The several dozen other articles that I have found in which this quotation appears all use this "Schlesinger once said" locution. None of them displays the slightest curiosity about the source of the quotation, or its context, or, indeed, its authenticity.

Assuming, for the sake of discussion, that the quotation is genuine, its terseness renders it difficult to evaluate. On what basis does Schlesinger think that Zinn is a polemicist? On what grounds does he think that he is not a historian? Does Schlesinger think that being a polemicist is in principle incompatible with being a historian, so that no polemicists are historians, or is there something about the specific kind of polemics in which Zinn engages that disqualifies him from meriting the title "historian"? We have no answers to these questions, or others like them. As we have seen, the arguments of others who have concluded that Zinn is a bad historian, or not a historian at all, have been fallacious. Perhaps Schlesinger's arguments, if only we had access to them, would be better. But perhaps they would not. Obviously, I am in no position to assess his arguments, since, so far as I can tell, no one has published them.

However, if we assume that Schlesinger's argument is that the taking of sides with regard to matters of history is unscholarly—it makes one a "polemicist," rather than a historian—then Zinn has a ready reply. His claim, discussed extensively in the previous chapter, is that the taking of sides is an unavoidable necessity in historical writing, since all such writing is necessarily selective (it is impossible to include every one of the literally infinite number of items that might be included), with the selection inevitably reflecting one sense of what is important and interesting at the expense of other possible perspectives. Further, the demand that historical writing be neutral, that it take no side, lends illegitimate support to a conservative, mainstream, status quo approach, for the simple reason that, while a selection that differs from that of previous historians will definitely be noticed, and will shine a spotlight on the values and political orientation that underlies it, a selection that simply reproduces the same choices that others have made can appear "objective," with the moral and political values inherent in it going unrecognized.

It is easy to make this point in connection with Schlesinger's own historical work, and Zinn has occasionally done so. Commenting on Schlesinger's Pulitzer Prize-winning book, *The Age of Jackson*, Zinn notes that "even after a war that should have made scholars more sensitive to issues of racial hatred, Schlesinger's book, emphasizing Jackson as an opponent of national banking interests, overlooked him as a racist, a slaveholder, a mutilator and killer of Indians" (CW 45).[154] Or again:

The leading books on the Jacksonian period, written by

respected historians (*The Age of Jackson* by Arthur Schlesinger; *The Jacksonian Persuasion* by Marvin Meyers), do not mention Jackson's Indian policy, but there is much talk in them of tariffs, banking, political parties, political rhetoric. If you look through high school textbooks and elementary school textbooks in American history you will find Jackson the frontiersman, soldier, democrat, man of the people—not Jackson the slaveholder, land speculator, executioner of dissident soldiers, exterminator of Indians. (APH 130)

Nor is this criticism anachronistic: "This is not simply hindsight (the word used for thinking back *differently* on the past). After Jackson was elected President in 1828…, the Indian Removal bill came before Congress and was called, at the time, 'the leading measure' of the Jackson administration and 'the greatest question that ever came before Congress' except for matters of peace and war" (APH 130).

And Schlesinger's indifference to the treatment of Indians is matched by his lack of concern for the treatment of blacks:

The folk vision of Andrew Jackson has always seen him as one of the great democratic presidents. Arthur Schlesinger, Jr., in his biography, reinforced this picture. He portrayed Jackson, along with Jefferson, as an early prototype of New Deal pluralistic liberalism, "a society in which no single group is able to sacrifice democracy and liberty to its own interests." Schlesinger did not, however, see the white man as such a group, or pay much attention to the anti-Negro aspect of Jackson's liberalism. It was not just that Jackson was himself a slaveholder; he urged Congress, in his message of December 1835, to pass a law to prohibit the circulation of Abolitionist literature in the Southern states. The law was not passed…, but Jackson's Postmaster General, and succeeding ones, simply closed their eyes to the fact that local postmasters in the South were removing antislavery literature from the mails.[155]

So now we see how this "historian/polemicist" game is played. Play up Jackson's pro-democracy actions while ignoring his anti-Indian and anti-black actions—you're a historian; call attention to those anti-Indian and anti-black policies—you have an axe to grind, you're a propagandist and a polemicist, not a historian. One has only to point out this double standard to reveal its absurdity. And yet, not one of the many anti-Zinn critics who mindlessly reproduce Schlesinger's (alleged) "polemicist, not a historian" quotation ever addresses these grotesque omissions in Schlesinger's work, or explains why their existence does not make him "a polemicist," rather than "a historian," or explains how, exactly, he is superior to Zinn in this regard, or, indeed, how he differs from him at all in any way other than being inferior to him (less fair, less comprehensive, less concerned with what is important, less philosophically sophisticated, less self-aware of his own biases and limitations). Because Schlesinger's biases and omissions are the same as those of his predecessors, they aren't recognized, and he is seen as unbiased, objective, and professional. Because Zinn's biases and omissions are different, he is seen as biased, a polemicist and propagandist, and as unprofessional.[156] But once this hidden double standard is exposed, it stands in need of a defense. Not one of Zinn's critics offers one, or shows the slightest awareness of the need to offer one, or gives even the most minimal indication of being capable of offering one.

Moreover, it is highly ironic that Schlesinger, of all people, would take it upon himself to lecture Zinn about the evils of partisanship and its alleged incompatibility with genuine historical scholarship, since it is Schlesinger, rather than Zinn, who temporarily abandoned academia in order to take a job in politics, serving as special assistant and "court historian" to

President John F. Kennedy. What is worse, by his own admission it is Schlesinger, rather than Zinn, who repeatedly did in that capacity what scholars, and especially historians, should never do—tell lies about historical events.

Zinn reports on one of these:

An item in *The New York Times*, November 25, 1965, read: "Arthur M. Schlesinger, Jr., said today he had lied to *The New York Times* in April 1961, about the nature and size of the Cuban refugee landing in the Bay of Pigs." Reminded by *The Times* that his statement of April 17, 1961, on the nature of the Bay of Pigs operation was contradicted by his book *A Thousand Days*, Schlesinger's response was: "Did I say that? Well I was lying. This was the cover story. I apologize...." (VLW 35)

And shortly before the launch of the Bay of Pigs invasion of Cuba, Schlesinger produced a remarkable memorandum, addressed to President Kennedy, in which he advocated a massive campaign of lying to cover up U.S. involvement in this illegal act of international aggression.[157] For example, after flattering the president, by declaring that "The character and repute of President Kennedy constitute one of our greatest national resources," so that "Nothing should be done to jeopardize this invaluable asset," Schlesinger advocates covering up Kennedy's knowledge of, and involvement in, the operation: "When lies must be told, they should be told by subordinate officials. At no point should the President be asked to lend himself to the cover operation." Further, "someone other than the President [should] make the final decision and do so in his absence—someone whose head can later be placed on the block if things go terribly wrong." Similarly, he urges U.S. representatives at the United Nations to tell lies to the entire world: "If our representatives cannot evade in debate the question whether the

CIA has actually helped the Cuban rebels, they will presumably be obliged, in the traditional, pre-U-2 manner, to deny any such CIA activity. (If Castro flies a group of captured Cubans to New York to testify that they were organized and trained by CIA, we will have to be prepared to show that the alleged CIA personnel were errant idealists or soldiers-of-fortune working on their own.)" And he gives advice on how to lie at press conferences, drawing up a list of answers to questions that reporters might ask:

Q. Sir, according to the newspapers, the rebel forces were trained in American camps and supplied by American agencies.

A. ...[S]o far as I can tell, this is a purely Cuban operation. I doubt whether Cuban patriots in exile would have to be stimulated and organized by the United States in order to persuade them to liberate their nation from a Communist dictator.

Q. Mr. President, is CIA involved in this affair?

A. ...I can assure you that the United States Government has no intention of using force to overthrow the Castro regime or of contributing force for that purpose unless compelled to do so in the interests of self-defense.

(Note that this memorandum was issued from the "Office of the Historian.")

But even so imaginative a liar as Schlesinger cannot figure out how to deny the illegality of the invasion, as the following exchange from his proposed press conference indicates:

Q. Mr. President, would you say that, so far as Cuba is concerned, the U.S. has been faithful to its treaty pledges against intervention in other countries? Would you say that it has resolutely enforced the laws forbidding the use

of U.S. territory to prepare revolutionary action against
another state?

A. ????

Kennedy followed Schlesinger's advice, saying at a press
conference, four days before the invasion, that "There will not be,
under any circumstances, an intervention in Cuba by the United
States armed forces."[158]

Once Schlesinger's career as a Machiavellian adviser to power
was over, he returned to academia, taking a position in 1966 as
the Albert Schweitzer Professor of the Humanities at the
Graduate Center of the City University of New York. How is this
possible? How can the history profession, of all professions, be so
contemptuous of historical truth as to welcome into its ranks an
admitted serial historical falsifier? As Noam Chomsky correctly
notes: "it is significant that such events provoke so little response
in the intellectual community—...that no one has said that there
is something strange in the offer of a major chair in the humanities to a historian who feels it to be his duty to persuade the
world that an American-sponsored invasion of a nearby country
is nothing of the sort."[159] In any case, none of the Zinn critics who
approvingly quote Schlesinger's (alleged) dismissal of Zinn say
anything about Schlesinger's record of lying about history, any
more than they explain why he, of all people, should be taken
seriously when he declares that another scholar, who is not an
admitted serial liar about history, and who has not worked as a
partisan for one political party, is "a polemicist, not a historian."

Kevin Mattson

Mattson is the Connor Study Professor of Contemporary History
at Ohio University, and the author of "History Lesson,"
published in *Democracy: A Journal of Ideas*.[160] Though this is ostensibly a review of APH and of C. Vann Woodward's *The Strange
Career of Jim Crow*, Mattson is content to denounce Zinn's book

without making any serious attempt to describe its contents or to address its arguments. As an example of his relentless question begging, consider the following passage:

> "There was never, for me as a teacher and writer," [Zinn]...explained, "an obsession with 'objectivity,' which I considered neither possible nor desirable." For Zinn, writing history was synonymous with doing politics. As he states in *A People's History*, there is an inevitable "taking of sides which comes from selection and emphasis in history." In other words, history can never be the disinterested pursuit of truth but is rather a radical project, from the very beginning an exercise in spin rather than scholarship.

Though his "in other words" locution suggests that he is offering an unproblematic and uncontroversial paraphrase of Zinn's remark, in *The Politics of History* Zinn had offered a series of arguments (discussed in the previous chapter) against the claim that a rejection of what is called "objectivity" must lead to any abandonment, or even lessening, of scholarly rigor. (For one thing, the use of political criteria in connection with the selection of topics is fully consistent with the rejection of political criteria when it comes to assessing evidence and determining truth.) Mattson simply ignores those arguments. Nor does Mattson offer any discussion of the meaning of the term "objectivity," as if it were the most straightforward of concepts. But Zinn's arguments depend on carefully disentangling from one another the many different things that are sometimes meant by that term.

Mattson also offers the curious claim that Arthur Schlesinger, Jr., despite his partisan activity as advisor to President John F. Kennedy, "never abandoned 'objectivity,' which he believed was an ideal 'towards which the historian must constantly strive.'" Mattson does not explain what this means, or how it can be squared with the fact that Schlesinger's book on Andrew Jackson says nothing about Jackson as "a racist, a slaveholder, a mutilator and killer of Indians," or about Jackson as someone who tried to pass a law making it illegal to distribute abolitionist literature in the southern states. Nor does Mattson explain how it can be reconciled with the many lies about history (not mere "spin") that Schlesinger told during his tenure as President Kennedy's advisor and "court historian" (see the discussion of Schlesinger above).

In short, Mattson's critique makes no contact with Zinn's work, and in particular fails to come to terms with any of his arguments about objectivity.

Benno Schmidt

Schmidt, who has been Professor of Constitutional Law at Columbia University, Dean of the law school there, and, subsequently, President of Yale University, is the author of an article, "Mitch Daniels's Gift to Academic Freedom," published in the *Wall Street Journal*.[161] Schmidt is somewhat coy in his defense of Daniels. He does not come right out and say that he agrees with Daniels, though he strongly implies it. His main points are that Daniels did not violate academic freedom, and that his emails have sparked a needed debate about the nature of academic freedom. The latter point may be granted, but that does not go to Daniels's credit—an irrational, unjustified attack on academic freedom can spark a needed debate about the nature of that concept. As to the former point, Schmidt's only support for it comes from his observation that in the wake of Daniels's anti-Zinn emails "there is currently no evidence that anything was done by him or his staff to act upon his heated remarks." But that should not go to Daniels's credit either, since he ordered that action be taken.

That Schmidt sympathizes with Daniels's perspective is revealed by his reference to "the biased, left-leaning, tendentious and inaccurate drivel that too often passes as definitive in

American higher education," and, even more clearly, by his claim that what has "essentially" happened "over the past 50 years" is that faculty have been "allowed to engage in indoctrination and professional irresponsibility without being held to account." But Schmidt offers no argument or evidence of any kind in support of such claims. Moreover, with regard to Zinn, Schmidt is here guilty of the fallacy of begging the question. Zinn's case is that mainstream history, the kind that was routinely taught more than 50 years ago (to use Schmidt's timeline), constituted indoctrination, and was irresponsibly biased and untruthful. Zinn offers his history as a corrective to such indoctrination. Of course, Schmidt does not engage this argument at all, but rather blithely assumes that the issue of indoctrination arises only with non-mainstream history.

Schmidt also misfires when he takes pains to argue that "politicians or outside groups" do not "violate academic freedom" when they criticize academics. Here he commits the straw man fallacy, since no one had claimed otherwise. The issue was the attempt to *ban* Zinn, not the mere fact that Daniels criticized him. Perhaps Schmidt was confused on this point by the fact, which he mentions, that the July 22, 2013 letter signed by 92 Purdue professors expressed concern that Daniels continued to criticize Zinn after the previously private emails (which were over three years old) had been made public. But the letter made clear that the source of this concern was not the criticism itself, but rather the fact that it was emanating from someone who both (1) had tried to ban Zinn's book and (2) was now the President of their university, with the ability to wield all of the power of that office.

Finally, note that Schmidt quotes favorably the statement that "respect for the truth" requires "avoiding bias in its various forms." That is an obvious falsehood—does respect for the truth require avoiding a bias (which means "leaning") for truth and against falsehood, for evidence and against wild guesswork, for logic and against fallacies, for peace and against war, for happiness and against misery, for fairness and against injustice?

Schmidt begs every significant question, and avoids contact with the most important arguments against the position he defends. Consequently, he makes no contribution to the debate over the Daniels–Zinn controversy.

Gabriel Schoenfeld

Schoenfeld, who holds a Ph.D. from Harvard University's Department of Government, was formerly senior editor of *Commentary* before serving as senior advisor to the 2012 Mitt Romney presidential campaign. He is the author of "An Honest History of Howard Zinn," published in the *New York Daily News*.[162]

Schoenfeld informs us that "Zinn certainly had his talents as a writer, but his strengths in that department are inversely proportionate to his fidelity to historical truth." Unfortunately, Schoenfeld does not succeed in supporting that judgment. For starters, and to his credit, he concedes that Zinn was not "a naked falsifier in the manner, say, of the historian and Holocaust denier David Irving." So, as it turns out, Zinn's alleged lack of fidelity to historical truth amounts to the charge that his account is one-sided, reductionistic, and tailored to support his political conclusions. To make that charge stick, it seems to me that Schoenfeld would have to point out instances in which Zinn has omitted crucial information that would undermine his conclusions. But Schoenfeld doesn't do that. Rather, he simply gives a few examples of things that Zinn says, and intermittently interrupts his presentation with the declaration that these prove his point.

Here are two of Schoenfeld's examples: (1) "The political philosopher John Locke is introduced by Zinn with the observation that his 'Second Treatise on Government,' which so heavily influenced our Founding Fathers, 'talked about government and political rights, but ignored the existing inequalities in property'—an unsurprising fact when one notes that Locke was 'a wealthy man, with investments in the silk trade and slave trade, income from loans and mortgages.'" (2) "Turning to relatively current events—the Reagan and Clinton presidencies— Zinn...finds a wealth of reasons to slam both. Thus under Reagan 'new requirements eliminated free school lunches for more than one million poor children,' while under Clinton 'the United States continued to supply lethal arms to some of the most vicious regimes in the world' while it took aim at social services even as it awarded 'huge contracts to military contractors and generous subsidies to corporations.'" Note that Schoenfeld does not explain what, specifically, is objectionable about Zinn's presentation in either case.

Next, Schoenfeld, like nearly all of the other Daniels defenders, cites the same quotations critical of Zinn, from the same authors that Daniels had used, without failing to reproduce his claim that some of these critics "identify with [Zinn's] political leanings."

Schoenfeld's article ends with these words:

Which brings us back to Mitch Daniels and his concern that the young people of Indiana not be "force fed a totally false version of our history." Daniels' worry was well-placed. "A People's History" was being employed by the state of Indiana as a textbook for summer courses for teachers to earn "professional development credit."

Removing it is not censorship; it is, rather, setting responsible academic standards—much like using Darwin and not the Bible in science class.

The only "astonishing and shocking" thing about this whole episode is that Daniels is being attacked for upholding critical standards. That is neither censorship nor an infringement of academic freedom. It is sanity. Daniels should be celebrated as an educator who is passionate about

American history and American freedom. Howard Zinn was in his own way an enemy of both.

Comments: (1) Though Schoenfeld here asserts twice that Daniels's attempt to remove Zinn's text would not constitute censorship, he gives no explicit argument in support of this conclusion. He seems to be implying an argument, however, and that is that if an act is describable as "setting responsible academic standards" or as "upholding critical standards," then it cannot be censorship. That's nonsense, on a par with saying that if an object is square it cannot also be brown. To see this, one need only consult standard dictionary definitions of censorship. Here are three: (a) "In modern times, censorship refers to the examination of books, periodicals, plays, films, television and radio programs, news reports, and other communication media for the purpose of altering or suppressing parts thought to be objectionable or offensive." —*Funk & Wagnalls New World Encyclopedia*; (b) "Official prohibition or restriction of any type of expression believed to threaten the political, social, or moral order. It may be imposed by governmental authority, local or national, by a religious body, or occasionally by a powerful private group." —*The Columbia Encyclopedia*, Sixth Edition. 2001; (c) "In its narrower, more legalistic sense, censorship means only the prevention by official government action of the circulation of messages already produced." —*Academic American Encyclopedia*.[163] So the suppression of a book by a government official counts as censorship, even if the motive for that act of censorship is to "set responsible academic standards."

(2) Schoenfeld, along with many other Daniels defenders, also completely ignores issues of process and governance—who should make decisions about academic standards, and how should those decisions be made. Should decisions about which history textbooks to use be made by history professors, who

possess doctoral degrees in history, who regularly engage in research and writing in the field of history, and who attend conferences in which they share and discuss with their colleagues each other's historical findings, or should the judgment of these scholars be overturned by governors who possess no demonstrated knowledge of, or competence in history, who have no degrees in that subject, and who have published no peer reviewed research in that field? And if there is to be some sort of process in which textbook decisions are to be evaluated in terms of their consistency with "respectable academic standards," should that be an open, democratic one, in which all concerned parties, representing a variety of points of view, can be heard, and have their arguments considered, or is it better for this to be handled privately, autocratically, by means of cranky emails between a governor and his yes-men subordinates?

To combine this point with the previous one, consider this analogy. Suppose that my doctor recommends that I undergo a certain surgical procedure. I decide not to follow his advice. So he breaks into my house, tranquilizes me, takes me, in my unconscious state, to his office, and performs the operation anyway. Even if the reason for performing the surgery was to "uphold medical standards," in the sense of doing what is best for me from a medical standpoint, this would still be an act of kidnap and assault, just as a governor's act of banning a textbook from use in the schools is still censorship, even if done to uphold academic standards. But now let's vary the example. Suppose, in this case, that I do take my doctor's advice, and agree to undergo the surgery. Suppose, further, that my doctor is fully licensed and in good standing, but that the surgery he wants to perform is controversial in the medical profession—some doctors would agree that it is a sound procedure, and appropriate for someone in my medical condition, while others strongly disagree, regarding it as "radical" and "dangerous." Suppose, finally, that the governor of my state, who is not a doctor and has no medical credentials, strongly adheres to the latter opinion. (He has read mischaracterizations of it by the likes of Roger Kimball, David Horowitz, and Daniel Flynn—if there are such people writing about medical issues.) He orders his subordinates to "ban" the procedure, and thus attempts to overturn the decision that I have made, and to usurp the authority of my doctor. I would think that most people, even if they agreed with the governor's opinion on the medical merits of the procedure in question, would have a problem with that. Schoenfeld fails to recognize that it even raises any issues.

(3) The analogy to Darwin and the Bible in a science class is an untenable one. The Bible postulates supernatural causes that are not accessible to the methods of science. It is not a science text at all, and no one takes it to be one. Zinn's book is a history text, and it utilizes no methods that are foreign to the standard practice of history. To teach Zinn in a history class is to use a history book that is controversial; to use the Bible in a science class is to use a book whose subject matter and purpose are external to those of the discipline for which it is being used.

(4) Schoenfeld also claims that Daniels's actions do not violate academic freedom. Why? He doesn't explicitly say, but he implies that the reason is that they are "sanity." This is fallacious for the same reason that his implicit argument about censorship is fallacious. One can violate academic freedom by imposing a "sane" position by force, bypassing the rights and responsibilities of others, such as faculty members.

(5) Schoenfeld says that "Daniels should be celebrated as an educator who is passionate about American history and American freedom." But since Daniels is also on record as wanting the "textbook of choice" in Indiana to be a book by fellow non-historian, fellow right-wing Republican politician, William Bennett, isn't it possible that he is more passionate about conservative indoctrination, and about shielding students' eyes from evidence and arguments that tell against his political

positions, than he is about American history? And what is this freedom of which Schoenfeld speaks? Is it freedom from reading? Freedom from thinking? Freedom from being able to pursue the critical examination of ideas with one's fellow students and one's teachers without gubernatorial interference?

(6) Schoenfeld ends by saying that "Howard Zinn was in his own way an enemy of both [American history and American freedom]." While one can gather, albeit only roughly, why Schoenfeld thinks that Zinn was an enemy of American history, one wonders: how was he an enemy of American freedom? Granted, he did interfere with southern segregationists when they attempted to deprive black Americans of their human rights. But how else did he interfere with, or oppose, American freedom? Schoenfeld does not say.

Rick Shenkman

Shenkman, a journalist, author, and former Associate Professor of History at George Mason University, is the founder of the History News Network website. He is the author of "The Left's Blind Spot," published at that website.[164]

He writes: "Like many left-wingers [Zinn] regularly calls attention to a long list of crimes American officials have committed against various groups and countries while celebrating the virtues of ordinary folks. But what he doesn't do is admit the obvious: that the ordinary people he is so eager to lionize have often turned a blind eye to what their government's leaders through the years have done in their name."

This is one of the few substantial criticisms that Shenkman offers. But he is wrong. Zinn often "admits" what Shenkman says he doesn't admit. Indeed, without explicitly saying so, and thus without retracting his criticism, Shenkman (inconsistently) concedes that Zinn not only does, after all, admit that ordinary people have often turned a blind eye to what their government's leaders have done in their name, but also offers an explanation for it:

> Not that The People are infallible. But in Zinn's accounts he hastens always to indicate that their mistakes are owing to their manipulation by elites. In the notorious case of Vietnam, for example, he notes that LBJ "used a murky set of events in the Gulf of Tonkin, off the coast of North Vietnam, to launch full-scale war." That ordinary people allowed themselves to be bamboozled by the president doesn't occur to Zinn. I do not mean to suggest that ordinary people should have been able to pierce through LBJ's lies—and they were lies, as we now know—about the events that transpired in the Tonkin Gulf. But their attitude was passive. Whatever the president said they believed. This was not LBJ's fault. This was their fault.

Note that Shenkman is claiming *both* that Zinn acknowledges that ordinary people sometimes fail to reject (or even actively support) the nefarious policies (such as the Vietnam war) of their leaders, explaining it by the claim that the people have been manipulated by elites, *and* that he refuses to acknowledge the failure of ordinary people to oppose such policies. That is a contradiction. One cannot present a theory explicitly as an explanation for a phenomenon when one refuses to acknowledge in the first place that the phenomenon to be explained even exists.

But is Zinn wrong? Do not wealthy and powerful elites control the mass media, and the political system? Are there not enormous temptations to try to do the best one can within the prevailing order, and enormous risks attached to the path of opposing and trying to change it? To be sure, Zinn does not excoriate ordinary people for failing to overcome these obstacles so as to achieve independence from the worldview of those who run the society. But it is implicit in his praise for the courage and morality of those who do achieve this that he thinks the others are, however understandably, doing the wrong thing.

Shenkman also charges that "Zinn's approach is self-contra-dictory. Many of the people who serve in top government posts have themselves emerged from the masses. When in their evolution should we therefore begin to say that they have made the transition from a blessed state of innocence to the ranks of the damned?"

There is no self-contradiction here, as Shenkman, with his talk of "evolution" and "transition" implicitly and unwittingly admits. Even if one waives any objection to Shenkman's cartoonish caricaturing of Zinn's views (e.g. "blessed state of innocence" and "ranks of the damned"), there is no contradiction in saying both that group A has a characteristic that group B lacks and that some of the members of group A were originally in group B.

One way this can happen is through "evolution" and "transition"—butterflies (group A) can fly; caterpillars (group B) can't, even though butterflies were once caterpillars. Frogs can hop; tadpoles can't, even though frogs were once tadpoles. Adult humans can talk, even though young human infants cannot.

Another way this can happen is through selection—one moves from one group to another precisely because one has character-istics or talents not generally found in the group from which one has emerged. The specific talents of brain surgeons, professional magicians, and Olympic gymnasts are extraordinarily rare within the general human population from which such individuals originally came. The same can be said about the height of NBA basketball centers and the weight of Japanese sumo wrestlers.

Yet another way it can happen is that movement from one class to another entitles one to privileges formally reserved for members of this new class. Those with drivers' licenses may legally drive; those without them may not, even though those with drivers' licenses have all emerged from the class of those lacking such licenses. Similarly, U.S. presidents have the right to command the U.S. armed forces; non-presidents lack this right, even though all presidents have come from the class of non-presidents. And so on endlessly.

Shenkman's claim that there is something contradictory and thus illogical about the conjunction of the two claims that, first, elites, but not ordinary people, tend to commit moral atrocities, and, second, that some members of the elite class originally came from the class of ordinary people, is sheer nonsense. Perhaps, just as it is only the extremely tall members of the class of ordinary people who have a chance to move from that class to that of NBA centers, so it is only those who are especially ruthless and immoral who have a chance of moving successfully into the ranks of the politically powerful (recall Machiavelli's conclusion that only those who know how to be "other than good" can succeed in the political realm). And it is indisputably true that one must have power before one can abuse it. So the difference between political elites and ordinary people in terms of their participation in nefarious political deeds can be partially explained on analogy with the difference between the class of those with and without access to cars in terms of their participation in aggressive or reckless driving behavior.

The Weekly Standard

An unsigned editorial in this publication, "Mitch vs. Zinn," asserts: "Daniels's supposed thoughtcrime is pointing out that Howard Zinn's *A People's History of the United States*, a popular left-wing text, is a fraudulent work of scholarship. When he found out an Indiana University summer institute for schoolteachers was awarding professional development credits for reading the book, Daniels called it 'a truly execrable, anti-factual piece of disinformation that misstates American history on every page.'"[165]

Comments: (1) The editorial misuses Orwell's concept of "thoughtcrime." One finds this ploy repeated endlessly by

Daniels's defenders. They claim that Daniels is being criticized for daring to criticize Zinn, when in fact the criticism is directed against his attempt to remove Zinn from classrooms and deny credit for classes that include Zinn, quite a different matter.

(2) Once again, those who champion the claim that Zinn is "anti-factual" cannot be bothered to get the facts right, and commit factual errors. The "truly execrable" quote was in Daniels's original email, issued before he was informed (in a subsequent email) that Zinn was being used in an Indiana University course. It is not true that he issued this statement "when he found out" about this. Sure, this is a trivial mistake, but the author makes it in a one-page discussion. Can any of Daniels's defenders discuss this issue for the mighty length of one page without committing demonstrable factual errors?

The editorial continues: "Daniels's opinion is spot-on, but don't take his word for it. The president of the National Association of Scholars, Peter Wood, runs down the recent criticism of Zinn's book...," and then the editorial quotes Wood quoting the same critics whom Daniels had quoted. Once again, the author of this editorial shows no evidence of having read Zinn's book, can't be bothered with making an original obser-vation about it, or finding and naming any specific errors in it, or, in this case, even finding critics of it who have not already been quoted by Daniels.

The editorial continues: "It's beyond dispute that Zinn's book isn't up to the kind of academic standards that justify it being taught as history, and the fact that Daniels thought public school teachers should receive no credit for reading it is hardly a scandal."

Comments: (1) It is not beyond dispute, and the editorial offers no evidence that it is. Quoting three critics who dislike the book is hardly sufficient. There are other historians of equal or greater eminence who disagree. The editorial ignores this fact.

(2) Once again, the scandal resides not in what Daniels

"thought," but in what he did—ordering that the book be banned, disqualified, gotten rid of. If Daniels had sent an email to his subordinates merely saying that he had a low opinion of Zinn's book and thought it should not be used as a textbook, there would have been no scandal.

The editorial continues: "The only possible reason one of the nation's biggest media outlets [presumably the reference here is to the Associated Press] is calling Daniels a 'censor' is that the left still feels it will lose credibility if the truth about Zinn becomes widely known."

No, the reason for this is that the facts fit the definition. If Daniels had undergone a radical political conversion prior to writing those emails, and had instead said that other history texts were crap, and should be disallowed for credit, and that Zinn's book should have been used instead, the outcry from me, and from other opponents of censorship, would have been the same.

The editorial concludes by mentioning the open letter to Daniels that 92 members of the Purdue faculty signed in which they criticize the Daniels emails. Though the tone of this letter is restrained and civil, as Daniels himself points out in his reply to it, the editorial accuses the letter of "hyperventilating" about the issue. The editorial's main response, however, is to quote *First Things* (no other information is given for this citation) as follows: "There are roughly 1,800 faculty at Purdue University, and just 90 of them signed this letter. There are 34 active full-time faculty in the History department, and just 15 of them signed it. There are 17 specialists in one branch or another of American history in that department, and just seven of them signed it."

Comments: (1) If the implication is supposed to be that the critics of Daniels on this issue represent only a small minority (about 5%) of the faculty, and that the rest, or at least most of them, do not object to his actions, such an inference is unreasonable for several reasons. First, with just a few exceptions, the letter circulated only among liberal arts faculty, so most professors were never given the opportunity to sign it. Second, because those behind this initiative wanted to get it out quickly, while the news of Daniels's emails was still fresh, many liberal arts faculty who were away for the summer, or for any other reason not immediately available, were given no opportunity to sign. Third, many professors, like many people in general, are cautious, timid, cowardly—not eager to confront with public criticism the most powerful person at the institution at which they are employed. Others simply wish to avoid entanglement in politics at all. So the fact that professors in this third category did not sign hardly proves that they are on Daniels's side. One way to think about this is to imagine that the situation were reversed. Suppose that, in response to the AP article and the ensuing controversy, supporters of Daniels had circulated a petition or open letter in support of his actions and had garnered just over 90 signatures. Would this prove that the rest of the faculty opposed his conduct?

(2) In the light of the fact that the open letter does not limit itself to raising concerns about academic freedom and censorship, but also explicitly defends Zinn's work as being worthy of study, it is odd that the editorial is so dismissive of the opinion of 90 professors, especially given that they include 15 historians, seven of whom are specialists in American history. If the three historians quoted in the editorial are supposed to be sufficient to show that it is "beyond dispute that Zinn's book isn't up to the kind of academic standards that justify it being taught as history," wouldn't the 15 Purdue historians, seven of whom specialize in American history, who disagree tend to cast doubt on that and, at the very least, show that the matter is not "beyond dispute"?

Peter Wood

Wood, an anthropologist, is President of the National Association of Scholars, a non-profit organization in the United States that combats what it regards as liberal and leftist bias in academia. He is the author of an article, "Why Mitch Daniels Was Right," published in *The Chronicle of Higher Education*.[166]

It begins as follows:

> The Associated Press broke a story on July 16 [2013] that Mitch Daniels, the president of Purdue University, wrote e-mails while the governor of Indiana attacking the use of Howard Zinn's book, *A People's History of the United States*, as "a truly execrable, anti-factual piece of disinformation that misstates American history on every page."
>
> My first response: good for Mr. Daniels. His comment, made on February 9, 2010—according to the date stamp on his e-mail—shows that he has a pretty clear grasp of both American history and Mr. Zinn's book.

To see the absurdity of Wood's comment, consider what we would be entitled to conclude from a freshman student's essay on Shakespeare that went something like this: "Shakespeare's plays are truly brilliant, with beautiful, poetic writing and keen insights into the human condition to be found on every page." Would it be reasonable to conclude that such a comment "*shows*" that the writer has "a pretty clear grasp of both English literature and Mr. Shakespeare's plays"? Of course not. It would not *show* that the student had ever even read a word of Shakespeare. To show that, to demonstrate an understanding of Shakespeare's texts, to justify the stated conclusion, one would have to go into details, gather evidence, construct an argument. Has Peter Wood, who was once a professor, never graded student papers or exams? Does he not understand that anyone can simply parrot statements gathered at second hand from others and offer broad stroke judgments, whether positive or negative, even without having attained anything close to "a pretty clear grasp" of the subject at hand? Does he fail to notice that Daniels, who claims that Zinn's book "misstates American history on every page," has yet to offer a single example of such a misstatement, in spite of the fact that, given the length of Zinn's book, there must be, if Daniels's claim is correct, nearly seven hundred such misstatements? Indeed, Daniels has not offered any original thoughts on Zinn, let alone something as substantial as a sustained engagement with Zinn's text, or a reasoned rebuttal to the arguments of any of Zinn's many admirers. Instead, all he gives us is short, sweeping denunciations, like the one just quoted, and, later, in response to criticism, quotations from a few scholars who have said harsh things about Zinn. One need not have "a pretty good grasp of both American history and Mr. Zinn's book" to provide that. Arrogance, a mean streak, and access to a search engine are sufficient.

Well, if Daniels does not offer any examples of Zinn's errors, or any reasoned arguments or evidence of any kind (aside from a few quotations of some other people's summary negative judgments), perhaps Wood, as Daniels's defender, can do better on this score. Here is what he says to support the claim that Daniels's evaluation of Zinn is fair and accurate: "Let's not take Daniels's word that [Zinn's book] is 'truly execrable' and amounts to 'disinformation.' We can instead consult, say" — and then, so help me, he proceeds to name and quote the same people that Daniels named and quoted (Sean Wilentz, Michael Kazin, Sam Wineburg, Oscar Handlin, and Michael Kammen, adding on his own just one name not on Daniels's list — David Greenberg).

Immediately after concluding his presentation of the quotations from six Zinn critics, Wood asserts: "That's more than enough to show that Governor Daniels's view is well supported by mainstream historians. It was not an eccentric judgment, let alone an ignorant one. The AP was able to find a Marxist English professor — Cary Nelson — to object to Daniels's characterization of *A People's History*, but the weight of scholarly opinion is on Daniels's side."

Comments: (1) Wood's sample is both small, at just six, and unrepresentative, since the six were selected precisely on the basis of the fact that they are harsh critics of Zinn. Such a sample is obviously insufficient to support the conclusion that "the weight of scholarly opinion is on Daniels's side," and Wood offers no other evidence in its support.

(2) Wood attempts to establish by innuendo ("The AP was able to find a Marxist English professor...") what he would not dare explicitly assert, namely, that there are not "mainstream historians" who admire Zinn as a historian. The fallout from the Daniels–Zinn controversy shows that there are many.

(3) Although the six scholars quoted do indeed criticize Zinn harshly, it is far from clear that any of them "support Governor Daniels's view." There is quite a distance between the claim of Sean Wilentz, that Zinn's book is "not particularly good history," and Daniels's wild and reckless claim that it "misstates American history on every page." Not even Oscar Handlin, by far the most severe of the critics Wood cites, is willing to go that far. And Sam Wineburg is as critical of traditional history textbooks as he is of Zinn's: "*A People's History* and traditional textbooks are mirror images that relegate students to similar roles as absorbers—not analysts—of information, except from different points on the political spectrum" (WIN 32).

(4) There is also quite a distance between the claim that Zinn's book presents "a very simplified view" (Wilentz), or that it "is stronger on polemical passion than historical insight" (Michael Kazin), and the conclusion that it should never be used in a classroom, or that its inclusion on the syllabus of a college course should result in the course "not be[ing] accepted for any credit by the state" (or, further, that such a decision should be made by a governor, with no discernible expertise in either history or education). And we know that at least three of the quoted critics (Wineburg, Kazin, and Kammen) agree with this point, as they have condemned Daniels's actions (as documented above). Since

Daniels and Wood like appeals to authority so much—and these authorities in particular—one wonders what they think of this. (They have been silent on this issue.)

(5) Many of these quoted criticisms are demonstrably false and incompetent (as discussed above).

Wood continues: "I side with Daniels. A governor worth his educational salt should be calling out faculty members who cannot or will not distinguish scholarship from propaganda."

But it is one thing to "call them out," to initiate a rational, public debate, so that a variety of arguments and points of view as to what should or should not be taught might be rationally considered. It is quite another for a governor to make this decision unilaterally and in secret, and to order that his view of what constitutes propaganda be implemented, all without discussion or debate.

Wood claims that "A governor has a responsibility to uphold academic standards as well as academic freedom. The movement to establish the Common Core State Standards in elementary and secondary education is premised on the idea that governors have a legitimate voice in saying what should be taught in schools. There is no bright-line distinction between saying what the substance of state standards should be and what should pass muster as a textbook."

I concur with John K. Wilson's rebuttal: "I'm dumbfounded at the fact that Wood sees 'no bright-line distinction' between a governor working with professional educators to create broad state standards, and a governor wanting to secretly order a statewide ban on the teaching of a book, even in post-graduate classes for teachers" (DOD).

"The central question," Wood writes, "is whether Mitch Daniels respects academic freedom. As often happens these days, that becomes a question of what 'academic freedom' means. If the term is set out…to mean something like the absolute right of a faculty member to teach whatever he wants regardless of

standards, the rights of students, the truthfulness of his statements, and the public interest in the integrity of higher
education, then sure, Daniels sacrificed academic freedom in
favor of other considerations." But of course, Wood goes on to
reject that construal of "academic freedom," regarding it, instead,
as "a principle that thrives only when it is sturdily woven
together with academic responsibility."

This sounds reasonable, but it ducks the central issue: who
decides? Should politicians make that call, as opposed to
scholars? Consider, for example, one of the values that Wood here
invokes, that of "the truthfulness of [a teacher's] statements."
Perhaps we can all agree that teachers should teach the truth,
rather than falsehoods. But the question of what is or is not true
is often controversial, and it is wise to regard even uncontroversial beliefs about what is true as having only a tentative status,
as being revisable in the light of new evidence or new consideration of old evidence. Accordingly, and for many other reasons as
well, it is advantageous to expose students to a variety of views
on controversial subjects (of which history certainly is one).
University professors must undergo a rigorous certification
process in order to receive a Ph.D. or comparable advanced
degree, and another one in order to receive tenure. While these
filtering processes are not perfect (some people of dubious
knowledge and ability do occasionally make it through), they are
adequate to insure that the great majority of professors have a
competent knowledge of the subjects they teach. Governors, by
contrast, attain their position by winning a popular election.
Moreover, one of the rationales for the (admittedly controversial)
tenure system is precisely to protect the integrity of free scholarly
research and teaching from the meddlesome intrusion of
powerful officials who might object to research findings or
teaching content for political reasons. Such protection is
especially necessary in highly ideological, value-laden, and
emotionally charged subjects, such as history. To say that Zinn's

book is propagandistic, and *therefore* it is right that a governor should be able to forbid its use for credit is (even if one grants the dubious premise) to ignore the broader question of what general system should be in place. If one's concern is to keep out false-hoods, bad theories, and bad textbooks, which system is more likely to do that—one in which credentialed experts, subject to evaluation by their peers (more senior scholars, who will decide whether they merit promotion and tenure) make the call (even granting that there will be some bad choices made), or one in which the final call is made by politicians? How would Peter Wood feel if a leftist governor declared a popular history text, written by a conservative and chosen by many conservative history professors, to be "propaganda," and then ordered that no class using it could be one in which students receive credit anywhere in the state? And yet, Wood concludes his article with the statement that Daniels "has a better grasp" of what academic freedom means than does "anyone who believes that real academic freedom is consistent with using *A People's History of the United States* as a text in anything other than a course on how propaganda works."

Consider what this means. Although hundreds, and perhaps thousands, of history professors and high school history teachers have made the decision that they think Zinn's text is worthy of inclusion in their curriculum, that his ideas and his presentation merit study, analysis, criticism, evaluation, they should not be allowed to act in accordance with this conclusion. Rather, the decision should be made by an elected official with no credentials in history, whose political philosophy differs radically from that of the author of the textbook in question, and whose preferred text is one written by another non-historian who shares the same political outlook as the elected official. *This, according to Wood, is what "academic freedom" means.*

Also, Wood, like Daniels, doesn't seem to grasp the fact that many professors use texts *critically* in their classes. I, for example, typically assign several texts in my classes, exposing the students to a variety of competing views, each of which the students are expected to evaluate critically. That point alone establishes the falsity of Wood's concluding claim, namely, that the only legitimate way in which Zinn's book could be used as a text would be in "a course on how propaganda works." As one commentator (in the online discussion to be found at the conclusion of Wood's article) wisely put it, "The relevant qualifying [criterion] should not be the quality of the book, but the quality of the instructor's *use* of the book" (emphasis added). Indeed, Carl Weinberg, the teacher whose course was named in the emails, spoke out via an article in *Inside Higher Ed*, explaining why *A People's History* was on his syllabus: "In designing that session, my aim was to help teachers appreciate the challenge of explaining how and why social movements develop. In addition to reading Zinn, the teachers were assigned a wide range of pieces based on social movement theories, some of which actually challenged aspects of Zinn's account as romantic and misleading.... So, by including Zinn, my aim was not to shove his views down teachers' throats—precisely the opposite.... After all, the purpose of education is to help people think for themselves. That is why censorship strikes at the heart of the educational mission."[167]

Sean Wilentz

Wilentz is the Sidney and Ruth Lapidus Professor of History at Princeton University. He is represented on Daniels's list of anti-Zinn quotations as follows: "'[Zinn's] view of history is topsy-turvy, turning old villains into heroes, and after a while the glow gets unreal.' Sean Wilentz, Princeton History professor." This quotation, taken from the *New York Times* obituary of Zinn (NYT), is truncated, leaving out Wilentz's more positive observation about Zinn: "What Zinn did was bring history writing out of the academy, and he undid much of the frankly biased and prejudiced views that came before it." And the more critical part that is quoted contains no reasoning to evaluate. We simply have the descriptive claim that Zinn's history "turns old villains into heroes," coupled with Wilentz's judgment that this creates an "unreal glow," whatever that means.

Slightly more substantive is Wilentz's contribution to a symposium on Zinn published in the *Los Angeles Times* shortly after Zinn's death (MIL):

> What he did was take all of the guys in white hats and put them in black hats, and vice versa.
>
> His view was that objectivity was neutrality, which I think is a formula for bad history. Objectivity is not neutrality; it is the deployment of evidence and building an argument based on historical logic. That's how we engage in rational discourse. To see history as a battleground of warring perspectives is to abandon the seat of reason.
>
> He saw history primarily as a means to motivate people to political action that he found admirable. That's what he said he did. It's fine as a form of agitation—agitprop—but it's not particularly good history.
>
> To a point, he helped correct mainstream popular conceptions of American history that were highly biased. But he ceased writing serious history. He had a very simplified view that everyone who was president was always a stinker and every left-winger was always great. That can't be true. A lot of people on the left spent their lives apologizing for one of the worst mass-murdering regimes of the 20th century, and Abraham Lincoln freed the slaves. You wouldn't know that from Howard Zinn.

Almost none of this qualifies as accurate, or even remotely intelligent, commentary on Zinn. Let's go through it, line by line.

"What he did was take all of the guys in white hats and put them in black hats, and vice versa." This is a caricature, a gross oversimplification of Zinn's work. Zinn puts Mark Twain in a white hat, and Adolf Hitler in a black one. Does Wilentz seriously think that, prior to Zinn, Twain was in a black hat, and Hitler a white one? There are plenty of other examples.

And there are many other persons whom Zinn places in neither a white nor a black hat, but rather a gray one. For example, Nat Turner is depicted as someone who fought for a just cause, the abolition of slavery, but who also murdered some innocent people, including children, in doing so (APH 174). Or again, consider Zinn's explanation of Thomas Jefferson's inability to "wean" himself from participating in the institution of slavery:

> Jefferson tried his best, as an enlightened, thoughtful individual might. But the structure of American society, the power of the cotton plantation, the slave trade, the politics of unity between northern and southern elites, and the long culture of race prejudice in the colonies, as well as his own weaknesses—that combination of practical need and ideological fixation—kept Jefferson a slaveowner throughout his life. (APH 89)

So, contrary to Wilentz's absurdly reductionistic description, Zinn's work acknowledges substantial moral ambiguity.

Finally, even if we confine our attention to those persons whose hats do take on a different color in Zinn's text, Wilentz's description of this as simply "what [Zinn] did" confuses end result with process. Zinn consistently applies certain explicitly defended principles of selection, which results in some figures who had worn white hats in traditional historical accounts ending up in black hats (and vice versa) in Zinn's. But that doesn't mean that Zinn simply "put them" in black hats. Unless Zinn's principles are indefensible, or he misapplies them, Columbus put *himself* in a black hat by murdering and enslaving Indians. Wilentz offers no argument that Zinn's principles are wrong, or that he misapplies them. Therefore, his assertion that Zinn "puts" Columbus in a black hat (as if this were Zinn's doing, rather than Columbus's) is gratuitous and question-begging.

"His view was that objectivity was neutrality, which I think is a formula for bad history. Objectivity is not neutrality; it is the deployment of evidence and building an argument based on historical logic. That's how we engage in rational discourse. To see history as a battleground of warring perspectives is to abandon the seat of reason." As discussed in the previous chapter, it is true that Zinn often is talking about "neutrality" when he writes of "objectivity." But nothing of substance turns on this. It is simply a matter of terminology. Zinn makes it abundantly clear what he is attacking when he attacks "objectivity," and it is certainly not "the deployment of evidence and building an argument based on historical logic." To the contrary, his own practice is thoroughly "objective" in that sense. And Zinn does not, in this or any other sense, "abandon the seat of reason." Nor is his practice of including previously excluded perspectives done in order to reduce history to "a battleground of warring perspectives," any more than is an insistence on hearing from both the prosecution and the defense in a criminal trial. Once the previously excluded perspectives are heard from, they must still be rationally evaluated in the light of relevant evidence. Zinn, as much as anyone, insists on that.

"He saw history primarily as a means to motivate people to political action that he found admirable. That's what he said he did. It's fine as a form of agitation—agitprop—but it's not particularly good history." Wilentz fails to point out that, as discussed in the previous chapter, these political considerations only come into play in connection with the selection of topics and questions—not in connection with the determination of answers, or with the handling of evidence. And why is it not good history? This is asserted, but neither explained nor defended.

"To a point, he helped correct mainstream popular conceptions of American history that were highly biased. But he ceased writing serious history. He had a very simplified view that everyone who was president was always a stinker and every left-winger was always great. That can't be true. A lot of people on the left spent their lives apologizing for one of the worst mass-murdering regimes of the 20th century, and Abraham Lincoln freed the slaves. You wouldn't know that from Howard Zinn."

Let's start with "every left-winger was always great." What is a "left-winger"? As we have seen, many of Zinn's critics like to make the point that "even leftists, like Arthur Schlesinger" criticize Zinn. So, if Schlesinger (and Oscar Handlin, and Michael Kazin, and the other "leftist" historians) are "left-wingers," Zinn makes it abundantly clear that he does not regard them as "always great." What about "liberal" U.S. presidents, such as Franklin Roosevelt, John Kennedy, Jimmy Carter, Bill Clinton, and Barack Obama? Are they, as many people maintain, "left-wingers"? No one can accuse Zinn of saying that they are "always great." Are Joseph Stalin, Fidel Castro, and Mao Zedong "left-wingers"? As we have seen, Zinn criticizes Stalin for "killing peasants for industrial progress in the Soviet Union," faults Castro for "imprisoning critics of the regime," and cites Mao's "bloody record of suppression." The only "left-wingers" who are treated wholly positively in APH are those activists who lacked political power, but who made their mark in political struggle for justice. Not holding office, they had no opportunity to do anyone significant political harm; and their private misbehavior (perhaps in their marriages, or in their treatment of their children, friends, or colleagues) would not rise to a level of significance sufficient to warrant inclusion in a work on the full sweep of American history—leaving their positive contributions as the only ones deserving of mention. So, to sum up: quite a few people who are widely regarded as "left-wingers" come in for severe criticism in Zinn's work. Those who are not criticized are those whose only actions meriting inclusion in a history text have been positive—

which is quite a different thing from saying that they did nothing negative that would have been worth noting in, say, a biography of them. Thus, nothing remains of the charge that Zinn's historical writings show that he had a "simplified view" according to which "every left-winger was always great."

What about the charge that, according to Zinn, "everyone who was president was always a stinker"—a "very simplified view" that "can't be true"? In the first place, this is a "very simplified view" of Zinn, and far more simplistic than is Zinn's view of *anything*. Zinn never says that "everyone who was president was a stinker," and he generally avoids statements, about anything, that are as vague and imprecise as that. Rather than calling any president a "stinker," Zinn points out, with specificity and documentation, cases in which presidents tell lies, commit crimes, kill innocent people, own slaves, overthrow democratically elected leaders, and so forth.

Second, even if a case could be made that Zinn regarded every president as "a stinker," note that Wilentz's charge is stronger than that, as he attributes to Zinn the view that "everyone who was president was *always* a stinker" (emphasis added)—a demonstrable falsehood. To say that every president did bad things is not to say that every president did *nothing but* bad things, and never did anything good.

Third, while Zinn makes neither the ridiculous statement that "everyone who was president was *always* a stinker" nor the milder, but unacceptably imprecise, claim that "everyone who was president was [on balance] a stinker," it would be a fair conclusion to draw from the things that he actually does say that he thinks that nearly all presidents have committed grossly immoral acts, showing, at best, a callous disregard for the rights and the lives of people who, often through no fault of their own, have stood in the way of their pursuit of power and profit. And while one might agree with Wilentz that "it can't be true" that a random collection of 44 individuals would include so many who were capable of acts of such depravity, the U.S. presidents are not a random collection, but rather a group of individuals who share several important characteristics in common—most notably, (1) having successfully survived a particularly arduous selection process, and (2) then having had access to tremendous economic, military, and political power. Political theorists from Plato to Machiavelli to Acton to contemporary political scientists have well understood why those who successfully seek such power tend to be those who are most prone to abuse it if they attain it, and that, in any case, power tends to corrupt. So the *a priori* dismissal of Zinn's nearly uniformly negative take on the morality of U.S. presidents as something that "can't be true" does not succeed. To make the case that he is wrong on this point, there is no shortcut. One must go through what he says about the various presidents and show that he is in error, or guilty of material omissions, or of basing his judgments on illegitimate or inappropriate criteria or standards, or something else similarly specific.

This underscores the astonishing intellectual laziness of Wilentz's entire critique. Zinn makes the point that all historical writing is necessarily selective; offers a critique of the selection principles on which traditional, mainstream accounts of U.S. history are implicitly based; articulates and defends an alternative set of selection principles; and employs them—with the result that many bad actions by U.S. presidents that are ignored in more mainstream texts are highlighted in Zinn's. A serious critique of Zinn would raise objections to his selection principles; or show that he misapplies them or applies them inconsistently; or show that he has his facts wrong, or that he makes some other kind of specific mistake. Wilentz, in radical contrast, ignores all of Zinn's theorizing, ignores his principles, and ignores his specific analyses, and instead serves up a number of false (or meaningless) generalizations—that Zinn's work gives off an "unreal glow," that "what he did was take all of the guys in white hats and put them in black hats, and vice versa," that "he had a very simplified view that everyone who was president was always a stinker and every left-winger was always great." We wouldn't accept a "critique" like this in a term paper for a freshman class.

Perhaps Zinn's harshest sustained statement about the moral malfeasance of a series of U.S. presidents is the following passage on presidential lying about war:

> Let's start with Harry Truman. He deceived the nation and the world when he described Hiroshima — which he had just devastated by atomic bomb — as "an important Japanese Army base." More than 100,000 civilians — men, women, and children — died in this city of 350,000.
>
> Truman also lied to the nation about our war in Korea, saying we were fighting for democracy (hardly, since South Korea was a military dictatorship). More than 50,000 Americans died there. And perhaps two million Koreans.
>
> Dwight D. Eisenhower lied about our spy flights over the Soviet Union, even after one flier on such a mission was shot down. He deceived the nation and the world about the U.S. involvement in the coup that overthrew a democratic government in Guatemala. That coup brought on a succession of military juntas that took tens of thousands of lives. Eisenhower deceived the nation about the U.S. role in subverting a government in Iran because it was offending multinational oil corporations. The United States put the Shah of Iran back on the throne, and his secret police tortured and executed thousands of his opponents.
>
> John F. Kennedy lied to the nation about U.S. involvement in the 1961 failed invasion of Cuba, telling a press conference: "I can assure you that the United States has no intention of using force to overthrow the Castro regime."
>
> Kennedy, Johnson, and Nixon all lied to the nation about

what was happening in Vietnam. Kennedy said the United States was not involved in the overthrow of Ngo Dinh Diem. And Kennedy repeatedly claimed that American fliers were not involved in the bombing of Vietnam, even though he sent two helicopter companies there as early as 1962, with the U.S. military dropping napalm shortly thereafter.

Johnson and Nixon both lied when they claimed only military targets were bombed (reporters knew the greatest number of deaths was among civilians). And Nixon deceived the nation about the secret bombing of Cambodia.

Reagan lied to the nation about his covert and illegal support of the contras in Nicaragua. He lied about the importance of Grenada in order to justify the 1983 invasion of that little island.

George Bush lied about the reasons for invading Panama in 1989, saying it was to stop the drug trade. In fact, the United States has allowed the drug trade to flourish. Bush also deceived the nation about his real interest in the Persian Gulf. He pretended to be anguished about the fate of Kuwait while he was actually more concerned about enhancing American power in Saudi Arabia and controlling the region's oil deposits.[168]

I trust that the reader will agree that this cannot be refuted simply by saying that it has an "unreal glow," or that it "can't be true." And the same point applies to Zinn's argument that every president of the United States, for a period of 100 years, violated his oath of office by failing to enforce the Fourteenth (equal protection of the law) and Fifteenth (voting rights—not to "be denied or abridged by the United States or by any State on account of race, color, or previous condition of servitude") Amendments to the U.S. Constitution: "The blacks were not allowed to vote in the South. Blacks did not get an equal protection of the laws. Every president of the United States for a hundred years, every president, Democrat or Republican, liberal or conservative, every president violated his oath of office. The oath of office says you will see to it that the laws are faithfully executed. Every president did not enforce the Fourteenth and Fifteenth Amendments, collaborated with Southern racism and segregation and lynching...."[169] Perhaps there is something to that "stinkers" theory, after all.

Moving on, what about Wilentz's point that "A lot of people on the left spent their lives apologizing for one of the worst mass-murdering regimes of the 20th century"? I take it that Wilentz finds fault with Zinn for failing to point this out, since it would refute his (alleged) view that "every left-winger was always great." Two points should suffice by way of reply: (1) Wilentz's (typically) exaggerated claim about "a lot of people on the left" is false; and (2) the non-exaggerated, and true, version of that claim is fully, and repeatedly, acknowledged by Zinn (see, for example, GM 123–7; DOI 275–6; and YCB 177–8).

While some American communists, especially during the 1920s, 30s, and 40s, were, indeed, apologists for the Soviet Union, I know of absolutely none of them who "spent their lives" on such apologetics. Rather, they mostly concentrated on domestic issues, and were usually a force for good in doing so. Bhaskar Sunkara makes this point forcefully in connection with Pete Seeger, the musician criticized so harshly by Moynihan (see above):

It's not that Seeger did a lot of good despite his longtime ties to the Communist Party; he did a lot of good because he was a communist.

This point is not to apologize for the moral and social catastrophe that was state socialism in the 20th century, but rather to draw a distinction between the role of communists when in power and when in opposition. A young worker in the Bronx passing out copies of The Daily Worker in 1938 shouldn't be conflated with the nomenklatura that oversaw labor camps an ocean away.

As counterintuitive as it may sound, time after time American communists like Seeger were on the right side of history—and through their leadership, they encouraged others to join them there.

Communists ran brutal police states in the Eastern bloc, but in Asia and Africa they found themselves at the helm of anti-colonial struggles, and in the United States radicals represented the earliest and more fervent supporters of civil rights and other fights for social emancipation. In the 1930s, Communist Party members led a militant anti-racist movement among Alabama sharecroppers that called for voting rights, equal wages for women and land for landless farmers. Prominent and unabashedly Stalinist figures such as Mike Gold, Richard Wright and Granville Hicks pushed Franklin D. Roosevelt's New Deal to be more inclusive and led the mass unionization drives of the era. These individuals, bound together by membership in an organization most ordinary Americans came to fear and despise, played an outsize and largely positive role in American politics and culture. Seeger was one of the last surviving links to this great legacy....

Stateside communists were the underdogs, fighting the establishment for justice—the victims of censorship and police repression, not its perpetrators....

Remarking on Seeger, Bruce Springsteen once said that "he'd be a living archive of America's music and conscience, a testament to the power of song and culture to nudge history along, to push American events towards more humane and justified ends."

In stark contrast to the role played by state socialists abroad, that's a good way to describe the legacy of the Communist Party at home....[170]

And finally, we arrive at the conclusion of Wilentz's remarks. Eager to prove how wrong Zinn is to (allegedly) hold the "very simplified view that everyone who was president was always a stinker," Wilentz triumphantly concludes his denunciation of Zinn with these words, which are illustrative of the general quality of his critique: "Abraham Lincoln freed the slaves. You wouldn't know that from Howard Zinn." I don't know about you, but I think that statement is refuted by the following passage from APH: "[I]t was Abraham Lincoln who freed the slaves" (171).[171] Perhaps Wilentz, the Sidney and Ruth Lapidus Professor of History at Princeton University, cannot derive the conclusion that "Abraham Lincoln freed the slaves" from Zinn's statement that "[I]t was Abraham Lincoln who freed the slaves." But the rest of us can.

Endnotes

Chapter 1: The Daniels–Zinn Controversy

1. Chris Sigurdson, "Trustees Elect Mitchell E. Daniels Jr. as Purdue's 12th President" (June 21, 2012); http://www.purdue.edu/newsroom/general/2012/120621KrachPresident.html

2. Kevin Kiley, "Purdue's Outsider," *Inside Higher Ed* (April 2, 2013); https://www.insidehighered.com/news/2013/04/02/purdues-mitch-daniels-challenging-higher-education-leadership; "Curriculum Vitae for Mitchell E. Daniels Jr.," http://www.purdue.edu/president/about/curriculum.html

3. Christy Hunter, "Daniels Has No Comment on Conflict of Interest Issue," *The Exponent Online* (June 25, 2012); http://www.purdueexponent.org/campus/article_94017752-3cb7-567d-aaff-dc9ca89520ca.html. See also Elle Moxley, "Daniels Will Have to Win Over Purdue's Faculty, Who Wanted an Academic" (June 27, 2012); http://indianapublicmedia.org/stateimpact/2012/06/27/daniels-will-have-towin-over-purdues-faculty-who-wanted-an-academic/

Some 7,000 members of the Purdue community responded to a survey ranking what credentials they thought were most important for the next president to have. Overwhelmingly, they wanted someone with qualifications equivalent to a full-time tenured professor.

Morris Levy, past president of the faculty senate, chaired the special advisory committee that conducted the survey. He says the leader of a research university needs the kind of experience you only get in a classroom or laboratory.

"People should not take this as some kind of elitist model that, unless you have a Ph.D., you're not qualified to work at Purdue," he says. "But when you have a creative force of thousands of people, you have to know how they work, why they work and how to empower them to work"....

Levy says it's disheartening that after the faculty senate conducted such an extensive survey—the first of its kind—the search committee decided to go another direction. He points out that the majority of the trustees were appointed by Daniels. None of them has worked in academia, either.

4. The emails themselves are available at EMA.

5. The quotation is from a January 27, 2010 email, obtained by the Associated Press through a public records request, that Daniels sent to Tony Bennett, Todd Huston, and David Shane, each of whom is briefly identified in the next paragraph. See Tom LoBianco, "Mitch Daniels Wanted to Replace Howard Zinn with Bill Bennett in History Curriculum," *Indianapolis Star* (August 8, 2013).

6. Daniels, speaking at a breakfast hosted by the *Christian Science Monitor*, asserted that his perspective on Zinn's work is in line with the "overwhelming judgment of historians" (as quoted in WAR).

7. Daniels, in communication with *Inside Higher Ed* (as quoted in JAS).

8. This quotation is from the first version of SPD, as originally posted on the Purdue University website on July 17, 2013. The current version is drastically shorter, and excludes all of the quotations from historians except for the one from Schlesinger. The reasons for this change will be discussed below. The longer version, quoted here, can be found in RIL.

9. Similarly, "academic freedom [does not] confer an entitlement to have one's work used in the K-12 public system" (JAS).

10. "Sophistry that claims that uniquely enlightened and altruistic governmental officials are the true agents of the public

interest must be exposed as defective in practice—look where it's gotten us—and immoral in theory, in its implicit denigration of Americans' capacity to look out for themselves and manage the risks that come with liberty" (KTR 196–7).

11. Indeed, he has asserted that "Protecting the educational standards of middle schoolers [is] to me an important duty of any governor" (RPF).

12. "A Statement from the Board of Trustees (July 17, 2013); http://www.purdue.edu/president/messages/130717-statement.html

13. Technically, this doesn't follow, since Daniels was referring to Purdue University, rather than Indiana University, when he spoke of "our campus." But none of his statements can be construed as implying that there is a difference between one university and another such as to justify handling these issues differently in one case than in another. Rather, the distinction he has consistently drawn in all of his after-the-fact explanations of his original emails has been between higher education and K-12 education.

14. http://www.merriam-webster.com/dictionary/censor

15. http://dictionary.reference.com/browse/censor?s=t

16. Bill Bigelow, "Indiana's Anti-Howard Zinn Witch-hunt" (July 18, 2013); https://zinnedproject.org/2013/07/indianas-anti-howard-zinn-witch-hunt/

17. "A People's History of Mitch Daniels" (August 8, 2013).

18. Margaret Fosmoe, "Zinn Book a Hot Read at Libraries," *South Bend Tribune* (August 13, 2013); http://www.south-bendtribune.com/news/local/article_4d61c53a-03aa-11e3-99e4-001a4bcf6878.html

19. http://www.britannica.com/topic/academic-freedom

20. See, for example, Donald F. Uerling, "Academic Freedom in K-12 Education," *Nebraska Law Review*, Vol. 79, No. 4 (2000), 956–75.

21. (July 19, 2013), emphasis added; http://blog.historian
s.org/2013/07/aha-statement-on-academic-freedom-and-
the-indiana-governor/

22. At a July 17, 2013 press conference (http://www.in
dystar.com/article/20130727/NEWS04/307270027/Flap-over-
academic-freedom-shows-Mitch-Daniels-faces-learning-
curve-Purdue-president), Daniels said that the academic
freedom that tenured professors enjoy does not
"immunize" them "from criticism for shoddy work...." But
no one has argued that tenure does or should immunize
one from criticism. Nor has anyone suggested that such
criticism by Daniels constitutes a violation of academic
freedom. Mere criticism is not the problem; it doesn't
violate academic freedom. Using one's authority as
Governor to order that a book be "disqualified" and "gotten
rid of" is the problem—it does violate academic freedom.
Daniels and many of his supporters repeatedly conflate this
elementary distinction. True, some of the criticism that
Daniels has received has been for his criticism of Zinn, and
not only for his attempt to censor him. But this criticism of
Daniels is not based on any claim that his criticisms of Zinn
violate anyone's rights or violate the principle of academic
freedom. Rather, it is simply directed to the merits of
Daniels's criticisms of Zinn. After all, just as "academic
freedom" does not immunize Zinn's work from criticism, so
does it not immunize that criticism *itself* from criticism—
including criticism that it is uninformed, factually in error,
and illogical (in short, that it is "shoddy"). See, on this
point, HCD: "No one objects to the fact that Daniels criticized Zinn's work. Daniels' attack on Zinn is so purely
political ('anti-American'), so dishonest ('purposely
falsified'), and so stupid ('phrenology') that it raises serious
questions about Daniels' ability to do or even understand
academic work."

23. Elle Moxley, "It's Official: Mitch Daniels Will Lead Purdue As University's Next President" (June 21, 2012); http://indianapublicmedia.org/stateimpact/2012/06/21/its-official-mitch-daniels-will-lead-purdue-as-universitys-next-president/

24. "Analysis: Public Records Key in Tony Bennett Grade-change Scandal," *Indianapolis Star* (August 4, 2013); http://www.indystar.com/story/news/politics/2013/08/04/na lysis-ublic-records-key-in-ony-ennett-grade-change-scandal/2616997/

25. He called Zinn "a distinguished scholar," stated that his chapter on the Vietnam War should be "required reading for a new generation of students," and concluded the review with this judgment: "Open-minded readers will profit from Professor Zinn's account, and historians may well view it as a step toward a coherent new version of American history" ("Majority Report," *New York Times Book Review* [March 2, 1980] BR3–BR4).

26. Ron Briley taught history at Sandia Preparatory School in Albuquerque, New Mexico, for 37 years. He is the author of three books, and editor or co-editor of two others. His teaching has earned recognition from the Organization of American Historians, the Society for History Education, the American Historical Association, and the National Council for History Education. See his "Thank You, Howard Zinn," *History News Network* (February 10, 2010); http://historynewsnetwork.org/article/122820

27. William H. Chafe is the Alice Mary Baldwin Professor Emeritus of History at Duke University and a past president of the Organization of American Historians. See "What Teachers and Students Are Saying" (January 20, 2011); http://zinnedproject.org/2011/01/what-teachers-are-saying/ (This article also contains laudatory quotations about Zinn from about 50 other teachers who teach Zinn's *A*

People's History of the United States.)

28. Carl Cohen is Professor of Philosophy at the University of Michigan. Reviewing Zinn's book, *Disobedience and Democracy*, in *The Nation* (December 2, 1968; in KRE, 179–89), he calls the book "extraordinary" and "splendid," finding that it is "crisp and biting, reflective and insightful, sympathetic and humane," and that it "deserves to be very widely read and very thoughtfully discussed" (KRE 181). Further, he judges it to be "a creative book, rich in insight and suggestion," and "so effective in opening our eyes and our minds that we profit more from considering [its] mistakes than from the muddy and superficial truths often encountered elsewhere" (KRE 187). Cohen also praises Zinn's writing, saying that "reading the book is a pleasure," owing to Zinn's "plain and beautiful" prose, that is also noteworthy for its rare "directness and candor" (188). Cohen finds Zinn himself to be "a compassionate and gentle man," a "perceptive critic of the American scene," and "a merciless enemy of hypocrisy and cruelty" — someone who "is good for us" (KRE 189).

29. Robert Cohen is Professor of Social Studies and Steinhardt Affiliated Professor in the History Department at New York University. See his WAZ and SWH.

30. Blanche Wiesen Cook is Distinguished Professor of History at John Jay College in the City University of New York, and is the author of *Eleanor Roosevelt: Volume One 1884–1933*, a Los Angeles Times Book Prize winning biography of Eleanor Roosevelt, as well as a second volume on Roosevelt, and one on Eisenhower. In her back cover blurb for Zinn's autobiography (YCB), she calls the book "important, inspiring, wise: like Howard Zinn's entire life."

31. Merle Curti was the Frederick Jackson Turner Professor of History at the University of Wisconsin, winner of the Pulitzer Prize in History for his book, *The Growth of*

American Thought, and a former president of the American Historical Association. A prestigious award, given annually by the Organization of American Historians for the best book in social, intellectual, and/or cultural history, is named in his honor (the Merle Curti Award). Reviewing Zinn's *The Politics of History* in the *Pacific Historical Review*, Vol. 40, No. 2 (May 1971), Curti praises Zinn for adding "several dimensions to the thought and work of the 'New Historians,'" marks several of the book's essays as "especially interesting and valuable," calls three of these "unforgettable" (227), credits Zinn with having "given us pointed and provocative...ways of regarding such problems as freedom, responsibility, the uses of violence, and academic neutrality" (228), and concludes his review with these words: "I think he has made a strong case for his position and that he has something to teach all of us. I earnestly hope that *The Politics of History* will not be disregarded" (228).

32. Susan Curtis, Professor of History at Purdue University, and author of three books in American history, is one of the two principal authors of the "Open Letter" to Daniels, signed by 92 Purdue professors, 16 of whom are historians, protesting his Zinn emails and expressing disagreement with his criticisms of Zinn (OLM). In an article on the Daniels–Zinn controversy (Jake Schmidt, "President Daniels Faces Controversy," *Purdue Exponent* [July 19, 2013), http://www.purdueexponent.org/campus/article_da8 298bc-4f9f-5aa2-801f-157cbf18edff.html), she is quoted as saying, "I read one of Zinn's essays in the very first college history course I took.... My professor helped us to examine his assumptions and research methods so we could understand why he reached conclusions different from other historians. I loved his work, but also felt empowered as I learned how to make sense of scholarly writings."

33. Kenneth C. Davis is a popular historian, and author of the million-selling *Don't Know Much About History*, revised edition (New York: HarperCollins, 2003). In that book he describes Zinn's *A People's History of the United States* as "revisionist history at its best," and says that it "serves as a useful and necessary corrective" to "traditional views" and "standard American historians" (635).

34. Peter Dreier is the E.P. Clapp Distinguished Professor of Politics at Occidental College. He names Zinn as one of *The 100 Greatest Americans of the 20th Century* (New York: Nation Books, 2012).

35. Ellen DuBois, Distinguished Professor of History at UCLA, writes that she is "very cheered by the continuing interest that young people have year after year in [Zinn's] version of history" (as quoted in MIL).

36. Mark A. Graber, University System of Maryland Regents Professor, and author of several major books on the U.S. Constitution, reviewing Zinn's *Declarations of Independence* in *Political Science Quarterly*, Vol. 107, No. 1 (Spring 1992), says that Zinn's book presents "for the most part...a successful crossexamination of American ideology," and suggests that its inclusion in a class's reading list would "enliven any introduction to American government or history" (188).

37. James Green, Professor of History and Labor Studies at the University of Massachusetts at Boston, and author of *Taking History to Heart* (University of Massachusetts Press, 2000), praises Zinn's "credibility and authority as a social critic"; refers to "his outstanding history as a chronicler and interpreter of social protest, and as a critical thinker," his "legendary work as a teacher at Boston University," and "his impressive accounts of the struggles against segregation in the American South and for peace in Vietnam"; praises the "readability" of *A People's History of the United*

States, and says that in that book Zinn "confidently surveys more than 500 years of history, drawing deftly on three decades of critical scholarship" ("Howard Zinn's History," *The Chronicle of Higher Education* [May 23, 2003]; https://chronicle.com/article/Howard-Zinns-History/9938/).

38. Jack P. Greene has been Andrew W. Mellon Professor in the Humanities at Johns Hopkins University's history department, a Distinguished Professor at the University of California, Irvine, and a visiting professor at the College of William and Mary, the University of Oxford, the Hebrew University of Jerusalem, the Ecole des Hautes Etudes en Sciences Sociales, University of Richmond, Michigan State University, and the Freie Universitat of Berlin. He has held fellowships from the John Simon Guggenheim Foundation, the Institute for Advanced Study, the Woodrow Wilson International Center for Scholars, the Center for Advanced Study in the Behavioral Sciences, the National Humanities Center, and the Andrew W. Mellon Foundation, among others. He is the author of at least eleven books in American history. In his "Foreword" to Zinn's *Postwar America: 1945–1971* (Indianapolis: Bobbs-Merrill, 1973), he calls that book an "extraordinarily powerful and moving reading of the recent American past" (x).

39. David Kennedy, a specialist in American history, is the Donald J. McLachlan Professor of History Emeritus at Stanford University and the Director of the Bill Lane Center for the American West. A winner of both the Bancroft Prize and the Pulitzer Prize for History, he credits Zinn's writings for persuading him that "there is this possibility of an alternative history that has been frustrated or thwarted," adding that "[m]y view of the New Deal was significantly affected by his and others' work" (as quoted in MIL).

40. James Levin, a scholar in the Department of Special Programs at the City University of New York, reviewed *A*

People's History of the United States in *Library Journal,* Vol. 105, No. 1 (January 1, 1980): "Howard Zinn has written a brilliant and moving history of the American people.... This book is an excellent antidote to establishment history, especially high school textbooks.... While the book is precise enough to please specialists, it should satisfy any adult reader. It will also make an excellent college text for basic history courses" (101).

41. James W. Loewen, a sociologist and historian who taught for over 20 years at the University of Vermont, is the author of several books on history, including the million-selling LMT. In his *Teaching What **Really** Happened: How to Avoid the Tyranny of Textbooks & Get Students Excited About Doing History* (New York: Teachers College Press, 2010), he argues that every middle school and high school U.S. history classroom should contain a few works on U.S. history other than the officially assigned textbook. For the most part, his recommendations are general—there should be "a selection of high school history textbooks.... Some should be old" (41). And there should be "at least one college-level textbook" (82). There are only two books that he recommends specifically by name. One of them is Zinn's *A People's History of the United States* (82).

42. Thaddeus Russell, an Occidental College historian, offers the judgment that "There was no better exemplar of [the] thoroughgoing, anti-statist left than Howard Zinn." Though Russell makes it clear that his own libertarian politics differ from Zinn's, he nonetheless lauds Zinn as a person of courage, principle, and commitment, and characterizes his *A People's History of the United States* as "a liberatory corrective to traditional American historiography" ("The Last Leftist," *Reason,* Vol. 44, No. 9 [February 2013, Vol. 44, Issue 9], 52–5).

43. Historian Robert C. Twombly, who formerly held the Walt

Whitman Chair in American Civilization at the University of Leiden (Netherlands), was one of the experts that Harper & Row asked to review Zinn's *A People's History of the United States* in manuscript, as part of that company's process of deciding whether or not to publish the book. Twombly pronounced the work "stunning, brilliant, original, and humane," called it "a much more accurate, realistic, and complete picture of life as actually lived in colonial America" than could be found in more traditional American history texts, praised the "rich...documentation" in which "[Zinn's] argument is solidly grounded," noted that he knows "of no other history of the United States...that gives such a full and careful picture of the way life was lived by people who are usually not the central figures in the story, that is, the American majority," and concluded by calling Zinn's book "a unique kind of American history" that "ought to be gotten into as many hands as possible" (as quoted in SWH 199–200).

44. Kelly Welch, a Villanova University criminologist, argues that Zinn's historical writings make an important contribution to the field of criminology. Her article, "Howard Zinn's Critical Criminology," *Contemporary Justice Review*, Vol. 12, No. 4 (December 2009), 485–503, concludes with these words: "Although Howard Zinn's primary academic disciplines are history and political science, it is apparent that the collection of his work, informed by extensive study and countless personal experiences, adds a unique and valuable perspective to the study of crime and justice in America. It may be instructive for those endeavoring to foster a significant proliferation of social justice" (502).

45. Henry West, Professor Emeritus of Philosophy at Macalester University, and author of numerous works in moral philosophy, called Zinn "the wisest commentator on public affairs that I have ever known or read" (as quoted in

DUB, 43–4).

46. Historian Donald Wright, of the University of New Brunswick, in "Howard Zinn, The People's Historian," *Labour/Le Travail*, Vol. 73 (Spring 2014), 265–77, praises Zinn's work. For example, he says of Zinn's essay, "A Speech for LBJ," that it "remains a brilliant and imaginative critique of American foreign policy and the war in Vietnam," and of "What War Looks Like," that it "is an equally brilliant critique of the rush to war against Iraq from the perspective of all those 'ordinary human beings who are not concerned with geopolitics and military strategy'" (273). The article concludes with these words: "[Zinn] was a rare and remarkable human being whose courage inspired a generation, making [a biographer's] problem everyone's problem: how does one write about Zinn without making the case for his sainthood?" (277).

47. Citations to Zinn's works can be found using the "Google Scholar" website's citation search engine. My "Howard Zinn" search (https://scholar.google.com/scholar?hl=en&as _sdt=0,15&q=%22Howard+Zinn%22), undertaken in August 2015, generated a list of Zinn's works together with a statement, for each one, as to how many times it had been cited. (One can also learn precisely which articles have cited any given Zinn work. For example, if one of Zinn's writings has been "cited by 208," clicking on the words "cited by 208" generates a list of those 208 publications.) My estimate of the number of citations to Zinn's works is conservative, both because I included only works solely authored by Zinn (and thus excluded citations to works that he co-wrote, edited or co-edited, or for which he merely wrote an "Introduction," and so forth), and because it is based on an extremely cautious extrapolation. I counted 6774 citations on the first 25 pages of lists that the search generated. Although the number of citations listed per page was

steadily declining the further I went into the search, there were 74 pages remaining when I stopped counting. I am confident that I would have found well over 226 citations on those remaining pages. My determination that relatively few of these citations were primarily critical is based on my energetic search, using this search engine and several others, for critical articles on Zinn that I might address in my chapter, to follow, in which I respond to criticisms of him.

48. http://in.gov/governorhistory/mitchdaniels/files/053009 _Rose-Hulman.pdf

49. "Does Zinn's Alternative History Teach Bad Lessons?," https://ed.stanford.edu/news/does-zinns-alternative-history-teach-bad-lessons

50. Even if Daniels's claim that he does not read *Reason* magazine is correct, it does not follow that he "never saw what [Moynihan] wrote." Published articles, or portions of them, tend to be re-published (often without attribution) on multiple websites. It is quite possible that Daniels, when he searched the Internet looking for anti-Zinn quotations that he could cite in support of his actions, came across Moynihan's words without knowing their original source.

Chapter 2: Bias and Objectivity in History

1. The basic facts of Zinn's life story are well documented. To date, his life has been chronicled in two biographies (DUB and JOY), an autobiography (YCB), and a feature-length documentary film (*Howard Zinn: You Can't Be Neutral on a Moving Train*, directed by Deb Ellis and Denis Mueller [First Run Features, 2004]). Many other essays by and about Zinn also discuss details of his life. See, for example, several of the pieces in AWS, and in Davis D. Joyce, ed., *Howard Zinn's Legacies* (Madison, WI: The Progressive, 2014). For Zinn's years at Spelman College, see LEF. Because most of the

biographical details that I will present are included in all (or at least most) of these published accounts of his life, I will provide specific documentation only for those few that are not.

2. http://www.nndb.com/honors/288/000043159/
   In addition to the quoted definition of the award, this site also lists Zinn as one of its recipients.

3. http://2012.republican-candidates.org/Daniels/Military.php

4. (Ithaca, New York: Cornell University Press, 2010).

5. Second edition (Chicago: Haymarket Books, 2013).

6. Second edition (Chicago: Haymarket Books, 2014).

7. Second edition (Chicago: Haymarket Books, 2014).

8. (New York: Harper Perennial, 2003).

9. Second edition (Chicago: Haymarket Books, 2014).

10. Second edition (Chicago: Haymarket Books, 2014).

11. YCB, paperback edition (Boston: Beacon Press, 2002).

12. Second edition (Chicago: Haymarket Books, 2014).

13. The one exception is KRE, which is still available as an electronic text.

14. Second edition (New York: Seven Stories Press, 2009).

15. Second edition (New York: Seven Stories Press, 2011).

16. Second edition (New York: Seven Stories Press, 2011).

17. (New York: Seven Stories Press, 2011).

18. (Boulder, CO: Paradigm Publishers, 2009).

19. Zinn, *Emma*, second edition (Chicago: Haymarket Books, 2014). This play is also included in THP.

20. This play is included in THP.

21. http://www.boston.com/ae/theater_arts/articles/2010/06/09/family_connections_divisions_in_zinns_venus/?camp=pm

22. Third edition (Chicago: Haymarket Books, 2014). It is also included in THP.

23. The linguist Noam Chomsky offers an analysis of Zinn's skills as a public speaker: "What has always been startling

to me...is Howard's astonishing ability to speak in exactly the right terms to any audience on any occasion, whether it is a rally at a demonstration, a seminar (maybe quite hostile, at least initially) at an academic policy-oriented graduate institution, an inner-city meeting, whatever. He has a magical ability to strike just the right tone, to get people thinking about matters that are important, to escape from stereotypes and question internalized assumptions, and to grasp the need for engagement, not just talk. With a sense of hopefulness, no matter how grim the objective circumstances. I've never seen anything like it" (from a July 29, 2000 email message to Joyce, as quoted in JOY 28).

24. Nearly everyone who writes about Zinn's personality emphasizes his personal warmth, his sunny disposition, his ready wit, his egalitarianism in treating everyone with respect, his casual manner, and his ability to put people at ease. "He is always ready with a smile," Joyce writes. "Even those who differ strongly with his ideology find it hard to dislike him. 'Everybody likes him,' proclaimed one of the secretaries in [his] department at Boston University..." (JOY 27). As one who observed him often, and in a variety of settings, during my undergraduate years at Boston University, I can personally testify to the accuracy of this characterization.

25. Joyce quotes a student of Zinn's at Boston University, who speaks of his "great respect and true love for people," and remarks that he was "never condescending," and "treats men and women exactly the same, all with the utmost respect" (JOY 90). Another student interviewed Zinn, and asked, "What do you ultimately want your students and the American people to know?" His reply: "I want them to know that they are capable of thinking things through for themselves, and capable of coming to their own judgments about right and wrong. Also, that the experts, the author-

ities, the people in power, the newscasters, and the teachers, should not be looked upon as authorities on important moral issues. People have to think for themselves and do for themselves" (JOY 91). And in another statement of his teaching philosophy, Zinn states: "[T]he most important single thing I wanted to develop in my students was a determination to look into things on their own, to not accept authority, including my own authority, to challenge me. I challenged them constantly to challenge me in class, to go and look up the things that I was talking about and bring in countervailing views.... They had to check up on things and investigate things for themselves" ("You Can't Be Neutral on a Moving Train," in FOH 68–9. Note: The source of this quotation is not Zinn's autobiography, but an interview-article with the same title).

26. I must admit, of course, that my claims about the reaction of other students to Zinn's teaching are based on anecdotal and impressionistic data, rather than rigorous science. But, for what it is worth, I must have discussed Zinn's teaching with a few dozen students of Zinn's over the course of my four years at B.U. (students often compare notes on courses and teachers), and I can only recall one negative comment about one of Zinn's classes—and even that one comment was directed at the students, rather than at Zinn (the complaint was that they were too uncritical of him, and failed to challenge him when they should). Even conservative students readily conceded that he was funny, knowledgeable, articulate, interesting, and fair—though dead wrong in his political convictions!

27. This quotation appears on a back cover blurb for YCB.

28. http://zinnedproject.org/why/howard-zinn-our-favorite-teacher/roger-ochoa/ Several other testimonials to Zinn's teaching can be found at http://zinnedproject.org/why/howard-zinn-our-favorite-teacher/

29. http://zinnedproject.org/why/howard-zinn-our-favorite-teacher/marian-wright-edelman/

30. "Remembering Howard Zinn" (May 5, 2011); http://www.huffingtonpost.com/marian-wright-edelman/remembering-howard-zinn_b_456128.html

     See also her *Lanterns: A Memoir of Mentors* (Boston: Beacon, 1999); her "Spelman College: A Safe Haven for a Young Black Woman," *The Journal of Blacks in Higher Education*, No. 27 (April 1, 2000), 118; and her contribution to "Remembering Howard Zinn," *The Nation* (February 15, 2010); http://www.thenation.com/article/remembering-howard-zinn?page=0,0

31. *Spelman Spotlight* (October 17, 1963), 4; as quoted in LEF 162.

32. Dolby, as quoted by Dave Bangert (from an interview), in his "What Would Howard Zinn Do?," *Lafayette Journal & Courier* (July 20, 2013); http://www.jconline.com/article/20130720/COLUMNISTS30/307200011/Howard-Zinn-Purdue-professor-Mitch-Daniels-controversy

33. http://zinnedproject.org/why/howard-zinn-our-favorite-teacher/stuart-shulman/

34. Chomsky comments on the rarity of this combination: "There are people whose words have been highly influential, and others whose actions have been an inspiration to many. It is a rare achievement to have interwoven both of these strands in one's life, as Howard Zinn has done. His writings have changed the consciousness of a generation, and helped open new paths to understanding history and its crucial meaning for our lives. He has always been on call, everywhere, a marvel to observe. When action has been called for, one could always be confident that he would be in the front lines, an example and trustworthy guide" ("Foreword" to JOY 13).

35. Duberman gives a few details about some of the occasions

in which Zinn was jailed. One jailing happened on May 4, 1971. Zinn was participating in the "May Day" protests in Washington, D.C., at the Capitol, when he "made the mistake of asking a policeman why he was beating up a long-haired young man." As a result, "after being beaten himself," Zinn "ended up in a one-person cell packed with half a dozen others. They stood for six hours in a pool of water several inches deep" (175). The very next day, however, an undaunted Zinn continued his political activities, speaking to a crowd of twenty-five thousand at an antiwar rally at the Boston Common. He was arrested and jailed again in July 1980, when he took part in a Washington, D.C. protest rally against the Reagan administration's policy of backing and training terrorist death squads in El Salvador, Guatemala, and Honduras. Zinn "and others were locked up in cells wretchedly hot and crowded; they had to take turns sitting. The first food was provided only after nine hours—two baloney sandwiches, two stale doughnuts, and a plastic cup of very sweet, lukewarm tea. The 'bed' was a perforated steel plate with no mattress, blanket, or pillow; there were roaches everywhere and the noise so loud that sleep proved impossible" (243–44). Granting Zinn's point that such experiences are merely highly unpleasant, rather than deeply tragic, one nonetheless wonders whether Mitch Daniels has ever taken on such pains in an effort to make his country better.

Incidentally, Mitch Daniels also has an arrest record. But unlike Zinn, Daniels's arrest was not for actions undertaken in pursuit of justice for others. Rather, he was arrested for drug possession, after police seized "enough marijuana to fill two size 12 shoe boxes" from the Princeton University dorm room that he shared with two other undergraduate students in 1970. Daniels was initially charged with possession of marijuana, LSD, and prescription drugs without a prescription, and with "maintaining a common nuisance by maintaining a place for the sale of narcotics." He eventually pled guilty to a disorderly person charge based on his marijuana use, and paid a $350 dollar fine. The other charges were dropped (Ben Smith, "Daniels' Drug Arrest" [February 10, 2011]); http://www.politico.com/blog s/bensmith/0211/Daniels_drug_arrest.html

36. Zinn's testimony, in full, is available in a book on the trial: NG 104–9. The passage quoted above is from 105 and 107.

37. "Howard Zinn in Vermont," *Green Mountain Daily* (February 2010), http://www.greenmountaindaily.com/di ary/5828/howard-zinn-in-vermont

38. See Zinn's "Testifying at the Ellsberg Trial" in ZR 420–6.

39. See, for example, Bob Herbert, "A Radical Treasure," *New York Times* (January 30, 2010); http://www.nytimes. com/2010/01/30/opinion/30herbert.html?pagewanted=print

[Zinn] was a historian with a big, engaging smile that seemed ever-present....

He was an unbelievably decent man who felt obliged to challenge injustice and unfairness wherever he found it. What was so radical about believing that workers should get a fair shake on the job, that corporations have too much power over our lives and much too much influence with the government, that wars are so murderously destructive that alternatives to warfare should be found, that blacks and other racial and ethnic minorities should have the same rights as whites, that the interests of powerful political leaders and corporate elites are not the same as those of ordinary people who are struggling from week to week to make ends meet?

Mr. Zinn was often taken to task for peeling back the rosy veneer of much of American history to reveal sordid realities that had remained hidden for too long. When writing about Andrew Jackson in his most famous book, "A People's History of the United States," published in 1980, Mr. Zinn said:

"If you look through high school textbooks and elementary school textbooks in American history, you will find Jackson the frontiersman, soldier, democrat, man of the people—not Jackson the slaveholder, land speculator, executioner of dissident soldiers, exterminator of Indians."

Radical? Hardly.

Mr. Zinn would protest peacefully for important issues he believed in—against racial segregation, for example, or against the war in Vietnam—and at times he was beaten and arrested for doing so. He was a man of exceptionally strong character who worked hard as a boy growing up in Brooklyn during the Depression. He was a bomber pilot in World War II, and his experience of the unmitigated horror of warfare served as the foundation for his lifelong quest for peaceful solutions to conflict....

He was a treasure and an inspiration. That he was considered radical says way more about this society than it does about him.

40. DUB 259–60; Daniel Gross, "Under the Volcano: Boston University in the Silber Age," *Lingua Franca*, Vol. 3 (November/December 1995), 44–53, as cited in JOY 89).

41. Zinn has made this point several times. For example, in a letter to the editor published in the *New York Times* (July 1, 2007), he writes: "I want...people to understand that ours is a beautiful country, but it has been taken over by men who have no respect for human rights or constitutional liberties. Our people are basically decent and caring, and our highest ideals are expressed in the Declaration of Independence, which says that all of us have an equal right to 'life, liberty and the pursuit of happiness.' The history of our country, I

point out in my book, is a striving, against corporate robber barons and war makers, to make those ideals a reality—and all of us, of whatever age, can find immense satisfaction in becoming part of that." Or again, in YCB (3): "[M]y love [is] for the *country*, for the people, not for whatever government happened to be in power." With regard to the charge that he is anti-American because he bashes America's heroes, Zinn replies that he celebrates plenty of heroes—but notes that they are often not the same ones celebrated in more conventional American history texts. Thus, in that same letter to the *New York Times*, he remarks, "My hero is not Theodore Roosevelt, who loved war and congratulated a general after a massacre of Filipino villagers at the turn of the century, but Mark Twain, who denounced the massacre and satirized imperialism." Or again, more expansively:

The Founding Fathers were not just ingenious organizers of a new nation (though they certainly were that) but also rich white slaveholders, merchants, bondholders, fearful of lower-class rebellion, or as James Madison put it, of "an equal division of property." Our military heroes—Andrew Jackson, Theodore Roosevelt—were racists, Indian-killers, war-lovers, imperialists. Our most liberal presidents— Jefferson, Lincoln, Wilson, Roosevelt, Kennedy—were more concerned with political power and national aggrandizement than with the rights of nonwhite people.

My heroes were the farmers of Shays' Rebellion, the black abolitionists who violated the law to free their brothers and sisters, the people who went to prison for opposing World War I, the workers who went on strike against powerful corporations, defying police and militia, the Vietnam veterans who spoke out against the war, the women who demanded equality in all aspects of life. (YCB 2–3)

The same point holds for Zinn's criticisms of some "heroes" of other cultures. For example, he tells of an Italian-American who said to him, at a lecture in which he criticized Columbus, "What are Italians going to do? Who are we going to celebrate?" Zinn responded, "Joe DiMaggio, Arturo Toscanini, Pavarotti, Fiorella LaGuardia, a whole bunch of wonderful Italians that we can celebrate" (WCP 14).

See also "Unsung Heroes" (in PGC 57–61), which is devoted entirely to the twin tasks of (a) challenging our admiration for a number of conventional, mainstream "heroes" of American history, and (b) calling attention to several currently neglected figures who might be more worthy of our admiration. As an example of (a), Zinn writes, "Shouldn't we...remind the admirers of Woodrow Wilson, another honored figure in the pantheon of American liberalism, that he insisted on racial segregation in federal buildings, attacked the Mexican coast, sent an occupation army into Haiti and the Dominican Republic, brought our country into the hell of World War I, and put antiwar protesters in prison" (59)? As an example of (b), Zinn makes a case for Fannie Lou Hamer, a Mississippi sharecropper who "was evicted from her farm and tortured in prison after she joined the civil rights movement," and who "became an eloquent voice for freedom" (59).

42. According to David Masciotra, "The slur 'anti-American' is symptomatic of the arrested development debilitating much of U.S. culture. Can any word but 'nonsense' describe the belief that an American who dedicated his life to teaching American youths, advocating for equality for African-Americans, wrestling for protections for American workers and struggling for peace for American soldiers hated his country ("Mitch Daniels Should Have Been More Open-Minded About Howard Zinn's Magnum Opus,"

Indianapolis Star [July 29, 2013]; http://truth-out.org/opinion/item/17846-mitch-daniels-should-have-been-more-open-minded-about-howard-zinns-magnum-opus?tmpl=component&print=1?

43. "Letter to Mandell Creighton, April 5, 1887," http://oll.libertyfund.org/titles/acton-acton-creighton-correspondence#lf1524_label_010

44. See especially Chapters 15–18. There are many translations and editions of *The Prince*.

45. This line of thought has been disputed by some recent thinkers, including Richard Rorty and Stanley Fish. I address their arguments in CP, and in "Rorty on Objectivity and Truth," in Randall E. Auxier and Lewis Edwin Hahn, eds., *The Philosophy of Richard Rorty* (Chicago: Open Court, 2010), 367–90. See also Rorty's "Reply to David Detmer" in the same volume, 391–3.

46. I discuss this extensively in CP.

47. See J. Anthony Blair, "What is Bias?," in Trudy Govier, ed., *Selected Issues in Logic and Communication* (Belmont, CA: Wadsworth, 1988), 93–103.

48. Thus, in OTO, Zinn writes: "I decided early that I would be biased in the sense of holding fast to certain fundamental values—the equal right of all human beings, whatever race, nationality, sex, religion, to life, liberty, the pursuit of happiness...I would always be biased (leaning toward) those ends, stubborn in holding to them" (30). See also DOI 49.

49. Coverage of Columbus in United States history textbooks may have improved somewhat in the wake of Zinn's famous discussion in APH, but there is no shortage of examples of treatments like Morison's in works published after that work. Catherine D. Lum (in *Know Your Zinn: Howard Zinn as a People's Public Intellectual* [B.A. thesis, Wesleyan University, 2012]; http://wesscholar.wesleya

n.edu/cgi/viewcontent.cgi?article=1887&context=etd_hon_t heses), compares Zinn's discussion of Columbus with that found in two more mainstream history textbooks: Lewis Paul Todd and Merle Curti, *Rise of the American Nation*, Liberty ed. (New York: Harcourt Brace Jovanovich, 1982); and James A. Henretta, Rebecca Edwards, and Robert O. Self, *America's History*, Seventh ed. (Boston: Bedford/St. Martin's, 2011). (Note that the original edition of APH appeared in 1980.) She points out that *Rise of the American Nation* makes no mention of Columbus's acts of mutilating, murdering, and enslaving the Arawaks. The text does mention that "Columbus called the dark-skinned people on the islands 'Indians'" (12), and states that "his voyages established Spain's claims in the Americas" (12–13). But there is no explanation to be found in the text as to how such "claims" were established, and certainly no hint that the process involved enslavement and violence. *America's History* does admit that Columbus "demanded tribute from the local Taino, Arawak, and Carib people," but neglects to explain what this really means. And it uses language similar to that of *Rise of the American Nation* in saying that Columbus "claimed the islands for Spain...and returned triumphantly to Spain" (25). Once again, all issues concerning the basis for the "claim," its moral legitimacy (or lack thereof), and its entanglement in violence and enslavement, are ignored. Moreover, as Lum points out, "this description of Columbus's conquest as 'triumphant' implies a heroic discourse rather than one tainted with criminality" (92). And Zinn himself, in a 1991 speech, notes that "in the long article on Columbus" in the *Columbia Encyclopedia* there is "no word about the atrocities committed by Columbus and his brothers and colleagues when he came here. If you look up the entry in the *Columbia Encyclopedia* under Las Casas, the Spanish priest who was a

harsh critic of what was being done to the natives on
Hispaniola, you will find that there's an entry on Las Casas,
fairly substantial, but nothing about his protests against
what was being done to the Arawaks on Hispaniola"
("1492–1992: The Legacy of Columbus" [a speech delivered
in Madison, Wisconsin, October 9, 1991], in HZS 79).

50. Zinn explains that the motive behind such an approach to
history is often not ideological political conservatism, but
rather a personal conservatism having to do with
conformity to established practices and aversion to
innovation and risk-taking: "[Historians and journalists]
often...will report on something because everyone else who
has written before has reported on it. And they will omit
something because it has always been omitted. In other
words, there is a conservative bias to history and a tendency
to emphasize what previous generations have emphasized.
The motive for that is safety, because the historian who
breaks the pattern causes stares and suspicions" ("The Use
and Abuse of History," in DOI 59).

51. Zinn has made this point many times. For example, in HPE
(27), he asserts that the historian "is not writing in an empty
field; thousands have preceded him and have weighted the
story in certain directions" (27). Similarly, in a 1998
interview with the Associated Press, Zinn notes that "The
orthodox viewpoint has already been done a thousand
times" (as quoted in R. Wolf Baldassarro, "Banned Books
Awareness: 'A People's History of the United States,'"
http://bannedbooks.world.edu/2013/07/28/banned-books-
awareness-a-peoples-history-of-the-united-states/). In his
autobiography he points out that his students "had had a
long period of political indoctrination before they arrived in
my class—in the family, in high school, in the mass media.
Into a marketplace so long dominated by orthodoxy I
wanted only to wheel my little pushcart, offering my wares

along with the others, leaving students to make their own choices" (YCB 8). Or again, a bit more dramatically: "My life has been devoted to rolling my little apple cart into the marketplace of ideas and hoping that I don't get run over by a truck" (as quoted in TIZ xxiv). (See also "A World Without Borders," in OZ, 134–5).

52. To be more precise, Zinn distinguishes "the people" from the "one percent of the nation" who own "a third of the wealth": "I am taking the liberty of uniting [the remaining] 99 percent as 'the people'" (APH 632). It seems likely that the recent Occupy Wall Street movement, with its "we are the 99 percent" movement, adopted this piece of rhetoric from Zinn's classic text.

53. See also DOI 48.

54. Diane Ravitch, former Assistant Secretary of Education in the administration of President George H. W. Bush, makes a similar argument: "In reality, every textbook has a point of view, despite a façade of neutrality; the authors and editors select some interpretations and reject others, choose certain events as important and ignore others as unimportant.... The pretense of objectivity and authority is, at bottom, just that: a pretense" (*The Language Police* [New York: Knopf, 2003], 134).

55. This essay is also available in ZR 499–508 (the quoted passage is from 502) and in OH 177–88 (the quoted passage is from 180). A slightly revised version of the piece appears as KFP 5–14 (the quoted passage is from 7–8). When quoting from this essay I will cite all of these sources, without bothering to mention the (slight and trivial) differences between the original version, as it appears online and in ZR and OH, and KFP (the revised version in POH). Zinn also discusses the Association of Asian Studies conference in TAV 31.

56. Equally absurdly, it often amounts to the demand that

historical writings, in order to avoid the charge of "propaganda," must be literally pointless. For as folk singer Pete Seeger observes, in the liner notes to his record album *Dangerous Songs!?* (Columbia, 1966; released on CD, 1997), "Any work…, from a Michelangelo painting to a Beethoven symphony to a play by Shaw, has a point to make. If we disagree with its point, we call the [work] 'propaganda.'

A lullaby is a propaganda song, in the opinion of the three-year-old who doesn't want to be put to sleep.

A hymn is a controversial song. Try singing one in the wrong church."

57.   Novick offers several examples of mainstream historians who in their professional work have taken sides on political issues even as they have simultaneously insisted that historians should not take sides on political issues. One example is that of Samuel Eliot Morison, the Harvard historian whose writing on Columbus was discussed above. In his 1950 presidential address to the American Historical Association he wrote that historians should refrain from judging the past or instructing the present, and should instead confine themselves to the humbler task of "simply explain[ing] the event exactly as it happened." And yet, in that same relatively short speech, Morison scolded some historians for having, in his judgment, "rendered the generation of youth which came to maturity around 1940 spiritually unprepared for the war they had to fight," and asserted that "Historians…are the ones who should have pointed out that war does accomplish something, that war is better than servitude" ("Faith of a Historian," *The American Historical Review*, Vol. 56, No. 2 [January 1951], 262, 265, 267; https://www.historians.org/about-aha-and-membership/aha-history-and-archives/presidential-addresses/samuel-eliot-morison). I would suggest, as an explanation for this contradiction, that Morison's

"patriotic" pro-war values may have seemed so natural and obvious to him as not to register in his mind as values at all, in radical contrast to the strange (from his point of view), and therefore noticeably subjective and partisan, anti-war values of the historians he criticized.

For a detailed examination of this phenomenon, see Jesse Lemisch, *On Active Service in War and Peace: Politics and Ideology in the American History Profession* (Toronto: New Hogtown Press, 1975); https://dl.dropboxusercontent.com/u/88737514/Lemisch_On%20Active%20Service%20in%20War%20and%20Peace.pdf

Lemisch documents that several leading American historians of the post-World War II era, such as Daniel Boorstin, Oscar Handlin, Samuel Eliot Morison, Allan Nevins, and Arthur Schlesinger, Jr., claimed that their work was "objective" and politically neutral in spite of the fact that they (a) often took political positions in their work and (b) harshly criticized other historians (typically those of a younger generation, who wrote in opposition to the war in Vietnam, or in support of civil rights, or against sanitized, absurdly upbeat descriptions of America's past) for "injecting politics" into their scholarship. Boorstin, for example, gave testimony before Congress in which he asserted that Communists, because of their political bias, should not be allowed to teach in American schools or even universities. But in that same testimony he also stated that his own opposition to communism had taken the form of an "attempt to discover and explain to students, in my teaching and in my writing, the unique virtues of American democracy" (67). Lemisch provides several similar examples, amply demonstrating that, to these mainstream historians, while there is somehow nothing political, nothing contrary to scholarly norms of neutrality and detachment, in their own use of historical scholarship to participate in the Cold War fight against communism, nonetheless historical works that champion any view lying outside of the spectrum of mainstream American political opinion are to be condemned, irrespective of their merits from the standpoint of considerations of evidential adequacy or logical rigor, as "biased," "propagandistic," "unscholarly," and "not objective."

58. Similar statements abound in Zinn's writings. For example, in DOI Zinn affirms his commitment to "scrupulous honesty in reporting on the past," and does so precisely in the context of explaining what is, and is not, meant by his rejection of "objectivity" (49). See also OTO 30, WCP 11, and CW 51.

59. Recall from the previous chapter that in a commencement address at the Rose-Hulman Institute Daniels, suffering from the delusion that scientists graduating from that institution would agree with him on the issue of global warming, called on them to apply their expertise to, and to take a stand on, that public policy issue. But when Zinn calls for historians to apply their expertise to controversial public issues, this is, somehow, an assault on the foundations of Purdue's entire research enterprise. In fairness to Daniels, there is no evidence that he understands that this is what Zinn's supposed rejection of "objectivity" and "the scientific method" amounts to. Thus, in this case, Daniels may be guilty only of ignorance and irresponsible recklessness (in publicly condemning a position he has made no effort to understand or to represent fairly), rather than hypocrisy.

60. With regard specifically to "the scientific method," a competent, fair-minded scholar who wished to charge Zinn with rejecting it would feel a need to address Zinn's explicit statement that his argument "does not aim to disengage history from the classical effort to be scientific" (IFE 2).

Note (a) that this statement appears in the book containing, as its first chapter, the essay that Daniels cites; and (b) that the context in which the quoted statement appears is precisely that of warning readers against possible misinterpretations of his intent.

61. See also CW 51, where Zinn states that history should not be used "as a buttress to any particular party, nation, or ideology." It is ironic that many of the critics who condemn Zinn as a "propagandist" because of his open allegiance to universal values have registered no similar objection to those historians who have celebrated Columbus, despite Zinn's demonstration that Columbus represented "the worst values of Western civilization: greed, violence, exploitation, racism, conquest, hypocrisy (he claimed to be a devout Christian)" (YCB 2). Such critics fail to acknowledge, and seem not to recognize, that the traditional treatment of Columbus involves even the slightest entanglement in values.

62. As Zinn points out, "a physiologist would be astonished if someone suggested that he starts from a neutral position as regards life or death, health or sickness" (UOS; ZR 505; KFP 12). Reflection on this pithy observation helps to establish several of Zinn's main points—the impossibility of the demand for neutrality (for what would it mean to demand that medical researchers remain neutral about the relative merits of the values of health and sickness?); the fact that widely accepted value-judgments tend not to be recognized as value-judgments at all (and thus, no one calls medical researchers "propagandists," even though they clearly take sides with regard to the values of life and death, and of health and sickness); that while a commitment to ultimate values will indeed influence one's choices as to which questions to ask, this value commitment need not influence one's answers to those questions (the commitment dictates

that one search for a cure, pursue the most promising leads toward that end, and so forth, but it does not dictate which proposed treatment genuinely is the cure—one needs evidence to establish that); and, in short, that a commitment to ultimate values need not compromise the objectivity (in the sense of accuracy, or scientific or scholarly rigor, or in any other defensible sense of that term) of one's research.

In support of these last two points, Zinn elsewhere comments, "Surely it is not necessary to violate the facts (hide them, or manufacture them) in order to focus on those which advance a vital human value. The distinction between instrumental and ultimate values in affecting accuracy...is important here. Neither the medical researcher working on curing disease nor the researcher working for some government on bacteriological warfare needs to distort the evidence (indeed, he had better not) to pursue his aim" ("The Philosophers," in POH 340).

63. In *Disobedience and Democracy* (New York: Vintage, 1968), Zinn writes: "While individual liberty can stand as a moral value on its own..., surely *the state*—except in totalitarian ideology—is an instrument, as Locke and Jefferson understood, for the achievement of human values (life, liberty, the pursuit of happiness, as Jefferson put it). And the state's needs, even its 'existence,' must be weighed against its capacity to achieve those values" (10).

64. Elsewhere in the same essay Zinn offers the following proposed list of "ultimate values": "peace, racial equality, economic security, freedom of expression" (HPE 23).

65. In a 1973 speech Zinn offers a similar example. One scientist, having been ordered to "figure out how to kill a million people with nerve gas," might agree to do so, on the grounds that it would be "unscientific" and contrary to the demands of objectivity to let his scientific work be colored by his personal "value judgments." But another scientist

might refuse the order and say, "I think I'll figure out how to make nerve gas harmless in case you use it." Zinn then makes the point that while these value-judgments determine which scientific project will be undertaken, they exert their influence before the work is done, not as it is being done. They do not in any way compromise the scientific rigor of a project once it has been chosen. Thus, the scientist who works on making nerve gas harmless can be "just as scientific" when he "does his technical work" as his colleague "who goes to work on nerve gas without a murmur." "But," Zinn adds, "he's being more human, it seems to me" (TAV 29). Though Zinn doesn't make the point here, he might well also have added that the decision to follow orders and work on making nerve gas even more deadly is every bit as much a value-laden decision as that of refusing such orders and choosing to work on rendering nerve gas harmless instead.

66. Novick makes a similar point when he remarks, "the physician is not less objective because of his or her commitment to the patient and against the germ" (NOV 303).

67. See also WCP 11, and DOI 6, for similar statements.

68. On this issue, see also HPE 18.

69. In "What is Radical History?," Zinn refers to those who reject his call for "value-laden historiography…despite my argument that this does not determine answers, only questions; despite my plea that aesthetic work, done for pleasure, should always have its place; despite my insistence that our work is value-laden whether we choose or not…" (POH 36). While Zinn's point in this passage is not to complain about the reception of his ideas, my point is that those ideas cannot be fairly or competently addressed without reference to the arguments that Zinn mentions here, and others like them. This is not to say, of course, that

Zinn's critics are obliged to agree with him. It is to say, however, that they are not entitled to beg the question and commit the straw man fallacy by rejecting his conclusions without confronting the arguments he marshals in their support, or by refuting a crude caricature of his position that takes no notice of the nuances of that position or the subtle distinctions that help to define it.

Chapter 3: Zinn's Critics

1. (New York: Columbia University Press, 1969).

2. "American Federation of Teachers' journal slanders historian Howard Zinn" (February 18, 2013); http://www. wsws.org/en/articles/2013/02/18/aftz-f18.html

3. "Defending Howard Zinn" (February 20, 2013), http://sys temicdisorder.wordpress.com/2013/02/20/defending-howard-zinn/

4. In a discussion of World War II Zinn states, "The enemy was evil. The enemy was unmistakably evil." Granted, his main point in this passage is that the United States also committed atrocities in that war (most notably the deliberate bombing of civilian populations), and that it is a mistake to suppose that since we were opposing evil we couldn't possibly be guilty of doing evil acts ourselves. But in the midst of making that point Zinn also emphasizes that "We didn't match the Holocaust. That's a unique event in World War II" (REE). Or again, in another speech, after making the point that a certain kind of propaganda works the same way in democratic countries as it does in totalitarian ones, Zinn hastens to add that this does not mean that "we are just like the Nazis. No, we are different." But he also makes such points as (a) that we are not as much different as we could and should be, (b) that the concepts "democratic" and "totalitarian" represent points on a spectrum, rather than a simple dichotomy, so that being

non-totalitarian is not sufficient to make one democratic, and (c) that we have "a ways to go" before we can say that we are fully at the "democratic" end of the spectrum. He adds, "We ought to recognize that.... I think it's important to have that kind of self-examination, that awareness of yourself, that awareness of your limitations, so you won't get too arrogant about who you are and what you're able to do" ("Overcoming Obstacles" [November 30, 2006], in HZS 210).

5. Zinn draws the distinction between (a) thinking that someone has not received a fair trial, and (b) thinking that he or she is factually innocent, many times, and in connection with many trials. For example, in a speech on "The Case of Sacco and Vanzetti," Zinn says, "one thing is for sure, whether they were guilty or not, they could not possibly get a fair trial in the atmosphere of the courtroom in 1920–21." He then makes the same point in connection with Mumia Abu-Jamal: "He's black, he's radical, he's poor. Is he going to get a fair trial? Again, it's not known for sure guilt or innocence" (CSZ 128). Note that in declaring his agnosticism with respect to the issue of the factual innocence or guilt of these individuals Zinn is not responding defensively to new information pointing to their guilt.

6. See Robert D. McFadden, "David Greenglass, the Brother Who Doomed Ethel Rosenberg, Dies at 92," *New York Times* (October 14, 2014); and "False testimony clinched Rosenberg spy trial," BBC News (December 6, 2001); http://news.bbc.co.uk/2/hi/americas/1695240.stm

7. See PA 35 for another good example of such evenhandedness in connection with World War II.

8. Historian Joseph A. Palermo offers a very different explanation for the success of APH. I invite the reader to consider whether it is more, or less, plausible than the explanations

offered by Wineburg and Kazin: "Zinn was...a gifted writer. He had the capacity to describe the plight of ordinary people in a compassionate and empathetic manner with clarity and emotion. He could convey irony in American history better than most writers and he was also very funny. These qualities contributed to the popularity of *A People's History* since people always respond positively to well-crafted writing. And young people in particular are tired of hearing that the 'truth' always can be found in some mushy middle somewhere" ("Mitch Daniels, Howard Zinn, and the Politics of History," [July 30, 2013]; http://www.huffingtonpost.com/joseph-a-palermo/mitch-daniels-howard-zinn_b_3677477.html).

9. https://zinnedproject.org/2011/01/what-teachers-are-saying/

10. (August 2, 2013); http://articles.latimes.com/2013/aug/02/opinion/la-oe-wineburg-daniels-zinn-20130802

11. See, for example, Mitchell J. Freedman, "The Cable, the footnote, and Howard Zinn" (August 6, 2013); http://mitchellfreedman.blogspot.com/2013/08/the-cable-footnote-and-howard-zinn.html

12. On this point see HPE 27–8.

13. "The Secret Word," *Boston Globe* (January 24, 1976), in ZR 224.

14. *Hiroshima: Breaking the Silence* (Westfield, NJ: Open Magazine Pamphlet Series, 1995), 6.

15. "Foreword" to *Marx in Soho* (Cambridge, MA: South End Press, 1999), xii.

16. "Eugene V. Debs," in PGC 234.

17. See, for example, DOI 271–5; "Anarchism," in ZR 648–50; and GM 124–7.

18. http://mpandgs.blogspot.com/2013/03/howard-zinn-ideology-and-faulty.html

19. Far worse (and equally evidence-free) invective can be

found all over the Internet. For example, a certain "pst 314," responding to another person's comment that Zinn had been part of the Civil Rights Movement, remarks: "Only because it was a way to attack America. He never cared about the civil rights of the millions murdered by commies or the billion terrorized and enslaved." And in response to the observation that Zinn "was very anti-war," the same bravely anonymous defamer counters: "No, he only objected to non-communists defending themselves from communist aggression and oppression. He was enthusiastically in favor of commies making war on everyone else" (http://althouse.blogspot.com/2010/01/if-you-want-to-read-real-history-book.html). Naturally, "pst 314" produces no evidence of any kind in support of these charges, cites no passages in which Zinn praises communist murder or aggression, and says nothing about the many passages, some of which are quoted above, in which Zinn straightforwardly condemns such atrocities. And with regard to pst 314's first comment, notice what it implies about Zinn's students at Spelman College, such as Alice Walker, Marian Wright Edelman, and Betty Stevens Walker. They clearly thought that Zinn respected them, cared about them, and wanted them to receive justice. How unperceptive they must have been, failing to realize that his true motivation for marching with them, being subjected to verbal abuse, going to jail, and risking (and ultimately losing) his job, was merely his hatred of "America." Moreover, leaving aside the issue of Zinn's motivations, one wonders what conception of "America" a person must have in order to be able to view the Civil Rights Movement as an attack on it. Are black Americans not part of "America"? Is "America" stronger when it is racist and segregationist, than when it is not?

20.　Further documentation of this point can be found in the previous chapter.

21. http://www.bu.edu/history/files/2011/01/westling.pdf
22. Further documentation of this point can be found in the previous chapter.
23. Further documentation of this point can be found in the previous chapter.
24. And incompetent scholars attract even more incompetent scholars as followers, who then pass on the original incompetent's errors to a wider audience on the Internet. Thus we find:

Of Zinn's scholarship in *A People's History of the United States*, Greenberg says:

> Zinn rests satisfied with what strikes him as the scandalous revelation that claims of objectivity often mask ideological predilections. Imagine! And on the basis of this sophomoric insight, he renounces the ideals of objectivity and empirical responsibility, and makes the dubious leap to the notion that a historian need only lay his ideological cards on the table and tell whatever history he chooses.

Lord, but I have heard this methodology set forth by undergraduates in courses past: "as long as I identify my point of view and find sufficient quotes that seem to lend authority, my work is done." Rather than reasoning and sound evidence that reflects a thorough consideration of the issue, support becomes a quote-hunt, the results of which are often cherry-picked, redefined, and decontextualized. (http://mpandgs.blogspot.com/2013/03/howard-zinn-ideology-and-faulty.html)

Yes indeed, it is annoying when undergraduates use such a defective methodology. But it is even sadder when their teachers commit the much more egregious error of uncritically accepting, and then passing on, someone else's damning indictment of a scholar without bothering to check whether that indictment is even to the slightest degree grounded in reality.

25. "Historians Respond to the New Republic's Diatribe Against Howard Zinn," Zinn Education Project (March 20, 2013); http://zinnedproject.org/2013/03/responsetonewrepublic/

26. http://historynewsnetwork.org/article/151106#Greenberg

27. Louis Jacobson, "Is book by Howard Zinn the 'most popular' high-school history textbook?," *Politifact* (April 15, 2015); http://www.politifact.com/truth-o-meter/statements/2015/apr/15/rick-santorum/book-howard-zinn-most-popular-high-school-history-/

28. Note that I am far more concerned with the substance of Greenberg's article—its factual errors and logical fallacies—than with its tone. In focusing briefly on his tone here, my point is to criticize Greenberg for violating *his* standards, not mine.

29. *The Greatest Show on Earth: The Evidence for Evolution* (New York: Free Press, 2010), 155. Of course, in Dawkins's text he refers to "those who oppose evolution."

30. https://www.amazon.com/David-J.-Bobb/e/B00FADYH6A/ref=sr_tc_2_0?qid=1484606448&sr=1-2-ent

31. http://www.wsj.com/articles/SB10001424127887324769704579008453713889352

32. See, for example, UOS; ZR 507; KFP 14; in which Zinn calls on scholars of all kinds to devote themselves to the task of *trying to figure out* how to make the world better, which is a very different thing from claiming to have the answers oneself:

Let the economists work out a plan for free food, instead of advising the Federal Reserve Board on interest rates. Let the political scientists work out insurgency tactics for the poor, rather than counter-insurgency tactics for the military.... Let the scientists figure out and lay before the public plans on how to make autos safe, cities beautiful, air pure. Let all social scientists work on modes of change instead of merely describing the world that is, so that we can make the necessary revolutionary alterations with the least disorder.

I am not sure what a revolution in the academy will look like, any more than I know what a revolution in the society will look like.

33. http://www.marygrabar.com/grabar_new/
34. http://theahi.org/about-us/people/fellows/
35. Mary Grabar, "Dissident Prof" (October 3, 2013); http://www.dissidentprof.com/latest-dispatches/168-howard-zinn-dissident-prof-read-in.html
36. Jerry Davich, "Attack on scholar 'indefensible,'" *Post Tribune* (September 22, 2013); http://posttrib.chicagotribune.com/news/davich/22651471-452/jerry-davich-former-governors-attack-on-scholar-indefensible.html#.VI4Mz1q4mu4
37. Zinn also discusses the Federalist Papers in FUT 122–3; and in DOI 152 and 235.
38. To be clear, in conceding that such a criticism is plausible, I am not saying that, in the final analysis, it is sound. To show that, one would have to make a case for it—a case that would be based on attention to the details of Zinn's texts, and would be respectful of considerations of evidence and logic. To my knowledge, no one to date has offered such a case.
39. Daniel Pye, "Retrospective: Interview with Howard Zinn (January 29, 2010); http://londonprogressivejournal.com/article/620/retrospective-interview-with-howard-zinn

40. https://www.washingtonpost.com/opinions/bill-oreilly-makes-a-mess-of-history/2015/11/10/03ef0d94-87d9-11e5-be8b-1ae2e4f50f76_story.html

41. http://www.realclearpolitics.com/video/2015/11/06/oreilly_vs_george_will_youre_a_hack_a_reagan_loyalist_who_doesnt_want_the_truth_to_be_told.html

42. For more on this, see Jon Wiener, "Radical Historians and the Crisis in American History, 1959–1980," in his *Professors, Politics and Pop* (New York: Verso, 1991), 175–216

43. See the discussion of Grabar above. In fairness to Paquette, however, it should be noted that the two pieces by Grabar that I analyze there were published after his two-part essay appeared. I speculate that her work on this topic may have been influenced by his. They obviously know one another, as both are affiliated with the Alexander Hamilton Institute for the Study of Western Civilization; and, as discussed above, she reproduces in her work the most spectacular scholarly atrocity found in his—that of rejecting a claim (that Mitch Daniels attempted to censor APH) without so much as acknowledging, let alone answering, the very evidence that establishes the truth of that claim.

44. Here Zinn is obviously offering yet another of his criticisms of the Soviet Union, the nation about which David Greenberg claims, as noted above, that Zinn "seems to have stayed silent."

45. Zinn elaborates on this point in a 1991 speech:

[T]he real argument is not about Columbus. The real argument goes across the centuries. The real argument is about Western civilization. The reason that people are so defensive about Columbus and anxious to maintain a glowing image of Columbus and what he did has nothing to do with Columbus. After all, it's really too late to do something about Columbus. He's not asking us for a letter of recommendation. The real point is now, and the people who are defending what Columbus did, what they really care about is now. What they really care about is what the discussion of Columbus says about...five hundred years that have elapsed since then. They are obviously worried that the casting of too harsh a light on what Columbus did might also cast a harsh light on all those events that followed Columbus.... It seems to me that there are certain key issues that are raised by the Columbus argument which need to be thought about. It's because of those issues, which are issues of today and not just issues of that time, because of the immediacy of those issues, that we reexamine what happened at that time and ask, what did it mean, and what does that tell us about the five hundred years since and about today?

One of those transcendental issues is conquest by violence.... [O]ne of those questions is about that long, long history of conquest by violence which Columbus ushered in in this hemisphere and to which then Spain and Portugal and the other European countries came, and the United States then joined that expansionist game that all the European powers were playing. The expansion of the United States followed very much the pattern set by Columbus, that is, the elimination of native peoples in order to find riches. (LOC 81–2)

46. And had he read further, he would have encountered other statements, like this one, of Zinn's refusal to judge individuals of the past by contemporary moral standards:

To say that the Declaration of Independence, even by its own language, was limited to life, liberty, and happiness for white males is not to denounce the makers and signers of the Declaration for holding the ideas expected of privileged males of the eighteenth century. Reformers and radicals, looking discontentedly at history, are often accused of expecting too much from a past political epoch—and sometimes they do. But the point of noting those outside the arc of human rights in the Declaration is not, centuries late and pointlessly, to lay impossible moral burdens on that time. It is to try to understand the way in which the Declaration functioned to mobilize certain groups of Americans, ignoring others. Surely, inspirational language to create a secure consensus is still used, in our time, to cover up serious conflicts of interest in that consensus, and to cover up, also, the omission of large parts of the human race. (APH 73)

47.   The source of this quotation, though Paquette fails to cite it, is Elizabeth Fox-Genovese, "Slavery, Race, and the Figure of the Tragic Mulatta; or, the Ghost of Southern History in the Writing of African-American Women," in Anne Goodwyn and Susan Van D'Elden Donaldson, eds., *Haunted Bodies: Gender and Southern Texts* (Charlottesville: University Press of Virginia, 1997), 467.

48.   Another prominent protestor was Antonio de Montesinos, a Spanish Dominican priest who denounced the Europeans in Haiti in 1511 for their treatment of American Indians (Joseph Schroeder, "Antonio Montesino," *Catholic Encyclopedia*); https://en.wikisource.org/wiki/Catholic_Encyclopedia_(1913)/Antonio_Montesino

49.   See, for example, "Columbus, the Indians, and Human Progress 1492–1992," in FTQ 121–44, especially 139–40.

50.   http://theahi.org/about-us/charter/

51.   That's the main point to be made about Horowitz's critique of Anton. But his characterization of the Radical Philosophy Association in this profile also serves as an example of his unscholarly sloppiness and penchant for factual error. He

offers no citation or evidence of any kind in support of what he says about this organization. It appears that the material quoted above about "broad social upheavals" and opposition to discrimination, environmental ruin, and the like, is taken from the group's website (though Horowitz appears to have cobbled together two statements that are quite distinct there, without indicating that he has done so, and, in any case, fails to provide a citation), but I can find no evidence on the website to support his other claims about what the group allegedly believes. My suspicion was initially aroused by his claim that the Association is a "group of Marxist professors," since (1) I personally know some members who are not Marxists, and (2) philosophical societies are generally non-sectarian, and typically attract members with a variety of views. Sure enough, if we check the Association's website we find the following: "Our members are from many nations and continue a variety of radical traditions including (but not limited to) feminism, phenomenology, Marxism, anarchism, post-structuralism, post-colonial theory and environmentalism" (http://www. radicalphilosophyassociation.org); and "The Radical Philosophy Association is a non-sectarian, international forum for the philosophical discussion of fundamental social change. Founded in 1982, the Association is open to anyone who shares the view that society should be built on cooperation rather than competition, and that social decision-making should be governed by democratic proce-dures" (http://www.pdcnet.org/pdc/bvdb.nsf/membership ?openform&memberjournal=pdc_rpa).

52. Ben Armbruster and Rob Savillo, "David Horowitz debunks David Horowitz: a *Media Matters* analysis of *The Professors*" (April 18, 2006); http://mediamatters.org/ research/2006/04/18/david-horowitz-debunks-david-horowitz-a-media-m/135442

Armbruster and Savillo's finding is also cited in a report by an organization called "Free Exchange on Campus" (FC iv). This is significant because an extremely lengthy and detailed article defending Horowitz's book against the "Free Exchange on Campus" report, and seemingly dedicated to refuting every one of its criticisms that it can, nonetheless explicitly declines to contest the "52 out of 100" finding, arguing instead that it fails to undermine Horowitz's thesis (LAK). I will respond to this defense below.

53. *One-Party Classroom: How Radical Professors at America's Top Colleges Indoctrinate Students and Undermine Our Democracy* (New York: Crown Forum 2009), 80.

54. http://www.lewisrgordon.com/teaching/syllabi/themes-in-existentialism.pdf

55. (Madison: The University of Wisconsin Press, 1989).

56. "D'Ho!" (February 22, 2006); https://www.insidehigh ered.com/views/2006/02/22/node_35635

57. See, for example, Jon Wiener, "Facing Black Students at Harvard: Stephan Thernstrom Takes a Stand," in *Historians in Trouble* (New York: The New Press, 2005), 58–69; and John K. Wilson, *The Myth of Political Correctness* (Durham, NC: Duke University Press, 1995), 17–20.

58. https://en.wikipedia.org/wiki/Noam_Chomsky#Recep tion_and_influence
I have removed the extensive documentation for these claims that is provided in the article.

59. The transcript of the screenplay is available at http://www.moviescriptsandscreenplays.com/BenandMatt/good willtrans.html

60. (Boston: South End Press, 1979). Chomsky has used the analytic device in question repeatedly in subsequent works.

61. *9-11* (New York: Seven Stories Press, 2002), 35.

62. A list of the 18 surveyed textbooks, including full biblio-

graphical information, can be found on pages 435–6 of LMT.

63. See Latin American Studies Association, *The Electoral Process in Nicaragua: Domestic and International Influences: The Report of the Latin American Studies Association Delegation to Observe the Nicaraguan General Election of November 4, 1984*; https://lasa-4.lasa.pitt.edu/members/reports/Elector alProcessNicaragua.pdf; Envio Team, "Nicaragua's 1984 Elections—A History Worth the Retelling," *Envio* No. 102 (1990); http://www.envio.org.ni/articulo/2578; Fairness & Accuracy in Reporting, "Lie: The Sandinistas Won't Submit to Free Elections" (October 1, 1987); http://fair.org/extra-online-articles/lie-the-sandinistas-wont-submit-to-free-elections/; and MC.

64. "Nicaragua"; https://www.hrw.org/legacy/reports/1989/WR 89/Nicaragu.htm

65. "Human Rights Watch World Report 1992—Nicaragua"; http://www.refworld.org/cgi-bin/texis/vtx/rwmain? page=publisher&publisher=HRW&type=&coi=NIC&docid= 467fca491e&skip=0

66. International Court of Justice, Case Concerning Military and Paramilitary Activities in and Against Nicaragua (Nicaragua v. United States of America), Affidavit of Edgar Chamarro (September 5, 1985); http://www.williamg-becker.com/chamorroaffidavit.pdf

67. Scott Jaschik, "Fact-Checking David Horowitz," *Inside Higher Ed* (May 9, 2006); https://www.insidehighered.com /news/2006/05/09/report

68. Alec Magnet, "Nine Professors At Columbia Are Deemed 'Dangerous,'" *New York Sun* (February 21, 2006); http://www.nysun.com/new-york/nine-professors-at-columbia-are-deemed-dangerous/27850/

69. Scott Jaschik, "Retractions From David Horowitz: Conservative critic of academe admits he has no evidence for two stories he uses to allege professorial bias," *Inside*

Higher Ed (January 11, 2006); https://www.insidehighered
.com/news/2006/01/11/retract

70. Third edition (New York: HarperPerennial, 1983), 108.

71. *George Washington on Leadership* (New York: Basic Books, 2008), 1.

72. "How Did Washington Make His Millions?," *Colonial Williamsburg Journal* (Winter 2013); http://www.history.o rg/Foundation/journal/winter13/washington.cfm

73. "U.S. National Unemployment by Political Party/ President," *Truthful Politics* (September 25, 2014); http://www.truthfulpolitics.com/http:/truthfulpolitics.com/ comments/u-s-national-unemployment-by-political-party-president/?utm_source=twitter&utm_medium=friendly%2 Blinks&utm_campaign=twitter%2Bfl%2Bplugin

74. Horowitz, as quoted in Nick Perry, "Peace class lands UW prof on list of 'most dangerous'" *Seattle Times* (February 28, 2006); http://old.seattletimes.com/html/education/2002833 474_dangerousprofs28m.html

75. Horowitz's "research" credit for his profile of Zinn goes to Daniel J. Flynn (TP 364), author of "Master of Deceit" (FLY). The two pieces overlap, and many of Horowitz's specific criticisms of Zinn are also to be found in Flynn's article. Criticisms that are not addressed in my discussion of Horowitz above can be found in my treatment of Flynn below.

76. Labor historian Dale McCartney also notices that "Kazin's review...oversimplifies" APH, as "a careful reading of Zinn's work reveals that he offers a considerably nuanced vision of his subjects." McCartney adds that although "Zinn's work is not academic history," he "clearly has the breadth of knowledge only possible through a life of study" ("Accessing History: The Importance of Howard Zinn," Seven Oaks [March 29, 2004]); http://www.faculty.umb.edu /gary_zabel/Courses/Morals%20and%20Law/06_zinn.html

77. I might add that Zinn shows in his work that he is perfectly aware of Manichaeism, and regards it as disdainfully as Kazin does. For example, he explicitly invokes that concept in pointing out that in war propaganda "enemy" nations and their leaders are presented as absolutely evil, and we, who are fighting them, are depicted as absolutely good, noble, and benevolent in doing so ("Just and Unjust Wars," in FTQ 109–10).

78. To give one more example, this time having to do with the content of textbooks, rather than of mass media news, and dealing with economics, rather than foreign affairs, two major studies of American history textbooks reveal that from the 1940s through the 1970s such textbooks typically said nothing about poverty in America, or about income distribution or inequality, or about economic classes, about labor struggles, or about the lives of laborers generally. The books depicted a classless society. See NAS; and Francis Fitzgerald, *America Revised: History Schoolbooks in the Twentieth Century* (New York: Vintage, 1980).

79. Leon Litwack (in "Trouble in Mind," *Journal of American History*, Vol. 74 [1987]), argues that "no group of scholars was more deeply implicated in the miseducation of American youth and did more to shape the thinking of generations of Americans about race and blacks than historians" (326, as quoted in NAS 62). Nash refers to the "pervasive racist consensus" of American historians that did not begin to be broken up until the civil rights movement of the 1960s. Imagine what the reaction would have been to an 1850s-era Zinn-like history textbook that argued that slavery was clearly and unambiguously evil, or a 1950s-era one that said the same thing about racism: "propaganda," "biased," "unbalanced," "not objective," "simplistic," "Manichean," "lacking in nuance and subtlety."

80. Historian Stuart Easterling cites another non-epistemic factor, class bias, in reaching a conclusion similar to mine on the issue of simplicity, complexity, and Manichaeism: [Historians'] class bias often undermines their analysis. This bias has gotten even worse over the past generation of Reaganism and neoliberalism. Academics will often extend their own partial middle-class stake in the oppressor's system—and its associated narrow self-interested cynicism—to everyone else, and particularly to oppressed people.

In the academy, expressing this class bias is unfortunately often made synonymous with being "nuanced" and "complex."

History certainly can be complicated, and merits serious study and debate. But to argue that Zinn overly simplifies things is inaccurate: *A People's History* is not a simple book, and his explanations for struggle and consent are not based on simple ideas or arguments....

To point out, as Zinn does, that in history there are people who wear black hats and those who wear white hats, who are opposed to and often in conflict with one other, is not overly simplifying. It is, in fact, clarifying.

It took a former worker and soldier, an activist and radical, to keep that insight alive within the historical profession—and society at large—during a difficult period for the left. For that gift alone, Zinn will be sorely missed. (EAS)

81. I exaggerate, but only slightly. Zinn provides extensive documentation for this point in APH. Here I quote just one passage:

A State Department list, "Instances of the Use of United States Armed Forces Abroad 1798–1945" (presented by

Secretary of State Dean Rusk to a Senate committee in 1962 to cite precedents for the use of armed force against Cuba), shows 103 interventions in the affairs of other countries between 1798 and 1895. A sampling from the list, with the exact description given by the State Department:

1852–53—Argentina—Marines were landed and maintained in Buenos Aires to protect American interests during a revolution.

1853—Nicaragua—to protect American lives and interests during political disturbances.

1853–54—Japan—The "Opening of Japan" and the Perry Expedition. [The State Department does not give more details, but this involved the use of warships to force Japan to open its ports to the United States.]

1853–54—Ryukyu and Bonin Islands—Commodore Perry on three visits before going to Japan and while waiting for a reply from Japan made a naval demonstration, landing marines twice, and secured a coaling concession from the ruler of Naha on Okinawa. He also demonstrated in the Bonin Islands. All to secure facilities for commerce.

1854—Nicaragua—San Juan del Norte. [Greytown was destroyed to avenge an insult to the American Minister to Nicaragua.]

1855—Uruguay—U.S. and European naval forces landed to protect American interests during an attempted revolution in Montevideo.

1859—China—For the protection of American interests in Shanghai.

1860—Angola, Portuguese West Africa—To protect American lives and property at Kissembo when the natives became troublesome.

1893—Hawaii—Ostensibly to protect American lives and property; actually to promote a provisional government under Sanford B. Dole. This action was disavowed by the United States.

1894—Nicaragua—To protect American interests at Bluefields following a revolution. (APH 298)

82. Zinn's letter (LET) and Kazin's reply both appear in *Dissent* (Summer 2004), 110.

83. Easterling's article also contains a powerful critique of Kazin's explanation of Americans' attitudes toward capitalism, which, as mentioned, differs substantially from Zinn's.

Stephen Bird, Adam Silver, and Joshua C. Yesnowitz similarly reject Kazin's claim that Zinn fails to explain why Americans have tended to accept the legitimacy of the oppressive aspects of the American system. They refer to "an array of conventional tools for dominance that Zinn actually outlines in his history," adding that "The use of force, intimidation, propaganda, xenophobia and nationalism, misinformation, and 'divide and conquer' strategies by dominant elites permeate his writing" ("Reassessing Zinn," in AWS 197).

84. "The Ludlow Massacre," in POH 101 (emphasis added).

85. "Introduction" to DOI 3 (emphasis added).

86. "Reflections on History," in FOH 1 (emphasis added).

87. For another example, see FUT 118.

88. For example, he writes, "I think some progressives have forgotten the history of the Democratic Party, to which people have turned again and again in desperate search for saviors, later to be disappointed. Our political history shows us that only great popular movements, carrying out bold actions that awakened the nation and threatened the Establishment, as in the thirties and the sixties, have been able to shake that pyramid of corporate and military power and at least temporarily change course" ("The Nobel's

Feeble Gesture" [January 2010], in HUP 219–20).

89. See Kazin's "Why Leftists Should Also Be Democrats," *Dissent* (Fall 2015); https://www.dissentmagazine.org /article/why-leftists-should-be-democrats

90. "The Obama Difference" (October 2008), in HUP 210.

91. Zinn makes this point explicitly on page 8 of "A Discussion with Howard Zinn," which appears in a "P.S." section appended to APH; in "Civil Disobedience in the Twenty-First Century," in HZS 227; and in "The Double Horror of 9/11," in PGC 75: "Nothing justifies killing innocent people."

92. "Michael Kazin on Roots of the Occupy Movement"; http://michaelkazin.com/article/michael-kazin-on-roots-of-the-occupy-movement/

93. "Economic Justice: The American Class System," in DOI 168–9. See also MIS, in which Zinn puts in Marx's mouth the remark, "capitalism has accomplished wonders unsurpassed in history—miracles of technology and science" (45). Whereas some of Marx's ideas receive criticism in this play (Marx returns in contemporary times and condemns them personally), such is not the case with his praise for capitalism.

94. March 14, 1997 interview with Davis D. Joyce in JOY 34–5.

95. On this point Zinn has been influenced by the thought of French existentialist philosophers, most notably Jean-Paul Sartre—yet another influence that Flynn's reductionist analysis omits. See, for example, "The New Radicalism" (ZR 632; OH 94) and "Freedom and Responsibility," in POH 284.

96. These last two points are also made by Ambre Ivol and Paul Buhle, in their "Legacies and Breakthroughs: The Long View on Zinnian History," in AWS 23–4.

97. See also Zinn's observation that "the Cultural Revolution in China" had been "murderous" (DOI 109).

98. http://genius.com/Todd-clear-tougher-is-dumber-annotated

99. "A Life in the Balance: The Case of Mumia Abu-Jamal" (February 17, 2000); https://web.archive.org/web/200 81212075045/http://www.amnesty.org/en/library/asset/AM R51/001/2000/en/dom-AMR510012000en.html

100. Nancy M. Cavender and Howard Kahane, *Logic and Contemporary Rhetoric*, 11th Edition (Belmont, CA: Wadsworth, 2010), 325–6.

101. See, for example, "Vietnam," which is Chapter Six of Handlin's *The Distortion of America*, Second Expanded Edition (New Brunswick, NJ: Transaction, 2015 [originally published 1981]).

102. Nick Thimmesch, "McGovern's Lead in College Faculties a Narrow One" (October 13, 1972); https://news.google.com /newspapers?nid=2519&dat=19721013&id=y85dAAAAIBAJ &sjid=b14NAAAAIBAJ&pg=785,2145416&hl=en

103. *The Mississippi Valley Historical Review,* Vol. 48, No. 4 (March 1962), 743–5.

104. Zinn makes this point often. For example, in an essay on the Holocaust, he writes (not in response to Handlin): "What happened to the Jews under Hitler is unique in its details, but it shares universal characteristics with many other events in human history" ("Respecting the Holocaust," in PGSU 107–8).

105. https://www.boundless.com/u-s-history/textbooks /boundless-u-s-history-textbook/slavery-freedom-and-the-struggle-for-empire-1750-1763-5/slavery-in-the-colonies-55/chesapeake-slavery-339-8551/

106. http://www.goodreads.com/book/show/18191085-legend-of-plough-jogger-the-chose-one

107. The complete text of the speech is available at http:// teachingamericanhistory.org/library/document/speech-at-chicago-illinois/

108. Vernon Burton, "The Movement Toward Civil Rights"; http://www.las.illinois.edu/news/lincoln/debates/

109. http://www.nps.gov/liho/learn/historyculture/debate4.htm

110. http://www.nps.gov/liho/learn/historyculture/debate5.htm

111. R. Sós, "Lincoln, Slavery, and Racism"; https://thehistoricpresent.wordpress.com/lincoln-slavery-and-racism/

112. "What Lincoln Said at Charleston...in Context (part three)" (February 12, 2011); https://cwcrossroads.wordpress.com/2011/02/12/what-lincoln-said-at-charleston-in-context-part-three/

113. These documents are both available in VAA 66–76.

114. We know this from an exchange between Zinn and Handlin (ZRH and HRZ) about Handlin's review of APH.

115. *Mandate for Change: The White House Years, 1953–1956* (Garden City, NY: Doubleday, 1963), 372.

116. "Fulgencio Batista"; http://www.ebooklibrary.org/articles/fulgencio_batista#Support_of_U.S._business_and_government

117. (Boston: Houghton Mifflin, 2002), 220.

118. http://www.latinamericanstudies.org/us-cuba/gardner-smith.htm

119. "The Reasons for Invading Cuba at the Bay of Pigs" (April 3, 1961); http://highered.mheducation.com/sites/dl/free/0072849037/35273/9_3.html

120. See, for example, Robert K. Brigham, *ARVN: Life and Death in the South Vietnamese Army* (Lawrence, KS: University Press of Kansas, 2006).

121. The textbooks are listed, with full bibliographical information, on pages 3–4 of TVR.

122. Pages 36–7 of TVR cite the specific textbooks from which these quotations and paraphrases are drawn.

123. Robert Buzzcano bases this conclusion on the contents of previously classified archives. For details, see his *Masters of War: Military Dissent and Politics in the Vietnam Era* (New

York: Cambridge University Press, 1996), 311–40.

124. I provide a long list of such quotations during the discussion of Greenberg above.

125. It is ironic that Handlin would raise the issue of "hatred of humanity" against Zinn, of all people, since he seemed unable to recognize such hatred when it actually was present in someone he supported: Richard Nixon. Consider, as a case in point, these excerpts of conversations between Nixon and Henry Kissinger (from tapes of private conversations, which their participants had never intended to share with the public, that were released by the National Archives in 2002): In an April 25, 1972 conversation Nixon suggests bombing dikes in North Vietnam, and then asks Kissinger, "Will that drown people?" Kissinger responds: "About two hundred thousand people." Apparently unsatisfied by the specter of such a small body count, Nixon counters: "No, no, no…. I'd rather use the nuclear bomb. Have you got that, Henry?" "That, I think, would just be too much," Kissinger replied, provoking this rejoinder from Nixon: "The nuclear bomb. Does that bother you?…I just want you to think big, Henry, for Christsakes." Continuing on this theme in a conversation in May, Nixon tells Kissinger: "The only place where you and I disagree…is with regard to the bombing. You're so goddamned concerned about the civilians and I don't give a damn. I don't care." But Kissinger reassures him that his only concern is about appearances, not something so trivial as the lives of innocent Vietnamese: "I'm concerned about the civilians because I don't want the world to be mobilized against you as a butcher" (as quoted in ELL 418–19. See also "Nixon had notion to use nuclear bomb in Vietnam" [February 2, 2002]; http://usatoday30.usatoday.com/news/w ashdc/2002/02/28/nixon-tapes.htm). The actual audiotapes of these conversations can be heard in the film *The Most*

Dangerous Man in America: Daniel Ellsberg and the Pentagon Papers, directed by Judith Ehrlich and Rick Goldsmith, First Run Features (2009). Whatever one may think about Howard Zinn, it is safe to say that we will never be hearing a recording of him saying that he doesn't "give a damn" about the killing of civilians.

126. This is a major theme of his autobiography, where Zinn records his reaction as a 19-year-old to reading Countee Cullen's poem, "Incident" (YCB 20–1—the poem is also reproduced, in full, in APH [444]); tells of his response to e.e. cummings's poem, "my father moved through dooms of love" (YCB 165); explains that reading the novels of Edgar Rice Burroughs at the age of eight, and those of Charles Dickens, at ten, were crucial events in his life (YCB 168–9); and relates the following anecdote about his teaching: "One semester I learned that there were several classical musicians signed up in my course. For the very last class of the semester I stood aside while they sat in chairs up front and played a Mozart quartet. Not a customary finale to a class in political theory, but I wanted the class to understand that politics is pointless if it does nothing to enhance the beauty of our lives. Political discussion can sour you. We needed some music" (YCB 201). And in an interview Zinn reveals that as a teenager,

It was people in the arts who had the greatest emotional effect on me. I'm thinking primarily of singers: Pete Seeger, Woody Guthrie, Paul Robeson…. [T]here was something special about the effect artists had on me—not only singers and musicians but poets, novelists, and people in the theater. It seemed to me that artists had a special power when they commented, either in their own work or outside their work, on what was happening in the world. There was a kind of force they brought into the discussion that mere prose could not match. The passion and emotion of poetry, music, and drama are rarely equaled in prose, even beautiful prose. I was struck by that at an early age ("Resistance and the Role of Artists," in OZ 65).

Zinn pursues this point in detail in several works, including the remainder of the interview just quoted (66–82) and the speech "Artists in Times of War" (in ATW 7–37). Zinn shows his range when discussing the arts in "Airbrushing History" (in OZ 105–30, and especially 124–30), in which he moves deftly from a discussion of a Greek play written in the fifth century B.C. (*The Persians* by Aeschylus) to an analysis of songs by the twentieth-century Americans Woody Guthrie and Bruce Springsteen. No one familiar with these writings could fail to appreciate the absurdity of Handlin's accusation that Zinn "lavishes indiscriminate condemnation upon all the works of man."

127. Actually, I am being slightly unfair to Handlin here, since four of Zinn's usages of the word "civilization" are to be found only in editions of APH that were published after the appearance of Handlin's review. So in the edition of APH that Handlin was reviewing, Zinn placed "civilization" within quotation marks 12.5 percent of the time (rather than 10 percent)—which still fails to come within shouting distance of "usually." The word "civilization" appears on the following pages of APH (I use the pagination of the 2015 edition, though I have verified that all of these usages, except for the last four—all on one page—also appear in identical form in the original, 1980, edition): 1, 9, 11, 12, 16, 17, 22, 26 (twice), 29, 104, 122, 127, 128, 137, 313, and 629 (four times). It is enclosed within quotation marks only on pages 104 and 128.

128. https://www.insidehighered.com/news/2013/07/18/mitch-daniels-renews-criticism-howard-zinn

(I have altered the quoted passage so as to correct obvious grammatical and typographical errors.)

129. (March 23, 1980), 7.

130. "Mitch Daniels Was Right," *National Review Online* (July 29, 2013); http://www.nationalreview.com/article/354614/mitch-daniels-was-right-editors

131. "Mitch Daniels Goes Too Far," *Minding the Campus* (July 18, 2013); http://www.mindingthecampus.org/2013/07/mitch_daniels_goes_too_far/

132. *National Review Online* (July 30, 2013); http://www.nationalreview.com/article/354691/daniels-vs-zinn-rich-lowry

133. "Annals of Censorship" (March 24, 2012); http://pjmedia.com/rogerkimball/2012/03/24/annals-of-censorship/

134. I am indebted to DOD for calling Kimball's inconsistency on this issue to my attention.

135. *The New Yorker* (February 3, 2010); http://www.newyorker.com/books/page-turner/zinns-history

136. I am not the only one to find this short piece unbearably condescending. Clement Lime writes:

I will never forget the appalling spectacle of Jill Lepore doing a snarky pirouette on Howard Zinn's grave in the pages of the *New Yorker*. The dirt was still fresh when Lepore penned a wistful commemoration not of Zinn's work, but of her relish at disabusing fresh-faced young coeds of their jejune Zinnfatuation upon arriving in Cambridge.

The point was all too clear: Zinn was cool for idealistic fourteen year olds and highly advanced toddlers, but once they get to Lepore's class...the scales fall from their eyes and they learn that life and history are far more complicated than the manichean fairy tale of *A People's History of the United States*. I try not to speak ill of the dead...but

Lepore has no such scruples when it comes to patting herself on the back ("David Greenberg Doesn't Hate Howard Zinn Because He Was a Bad Scholar, but Because He Was a Radical," *Tropics of Meta* (March 22, 2013); https://tropicsofmeta.wordpress.com/2013/03/22/david-greenberg-doesnt-hate-howard-zinn-because-he-was-a-bad-scholar-but-because-he-was-a-radical-2/

And another commentator (identified only as "Mike, Brit in Exile") remarks as follows:

Lepore not only shows contempt for Zinn, but patronizes her students who (bless 'em) come to class full of naive enthusiasm for Zinn, before they are put right by the superior, more nuanced analysis of the Ivy League professor.

If I may paraphrase Phil Ochs, I can imagine Lepore singing:

Once I was young and impulsive
I wore every conceivable pin
Even went to socialist meetings
Read everything by Howard Zinn
But I've grown older and wiser
And that's why I'm turning you in
So love me, love me, love me, I'm a liberal
(http://louisproyect.org/2010/02/04/howard-zinns-detractors/)

137. Nathalie Malinarich, "Flashback: The Berlin disco bombing," BBC News Online (November 13, 2001); http://news.bbc.co.uk/2/hi/europe/1653848.stm

138. "Johnson Replies" (in the "Letters" section), *The Nation*

(December 10, 2001), 2; http://www.thenation.com/article/letters-296/
See also Michael Moran, "Bin Laden comes home to roost: His CIA ties are only the beginning of a woeful story," http://www.nbcnews.com/id/3340101/t/bin-laden-comes-home-roost/#.VreiclI4n-Y

139. "The struggle against terrorism cannot be won by military means," *The Guardian* (July 8, 2005); http://www.theguardian.com/uk/2005/jul/08/july7.development

140. For further documentation, see Stephen Rosskamm Shalom, *Imperial Alibis* (Boston: South End Press, 1993), 92–9.

141. https://www.kennedy-center.org/programs/specialevents/honors/history.cfm

142. https://www.arts.gov/honors/medals/pete-seeger

143. http://songwritershalloffame.com/exhibits/era

144. https://rockhall.com/inductees/pete-seeger/

145. http://www.footballfoundation.org/Programs/CollegeFootballHallofFame/SearchDetail.aspx?id=10080

146. http://www.theaterhalloffame.org/members.html#QR

147. http://www.walkoffame.com/paul-robeson

148. https://www.nelsonmandela.org/omalley/index.php/site/q/03lv01538/04lv01539/05lv01562/06lv01571.htm

149. http://www.simplyscripts.com/oscar_winners.html

150. Beth L. Savage, ed., *African American Historic Places* (New York: Wiley, 1994), 277.

151. Sam Roberts, "Rosenberg Case Open and Shut?," *New York Times* (September 18, 2008); http://cityroom.blogs.nytimes.com/2008/09/18/podcast-rosenberg-case-open-and-shut/

152. (Northampton, MA: Olive Branch Press, 2004). Zinn's blurb is on page i.

153. (Northampton, MA: Olive Branch Press, 2007). Zinn's blurb is on the back cover.

154. See also the interview with Zinn in PAC 282–3.

155. "Liberalism and Racism," in POH 170. Zinn provides an endnote citation for his quotation from Schlesinger ("a society in which..."): *The Age of Jackson* (Little, Brown, 1946), 522.

156. Though he is not specifically addressing Schlesinger, or Schlesinger's (alleged) criticism of him, Zinn himself comments on this issue in an interview: "They'll say you're not a scholar, you're a journalist. Or you're not a scholar, you're a propagandist, because you have a point of view. They don't have a point of view.... Of course, they really do. They have an agenda. But they don't say it. They may not even know they have an agenda. The agenda is obedience. The agenda is silence. The agenda is safety. The agenda is 'Don't rock the boat'" ("How Social Change Happens," in FOH 38).

157. "Memorandum from the President's Special Assistant to President Kennedy," U.S. Department of State, Office of the Historian (April 10, 1961); https://history.state.gov/historicaldocuments/frus1961-63v10/d86
Zinn discusses this memorandum in DOI 20; in CW 50; and in "A People's History of the United States," in ODE 70–1. (Note: this last item is different from the book, and from the previously cited Reed College lecture, both of which have the same title.)

158. An audio recording of this press conference is available at http://www.jfklibrary.org/Asset-Viewer/Archives/JFKWHA-022.aspx

159. "The Responsibility of Intellectuals," in *American Power and the New Mandarins* (New York: The New Press, 2002 [originally published 1969]), 325.

160. No. 3 (Winter 2007); http://democracyjournal.org/magazine/3/history-lesson/

161. (July 30, 2013); http://www.wsj.com/news/articles/SB10001424127887324809004578637713582677352?mod=WSJ_Opinio

n_LEADTop&mg=reno64-wsj&url=http%3A%2F%2Fonline
.wsj.com%2Farticle%2FSB10001424127887324809004578637
713582677352.html%3Fmod%3DWSJ_Opinion_LEADTop

162. (July 26, 2013); http://www.nydailynews.com/opinion/h
onest-history-howard-zinn-article-1.1410091

163. All of these quotations are taken from http://media.ok
state.edu/faculty/jsenat/censorship/defining.htm

164. (February 9, 2010); http://historynewsnetwork.org/article
/50997

165. Vol. 18, No. 44 (August 5, 2013); http://www.weeklystan
dard.com/articles/mitch-vs-zinn_741013.html

166. (July 18, 2013); http://chronicle.com/blogs/conversation/20
13/07/18/why-mitch-daniels-was-right/

167. Allen Mikaelian, "The Mitch Daniels Controversy: Context
for the AHA Statement" (September 2013); http://www.hist
orians.org/publications-and-directories/perspectives-on-
history/september-2013/the-mitch-daniels-controversy-
context-for-the-aha-statement

168. "There Are Lies," and There Are Lies, *The Progressive*
(November 1998); http://www.thirdworldtraveler.com/Zi
nn/ThereAreLies.html
A slightly different version of this article is available as "On
Presidential Liars," in *On History* (New York: Seven Stories,
2001), 50–2. Zinn makes a similar point about some earlier
presidential liars about war—James Polk, William
McKinley, and Woodrow Wilson—in "Confronting
Government Lies," in HZS 147–8.

169. "Three Holy Wars," in HZS 293. See also "History Matters,"
in HZS 174; "The Bill of Rights," in FTQ 64 (also in ZR 416);
PAC 278; and DOI 240.

170. "In defense of Pete Seeger, American communist,"
Aljazeera America (January 29, 2014); http://america.aljaz
eera.com/opinions/2014/1/peet-seeger-communistpartyac-
tivism.html

171. Zinn more than once makes the point that Lincoln freed the slaves, though his second statement to that effect is not as direct as the first: "In 1859, John Brown was hanged, with federal complicity, for attempting to do by small-scale violence what Lincoln would do by large-scale violence several years later—end slavery" (APH 171).

Index

Abu-Jamal, Mumia, 343-351, 355, 547

academic freedom, 20-21, 27, 30, 36-42, 235-236, 272, 276-277, 287, 439-441, 482-483, 486, 488-489, 499-502, 515, 517

Acton, Lord (John Dalberg-Acton), 92, 508

Adams, John, 408-409

Aeschylus, 569

Alperovitz, Gar, 171, 242

American Historical Association, The, 39-40, 44-45, 63, 194, 225, 248-249, 306, 433-434, 436, 518-520, 540

Anthony, Susan B., 242

"anti-Americanism", 60-62, 78, 80, 89-96, 110, 203-204, 359, 401-402, 412-413, 415, 417-418, 430, 473-474, 534-535

Anton, Anatole, 273-278, 290, 555

appeal to authority, 43-44, 51-52, 54-56, 247-250, 324-325, 383-384, 453, 499

appeal to consensus, 19-20, 53-56

Aptheker, Herbert, 242

atomic bombs dropped on Japan, 170-174, 195-197, 202-204, 309, 473, 509

Baez, Joan, 364-365, 430-432, 438, 450, 462

Bailyn, Bernard, 242

Baldwin, Hanson, 196-197

Barnet, Richard, 242

Batista, Fulgencio, 385, 397-402, 448-449

Beard, Charles, 179, 242

Beatles, The, 290-291

Beauvoir, Simone de, 242, 337

Becker, Carl, 242

Behan, Brendan, 412-413

Bellamy, Edward, 242

Bennett, William, 17, 489

Bernstein, Barton, 242

Berrigan brothers (Daniel and Philip), 364-365

bias, 60, 64, 96-113, 119-126, 131-133, 138-140, 184, 247, 263, 272-273, 296, 312, 357-358, 361, 363-364, 428, 437, 444-447, 477, 483-484, 503, 506, 536, 538, 541-542, 560-561

bin Laden, Osama, 327, 329, 455-460

Bird, Stephen, 563

Bobb, David J., 235-237

Bogle, Charles, 151

Bond, Horace Mann, 144

Boorstin, Daniel, 541

Bradford, William, 386

Briley, Ron, 45, 518

Brookhiser, Richard, 306

Bross, Kristina, 38-39, 48-49

Burroughs, Edgar Rice, 568

Bush, George H. W., 306, 510, 539

Bush, George W., 241, 274, 276, 303, 330-331, 472

Camus, Albert, 107, 109

Carter, Jimmy, 112, 308, 506

Castro, Fidel, 339-341, 354, 359, 397, 399-400, 460, 479, 506, 510

Cave, Alfred A., 360-363

censorship, 20, 27, 33-35, 37, 42, 238, 251-253, 259, 366, 429-433, 435-436, 438-439, 449, 485-488, 494-495, 502, 512

Chafe, William H., 45, 518

Chamorro, Edgar, 300

Chomsky, Noam, 287-295, 311, 480, 527-528, 530, 557

Churchill, Ward, 272

civil disobedience, 64, 72, 79-83

Clear, Todd, 341-343

Clinton, Bill, 331, 341-343, 458, 485, 506

Coffey, Ralph J., 192

Cohen, Carl, 45, 519

Cohen, Robert, 45, 189-193, 237, 519

Colapinto, David, 76-77

Coll, Steve, 455-457, 459-460

Collier, Peter, 295

Columbus, Christopher, 98-107, 109, 111, 113, 117-118, 130, 186, 202, 265-266, 269-271, 296-297, 311, 333, 335, 380, 385-386, 413, 427, 442, 447-448, 505, 535-538, 543, 553-554

Conkin, Paul K., 46-47

Cook, Blanche Wiesen, 45, 519

Cook, Robin, 458-459

Cullen, Countee, 568

cummings, e. e., 568

Curti, Merle, 45, 519-520, 536-537

Curtis, Susan, 38-39, 45, 48-49, 520

Damon, Matt, 291

Daniels, Mitch, 2-3, 5, 17-43, 45-64, 80, 84-86, 89, 91-92, 94, 96-98, 101-102, 113-115, 118, 126-129, 131, 134, 137, 140-142, 192-193, 195, 198-200, 224, 235-238, 246-247, 249-251, 253-259, 308, 315, 324-325, 332, 338, 378, 402, 417, 420, 429-430, 432-437, 439-443, 474, 482-489, 492-503, 514-518, 520, 526, 531-532, 542-543, 553

Darrow, Clarence, 242, 376

Davich, Jerry, 238

Davidson, Basil, 242
Davis, Kenneth C., 45, 521
Dawkins, Richard, 234
Debs, Eugene, 201, 242
Degler, Carl, 306
Dickens, Charles, 568
Diem, Ngo Dinh, 84, 396, 510
Doctorow, E. L., 274, 276
Dolack, Pete, 151-152
Dolby, Nadine, 77
Douglas, Stephen, 389-393
Douglass, Frederick, 181, 242
Dreier, Peter, 45, 521
Duberman, Martin, 44-45, 70, 78, 80, 86-87, 194, 206, 208-209, 214-218, 226-228, 231-233, 248, 429, 443, 530-531
DuBois, Ellen, 45, 521
Du Bois, W. E. B., 242, 461-462, 464-467
Dylan, Bob, 365, 431, 462

Easterling, Stuart, 315-316, 560-561, 563
Edelman, Marian Wright, 75-76, 549
Eisenhower, Dwight D., 397, 401, 509-510
Ellsberg, Daniel, 83-84, 405
Evangelista, Matthew, 305

Fish, Stanley, 536
Fisk, Robert, 329
Flynn, Daniel J., 240, 332-378, 430, 442-443, 559, 564
Fogel, Robert, 242
Foner, Eric, 44, 192-193, 197-199, 242, 301-302, 304-305, 518
Foner, Philip, 242, 420-422
Ford, Gerald, 460-461
Fox-Genovese, Elizabeth, 555
Franklin, Benjamin, 389
Franklin, John Hope, 242
"frankly speaking", 417-419
freedom of expression, 65-67
Friedman, Milton, 435
Froude, James Anthony, 222-224

Gallie, W. B., 114
Gardner, Andrew G., 306
Gardner, Lloyd, 242
Genovese, Eugene D., 224-225, 240, 246-250, 256, 333
Goldman, Emma, 69, 242, 324
Goodman, Walter, 69
Gordon, Lewis, 283-283
Gore, Al, 325
Grabar, Mary, 237-247, 249-250, 256, 553
Graber, Mark A., 45, 521
Green, James, 45, 521-522
Greenberg, David, 200-235, 497-498, 550-551, 553
Greene, Jack P., 45, 522
Greenglass, David, 176
Greenglass, Ruth, 176

Griffin, David Ray, 471-472
Guthrie, Woody, 568-569
Gutman, Herbert, 242

Hamby, Alonzo, 242
Hamer, Fannie Lou, 535
Hamilton, Alexander, 242, 430-432, 438, 450
Handlin, Oscar, 20, 46-47, 50, 57-59, 193, 197, 378-417, 428, 430, 440, 448-451, 453, 497-498, 506, 541, 563, 566-567, 569
Heidegger, Martin, 283
Herbert, Bob, 532-533 A
Herman, Edward S., 293, 311
Hersey, John, 203
Hirohito, Emperor, 171, 195-196
Hitler, Adolf, 104-105, 150, 170, 206, 353, 453, 504, 565
Ho Chi Minh, 84, 397
Hofstadter, Richard, 242
Horowitz, David, 240, 271-308, 338-339, 341, 441-443, 555-557, 559
Horwitz, Jamie, 303
Hughes, Langston, 242, 416
Hume, David, 134
Hussein, Saddam, 367

Irving, David, 472-473, 484

Jackson, Andrew, 107, 365, 378,

451, 453, 467, 476-477, 482, 532-534
Jaschik, Scott, 301-302
Jefferson, Thomas, 268-269, 420-422, 476-477, 504, 534, 544
Jennings, Francis, 242, 357, 381, 386
Jerne, Niels Kaj, 289
Johnson, Chalmers, 457-458
Johnson, Lyndon, 490, 510
Jones, Mother, 242, 324
Joyce, Davis D., 45, 336, 443, 528

Kammen, Michael, 52, 228, 420-429, 497, 499
Kant, Immanuel, 221
Kazin, Michael, 19-20, 52, 58, 180, 193, 197, 240, 244, 308-332, 429, 433-435, 453, 497-499, 506, 547-548, 559, 563
Keller, Helen, 181
Kennedy, David, 45, 522
Kennedy, John F., 107, 399-401, 478-480, 482, 506, 510, 534, 573
Kennedy, Louise, 69
Khrushchev, Nikita, 206
Kierkegaard, Søren, 282
Kimball, Roger, 65, 430, 435, 438-451
King, Martin Luther, Jr., 181
Kissinger, Henry, 567

Koestler, Arthur, 206
Kohn, Stephen, 77
Kolko, Gabriel, 242
Kovic, Ron, 464
Kuklick, Bruce, 46
Kysia, Alison, 152, 170

LaFeber, Walter, 242
Laksin, Jacob, 275-280, 290,
    301, 305
Las Casas, Bartolomé de, 99-
    100, 270, 380, 386, 537-538
Leibowitz, Samuel, 376-377
Lemisch, Jesse, 225-226, 541-
    542
Leo, John, 433
Lepore, Jill, 451-453, 570-571
Levin, James, 45, 522-523
Levine, Lawrence, 242
Lime, Clement, 570-571
Lincoln, Abraham, 107, 112,
    385, 389-393, 448, 504, 506,
    513, 534, 574-575
Linder, Douglas O., 375-377
Little, Ann M., 418-419
Litwack, Leon, 560
LoBianco, Tom, 25, 42, 251,
    253-256, 432
Locke, John, 485, 544
Loewen, James W., 45, 297,
    369-370, 523
Lowry, Rich, 433-438
Lum, Catherine D., 536-537
Lynd, Staughton, 225-226, 248-

249
Lyons, John, 288

Machiavelli, Niccolò, 92, 480,
    492, 508
Madison, James, 241-242, 534
Magnet, Alec, 301
Maharaji, Guru, 290-291
Maharishi Mahesh Yogi, 290-
    291
Manichaeism, 308-313, 354-355,
    434, 466-467, 559-560, 570
Manley, Albert, 63, 226-228,
    245
Mao Zedong, 339-341, 506
Marcuse, Herbert, 208, 242
Marx, Karl, 239, 332, 335-338,
    355-357, 564
Masciotra, David, 535-536
Mattson, Kevin, 481-482
Mazelis, Fred, 151
McCartney, Dale, 559
McCue, James A., 389
McCullough, Jack, 83
McKinley, William, 574
McLemee, Scott, 285
Meeropol, Robert, 468
Milk, Harvey, 241
Miller, Arthur, 416
Montesinos, Antonio de, 555
Montgomery, David, 242
Moore, Michael, 302
"moral equivalence", 351-355
Morgan, Edmund, 242, 386

Morison, Samuel Eliot, 101-102, 104-105, 335, 442, 536, 540-541
Moscone, George, 241
Moynihan, Michael C., 57-58, 244, 434, 453-474, 526
Mozart, Wolfgang Amadeus, 568

Nader, Ralph, 325
Nash, Gary, 242, 560
National Review, Editors of The, 429-433, 438, 450
Nelson, Cary, 498
Nishitani, Keiji, 283
Nixon, Richard, 384, 453, 510, 567
Novick, Peter, 114, 248-249, 428-429, 540, 545

Obama, Barack, 111, 439, 506
objectivity, 4-5, 43, 60, 64, 107, 112-140, 186-187, 213, 221-225, 231-232, 239, 266, 296, 312, 339, 428-429, 437-440, 475, 477, 481-482, 503, 505, 539, 542-544, 550; as accuracy/as neutrality/as centrism (threefold distinction), 115-129, 139, 222
Ochoa, Roger, 74-75
Ochs, Phil, 571
Offner, Arnold, 242

Oldham, John, 360-361
O'Reilly, Bill, 247
Ortega, Daniel, 299-300

Paine, Thomas, 408-409
Painter, Nell, 242
Palermo, Joseph A., 547-548
Paquette, Robert, 251-271, 553, 555
Parker, Theodore, 408-410
patriotism, 2, 95-96
Patterson, Bill, 190-191
Pearl Jam, 290
Peck, Jedediah, 389
Pentagon Papers, The, 83-84, 396, 405-406, 408
Pequot War, 333, 357-364
Pike, Douglas, 381, 407-408
plagiarism, 56-59
Plato, 71-72, 508
Plotnikoff, David, 56-57
Polk, James K., 574

Qaddafi, Muammar, 453-455

Rage Against the Machine, 290
Rather, Dan, 367
Ravitch, Diane, 539
Reagan, Ronald, 77, 81, 247, 301, 307-308, 338-339, 366, 373, 454, 485, 510, 531, 560-561
Reynolds, Malvina, 462
Robeson, Paul, 462-463, 465-

467, 568
Roosevelt, Franklin D., 107, 112, 166-168, 309-310, 355, 506, 512, 534
Roosevelt, Theodore, 534
Rorty, Richard, 536
Rosenberg, Ethel, 174-177, 468-469
Rosenberg, Julius, 174-177, 467-469
Russell, Thaddeus, 45, 523
Russett, Bruce, 242, 355

Sacco, Nicola, 547
Sartre, Jean-Paul, 72, 282, 564
Schlesinger, Arthur M., Jr., 19, 57-58, 197, 242, 398, 400, 428, 430, 434-435, 453, 474-482, 506, 515, 541, 573
Schmidt, Benno, 482-484
Schoenfeld, Gabriel, 484-489
Seeger, Pete, 461-462, 466-467, 511-513, 540, 568
Sepúlveda, Juan Ginés de, 270
Sheeler, Charles, 422, 424-425
Shenkman, Rick, 489-492
Sherwin, Martin, 171, 196
Shulman, Stuart W., 77-78
Silber, John, 70-71, 87-88, 207-209, 214, 219, 221, 245, 418-419
Silver, Adam, 563
Simpson, Brooks D., 393
Smith, Earl, 397, 399-400

Smith, Page, 242
Smith, Walter Bedell, 395-396
Sobell, Morton, 175-177, 467-469
Speckled Snake, 364-365
Springsteen, Bruce, 513, 569
Stalin, Joseph, 205-207, 467, 506
Stampp, Kenneth, 242
Stone, I. F., 242
Stone, John, 360-361
Summers, Lawrence, 285-287
Sunkara, Bhaskar, 511-513

Thernstrom, Abigail, 287
Thernstrom, Stephan, 285-287
Togo, Shigenori, 195-197
Truman, Harry, 509
Trumbo, Dalton, 461-464, 466-467
Turner, Nat, 504
Twain, Mark, 181, 416, 504, 534
Twombly, Robert C., 45, 523-524

values: in historical writing and research, 104-109, 116-118, 125-126, 129, 136-139, 233, 280-282, 441-442, 445-446, 475-478, 501, 540-543; ultimate/instrumental distinction, 5, 109-110, 130, 132-135, 139, 213, 225, 262-265, 446, 536, 543-545; universal/parochial distinction, 5, 109, 130-132, 135-136, 139, 225, 269-270, 446, 536

Van Dusen, Hugh, 64-65

Vanzetti, Bartolomeo, 547

Vietnam war, 63-64, 67, 79-80, 83-84, 90, 106, 112, 118-119, 129, 137, 184-185, 198, 210, 213-214, 248, 266, 311, 385-386, 393-397, 402-408, 443, 448-449, 473, 490, 510, 518, 541, 566-567

Vogel, Virgil, 386

Walker, Alice, 73-74, 86, 549

Walker, Betty Stevens, 76, 549

Washington, George, 268-269, 301, 306-307, 338-339, 373

Weekly Standard, The, 492-496

Weil, Simone, 161-165

Weinberg, Carl, 502

Weissberg, Josh, 192

Welch, Kelly, 45, 524

West, Cornel, 272, 283-285

West, Henry, 45, 79, 524-525

West, Pat, 79

Westling, Jon, 221

Westmoreland, William, 405

Wheeler, Earle, 405

White, Dan, 241

White, Shannon, 192

Wiener, Jon, 202

Wieseltier, Leon, 284

Wilentz, Sean, 57, 197, 434, 453, 497-499, 502-513

Will, George, 247

Williams, Robin, 291

Williams, Walter, 279

Williams, William Appleman, 381, 384

Wilson, John K., 40-41, 50-52, 280, 285, 439, 499-500, 570

Wilson, Woodrow, 107, 534-535, 574

Windschuttle, Keith, 294-295

Wineburg, Sam, 20, 52, 56-59, 142-200, 429, 497-499, 547-548

Witten, Edward, 253

Wittner, Lawrence, 144

Wood, Peter, 493, 496-502

World War II, 143-153, 156, 158-159, 161-174, 195-197, 202-204, 309-310, 509

Wright, Donald, 45, 525

Yesnowitz, Joshua C., 563

Zinn, Howard: activism of, 78-80, 530-532; as alleged conspiracy theorist; 19, 58, 308, 316-324, 471-472; as expert witness, 80-84; as public speaker; 69-70, 527-528; as teacher, 70-78, 528-529; awards received by, 84-86; biographical sketch of, 62-89; critics of, 2-5, 19-20, 50-52, 140-513; on China,

, 417-418,
, 339-341,
149, 506; on
_ -guez incident, 460-
461; on the Soviet Union,
204-207, 230, 265, 411, 413-
415, 417-418, 467, 506, 553; on
the terrorist attacks of
September 11, 2001, 326-331,
351-353, 358-359, 564; *People's
History of the United States, A*,
1-3, 17-22, 35-36, 46, 57-58,
60, 64-65, 69, 85, 96, 98-103,
106-112, 142-159, 161-183,

185-202, 205, 229-230, 234-
237, 241-247, 250-251, 256-
262, 265-267, 275, 296, 300,
306-310, 314-319, 321-323,
325-327, 330-345, 354-355,
358-361, 363-382, 385-391,
393-424, 426-433, 438-440,
443-444, 448, 450-451, 455,
460-470, 473, 476, 481, 492-
502, 504, 506, 513, 518-519,
521-524, 532-533, 536-537,
539, 547-548, 550, 553, 555,
559, 561-564, 566, 568-570,
574-575; writings of, 63-69

Zero Books
CULTURE, SOCIETY & POLITICS

Contemporary culture has eliminated the concept and public figure of the intellectual. A cretinous anti-intellectualism presides, cheer-led by hacks in the pay of multinational corporations who reassure their bored readers that there is no need to rouse themselves from their stupor. Zer0 Books knows that another kind of discourse - intellectual without being academic, popular without being populist - is not only possible: it is already flourishing. Zer0 is convinced that in the unthinking, blandly consensual culture in which we live, critical and engaged theoretical reflection is more important than ever before.

If you have enjoyed this book, why not tell other readers by posting a review on your preferred book site. Recent bestsellers from Zero Books are:

In the Dust of This Planet
Horror of Philosophy vol. 1
Eugene Thacker
In the first of a series of three books on the Horror of Philosophy, *In the Dust of This Planet* offers the genre of horror as a way of thinking about the unthinkable.
Paperback: 978-1-84694-676-9 ebook: 978-1-78099-010-1

Capitalist Realism
Is there no alternative?
Mark Fisher
An analysis of the ways in which capitalism has presented itself as the only realistic political-economic system.
Paperback: 978-1-84694-317-1 ebook: 978-1-78099-734-6

Rebel Rebel
Chris O'Leary

y single song. Everything you want to know, everything you didn't know.
Paperback: 978-1-78099-244-0 ebook: 978-1-78099-713-1

Cartographies of the Absolute
Alberto Toscano, Jeff Kinkle

An aesthetics of the economy for the twenty-first century.
Paperback: 978-1-78099-275-4 ebook: 978-1-78279-973-3

Malign Velocities
Accelerationism and Capitalism
Benjamin Noys

Long listed for the Bread and Roses Prize 2015, *Malign Velocities* argues against the need for speed, tracking acceleration as the symptom of the on-going crises of capitalism.
Paperback: 978-1-78279-300-7 ebook: 978-1-78279-299-4

Meat Market
Female flesh under Capitalism
Laurie Penny

A feminist dissection of women's bodies as the fleshy fulcrum of capitalist cannibalism, whereby women are both consumers and consumed.
Paperback: 978-1-84694-521-2 ebook: 978-1-84694-782-7

Poor but Sexy
Culture Clashes in Europe East and West
Agata Pyzik

How the East stayed East and the West stayed West.
Paperback: 978-1-78099-394-2 ebook: 978-1-78099-395-9

Romeo and Juliet in Palestine
Teaching Under Occupation
Tom Sperlinger
Life in the West Bank, the nature of pedagogy and the role of a
university under occupation.
Paperback: 978-1-78279-637-4 ebook: 978-1-78279-636-7

Sweetening the Pill
or How we Got Hooked on Hormonal Birth Control
Holly Grigg-Spall
Has contraception liberated or oppressed women? *Sweetening
the Pill* breaks the silence on the dark side of hormonal
contraception.
Paperback: 978-1-78099-607-3 ebook: 978-1-78099-608-0

Why Are We The Good Guys?
Reclaiming your Mind from the Delusions of Propaganda
David Cromwell
A provocative challenge to the standard ideology that Western
power is a benevolent force in the world.
Paperback: 978-1-78099-365-2 ebook: 978-1-78099-366-9

Readers of ebooks can buy or view any of these bestsellers by clicking on the live link in the title. Most titles are published in paperback and as an ebook. Paperbacks are available in traditional bookshops. Both print and ebook formats are available online.

Find more titles and sign up to our readers' newsletter at
http://www.johnhuntpublishing.com/culture-and-politics

Follow us on Facebook at https://www.facebook.com/ZeroBooks
and Twitter at https://twitter.com/Zer0Books